Now You're Talking!

**ALL YOU NEED
TO GET YOUR
FIRST HAM
RADIO
LICENSE**

5th Edition

Edited by	**Larry D. Wolfgang, WR1B**
Contributing Editors	**R. Dean Straw, N6BV** **Dana G. Reed, W1LC** **R. Jan Carman, K5MA**
Editorial Assistants	**Maty Weinberg, KB1EIB** **Helen Dalton, KB1HLF**
Production Staff	**David Pingree**, N1NAS, Senior Technical Illustrator: **Jodi Morin**, KA1JPA, Assistant Production Supervisor: Layout **Kathy Ford**, Proofreader **Sue Fagan**, Graphic Design Supervisor: Cover Design **Michael Daniels**, Technical Illustrator **Michelle Bloom**, WB1ENT, Production Supervisor: Layout

ARRL *The national association for* **AMATEUR RADIO**
225 Main Street, Newington, CT 06111-1494

This book may be used for Technician license exams given beginning July 1, 2003. The Technician (Element 2) question pool in this book is expected to be used for exams given until July 1, 2007. (This ending date assumes no FCC Rules changes to the Amateur Radio license structure or privileges for this license class, which would force the VEC Question Pool Committee to modify this question pool.) *QST* and **ARRLWeb** (**www.arrl.org**) will have news about any Rules changes.

We strive to produce books without errors. Sometimes mistakes do occur, however. When we become aware of problems in our books (other than obvious typographical errors that should not cause our readers any problems) we post an Adobe Portable Document Format (PDF) file on **ARRLWeb**. If you think you have found an error, please check **www.arrl.org/notes** for corrections. If you don't find a correction there, please let us know, either using the Feedback Form in the back of this book or by sending an e-mail to **pubsfdbk@arrl.org**.

Foreword

You are about to enter the wonderful world of Amateur Radio! This hobby is truly all about the very best things in life: great friends, devotion to public service, intellectual and scientific curiosity, exploration and just plain fun.

I was a member of the crew of STS-78 aboard Space Shuttle Columbia, which flew in June 1996. The other crew members and I enjoyed the tremendous honor and pleasure of talking from space with so many friends in Amateur Radio around the world. During that time I couldn't help but reflect on all the deeply personal and emotional moments Amateur Radio had brought to me. I have many fond memories of my own great mentor in the traditions and ethics of Amateur Radio, my "Elmer," Mr Bill Brown, W4NIW (now a Silent Key — but he will live forever in my heart). I remember the sheer exhilaration of listening to signals from around the world as a young boy in a darkened room with the glow of a tube radio my dad helped me build. As a teenager I talked with Senator Barry Goldwater and King Hussein of Jordan on the radio and didn't realize who they were until I looked up their call signs later. Sitting on St. Peter and St. Paul Rocks on a DXpedition in the middle of the Atlantic Ocean with my friends Al, K8CW; Stu, WA2MOE; Phillip, PY2CPU and Jacinto, PY2BZD, I was in awe of a place where Charles Darwin had visited on the voyage of the Beagle. I experienced these same wonderful feelings while talking from space to the great fraternity of ham operators around the world.

There is no greater feeling for a person in space than the warm personal contact with another human being on Earth. It will be so important for us to be able to communicate with one another in this way as we fulfill our planet's destiny in space. I am absolutely sure that wherever we travel in our universe, whether it is on the International Space Station, back to the lunar surface to live or even to Mars, there will be Amateur Radio and fellow hams reaching out like they always do.

There is truly something for everyone in this fantastically diverse world of Amateur Radio. I am always amazed with the many activities Amateur operators get involved in: building, testing, contests, clubs, computers, public service, satellites and so many more.

What a great thing it is that anywhere we go, be it on Earth or in space, we can always call CQ and reach out with our first names and call signs to all our fellow human beings of the Earth!

I hope I have my chance to talk with you!

73,

Chuck, N4BQW

Mission Specialist Charles E. Brady, Jr

Preface

Welcome to the exciting world of Amateur Radio! You are about to join nearly 700,000 licensed Amateur Radio operators in the United States and nearly three million people around the world who call themselves "hams." Hams are found in virtually every country in the world. They have earned the special privilege of being able to communicate directly with one another, by radio, without regard to the geographic and political barriers that so often limit our understanding of the world.

There are many important reasons why governments allow Amateur Radio operators to use valuable radio frequencies for personal communications. As a licensed Amateur Radio operator, you will become part of a large group of trained communicators and electronics technicians. You will be an important emergency communications resource for your neighbors and fellow citizens. Who knows when you may find yourself in the situation of having the only communications link outside your neighborhood? Whether you are caught in a flood, earthquake or other natural disaster or answering a call from someone else, you can provide the knowledge and resources to help.

Whether across town or across the sea, hams are always looking for new friends. So wherever you may happen to be, you are probably near someone — perhaps a whole club — who would be glad to help you get started. If you need help contacting hams, instructors, Volunteer Examiners or clubs in your area, contact us here at ARRL Headquarters. We'll help you get in touch with someone near you. (See the contact information at the bottom of this page.)

When you pass that exam and enter the exciting world of Amateur Radio, you'll find plenty of activity to keep you busy. You'll also find plenty of friendly folks who are anxious to help you get started. Amateur Radio has many interesting areas to explore. You may be interested in one particular aspect of the hobby now, but be willing to try something new occasionally. You'll discover a world of unlimited potential!

Most of the active radio amateurs in the United States are members of ARRL. The hams' own organization since 1914, ARRL is truly the national association for Amateur Radio. We provide training materials and other services, and represent our members nationally and internationally. *Now You're Talking!* is just one of the many ARRL publications for all levels and interests in Amateur Radio. You don't need a ham license to join. If you're interested in ham radio, we're interested in you. It's as simple as that! We have included an invitation for you to join ARRL at the back of this book.

David Sumner, K1ZZ
Executive Vice President
Newington, Connecticut
March 2003

Now You're Talking! ON THE WEB

WWW.ARRL.ORG/NYT

Visit *Now You're Talking!*'s home on the web for additional resources as you prepare for your first Amateur Radio license:

- Find a local radio club
- Locate a testing site
- Take a practice test

- Ask a question
- BONUS CHAPTER "Selecting Your Equipment"
- ARRL Membership & FREE Book Coupon

New Ham Desk
ARRL Headquarters
225 Main Street
Newington, CT 06111-1494
(860) 594-0200

Prospective new amateurs call:
800-32-NEW-HAM (800-326-3942)
You can also contact us via e-mail: **newham@arrl.org**
or check out **ARRLWeb: www.arrl.org/**

Contents

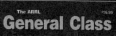

Your First Ham Radio License

The Technician license is the entry-level license for most newcomers to Amateur Radio. In fact, there are more Technician licensees now than any other license class. There is no Morse code exam required to earn a Technician class license. Earn the Technician license by passing a single 35-question written exam covering basic Rules, operating practices and electronics theory.

Technician licensees have full VHF and UHF privileges granted to higher-class licensees, but *no* HF privileges. Any Technician licensee who passes a 5-wpm Morse code test can take one small step up the ladder, though. A Technician licensee with credit for passing the Morse code exam will earn privileges on four of the HF bands — the same privileges held by those with a valid Novice license. No new Novice licenses have been issued since April 15, 2000.

Upgrading to a General class license requires passing a 5 word-per-minute Morse code exam and a more advanced 35-question written exam. The General class license includes privileges on the nine medium and high frequency bands. The third and final step on the Amateur Radio license ladder is the Amateur Extra class license. To earn this license, with full amateur privileges on all amateur bands, you will have to pass an additional 50-question written exam. This exam covers the finer points of the FCC Rules as well as more advanced operating practices and electronics principles. No additional Morse code exam is required, however.

Any holder of a Technician license who passes the 5 wpm code test is issued a *Certificate of Successful Completion of Examination* (CSCE) and is immediately granted "Novice" operating privileges on the HF bands.

WANT MORE INFORMATION?

Looking for more information about ham radio in your local area? Interested in taking a ham radio class? Ready for your license exam? Call 1-800-32 NEW HAM (1-800-326-3942). Do you need a list of ham radio clubs, instructors or examiners in your local area? Just let us know what you need! You can also contact us via e-mail:

newham@arrl.org

or check out our World Wide Web site:

www.arrl.org/

Find some special content just for *Now You're Talking!* readers at

www.arrl.org/NYT

You can even write to us at:
New Ham Desk
ARRL Headquarters
225 Main Street
Newington, CT 06111-1494

How to Use This Book

You're about to begin an exciting adventure: a fun-filled journey into the world of Amateur Radio. *Now You're Talking!* is *the* study guide to help you reach your goal. This book introduces you to basic radio theory in an easily understood style. You'll also learn Federal Communications Commission (FCC) rules and regulations—just as the FCC requires. You will learn enough to pass your Technician written exam with ease. ARRL cares much more about you and your future in Amateur Radio than to stop there! We won't abandon you once your new "ticket" is in hand.

Now You're Talking! is also a pathway to a successful beginning after you've passed your license exam. In this book you'll find the practical knowledge needed to become an effective communicator. We all hope you will take enough pride in the achievement of earning your license to be a considerate communicator as well.

But that's all a few weeks and a few pages down the line. To ensure your success and head you in the right direction toward your first on-the-air contact, here's how to use this book to your best advantage.

Now You're Talking! has been designed and written by a staff with a great deal of experience, backed by decades of Amateur Radio tradition. This book provides everything you'll need to learn — and understand — what you should know to operate an Amateur Radio station. We explain all the rules and regulations required of Technician candidates, not only to pass the test, but to operate properly (legally) once your license is hanging proudly in your shack.

Self Study or Classroom Use?

We designed *Now You're Talking!* both for self study and for classroom use. An interested student will find this book complete, readable and easy to understand. Read carefully, and test yourself often as you study. Before you know it, you'll be ready to pass that exam!

Why deprive yourself of the company of fellow beginners and the expertise of those "old-timers" in your hometown, though? *Now You're Talking!* goes hand-in-hand with a very effective ARRL-sponsored training program run by over 6000 volunteer instructors throughout the United States. If you would like to find out about a local class, just contact the New Ham Desk at ARRL Headquarters—we'll be happy to assist. (Our phone number and e-mail address were listed earlier.)

Hams are very social animals who derive a great deal of pleasure from helping a newcomer along the way. The most effective learning situation is often the one you share with others. There are knowledgeable people to turn to when you have a question or problem. Fellow students can quiz one another on basic electronics concepts and operating practices. It doesn't matter if you're studying on your own or joining a class, though. Use *Now You're Talking!* to study for your Technician exam and you'll be on the air in no time at all.

Using This Book

Now You're Talking! presents the material in easily digested and well-defined "bite-sized" sections. You will be directed to turn to the question pool in Chapter 11 as you complete a section of the material.

This review will help you determine if you're ready to move on. It will also highlight those areas where you need a little more study. In addition, this approach takes you through the entire question pool. By the time you complete the book, you will be familiar with all the questions used to make up your test. Please take the time to follow these instructions. Believe us, it's better to learn the material correctly the first time than to rush ahead, ignoring weak areas and unresolved questions.

Every page of Chapters 1 through 10 presents information you'll need to pass the exam and become an effective operator. We have used **bold type** to highlight many important terms and key words in the text. The Appendix includes a **Glossary of Key Words**, where you can find clear definition of these terms. Pay attention to diagrams, photographs, sketches and captions; they contain a wealth of information you should know. You'll also find a few anecdotes and "mini-articles" (called Sidebars) that will help put the tradition of Amateur Radio in perspective. Our roots go back to the beginning of the 20th Century, and our community service continues even as you read this.

Start at the beginning. The Introduction summarizes the fun you will have when you earn your license and join the thousands of other active radio amateurs. Chapter 1 explains the need for international and national regulation. It describes the regulating bodies and the relevant sections of Part 97 of the FCC Rules and Regulations.

Chapters 2 through 10 teach basic radio theory and amateur practices in well-defined sections. Study the material in each section carefully. It explains the theory you'll need to answer the questions in Chapter 11.

Study the material presented in this book and follow the instructions to review the exam questions. You'll cover small sections of the text and a few questions at a time. This is the best way to determine how well you understand the most important points. The text explains the theory in straightforward terms, so you shouldn't have any problems. Review the related sections if you have any difficulty, and then go over the questions again. In this way, you will soon be ready for your exam. Before you know it, you'll be on the air!

Don't be afraid to ask for help if you don't understand something, though. If you're participating in a class taught by an ARRL-registered instructor, you'll have the chance to ask the experts for help. Ask your instructor about anything you are having difficulty with. You may also find it helpful to discuss the material with your fellow students. If you're not in a class and run into snags, don't despair! The folks at the New Ham Desk at ARRL Headquarters will be happy to put you in touch with an Amateur Radio operator in your area who can help answer your questions.

Most people learn more when they are actively involved in the learning process. Turning to the questions and answers when directed in the text helps you be actively involved. Fold the edge of the question-pool pages to cover the answer key and page-reference information. Check your answers after you study each group of questions, and review the appropriate text for any questions you get wrong. Paper clips make excellent place markers to help you keep your spot in the text and the question pool.

Before You Take Your Test

If you need help in locating someone to administer a Technician test, or for a schedule of Volunteer Examiner test sessions in your area, write to the ARRL/VEC Office, ARRL Headquarters, 225 Main St, Newington, CT 06111-1494. If you need help locating a ham, instructor or club, contact the New Ham Desk at ARRL Headquarters as listed earlier. We can put you in touch with examiners, instructors and clubs in your area! *ARRLWeb* also includes exam and club search sections to help you find local hams on line. Go to **http://www.arrl.org** and follow the site index to "clubs" or "exams" for the information you need.

Give *Now You're Talking!* a chance to guide you the way it was intended — by following these instructions. You'll soon be joining us on the air. Each of us at the ARRL Headquarters and the entire ARRL membership wishes you the very best of success. We are all looking forward to that day in the not-too-distant future when we hear your signal on the ham bands. 73 (best regards) and good luck!

DISCOVERING AMATEUR RADIO

Join us for a fascinating journey through the wonderful world of Amateur Radio.

How did you first hear about Amateur Radio? That evening news report about the Amateur Radio operators who relayed messages after a devastating hurricane or terrible earthquake? The funny-looking antenna in your neighbor's yard? A birthday greeting via Amateur Radio from your uncle who lives clear across the country? Or maybe you heard about hams who helped school students talk to astronauts aboard the International Space Station?

Obviously, you know something about amateur (ham) radio; you have this book. But you want to know more. *Now You're Talking!* will introduce you to the wonderful hobby of Amateur Radio. It will answer your many questions on the subject, and lead you to your first license.

What Can I Do As a Ham?

Ham radio offers so much variety, it would be hard to describe all its activities in a book twice this size! Most of all, ham radio gives you a chance to meet other people who like to communicate. That's the one thing all hams have in common. You can communicate with other hams on a simple hand-held radio that fits in your pocket. Thanks to "repeater stations" (*repeaters*) operated by local ham clubs, your range with a tiny hand-held radio or "HT" may be 50 miles or more.

Repeaters also make it possible for mobile ham stations to keep in touch. Mobile operating is very popular during commuting hours. There's usually someone to talk to on a repeater. Most people would like to do something to help their communities. Someday, you may spot another motorist who needs help, and use the repeater telephone link to call the police. Or, your repeater club may provide communications for a parade, foot race, or even during an emergency like a flood. Best of all, you'll be meeting other people nearby who are as excited about Amateur Radio personal communications as you are.

Imagine talking to a missionary operating a battery-powered station deep in the Amazon jungle, or a sailor attempting an around-the-world solo journey! You can talk to hams all over the world in many ways. The most popular way is by bouncing your signal off the ionosphere, a layer in the upper atmosphere. Other hams like to use the OSCAR satellites. OSCAR means Orbiting Satellite Carrying Amateur Radio. Hams have designed and built more than 50 OSCARs since 1961. If you like a challenge, you can even bounce your signals off the moon. It's possible to contact other hams in more than 100 countries by this method, as strange as it sounds!

How do you talk to these other hams? Well, you can use voice, of course, but there are other ways as well. Maybe you've tried computer-to-computer conversations over the telephone lines. As a ham, you can have similar conversations with other hams around the world. The best part is, you don't have to pay for the call! Not even an Internet Service Provider needed.

The earliest radio communication was done with Morse code. You don't have to know the code to become a ham anymore, but many hams still enjoy using this funny language. To them, the beeping of Morse code is like listening to a favorite song.

Maybe you're interested in photography or video. Many hams have television equipment, including color systems. Hams led the way in *slow-scan television*, which lets you send color photographs, slides and artwork to other hams thousands of miles away.

How about radio-controlled models? Yes, many hams enjoy using exclusive ham frequencies to fly gliders and powered planes, or pilot graceful sailboats. The Technician class amateur license (with no Morse code exam)

Be On the Frontier of Technological Advances

For nearly 100 years, hams have carried on a tradition of learning by doing. From the earliest days of radio, hams have built their transmitters from scratch, wrapping strands of copper wire salvaged from Model T automobiles around oatmeal boxes. Through experimenting with building their own equipment, hams have pioneered advances in technology such as the techniques for single sideband voice. Hams were the first to bounce signals off the moon to extend signal range. Amateurs' practical experience has led to many technical refinements and cost reductions beneficial to the commercial radio industry. The photo at the right shows a complete amateur television (ATV) transmitter constructed in a small package. This photo is from a project described in the November 1996 issue of *QST*.

is all you need to join them.

If you like to work on electronic circuits, ham radio gives you the chance to build your own transmitters and receivers, and actually use them to talk to other people. Even if you'd just like to plug in a radio and go on the air, you might enjoy building some part of your station, from scratch or from a kit.

Unlike shortwave or scanner listening, Amateur Radio doesn't make you sit on the sidelines. When East and West Germany became one country, hams didn't have to learn about it from the TV news: they talked directly to hams in both halves of the country! Instead of listening to police calls on Halloween, you can join your club's "Goblin Watch," and help make the streets safer for Trick-or-Treaters.

Ham radio operators are proud of their hobby. That's why you see so many license plates with ham call signs. Communicating on the air isn't all we do, though. We get together at club meetings, hamfests and conventions. To welcome newcomers we sponsor thousands of classes each year to help anyone who's interested join our great hobby.

Getting Started With a License

You can earn one of three classes of Amateur Radio license in the United States. All US amateur licenses have 10-year terms and are renewable. The Federal Communications Commission (FCC) issues licenses. There is no license fee. Although you can take the exams and start right out at the highest class, most beginners enter Amateur Radio with a Technician license.

When Amateur Radio operators want to communicate with someone, they select from the many frequencies set aside for Amateur Radio use. You can think of a frequency as the spot on a dial where your radio receiver (or transmitter) is set to operate. For example, suppose you want to listen to your favorite FM broadcast radio station. You set your FM receiver dial to the frequency for that station, perhaps 92.5. The Federal Communications Commission (FCC) designates certain ranges of frequencies for Amateurs. These are called bands. Each band has characteristics that make it suitable for communications over

certain distances. For example, some bands are most-suited for local communications, perhaps a hundred miles or less. Other bands provide communications out to a few hundred miles while still others might be used to communicate over thousands of miles and around the world.

With each higher class of Amateur Radio license, you will be allowed to use more of the Amateur frequency bands or a wider range of frequencies within those bands. When we talk about these bands, we often use a series of numbers to identify individual bands. For example, as a new Technician licensee, you will probably make your first contacts on the 2-meter band, or perhaps the 70-centimeter band. We also use more general terms to describe groups of these frequency bands. Some of these general terms are medium frequency (MF), high frequency (HF), very high frequency (VHF) and ultra high frequency (UHF). There are other general groupings, but these are the most common names you will see. As you study this book you will learn more about the characteristics of the various bands and the types of communications that Amateur Radio operators use.

The Technician License

If you are ready to get started in Amateur Radio right now, the Technician license is for you. To receive a Technician license you have to pass a 35-question written exam (Element 2). The exam covers FCC regulations, basic electronics theory and operating practices. A passing grade is 74%, or at least 26 correct answers out of the 35 questions.

Technician licensees are granted full amateur privileges on the extensive VHF, UHF and microwave amateur bands, including the Amateur Radio satellite bands. Yes, with a Technician license you can talk to other amateurs around the world via satellite! Technician licensees can use the popular 2-meter band, where thousands of amateur-owned repeater stations provide solid communications over large areas.

Teams of Volunteer Examiners (VEs), who are accredited by a Volunteer Examiner Coordinator (VEC), give the Technician license exam (as are all amateur license exams). Thousands of exam sessions are held each year, so you shouldn't have to travel far or wait long to take one. Contact the ARRL/VEC Office for information on exam sessions near you. Call 860-594-0300, send e-mail to vec@arrl.org, search for exam listings on *ARRLWeb* at **www.arrl.org/arrlvec/examsearch.phtml** or write to ARRL/VEC, 225 Main St, Newington, CT 06111-1494.

If you start out as a Technician and then decide you'd also like to use the high-frequency bands, you can upgrade your license. Why would you want to do that? Well, the high-frequency (HF) bands offer the ability to talk to other radio amateurs around the world, without the use of satellites. On these frequencies, radio signals that go up into the upper regions of our Earth's atmosphere are bent back towards the Earth, and they can return hundreds or thousands of miles away.

One step in the upgrade process is to pass a 5-wpm Morse code exam. When you pass the Morse code exam you will be allowed to operate on portions of four HF bands using Morse code. You will also be allowed to operate on one band using digital (computer-based) communications as well as voice. These portions of the HF bands are known as the Novice bands because that was the name of a previous class of license issued by the FCC. No new Novice licenses are being issued, but the old licenses can still be renewed. An international treaty requires knowledge of Morse code for any Amateur Radio operators who are using the HF bands. You can think of passing

the Morse code exam as a way to obtain a Morse code endorsement for your Technician class license, granting you the authority to operate on the Novice bands.

The Morse code and many abbreviations such as "Q signals" are understood internationally. This makes Morse code the ideal language for communicating with hams in foreign countries. Plenty of stations in other countries operate in the Novice bands. Quite a few US hams have even contacted hams in more than 100 different countries using only these Novice license privileges. Your new privileges will begin the day you pass the exam. You will learn more about the Technician-license privileges as you study this book.

For help learning Morse code we recommend *Your Introduction to Morse Code*, a package of two audio CDs or two audio cassettes that teach you the code, letter by letter. When you know the code, this package gives you practice at the 5 wpm speed required for the Morse code exam. The ARRL also offers *Ham University,* a computer program that will help you learn Morse code.

You can take two more steps to upgrade your license. By passing another 35-question exam (Element 3) about FCC Rules, more advanced electronics theory and operating practices you can earn a General class license. You must also pass the 5-wpm Morse code exam if you want to go directly from your Technician license to a General class license. With the General class license, you gain operating privileges on nine medium and high-frequency bands. The General class license gives you voice privileges on eight of those bands as well as allowing you to operate with up to 1500 watts of power on them.

The last upgrade step you can take is to earn the Amateur Extra class license. This one requires that you pass a 50-question written exam about FCC Rules, advanced electronics principles and operating practices. With the Extra class license comes full amateur privileges on all bands.

We Come From All Walks Of Life

Having fun communicating with other hams and experimenting with antennas and radio circuits — that's what Amateur Radio is all about. That's why people from all walks of life become hams. Young or old, we all enjoy the thrill of meeting and exchanging ideas with people from across town or from the other side of the Earth. The excitement of building a new project or getting a circuit to work properly and then using that project to talk with someone "over the air" is almost beyond description.

Hams all over the world affectionately call the place where they operate their radio the "shack." This can be a corner of a basement or bedroom. It may be an entire room or equipment set on the kitchen table to operate and stored in a cabinet when not in use. The equipment might include a transmitter for sending and a receiver for listening or a single piece of equipment called a transceiver designed to do both jobs. Many hams have an antenna outside, hung from a tree or some other support. Hams can talk with a friend in the next town one minute and with a ham halfway around the world the next.

Each Amateur Radio station has its own distinctive call sign. The Federal Communications Commission (FCC) issues these call signs. Ham radio operators are so proud of their call signs that the two often become inseparable in the minds of friends.

Patty, KD4WUJ, of Georgia enjoys getting on the air. Many of the hams who talk to Patty don't know that she also goes by the name Patty Loveless, nor that she is a country music superstar. Thousands of hams have made contacts with Joe, NK7U, who is a very active contest operator. Some of them remember that Joe Rudi used to roam the outfield in an Oakland A's uniform. There are many other celebrity hams who are active on the air. After you've talked with Joe, WB6ACU, you may want to listen to some music by The Eagles, with Joe Walsh on vocals and guitar. Over 80 astronauts have their ham licenses, and they love to take ham radio equipment along with them into space. In fact, Amateur Radio is a permanent part of the International Space Station.

Age Is No Barrier

Age is no barrier to getting a ham license and joining in the fun. There are hams of all ages, from five years to more than 80 years. Samantha Fisher received her Technician license at age 9. Known to her ham friends as KA1VBQ, she enjoys talking on 10 meters.

Then there's Luke Ward, KO4IQ, of Alexandria, Virginia, who was licensed at age 7. Luke upgraded to General at age 8, and became an Amateur Extra class licensee when he turned 11. Luke hopes to experiment with "moonbounce" — reflecting VHF/UHF signals off the moon to communicate over long distances.

Like many hams, Dan Broniatowski, N8QWI, enjoys chasing DX from his Cleveland Heights, Ohio, station. Dan was licensed at the age of 10, and received his General license less than a year later.

Of course, young people aren't the only ones who are active radio amateurs. Involved in many hobbies, Evelyn Fox of Merrimac, Wisconsin, played contract bridge with her AARP (American Association of Retired Persons) group on the 40-meter band.

Evelyn was over 75 years old when she became interested in Amateur Radio. That didn't stop her from taking on the job of learning radio theory and the international Morse code. She found the theory a pleasant challenge. She joined a club, attended its classes, and became WB9QZA. Not bad for someone who knew nothing about electronics when she first got started.

Bill Bliss, KD6AHF received his first ham license about 3 weeks before his birthday. So what, you say? He was 82 years old on that birthday! Bill says, "Some think that a bit old to start ham radio, but I have the rest of my life to enjoy it."

Herb Kline is

DALE V. GUADIER, K4DG

EMORY GORDY JR, W4WRO

flying doctors. He worked out of a small village on the north slope of Mount Kilimanjaro in Kenya. Pete was bitten by an OSCAR bug, but couldn't do anything about it while on medical duty. He attacked it with great pleasure, however, when he was off duty.

Somebody gave Pete an old radiotelephone, a vacuum tube and some coaxial cable. The doctor added empty aspirin tins and a quartz crystal from his airplane radio. Right out there in the African bush, he fired up a homemade transmitter, built on the aspirin tins. Then he talked to the world through OSCAR, an Orbiting Satellite Carrying Amateur Radio.

Pete proved something with his homemade gear: You don't need a shack full of the latest commercial equipment to have fun on the air. New hams find this out every day. Tom Giugliano, WA2GOQ, of Brooklyn, New York, contacted 26 states using a pre-World War II transmitter and receiver. He used a simple homemade wire antenna. Other hams have bridged the oceans to contact hams in Europe and Japan using simple equipment running less than 1 watt of power. As a Technician licensee with credit for the 5 wpm Morse code exam, you'll be permitted to run 200-watts output on the HF bands. That's more than enough to contact other hams around the world. On the VHF, UHF and microwave bands, Technicians are allowed to use 1500-watts output, although that much power is rarely needed or used.

There was a time, many years ago, when no commercial equipment was available. The earliest hams, beginning nearly 100 years ago, tried to find more efficient ways of communicating with each other. All early radio sets were "home brew" (home built) and were capable only of communication over several miles. Some transmitters were nothing more than a length of copper wire wrapped around an oatmeal box, attached to a few other basic parts and a wire antenna. Often the transmissions were one-way, with one transmitting station broadcasting

further proof that it's never too late to become a ham. Herb, KB2QGD, of Adams, New York passed his first license exam just before his 83rd birthday. Herb likes to operate CW (Morse code). He also started learning about computers after earning his Amateur Radio license.

"Brewing It" At Home

Ham radio operators pop up in some of the least expected places. Dr. Peter Pehem, 5Z4JJ, was one of Africa's

---

Some Early Amateur Ingenuity

One young lad of seventeen, known to possess an especially efficient spark, CW and radio telephone station, was discovered to be the son of a laboring man in extremely reduced circumstances. The son had attended grammar school until he was able to work, and then he assisted in the support of his family. They were poor indeed. Yet despite this the young chap had a marvelously complete and effective station, installed in a miserable small closet in his mother's kitchen. How had he done it? The answer was that he had constructed every last detail of the station himself. Even such complicated and intricate structures as head telephones and vacuum tubes were homemade! Asked how he managed to make these products of specialists, he showed the most ingenious construction of headphones from bits of

wood and wire. To build vacuum tubes he had found where a wholesale drug company dumped its broken test tubes, and where the electric light company dumped its burned-out bulbs, and had picked up enough glass to build his own tubes and enough bits of tungsten wire to make his own filaments. To exhaust the tubes he built his own mercury vacuum pump from scraps of glass. His greatest difficulty was in securing the mercury for his pump. He finally begged enough of this from another amateur. And the tubes were good ones — better than many commercially manufactured and sold. The greatest financial investment that this lad had made in building his amateur station was 25 cents for a pair of combination cutting pliers. His was the spirit that has made Amateur Radio
— Clinton B. Desoto, in *200 Meters and Down*

to several receive-only stations. Over the years, hams have continually looked for ways to transmit farther and better. They are constantly developing and advancing the state of the communications art in their quest for more effective ways of communicating.

Peering Back Through Time

It all started on a raw December day in 1901. Italian inventor and experimenter Guglielmo Marconi launched the Age of Wireless from an abandoned barracks at St John's, Newfoundland. He listened intently for a crackling series of buzzes, the letter S in international Morse code, traversing the 2000 miles from Cornwall, England. That signal was the culmination of years of experimentation. News of Marconi's feat stimulated hundreds of electrical hobbyists to build their own "wireless" equipment. They became the first hams.

Later, Marconi set up a huge station at Cape Cod that was unlike anything today's ham has experienced. Marconi's 3-foot-diameter spark-gap rotor fed 30,000 watts of power to a huge antenna array suspended from four 200-foot towers on the dunes at South Wellfleet, Massachusetts.

By 1914, Marconi had set up a station and antennas for daily transmission across the Atlantic. At the same time, Amateur Radio operators all over America were firing up their own homebuilt transmitters. Soon, several hundred amateurs across the country joined Hiram Percy Maxim in forming the American Radio Relay League (ARRL), based in Hartford, Connecticut. These amateurs set up a series of "airborne trunk lines" through which they could relay messages from coast to coast. If you're interested in learning more about the history of Amateur Radio, you'll enjoy *200 Meters and Down* by Clinton B. DeSoto. This book is available directly from the ARRL. *Fifty Years of ARRL* is also an interesting account of the ARRL's first half century, but that book is out of print. Perhaps you can borrow a copy from a ham in your area.

There were more hams experimenting all the time. Commercial broadcasting stations began to spring up after World War I. This brought a great deal of confusion to the airwaves. Congress created the Federal Radio Commission in 1927 to unravel the confusion and assign specific frequencies for specific uses. Soon amateurs found themselves with their own frequency bands.

Continued experimentation over the years has brought us tubes, transistors and integrated circuits. Equipment has grown smaller and more sophisticated. In the early days of radio communications, equipment was large and heavy. Sometimes it would take a roomful of equipment to accomplish what can now be done with the circuitry in a tiny box.

We Pitch In When Needed

Traditionally, amateurs have served their countries in times of need. During wartime, amateurs have patriotically taken their communications skills and technical ability into the field. During natural disasters, when normal channels of communication are interrupted, hams provide an emergency communications system. Practically all radio transmitters operating in the United States provide some public service at one time or another. Hams don't wait for someone to ask for their help; they pitch in when needed. They provide communications on March of Dimes walk-a-thons, help plug the dikes when floods threaten and warn of approaching hurricanes. Hams bring assistance to sinking ships, direct medical supplies into disaster areas, and search for downed aircraft and lost children.

Amateur Radio operators recognize their responsibility to provide these public-service communica-

KIT LAMMERS

Mark Hill, KD6ZEK, Communications Unit Leader, acting as a human repeater during a recent prescribed fire exercise.

tions. They train in various ways to be effective communicators in times of trouble. ARRL even offers a series of three emergency communications courses as part of a Continuing Education/Certification program. These classes (and others in the CCE program) are taught over the Internet.

Broken Arrow, Oklahoma, a town of 75,000, experienced a city-wide telephone outage on December 23, 2002. A request went out for amateurs to assist with emergency communications at the local Emergency Operations Center and three area hospitals. Hams from the Broken Arrow Amateur Radio Club responded to the call, staffing positions at the Broken Arrow EOC and three hospital emergency rooms.

Every day, amateurs relay thousands of routine messages across the country. They send many of these messages through "traffic nets" devoted to developing the skill of sending and receiving messages efficiently. (A net is a gathering of hams on a single frequency for some specific purpose. In this case the net's purpose is to "pass traffic" — relay messages.) This daily operation helps prepare hams for real emergencies. Also, each June thousands of hams across the country participate in the ARRL Field Day. They set up portable stations, including antennas, and use emergency power. Relaying messages and operating on Field Day helps hams to test their emergency communications capabilities and to help them identify problems that could arise in the event of a disaster.

MAYDAY — We're Going Down

In September 1991, a Pacific storm caught two boats, the *Molly Sue* and the *Dauntless*, eastbound from Hawaii to California. The *Molly Sue* and the *Dauntless* had intended to travel together, but the *Dauntless*, a 65-foot schooner, outran the other boat by 500 miles in the storm, out of maritime radio range.

The storm's winds ripped the *Molly Sue*'s sails and broke her halyard, injuring a crewmember in the process — injuries that appeared serious. Alerted by hams operating on the California-Hawaii net, with whom the *Molly Sue*'s skipper was in contact, the Coast Guard diverted a freighter to help. Unfortunately, the *Molly Sue* needed new sails. A local ham picked up a set of sails from the skipper's home in San Diego, and delivered them to the Coast Guard. The Coast Guard parachuted the sails to the *Molly Sue*.

Meanwhile, the *Dauntless*, back in radio range, reported she was taking on water and running out of fuel. The net relayed this word to the Coast Guard, and the *Dauntless* was towed to San Francisco. The *Molly Sue*, fitted with new sails, arrived safely in San Diego.

An FCC official commended the hams on the net for their "shining example of the communications skills, dedication and public spirit of the amateur service."

In Quakes, Tornadoes, Fires And Floods: Hams Are There

In February 2000, a major tornado leveled a housing development in Camilla, Georgia. Other storms in the area also tore roofs from houses and flattened mobile homes. The storms caught many residents by surprise since warnings were not issued until after they'd already gone to bed for the night. At least 22 people were killed and over 100 were injured. More than 500 families lost their homes. Thousands were left without power in Georgia and elsewhere. The storm that wreaked havoc on Georgia was part of a system that also struck Arkansas, Tennessee, Mississippi and Alabama before moving into Georgia, northeastern Florida and the Carolinas.

With telephone lines gone and no communications into the area, hams responded to set up communications links in shelters and provide other vital communications.

Thousands of inquiries came in to ARRL Headquarters and to individual hams across the country. Friends, relatives and business associates worried about people in the affected area.

Why did they choose to ask Amateur Radio operators to help them? Over the decades, hams have volunteered their services in times of emergency to relay vital information to and from stricken areas. With local power and telephone communications knocked out, hams get to work. Using amateur stations that fit in briefcases, they relay messages between residents and their worried relatives and friends outside the stricken area. These tiny stations often include a hand-held Amateur Radio transceiver, a lap-top computer and a radio modem called a terminal-node controller, or TNC. Local hams go back to their regular routine of working and spending time with their families only after workers restore regular communications channels.

The summer of 1993 is one that won't soon be forgotten across the middle of the US. In early April heavy rain caused rivers and streams to rise. Crews were laying sandbags along some stretches of the mighty Mississippi to fend off the rising water. In June, many Field Day plans turned to real emergency communications events as flooding occurred along the Minnesota River in the St. Peter, Minnesota area. The rain continued through July, and people in Kansas, Kentucky, Iowa, Illinois, Missouri, Minnesota and Wisconsin were affected. It was September before all the floodwaters had retreated. Through it all, Amateur Radio operators were there, providing vital emergency communications and helping coordinate sand bagging and rescue efforts. In Saint Charles county Missouri, hams operated from the emergency operations cen-

This used to be a pickup truck—before a tornado wrapped it around a tree.

Public service has been a ham tradition since the very beginning. Whether it's a walk-a-thon, the Olympic Torch Run or the aftermath of a hurricane, tornado or other disaster, hams are always there to help with communications, which they provide at no cost to the group involved. Here, Mark Dieterich, N2PGD checks the volunteer communicator shift schedule. Simone Lambert, KA1YVF handles schedule management from the World Trade Center Disaster Relief Communications site.

ter (EOC) 24 hours per day from July 2 through August 20. Volunteers came from across the country to relieve weary radio operators and help wherever needed.

Terrorists struck our country on September 11, 2001 in a way that most of us would never have imagined. Within 5 minutes of the first plane attack on the World Trade Center, the New York City Amateur Radio Emergency Service (ARES) group was activated! Hundreds of Amateur Radio operators answered the call for assistance. The net was on the air continuously, with operators taking turns in shifts for two weeks.

Radio amateurs help when the emergency is outside the US, too. In September 1989, Hurricane Hugo did terrible damage to island nations in the Caribbean, and Puerto Rico. Most of the islands were completely cut off from the outside world; all normal means of communication were destroyed. Through volunteer Amateur Radio networks, shipments of relief and medical supplies were coordinated. Island residents were able to contact loved ones on the mainland and other islands. Amateur Radio "jump teams" even sped to the affected areas to help restore communications.

No Barriers To Enjoying Ham Radio

Amateur Radio holds no roadblocks for people with disabilities. Many people who are unable to walk, see or talk are able to enjoy their Amateur Radio hobby, conversing with friends in their hometown or across the world. Some local ham clubs even take classes to a home to help a person with a disability discover ham radio.

Although unable to leave his bed, Otho Jarman was able to earn his ham license. Bill Haney, KE3CO, (then WA6CMZ) helped Otho learn the Morse code and pass his license exam through such a club program. Bill spent one hour each week teaching Otho the code, and in seven weeks he passed his license exam. Other members of the Barstow (California) Amateur Radio Club helped Otho put his station together. They obtained equipment for him and constructed antennas.

Soon, Otho, WB6KYM, was on the air talking with hams in Mozambique, Nicaragua and Puerto Rico. He could communicate with the world from his bed. Sixteen years earlier, at age 22, Otho had broken his spine when he dove into a reservoir to rescue a drowning child. Although interested in Amateur Radio for years, he had not had an opportunity to learn about it until the club came along. Now he monitors local frequencies from 7 AM to 10 PM, often just chatting or giving directions to motorists.

"Amateur Radio can take a disabled person out of his living room, out of his bed or out of his wheelchair, and put him in the real world," Otho says.

The Courage Center, of Golden Valley, Minnesota, sponsors the HANDI-HAM system to help people with physical disabilities obtain amateur licenses. The system provides materials and instruction to persons with disabilities interested in obtaining ham licenses. The Center also provides information to other hams, "verticals," who wish to help people with disabilities earn a license. Write to:

Courage HANDI-HAM System
Courage Center
3915 Golden Valley Road
Golden Valley, MN 55422

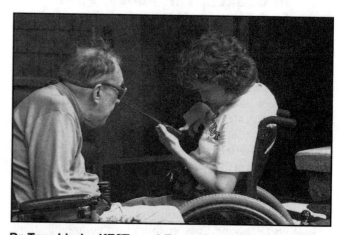

Dr Tom Linde, KZØT, and Tracy Schramm, KCØHXU, program a hand-held radio at a Handi-Hams Radio Camp session.

Now You're Talking!

Once you've earned your Technician license, you can join the millions of other hams on the air. Then you'll begin to experience the thrill of Amateur Radio firsthand. As a ham, you can contact other hams in your town and around the world. You can talk into a microphone to use either single sideband (SSB) or frequency modulation (FM) to communicate. If you want, you can experience the thrill of using the international Morse code (called "CW" by hams). You can even communicate by packet radio or radioteletype using a computer. You can do all this on parts of special frequency bands set aside by the FCC for Amateur Radio operators.

For your first contact, you may choose to listen to the local repeaters, hoping to hear another ham. Perhaps you will decide to transmit: "KB1DCO listening." Suddenly you'll hear your own call coming back! It's hard to describe the excitement. Someone else is sending your call sign back to let you know that they hear you and want to make contact.

Operating with SSB or CW, perhaps you will tune around looking for a station calling "CQ" (calling for any station to make contact). Maybe you'll even try calling a CQ on your own. Each time you send a CQ, you'll wonder who will answer. It could be a ham in the next town, the next state or clear across the country. The whole world is full of hams to talk to.

You can do many wonderful things as a ham. After you have been on the air for a while, you'll be known as one of the regulars on the band. It's surprising how many people from all over you'll recognize and who will recognize you. Many a fast friendship has developed through repeated on-the-air contacts.

Soon you'll be collecting contacts with different states and exchanging QSL cards (postcards) with other hams you've talked to. These special cards commemorate each contact. They also serve as proof of the contact as you begin working toward some of the awards issued by the ARRL. [The Worked All States (WAS) award is one

There are many hobbies within the hobby of Amateur Radio. Some hams collect QSL cards and awards. Others love the thrill of talking to rare DX stations in foreign lands, while still others enjoy exchanging pictures by slow-scan television. You'll find one or more of these pastimes enjoyable, and in time you'll probably try most of them.

popular example.] You'll learn more about the special language and abbreviations that hams use as you study. Chapter 6 has a list of common "Q signals" used by most hams, for example.

There is a certain intrigue about DX (long-distance communication) that catches many hams. Talking to hams from other lands can be quite an experience. After all, foreign hams are people just like you who enjoy finding out about other people and places! Also, hams in other countries often speak enough English to carry on a limited conversation, so you'll have little problem there. Whether you stay a Technician, add Morse code credit to your license or upgrade to General or Amateur Extra, Amateur Radio offers many opportunities to contact DX stations.

If you enjoy a little competition, perhaps you'll like on-the-air contesting. The object of a contest is to work as many people in as many different areas as possible in a certain time. Each year, the ARRL sponsors a number of contests and operating events. Several of these events have provisions to encourage beginning operators. For example, the Field Day rules (always the fourth full weekend in June) include a provision for a station that encourages clubs to involve beginners. The club can add a "free" VHF/UHF station without affecting their entry category. There are even contests specifically for VHF/UHF operators, where Technician class operators have all operating privileges. All these events give you the chance to contact old friends and make new ones. You might work some new states or countries, and if you use Morse code you will increase your code speed. You are certain to improve your general operating skills and ability. Most of all, though, you will have fun.

Other Modes

Technician-class licensees may use just about every type of communication available to Amateur Radio operators. You should become familiar with these modes. In addition to voice and Morse code, you may want to investigate some of the less traditional modes.

With slow-scan television (SSTV), hams send still photos to each other, one frame at a time. It takes between 20 seconds to two minutes for the bright band of light to creep down the screen and paint a complete color picture. (Your home TV makes 30 complete pictures per second.) SSTV pictures may be transmitted with a hand-held radio and even over repeaters (with the repeater owner's permission, of course). They can also be sent around the world using shortwave (HF) ham transmitters. Many hams use computer software and adapters to enjoy the fun of SSTV even without a video camera. Facsimile (fax) is a means of sending drawings, charts, maps, graphs and pictures. You can even play games over the air by transmitting fax pictures of each move.

Amateurs even exchange amateur television (ATV)

Clarence, AB2BP, had little interest in Amateur Radio — until he realized that amateur television (ATV) could add a new viewpoint to his other hobby of radio-controlled flying.

or "fast scan TV" pictures on some UHF bands. That's TV using the same standards as your "regular" home TV. Full moving-picture video by Amateur Radio is great for public service communications as well as general fun!

Using the "digital" modes, a ham can type out a message and send it over the air to a friend's station. Even if the friend is away, her radioteletype system can receive and hold the message until she returns. Early digital systems used mechanical machines cast off by news services. Today, many hams use personal computer systems. These display the message silently on a TV screen rather than using roll after roll of paper with noisy, clacking typewriter keys. There are a growing number of modern computer-controlled systems capable of relaying messages and storing them for later reception by the intended ham.

Ham Satellites

Hams use satellites to communicate in voice, code, radioteletype and packet radio around the world. Long-distance telephone, radio and TV broadcasters also use communications satellites to relay signals around the world. Hams are special, though, because their satellites are known as OSCARs (Orbiting Satellites Carrying Amateur Radio), which were designed and built by amateurs!

Some schools use the OSCARs to instruct students in science and math. No license is needed to listen, so many students across the country have eavesdropped on Amateur Radio transmissions. A receiver and an antenna are all you need to introduce students to the exciting world of space technology. Many Amateur Radio clubs have worked with school systems to schedule a contact with astronauts onboard the International Space Station. How exciting would it be to talk to an astronaut live by Amateur Radio? Many students have found out first hand!

What Are You Waiting For?

You can operate in any of these exciting modes when you become an Amateur Radio operator. Take the time to explore the adventure of ham radio! As a new or prospective amateur operator, you will begin to discover the wide horizons of your new pastime. You will learn more about the rich heritage we all share. Take this sense of pride with you, and follow the Amateur's Code.

When It's Time To Upgrade

ARRL has all the study materials you will ever need for any Amateur Radio license exam. Always complete. Always accurate. Always up to date. Whether you are preparing to study for your General license exam or for the Amateur Extra exam, there is an *ARRL License Manual* ready to help. *The ARRL General Class License Manual* and *The ARRL Extra Class License Manual* are completely revised when those new question pools are released by the VEC Question Pool Committee. *ARRL's Tech Q & A*, *ARRL's General Q & A* and *ARRL's Extra Q &A* provide convenient question and answer format study guides.

Be sure you have the latest study materials, covering the current question pool, no matter which license exam you are preparing to take. Call the ARRL Publications Sales Staff for assistance with placing your order (888-277-5289 toll-free) or check out *ARRLWeb* for a complete catalog and on-line ordering: **www.arrl.org/**

When you are ready to learn Morse code, check out the ARRL's line of Morse code training products, too. Available as a set of two audio CDs or two cassette tapes, *Your Introduction to Morse Code* teaches you all the characters needed for your 5 wpm Morse code exam. If you prefer to use your IBM-PC compatible computer to learn Morse code, then you will want a copy of the *Ham University* program, available from ARRL.

The Amateur's Code

The Radio Amateur is:

CONSIDERATE . . .
never knowingly operates in such a way as to lessen the pleasure of others.

LOYAL . . .
offers loyalty, encouragement and support to other amateurs, local clubs, and the ARRL, through which Amateur Radio in the United States is represented nationally and internationally.

PROGRESSIVE . . .
with knowledge abreast of science, a well-built and efficient station and operation above reproach.

FRIENDLY . . .
slow and patient operating when requested; friendly advice and counsel to the beginner; kindly assistance, cooperation and consideration for the interests of others. These are the hallmarks of the amateur spirit.

BALANCED . . .
radio is an avocation, never interfering with duties owed to family, job, school, or community.

PATRIOTIC . . .
station and skill always ready for service to country and community.

The original Amateur's Code was written by Paul M. Segal, W9EEA, in 1928.

Table 1—Technician Class (Element 2) Syllabus

(Required for all operator licenses.)

SUBELEMENT T1 - FCC Rules
[5 Exam Questions — 5 Groups]

T1A   Definition and purpose of Amateur Radio Service, Amateur-Satellite Service in places where the FCC regulates these services and elsewhere; Part 97 and FCC regulation of the amateur services; Penalties for unlicensed operation and for violating FCC rules; Prohibited transmissions.

T1B   International aspect of Amateur Radio; International and domestic spectrum allocation; Spectrum sharing; International communications; reciprocal operation; International and domestic spectrum allocation; Spectrum sharing; International communications; reciprocal operation.

T1C   All about license grants; Station and operator license grant structure including responsibilities, basic differences; Privileges of the various operator license classes; License grant term; Modifying and renewing license grant; Grace period.

T1D   Qualifying for a license; General eligibility; Purpose of examination; Examination elements; Upgrading operator license class; Element credit; Provision for physical disabilities.

T1E   Amateur station call sign systems including Sequential, Vanity and Special Event; ITU Regions; Call sign formats.

SUBELEMENT T2 — Methods of Communication
[2 Exam Questions — 2 Groups]

T2A   How Radio Works; Electromagnetic spectrum; Magnetic/Electric Fields; Nature of Radio Waves; Wavelength; Frequency; Velocity; AC Sine wave/Hertz; Audio and Radio frequency.

T2B   Frequency privileges granted to Technician class operators; Amateur service bands; Emission types and designators; Modulation principles; AM/FM/Single sideband/upper-lower, international Morse code (CW), RTTY, packet radio and data emission types; Full quieting.

SUBELEMENT T3 - Radio Phenomena
[2 Exam Questions - 2 Groups]

T3A   How a radio signal travels; Atmosphere/troposphere/ionosphere and ionized layers; Skip distance; Ground (surface)/sky (space) waves; Single/multihop; Path; Ionospheric absorption; Refraction.

T3B   HF vs. VHF vs. UHF characteristics; Types of VHF-UHF propagation; Daylight and seasonal variations; Tropospheric ducting; Line of sight; Maximum usable frequency (MUF); Sunspots and sunspot Cycle, Characteristics of different bands.

SUBELEMENT T4 — Station Licensee Duties
[3 Exam Questions — 3 Groups]

T4A   Correct name and mailing address on station license grant; Places from where station is authorized to transmit; Selecting station location; Antenna structure location; Stations installed aboard ship or aircraft.

T4B   Designation of control operator; FCC presumption of control operator; Physical control of station apparatus; Control point; Immediate station control; Protecting against unauthorized transmissions; Station records; FCC Inspection; Restricted operation.

T4C   Providing public service; emergency and disaster communications; Distress calling; Emergency drills and communications; Purpose of RACES.

SUBELEMENT T5 - Control Operator Duties
[3 Exam Questions — 3 Groups]

T5A   Determining operating privileges, Where control operator must be situated while station is locally or remotely controlled; Operating other amateur stations.

T5B   Transmitter power standards; Interference to stations providing emergency communications; Station identification requirements.

T5C   Authorized transmissions, Prohibited practices; Third party communications; Retransmitting radio signals; One way communications.

SUBELEMENT T6 - Good Operating Practices
[3 Exam Questions — 3 Groups]

T6A   Calling another station; Calling CQ; Typical amateur service radio contacts; Courtesy and respect for others; Popular Q-signals; Signal reception reports; Phonetic alphabet for voice operations.

T6B   Occupied bandwidth for emission types; Mandated and voluntary band plans; CW operation.

T6C   TVI and RFI reduction and elimination, Band/Low/High pass filter, Out of band harmonic Signals, Spurious Emissions, Telephone Interference, Shielding, Receiver Overload.

SUBELEMENT T7 Basic Communications Electronics
[3 Exam Questions — 3 Groups]

T7A   Fundamentals of electricity; AC/DC power; units and definitions of current, voltage, resistance, inductance, capacitance and impedance; Rectification; Ohm's Law principle (simple math); Decibel; Metric system and prefixes (e.g., pico, nano, micro, milli, deci, centi, kilo, mega, giga).

T7B   Basic electric circuits; Analog vs. digital communications; Audio/RF signal; Amplification.

T7C   Concepts of Resistance/resistor; Capacitor/capacitance; Inductor/Inductance; Conductor/Insulator; Diode; Transistor; Semiconductor devices; Electrical functions of and schematic symbols of resistors, switches, fuses, batteries, inductors, capacitors, antennas, grounds and polarity; Construction of variable and fixed inductors and capacitors.

SUBELEMENT T8 - Good Engineering Practice
[6 Exam Questions - 6 Groups]

T8A   Basic amateur station apparatus; Choice of apparatus for desired communications; Setting up station; Constructing and modifying amateur station apparatus; Station layout for CW, SSB, FM, Packet and other popular modes.

T8B   How transmitters work; Operation and tuning; VFO; Transceiver; Dummy load; Antenna switch; Power supply; Amplifier; Stability; Microphone gain; FM deviation; Block diagrams of typical stations.

T8C   How receivers work, operation and tuning, including block diagrams; Super-heterodyne including Intermediate frequency; Reception; Demodulation or Detection; Sensitivity; Selectivity; Frequency standards; Squelch and audio gain (volume) control.

T8D   How antennas work; Radiation principles; Basic construction; Half wave dipole length vs. frequency; Polarization; Directivity; ERP; Directional/non-directional antennas; Multiband antennas; Antenna gain; Resonant frequency; Loading coil; Electrical vs. physical length; Radiation pattern; Transmatch.

T8E   How transmission lines work; Standing waves/SWR/SWR-meter; Impedance matching; Types of transmission lines; Feed point; Coaxial cable; Balun; Waterproofing Connections.

T8F   Voltmeter/ammeter/ohmmeter/multi/S-meter, peak reading and RF watt meter; Building/modifying equipment; Soldering; Making measurements; Test instruments.

SUBELEMENT T9 - Special Operations
[2 Exam Questions — 2 Groups]

T9A   How an FM Repeater Works; Repeater operating procedures; Available frequencies; Input/output frequency separation; Repeater ID requirements; Simplex operation; Coordination; Time out; Open/closed repeater; Responsibility for interference.

T9B   Beacon, satellite, space, EME communications; Radio control of models; Autopatch; Slow scan television; Telecommand; CTCSS tone access; Duplex/crossband operation.

SUBELEMENT T0 - Electrical, Antenna Structure and RF Safety Practices
[6 Exam Questions - 6 Groups]

T0A   Sources of electrical danger in amateur stations: lethal voltages, high current sources, fire; avoiding electrical shock; Station wiring; Wiring a three wire electrical plug; Need for main power switch; Safety interlock switch; Open/short circuit; Fuses; Station grounding.

T0B   Lightning protection; Antenna structure installation safety; Tower climbing Safety; Safety belt/hard hat/safety glasses; Antenna structure limitations.

T0C   Definition of RF radiation; Procedures for RF environmental safety; Definitions and guidelines.

T0D   Radiofrequency exposure standards; Near/far field, Field strength; Compliance distance; Controlled/Uncontrolled environment.

T0E   RF Biological effects and potential hazards; Radiation exposure limits; OET Bulletin 65; MPE (Maximum permissible exposure).

T0F   Routine station evaluation.

FEDERAL COMMUNICATIONS COMMISSION'S RULES

After your license exam, you will anxiously watch the Volunteer Examiners grade your test. You will be all smiles when they announce that you have passed your exam!

Part 97 of the Federal Communication Commission's Rules govern the Amateur Radio Service in the United States. Each Amateur Radio license exam includes questions covering sections of these rules. There are five questions from the FCC Rules section of the Technician class exam. This chapter of *Now You're Talking!* describes the rules covered by those questions.

This book does not include a complete listing of the Part 97 Rules. The FCC modifies Part 97 on an irregular basis, and it would be impossible to keep an up-to-date set of rules in a book designed to be revised with the release of a new Technician Question Pool every four years. We do recommend, however, that every Amateur Radio operator have an up-to-date copy of the rules in their station for reference. *The ARRL's FCC Rule Book* contains the complete text of Part 97, along with detailed explanations of all the regulations. *The ARRL's FCC Rule Book* is updated as necessary to keep it current with the latest rules changes.

The five rules questions on your Technician license exam will come from five exam-question groups. Each group forms a subelement section on the syllabus or study guide, and the question pool. The five groups are:

T1A Definition and purpose of Amateur Radio Service, Amateur-Satellite Service in places where the FCC regulates these services and elsewhere; Part 97 and FCC regulation of the amateur services; Penalties for unlicensed operation and for violating FCC rules; Prohibited transmissions.

T1B International aspect of Amateur Radio; International and domestic spectrum allocation; Spectrum sharing; International communications; reciprocal operation; International and domestic spectrum allocation; Spectrum sharing; International communications; reciprocal operation.

T1C All about license grants; Station and operator license grant structure including responsibilities, basic differences; Privileges of the various operator license classes; License grant term; Modifying and renewing license grant; Grace period.

T1D Qualifying for a license; General eligibility; Purpose of examination; Examination elements; Upgrading operator license class; Element credit; Provision for physical disabilities.

T1E Amateur station call sign systems including Sequential, Vanity and Special Event; ITU Regions; Call sign formats.

When you tune an AM or FM broadcast radio to your favorite station, you select a specific spot on the tuning dial. There are many stations spread across that dial. Each radio station occupies a small part of the entire range of "electromagnetic waves." Other parts of this range, or spectrum, include microwaves, X-rays and even infrared,

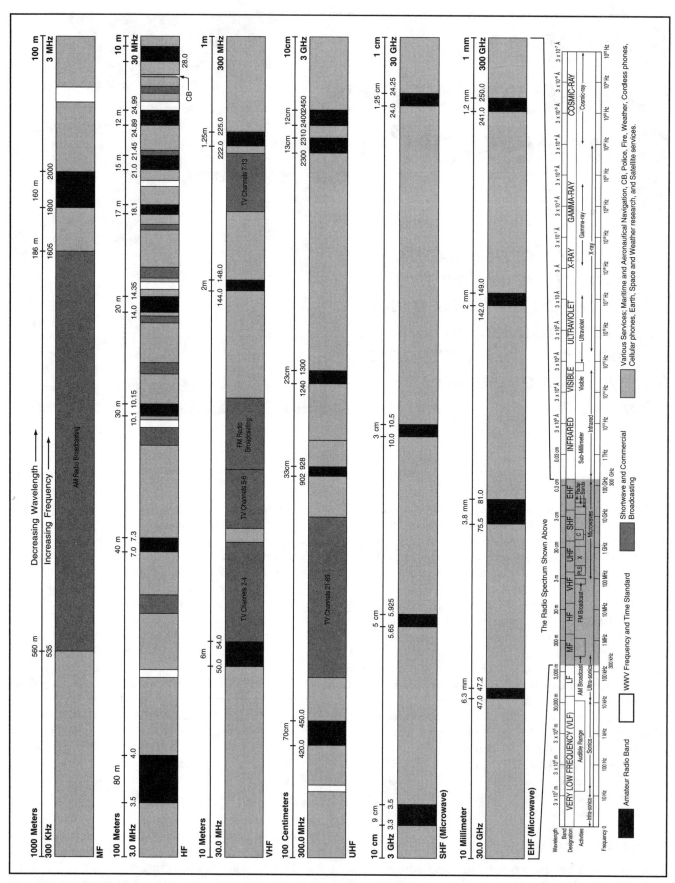

Figure 1.1 — This chart shows the electromagnetic spectrum of radio frequencies. It starts with the AM Standard Broadcast Band, through the radio frequencies, X-rays and gamma rays. Amateur Radio operations use a small, but significant, portion of these frequency bands. The amateur bands are represented as short bars on the graph.

ultraviolet and visible light waves. When Amateur Radio operators talk about picking an operating **frequency**, they are selecting a spot on their tuning dial. That is one way you can think about a simple definition of *frequency*. (Throughout this book you will find words printed in **boldface type**. These are important terms, which we call key words. They are usually printed in boldface type the first time they are used in the text. There is a simple definition of the term in the text. These key words have also been collected in a Glossary of Key Words in the Appendix to the book. You may find it helpful to review the definitions in the Glossary of Key Words as final preparation for your exam.)

Figure 1.1 shows the electromagnetic spectrum from below the radio range all the way through the X-rays. Amateur Radio occupies only a small part of the total available space. Countless users must share the electro-magnetic spectrum.

You may be thinking: "Who decides where Amateur Radio frequencies will be, and where my favorite FM broadcast station will be?" That's a good question, and the answer has several parts.

Radio signals travel to distant corners of the globe, so there must be a way to prevent total chaos on the bands. The International Telecommunication Union (ITU) has the important role of dividing the entire range of communications frequencies between those who use them. Many radio services have a need for communications frequencies. These services include commercial broadcast, land mobile and private radio (including Amateur Radio). ITU member nations decide which radio services will be given certain bands of frequencies, based on the needs of the different services. This process takes place at ITU-sponsored World Radio Conferences (WRCs).

Why is there Amateur Radio?

In the case of Amateur Radio, the ITU has long recognized that hams are invaluable in times of emergency or disaster. The ITU makes frequency allocations on an international basis. The Federal Communications Commission (FCC) decides the best way to allocate frequency bands to those services using them in the US. The FCC is the governing body in the United States when it comes to Amateur Radio. Title 47 of the Code of Federal Regulations governs all telecommunications in the US. It includes Parts 0 through 300. An entire part of the FCC Rules is devoted to the amateur service — Part 97. The amateur service rules in Part 97 describe station operation standards, technical standards and emergency communications. As you learn more about Amateur Radio, you'll become more familiar with Part 97.

To gain the privilege of sending a radio signal over the airwaves in the US, you must pass a license exam. To earn a Technician license, you will need to pass a 35-question exam covering basic radio theory and FCC regulations. There is no Morse code requirement for the Technician exam. You can earn a higher-class license, with more privileges, by passing an exam in the Interna-

In the days before the giant eruption that demolished vast areas around the Mount St. Helens volcano in Washington, volunteer amateurs monitored its behavior. Hams are ready to do whatever they can when someone needs their communications services. Because of the suddenness and extent of that eruption, two hams lost their lives while helping to monitor the volcano.

tional Morse code. By passing the 5 word-per-minute Morse code exam you will be allowed to operate on portions of four of the amateur high frequency (HF) bands. By passing more difficult written exams you can earn the General class and then the Amateur Extra class license. Right now, though, you are interested in getting started with Amateur Radio, and this book will prepare you to earn your first Amateur Radio license.

The Five Principles

In Section 97.1 of its Rules, the FCC describes the basis and purpose of the amateur service. It consists of five principles:

97.1(a) Recognition and enhancement of the value of the amateur service to the public as a voluntary non-commercial communication service, particularly with respect to providing emergency communications.

The best-known aspect of Amateur Radio may be our ability to provide life-saving emergency communications. Normal communications channels often break down during hurricanes, earthquakes, tornadoes, forest fires, airplane crashes and other disasters. Amateur Radio is frequently the first available means of contact with the outside world from the affected area. Red Cross and other civil-defense agencies rely heavily on the services of volunteer radio amateurs.

One of the more noteworthy aspects of Amateur Radio is its noncommercial nature. In fact, amateurs may not accept any form of payment for operating their radio stations. (There is one limited exception to this rule, which we will explain later.) This means that hams make their services available free of charge. This is true whether they are assisting a search-and-rescue operation in the Sierra Nevada, relaying Health-and-Welfare messages from a disaster-stricken Caribbean island or providing communications assistance at the New York City Marathon. Talk about value!

Why do hams work so hard if they can't be paid? It gives them an immense feeling of personal satisfaction! It's like the good feeling you get when you lend a hand to an elderly neighbor, only on a much grander scale. Hams operate their stations only for personal satisfaction and enjoyment. They don't talk about business matters on the air. (FCC rules don't allow business communications over Amateur Radio.)

97.1(b) Continuation and extension of the amateur's proven ability to contribute to the advancement of the radio art.

In the early days of radio there were no rules, but in 1912 Congress passed a law to regulate the airwaves. Amateurs had to keep to a small range of frequencies (known as "short waves"). There they would remain "out of the way" — everyone knew that radio waves couldn't travel very far at those frequencies. Ha! Amateurs soon

overcame the restrictions. They were among the first to experiment with radio propagation, the study of how radio waves travel through the atmosphere. When vacuum tubes became available, amateurs began to develop much-improved radio communication circuits.

Today, the traditions and spirit in Amateur Radio remain. Amateurs continue to experiment with state-of-the-art technologies. Advancement of the radio art takes a major portion of an amateur's energies. The FCC promotes this amateur experimentation and technical development by establishing rules that are consistent with amateur techniques.

97.1(c) Encouragement and improvement of the amateur service through rules which provide for advancing skills in both the communications and technical phases of the art.

Along with some of the technical aspects of the service, amateurs also hold special training exercises in preparation for communications emergencies. Simulated Emergency Tests and Field Days, where amateurs practice communicating under emergency conditions, are just two ways amateurs sharpen their operating skills.

97.1(d) Expansion of the existing reservoir within the amateur radio service of trained operators, technicians and electronics experts.

Self-training, station operating standards, intercommunication and technical investigation are all-important parts of the amateur service. We need more amateurs who are experienced in communications methods, because they are a national resource to the public.

97.1(e) Continuation and extension of the amateur's unique ability to enhance international goodwill.

People of all ages enjoy the thrill of communicating by Amateur Radio. This photo shows Iris, ZS2AA, age 93, and Elaine, ZR2ELF, age 12, two hams in South Africa.

Hams are unique, even in this time of worldwide jet travel. They journey to the far reaches of the earth and talk with amateurs in other countries every day. They do this simply by walking into their ham shacks. International peace and coexistence are very important today. Amateurs represent their countries as ambassadors of goodwill. Amateur-to-amateur communications often cross the cultural boundaries between societies. Amateur Radio is a teacher in Lincoln, Nebraska, trading stories with the headmaster of a boarding school in a London suburb. It is a tropical-fish hobbyist learning about fish in the Amazon from a missionary stationed in Brazil. Amateur Radio is a way to make friends with other people everywhere.

To summarize, the five principles on which the amateur service is based are to recognize the value of emergency communication skills, advance the radio art,

improve communication and technical skills, to increase the number of trained radio operators and electronics experts, and to improve international goodwill. These five principles provide the basis and purpose for the amateur service, as set down by the FCC. These principles place a large responsibility on the amateur community — a responsibility you will share. It is the Commission's duty to ensure that amateurs are able to operate their stations properly, without interfering with other radio services. All amateurs must pass an examination before the FCC will issue a license authorizing amateur station operation. It's a very serious matter.

While the FCC expects you to operate your station properly, the construction of your station is up to you. There are no FCC requirements for amateur station construction.

The Amateur Service

The FCC defines some important terms in Section 97.3 of the amateur rules. The **amateur service** is "A radiocommunication service for the purpose of self-training, intercommunication and technical investigations carried out by amateurs, that is, duly authorized persons interested in radio technique solely with a personal aim and without pecuniary interest." **Pecuniary** means related to money or other payment. In other words, you can't be paid for operating your station or providing a communications service for some individual or group. (There is one exception. A club station operator — such as at ARRL's W1AW — may be paid while the station transmits information bulletins of interest to Amateur Radio operators.) Pecuniary means more than money. You can't trade a communications service from your Amateur Radio station in return for other types of service or materials, either. Amateurs learn various communication skills on their own, and carry out technical experiments in electronics and radio principles.

An **amateur operator** is a person who has been granted a license in the amateur service. In the United States, the Federal Communications Commission issues these licenses. A US amateur license allows you to operate wherever the FCC regulates the amateur service. That includes the 50 states as well as any territories under US government control. An amateur operator performs communications in the amateur service.

How does the FCC define an **amateur station**? "A station licensed in the amateur service, including the apparatus necessary for carrying on radiocommunications." The person operating an amateur station has an interest in self-training, intercommunication and technical investigations or experiments.

An Amateur Radio license is really two licenses in one — an *operator license* and a *station license*. The operator license is one that lets you operate a station within your

authorized privileges on amateur-service frequencies. You must have an amateur license to operate a transmitter on amateur service frequencies. This license is your permission to control the transmissions of an amateur station.

The station license authorizes you to have an amateur station and its associated equipment. It also lists the call sign that identifies that station. The FCC calls this license an amateur **operator/primary station license**. One piece of paper includes both the operator and the station license. **Figure 1.2** shows an actual Amateur Radio license document.

The operator license portion lists your license class and gives you the authority to operate an amateur station. The station license portion includes the address of your

This gentleman brought his 10-GHz microwave station to the summit of Mount Monadnock in New Hampshire to take part in an ARRL-sponsored contest. Many hams enjoy operating away from the comforts of home.

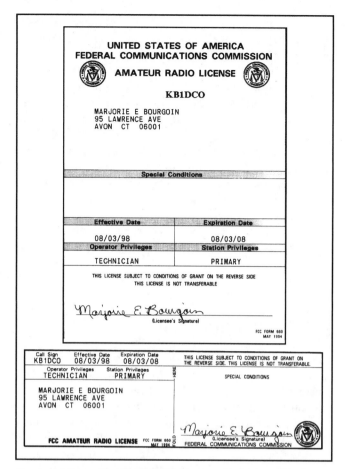

Figure 1.2 — An FCC Amateur Radio license is actually two licenses in one — the station license and the operator's license. The printed license document also comes in two parts. One part is suitable for framing and display in your station. The other can be folded in half and carried in your wallet.

primary, or main, Amateur Radio station. The station license also lists the call sign of your station. It is your written authorization for an amateur station.

Your Amateur Radio license is valid as soon as the FCC posts the information about your license in their electronic database. You don't have to wait for the actual license document to arrive in the mail before you begin to transmit. You can check the FCC database on one of the Internet license "servers" (or someone else can check it for you). There is a call sign lookup service on *ARRLWeb*: **www.arrl.org/fcc/fcclook.php3**. The processing time depends on how quickly the examiners return the paperwork to the Volunteer Examiner Coordinator, and the number of applications that VEC as well as the FCC have to process. Normally you should expect it to take one to two weeks to process the paperwork for your license application, although it can take longer.

It is a good idea to make a copy of your license and carry it in your wallet or purse after it arrives in the mail. You are using the *operator license* portion when you serve as the control operator of a station.

You should also post your original license, or a photocopy of it, in your station after it arrives in the mail. You will be proud of earning the license, so display it in your station. A copy of the license on the wall also makes your station look more "official."

Amateur licenses are printed on a laser printer, and issued in two parts (Figure 1.2). One part is small enough to carry with you; the other can be framed and displayed in your shack. This means you can carry your license *and* display it! Laser ink can smear or lift off the paper, so it's a good idea to laminate your wallet copy. If you put the large part behind glass in a frame the ink can lift off. Clear plastic Con-Tac® or similar material is inexpensive and available in most department stores.

If the small part is too large for your wallet, you can make a reduced-size copy on a photocopier. If you carry a copy, you can leave your original safely at home. Although you can legally carry a copy, your original license must be available for inspection by any US government official or FCC representative. Don't lose the original license!

The FCC issues all licenses for a 10-year term. You should always renew your license for another 10 years before it expires. About 60 to 90 days before the present one expires, you should apply for your license renewal. If your license is issued in September 2003, it expires in September 2013. It's a good idea to form the habit of looking at the expiration date on your license every now and then. You'll be less likely to forget to renew the license in time. Use an FCC Form 605 to apply for a license renewal. Always attach a photocopy of your current license. You can also ask one of the Volunteer Examiner Coordinators' offices to file your renewal application electronically if you don't want to mail the form to the FCC. You must still mail the form to the VEC, however. The ARRL/VEC Office will electronically file application forms for any ARRL member free of charge. You can also file for your license renewal using the FCC Universal Licensing System on the World Wide Web.

If you do forget to renew your license, you have up to two years to apply for a new license. After the two-year **grace period**, you will have to take the exam again. Your license is not valid during this two-year grace period, however. You may not operate an amateur station with an expired license. All the grace period means is that the FCC will renew the license if you apply during that time.

If your license is lost, mutilated or destroyed, request a new one from the FCC. A Form 605 isn't required; a letter will do. Be sure to explain why you are requesting a new license. (You don't have to explain that your dog ate your license — just that it was destroyed.)

The FCC has a set of detailed instructions for the Form 605, which are included with the form. To obtain a new Form 605, call the FCC Forms Distribution Center at 800-418-3676. You can also write to: Federal Communications Commission, Forms Distribution Center, 9300 E. Hampton Drive Capital Heights, MD 20743 (specify "Form 605" on the envelope). The Form 605 also is avail-

FCC 605
Main Form

Quick-Form Application for Authorization in the Ship, Aircraft, Amateur, Restricted and Commercial Operator, and General Mobile Radio Services

Approved by OMB
3060 - 0850
See instructions for public burden estimate

1) Radio Service Code: **HA**

Application Purpose (Select only one) (**MD**)

2) NE – New   RO – Renewal Only   WD – Withdrawal of Application
MD – Modification   RM – Renewal / Modification   DU – Duplicate License
AM – Amendment   CA – Cancellation of License   AU – Administrative Update

3) If this request if for Developmental License or STA (Special Temporary Authorization) enter the appropriate code and attach the required exhibit as described in the instructions. Otherwise enter 'N' (Not Applicable).   (**N**) D S N/A

4) If this request is for an Amendment or Withdrawal of Application, enter the file number of the pending application currently on file with the FCC.   File Number

5) If this request is for a Modification, Renewal Only, Renewal / Modification, Cancellation of License, Duplicate License, or Administrative Update, enter the call sign (serial number for Commercial Operator) of the existing FCC license. If this is a request for consolidation of DO & DM Operator Licenses, enter serial number of DO. Also, if filing for a ship exemption, you must provide call sign.   Call Sign/Serial #   **WR1B**

6) If this request is for a New, Amendment, Renewal Only, or Renewal Modification, enter the requested expiration date of the authorization (this item is optional).   MM   DD

7) Does this filing request a Waiver of the Commission's rules? If "Y", attach the required showing as described in the instructions.   (**N**) Yes No

8) Are attachments (other than associated schedules) being filed with this application?   (**N**) Yes No

Applicant/Licensee Information

9) FCC Registration Number (FRN): **0003-3573-99**

10) Applicant/Licensee legal entity type: (Select One)
☑ Individual ☐ Unincorporated Association ☐ Trust ☐ Government Entity
☐ Consortium ☐ Corporation ☐ Limited Liability Company
☐ Limited Partnership ☐ General Partnership ☐ Limited Liability Partnership
☐ Other (Description of Legal Entity)

11) First Name (if individual): **Larry**   MI: **D**   Last Name: **Wolfgang**   Suffix:

12) Entity Name (if other than individual):

13) If the licensee name is being updated, is the update a result from the sale (or transfer of control) of the license(s) to another party and for which proper Commission approval has not been received or proper notification not provided?   (**N**) Yes No

14) Attention To:

15) P.O. Box: And/Or   16) Street Address: **225 Main Street**

17) City: **Newington**   18) State: **CT**   19) Zip Code/Postal Code: **06111**   20) Country: **USA**

21) Telephone Number: **860-594-0200**   22) FAX Number:

23) E-Mail Address: **wr1b@arrl.net**

Ship Applicants/Licensees Only
24) Enter new name of vessel:

Aircraft Applicants/Licensees Only
25) Enter the new FAA Registration Number (the N-number):
NOTE: Do not enter the leading "N".

FCC 605 – Main Form
July 2005 - Page 1

Fee Status
26) Is the applicant/licensee exempt from FCC application Fees?   (**N**) Yes No
27) Is the applicant/licensee exempt from FCC regulatory Fees?   (**N**) Yes No

General Certification Statements

1) The applicant/licensee waives any claim to the use of any particular frequency or of the electromagnetic spectrum as against the regulatory power of the United States because of the previous use of the same, whether by license or otherwise, and requests an authorization in accordance with this application.

2) The applicant/licensee certifies that all statements made in this application and in the exhibits, attachments, or documents incorporated by reference are material, are part of this application, and are true, complete, correct, and made in good faith.

3) Neither the applicant/licensee nor any member thereof is a foreign government or a representative thereof.

4) The applicant/licensee certifies that neither the applicant/licensee nor any other party to the application is subject to a denial of Federal benefits pursuant to Section 5301 of the Anti-Drug Abuse Act of 1988, 21 U.S.C. § 862, because of a conviction for possession or distribution of a controlled substance. **This certification does not apply to applications filed in services exempted under Section 1.2002(c) of the rules, 47 CFR § 1.2002(c).** See Section 1.2002(b) of the rules, 47 CFR § 1.2002(b), for the definition of "party to the application" as used in this certification.

5) Amateur or GMRS applicant/licensee certifies that the construction of the station would NOT be an action which is likely to have a significant environmental effect (see the Commission's rules 47 CFR Sections 1.1301-1.1319 and Section 97.13(a) rules (available at web site http://wireless.fcc.gov/rules.html).

6) Amateur applicant/licensee certifies that they have READ and WILL COMPLY WITH Section 97.13(c) of the Commission's rules (available at web site http://wireless.fcc.gov/rules.html) regarding RADIOFREQUENCY (RF) RADIATION SAFETY and the amateur service section of OST/OET Bulletin Number 65 (available at web site http://www.fcc.gov/oet/info/documents/bulletins/).

Certification Statements For GMRS Applicants/Licensees

1) Applicant/Licensee certifies that he or she is claiming eligibility under Rule Section 95.5 of the Commission's rules.

2) Applicant/Licensee certifies that he or she is at least 18 years of age.

3) Applicant/Licensee certifies that he or she will comply with the requirement that use of frequencies 462.650, 467.650, 462.700 and 467.700 MHz is not permitted near the Canadian border North of Line A and East of Line C. These frequencies are used throughout Canada and harmful interference is anticipated.

4) Non-Individual applicants/licensees certify that they have NOT changed frequency or channel pairs, type of emission, antenna height, location of fixed transmitters, number of mobile units, area of mobile operation, or increase in power.

Certification Statements for Ship Applicants/Licensees (Including Ship Exemptions)

1) Applicant/Licensee certifies that they are the owner or operator of the vessel, a subsidiary communications corporation of the owner or operator of the vessel, a state or local government subdivision, or an agency of the US Government subject to Section 301 of the Communications Act.

2) This application is filed with the understanding that any action by the Commission thereon shall be limited to the voyage(s) described herein, and that apart from the provisions of the specific law from which the applicant/licensee requests an exemption, the vessel is in full compliance with all applicable statues, international agreements and regulations.

Signature
28) Typed or Printed Name of Party Authorized to Sign
First Name: **Larry**   MI: **D**   Last Name: **Wolfgang**   Suffix:
29) Title:
Signature: *Larry D Wolfgang*   30) Date: **7/14/05**

Failure to Sign This Application May Result In Dismissal Of The Application And Forfeiture Of Any Fees Paid

WILLFUL FALSE STATEMENTS MADE ON THIS FORM OR ANY ATTACHMENTS ARE PUNISHABLE BY FINE AND/OR IMPRISONMENT (U.S. Code, Title 18, Section 1001) AND / OR REVOCATION OF ANY STATION LICENSE OR CONSTRUCTION PERMIT (U.S. Code, Title 47, Section 312(a)(1)), AND / OR FORFEITURE (U.S. Code, Title 47, Section 503).

FCC 605 – Main Form
July 2005 - Page 2

Figure 1.3 — Portions of an FCC Form 605, showing the sections you would complete for a modification of your license, such as a change of address. Note that FCC Form 605 is not used as the application for a new license submitted to the Volunteer Examiners at an exam session. The National Conference of Volunteer Examiner Coordinators developed the NCVEC Quick Form 605 for use at exam sessions. That form collects additional information needed to process the exam results.

able from the FCC's fax on demand service. Call 202-418-0177 and ask for form number 000605. Form 605 also is available via the Internet. The World Wide Web location is: **www.fcc.gov/formpage.html** or you can receive the form via ftp to: **ftp.fcc.gov/pub/Forms/Form605**.

The ARRL/VEC has created a package that includes the portions of Form 605 that are needed for amateur applications, as well as a condensed set of instructions for completing the form. Write to: ARRL/VEC, Form 605, 225 Main Street, Newington, CT 06111-1494. (Please include a large business sized stamped, self-addressed envelope with your request.) **Figure 1.3** is a sample of those portions of an FCC Form 605 that you would complete to submit a change of address to the FCC.

Most of the form is simple to fill out. You will need to know that the Radio Service Code for box 1 is HA for Amateur Radio. (Just remember HAM radio.) You will have to include a "Taxpayer Identification Number" on the Form. This is normally your Social Security Number. If you don't want to write your Social Security Number on this form, then you can register with the ULS as described above. Then you will receive a ULS Registration Number from the FCC, and you can use that number instead of your Social Security Number on the Form. Of course, you will have to supply your Social Security Number to register with the ULS.

The telephone number, fax number and e-mail address information is optional. The FCC will use that information to contact you in case there is a problem with your application.

Page two includes six General Certification Statements.

Statement five may seem confusing. Basically, this statement means that you do not plan to install an antenna over 200 feet high, and that your permanent station location will not be in a designated wilderness area, wildlife preserve or nationally recognized scenic and recreational area.

The sixth statement indicates that you are familiar with the FCC RF Safety Rules, and that you will obey them. Chapter 10 includes detailed information about those rules.

[This is a good time to take a break from reading the text, and to turn to Chapter 11 and study the questions that cover this material in the Technician question pool. Before you turn to Chapter 11, though, it may be helpful to understand a bit about the numbering system used for these questions. The numbers match the study guide or syllabus printed at the end of the Introduction. The syllabus forms a type of outline, and the numbering system follows this outline format. There are ten subelements, labeled T1 through T0.

Each subelement is further divided into question groups. These groups represent the number of questions to be selected from each subelement. There are five questions on the exam from subelement T1, FCC Rules. So there are 5 question groups labeled T1A through T1E. Individual questions end with a two-digit number, such as T1A01, T1B08, T1E12 and so on.

Now you should study questions T1A01, T1A02 and T1A03. Also study question T1C01 and questions T1C03 through T1C06, T1C08 and T1C11. Review this section if you have difficulty with any of these questions.]

Amateur License Classes

Anyone earning a new Amateur Radio license can earn one of three license classes — Technician, General and Amateur Extra. These vary in degree of knowledge required and **frequency privileges** granted. (*Frequency privileges* refers to permission from the FCC to use a specific range of frequencies, based on your Amateur Radio license.) Higher-class licenses have more comprehensive examinations. In return for passing a more difficult exam you earn more frequency privileges.

The FCC refers to the various exams for Amateur Radio licenses as exam *Elements*. For example, exam Element 1 is the 5 word-per-minute (wpm) Morse code exam. Element 2 is the Technician written exam. **Table 1.1** lists the Amateur license classes you can earn, along with a brief description of the exam requirements and the operator privileges.

The table shows that you must pass exam Element 2 for the Technician license. The Element 2 written exam

covers basic FCC Rules and operating procedures, along with basic electronics theory. The purpose of Element 1 is to prove your ability to send and receive messages using the international Morse code at a speed of 5 words per minute.

Technician licensees also can pass an exam to demonstrate their knowledge in International Morse code at 5 wpm. With proof of passing the Morse code exam, a Technician licensee gains some frequency privileges on four of the amateur high frequency (HF) bands. This license was previously called the Technician Plus license, and many amateurs will refer to it by that name.

There are also several other amateur license classes, but the FCC is no longer issuing new licenses for these classes. The Novice license was long considered the beginner's license. Exams for this license were discontinued as of April 15, 2000. The FCC also stopped issuing new Advanced class licenses on that date. They will con-

Table 1-1

Amateur Operator Licenses†

Class	Code Test	Written Examination	Privileges
Technician		Basic theory and regulations. (Element 2)*	All amateur privileges above 50.0 MHz.
Technician With Morse Code Credit	5 wpm (Element 1)	Basic theory and regulations. (Element 2)*	All "Novice" HF privileges in addition to all Technician privileges.
General	5 wpm (Element 1)	Basic theory and regulations; General theory and regulations. (Elements 2 and 3)	All amateur privileges except those reserved for Advanced and Amateur Extra class; see Table 1-2.
Amateur Extra	5 wpm (Element 1)	All lower exam elements, plus Extra-class theory (Elements 2, 3 and 4)	All amateur privileges.

†A licensed radio amateur will be required to pass only those elements that are not included in the examination for the amateur license currently held.

*If you have a Technician-class license issued before March 21, 1987, you also have credit for Elements 1 and 3. You must be able to prove your Technician license was issued before March 21, 1987 to claim this credit.

tinue to renew previously issued licenses, however, so you will probably meet some Novice and Advanced class licensees on the air.

The first step on the Amateur Radio license ladder is a Technician license. The FCC issues these "beginner's" licenses to those who demonstrate the ability to operate an Amateur Radio transmitter safely and properly.

The written Technician exam covers some very basic radio fundamentals and knowledge of some of the rules and regulations in Part 97. With this book and a little study you'll soon be ready to pass the Technician exam.

Each step up the Amateur Radio license ladder requires the applicant to pass the lower exams. So if you want to start out as a General class or even an Amateur Extra class licensee, you must also pass the Technician written exam.

Anyone (except an agent or representative of a foreign government) is eligible to qualify for an Amateur Radio operator license. There is no age requirement. To hold an Amateur Radio station license, you must have a valid operator license. (Remember, both licenses are printed on the same piece of paper.)

A Technician license gives you the freedom to develop operating and technical skills through on-the-air experience. These skills will help you upgrade to a higher class of license, with additional privileges.

As a Technician, you can use a wide range of frequency bands — all amateur bands above 50 MHz, in fact. You'll use repeaters, packet radio and orbiting satellites to relay your signals over a wider area. You can provide public service through emergency communications and message handling.

By passing the 5-wpm Morse code test you will have a *Technician license with Morse code credit*. With this license you will gain "Novice" privileges below 30 MHz. When you pass the Morse code exam you will gain fre-

quency privileges on four of the high frequency (HF) bands. On those bands you can communicate directly with other amateur stations in the exotic reaches of the world. You can enhance international goodwill by making friends with amateurs around the world. When you pass the Morse code exam you will receive a Certificate of Successful Completion of Examination (CSCE) from the Volunteer Examiners (VE) who conduct the exam session. The CSCE proves that you passed the Morse code exam, and allows you to operate on the four HF Novice subbands that normally provide direct worldwide communication.

There are no FCC Rules that limit the distance over which you can communicate by Amateur Radio. The world is literally at your fingertips! The VHF and UHF bands available to a Technician licensee are often considered to be local communications bands, but there are ways to communicate over great distances on these bands. The HF bands are normally considered to be long-distance bands. Each band has its own characteristics, and you can have a lot of fun learning about the practical communications distances of each band.

As you gain operating experience, you will probably want to earn greater operating privileges. You will prepare for a higher-class license exam — the gateway to more frequencies and modes. Don't get the idea that a Technician license is so limited that you can't enjoy the full range of amateur activities, though. You will be allowed to use all of the major operating modes on the VHF and UHF bands. You can even send messages for your unlicensed friends (called **third-party communications**) or allow them to talk over your radio (more on this later). As you upgrade, however, you will gain access to more operating frequencies, and you will even be able to help prepare and administer Amateur Radio license exams!

There is a real thrill to having more frequencies avail-

Table 1.2

Technician Amateur Bands By Range and Wavelength

VHF Wavelength	UHF	SHF	EHF
6 meters	70 centimeters	9 centimeters	6 millimeters
2 meters	33 centimeters	5 centimeters	4 millimeters
1¼ meters	23 centimeters	3 centimeters	2.5 millimeters
	13 centimeters	1.2 centimeters	2 millimeters
			1 millimeter

able to talk with other amateurs on the far side of the globe. That is a powerful incentive to upgrade to the General class license. You will have to pass a 5-wpm Morse code exam and another 35-question theory and rules exam to earn the General class license. The General class license gives voice privileges on nine high-frequency (HF) bands and one medium frequency (MF) band. These bands typically carry signals over great distances. In addition there is one HF band exclusively for Morse code, radioteletype and other "digital" (computer) modes. For this reason, the General class license is very popular.

As you progress and mature in Amateur Radio, you will develop specialized interests in such exciting modes as amateur television and satellite communication. You'll also want even more privileges, and that is where the Amateur Extra license comes in. To obtain one of these, you must pass a 50-question exam on the more technical aspects of the hobby.

To qualify for a higher-class license, you must pass the theory exam for each level up to that point. For example, suppose you want to go from Technician directly to Amateur Extra. You will have to pass the General theory exam as well as the Amateur Extra test. You will also have to pass the 5-wpm code test. In fact, you could take the Technician through Extra exams all at the same exam session.

With Technician license in hand, you'll be able to operate on all the very high frequency (VHF), ultra high frequency (UHF), super high frequency (SHF) and extra high frequency (EHF) bands allocated to the amateur service — and there are a lot of them! (The SHF and EHF bands are often called microwave bands.) **Table 1.2** lists the approximate **wavelength** for the Technician bands. Wavelength refers to the distance the radio wave will travel during one complete cycle of the wave. You will learn more about this definition in Chapter 2. You will learn the specific frequency limits of the Technician bands later in this chapter. For a complete list of all the amateur bands, see *The ARRL's FCC Rule Book*.

The Technician Exam

The Technician class exam consists of a 35-question written test, Element 2. Chapter 11 of this book contains every question in the question pool from which your exam will be composed. If you study this book carefully, you will easily pass the Technician class exam. If you wish to qualify for the Technician license with Morse code credit, you'll also have to pass Element 1; the 5-wpm Morse code exam. In that case you'll need a computer program, cassette tapes or audio CDs that teach international Morse code. The ARRL offers a set of two cassettes or audio CDs called *Your Introduction to Morse Code*. The ARRL also offers the *Ham University* program for IBM-PC and compatible computers.

A Question Pool Committee selected by the **Volunteer Examiner Coordinators (VECs)** maintains the question pools for all amateur exams. A VEC is an organization that has made an agreement with the FCC to coordinate Amateur Radio license examinations by using **Volunteer**

Examiners (VEs). A VE is a licensed Amateur Radio operator who volunteers to help give amateur license exams. The VECs must certify that their Volunteer Examiners meet FCC requirements, and that all test sessions are conducted to FCC standards. The FCC allows VEs to select the questions for an amateur exam, but they must use the questions exactly as the VEC Question Pool Committee releases them. If you attend a test session coordinated by the ARRL/VEC, your test most likely will be designed by the ARRL/VEC, or by a computer program designed by the ARRL/VEC. The questions and answers will be exactly as they are printed in Chapter 11.

Finding an Exam Opportunity

To determine where and when an exam will be given, contact the ARRL/VEC Office, or watch for announcements in the Hamfest Calendar and Coming Conventions columns in *QST*. Many local clubs sponsor exams, so they

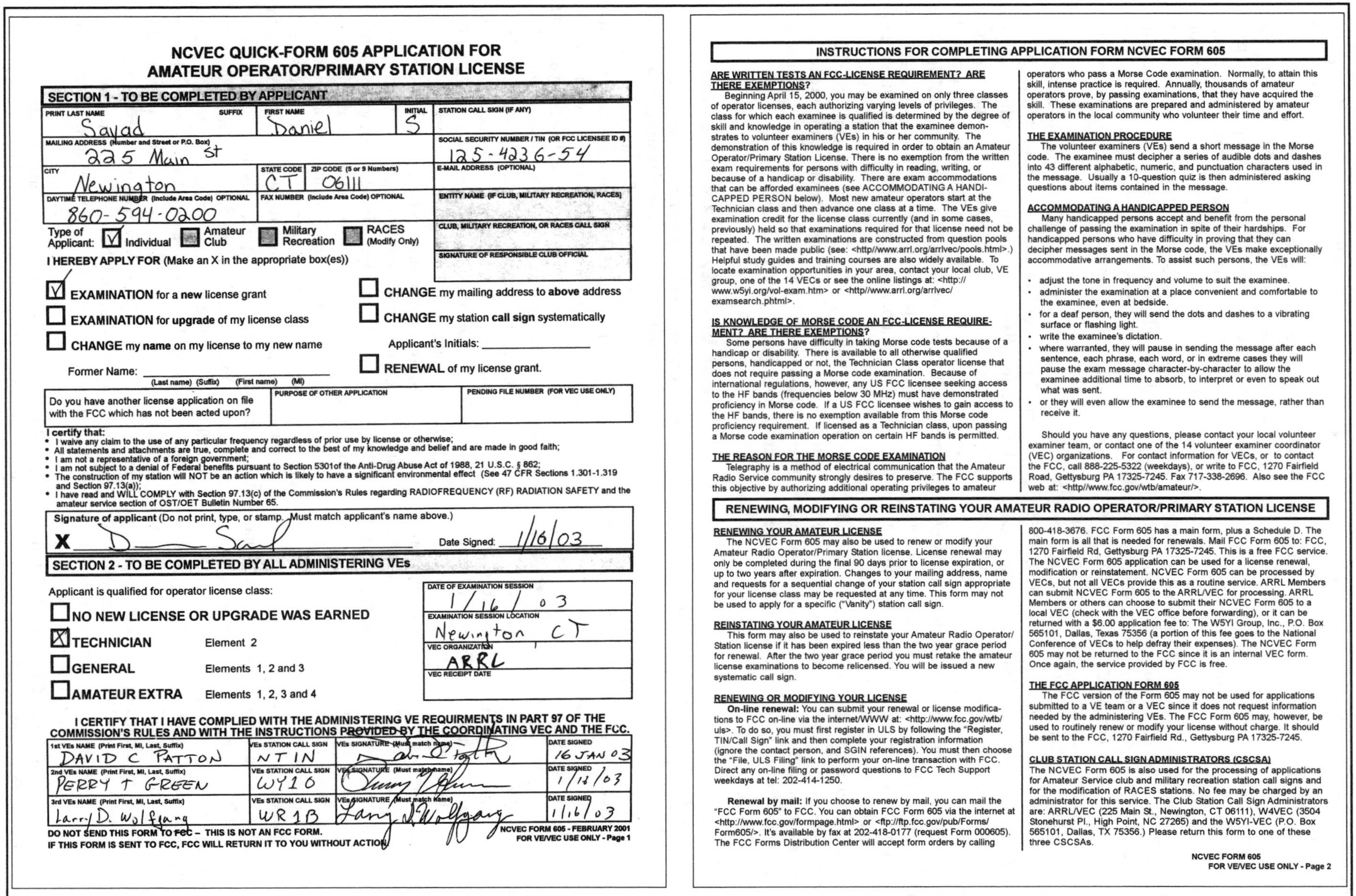

NCVEC QUICK-FORM 605 APPLICATION FOR AMATEUR OPERATOR/PRIMARY STATION LICENSE

SECTION 1 - TO BE COMPLETED BY APPLICANT

PRINT LAST NAME	SUFFIX	FIRST NAME	INITIAL	STATION CALL SIGN (IF ANY)
Sayad		Daniel	S	

MAILING ADDRESS (Number and Street or P.O. Box)			SOCIAL SECURITY NUMBER / TIN (OR FCC LICENSEE ID #)
225 Main St			125-4236-54
CITY	STATE CODE	ZIP CODE (5 or 9 Numbers)	E-MAIL ADDRESS (OPTIONAL)
Newington	CT	06111	
DAYTIME TELEPHONE NUMBER (Include Area Code) OPTIONAL	FAX NUMBER (Include Area Code) OPTIONAL		ENTITY NAME (IF CLUB, MILITARY RECREATION, RACES)
860-594-0200			

Type of Applicant: [X] Individual [ ] Amateur Club [ ] Military Recreation [ ] RACES (Modify Only)

CLUB, MILITARY RECREATION, OR RACES CALL SIGN

SIGNATURE OF RESPONSIBLE CLUB OFFICIAL

I HEREBY APPLY FOR (Make an X in the appropriate box(es))

- [X] **EXAMINATION** for a **new** license grant
- [ ] **EXAMINATION** for **upgrade** of my license class
- [ ] **CHANGE** my **name** on my license to my new name

Former Name: ____________ (Last name) (Suffix) (First name) (MI)

- [ ] **CHANGE** my mailing address to **above** address
- [ ] **CHANGE** my station **call sign** systematically

Applicant's Initials: ____________

- [ ] **RENEWAL** of my license grant.

Do you have another license application on file with the FCC which has not been acted upon?	PURPOSE OF OTHER APPLICATION	PENDING FILE NUMBER (FOR VEC USE ONLY)

I certify that:

- I waive any claim to the use of any particular frequency regardless of prior use by license or otherwise;
- All statements and attachments are true, complete and correct to the best of my knowledge and belief and are made in good faith;
- I am not a representative of a foreign government;
- I am not subject to a denial of Federal benefits pursuant to Section 5301of the Anti-Drug Abuse Act of 1988, 21 U.S.C. § 862;
- The construction of my station will NOT be an action which is likely to have a significant environmental effect (See 47 CFR Sections 1.301-1.319 and Section 97.13(a));
- I have read and WILL COMPLY with Section 97.13(c) of the Commission's Rules regarding RADIOFREQUENCY (RF) RADIATION SAFETY and the amateur service section of OST/OET Bulletin Number 65.

Signature of applicant (Do not print, type, or stamp. Must match applicant's name above.)

X D Sayad Date Signed: 1/16/03

SECTION 2 - TO BE COMPLETED BY ALL ADMINISTERING VEs

Applicant is qualified for operator license class:

- [ ] NO NEW LICENSE OR UPGRADE WAS EARNED
- [X] TECHNICIAN Element 2
- [ ] GENERAL Elements 1, 2 and 3
- [ ] AMATEUR EXTRA Elements 1, 2, 3 and 4

DATE OF EXAMINATION SESSION
1/16/03
EXAMINATION SESSION LOCATION
Newington, CT
VEC ORGANIZATION
ARRL
VEC RECEIPT DATE

I CERTIFY THAT I HAVE COMPLIED WITH THE ADMINISTERING VE REQUIRMENTS IN PART 97 OF THE COMMISSION'S RULES AND WITH THE INSTRUCTIONS PROVIDED BY THE COORDINATING VEC AND THE FCC.

VEs NAME (Print First, MI, Last, Suffix)	VEs STATION CALL SIGN	VEs SIGNATURE (Must match name)	DATE SIGNED
1st: DAVID C PATTON	NT1N	David C Patton	16 JAN 03
2nd: PERRY T GREEN	WY1O	Perry T Green	1/16/03
3rd: Larry D. Wolfgang	WR1B	Larry D Wolfgang	1/16/03

DO NOT SEND THIS FORM TO FCC – THIS IS NOT AN FCC FORM.
IF THIS FORM IS SENT TO FCC, FCC WILL RETURN IT TO YOU WITHOUT ACTION.

NCVEC FORM 605 - FEBRUARY 2001
FOR VE/VEC USE ONLY - Page 1

INSTRUCTIONS FOR COMPLETING APPLICATION FORM NCVEC FORM 605

ARE WRITTEN TESTS AN FCC-LICENSE REQUIREMENT? ARE THERE EXEMPTIONS?

Beginning April 15, 2000, you may be examined on only three classes of operator licenses, each authorizing varying levels of privileges. The class for which each examinee is qualified is determined by the degree of skill and knowledge in operating a station that the examinee demonstrates to volunteer examiners (VEs) in his or her community. The demonstration of this knowledge is required in order to obtain an Amateur Operator/Primary Station License. There is no exemption from the written exam requirements for persons with difficulty in reading, writing, or because of a handicap or disability. There are exam accommodations that can be afforded examinees (see ACCOMMODATING A HANDICAPPED PERSON below). Most new amateur operators start at the Technician class and then advance one class at a time. The VEs give examination credit for the license class currently (and in some cases, previously) held so that examinations required for that license need not be repeated. The written examinations are constructed from question pools that have been made public (see: <http//www.arrl.org/arrlvec/pools.html>.) Helpful study guides and training courses are also widely available. To locate examination opportunities in your area, contact your local club, VE group, one of the 14 VECs or see the online listings at: <http://www.w5yi.org/vol-exam.htm> or <http//www.arrl.org/arrlvec/examsearch.phtml>.

IS KNOWLEDGE OF MORSE CODE AN FCC-LICENSE REQUIREMENT? ARE THERE EXEMPTIONS?

Some persons have difficulty in taking Morse code tests because of a handicap or disability. There is available to all otherwise qualified persons, handicapped or not, the Technician Class operator license that does not require passing a Morse code examination. Because of international regulations, however, any US FCC licensee seeking access to the HF bands (frequencies below 30 MHz) must have demonstrated proficiency in Morse code. If a US FCC licensee wishes to gain access to the HF bands, there is no exemption available from this Morse code proficiency requirement. If licensed as a Technician class, upon passing a Morse code examination operation on certain HF bands is permitted.

THE REASON FOR THE MORSE CODE EXAMINATION

Telegraphy is a method of electrical communication that the Amateur Radio Service community strongly desires to preserve. The FCC supports this objective by authorizing additional operating privileges to amateur operators who pass a Morse Code examination. Normally, to attain this skill, intense practice is required. Annually, thousands of amateur operators prove, by passing examinations, that they have acquired the skill. These examinations are prepared and administered by amateur operators in the local community who volunteer their time and effort.

THE EXAMINATION PROCEDURE

The volunteer examiners (VEs) send a short message in the Morse code. The examinee must decipher a series of audible dots and dashes into 43 different alphabetic, numeric, and punctuation characters used in the message. Usually a 10-question quiz is then administered asking questions about items contained in the message.

ACCOMMODATING A HANDICAPPED PERSON

Many handicapped persons accept and benefit from the personal challenge of passing the examination in spite of their hardships. For handicapped persons who have difficulty in proving that they can decipher messages sent in the Morse code, the VEs make exceptionally accommodative arrangements. To assist such persons, the VEs will:

- adjust the tone in frequency and volume to suit the examinee.
- administer the examination at a place convenient and comfortable to the examinee, even at bedside.
- for a deaf person, they will send the dots and dashes to a vibrating surface or flashing light.
- write the examinee's dictation.
- where warranted, they will pause in sending the message after each sentence, each phrase, each word, or in extreme cases they will pause the exam message character-by-character to allow the examinee additional time to absorb, to interpret or even to speak out what was sent.
- or they will even allow the examinee to send the message, rather than receive it.

Should you have any questions, please contact your local volunteer examiner team, or contact one of the 14 volunteer examiner coordinator (VEC) organizations. For contact information for VECs, or to contact the FCC, call 888-225-5322 (weekdays), or write to FCC, 1270 Fairfield Road, Gettysburg PA 17325-7245. Fax 717-338-2696. Also see the FCC web at: <http//www.fcc.gov/wtb/amateur/>.

RENEWING, MODIFYING OR REINSTATING YOUR AMATEUR RADIO OPERATOR/PRIMARY STATION LICENSE

RENEWING YOUR AMATEUR LICENSE

The NCVEC Form 605 may also be used to renew or modify your Amateur Radio Operator/Primary Station license. License renewal may only be completed during the final 90 days prior to license expiration, or up to two years after expiration. Changes to your mailing address, name and requests for a sequential change of your station call sign appropriate for your license class may be requested at any time. This form may not be used to apply for a specific ("Vanity") station call sign.

REINSTATING YOUR AMATEUR LICENSE

This form may also be used to reinstate your Amateur Radio Operator/Station license if it has been expired less than the two year grace period for renewal. After the two year grace period you must retake the amateur license examinations to become relicensed. You will be issued a new systematic call sign.

RENEWING OR MODIFYING YOUR LICENSE

On-line renewal: You can submit your renewal or license modifications to FCC on-line via the internet/WWW at: <http://www.fcc.gov/wtb/uls>. To do so, you must first register in ULS by following the "Register, TIN/Call Sign" link and then complete your registration information (ignore the contact person, and SGIN references). You must then choose the "File, ULS Filing" link to perform your on-line transaction with FCC. Direct any on-line filing or password questions to FCC Tech Support weekdays at tel: 202-414-1250.

Renewal by mail: If you choose to renew by mail, you can mail the "FCC Form 605" to FCC. You can obtain FCC Form 605 via the internet at <http://www.fcc.gov/formpage.html> or <ftp://ftp.fcc.gov/pub/Forms/Form605/>. It's available by fax at 202-418-0177 (request Form 000605). The FCC Forms Distribution Center will accept form orders by calling 800-418-3676. FCC Form 605 has a main form, plus a Schedule D. The main form is all that is needed for renewals. Mail FCC Form 605 to: FCC, 1270 Fairfield Rd, Gettysburg PA 17325-7245. This is a free FCC service. The NCVEC Form 605 application can be used for a license renewal, modification or reinstatement. NCVEC Form 605 can be processed by VECs, but not all VECs provide this as a routine service. ARRL Members can submit NCVEC Form 605 to the ARRL/VEC for processing. ARRL Members or others can choose to submit their NCVEC Form 605 to a local VEC (check with the VEC office before forwarding), or it can be returned with a $6.00 application fee to: The W5YI Group, Inc., P.O. Box 565101, Dallas, Texas 75356 (a portion of this fee goes to the National Conference of VECs to help defray their expenses). The NCVEC Form 605 may not be returned to the FCC since it is an internal VEC form. Once again, the service provided by FCC is free.

THE FCC APPLICATION FORM 605

The FCC version of the Form 605 may not be used for applications submitted to a VE team or a VEC since it does not request information needed by the administering VEs. The FCC Form 605 may, however, be used to routinely renew or modify your license without charge. It should be sent to the FCC, 1270 Fairfield Rd., Gettysburg PA 17325-7245.

CLUB STATION CALL SIGN ADMINISTRATORS (CSCSA)

The NCVEC Form 605 is also used for the processing of applications for Amateur Service club and military recreation station call signs and for the modification of RACES stations. No fee may be charged by an administrator for this service. The Club Station Call Sign Administrators are: ARRL/VEC (225 Main St., Newington, CT 06111), W4VEC (3504 Stonehurst Pl., High Point, NC 27265) and the W5YI-VEC (P.O. Box 565101, Dallas, TX 75356.) Please return this form to one of these three CSCSAs.

NCVEC FORM 605
FOR VE/VEC USE ONLY - Page 2

Figure 1.4 — The left side shows a completed NCVEC Quick Form 605, as used by Volunteer Examiner Coordinators for candidates at exam sessions. Note that the NCVEC Quick Form 605 should not be submitted to the FCC for license renewals or modifications. It can be submitted to VECs for electronic filing with the FCC, though. The right side shows the instructions on the back of the form.

nities. ARRL officials such as Directors, Vice Directors and Section Managers receive notices about test sessions in their area. See pages 15 and 16 in the latest issue of *QST* for names and addresses.

All Amateur Radio exams are given by VEs who operate under the guidance of one of the VEC organizations. If you have any trouble locating examiners, go to the Exam Search section of *ARRLWeb*: **www.arrl.org/arrlvec/examsearch.phtml**. If you do not have Internet access, write to: ARRL/VEC Office, ARRL Headquarters, 225 Main Street, Newington, CT 06111-1494. We will refer you to someone near you who can arrange your test. We will also supply a list of ARRL/VEC Volunteer Exam sessions in your area. The ARRL/VEC oversees the thousands of ARRL Volunteer Examiners, arranges and publishes exam schedules and inspects application forms before they are submitted to the FCC.

To register for an exam, send a completed NCVEC Quick Form 605 to the VE Team responsible for the exam session if preregistration is required. Otherwise, bring the form to the session. The Volunteer Examiner Team will have copies of this form available at the test session, and some Teams prefer to have you complete the form at the session. Registration deadlines, and the time and location of the exams, are mentioned prominently in publicity releases about upcoming sessions.

Filling Out Your NCVEC Quick Form 605

What's next? A bit of paperwork! All applications for new amateur licenses are made on an NCVEC Quick Form 605. See the information earlier in this chapter for detailed information about getting a copy of this Form. **Figure 1.4A** shows an NCVEC Quick Form 605 completed for a successful Technician applicant.

You should complete the top half of the form, Section 1, as shown. You must supply a "Taxpayer Identification Number" or TIN, which is usually your Social Security Number. Some people may be uncomfortable listing their Social Security Number on a form that others may read. There is a way around this problem. You can register with the FCC's Universal License System and obtain a registration number from the FCC. In that case, you can list your registration number rather than your Social Security number on the Form 605.

Telephone and fax numbers, as well as an e-mail address are optional items. This information is helpful in case there are any questions about your application.

Check the box next to "EXAMINATION for **new** license grant" if you don't already have a license. If you already have a license and are taking an exam to upgrade your license, then check that box. Do *not* use the NCVEC Quick Form 605 to submit change of address information or a license renewal application to the FCC. If you have another Form 605 waiting for the FCC to process it, then list the information on this form.

Just before your signature there is a list of six general certification statements. When you sign and date your Form 605, you are stating that those statements are true.

The fifth statement may seem a little confusing. Basically, this statement means that you do not plan to install an antenna over 200 feet high, and that your permanent station location will not be in a designated wilderness area, wildlife preserve or nationally recognized scenic and recreational area.

The sixth statement indicates that you are familiar with the FCC RF Safety Rules, and that you will obey them. Chapter 10 includes detailed information about those rules.

Be sure to sign and date your application.

Your Volunteer Examiners will fill out Section 2, the Administering VE's report, on the bottom half of the Form 605. That is where the examiners certify that you have passed the exam. They will check the appropriate box and fill out the information about the exam session. The three Volunteer Examiners will print their names, call signs and the date of the exam, and sign the form on the lines at the bottom.

The back of the NCVEC Quick Form 605 includes instructions and information about exam procedures. There is also information about how to modify or renew your license. See Figure 1.4B.

What Will My Exam Be Like?

Three amateurs with General class licenses or higher, who are accredited by a **Volunteer Examiner Coordinator (VEC)** can give the test for a Technician license. A VEC is an organization that has an agreement with the FCC to coordinate the work of volunteers who give license exams. The examiners must be at least 18 years old and must not be relatives of anyone taking the exam. The exams can be given at the convenience of the candidates and the examiners, at any location they agree to. (All rules of the VEC program must be followed.) *The ARRL's FCC Rule Book* contains details on the VE program.

A **Volunteer Examiner (VE)** is someone who volunteers to test others for amateur licenses. There is probably an active Volunteer Examining Team somewhere in your area. These teams conduct tests for all classes of Amateur Radio licenses. The Volunteer Examiners give Technician exams at all of their regular exam sessions.

By the time examination day rolls around, you should have already prepared yourself. This means getting your schedule, supplies and mental attitude ready. Plan your schedule so you'll get to the examination site with plenty of time to spare. There's no harm in being early. In fact, you might have time to discuss hamming with another applicant, which is a great way to calm pretest nerves. Try not to discuss the material that will be on the examination as this may make you even more nervous. By this time, it's too late to study anyway!

What supplies will you need? First, be sure you bring your current *original* Amateur Radio license, if you have one. Also bring the *original* Certificate of Successful Completion of Examination (CSCE) if you have one of those for some of the exam elements. Also be sure to bring a photocopy of your license and CSCE. Bring along several sharpened number 2 pencils and two pens (blue or black ink). Be sure to have a good eraser. A pocket calculator may also come in handy. You may use a programmable calculator if that is the kind you have, but take it into your exam "empty" (cleared of all programs and constants in memory). Don't program equations ahead of time because you may be asked to demonstrate that there is nothing in the calculator's memory.

The VE Team is required to check two forms of identification before you enter the test room. This includes your *original* Amateur Radio license (if you have one). A photo ID of some type is best for the second form, but is not required by FCC. Other acceptable forms of ID include a driver's license, a piece of mail addressed to you, a birth certificate or some other such document.

The following description of the testing procedure applies to exams coordinated by the ARRL/VEC, although many other VECs use a similar procedure.

Code Tests

If you are planning to take the Morse code exam and gaining the additional privileges granted to Technicians who have passed a 5-wpm code test, this information will be of special interest to you. Even if you don't plan to take the Morse code exam right away, this section will help you understand the testing procedures.

The code test is normally given first. The examiners will send a bit more than five minutes of 5-word-per-minute code, and then test your copy. (The FCC requires that the text of the message be at least 5 minutes long.) The test usually takes one of two forms. The examiners may ask you 10 questions based on the contents of the transmission, and you must answer 7 of the 10 questions correctly. These questions will have a fill-in-the-blank format. The examiners may check your answer sheet for one minute of perfect ("solid") copy. For purposes of timing Morse code messages, a "word" means 5 letters. At 5 wpm, the requirement is for 25 characters in a row with no errors. If you don't plan to take the code exam, you will be asked to sit quietly while the other candidates take the test.

Before you take the code test, you'll be handed a piece of paper to copy the code as it's sent. The test will begin with about a minute of practice copy. Then comes the actual test. You are responsible for knowing the 26 letters of the alphabet, the numerals 0 through 9, the period, comma, question mark, as well as some procedural signals: $\overline{AR}$, $\overline{SK}$, $\overline{BT}$ (or double dash =) and $\overline{DN}$ (fraction bar /). You may copy the entire text word for word, or just take notes on the content. At the end of the transmission, the examiner will hand you 10 questions about the text. Simply fill in the blanks with your answers. (You must spell each answer exactly as it was sent.) If you get at least 7 correct, you pass! Alternatively, the exam team has the option to look at your copy sheet. If you have one minute of solid copy, they can certify that you passed the test on that basis. The format of the test transmission is similar to one side of a normal on-the-air amateur conversation.

A sending test may not be required. The Commission has decided that if applicants can demonstrate receiving ability, they most likely can also send at that speed. But be prepared for a sending test, just in case! Subpart 97.503(a) of the FCC Rules says, "A telegraphy examination must be sufficient to prove that the examinee has the ability to send correctly by hand and to receive correctly by ear texts in the international Morse code at not less than the prescribed speed ...". So the Element 1 exam is a test of your Morse code comprehension at 5 words-per-minute.

The volunteer examiners can use a variety of methods to accommodate an applicant with a physical disability. For example, they could use a vibrating surface or a flashing light to give the Morse code exam.

When you pass the Morse code exam, you will be issued a Certificate of Successful Completion of Examination (CSCE) for Element 1. Make sure you keep this paper in a safe place. Along with your actual Technician license, it serves as authorization to operate on the HF "Novice" bands. That proof is good for as long as you hold your Technician class license.

You can also use your CSCE as proof that you passed the Morse code exam for credit to complete an upgrade to a General class license. That credit is only valid for 365 days from the date on the form. After that you will have to pass the code exam again to upgrade to General. That should be some incentive to study for your General class written exam right away!

There are several documents that you can present to the examiners to receive credit for the Element 1 Morse code exam. If you ever held a Novice license, show the original license and give a photocopy to the examiners. You can also show a page from an old edition of *The Radio Amateur's Callbook* or another call sign listing to prove that you held that license. A Technician license issued before February 14, 1991 will also give you credit for having passed the Element 1 exam. This is a good reason to save your old license documents after they expire. You may want it to prove that you passed an exam some time in the future. Finally, if you have a current commercial radiotelegraph license or permit (or if it is expired less than 5 years) you can also present that document to receive credit for the Morse code exam. In any of these cases, bring the original to show, and a photocopy to give to the examiners to submit with your application.

Written Tests

The written test consists of 35 questions on basic operating practices, rules and regulations, and basic radio theory. To pass, you must correctly answer 26 of the 35 questions on your exam. There are ten subelements, or divisions, for the Technician exam. The Technician Syllabus printed in Table 1 at the end of the Introduction chapter lists the ten subelements and the topics covered by each one.

Your exam must include 35 questions taken from the pool of questions as released by the Volunteer Examiner Coordinators' Question Pool Committee, and printed in Chapter 11 of this book. Your examiners should choose one question from each of the 35 question-pool subsections. The questions and answers must be used exactly as they are printed in Chapter 11, although the order of the answer positions A, B, C and D may be scrambled.

The examiner will give each applicant a test booklet, an answer sheet and scratch paper. After that, you're on your own. The first thing to do is read the instructions. Be sure to sign your name every place it's called for. Do all of this at the beginning to get it out of the way.

Next, check the examination to see that all pages and questions are there. If not, report this to the examiner immediately. When filling in your answer sheet, make sure your answers are marked next to the numbers that correspond to each question.

Go through the entire exam, and answer the easy questions first. Next, go back to the beginning and try the harder questions. The really tough questions should be left for last. Guessing can only help, as there is no additional penalty for answering incorrectly.

If you have to guess, do it intelligently: At first glance, you may find that you can eliminate one or more "distracters." Of the remaining responses, more than one may seem correct; only one is the best answer, however. To the applicant who is fully prepared, incorrect distracters to each question are obvious. Nothing beats preparation!

After you've finished, check the examination thoroughly. You may have read a question wrong or goofed in your arithmetic. Don't be overconfident. There's no rush, so take your time. Think, and check your answer sheet. When you feel you've done your best and can do no more, return the test booklet, answer sheet and scratch pad to the examiner.

The Volunteer-Examiner Team will grade the exam while you wait. The passing mark is 74%. (That means no more than 9 incorrect answers on the Element 2 exam.) You will receive a Certificate of Successful Completion of Examination (CSCE) showing all exam elements that you pass. If you are already licensed, and you pass the exam elements required to earn a higher class of license, the CSCE authorizes you to operate with your new privileges. When you use these new privileges, you must sign your call sign, followed by the slant mark ("/"; on voice, say "stroke" or "slant") and a special designator. For Technicians upgrading to General, this designator is "AG." There is one exception to this rule: If you have a Technician license and then pass the 5-wpm code test, you do not have to use an indicator when you use your new privileges.

If you pass only some of the exam elements required for a license, you will still receive a CSCE. That certificate shows what exam elements you passed, and is valid for 365 days. Use it as proof that you passed those exam elements so you won't have to take them over again next time you try for the license.

[This is a good time to take a break your studies in this chapter. Turn to Chapter 11 and study questions T1C02 and T1C10. Also study questions T1D01 through T1D11. Review this section if you have difficulty answering any of those questions.]

Frequency Privileges

You learned earlier in this chapter that the Federal Communications Commission sets the specific radio regulations for the United States. The International Telecommunication Union (ITU) coordinates the regulations around the world. The ITU is an agency of the United Nations. The ITU divides the world into three regions, as shown in **Figure 1.5**. ITU Region 1 comprises Africa, Europe, Russia and parts of the Middle East. ITU Region 2 comprises North and South America as well as the Caribbean Islands and Hawaii. Alaska is in ITU Region 2. ITU Region 3 comprises Australia, China, India and parts of the Middle East. Region 3 also includes many islands in the Pacific Ocean, such as American Samoa, the Northern Mariana Islands, Guam and Wake Island.

Amateur Radio operators have different frequency privileges for many of the bands, depending on the ITU Region in which they are operating. US amateurs will

Table 1.3

VHF and UHF Technician Amateur Bands
ITU Region 2

Band (Wavelength)	Frequency Limits
VHF Range	
6 meters	50 - 54 MHz
2 meters	144 - 148 MHz
1.25 meters	219 - 220 MHz
1.25 meters	222 - 225 MHz
UHF Range	
70 centimeters	420 - 450 MHz
33 centimeters	902 - 928 MHz
23 centimeters	1240 - 1300 MHz
13 centimeters	2300 - 2310 MHz
13 centimeters	2390 - 2450 MHz

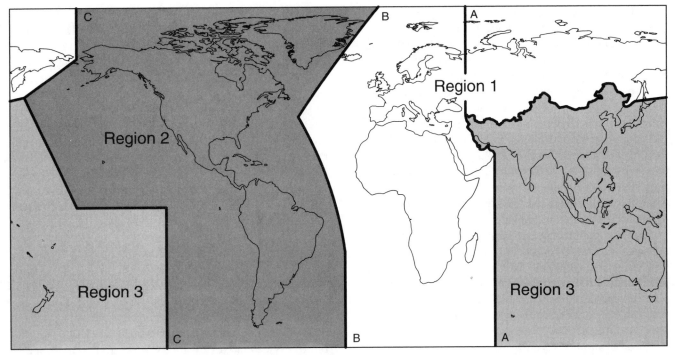

Figure 1.5 — This map shows the world divided into three International Telecommunication (ITU) Regions.

normally be using the privileges for ITU Region 2. There are certain times when they will have to follow the privileges for one of the other regions, though. For example, if you are operating from your sailboat and cross into Region 1 or Region 3, then you will have to follow the privileges for the appropriate region.

Table 1.3 shows the VHF and UHF Technician bands, with their frequency limits. For a complete list of the frequencies of all the amateur bands, see *The ARRL's FCC Rule Book*. You should study the list of bands and frequencies in Table 1.3 so you will know your frequency privileges on those bands.

Frequency Sharing

If we are to make the best use of the limited amount of available spectrum, there must be ways to ensure that harmful interference is kept to a minimum. If two amateur stations want to use the same frequency, both stations have an equal right to do so. The FCC encourages efficient, interference-free sharing of the ham bands by limiting transmitter output power, by assigning services either *primary* or *secondary* status on a frequency band and by encouraging repeaters to be *coordinated* (operating frequencies are recommended by a regional group organized for this purpose).

The FCC has the authority to modify the terms of your amateur license any time they determine that such a modification will promote the public interest, convenience and necessity. This might occur, for example, if your station causes interference to another station with a primary allocation and you are unable to resolve the interference. In that case they might place time, power or fre-

quency restrictions on your station. (Don't panic, though! Such action is very rare.)

Primary and Secondary Allocations

The basic frequency-sharing principle is straightforward: Where a band of frequencies is allocated to different services of the same category, the basic principle is the *equality of right to operate*. "Category" refers to whether the station operators are part of a primary service or a secondary service. A radio service that is designated as the **primary service** on a band is protected from interference caused by other radio services. A radio service that is designated as the **secondary service** must not cause harmful interference to, and must accept interference from, stations in a primary service. The amateur service has many different frequency bands. Some of them are allocated on a primary basis and some are secondary.

By sharing our frequencies with several other services, including the US military, hams can have the use of a greater amount of spectrum than would otherwise be the case. If you are operating on a band on which the amateur service has a secondary allocation, and a station in the primary service causes interference, you should change frequency immediately. You may also be interfering with the other station, and that is prohibited by Part 97 of the FCC Rules. *The ARRL's FCC Rule Book* shows which amateur bands are primary allocations and which are secondary.

All of the UHF bands and those with higher frequencies (shorter wavelengths) have some type of sharing arrangements. Some of these sharing arrangements apply to stations in certain geographic areas but not others. Before you operate on the UHF bands, you should be familiar with the specific sharing arrangements for the band you want to operate. *The ARRL's FCC Rule Book* is a good place to check. You can also ask other operators in your area for information.

For example, if you want to operate in the 420 to 430 MHz segment of the 70-centimeter band you should be aware of several limitations. If you live within about 50 miles of the Canadian border you may be north of "Line A." The sharing requirements of Section 97.303(f)(1) say "No amateur station shall transmit from north of Line A in the 420 - 430 MHz segment." That means if you are operating from a location north of Line A, you are limited to the 430 to 450 MHz section of the 70-centimeter band. There are further restrictions around certain military bases as well. Depending on the base, the restrictions apply to sta-

tions in a radius of from 50 miles to as much as 200 miles.

One special sharing arrangement is worth additional comment. Amateurs have a secondary allocation at 219 to 220 MHz. Amateur use of this band segment is limited to stations acting as packet radio network relay stations in point-to-point fixed digital message systems. Stations are limited to 50 watts **peak envelope power (PEP)** output when operating on this band. (**Peak envelope power** is a measure of the average power output of a radio transmitter at the largest amplitude peak. You will learn more about power and PEP in Chapter 2.) Before you can operate such a station in this band you must meet several requirements. The Rules in Section 97.303(e) give the details of these requirements. You must give written notice to the ARRL about any such operation at least 30 days prior to making any transmissions on the band. You must make sure you are not within certain distances of Automated Maritime Telecommunications Systems (AMTS) stations unless you obtain their permission.

Amateur stations using the 219 to 220 MHz band must not cause harmful interference to stations of any radio service that has a primary allocation on this band or adjacent frequencies. Such services include the AMTS stations, television stations broadcasting on channels 11 or 13 and Interactive Video and Data Service systems.

[Before moving along to the next section, turn to Chapter 11 and review questions T1B01 through T1B09, T1B11, T1B13 and T1B15. Also study questions T1E04, T1E05 and T2B14. Study this section again if you have difficulty with any of these questions.]

You Have A License!

Well, the big day has finally arrived — the FCC has granted your license and you found your new call sign listed on one of the internet call sign servers (or your license arrived in the mail)! You have permission to operate an amateur station. Now you are ready to put your very own amateur station on the air!

As the proud owner of a new Amateur Radio ticket, you'll soon be an "on-the-air" person instead of an "off-the-air" person. You probably can't wait to make your first contact! You'll be putting all the information you had to learn for the exam to good use.

Call Signs

The FCC issues call signs on a systematic basis. When they process your application, you get the next call sign to come out of the computer. Your call sign identifies your station. You have the only Amateur Radio station in the world with this call sign. You must transmit your call sign

to identify your Amateur Radio station when you are on the air operating.

The first letter of a US call will always be A, K, N or W. These letters are assigned to the United States as amateur call-sign prefixes. After the first one or two letters there will be number and then one to three letters. The letters before the number make up the call sign *prefix*, and the letters after the number are the *suffix*. Other countries use different prefixes — LA2UA is a Norwegian call sign, VE3BKJ is a call sign from Canada and VU2HO is from India.

The number in a US call sign shows the district where the call was first issued. **Figure 1-6** shows the 10 US call districts. Every US amateur call sign includes a single-digit number, 0 through 9 corresponding to these call districts. Amateurs may keep their calls when they move from one district to another. This means the number is not always an indication of where an amateur is. It tells only where he or she was living when the license was first

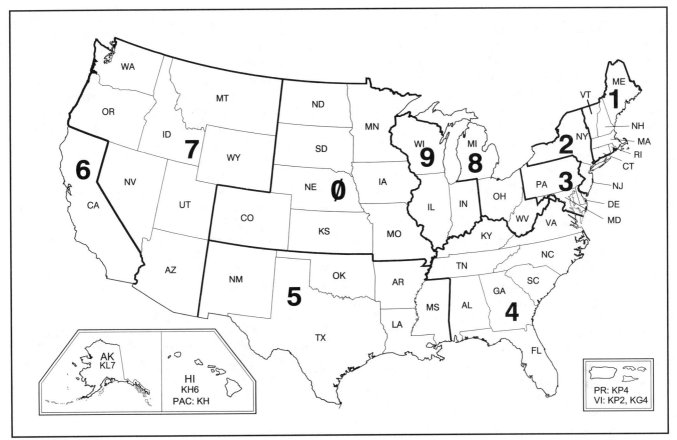

Figure 1.6 — The 10 US call districts. An amateur holding the call sign K1STO lived in the first district when the FCC assigned her that call. Alaska is part of the seventh call district, but has its own set of prefixes: AL7, KL7, NL7 and WL7. Hawaii, part of the sixth district, has the AH6, KH6, NH6 and WH6 prefixes.

first issued. For example, WB3IOS received her license in Pennsylvania, in the third call district, but she now lives in Connecticut, the first district.

US Amateur call signs can have several different formats. Technician and General class call signs might have a "one-by-three" format — a letter followed by a number and then three more letters. These are called "Group C" call signs. They may also have a "two-by-three" format. These are called "Group D" call signs, which are intended for Novice licenses and club station call signs. (The FCC is not issuing any new Novice licenses.) As all of the Group C call signs in a call area are issued, then Technician and General class licensees will receive Group D call signs. Examples of Technician call signs are N1NAG, KB1DCO and KB3TMJ.

Call signs with a "one-by-two" or "two-by-one" format are reserved for Amateur Extra class licensees. These are called "Group A" call signs. N6BV and WR1B are examples of Extra class call signs. Group B call signs have a "two-by-two" format. These call signs are intended

for Advanced class licensees. The FCC is no longer issuing new Advanced class licenses. AA1GW is an example of a Group B call sign. As all the Group A call signs are all issued then the FCC issues Group B call signs to Amateur Extra class licensees.

In addition to the automatic sequential call sign system, the FCC has a way for Amateurs to select their own call sign. This is called the Vanity Call Sign system. Vanity call sign choices must take the same format as a sequential call sign for your license class. As a Technician licensee, you would be eligible to select a "one-by-three" or a "two-by-three" format call sign of your choice. You can select a call sign that is not currently assigned to another station. Call signs with the operator's initials for the suffix are popular.

The FCC does not charge a fee to issue an Amateur Radio license. They do charge a fee to help recover the costs of administering the vanity call sign system, however. The fee for filing a vanity call sign application in 2005   is $21.90 for the ten-year term of the license. This fee is adjusted each year, so you may be paying a different amount when it comes time to renew your license. You can find more information about the Vanity call sign program on ARRLWeb at **www.arrl.org** and also on the FCC Web site at **www.fcc.gov**.

If you would like to change your call sign, but don't want to pay the vanity fee, you can apply for a different call sign from the sequential call sign system. One simple way to do this is to complete an NCVEC Quick Form 605 and check the box to "Change my station call sign systematically." Initial the line next to this box and submit the application to a Volunteer Examiner Coordinator to file for you. See Figure 1.4. The VEC may charge a fee for this service. The ARRL/VEC will file your application electronically for ARRL members for free. There is a small fee for nonmembers.

Once you have a call sign, you may keep it as long as you want to (unless your license expires or is revoked). In other words, there's no requirement to change your call sign when you upgrade to a higher license class. The FCC gives amateurs their choice in this matter.

Amateur Radio clubs can also obtain a station call sign. The club must name one member as the license trustee, to have primary responsibility for the license. The club must apply for the license through an FCC-approved Club Station Call Sign Administrator. The Call Sign Administrator collects the required information and sends it to the FCC in an electronic file. The ARRL/VEC, W4VEC and W5YI-VEC are Club Station Call Sign Administrators.

The FCC has one more system for assigning Amateur Radio call signs. Individuals or club groups who plan to operate an amateur station to commemorate a special event can apply for a Special-Event Call Sign. These special "one-by-one" format call signs can help call attention to the on-the-air operation at the special event. These call signs are issued for a short-term operation, normally 15 days or less. Any licensed amateur is allowed to apply for a Special-Event Call Sign. The FCC-approved Special-Event Call Sign Administrators coordinate these call signs. The ARRL/VEC, Laurel (Maryland) Amateur Radio Club, W4VEC and W5YI-VEC are Special-Event Call Sign Administrators.

[You should turn to Chapter 11 now, and study questions T1E01 through T1E03 and T1E06 through T1E12. Review this section if you have any difficulty with any of these questions.]

Operating Guidelines

Part 97 of the FCC Rules provide quite a bit of guidance about what you can and cannot do as an Amateur Radio operator. Of course every possible situation can't be covered, so you will have to use good judgement in your operating practices. You should be familiar with the specific requirements of the Rules, and always try to operate within the intent of those Rules. As an Amateur Radio operator, you are always responsible for the proper operation of your Amateur Radio station.

Points of Communications

Who can you talk to with your new license? The FCC defines "points of communication" to specify the kinds of radio stations with which you may talk. It's pretty simple, actually: *You may converse with all amateur stations at any time.* This includes amateurs in foreign countries, unless either amateur's government prohibits the communications. (There are a few countries in the world that do not allow Amateur Radio. There are also times when a government will not allow its amateurs to talk with people in other countries.)

It is interesting to note that many countries make arrangements for Amateurs from other countries to operate Amateur Radio while they are visiting. This is called **reciprocal operating authority**. Some of the agreements require a separate document from the government you are visiting. Other times you can simply show up and operate. For example, the US and Canada have an agreement that Amateur Radio operators from those two countries can simply cross the border and operate. Of course we must follow the rules of the country we are visiting.

The FCC must authorize any communication with stations not licensed in the amateur service. An example of such authorization is when amateur stations communicate with military communications stations on Armed Forces Day each year.

Another example of amateurs communicating with non-amateur stations is during Radio Amateur Civil Emergency Service (RACES) operation. During an emergency, a registered RACES station may conduct civil-defense communications with US Government stations authorized to conduct civil-defense communications.

Speaking of emergencies, FCC rules also permit you to communicate with other radio services if it is the only way you have to get help in an emergency situation. Section 97.403 of the Rules defines a **communications emergency** as "communication needs in connection with the immediate safety of human life and immediate protection of property when normal communications systems are not available." So you are allowed to communicate with stations in other radio services during a communications emergency.

There are many examples of times when personal property or lives are in immediate danger. You may use Amateur Radio to call for help in such a situation, even though you seem to be violating other rules. Just be sure you really have an emergency situation first. For example, the Part 97 Rules allow you to call for help on frequencies outside of your license privileges, and even on frequencies outside of the amateur bands if that is what it takes to establish the communications you need.

Broadcasting

Amateur Radio is a two-way communications service. Amateur Radio stations may *not* engage in **broadcasting**. Broadcasting normally means the transmission of information intended for reception by the general public. There are also restrictions regulating **one-way communications** or transmissions of information of general interest to other amateurs. Amateur stations may transmit one-way signals while in beacon operation or radio-control operation.

Since normal restrictions are suspended when life or property is in immediate danger, one-way transmissions are not considered broadcasting (which is not allowed) under emergency conditions. (You will learn more about emergency communications later in this book.)

Business Communications

Amateur communication is noncommercial radio communication between amateur stations, solely with a personal aim and without **pecuniary** interest or business reasons. *Pecuniary* refers to payment of any type.

This definition tells us that amateur operators should not conduct any type of business communications. You may not conduct communications for your own business, or for your employer. You can, however, use your Amateur Radio station to conduct your own personal communications. This includes using the autopatch on your local repeater for such personal calls as making an appointment or ordering food. (In 1993, the FCC amended the business communications rules in Section 97.113 to allow such communication. Prior to this rule change, such calls would have been considered "illegal business communications." Some repeater owners may not like you making such calls on their repeater. Please respect the owner's wishes.)

Of course you can also use the autopatch to call a garage for help when your car breaks down in the middle of a busy expressway. This is an emergency, because your property (car), and possibly your life, are in immediate danger. In an emergency, you can use Amateur Radio in any way possible to call for help.

No one can use an amateur station for monetary gain. You must not accept payment in any form for the use of your station at any time. This also means you may not accept payment for transmitting a message for anyone, such as in third-party communication. Payment means more than just money here. It refers to any type of compensation, which would include materials or services of any type. That is why the FCC uses the words *pecuniary interest* when stating that you can't be paid for operating your station.

There are two exceptions to this rule. A club station intended primarily for transmitting Morse code practice and information bulletins of interest to all amateurs may employ a paid control operator as long as certain conditions are met. That person can be paid to serve as the control operator only when the station is actually transmitting code practice or bulletins. The code practice and bulletins must last at least 40 hours per week. The station must transmit on at least six medium and high-frequency bands, and the schedule of transmissions must be published 30 days in advance. This exception allows the ARRL to pay a control operator for W1AW, the station at ARRL Headquarters in Newington, Connecticut, for example. The station is dedicated to Hiram Percy Maxim, the ARRL's first president. The W1AW operator can't make general contacts with other hams after the code-practice sessions, however.

The second exception is that teachers may use Amateur Radio stations as part of their classroom instruction at an educational institution. This permits a science teacher to use an amateur station to demonstrate satellite communications or a geography teacher to establish contact with an amateur in another part of the country to describe local terrain or weather conditions.

Another common question about the "no business" rule is whether it is okay to buy and sell Amateur Radio equipment over the air. The best way to answer this question is by taking a look at what the Rules say. Section 97.113(a) says, "No amateur station shall transmit: (3) Communications in which the station licensee or control operator has a pecuniary interest, including communications on behalf of an employer. Amateur operators may, however, notify other amateur operators of the availability for sale or trade of apparatus normally used in an amateur station, provided such activity is not conducted on a regular basis."

So if you decide to upgrade your station equipment and want to sell your old rig to another ham, go right ahead and mention it on the air. (Many hams prefer to "close" the deal off the air, in person or over the telephone.) Just when does such activity become "regular?" Well, if you find that you are buying or selling gear every week or so, and it is almost always passed on at a profit, you have probably crossed that line. If the local ham dealer starts referring to you as "the competition" you have definitely gone too far!

Many clubs hold "swap nets" on local repeaters and you will find lots of "For Sale" notices posted on your local packet radio bulletin board. Keep in mind, however, that this is for Amateur Radio equipment and not the rest of your household belongings, including the "kitchen sink!"

Other Assorted Rules

Under FCC Rules, amateurs may not transmit music of any form. This means you can't transmit your band's practice session or play the piano for transmission over the air. It also means you can't play a song from your favorite tape or CD for your friend to hear. You should take care not to transmit *unintentional* music, either. For example, this could happen if you have a broadcast radio playing in the background when you pick up the microphone to talk with someone. There is one exception to the "No Music" rule. If you obtain special permission from NASA to retransmit the audio from a space shuttle mission or the International Space Station for other amateurs to listen, and during that retransmission NASA or the astronauts play some music over the air, you won't get in trouble.

Amateurs may not use obscene or indecent language. Remember that anyone, of any age, can hear your transmission if they happen to be tuned to your transmitting frequency. Depending on your operating frequency and other conditions, your signals can be heard around the world. While there is no list of "banned words" or other specific list, you should avoid any questionable language. The FCC Rules simply state [97.113(a) No amateur station shall transmit: (4) ...obscene or indecent words or language...] Avoid using any words that some people might find offensive or that young children should not hear.

You can't use codes or ciphers to obscure the meaning of transmissions. This means you can't make up a "secret" code to send messages over the air to a friend. Control signals transmitted for remote control of model craft are not considered codes or ciphers. Neither are telemetry signals, such as a satellite might transmit to tell about its condition. A space station —satellite — control operator can use specially coded signals to control the satellite.

Amateurs may not cause **malicious (harmful) interference** to other communications of any type, amateur or non-amateur. You may not like the other operator's practices, or you may believe he or she is violating the rules. You have no right to interfere with their communications, however. You may never deliberately interfere with another station's communications. Repeatedly transmitting on a frequency already occupied by other amateurs, such as in a net operation, is a form of harmful or malicious interference.

Some Amateur Radio transceivers can transmit on frequencies outside of the amateur bands. You should not use such a radio to transmit signals on other frequencies. Such transmissions, even if sent as a "joke" can cause serious harmful interference. For example, if someone were to transmit on police frequencies, that transmission might block real police calls that could involve an emergency.

Amateurs may not transmit **false or deceptive signals**, such as a distress call when no emergency exists.

You must not, for example, start calling **MAYDAY** (an international distress signal) unless you are in a life-threatening situation.

Amateurs are required to transmit their station call signs for station identification. If you do not transmit your call sign as required, you have transmitted an *unidentified* communication. You will learn more about the station identification rules in Chapter 5 of this book.

Remote Control of Model Craft

Amateurs are permitted to use radio links to control model craft. This is called "telecommand" (control) of model craft. Most model control activity takes place on the 6-meter band, so you would need a Technician license to participate in this activity. Remote control operation is permitted with these restrictions:

- station identification is not required for transmissions directed only to the model craft. The control transmitter must have a label indicating the station's call sign and the licensee's name and address.
- control signals are not considered codes and ciphers. (Amateurs may not generally make up "secret codes" that will hide the meaning of their communications.)
- transmitter power cannot exceed 1 watt.

Space Stations and Earth Stations

The FCC defines a **space station** as "An amateur station located more than 50 kilometers (km) — about 30 miles — above the Earth's surface." This obviously includes amateur satellites, and also includes any operation from the Space Shuttle, the International Space Station and any future operations by astronauts in space. Any licensed ham can be the licensee or control operator of a space station. Likewise, any licensed amateur may operate through or communicate with a space station, as long as their transmissions take place on frequencies available for that license class.

Orbiting Satellites Carrying Amateur Radio (OSCARs) relay signals between amateur operators on the Earth (**Earth stations**). In that case, the satellite itself does not have to transmit a station call sign. Operators transmitting to the satellite do have to transmit their call signs, however!

Earth stations are stations located on the Earth's surface, or within 50 km of it. They are intended for communications with **space stations** or with other Earth stations by means of one or more objects (satellites) in space. Any amateur can be the control operator of an Earth station, subject to the limitations of his license class. Some specific transmitting frequencies are authorized for Earth stations. These are located in the 40, 20, 17, 15, 12, 10 and 2-meter bands, in the 23- and 70-cm bands, and in all other amateur bands that are higher in frequency. There are no frequencies available for

Earth stations in the 6-meter band, however. A complete list appears in *The ARRL's FCC Rule Book.*

Official Notices of Violation

The FCC is the agency in charge of maintaining law and order in radio operation in the US. The International Telecommunication Union (ITU) sets up international rules that the government telecommunication agencies of each country follow. Both sets of rules provide the basic structure for Amateur Radio in the United States.

Suppose you receive an official notice from the FCC informing you that you have violated a regulation. Now what should you do? Simple: Whatever the notice tells you to do. Usually this will involve some station modification and making a response to the FCC about what corrective steps you have taken.

There exists a philosophy in Amateur Radio that is deeply rooted in our history. This philosophy is as strong now as it was in the days of the radio pioneers. We are talking about the *self-policing* of our bands. Over the years, amateurs have become known for their ability to maintain high operating standards and technical skills.

We do this without excessive regulation by the FCC. The Commission itself has praised the amateur service for its tradition of self-policing. Perhaps the underlying reason for this is the amateur's sense of pride, accomplishment, fellowship, loyalty and concern. Amateur Radio is far more than just a hobby to most amateurs.

As a new or prospective amateur operator, you will begin to discover the wide horizons of your new pastime. You will learn more about the rich heritage we all share. Take this sense of pride with you, and follow the Amateur's Code. (The Amateur's Code is printed at the end of the Introduction chapter.)

[Now it's time to turn to Chapter 11 again, and study a few more questions. You should be able to answer questions T1A04 through T1A16. Also study questions T1B12, T1B14, T1C07 and T1C09. You should also be able to answer question T5C02. Review this section if you have difficulty with any of these questions.

Congratulations. That completes your study of the material in the FCC Rules subelement of the Technician question pool.]

METHODS OF COMMUNICATION

As an Amateur Radio operator, you will find many ways to communicate with other operators. You can choose an operating frequency from the many bands available. You also can select an operating mode, from voice to Morse code, radioteletype or even television.

Your Element 2, Technician license exam will include two questions from the Methods of Communication material in this chapter. Those questions will come from the two groups of questions covered by syllabus topics T2A and T2B:

T2A Magnetic/Electric Fields; Wavelength; Frequency; Velocity; ac Sine wave/Hertz; Audio and Radio frequency.

T2B Frequency privileges granted to Technician class operators; Amateur service bands; Emission types and designators; Modulation principles; AM/FM/Single sideband/upper-lower, international Morse code (CW), RTTY, packet radio and data emission types.

Be sure to turn to Chapter 11 and study the appropriate questions when the text directs you there. This will help you check your progress and help you decide if you need a little extra study time on certain topics. This book will teach you everything you need to know to pass your Technician license exam. Of course there is much more to learn about every topic in the book. To learn more about a particular topic you may want to read more-advanced texts. ARRL's *Understanding Basic Electronics*, *The ARRL Handbook*, *The ARRL Antenna Book*, *The ARRL Operating Manual* and many other specialized books can satisfy your urge to learn more. After you have your license in hand you can "learn by doing" as well as by reading books.

Direct and Alternating Current

In this section, you will learn what we mean by *direct current* and *alternating current*. You will also learn the meaning of some important terms that go along with alternating current, such as *frequency* and *wavelength*.

Two Types of Current

In **direct current**, known as **dc** for short, the electrons flow in one direction only — from negative to positive. Batteries are the most common source of direct current. Lead-acid car batteries, nickel-cadmium (NiCd) rechargeable batteries and alkaline batteries are all examples. We can also get dc from a solar panel.

Using a water-flow analogy, we normally think of water flowing in one direction through pipes. But water could actually flow in either direction through a pipe. We know that water can flow in more than one direction. The tides in the ocean are a good example of water flowing in one direction, then reversing and flowing in the opposite direction.

There is a second kind of electricity called **alternating current**, or **ac**. In ac, the terminals of the power supply change from positive to negative to positive voltage and so on. Because the poles change and electrons always flow from negative to positive, ac flows first in one direction, then the other. The current *alternates* in direction. The basic unit of electric current is the ampere, abbreviated A.

We call one complete round trip a *cycle*. The **frequency** of the ac is the number of complete cycles, or alternations, that occur in one second. We measure frequency in hertz (abbreviated Hz). Frequency is a measure of the number of times in one second the alternating current flows back and forth. One cycle per second is 1 Hz. 150 cycles per second is 150 Hz. One thousand cycles per second is one kilohertz (1 kHz). One million cycles per second is one megahertz (1 MHz). If a radio wave makes 3,725,000 cycles in one second, this means it has a frequency of 3,725,000 hertz (Hz), 3725 kilohertz (kHz) or 3.725 megahertz (MHz).

More AC Terminology

Batteries provide direct current. To make an alternating current from this direct-current source, you would have to switch the polarity of the voltage source rapidly.

> The basic unit of frequency is the hertz. This unit is named in honor of Heinrich Rudolf Hertz (1857-1894). This German physicist was the first person to demonstrate the generation and reception of radio waves.

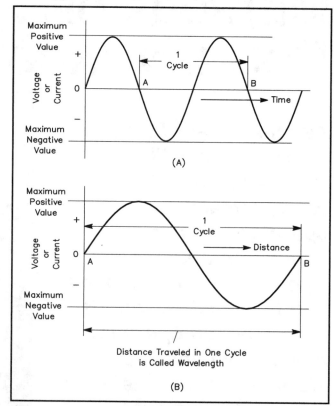

Figure 2.1 — The sine wave is one way to show alternating current. Let's follow one cycle on Part A, starting on line "0" at point A, indicated near the center of the graph. The wave goes in a negative direction to its most negative point, then heads back up to zero. After the wave goes through zero, it becomes more and more positive, reaches the positive peak, then goes back to zero again. This is one full cycle of alternating current. Part B shows that one wavelength is a measure of the distance the wave will travel during one complete cycle.

Imagine trying to turn the battery around so the plus and minus terminals changed position very rapidly. This would not be a very practical way to produce ac! You must have a power supply in which the polarity is constantly changing. The terminals must be positive and negative one moment, and then negative and positive, constantly switching back and forth.

The power company has a more practical way to create ac: They use a large machine called an *alternator* to produce power at their generating stations. The ac supplied to your home goes through 60 complete cycles each second. Thus, the electricity from the power company has a frequency of 60 Hz.

This 60-hertz ac electricity builds to a peak current or voltage in one direction, then decreases to zero and reverses to build to a peak in the opposite direction. If you plot these changes on a graph, you get a gentle

Why Use Alternating Current in Our Homes?

Why do power companies use alternating current in the power lines that run to your home? One important reason is so they can use transformers to change the voltage. This allows the company to use an appropriate voltage for each part of their distribution system. In this way the power company can minimize the power losses in the transmission lines. The generator at the power station produces ac by moving a wire (actually many turns of wire) through a magnetic field in an alternator. The resulting output has a relatively low voltage. Why don't the power companies send this directly through the power lines to your house? At first, this seems like a good idea. It would eliminate the many transformers and power stations that often clutter our landscape.

The answer can be found in Ohm's Law. Even a very good conductor, such as the copper used in the power company's high-voltage lines, has a certain amount of resistance. This factor becomes very important when we consider the very long distances the generated electricity must travel.

Remember that the voltage drop across a resistance is given by the formula E = IR, where I is the value of current and R is the value of resistance. If we can reduce either the resistance of the wire or the value of the current through the wire, we can reduce the voltage drop. The resistance of the wire is relatively constant, although we can reduce it somewhat by using a very large diameter wire. If we increase the voltage, a smaller current will be required for the same power transfer from the generating station to your home.

Using a very high voltage also provides more "overhead." If the power company starts with 750,000 volts, and the voltage has dropped to 740,000 volts by the time it reaches the first substation, they just use a transformer rated for 740,000-V input to give the desired output. If they send 50,000 volts on to the next substation, there is still plenty of overhead. By the time it gets to the power lines outside your house, the voltage has been stepped down to around 3000 volts. A pole transformer then steps it down further to 240 volts to supply power to your house. This voltage is normally split in half to provide two 120-V circuits to your house.

up-and-down curve. We call this curve a *sine wave*. **Figure 2.1A** shows two cycles of a sine wave ac signal. Alternating current can do things direct current can't. For instance, a 120-V ac source can be increased to a 1000-V source with a *transformer*. Transformers can change the value of an ac voltage, but not a dc voltage. The power company supplies 120-V ac and 240-V ac to your house.

Frequency and Wavelength

From the discussion of the frequency of an ac signal, you must realize that alternating currents and voltages can change direction at almost any rate imaginable. Some signals have low frequencies, like the 60-Hz-ac electricity the power company supplies to your house. Other signals have higher frequencies; for example, radio signals can alternate at more than several million hertz.

If we know the frequency of an ac signal, we can use that frequency to describe the signal. We can talk about 60-Hz power or a 3725-kHz radio signal. **Wavelength** is another quality that can be associated with every ac signal. As its name implies, wavelength refers to the distance that the wave will travel through space in a single cycle. See Figure 2.1.

We hear sounds because of vibrations or changes in the air pressure that reaches our eardrums. We can't actually hear electromagnetic waves or signals at any frequency. If the signal has cycles that repeat at 20 times per second to 20,000 times per second, however, we call that signal an **audio frequency (AF) signal**. An AF signal is an ac signal that has a frequency in the range of 20 Hz to 20,000 Hz. Signals in this frequency range will produce sounds when they are connected to a speaker.

Radio frequency (RF) waves are electromagnetic waves or cycles that repeat more than 20,000 times per second. All electromagnetic waves travel though space at the speed of light, 300,000,000 meters per second (3.00×10^8 m/s). We use the lower-case Greek letter lambda (λ) to represent wavelength.

The faster a signal alternates, the less distance the signal will be able to travel during one cycle. There is an equation that relates the frequency and the wavelength of a signal to the speed of the wave:

$$c = f \lambda \qquad \text{(Equation 2.1)}$$

where:
  c is the speed of light, 3.00×10^8 meters per second
  f is the frequency of the wave in hertz
  λ is the wavelength of the wave in meters

We can solve this equation for either frequency or

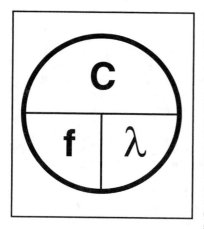

Figure 2.2 — This simple diagram will help you remember the frequency and wavelength equations. To find any quantity if you know the other two, simply cover the unknown quantity with your hand or a piece of paper. The positions of the remaining two symbols show if you have to multiply (when they are side by side) or divide (when they appear one over the other as a fraction).

wavelength, depending on which quantity we want to find.

$$f = \frac{c}{\lambda}$$ (Equation 2.2)

and

$$\lambda = \frac{c}{f}$$ (Equation 2.3)

From these equations you may realize that as the frequency increases the wavelength gets shorter. **Figure 2.2** is a simple diagram that will help you remember the frequency and wavelength relationships. As the frequency decreases the wavelength gets longer. Suppose you are transmitting a radio signal on 225 MHz. What is the wavelength of this signal? We can use Equation 2.3 to find the answer. First we must change the frequency to hertz:

225 MHz = 225,000,000 Hz.

Then we use this value in Equation 2.3.

$$\lambda = \frac{c}{f} = \frac{3.00 \times 10^8 \frac{m}{s}}{225 \times 10^6 \, Hz}$$

$$\lambda = \frac{300,000,000 \frac{m}{s}}{225,000,000 \, Hz}$$

This frequency is in the band we often call the 1.25-meter band. When we refer to an amateur band by a wavelength, we normally use round numbers that are easier to remember, so this answer doesn't exactly match the common name for this band.

As another example, what is the wavelength of a signal that has a frequency of 144.25 MHz? (144.25 MHz = 144, 250,000 Hz.)

$$\lambda = \frac{c}{f} = \frac{3.00 \times 10^8 \frac{m}{s}}{144.25 \times 10^6 \, Hz}$$

$$\lambda = \frac{300,000,000 \frac{m}{s}}{144,250,000 \, Hz}$$

This frequency is in the popular 2-meter band.

Notice that higher-frequency signals have shorter wavelengths. Lower-frequency signals have longer wavelengths. As you increase a signal frequency the wavelength gets shorter. As a signal's wavelength increases, the frequency goes down.

Radio signals cover a very wide range of frequencies. We divide the RF spectrum into several groups for easier reference. For example, the bands between 300 kHz and 3 MHz are called medium frequency (MF) bands. The high frequency (HF) bands fall between 3 MHz and 30 MHz. The bands between 30 MHz and 300 MHz are called the very high frequency (VHF) bands and those between 300 MHz and 3000 MHz (3 gigahertz or GHz) are the ultra high frequency (UHF) bands. The bands from 3 GHz to 30 GHz are called the super high frequency (SHF) bands and those between 30 GHz and 300 GHz are called extremely high frequency (EHF) bands. Above that, we have infrared and visible light. Notice that the popular 2-meter band, with frequencies between 144 and 148 MHz, is in the VHF range. So in addition to the frequency and wavelength of a radio wave, we can also use these band ranges to identify the RF signal.

[Congratulations! You have learned some very important electronics concepts. Before going on to the next section, turn to Chapter 11 and study questions T2A01, T2A03, T2A04, T2A06 through T2A12 and T2A14 through T2A16. Also study questions T7A01 through T7A03, T7A05 and T7B05 through T7B09. Come back to this section for a review if you are still a little uncertain about any of these questions.]

Technician Privileges

When operating, you must stay within your assigned frequency bands. Amateurs usually refer to these frequency bands by their wavelength. Each band is further divided into subbands for the different classes of license. The bands are also divided into segments for various emission modes, or types of signals from the transmitter.

We use the metric system of measurement in electronics. Chapter 7 includes a full explanation of the metric system and terms like kilo, mega and centi that we have used here. For now it is important that you know that kilohertz and megahertz are measures of the frequency of a radio signal. The hertz (Hz) is the basic unit of frequency. Kilo means thousand and mega means million. We can list any of the amateur frequency bands in either kilohertz or megahertz. For example, the 15-meter Novice band can be written either as 21.100 to 21.200 MHz, or 21,100 to 21,200 kHz and the 10-meter band can be written either as 28.100 to 28.500 MHz or 28,100 to 28,500 kHz.

Emission Privileges

Amateur operators transmit a wide variety of signals. These include Morse code, radioteletype, several types of voice communications and even television pictures. An **emission** is any radio-frequency (RF) signal from a transmitter.

There is a system for describing the various types of signals (or emissions) found on the amateur bands. Different modes are given identifiers, called emission types.

You should be familiar with the various emission types. The FCC lists the **emission privileges** for each license class by giving the emission types each may use. An emission privilege is FCC permission to use a particular emission type, such as Morse code or single-sideband phone. As a Technician, you will be permitted to use all of the emission types on at least one frequency band. The emission types defined by the FCC are:

- CW — Morse code telegraphy.
- Data — Computer communications modes, often called *digital communications* because digital computers are used.
- Image — Television and facsimile communications.
- MCW — (Tone-modulated CW) Morse code telegraphy using a keyed audio tone.
- Phone — Speech (voice) communications.
- Pulse — Communications using a sequence of controlled signal variations.
- RTTY — Narrow-band direct-printing telegraphy communications (received by automatic techniques). Since digital computers are often used on radioteletype (RTTY), these signals are also often called *digital communications*.
- SS — Spread-spectrum communications in which the signal energy is spread across a wide bandwidth.
- Test — Transmissions containing no information.

On 80, 40 and 15 meters, Technician licensees with Morse code credit may transmit only Morse code (CW). The transmitter produces this Morse code signal by *keying* (switching on and off) the signal from a continuous-wave (CW) transmitter. On 10 meters, Technician licensees with Morse code credit may use CW from 28.1 to 28.5 MHz. Technicians with Morse code credit may also transmit radioteletype (RTTY) and data from 28.1 to 28.3 MHz, and single-sideband phone from 28.3 to 28.5 MHz. **Table 2.1** summarizes the amateur band limits and operating modes for each license class. Morse code (CW) is the only emission type that can be used on any amateur frequency. Technician class licensees may use FM phone emissions on all the VHF and UHF bands. There are no FM phone emission privileges on any of the HF bands for Technicians with Morse code credit, however.

Hams often describe radioteletype (RTTY) and packet radio or other data emissions as *digital communications*. These are signals intended to be received and printed or displayed on a computer screen automatically. Information transferred directly from one computer to another is an example of digital communications. Data emissions also include telemetry and telecommand communications. Telemetry refers to signals sent from a remote location, such as a satellite, to provide information about the station and operating conditions. Telecommand communications are signals sent to a remote station, such as a satellite, to control the station.

Frequency Privileges

As you can see from Table 2.1, Technician class operators enjoy *all frequency privileges* allocated to the amateur service *above 50 MHz*. Technician class amateurs can operate on all authorized frequencies, using all authorized modes, on the VHF, UHF and microwave amateur bands, as can General and Amateur Extra class licensees. They may use up to 1500-watts peak envelope power (PEP) output on these bands. In addition, Technicians who pass a 5-wpm code test gain the same emission privileges that Novice licensees have on the four HF Novice bands. Novice and Technician with Morse code operators are limited to 200 watts PEP output on the HF bands. These bands are:

- On the 80-meter band, 3675 to 3725 kHz, CW only.
- On the 40-meter band, 7100 to 7150 kHz, CW only.*
- On the 15-meter band, 21,100 to 21,200 kHz, CW only.
- On the 10-meter band, 28.1 to 28.3 MHz, CW, RTTY and data; and 28.3 to 28.5 MHz, CW and SSB phone.

*In ITU Region 2 only. ITU Region 2 comprises all of North America, the Caribbean and the Eastern Pacific, including Hawaii. Chapter 1 has more information about the ITU Regions.

Table 2.1

US Amateur Bands

ARRL *The national association for* **AMATEUR RADIO**

June 1, 2003   Novice, Advanced and Technician Plus Allocations

New Novice, Advanced and Technician Plus licenses are no longer being issued, but *existing* Novice, Technician Plus and Advanced class licenses are unchanged. Amateurs can continue to renew these licenses. Technicians who pass the 5 wpm Morse code exam *after* that date have Technician Plus privileges, although their license says Technician. They must retain the 5 wpm Certificate of Successful Completion of Examination (CSCE) as proof. The CSCE is valid indefinitely for operating authorization, but is valid only for 365 days for upgrade credit.

160 METERS

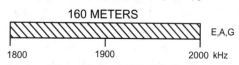

E,A,G

Amateur stations operating at 1900-2000 kHz must not cause harmful interference to the radiolocation service and are afforded no protection from radiolocation operations.

80 METERS

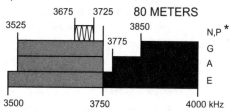

N,P *
G
A
E

60 METERS

General, Advanced, and Amateur Extra licensees may use the following five channels on a secondary basis with a maximum effective radiated power of 50 W PEP relative to a half wave dipole. Only upper sideband suppressed carrier voice transmissions may be used. The frequencies are 5330.5, 5346.5, 5366.5, 5371.5 and 5403.5 kHz. The occupied bandwidth is limited to 2.8 kHz centered on 5332, 5348, 5368, 5373, and 5405 kHz respectively.

40 METERS

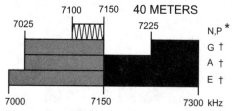

N,P *
G †
A †
E †

† Phone and Image modes are permitted between 7075 and 7100 kHz for FCC licensed stations in ITU Regions 1 and 3 and by FCC licensed stations in ITU Region 2 West of 130 degrees West longitude or South of 20 degrees North latitude. See Sections 97.305(c) and 97.307(f)(11). Novice and Technician Plus licensees outside ITU Region 2 may use CW only between 7050 and 7075 kHz. See Section 97.301(e). These exemptions do not apply to stations in the continental US.

30 METERS

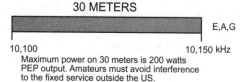

E,A,G

Maximum power on 30 meters is 200 watts PEP output. Amateurs must avoid interference to the fixed service outside the US.

20 METERS

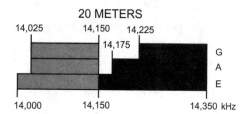

G
A
E

17 METERS

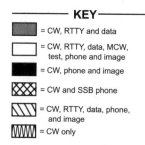

E,A,G

15 METERS

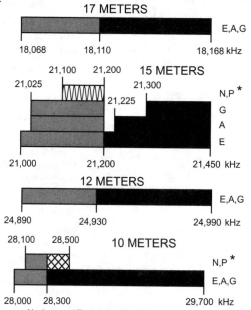

N,P *
G
A
E

12 METERS

E,A,G

10 METERS

N,P *
E,A,G

Novices and Technician Plus Licensees are limited to 200 watts PEP output on 10 meters.

6 METERS

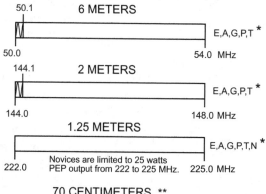

E,A,G,P,T *

2 METERS

E,A,G,P,T *

1.25 METERS

E,A,G,P,T,N *

Novices are limited to 25 watts PEP output from 222 to 225 MHz.

70 CENTIMETERS **

E,A,G,P,T *

33 CENTIMETERS **

E,A,G,P,T *

23 CENTIMETERS **

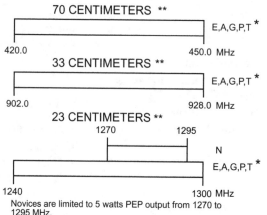

N
E,A,G,P,T *

Novices are limited to 5 watts PEP output from 1270 to 1295 MHz.

US AMATEUR POWER LIMITS

At all times, transmitter power should be kept down to that necessary to carry out the desired communications. Power is rated in watts PEP output. Unless otherwise stated, the maximum power output is 1500 W. Power for all license classes is limited to 200 W in the 10,100-10,150 kHz band and in all Novice subbands below 28,100 kHz. Novices and Technicians are restricted to 200 W in the 28,100-28,500 kHz subbands. In addition, Novices are restricted to 25 W in the 222-225 MHz band and 5 W in the 1270-1295 MHz subband.

Operators with Technician class licenses and above may operate on all bands above 50 MHz. For more detailed information see *The ARRL FCC Rule Book.*

━━ KEY ━━

▓ = CW, RTTY and data

☐ = CW, RTTY, data, MCW, test, phone and image

■ = CW, phone and image

▧ = CW and SSB phone

▨ = CW, RTTY, data, phone, and image

▒ = CW only

E = EXTRA CLASS
A = ADVANCED
G = GENERAL
P = TECHNICIAN PLUS
T = TECHNICIAN
N = NOVICE

*Technicians who have passed the 5 wpm Morse code exam are indicated as "P".

**Geographical and power restrictions apply to all bands with frequencies above 420 MHz. See *The ARRL FCC Rule Book* for more information about your area.

All licensees except Novices are authorized all modes on the following frequencies:

2300-2310 MHz
2390-2450 MHz
3300-3500 MHz
5650-5925 MHz
10.0-10.5 GHz
24.0-24.25 GHz
47.0-47.2 GHz
75.5-76.0, 77.0-81.0 GHz
119.98-120.02 GHz
142-149 GHz
241-250 GHz
All above 300 GHz

For band plans and sharing arrangements, see *The ARRL FCC Rule Book.*

Technician class licensees may operate on the VHF and UHF bands listed below, plus several others that are higher in frequency. For a complete list of amateur frequency privileges, including the microwave bands where frequency is measured in gigahertz, see *The ARRL's FCC Rule Book*. All Technician class and higher licensees have these privileges. Note that the frequencies listed here are for ITU Region 2 only. If you will be operating from an area in ITU Regions 1 or 3 you must check the frequency limits for those Regions in the FCC Rules.

- On the 50-MHz (6-meter) band: On 50.0 to 50.1 MHz, only CW is allowed. On 50.1 MHz to 54.0 MHz all emission types except pulse — CW, RTTY, data, MCW, test, phone and image — are authorized.
- On the popular 144-MHz (2-meter) band: 144.0 to 144.1 MHz, CW only. 144.1 to 148 MHz, all emission types (except pulse, but including image transmissions). Although the 2-meter band is best known for repeater and packet operation, hams also use it for such *weak-signal activities* as meteor scatter, moonbounce and aurora.
- On the 222-MHz (1.25-meter) band: all emission types (except pulse) from 222.0 to 225.0 MHz.
- On the 420-MHz (70-cm) band: all emission types (except pulse) from 420 to 450 MHz. This band is popular for image communications because it is the lowest frequency band where fast-scan TV (FSTV) — also known as Amateur TV (ATV) — can be transmitted. This mode uses the same standards as broadcast TV, with full-motion video.
- On the 902-MHz (33-cm) band: all emission types from 902 to 928 MHz.
- On the 1240-MHz (23-cm) band: all emission types (except pulse) from 1240 to 1300 MHz.
- On the 2300-MHz (13-cm) band: all emission types from 2300 to 2310 and 2390 to 2450 MHz.

You have learned about some common Amateur Radio communication methods. The signals you transmit from your station to communicate using the various operating modes are called emission types. In the next section you will learn about some of the ways the emissions are produced. You will also learn the FCC names for these emissions.

Common Emission Types

All radio transmissions begin with a steady radio frequency signal. This unmodulated radio wave (a steady signal with no information included) is called a test emission. This type of radio signal doesn't communicate any information, except perhaps that someone is testing their transmitter. See **Figure 2.3**. We want to use a radio signal to communicate information, and to do this we have to add the information to the signal somehow. This process of combining an information signal with a radio signal is called modulation. The simplest form of modulation is to turn the radio signal on and off. CW, also called international Morse code, is transmitted by on/off keying of a radio-frequency signal. This is demonstrated whenever you use a key to send CW. To send CW, you press a lever. To stop sending, you let up on the lever. Code is either on or off. By controlling the on/off patterns of the radio signal, you are sending information by Morse code. What could be simpler? **Figure 2.4** shows a radio signal that has been keyed on and off to produce the Morse code character C.

Any voice mode used for communication is known as a phone emission under FCC Rules. AM, SSB and FM voice are all phone emission types.

What does single-sideband (SSB) mean? Begin with a steady radio frequency (RF) signal such as you would get by pressing the key of a Morse code transmitter and just holding it down. This is called the RF carrier. Then combine this signal with a voice signal from a microphone. The process of combining such an RF carrier with any information signal is called modulation. If we use amplitude modulation, the resulting signal has two side-

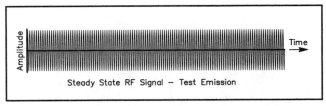

Figure 2.3 — A constant amplitude, steady RF signal is a test emission. There is no information included with a test emission signal.

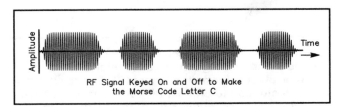

Figure 2.4 — Keying an RF signal on and off to send Morse code produces a CW transmission. This example shows the RF output for the letter C – dah di dah dit.

bands, one higher in frequency than the carrier frequency and one lower in frequency than the carrier frequency. These are called the upper sideband and the lower sideband. For a single-sideband voice signal, the carrier and one of the sidebands is removed, and only one sideband is transmitted. See **Figure 2.5**. The RF carrier is the signal that we modulate to produce a radiotelephone signal.

SSB is the most common voice mode on HF. You can use either the lower sideband or the upper sideband to transmit an SSB signal. Amateurs normally use the upper sideband for 10-meter phone operation. When SSB is used on the VHF and UHF bands, hams normally use the upper sideband (USB).

Most Technician class amateurs use frequency modulated (FM) phone more than any other mode. Nearly all VHF and UHF voice repeaters use FM phone. A practical FM transmitter varies the carrier frequency or phase to produce the modulated signal. **Figure 2.6** shows an RF carrier signal that varies in frequency with the voice modulating signal.

FM is well suited to mobile operation, which is a common use for VHF/UHF repeaters. A good signal will quiet any background noise. That is why we say such signals are "full quieting." Amateurs also use a variety of digital communications modes. Generally, digital communications refers to a type of communication that uses computers to send and receive signals through a radio transceiver.

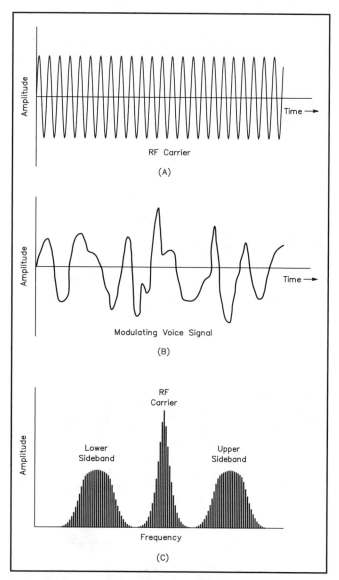

Figure 2.5 — A single-sideband (SSB) signal is formed by combining an RF carrier signal (A) with a voice or other information signal (B). The resulting signal includes the original RF carrier as well as two sidebands, one on either side of the carrier. The upper and lower sidebands are shown at C. To transmit an SSB signal, one of the sidebands and the RF carrier are removed in the transmitter, and the remaining sideband is transmitted.

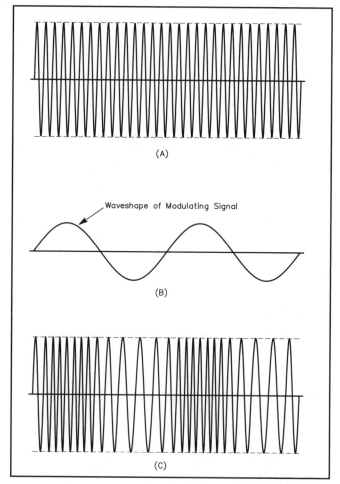

Figure 2.6 — This drawing shows a graphical representation of frequency modulation. In the unmodulated carrier at A, each RF cycle takes the same amount of time to complete. When the modulating signal at B is applied, the carrier frequency is increased or decreased according to the amplitude and polarity of the modulating signal, as shown by Part C.

Packet radio, which sends the information in short bursts, or packets, is called a data emission. The receiving station acknowledges each packet. Your radio will transmit for a short time, then listen for a brief instant before transmitting again while you type on the keyboard. The name packet radio comes from the way the information, such as computer data files or digital information, is organized into small pieces or packets.

Packet radio communications is designed primarily as a link between two stations. When your packet radio station is *connected* to another packet station, it means that one station is transmitting to the other, and the receiving station is acknowledging that the data is being received correctly.

Packet radio signals are generally produced by feeding an audio signal that switches between two audio tones into the microphone input of an FM transmitter. This results in a signal called audio frequency shift keying, or AFSK.

Another type of digital communications is called radioteletype, or RTTY. RTTY signals consist of a constant transmitted signal while you type on the keyboard. When you stop typing and give the command for your station to stop transmitting, then you can listen for the other station's reply. RTTY can only be used to transmit and receive text.

Shifting the transmitter RF carrier frequency between two frequencies produces RTTY signals. Some HF transceivers allow a signal to automatically shift the carrier frequency for RTTY transmissions. Others use audio tones fed into the microphone input of an SSB transceiver. The end result is the same, however. The transmitted RF simply shifts between two carrier frequencies. In either case, this system is called frequency shift keying, or FSK.

Packet is more commonly used on VHF and UHF while RTTY is more often used on HF. Technically there is no reason any of these modes could not be used on any band. In fact, there are forms of packet used on HF and some operators use RTTY on the VHF and UHF bands.

There are many new digital communications systems being developed. One very popular system is called PSK31. This has proven to be a reliable communications method for keyboard to keyboard (computer) communications. It works very well with low power transmitters, and it has a very narrow bandwidth. A typical PSK31 digital communications signal has a bandwidth of approximately 31 Hz.

Modern data-transmission techniques provide high-speed communications. These systems also provide very reliable communications. A computer system can be set up to automatically send and receive the data. Data communications systems use some form of error checking to ensure that the information was received correctly.

[Now turn to Chapter 11 and study question T1B10. Also study questions T2A13 and T2B01 through T2B13. Also study questions T2B15 through T2B17. Review this section if you have any difficulty with those questions.]

RADIO PHENOMENA

3

The sun has a large effect on long-distance radio communication on Earth. Solar flares, like the ones shown here, as well as sunspots, can make long-distance communication possible—or impossible.

All living things on Earth exist because of the **atmosphere** that surrounds our planet. The atmosphere not only supplies us oxygen to breathe, but also shields us from the harmful effects of radiation from the Sun.

The word *atmosphere* is made up of a Greek word, *atmos*, meaning "vapor" and a Latin word, *sphaera*, meaning "sphere." The Earth's atmosphere is literally a "sphere of vapor" surrounding the planet. The atmosphere reaches a height of almost 400 miles above the Earth, and is made up of three main regions. See **Figure 3.1**.

- The **troposphere**, is the region near the Earth where all our weather occurs. The troposphere reaches a height of about 7 miles. In this region clouds form and temperature decreases rapidly with altitude. The Greek root word for troposphere is *trope*, meaning "to change," bringing new meaning to an old saying about New England weather: "If you don't like the weather now, just wait a minute."
- The **stratosphere**, ranging from about 6 to 30 miles high, is where atmospheric gases "spread out" horizontally, as the Latin root word *stratus* implies. The high-speed jet stream travels in the stratosphere, influencing the weather in the troposphere below.
- The **ionosphere**, from about 30 to 400 miles high, is where solar radiation creates *ions*. Only about 1% of the Earth's atmospheric gases are found in the ionosphere, despite its large area. The ionosphere, however, is of great interest to hams wanting to communicate long distances. We'll study various aspects of HF radio-wave propagation through the ionosphere in this chapter.

There will be two questions on your Technician license exam from this Radio Phenomena chapter. These questions will come from the two groups in Subelement T3 of the Technician class question pool:

T3A How a radio signal travels; Atmosphere/ troposphere/ionosphere and ionized layers; Skip distance; Ground (surface)/sky (space) waves; Single/multihop; Path; Ionospheric absorption; Refraction.

T3B HF vs. VHF vs. UHF characteristics; Types of VHF-UHF propagation; Daylight and seasonal variations; Tropospheric ducting; Line of sight; Maximum usable frequency (MUF); Sunspots and sunspot Cycle, Characteristics of different bands.

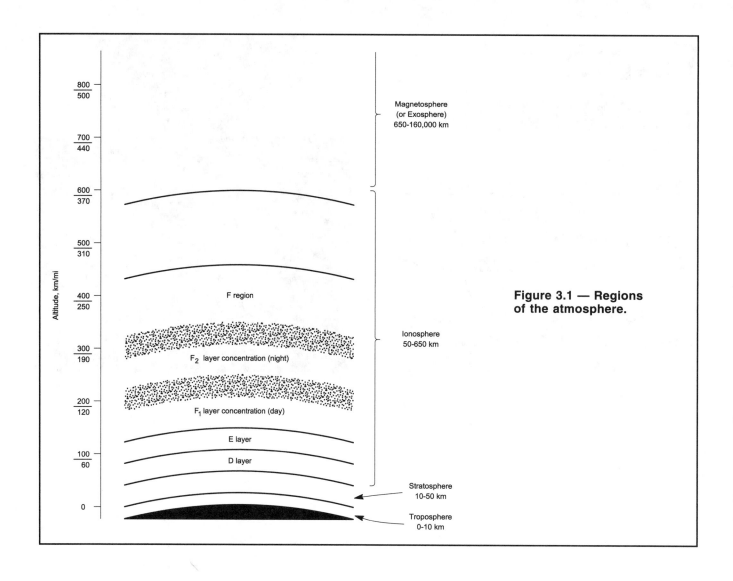

Figure 3.1 — Regions of the atmosphere.

Propagation: How Signals Travel

Amateurs enjoy the privilege of using many different frequency bands. Some of these are scattered throughout the **high frequency (HF)** spectrum, and others extend across the **very high frequency (VHF)** and **ultra high frequency (UHF)** bands.

Some of the bands work better during the day, and some work better at night. Some frequencies are good for long-distance communications, and others provide reliable short-range communications. Amateurs who want to work a certain part of the country or world need to know which frequency to use and when to be there. Experience, combined with lots of careful listening, is a good way to gain this knowledge. In this chapter we will cover the basic ways that radio waves travel from one place to another, and help you begin to learn about propagation.

Radio waves generally travel to their destination in four ways:

- They can travel directly from one point to another.
- They can travel along the ground, bending slightly to follow the curvature of the Earth for some distance.
- They can be trapped in a layer of the Earth's atmosphere, traveling a longer distance than normal before coming back to the Earth's surface.
- They can be refracted — or bent — back to Earth by the ionosphere. (The ionosphere is a layer of charged particles — called ions — in the Earth's outer atmosphere. These ionized gases make long-distance radio contacts possible on the HF bands.)

The study of how radio waves travel from one point to another is the science of **propagation**. Radio-wave propagation is a fascinating part of ham radio. Let's take a look at the different ways radio waves travel.

Propagation on the High Frequency (HF) Bands

Technician licensees who have passed a 5 wpm Morse code exam have privileges on four high frequency (HF) bands. These bands are often called the "Novice bands." Although the FCC no longer issues Novice licenses, those licenses can still be renewed, so there are still amateurs who hold that license class.

Table 3.1 summarizes the HF privileges granted to radio amateurs. When you upgrade to a General class license you will be able to operate on all of these bands. We often refer to amateur bands by approximate wavelength rather than frequency. When you hear someone refer to the "15-meter band," 15 meters is the approximate wavelength of a 21-MHz signal. During a typical day, you can reach any part of the world using one of the Novice bands.

Ground-Wave Propagation

In **ground-wave propagation**, radio waves travel along the Earth's surface, even over hills. They follow the curvature of the Earth for some distance. AM broadcasting signals travel by way of ground-wave propagation during the day. Ground wave works best at lower frequencies. During the day you might have an 80-meter contact with a station a few miles away, on the other side of a hill. For that contact, you are using ground-wave propagation.

Ground-wave propagation on the HF ham bands means relatively short-range communications. Stations at the high-frequency end of the Medium Frequency (MF) AM broadcast band (the 1600-kHz end) generally carry less than a hundred miles during the day. Stations near the low-frequency end of the dial (540 kHz) can be heard up to 100 miles or so away. Amateur Radio frequencies are higher than the AM broadcast band, so the ground-wave range is even shorter.

Sky-Wave Propagation by Means of the Ionosphere

The Earth's upper atmosphere (from 25 to 200 miles high) consists mainly of oxygen and nitrogen. There are traces of hydrogen, helium and several other gases. The atoms making up these gases are electrically neutral: They have no charge and exhibit no electrical force outside their own structure. The gas atoms absorb **ultraviolet (UV) radiation** and other radiation from the sun, which knocks electrons out of the atoms. These electrons are negatively charged particles, and the remaining portions of the gas atoms form positively charged particles. The positive and negative particles are called *ions*. The process by which ions are formed is called *ionization*. **Figure 3.2** illustrates this process.

When ionized by solar radiation, this region, called the **ionosphere**, can **refract** (bend) radio waves. If the wave is bent enough, it returns to Earth. If the wave is not bent enough, it is lost as it travels off into space. The

Table 3.1

Medium/High-Frequency Ham Bands, with Privileges for Technicians with Morse Code Credit

MF/HF Bands

For Full Amateur Privileges (MHz)	Privileges for Technicians with Morse Code Credit	Band (Meters)
1.8 to 2.0	None	160
3.5 to 4.0	3.675 to 3.725	80
7.0 to 7.3	7.1 to 7.15	40
10.10 to 10.15	None	30
14.00 to 14.35	None	20
18.068 to 18.168	None	17
21.00 to 21.45	21.1 to 21.2	15
24.890 to 24.990	None	12
28.00 to 29.70	28.1 to 28.5	10

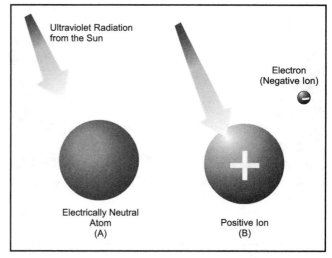

Figure 3.2 — Ultraviolet and other radiation from the sun strikes the atoms of the various gases in the Earth's upper atmosphere. When an electron is knocked free from an electrically neutral atom, positive and negative ions are formed. This upper region of the atmosphere is called the ionosphere.

highest frequency where a radio wave transmitted straight upwards into the ionosphere will be reflected back down to the Earth is called the **critical frequency**.

Ham radio contacts of up to 2500 miles are possible with one *skip* off the ionosphere. Worldwide communications using several skips (or **multi-hops**) can take place if conditions are right, especially when radio waves are launched at low takeoff angles into the ionosphere. This is the way long-distance radio signals travel.

Two factors determine **sky-wave propagation** possibilities between two points: the *frequency* in use and the level of *ionization*. The higher the frequency of the radio wave, the less it is bent by the ionosphere. The highest frequency at which the ionosphere bends radio waves back to a desired location on Earth is called the **maximum usable frequency (MUF)**. The MUF for communication between two points depends on solar radiation strength and the time of day. Radio waves that travel beyond the horizon by refraction in the ionosphere are called *sky waves*. Sky-wave propagation takes place when a signal is returned to Earth by the ionosphere.

Ionization of the ionosphere results from the sun's UV radiation striking the upper atmosphere. It is greatest during the day and during the summer. The amount of radiation coming from the sun varies through the day, season and year. This radiation is closely related to visible **sunspots** (grayish-black blotches on the sun's surface). See **Figure 3.3**. Hams interested in long-distance communication always know what part of the **sunspot cycle** we are in. Sunspots vary in number and size over an 11-year cycle. More sunspots usually mean more ionization of the ionosphere. As a result, the MUF tends also to be higher when there are more sunspots.

By contrast, when sunspots are low, solar radiation — and thus the MUF — is lower. That is why HF communication is degraded during times of low sunspot activity and enhanced during times of greater sunspot activity.

Skip propagation has both a maximum range limit and a minimum range limit. That minimum is often greater than the ground-wave range. There is an area between the maximum ground-wave distance and the minimum skip distance where radio signals on a particular frequency will not reach. This "dead" area is called the **skip zone**. **Figure 3.4** illustrates the difference between ground-wave and skip propagation. The drawing also shows the concept of skip zone and skip distance. Some radio signals may not be bent enough to bring them back to Earth.

Regions in The Ionosphere

Several ionized regions appear at different heights in the atmosphere. Each region has a central region where the ionization is greatest. The intensity of the ionization decreases above and below this central area in each region. See **Figure 3.5**.

The ionosphere consists of several regions of charged

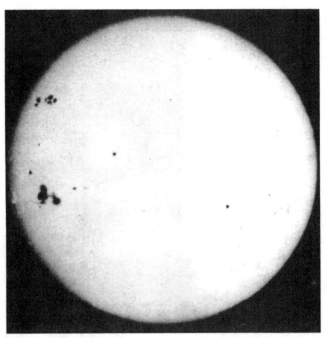

Figure 3.3 — Cool sunspots allow hot propagation on Earth!

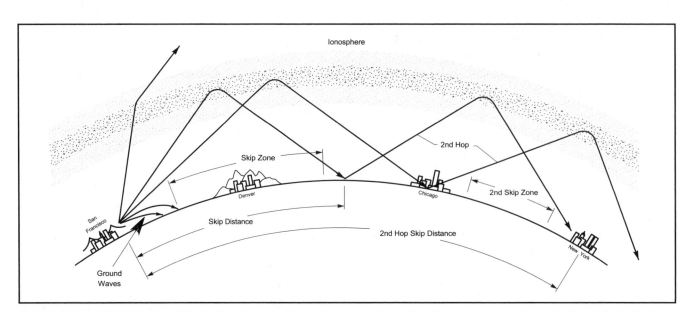

Figure 3.4 — This drawing illustrates how radio waves travel into the ionosphere and are bent back to Earth. Ground waves, skip distance and skip zone are all shown on the drawing.

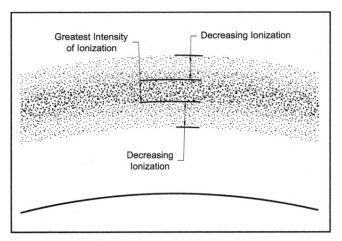

Figure 3.5 — This drawing shows a cross section of one region of the ionosphere. The intensity of the ionization is greatest in the central region and decreases above and below the central region.

particles. These regions have been given letter designations, as shown in **Figure 3.6**. Scientists started with the letter D just in case there were any undiscovered lower regions. None have been found, so there is no A, B or C region.

D Region

The **D region**: The lowest region of the ionosphere affecting propagation is the D region. This region is in a relatively dense part of the atmosphere about 35 to 60 miles above the Earth. When the atoms in this region absorb sunlight and form ions, the ions don't last very long. They quickly recombine with free electrons to form neutral atoms again. The amount of ionization in this region varies widely. It depends on how much sunlight hits the region. At noon, D-region ionization is maximum or very close to it. By sunset, this ionization disappears.

The D region is ineffective in refracting or bending high-frequency signals back to Earth. The D region's

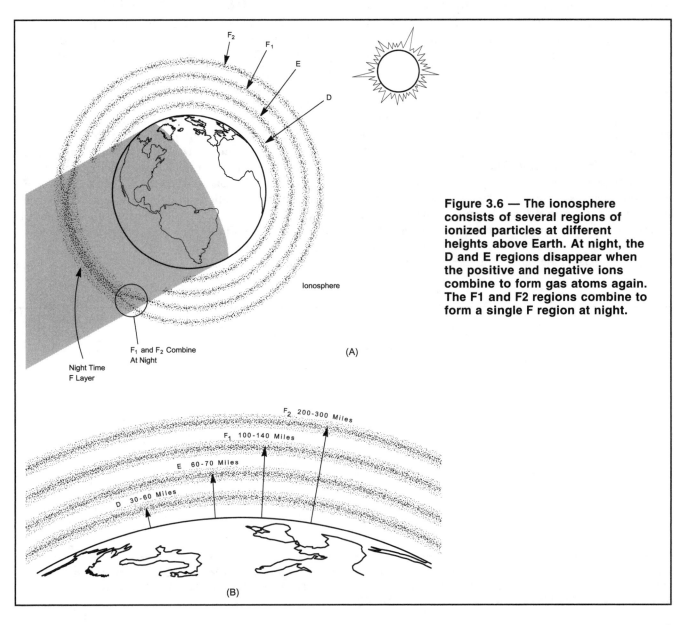

Figure 3.6 — The ionosphere consists of several regions of ionized particles at different heights above Earth. At night, the D and E regions disappear when the positive and negative ions combine to form gas atoms again. The F1 and F2 regions combine to form a single F region at night.

major effect is to absorb energy from radio waves. As radio waves pass through the ionosphere, they give up energy. This sets some of the ionized particles into motion. Effects of absorption on lower frequencies (longer wavelengths) are greater than on higher frequencies.

Absorption also increases when there is more ionization. The more ionization, the more energy the radio waves lose passing through the ionosphere. Absorption is most pronounced at midday. It is responsible for the short daytime communications ranges on the lower-frequency amateur bands (160, 80 and 40 meters).

E Region

The next region of the ionosphere is the **E region**, at an altitude of about 60 to 70 miles. At this height, ionization produced by sunlight does not last very long, again due to rapid recombination of ions with free electrons. The E region is thus useful for bending radio waves only when it is in sunlight. Like the D region, the E region reaches maximum ionization around midday. By early evening the ionization level is very low. The ionization level reaches a minimum just before sunrise, local time. Using the E region, a radio signal can travel a maximum distance of about 1250 miles in one hop.

F Region

The **F region**: This is the region of the ionosphere most responsible for long-distance amateur communication. The F region is very large. It ranges from about 100 to 310 miles above the Earth. The height depends on season, geographic latitude, time of day and solar activity. Ionization reaches a maximum shortly after noon local standard time. It tapers off very gradually toward sunset. At this altitude, the ions and electrons recombine very slowly because there aren't many of them around. The F region thus remains ionized during the night, reaching a

minimum just before sunrise. After sunrise, ionization increases rapidly for the first few hours. Then it increases slowly to its noontime maximum.

During the day, the F region often splits into two parts, F1 and F2. The central part of the F1 region forms at an altitude of about 140 miles. For the F2 region, the central region forms at about 200 miles above the Earth. These altitudes vary with the season of the year and other factors. At noon in the summer the F2 region can reach an altitude of 300 miles. At night, these two regions recombine to form a single F region slightly below the higher altitude. The F1 region does not have much to do with long-distance communications. Its effects are similar to those caused by the E region. The F2 region is responsible for almost all long-distance communication on the amateur HF bands. A one-hop radio transmission travels a maximum of about 2500 miles using the F2 region.

HF Scatter Modes

All electromagnetic-wave propagation is subject to **scattering** influences. These alter idealized patterns to a great degree. The Earth's atmosphere, ionospheric regions and any objects in the path of radio signals scatter the energy. Understanding how scattering takes place helps us use these propagation modes to our advantage.

There is an area between the outer limit of ground-wave propagation and the point where the first signals return from the ionosphere. We studied this area, called the *skip zone*, earlier in this chapter. Look back at Figure 3.4. The skip zone is often described as if communications between stations in each other's skip zone were impossible. Actually, some of the transmitted signal is scattered in the atmosphere, so the signal can be heard over much of the skip zone.

You can observe a complex form of scatter when you

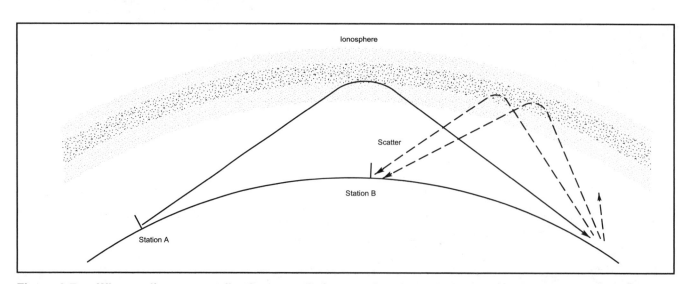

Figure 3.7 — When radio waves strike the ground after passing through the ionosphere, some of the signal may reflect back into the ionosphere. If some of the signal is reflected back toward the transmitting station, some of the energy may be scattered into the skip zone.

are working very near the MUF. The transmitted wave is refracted back to Earth at some distant point. This may be an ocean area or land mass. A portion of the transmitted signal reflects back into the ionosphere. Some of this signal comes toward the transmitting station. The reflected wave helps fill in the skip zone, as shown in **Figure 3.7**.

Scatter signals are generally weak and subject to echoes and distortion, because the signal may arrive at the receiver from many different directions. This type of scatter propagation is usable from just beyond the local range out to several hundred miles. Under ideal conditions, scatter propagation is possible over 3000 miles or more. This form of propagation is sometimes called "backscatter," but the term "sidescatter" is more descriptive of what probably happens on such long paths.

[You should turn to Chapter 11 now and study questions T3A01 through T3A09, T3A11 and T3A12. Then study questions T3B07, T3B08 and T3B11 to T3B13. Review this section on HF propagation if any of these questions give you difficulty.]

VHF/UHF Propagation Characteristics

Because HF radio waves can so easily travel long distances, even with low transmitter power, short-range communication is best carried out on the VHF and UHF bands. This prevents unnecessary interference to other hams using the HF bands. In particular, UHF radio waves do not travel by means of sky wave propagation through the ionosphere.

Line-of-Sight Propagation

Line-of-sight propagation occurs when signals travel in a straight line from the transmitting antenna to the receiving antenna. These *direct waves* are useful mostly in the very high frequency (VHF) and ultra high frequency (UHF) ranges. (As a Technician licensee, you will have full access to the amateur bands in the VHF and UHF range.) TV and FM radio broadcasts (those that are broadcast to your TV or radio antenna instead of through a cable) are examples of signals that are received as direct waves. When you transmit on a local repeater frequency, direct waves generally travel in a straight line to the repeater. The repeater sends the signals, in a straight line, to other fixed, portable and mobile stations. When you use a hand-held transceiver to communicate with another nearby ham, your signals also travel in a straight line. See **Figure 3.8**.

When you operate on the VHF and UHF bands you usually will be contacting nearby stations — within 100 miles or so. The signal travels directly between stations, so if you're using a directional antenna, you normally point it toward the station you are trying to contact. VHF and UHF signals, however, are easily reflected by buildings (especially metal-framed ones), hills and even airplanes. Some of your signal reaches the other station by a direct path and some may be reflected. When such **reflections** occur, it is possible to contact other stations by pointing your antenna toward the reflecting object, rather than directly at the station you're trying to contact.

Reflections can cause problems for mobile operation, as the propagation path is constantly changing. The direct and reflected waves may first cancel and then reinforce each other. This causes a rapid fluttering sound called *picket fencing*.

Tropospheric Bending and Ducting

We've been focusing on the VHF and UHF bands for short-range local communications. However, for many years amateurs have been using VHF/UHF for DX contacts well beyond local, line-of-sight coverage.

As radio waves travel through the troposphere, there will always be some signal loss. For any particular path through the troposphere, the signal loss increases as the frequency increases. Amateurs commonly use SSB or CW as **weak-signal modes** for VHF/UHF DX work — as opposed to "strong-signal modes," such as local FM or packet radio.

The **visible horizon** is the most distant point you can see when the sky is clear. It is limited by the height of the observer above ground. You can see farther if you climb a ladder or go up an observation tower. From the top of a mountain you can see much farther than the 8 or 9 miles you can see over flat ground or water.

As described earlier, the troposphere consists of atmospheric regions close to the Earth's surface. Slight bending of VHF/UHF radio waves occurs in the troposphere. This will cause signals to return to Earth somewhat beyond the geometric horizon, and allows you to contact stations that are somewhat farther away than would otherwise be possible. This radio-path horizon is generally about 15 percent farther away than the true horizon. See **Figure 3.9**. **Tropospheric bending** is evident over a wide range of frequencies. It is most useful in the VHF/UHF region, especially at 144 MHz and above.

Radio signals can also be trapped in the troposphere, traveling a longer distance than normal before coming

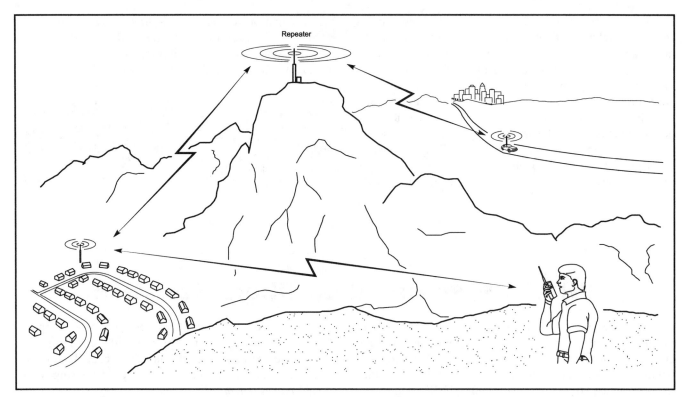

Figure 3.8 — VHF and UHF radio signals usually travel in a straight line, from one antenna to another. This is the type of radio signal propagation you normally use to communicate with someone over a repeater or by direct contact between two radios.

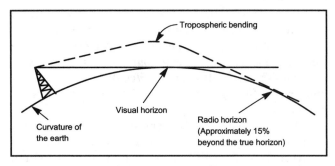

Figure 3.9 — Under normal conditions, tropospheric bending causes radio waves to return to Earth beyond the visible horizon.

back to the Earth's surface. Usually the warmest air in the troposphere is close to the Earth, and the temperature decreases as you go higher. The air pressure also usually decreases as you go higher. Instead of gradual changes in air temperature, pressure and humidity, sometimes distinct regions may form in the troposphere. Adjacent regions having significantly different densities will bend radio waves passing between regions. (In the same way, light is bent when it passes from air into water. That's why

a spoon in a glass of water seems to bend where it enters the water.)

Sometimes, especially during the spring, summer and fall months, it is possible to make VHF and UHF contacts over long distances — up to 1000 miles or more. This occurs during certain weather conditions that cause *tropospheric enhancement* and **tropospheric ducting**. It is most useful in the VHF/UHF region, especially at 144 MHz and above. When such "tropo" openings occur, the VHF and UHF bands are filled with excited operators eager to work **DX**. Under normal conditions, the temperature of the air gradually decreases with increasing height above ground. When there's a stable high-pressure system, a mass of warm air may overrun cold air. When warm air covers cold air, we have a **temperature inversion**. Radio waves can be trapped below the warm air mass. They can travel great distances with little loss. The area between the Earth and the warm air mass is known as a **duct**. See **Figure 3.10**.

Tropospheric ducting is the most common type of enhanced propagation at UHF. Ducts usually form over water, though they can form over land as well. A widespread temperature inversion formed over an ocean may help your VHF or UHF signals travel several hundred miles. Tropospheric ducting supports contacts of 950 miles or more over land and up to 2500 miles over oceans.

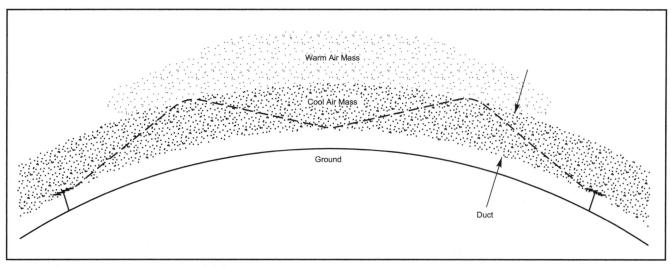

Figure 3.10 — When a cool air mass is overrun by a mass of warmer air, a "duct" may be formed, allowing VHF and UHF radio signals to travel great distances with little attenuation, or signal loss.

VHF/UHF Signals Through the Ionosphere

Sporadic E, or "E skip," is a type of sky-wave propagation that allows long-distance communications on the VHF bands (6 meters, 2 meters and 222 MHz) through the E region of the ionosphere. Although, as its name implies, sporadic E occurs only sporadically, during certain times of the year, it is the most common type of VHF ionospheric propagation.

During the summer, even when we are at a low point on the 11-year sunspot cycle, the 6-meter band (50 MHz) often experiences sporadic-E propagation. As a Technician licensee, your best chance of experiencing sky-wave propagation will occur on the 6-meter band.

[Congratulations! You have completed all the material about radio-wave propagation on your Technician class license exam. Before you go on to Chapter 4, turn to Chapter 11 and study questions T3A10, T3B01 to T3B06, T3B09 and T3B10. Review the material in this VHF/UHF-propagation section if you have difficulty with these questions.]

STATION LICENSEE DUTIES

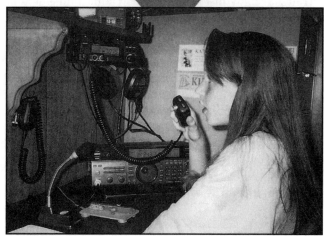

4

When you pass your Technician exam, you will be anxious to start using your new privileges. You are responsible for operating your station within the Rules. You will also want to continue the Amateur Radio tradition of service in the public interest.

In this chapter you will learn the responsibilities that every station licensee should know and follow. Hams in the US enjoy many operating and frequency privileges that cannot be taken for granted. Those privileges are not available in many places around the globe. You should be familiar with the overall licensing process, basic station setup and access, and operating rules. The public service aspect of Amateur Radio — especially emergency communications — is very important. It is the primary reason that we enjoy the amount of operating freedom that we do. The three questions on your Technician license exam about station licensee duties will come from three exam question groups. The three groups are:

T4A Correct name and mailing address on station license grant; Places from where station is authorized to transmit; Selecting station location; Antenna structure location; Stations installed aboard ship or aircraft.

T4B Designation of control operator; FCC presumption of control operator; Physical control of station apparatus; Control point; Immediate station control; Protecting against unauthorized transmissions; Station records; FCC Inspection; Restricted operation.

T4C Providing public service; emergency and disaster communications; Distress calling; Emergency drills and communications; Purpose of RACES.

The Application

Form 605 provides important information about your license application. This form provides the **Federal Communications Commission (FCC)** with a mailing address where they can contact you with any questions about your station or operation. If you move, or your address changes for any reason, use an FCC Form 605 to notify them of your new address. (Chapter 1 has detailed information about FCC Form 605 and how to complete it. See Figure 1.3.) It is important that you receive any mail sent to you by the FCC. If you don't respond to an FCC letter concerning a rules violation, you may be fined or your license may be suspended or revoked! Send the completed Form 605 to the FCC in Gettysburg, PA, and attach a photocopy of your license. Then FCC will be able to write to you if necessary.

You can also change your address records with the FCC by filing the information using the **Universal Licensing System (ULS)** on the World Wide Web. Go to **wireless.fcc.gov/uls/** and click the " Online Filing button.

If you do not already have a unique FCC Registration Number (FRN) you will first have to register with the Commission Registration System (CORES) and obtain an FRN. The instructions on the Web will lead you through the necessary steps. If you are not sure if you have an FRN, use the Search Licenses option on this Web page to look up your call sign. The system will show your FRN, if you have one. Follow the directions on the FCC Web site to fill out an on-line version of the 605 Form.

Your License

In Chapter 1 you learned that your Amateur Radio license is really two licenses in one. The **operator license** portion lists your license class and gives you the authority to operate an amateur station. The **station license** portion includes the address of your primary, or main, Amateur Radio station. **Figure 4.1** shows the two pieces of a printed

FCC license. Both of these pieces of paper include the station license and the operator license. The station license lists the call sign of your station and your primary station location. This is your written authorization for an amateur station. You can operate an amateur station at locations other than the one listed for your primary loca-

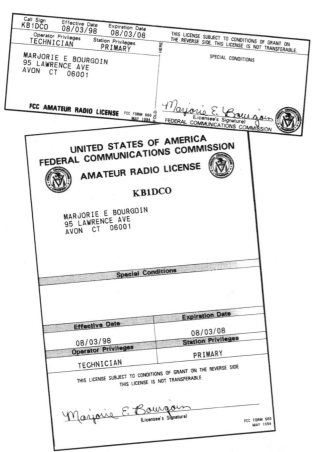

Figure 4.1 — An FCC Amateur Radio license consists of two parts — the station license and the operator license. The two pieces of paper shown here each represent a station license and an operator license. You can carry the smaller section in your wallet for portable or mobile operation. You can post the larger section at your main operating position, or "shack."

An avid outdoorsman, Luigi, IC8GVV, always carries his hand-held radio when he climbs the cliffs near his home on the Isle of Capri. He used his radio to call for help when his climbing partner fell and broke a wrist.

tion, however. For example, you might operate a portable station somewhere away from home, or a mobile station while you are riding in a vehicle. In fact, your amateur license authorizes you to operate a station anywhere that the FCC regulates the amateur service. In addition to the 50 states, this also means US possessions such as certain Pacific islands and onboard ships registered in the US even while sailing in international waters.

Owners of private property may restrict you from operating while you are on their property, of course. For example, you may find that when you go to enter an amusement park or other public attraction, the security people won't allow you to carry your VHF or UHF hand-held radio along. They may not understand Amateur Radio, and may have other security concerns.

You might also wonder if you would be allowed to operate your radio while on board a commercial airplane or even on board a ship. The answer is a qualified yes. The FCC Rules specify that the pilot or master of the ship must approve your station. Section 97.11 lists some other qualifications for such an operation. For example, you may not operate your station while the airplane is operating under "Instrument Flight Rules." You may not operate using the normal communications equipment of the ship or aircraft. You will have to use separate Amateur Radio equipment to operate on the ham bands. The practical answer to this question is that you will probably not be allowed to use your radio on a commercial airplane. With prior arrangements you will have a better chance of getting permission to operate Amateur Radio onboard a ship.

[Now turn to Chapter 11 and study questions T4A01 through T4A06 and T4A10. Review this section if you are uncertain of the answers to any of those questions.]

Antenna Structure Location

An important restriction designed to protect others is an antenna-height limitation. You may not build an **antenna structure** (this includes the radiating elements, tower supports or any other attachments) that is over 200 feet high, unless you first register with and obtain FCC approval. Also, if the antenna structure height exceeds 200 feet, you are required to notify the Federal Aviation Administration (FAA). Generally, the height of an antenna structure may also be further limited under Section 97.15 and Part 17 of the FCC Rules if you live within four miles of an airport. You can check *The ARRL's FCC Rule Book* if you think you may be affected by the airport limitation.

You must choose the location of your transmitting antenna carefully. Objects in the vicinity may negatively affect the performance of the antenna or raise other safety or operating concerns. Nearby structures – especially metal ones – can seriously detune and degrade antenna performance. Antenna height above average terrain (ground) and the distance of the antenna from the transmitter are also important considerations. Antenna height is important to obtain the best performance from the antenna and also to keep the radiating element(s) away from humans and animals whenever possible. The distance of the antenna from the transmitter is important for several reasons. First, you want the antenna to be far enough away from people so it is not a safety hazard. (You will learn more about this in Chapter 10.) If your antenna is too far from your transmitter, though, you will need a long feed line to reach the antenna. This adds to the cost of the installation. It can also result in significant signal loss in the feed line. Feed lines do not have any polarization characteristics. Therefore, the feed-line polarization is not an important consideration when selecting an antenna location.

[This is another good time to take a break from studying the text. Make sure you understand the material and can answer the questions that may appear on your exam. Turn to Chapter 11 and review questions T4A07 through T4A09. If you have any difficulty with those questions study this section of the text again.]

The Control Operator

A **control operator** is an "amateur operator designated by the licensee of a station to be responsible for the transmissions from that station to assure compliance with the FCC Rules." In effect, the control operator operates the Amateur Radio station. Only a licensed ham may be the control operator of an amateur station. If another licensed radio amateur operates your station with your permission, he or she assumes the role of control operator.

If you let an amateur with a higher-class license than yours control your station, he or she may use any operating privileges allowed by the higher-class license. They must follow the proper station identification procedures. If you are the control operator at the station of an amateur who has a higher class of license than yours, you can use only the privileges allowed by your license.

Any amateur operator may designate another licensed

operator as the control operator, to share the responsibility of station operation. The FCC holds both the control operator and the station licensee responsible for proper operation of the station. If you are operating your own Amateur Radio station, then you are the control operator at that time.

A control operator must be present at the station **control point** whenever a transmitter is operating. (The FCC defines control point as "the location at which the control operator function is performed.") This means that you may not allow an unlicensed person to operate your radio transmitter while you are not present. There is one time when a transmitter may be operated without a control operator being present, however. Some types of stations, such as repeater stations, may be operated by automatic control. In this case there is no control operator at the transmitter control point. A control operator can control any number of transmitters.

Your Technician license authorizes you to be the control operator of an amateur station in the Technician frequency bands. This means you can be the control operator of your own station or someone else's station. In either case, you are responsible to the FCC for the proper operation of the station.

If you allow another licensed ham to operate your station, you are still responsible for its proper operation. You are always responsible for the proper operation of your station. Your primary responsibility as the station licensee is to ensure the proper operation of your station. Unless your station records show that another amateur was the control operator of your station at a certain time, the FCC will assume that you were the only control operator.

Station Records

Your **station records** include any written documentation about your amateur station and your on-the-air operating. Most hams keep a **station logbook**, which includes the details about their station operation. A logbook can be used to help answer questions about your station. It can also help you troubleshoot interference-related problems or complaints. What kind of station records should you keep? The FCC does not *require* you to keep any particular information about the operation of your station. Many amateurs find it helpful to keep a logbook with certain information about the operation of their station. A logbook is useful for recording dates, calls, names and locations of those stations you contact. When you confirm contacts by sending "QSL cards" (see Chapter 6) a logbook is a convenient way to keep track of these exchanges. Your log will provide a useful and interesting history, if you choose to keep one. **Figure 4.2** shows an example of the information many amateurs keep in a logbook.

There are commercially prepared logbooks, such as the *ARRL Log Book*, or you can use a notebook or other form that you prepare for your own use. Many amateurs find it helpful to use one side of a page to log amateur contacts and the back of the page to record information about station equipment, changes and other information. Many amateurs also use computer programs to keep their station log information. There are several excellent programs that will help track your progress toward various operating awards. Some of the programs will even print the application forms for those awards.

It isn't necessary to use a station logbook. If you don't, though, it will not be possible to show when someone else has been the control operator of your station. Whenever you give someone else permission to be the control operator at your station, enter the other person's name and call sign, and the time, date and frequencies used, in your logbook.

FCC Inspections

The FCC can conduct an inspection of your amateur station at any time. You must make both the station and any station records available for inspection upon request by an FCC representative. If the FCC decides that it would "promote the public interest, convenience and necessity," they may modify the terms of your station license. For example, suppose a spurious emission from your station is causing interference to nearby radio or television receivers of good engineering design. The FCC can impose operating restrictions on your station. These restrictions may include a requirement to discontinue operation on frequencies causing interference during certain evening hours and on Sunday mornings (local time). Section 97.121 of the FCC Rules says that these restrictions apply between 8 PM and 10:30 PM local time daily and from 10:30 AM to 1 PM on Sunday.

Station Access

It is important to keep any unauthorized persons from using your Amateur Radio station. This is both a safety concern and a requirement of the FCC Rules. You can install a key-operated on/off switch in the main ac-power line to your station equipment. With the switch turned off and the key in your pocket, you will be sure no one can use your station. In a mobile installation, disconnect the microphone and remove it when you leave the vehicle. This is an easy way to prevent unauthorized operation.

[Before you go on to the next section, you should turn to Chapter 11 and study questions T4B01 through T4B13. If you have difficulty with any of these questions, review the material in this section.]

DATE	FREQ.	MODE	POWER	TIME	STATION WORKED	REPORT SENT	REPORT REC'D	TIME OFF	COMMENTS QTH / NAME / QSL VIA	QSL S	QSL R
16 NOV	146.73	FM	5	1725	WB3IOS	59	59	1740	Bozrah, CT Jean	X	X
18 NOV	50.12	PACKET	50	2123	N3KFC			2123	Hazleton, PA Jack METEOR SCATTER!	X	X
19 NOV	147.585	PACKET	25	0326	WB8IMY				Wallingford, CT Steve METEOR SCATTER?	X	X
22 NOV	145.45	FM	5	1655	KB1DCO	59	59	1703	Newington, CT Margie	X	X
22 NOV	28.125	CW	100	1804	XZ1A	599	179	1804	MYANMAR! Bill K5FUV	X	X
22 NOV	28.035	CW	100	2002	KC4AAA	469	599	2003	SOUTHPOLE! Big Pileup		X
22 JAN	50	Phone	50	2335	K3MQH	FN31	FMA		ARRL JANUARY VHF CONTEST	X	
23 JAN	50	Phone	50	0040	W1XM	FN31	FN55		"	X	
23 JAN	144	Phone	75	1944	VE2SMG	FN31	FN35		"	X	X
23 JAN	222	Phone	50	1945	VE2SMG	FN31	FN35		"	X	X
23 JAN	420	Phone	150	1946	VE2SMG	FN31	FN35		"	X	X
21 JUNE	2m/70cm	FM	25	1605	N1JEZ	59	59	1610	Mike - via UO-14	X	
				1611	AA1GW	59	59	1612	Joe in Newington, CT - UO-14	X	X
25 JUNE	15m/10m	SSB	50	2235	G4FHA	57	56	2241	Flos near London - via RS-13	X	
26 JUNE	2m/70cm	FM	25	1550	WB8ISZ	59	59	1553	Dave in Dayton - AO-27	X	
29 JUNE	70cm/2m	SSB	150	0104	S92DX	55	57	0105	Sao Tome DXpedition OSCAR 10	X	

Figure 4.2 — Most amateurs keep a station logbook to record information about each contact.

Emergency Communications

The FCC encourages licensed hams to assist in emergency situations. There are even Rules to get around the Rules that apply at all other times! Section 97.401(a) says:

"When normal communication systems are overloaded, damaged or disrupted because a disaster has occurred, or is likely to occur … an amateur station may make transmissions necessary to meet essential communication needs and facilitate relief actions."

This is a definition of **emergency communications**. The FCC recognizes that "amateurs may provide essential communications in connection with the immediate safety of human life and immediate protection of property when normal communication systems are not available." The Rules go on to say:

97.405 Station in distress.

(a) No provision of these rules prevents the use by an amateur station in distress of any means at its disposal to attract attention, make known its condition and location, and obtain assistance.

(b) No provision of these rules prevents the use by a station, in the exceptional circumstances described in paragraph (a), of any means of radiocommunication at its disposal to assist a station in distress.

If you're in the middle of a hurricane, forest fire or blizzard, and you offer your communications services to the local authorities, you can do whatever you need to do to help deal with the emergency. This includes allowing a physician to operate your radio or helping the Red Cross to assess damages.

Other cases may not be as clear cut. Suppose you

Hurricane debris on St Maarten. Note the "Emergency Dial 911" sign on the downed telephone pole!

hear a ship at sea sending a distress call on a frequency outside of your license privileges or even outside of a ham band. Can you call the ship and offer assistance? If it appears that no other station is able to provide the required communications, yes, you can. If you came across a serious auto accident (or were involved in one) and you were unable to obtain help on a ham band, could you transmit outside of the ham band where you hear another station operating? Again, the answer is a qualified yes. Be sure you have a *real* emergency and that you have no other way to obtain the necessary help.

In the wake of a major disaster, the FCC may suspend or change its Rules to help deal with the immediate problem. Part 97 says that when a disaster disrupts normal communications systems in a particular area, the FCC may declare a **temporary state of communication emergency**. This declaration will set forth any special conditions or rules to be observed during the emergency. Amateurs who want to request that such a declaration be made should contact the FCC Engineer in Charge in the area concerned.

Distress Calls

If you should require immediate emergency help, and you're using a voice (telephony) mode, call **MAYDAY**. Use whatever frequency offers the best chance of getting a useful answer. "MAYDAY" is from the French *m'aidez* (help me). On CW (telegraphy), use $\overline{\text{SOS}}$ to call for help. Repeat the appropriate call a few times, and pause for any station to answer. Identify the transmission with your call sign. Stations that hear the call sign will realize that the MAYDAY or $\overline{\text{SOS}}$ is legitimate. Repeat this procedure for as long as possible, or until you receive an answer. In a life or property-threatening emergency, you may send a distress call on *any* frequency, even outside the amateur bands, if you think doing so will bring help faster.

Be ready to supply the following information to the stations responding to an $\overline{\text{SOS}}$ or MAYDAY call:

- *The location of the emergency*, with enough detail to permit rescuers to locate it without difficulty.
- *The nature of the distress.*
- *The type of assistance required* (medical, evacuation, food, clothing or other aid).
- *Any other information* to help locate the emergency area.

If you receive a distress signal, you are also allowed to transmit on *any* frequency to provide assistance. What if you happen to be in contact with another station when an emergency call for help is heard on your frequency? You should immediately stop your QSO and take the call! To make a distress call during an ongoing repeater conversation, the proper procedure is to say "BREAK" once, followed by your call sign. (On some repeaters, operators may say "BREAK" when they want to join a conversation. In general, you should try to avoid using that practice. If you hear someone say "BREAK" you should immediately answer them and stand by for their emergency communications.)

Emergency Operations

When cities, towns, counties, states or the federal government call for emergency communications, amateurs answer. They put their mobile and portable radio equipment into service, using alternatives to commercial power. Generators, car batteries, windmills or solar energy can provide power for equipment during an emergency, when normal ac power is often out of service. Many amateurs have some way to operate their station without using commercial ac power. Power lines are often knocked down and areas lose power during a natural disaster such as a hurricane, tornado, earthquake or ice storm.

A dipole antenna is the best choice for a portable HF

station that can be set up in emergencies. It can be installed easily, and wire is light and portable. Carry an ample supply of wire and you'll be ready to go on the air at any time and any place.

If you're planning to use a battery-powered hand-held transceiver, bring along at least one spare, *charged* battery pack. One of the most important accessories you can have for your hand-held radio is several extra battery packs. Just be sure you keep them charged. Many hams have found that a battery pack that holds regular alkaline batteries is also an excellent accessory. Alkaline batteries are available anywhere. They have a long shelf life and will last longer than a single charge in a rechargeable battery pack.

A hand-held transceiver is a very useful piece of equipment. It can be used in a variety of emergency situations. You can use such a radio at home, in your car and you can take it just about anywhere. You can carry it along on an emergency search and rescue mission, use it for communications from an emergency shelter or take it into the field for making damage reports to government officials.

Tactical Communications

Tactical communications is first-response communications in an emergency involving a few people in a small area. This type of communications is unformatted and seldom written. It may be urgent instructions or requests such as "Send an ambulance," or "Who has the medical supplies?"

Tactical communications often use 2-meter repeater net frequencies or the 146.52-MHz simplex calling frequency. Compatible mobile, portable and fixed-station equipment is plentiful and popular for these frequencies.

Tactical communications is particularly important when working with local government and law-enforcement agencies. Use the 12-hour local-time system for times and dates when working with relief agencies. Most may not understand the 24-hour system or Coordinated Universal Time (UTC).

Make tactical communications efficient by using **tactical call signs**. They describe a function, location or agency. Their use promotes coordination with individuals or agencies that are monitoring. When operators change shifts or locations, the set of tactical call signs remains the same. Amateurs may use such tactical call signs as *parade headquarters*, *finish line*, *Command Post*, *Weather Center* or *Net Control*. This procedure promotes efficiency and coordination in public-service communication activities. Tactical call signs do not fulfill the identification requirements of Section 97.119 of the FCC Rules, however. Amateurs must also identify their station operation with their FCC-assigned call sign. Identify at the end of the operation and at least every 10 minutes during the operation.

Health-and-Welfare Traffic

There can be a large number of messages to handle during a disaster. Phone lines still in working order are often overloaded. They should be reserved for emergency use by those people in peril. Shortly after a major disaster, **Emergency traffic** messages leave the disaster area. These have life-and-death urgency or are for medical help and critical supplies. Handle them first! Next is **Priority traffic**. These are emergency-related messages, but not as important as Emergency messages. **Health-and-Welfare traffic** pertains to the well being of people in the disaster area. Friends and relatives of those who may have been injured or evacuated want to know if their loved ones are okay. Health-and-Welfare traffic provides information to those waiting outside the disaster area.

Hams inside disaster areas cannot immediately find out about someone's relative when their own lives may be threatened — they are busy handling emergency messages. After the immediate emergency subsides, concerned friends and relatives of possible victims can send Health-and-Welfare inquiries into the disaster area.

RACES

The FCC Rules establish the **Radio Amateur Civil Emergency Service (RACES)** as a communications service within the Amateur Radio Service. RACES provides communications assistance to civil defense organizations in times of need. RACES is a part of the amateur service that provides radio communications only for civil defense purposes. It is active *only* during periods of local, regional or national civil emergencies.

You must be registered with the responsible civil defense organization to operate as a RACES station or participate in RACES drills. RACES stations may not communicate with amateurs not operating in a RACES capacity. Only civil-preparedness communications can be transmitted during RACES operation. These are defined in section 97.407 of the FCC regulations. Rules permit tests and drills for a maximum of one hour per week. All test and drill messages must be clearly identified as such.

The **Amateur Radio Emergency Service (ARES)** is sometimes confused with RACES. ARES is sponsored by ARRL, and presents a way for local amateurs to provide emergency communications while working with groups such as the American Red Cross and local Emergency Operations Centers.

[Congratulations! You have studied all of the material about station licensee requirements and duties for your Technician class license exam. Before you go on to Chapter 5, turn to Chapter 11 and study questions T4C01 through T4C14. Review this section if you have difficulty with any of these questions.]

CONTROL OPERATOR DUTIES

Your Amateur Radio experience will be fun and exciting as you make new friends on the air. You will want to operate your station properly. You must understand the FCC Rules about control operators.

In this chapter, we will review the control operator duties for proper station operation. This includes control operator privileges and the presence of a control operator. You will also learn about the procedures for operating other amateur stations. We will review transmitter power standards, identification requirements, and interference issues to both emergency and general communications. We will also cover third-party communications, retransmission of signals and prohibited practices. The three control operator duties questions on your Technician license exam will come from three exam groups. The three groups are:

T5A Determining operating privileges, Where control operator must be situated while station is locally or remotely controlled; Operating other amateur stations.

T5B Transmitter power standards; Interference to stations providing emergency communications; Station identification requirements.

T5C Authorized transmissions, Prohibited practices; Third party communications; Retransmitting radio signals; One way communications.

The Control Operator

As we learned in Chapter 4, the **control operator** is an amateur operator designated by the licensee of a station to be responsible for station transmissions. Suppose that you are the control operator and hold a Technician class license at the station of another amateur with a higher-class license than yours (a General, Advanced or Amateur Extra class.) You can use only the privileges allowed by *your* license! On the other hand, if you let another amateur with a higher-class license than yours control your station, any privileges allowed by his or her license are permitted. They're permitted—as long as proper identification procedures are followed.

Any amateur operator may designate another licensed operator as the control operator. They share the responsibility of station operation. The FCC holds both the control operator and the station licensee responsible for proper operation of the station. If you are operating your own Amateur Radio station, then you are the control operator at that time.

A control operator must be present at the station **control point** whenever a transmitter is operating. The control point is simply the location where the control operator function is performed. A control operator can control any number of transmitters. This means that you may not allow an unlicensed person—even a family member—to operate your radio transmitter while you are not present. They must first be licensed before they're allowed to be control operators. There is one exception where a control operator is not required to be present, however. A **repeater station** may be operated by automatic control. A repeater station is an amateur station that automatically retransmits the signals of other stations. In this case there is typically no control operator at the transmitter control point. What if you wanted to set up your dual-band mobile transceiver as a crossband repeater? In this instance, a control operator *is* required at the system's control point.

Your Technician license authorizes you to be the control operator of an amateur station in the Technician frequency bands. This means you can be the control operator of your own station or someone else's station. In either case, you are responsible to the FCC for the proper operation of the station. You may operate any amateur equipment provided that you do so within *your* amateur license privileges.

If you allow another licensed ham to operate your station, you are still responsible for its proper operation. You are always responsible for the proper operation of your station. Your primary responsibility as the station licensee is to ensure proper station operation. What if your station records do not show that another amateur was the control operator of your station at a certain time? In this case, the FCC will assume that you were the only control operator!

Keep your operation "above board" — set an operating example that will make you proud. You should be familiar with the basic operating and technical rules covered in the FCC's Regulations. These FCC Regulations are known as Part 97 and they govern the Amateur Radio Service. You will also find a detailed list of your operating privileges in Part 97. You should also know the standard operating practices used for the various modes you operate. Other chapters in this book have detailed information about operating and the various modes you'll want to sample. In this section we will review the control operator's duties and guidelines for good operation.

Preventing Interference to Emergency Communications

When an emergency communication *is in progress*, it is important to use good judgment. You don't want to be an obstacle to the emergency, relief or recovery effort. Unless you can be of needed assistance, it is essential to resist being a microphone or key hog! Sometimes even a minor delay in exchanging needed information could mean the difference between life or death, or serious injury to others. Let's suppose you are helping in a communications emergency that is being handled by a net control operator. How can you best minimize interference to the net once you have checked in? An effective solution is to not transmit until you are asked to by the net operator. This act of self-restraint helps to avoid station **doubling**. Doubling occurs when two or more operators transmit at the same time on the same frequency. You can help prevent needless confusion to a scenario where literally seconds can matter! While FCC rules permit a broad standard of operating flexibility for emergency communications, they must not be taken lightly. Transmitting on a police frequency as a joke, for example, is harmful interference. A large penalty is the likely result of such an act! Such interference can block police calls that might be an emergency, and interrupt police communications.

Preventing Interference in General

Let's consider another example of possible interference. Say you are using a frequency within a band assigned to the amateur service on a secondary basis. Soon, a station assigned to the primary service on that same band actually causes interference. What action should be taken? The answer may surprise you. As a secondary service operation, *YOU* should change frequencies! You may be causing harmful interference to the other station with primary service status, in violation of FCC rules.

[Before you go on to the next section, you should turn to Chapter 11 and study questions T5A01 through T5A10 and questions T5B09, T5B11 and T5B12. Also study question T5C12. Review this section if you have difficulty with any of those questions.]

Time Out for Station Identification

FCC regulations are very specific about station identification. You must identify your station every ten minutes or less during a contact and at the end of the contact. You do not have to identify with every transmission during a conversation with another ham or group of hams, though. Identify your station by transmitting the station call sign listed on your license at the required intervals.

It doesn't matter if you are operating from your home station, from a portable location or in a vehicle as a mobile station. It doesn't matter what mode you are operating. You must always identify your station every ten minutes when you are operating.

You don't *have* to transmit your call sign at the *beginning* of a contact. In most cases it will help you establish the communications, though. Unless you give your call sign, the other stations may not know who you are! When you take part in a net, or talk with a group of hams regularly, they may learn to recognize your voice. Then you may not have to give your call sign for them to know who you are.

You do not have to transmit both call signs when you are talking with another ham — only your own. The exception is in cases of **third-party communications** with a station in a foreign country. (You'll learn more about third-party communications later in this chapter.) Then you do have to transmit both call signs at the end of the contact.

Let's look at an example of how to identify an Amateur Radio station properly. WB8IMY and WR1B have been in communication for 45 minutes and are now signing off. Each operator has already transmitted his call four times (once after each 10-minute interval). Each should now transmit his call one more time as they sign off, for a total of five times during the QSO. (*QSO* means a two-way contact or communication with another ham.)

What if the QSO had lasted only eight minutes? Each station would be required to transmit their call sign only once (at the end of the communication). You may identify more often than this to make it easier to communicate on a crowded band. But the rules specify only that you identify every 10 minutes, and at the end of a contact. On voice, identification is simply "this is WB8IMY." In Morse code, use DE WR1B ("DE" means *from* in French).

Suppose you have a Technician license and also have a Certificate of Successful Completion of Examination (CSCE). The CSCE shows that you have credit for passing the Morse code exam. What special identification procedures must you follow when you operate on the HF bands? No special procedure is needed. Just give your call sign as described here.

By the way, Morse code is the one emission mode that may always be used to transmit your station identification. It doesn't matter what frequency you are operating on, or what mode you are using for the communication. You may use Morse code to send your station identification.

You can use any language you want to communicate with other amateurs. Amateur Radio gives you a great opportunity to practice your "foreign" language skills. You can find other hams that speak the language you are learning. They will usually be very helpful with questions you may have. You will find they are quite pleased that you would try to speak with them in their native language! When you give your station identification, however, you must use English.

The FCC recommends that you use a phonetic alphabet as an aid to station identification. The International Telecommunication Union (ITU) phonetic alphabet uses words that are internationally recognized substitutes for letters. This makes it easier to understand the letters. You will learn the ITU phonetic alphabet and how to use it in Chapter 6 of this book.

There are two exceptions to the station identification rules. The first exception is when you are transmitting signals to control a model craft—a plane or boat. This control or **telecommand operation** is a permissible one-way transmission. This type of transmission is to start, change or end functions of a device. The device is usually some distance from the transmitter. The model craft's control transmitter must be labeled, however. The label must contain the station licensee's name, address and call sign. Also, the model craft's control transmitter power cannot exceed one watt. The second exception to station identification is for a **space station**. A space station is an Amateur Radio station located more than 50 km above the Earth's surface. An OSCAR (Orbiting Satellite Carrying Amateur Radio) satellite itself, for example, does not have to transmit a station call sign. Operators transmitting to the satellite must transmit their call signs, however.

[Go to Chapter 11 and study questions T5B01 through T5B04, T5B08, T5B10 and T5C07. Review this section as needed.]

Prohibited Practices

Under FCC Rules, you must clearly make known the source of your transmissions to anyone receiving them. The rules prohibit **unidentified communications or signals**. These are signals where the transmitting station's call sign is not included. Be sure you understand the proper station identification procedures, so you don't violate this rule. You should not press the push-to-talk button on your radio or microphone without giving your call sign. Don't just press the mike button to send a signal to test repeater access. Give your call sign, too.

What if you answer someone on the air and complete your communication without giving your call sign? These are both examples of unidentified communications (or unidentified signals or transmissions), and they're illegal.

No station may transmit as the station call any call not authorized to that station. You can't make up a call sign or use someone else's call sign without their permission!

FCC rules also prohibit the transmission of **false or deceptive signals**. These are transmissions intended to mislead or confuse those who receive them. As an example, it is illegal for you to pretend there is an emergency and transmit MAYDAY! Further, you must always avoid deliberately interfering with another station's communications. For example, you must not repeatedly transmit on a frequency already occupied. It could be over a group of amateurs in a net, or just two hams already in a QSO. Each of these is an example of harmful or malicious interference.

Permitted One-Way Transmissions

Emergency communications, remote control of a model craft and beacon operation are all examples of permitted **one-way communications**. These are transmissions that are not intended to be answered. The FCC strictly limits the types of one-way communications allowed on the amateur bands. Part 97 also allows the following kinds of one-way amateur communications:

• brief transmissions necessary to make adjustments to a station;

• brief transmissions necessary to establishing two-way communications with other stations;

• transmissions necessary to assisting persons learning, or improving proficiency in, the international Morse code; and

• transmissions necessary to disseminate information bulletins (these are to be directed only to amateurs and must consist solely of subject matter of direct interest to the amateur service).

Transmitter Power

When you consider how much transmitter power to use, the main FCC Rule is Section 97.313 (a). "An amateur station must use the minimum power necessary to carry out the desired communications." What this means is simple — if you don't need 200 W to contact someone, don't use it! For example, suppose you contact another amateur station. You learn that your signals are extremely strong and loud, and perfectly readable. You should turn down your transmitter output power in that case.

Transmitter power is measured in watts of **peak envelope power (PEP)** output at the antenna terminals of the transmitter or amplifier. The FCC defines peak envelope power as "the average power supplied to the antenna transmission line by a transmitter during one RF cycle at the crest of the modulation envelope." This sounds pretty technical, but it isn't too difficult to understand the basic principle. The *modulation envelope* refers to the way the information signal varies the transmitter output. Think of it as increasing and decreasing the transmitted signal. All we have to do is find the highest point, or maximum output-signal level. Then we look at one cycle of the radio-frequency (RF) signal. We next measure the average power during that time. **Figure 5.1** illustrates this measurement on a radio-signal waveform. You might use a *wattmeter* to make that measurement for you, and the meter will do all the work. So you just have to read a meter scale or read the numbers off a digital display.

Technician and higher-class operators may operate with a *maximum* **peak envelope power (PEP)** output of 1500 W. Notice that the word *maximum* is emphasized. There are some exceptions to the maximum power rules:

• All who are authorized to operate in the 80, 40 and 15-meter Novice subbands may use a maximum of 200 watts PEP.

• Technicians who are authorized to operate on the Novice bands (those who have passed a 5-wpm code test) are also limited to 200 W PEP on the 10-meter Novice sub band, 28.1 to 28.5 MHz.

• All amateurs are limited to 200 W PEP on the 30-meter band (10.1-10.15 MHz). You will be able to use this band when you upgrade to General class.

• Stations in beacon operation are limited to 100 W PEP output.

• Stations operating near certain military installations may use a maximum of 50 W PEP on the 450-MHz band.

The rules limit the maximum transmitter *output* power in the amateur service to 1500 W PEP. Amateurs rarely use more than a couple of hundred watts on the VHF and UHF bands. An exception would be a challenging attempt like "moonbounce" — bouncing a signal off the moon. Such activities may require increased power levels for success.

[Before continuing, turn to Chapter 11 and review questions T5B05 through T5B07. Also study questions T5C01 and T5C08 through T5C11. Review this section as necessary.]

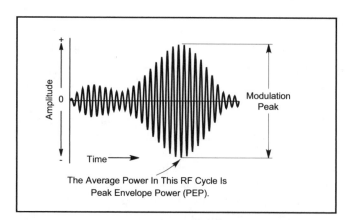

Figure 5.1 — This drawing represents a modulated RF waveform. The peak envelope power (PEP) of this signal is calculated or measured by finding the average power of one RF cycle that occurs at the modulation peak.

Third-Party Communications

A message sent between two amateur stations for someone else is **third-party communications**. (Many hams call it *third-party traffic*.) For example, sending a message from your mother-in-law to her relatives elsewhere is third-party communications. The control operator of one station (the first party) sends communications to the control operator of another station (the second party) for someone else (the third party). Third-party messages include those that are in any way originated by or for a third party, and transmitted by an amateur station either live or delayed. They can include spoken, written, keystroked, keyed, and/or photographed material.

Third-party communications of a personal nature is okay. Passing along messages involving business matters is not! The Amateur Service is not the place to conduct business. Therefore, you may not receive any type of payment in return for transmitting or receiving third-party communication.

You can pass third-party messages to other stations in the United States. Outside the US, FCC Rules strictly limit this type of communication. You may only communicate with those countries that have **third-party communications agreements** with the US. The agreement is an understanding between the United States and another country. It allows amateurs in both countries to participate in third-party communications. In general, you should consider that international third-party communication is prohibited, except when:

- communicating with a person in a country with which the US shares a third-party agreement, or
- in cases of emergency where there is an immediate threat to lives or property, or
- the third party is eligible to be a control operator of the station.

In many countries, the government operates the telephone system and other communications lines. You can imagine why these governments are reluctant to allow their amateur operators to pass messages. They would be in direct competition with the government-operated communications system.

The ARRL monthly journal, *QST*, periodically publishes a list of countries with which the US has a third-party communications agreement. The list does change, and sometimes there are temporary agreements to handle special events. Check such a list, or ask someone who knows, before you try to pass a message to another country. **Table 5.1** is a list of countries with which the US had third-party communications agreements as this book was being printed.

You may allow an unlicensed person to participate in Amateur Radio communications from your station. This is **third-party participation**. It is another form of third-party communications.

From October 1955 *QST*

You (as control operator) must always be present to make sure the unlicensed person follows all the rules. This is how you can allow your family members and friends to enjoy some of the excitement of Amateur Radio. They can speak into the microphone or even send Morse code messages on a keyboard, as long as you are present to control the radio. They can also type messages on your computer keyboard to talk with someone using packet radio or radioteletype.

What should you do if you are allowing your non-amateur sister to use your station, and a foreign station breaks in to talk to her? You should have your sister wait while you find out if the US has a third-party agreement with the foreign station's government.

There is another important rule to keep in mind about third-party participation. What if the unlicensed person was an amateur operator whose license was suspended or revoked by the FCC? That person may not participate in any amateur communication! You can't allow that person to talk into the microphone of your transmitter or operate your Morse code key or computer keyboard.

[Now turn to Chapter 11 and study questions T5C03 through T5C06. Review this section if any of these questions give you difficulty. Then move on to Chapter 6.]

Table 5.1

International Third-Party Traffic — Proceed With Caution

Occasionally, DX stations may ask you to pass a third-party message to a friend or relative in the States. This is all right as long as the US has signed an official third-party traffic agreement with that particular country, or the third party is a licensed amateur. The traffic must be noncommercial and of a personal, unimportant nature.

US Amateurs May Handle Third-Party Traffic With:

C5	The Gambia	J6	St Lucia	VK	Australia
CE	Chile	J7	Dominica	VR6*	Pitcairn Island
CO	Cuba	J8	St Vincent and the Grenadines	XE	Mexico
CP	Bolivia	JY	Jordan	YN	Nicaragua
CX	Uruguay	LU	Argentina	YS	El Salvador
D6	Federal Islamic Republic	OA	Peru	YV	Venezuela
	of the Comoros	PY	Brazil	ZP	Paraguay
DU	Philippines	TA	Turkey	ZS	South Africa
EL	Liberia	TG	Guatemala	3DAØ	Swaziland
GB	United Kingdom	TI	Costa Rica	4U1ITU	ITU Geneva
HC	Ecuador	T9	Bosnia-Herzegovina	4U1VIC	VIC, Vienna
HH	Haiti	V2	Antigua and Barbuda	4X	Israel
HI	Dominican Republic	V3	Belize	6Y	Jamaica
HK	Colombia	V4	St Christopher and Nevis	8R	Guyana
HP	Panama	V6	Federated States of Micronesia	9G	Ghana
HR	Honduras	V7	Marshall Islands	9L	Sierra Leone
J3	Grenada	VE	Canada	9Y	Trinidad and Tobago

Notes:

*Since 1970, there has been an informal agreement between the United Kingdom and the US, permitting Pitcairn and US amateurs to exchange messages concerning medical emergencies, urgent need for equipment or supplies, and private or personal matters of island residents.

Please note that the Region 2 Division of the International Amateur Radio Union (IARU) has recommended that international traffic on the 20 and 15-meter bands be conducted on the following frequencies:

14.100-14.150 MHz   21.150-21.200 MHz
14.250-14.350 MHz   21.300-21.450 MHz

The IARU is the alliance of Amateur Radio societies from around the world; Region 2 comprises member-societies in North, South and Central America, and the Caribbean.

Note: At the end of an exchange of third-party traffic with a station located in a foreign country, FCC-licensed amateurs must also transmit the call sign of the foreign station as well as their own call sign.

GOOD OPERATING PRACTICES

The operating world is rich and varied. As you operate and try new modes, you'll become more proficient on the air.

With your ham license, you can relax and enjoy a conversation (a ragchew) with another ham. You can send and receive messages anywhere in North America via the National Traffic System (handle third-party messages, or *traffic*). You can contact large numbers of stations in a very short time in competition with other hams (enter *contests*). You can try to contact hams in as many different countries or distant places as possible (chase **DX**). These are just a few of the activities that Amateur Radio operators enjoy.

In this chapter, we'll give you some tips for operating with your new Technician license — on phone using single sideband; on some digital modes; and using Morse code (CW). Then we'll take a look at some other operating modes you may want to try. We will even consider some of the problems you may experience with your new ham station, and find ways to solve those problems.

There will be three questions on your Technician class exam taken from the material in this chapter. Those questions will come from the following three question topics from the Element 2 syllabus:

T6A Calling another station; Calling CQ; Typical amateur service radio contacts; Courtesy and respect for others; Popular Q-signals; Signal reception reports; Phonetic alphabet for voice operations.
T6B Occupied bandwidth for emission types; Mandated and voluntary band plans; CW operation.
T6C TVI and RFI reduction and elimination, Band/Low/High pass filter, Out of band harmonic Signals, Spurious Emissions, Telephone Interference, Shielding, Receiver Overload.

Operating Skill

Poor operating procedure is ham radio's version of original sin. It is a curse that will not go away. Hams refer to these poor operators as *lids*. No one wants to be a lid or to have a conversation with a lid. Calling someone a lid is the ultimate insult. (Don't do it on the air. Just be sure your operating practices are such that no one *wants* to call *you* a lid.)

It is actually easier to be a good operator than to fall prey to sloppy habits. You can transmit a message without needless repetition and without unnecessary identification. Good operating makes hamming more fun for everyone. For example, on **CW (Morse code)**, you don't have to spell out each and every word to have a conversation.

Clearly, the initial glamour of Amateur Radio is the opportunity to talk to people who share a common bond, the hobby of ham radio. It doesn't matter if they're across town or in another country. Technician licensees who have credit for passing the Morse code exam, to gain

"Novice privileges," have plenty of chances to work DX (contact distant stations — usually in other countries) on the 10- and 15-meter HF ham bands (28.1 to 28.5 MHz and 21.1 to 21.2 MHz). The 40- and 80-meter Novice HF bands (7.1 to 7.15 MHz and 3.675 to 3.725 MHz) also provide good DX opportunities at times, as well as long-distance communications across the US. The VHF and UHF bands are useful primarily for shorter-range contacts. Satellites provide a good opportunity for Technician class licensees to talk with stations in other countries and over longer distances than normal FM repeater contacts. In addition, there are some conditions in the Earth's atmosphere that will help you contact stations hundreds of miles away. You learned about *propagation* — how radio signals travel — in Chapter 3.

Certain segments of each band are set aside for various kinds of operation. For instance, the six-meter band "DX Window" is 50.100 – 50.125 MHz. By agreement, USA stations only work DX (non-USA stations) in this band segment. Most of these frequency segments are part of the ARRL and International Amateur Radio Union (IARU) Band plans. Band plans are voluntary agreements between operators about how to use a particular band, rather than FCC regulations. Good operators are familiar with the band plans and try to follow them.

Chapter 8 presents information on antennas for all types of locations. Once you choose the frequency bands on which you want to operate, you'll need to install an antenna that will get you on the air. The success of your antenna installation will be evident once you actually begin making contacts: Either they'll hear you or they won't. You won't need a beam antenna to work DX. At times of high sunspot activity, many hams report outstanding results using dipoles or converted CB antennas. Your goal is to put the best possible signal on the air. Of course, this will vary depending on your location and your budget. Don't worry about competing with the ham down the street who has a huge antenna atop a 70-foot tower.

In Amateur Radio, it's important to enjoy and take pride in your own accomplishment. You've heard it said "It's what you do with what you've got that really counts." That is especially true in Amateur Radio. To make up for any real or imagined lack of equipment, concentrate on improving your own operating ability.

Good operating skills can be like making your signal ten times stronger! Hams say it is like adding 10 dB to your signal. (More detailed operating information can be found in *The ARRL Operating Manual*. This book is available from your local radio dealer or directly from ARRL.)

The first rule of good operating practice is to always *listen* before you transmit! This may seem so obvious that we wouldn't even have to mention it. A few seconds of listening will help ensure that you don't interfere with a conversation (QSO) in progress. If the frequency sounds clear, make a brief call or ask if the frequency is clear. You may have just heard the pause between two parts of the contact.

Another good rule for Amateur Radio contacts is to talk as you would during a face-to-face conversation. When you meet someone for the first time, you introduce yourself once; you don't repeat your name over and over again. An exception would be if the other person is hard of hearing or you're meeting in a noisy place. Even then you would only repeat if the person couldn't hear you. To call another station when the frequency is not in use, just give both calls. For, example, "WR1B, this is WB3IOS." When you are on the air, the other operator will tell you if she can't hear you clearly.

Now, let's take a look at some guidelines that will help you get accustomed to operating your new radio with your new privileges.

SSB Voice Operating

Operating **single sideband (SSB)** voice is a bit different than using FM **phone** on a repeater. The procedures described here apply to voice operation on the "weak-signal" SSB frequencies on the VHF/UHF bands and on 10-meter single sideband (SSB).

What does single-sideband (SSB) mean? Begin with a steady radio frequency (RF) signal such as you would get by pressing the key of a Morse code transmitter and just holding it down. This signal is called the *RF carrier*. Then combine this signal with a voice signal from a microphone. The process of combining such an RF carrier with any information signal is called *modulation*. (Actually, keying the RF carrier to form Morse code is a form of modulation.) If we use *amplitude* modulation, the resulting signal has two **sidebands**, one higher in frequency than the carrier frequency and one lower in frequency than the carrier frequency. These are called the *upper sideband* and the *lower sideband*. For a single-sideband voice signal, the carrier and one of the sidebands is removed, and only one sideband is transmitted. See **Figure 6.1**. The RF carrier is the signal that we modulate to produce a radiotelephone signal.

SSB is the most common voice mode on HF. You can use either the *lower sideband* or the *upper sideband* to transmit an SSB signal. Amateurs normally use the upper sideband for **phone** operation on frequencies higher than 14 MHz. This includes the VHF and UHF bands.

Operating techniques and procedures vary for different modes, and even a little from band to band. A great way to become familiar with new techniques is to spend

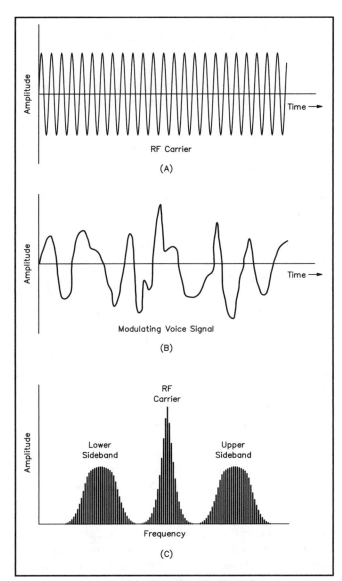

Figure 6.1 — A single-sideband (SSB) signal is formed by combining an RF carrier signal (A) with a voice or other information signal (B). The resulting signal includes the original RF carrier as well as two sidebands, one on either side of the carrier. The upper and lower sidebands are shown at C. To transmit an SSB signal one of the sidebands and the RF carrier are removed in the transmitter, and the remaining sideband is transmitted.

time listening. Be discriminating, though. Take a few moments to understand the techniques used by the proficient operators — the ones who are the most understandable and who sound the best. Don't simply mimic whatever you hear. This is especially true if you're going on the air for the first time.

Whatever band or mode you are using, there are three fundamental things to remember. These apply for any type of voice operating you might try. The first is that courtesy costs very little. It is often rewarded by bringing out the best in others. Second, the aim of each radio contact should

be 100% effective communication. A good operator is never satisfied with anything less. Third, your "private" conversation with another station is actually open to the public. Many amateurs are uncomfortable discussing controversial subjects over the air. Also, never give any confidential information on the air. You never know who may be listening.

Keep it Plain and Simple

Although it does not require the use of any codes or special abbreviations, proper voice procedure is very important. Voice operators *say* what they want to have understood. CW operators abbreviate so they don't have to spell it out. One advantage of voice operation is speed: a typical voice QSO takes place at between 150 and 200 words per minute. Whether you're working a DX operator who may not fully understand our language, or talking to your friend down the street, speak slowly and clearly. That way, you'll have fewer requests to repeat information.

Avoid using CW abbreviations and prosigns such as "HI" and "K" for voice communications. Also, Q signals (QRX, QRV and so forth) are for CW, not voice, operation. (You will learn about proper CW operating techniques later in this chapter.) You may hear operators using Q signals such as QSL, QSO and QRZ on voice, but you should generally avoid using them on voice modes. Abbreviations are used on CW to say more in less time, to improve the efficiency of your communications. On voice, you have plenty of time to say what you mean. On CW, for example, it's convenient to send "K" at the end of a transmission. On voice, it takes less than a second to say "go ahead."

Use plain language and keep jargon to a minimum. In particular, avoid the use of "we" when you mean "I" and "handle" or "personal" when you mean "name." Also, don't say "that's a roger" when you mean "that's correct." Taken individually, any of these sayings is almost harmless. Combined in a conversation, however, they give a false-sounding "radioese" that is actually less effective than plain language.

If the other operator is having difficulty copying your signals you should use the standard International Telecommunication Union (ITU) **phonetic alphabet**, detailed in **Table 6.1**. Use the words in the phonetic alphabet to spell out the letters in your call sign, your name or any other piece of information that might be confused if the letters are not received correctly. This phonetic alphabet is generally understood by hams in all countries.

Initiating a Contact

There is no point in wasting words, and that includes when you are trying to make a radio contact. Hams establish a contact when one station calls **CQ** and another replies. **CQ** literally means "Seek you: Calling any station." You can usually tell a good ham by the length of the CQ

Table 6.1

Standard ITU Phonetics

Letter	Word	Pronunciation
A	Alfa	**AL** FAH
B	Bravo	**BRAH** VOH
C	Charlie	**CHAR** LEE
D	Delta	**DELL** TAH
E	Echo	**ECK** OH
F	Foxtrot	**FOKS** TROT
G	Golf	GOLF
H	Hotel	HOH **TELL**
I	India	**IN** DEE AH
J	Juliett	**JEW** LEE ETT
K	Kilo	**KEY** LOH
L	Lima	**LEE** MAH
M	Mike	MIKE
N	November	NO **VEM** BER
O	Oscar	**OSS** CAH
P	Papa	PAH **PAH**
Q	Quebec	KEH **BECK**
R	Romeo	**ROW** ME OH
S	Sierra	SEE **AIR** RAH
T	Tango	**TANG** GO
U	Uniform	**YOU** NEE FORM
V	Victor	**VIK** TAH
W	Whiskey	**WISS** KEY
X	X-Ray	**ECKS** RAY
Y	Yankee	**YANG** KEY
Z	Zulu	**ZOO** LOO

Note: The **boldfaced** syllables are emphasized. The pronunciations shown in this table were designed for those who speak any of the international languages. The pronunciations given for "Oscar" and "Victor" may seem awkward to English-speaking people in the US.

call. A good operator sends short calls separated by concentrated listening periods. Long CQs drive away more contacts than they attract!

Before calling CQ, it is important to find a frequency that appears unoccupied by any other station. This may not be easy, particularly during crowded band conditions. Listen carefully — perhaps a weak DX station is on frequency. If you're using a beam antenna, rotate it to make sure the frequency is clear. If, after a reasonable time, the frequency seems clear, ask if the frequency is in use, then sign your call. "Is the frequency in use? This is KA1IFB." If, as far as you can determine, no one responds, you are ready to make your call.

Keep your CQ calls short. Long calls are considered poor operating technique. You may interfere with stations already on frequency who didn't hear your initial frequency check. Also, stations intending to reply to the call may become impatient and move to another frequency. If two or three calls produce no answer, it may be that there is too much noise or interference, or that atmospheric conditions are not favorable. At that point, change frequency and try again. If you still get no answer, try looking around and answer someone else's CQ. Here's an example of a CQ call:

"CQ CQ Calling CQ. This is KB1AFE, Kilo Bravo One

Alfa Foxtrot Echo, KB1AFE calling CQ and standing by."

Notice that the operator used the International Telecommunication Union standard phonetic alphabet to spell out her call sign. This ensures that her call sign will be understood and letters won't be confused for other letters. There is no need to say what band is being used or to add other information.

The format of this CQ call is a "3 × 3" call. This refers to calling CQ three times, then giving your call sign three times. There are two ways to initiate an SSB voice contact: *call* CQ or *answer* a CQ. At first, you may want to tune around and find another station to answer. If activity on a band seems low, a CQ call may be worthwhile.

When replying to a CQ, say both call signs clearly. It's not necessary to sign the other station's call phonetically. You should always sign yours with standard phonetics, however. Remember to keep calls short. Say the call sign of the station you are calling only once. Follow with your call sign, repeated phonetically, several times. For example, "W1AW, this is KA3HAM, Kilo Alfa Three Hotel Alfa Mike, KA3HAM, over." Depending on conditions, you may need to give your call phonetically several times. Repeat this calling procedure as required until you receive a reply or until the station you are calling has come back to someone else.

Listening is very important. If you're using *PTT* (push-to-talk), be sure to let up on the transmit button between calls so you can hear what is going on. With *VOX* (voice operated switch), you key the transmitter simply by talking into the microphone. VOX operation is helpful because, when properly adjusted, it enables you to listen between words. Remember: It is extremely poor practice to make a long call without listening. Also, don't continue to call after the station you are trying to contact replies to someone else. Wait for the contact to end before trying again, or try another spot on the band.

Conducting the QSO

Once you've established contact, it is no longer necessary to use the phonetic alphabet for your call sign or to give the other station's call. FCC regulations say that you need to give your call only every 10 minutes and at the conclusion of the contact. (The exception is when handling international third-party traffic. Then, you must sign both calls.) This allows you to enjoy a normal two-way conversation without the need for continual identification. Use "over" or "go ahead" at the end of a transmission to indicate that it's the other station's turn to transmit. (During FM repeater operation, it is obvious when you or the other station stops transmitting because you will hear the repeater carrier drop. In this case it may not be necessary to say "over.")

Aside from signal strength, most hams exchange name, location and equipment information (especially antennas!). Once these routine details are out of the way, you can talk about your families, the weather, your occupation or any appropriate subject.

Working DX

The 6 and 2 meter bands can provide some excellent band openings for SSB and CW **DX** contacts. DX can mean a contact with any distant station. Most operators understand DX to mean a contact with a station in another country, no matter how near or far that may be. Really, it's a relative term, though. On the VHF/UHF bands, where we normally expect the contacts to be limited to your local area, talking with a station 100 miles away might become DX.

During the years of maximum sunspot activity, 10-meter worldwide communication on a daily basis is commonplace. (Chapter 3 discusses the effects of sunspots on radio-wave propagation.) Ten meters is an outstanding DX band when conditions are right. A particular advantage of 10 meters for DX work is that effective beam-type antennas tend to be small and light, making for relatively easy installation.

With a Technician class license you won't be able to take advantage of these excellent conditions on the HF bands, unfortunately. This is one reason to pass the 5 wpm Morse code exam. With a Technician license and credit for Morse code you will gain access to the "Novice" HF bands. You can still have plenty of fun on the VHF and UHF bands with your Technician license, of course.

There are a few things to keep in mind when you contact amateurs from outside the United States. While many overseas amateurs have an exceptional command of English (which is especially remarkable since few US amateurs understand foreign languages), they may not be familiar with many of our local sayings. Because of the language differences, some DX stations are more comfortable with the "bare-bones" type contact, and you should be sensitive to their preferences.

During unsettled band conditions it may be necessary to keep the contact short in case fading or interference occurs. Take these factors into account when expanding on a basic contact. Also, during a band opening on 10 meters or on VHF, it is crucial to keep contacts brief. This allows many stations to work whatever DX is coming through.

When the time comes to end the contact, end it. Thank the other operator (once) for the pleasure of the contact and say good-bye: "This is WB3IOS, clear." This is all that is required. Unless the other amateur is a good friend, there is no need to start sending best wishes to everyone in the household including the family dog! Nor is this the time to start digging up extra comments on the contact which will require a "final final" from the other station (there may be other stations waiting to call in).

Tips for Better SSB Operating

- *Listen with care.* It is natural to answer the loudest station that calls, but sometimes a weaker signal may provide a more interesting contact. Not all amateurs can run high power, and sometimes the weaker signal

may be from a more-distant station. Don't reward an operator who has cranked up the transmitter gain to the point of being difficult to understand, especially if a station with a nice sounding signal is also calling.

- *Use VOX or PTT.* If you use VOX, don't defeat its purpose by saying "aah" to keep the transmitter on the air. If you use PTT, let go of the mike button every so often to make sure you are not "doubling" with the other station. A QSO should be an interactive conversation. Don't do all the talking.

- *Take your time.* The speed of voice transmission (with perfect accuracy) depends almost entirely on the skill of the two operators concerned. Use a rate of speech that allows perfect understanding. The operator on the other end should have time to record important details of the contact. If you go too fast, you'll end up repeating a lot of information.

- *Use standard phonetics* to make your call sign easier to understand.

Sampling Various Other Modes

With a Technician license you can sample virtually every type of Amateur Radio operating activity. Even without passing a Morse code exam you can use CW on the VHF and UHF bands. You can also use single sideband (SSB) voice on those bands. There are segments of each band dedicated to CW operation as well as other "weak signal" operation such as SSB. You can sample amateur television (ATV), Earth-Moon-Earth (EME or moonbounce) communication, amateur satellites and packet radio. The only type of operating that you can't experience is on the high-frequency (HF) bands. There is certainly no reason to feel confined to FM voice on 2 meters!

Your selection of station equipment should be guided by the type of operating you want to try. If you want to create an effective weak-signal station, for example, you will want to look for a multi-mode VHF transceiver rather than just an FM rig. You'll also want to put up some type of directional antenna that you can rotate to point at other stations rather than one that sends signals equally well in all directions.

If amateur television (ATV) sounds interesting, you can sample the activity in your area with a cable-ready TV receiver connected to a good outside beam antenna for the 70-cm (420 to 450-MHz) amateur band. Tune the TV to cable channels 57 through 61. These cable channels are not the same as the UHF broadcast channels 57 to 61. Cable channel 57 is 421.25 MHz, and each channel is 6 MHz higher in frequency.

[Before going on to the next section, turn to Chapter 11 and study questions T6A01 through T6A03, T6A07, T6A09, T6A10, and T6A12. Also study question T6B06. Review this section if you have difficulty with any of these questions.]

Operating CW

Even if you don't think you will ever touch a Morse code key, don't pass up the information in this section. There is a special feeling of accomplishment that comes from a Morse code conversation. This is especially true if that conversation takes place using an inexpensive radio that you built yourself! There are many similarities between CW and voice operation. Remember, you can operate CW on the VHF and UHF bands with your Technician license. You don't have to pass a CW exam before you can operate this mode! Passing the CW exam gives you access to the Novice HF bands.

An unmodulated carrier wave (a steady signal with no information included) is called a test emission. **CW**, also called international **Morse code**, is transmitted by on/off keying of a radio-frequency signal. This is demonstrated whenever you use a key to send CW. To send code, you press a lever. To stop sending, you let up on the lever. Code is either on or off. What could be simpler?

Calling CQ

Morse code CQ calls should follow the same general procedure as an SSB CQ. Generally, a "3 × 3" call is more than sufficient. Here's an example:

CQ CQ CQ DE KA7XYZ KA7XYZ KA7XYZ K

As you remember, "3 × 3" refers to calling CQ three times, followed by your call sign three times. **DE** is a Morse code abbreviation that means"from" or "this is." Perhaps the best way to get started is to listen for someone else's CQ. Listen between 50.0 and 50.1 MHz on 6 meters or between 144.0 and 144.1 MHz on 2 meters for CW activity. You are most likely to hear some activity on these bands during a VHF contest or during Field Day. Weekends and evenings are other good times to listen. The HF Novice bands are usually alive with signals, however. When you decide to call CQ yourself, follow the first rule of operating: Always listen before you transmit, even if the frequency appears clear. To start, send QRL? ("Is this frequency in use?"). If you hear a C ("yes") in reply, then try another frequency. It is not uncommon to hear only one of the stations in a QSO. A frequency may seem clear even though there is a contact in progress. It's the worst of bad manners to jump on a frequency that's already busy. Admittedly, the Novice bands, especially 40 and 80 meters, are often crowded. Even so, if you listen first you'll avoid interfering with an in-progress QSO.

Whatever you do, be sure to *send at a speed you can reliably copy*. Sending too fast will surely invite disaster! This is especially true when you call CQ. If you answer a CQ, answer at a speed no faster than that of the sending station. Don't be ashamed to send PSE QRS (please send more slowly).

You will learn the meaning of many other **Q signals**

as you gain operating experience. QTH means "location." Followed by a question mark, it asks, "What is your location?" QSL means "I acknowledge receipt" (of a message or information). A **QSL card** is a written confirmation of an amateur contact. QSY means "change frequency" and QRS means "send more slowly." **Table 6.2** lists many common **Q signals**. Although hams use some Q signals in face-to-face conversations, when you're on the air, use them on CW only. On voice, say what you mean.

As you gain experience, you will develop the skill of sorting out the signal you want from those of other stations. Space in the ham bands is limited. Make sure your QSO takes up as little of it as possible to avoid interfering with other QSOs. When you tune in the other station, adjust your receiver for the strongest signal and the "proper" tone for your radio. This will usually be between 500 and 1000 Hz. If you tune your radio for a tone that is different from the design frequency, your transmitted frequency may not be the same as the station you are trying to contact. The other station may not hear your signal, and you may cause interference to stations on a nearby frequency.

Working "Split"

There is an exception to the zero-beat rule. Sometimes a DX station has a "pileup" of stations trying to make contact. If they are all calling on the DX station's frequency, no one (including the DX station!) can copy anything. Under these conditions, the DX station may choose to work *split*. When you hear a DX station, but you never hear anyone else calling or working him, chances are he's working split. Listen to the directions given by the DX operator. Chances are he or she will say something like "U 5" or "U 10." This is telling you to call the DX station 5 or 10 kHz higher (Up) in frequency. Tune higher in the band, and look for the pileup. It should be easy to find. DX stations work split when operating SSB, too. (For more helpful hints on working DX, see *The ARRL Operating Manual*.)

For amateurs to understand each other, we must standardize our communications. You'll find, for instance, that most hams use abbreviations on CW. Why? It's faster to send a couple of letters than it is to spell out a word. But there's no point in using an abbreviation if no one else understands you. Over the years, amateurs have developed a set of standard abbreviations (**Table 6.3**). If you use these abbreviations, you'll find that everyone will understand you, and you'll understand them. In addition to these standards, we use a set of **procedural signals**, or **prosigns**, to help control a contact. See Table 6.3.

Answering a CQ

What about our friend KA7XYZ? In our last example

Table 6.2

Q Signals

These Q signals are the ones used most often on the air. (Q abbreviations take the form of questions only when they are sent followed by a question mark.)

QRG   Your exact frequency (or that of ___) is ____kHz. Will you tell me my exact frequency (or that of _____)?

QRL   I am busy (or I am busy with ____). Are you busy?

QRM   Your transmission is being interfered with ____ (1. Nil; 2. Slightly; 3. Moderately; 4. Severely; 5. Extremely.) Is my transmission being interfered with?

QRN   I am troubled by static ____. (1 to 5 as under QRM.) Are you troubled by static?

QRO   Increase power. Shall I increase power?

QRP   Decrease power. Shall I decrease power?

QRQ   Send faster (____wpm). Shall I send faster?

QRS   Send more slowly (____wpm). Shall I send more slowly?

QRT   Stop sending. Shall I stop sending?

QRU   I have nothing for you. Have you anything for me?

QRV   I am ready. Are you ready?

QRX   I will call you again at ___hours (on ___kHz). When will you call me again?

QRZ   You are being called by ____ (on ___kHz). Who is calling me?

QSB   Your signals are fading. Are my signals fading?

QSK   I can hear you between signals; break in on my transmission. Can you hear me between your signals and if so can I break in on your transmission?

QSL   I am acknowledging receipt. Can you acknowledge receipt (of a message or transmission)?

QSN   I did hear you (or ___) on ___kHz. Did you hear me (or ___) on ____kHz?

QSO   I can communicate with ____ direct (or relay through ___). Can you communicate with ___ direct or by relay?

QSP   I will relay to ___. Will you relay to ___?

QST   General call preceding a message addressed to all amateurs and ARRL members. This is in effect "CQ ARRL."

QSX   I am listening to ___ on ___kHz. Will you listen to ___on ___kHz?

QSY   Change to transmission on another frequency (or on ___kHz). Shall I change to transmission on another frequency (or on ___kHz)?

QTB   I do not agree with your counting of words. I will repeat the first letter or digit of each word or group. Do you agree with my counting of words?

QTC   I have ___messages for you (or for ___). How many messages have you to send?

QTH   My location is ____. What is your location?

QTR   The time is ____. What is the correct time?

---

he was calling CQ. What happened? Another ham, N2SN, heard him and answered the CQ:

KA7XYZ KA7XYZ DE N2SN N2SN $\overline{AR}$

Notice the "2 × 2" format. N2SN sent the call sign of the station he was calling twice, then sent DE, then sent his call sign twice. If KA7XYZ thought he heard someone calling him, but wasn't quite sure, he would send:

QRZ? DE KA7XYZ $\overline{AR}$

The Q signal "QRZ?" means "who is calling me?" In that case, N2SN will send his call sign again, usually two or three times.

Use the prosign $\overline{AR}$ (the letters A and R run together with no separating space) in an initial call to a specific station before officially establishing contact. When calling CQ, use the prosign **K**, because you are inviting any station to reply. ("K" means "Any station go ahead and transmit.") KA7XYZ comes back to N2SN in a to-the-point manner (one you should copy).

N2SN DE KA7XYZ R GE UR RST 599 DENVER CO $\overline{BT}$ NAME BOB HW BK

In this transmission, **RST** refers to the standard *readability*, *strength* and *tone* system of reporting signal reception.

Exchanging Signal Reports — The RST System

You'll exchange a signal report in nearly every Amateur Radio QSO. Don't spend a lot of time worrying about what signal report to give to a station you're in contact with. The scales are simply a general indication of how you are receiving the other station. As you gain experience with the descriptions given in **Table 6.4**, you'll be more comfortable estimating the proper signal report.

A report of RST 368 would be interpreted as "Your signal is readable with considerable difficulty, good strength, with a slight trace of modulation." The tone report is a useful indication of transmitter performance. When the RST system was developed, the tone of amateur transmitters varied widely. Today, a tone report of less than 9 is cause to ask a few other amateurs for their opinion of the transmitted signal. Consistently poor tone reports means your transmitter has problems.

Signal reports on SSB are two-digit numbers using the RS portion of the RST system. No tone report is required. The maximum signal report would be "five nine" — that is, readability 5, strength 9. (See Table 6.4) A signal report of "five seven" means your signal is perfectly readable and moderately strong. On the other hand, a signal report of "three three" would mean that the other operator is only able to understand your signal with considerable difficulty

Table 6.3

Some Common Abbreviations Used on CW

Although abbreviations help to cut down unnecessary transmission, it's best not to abbreviate unnecessarily when working an operator of unknown experience.

AA	All after	GN	Good night	SASE	Self-addressed, stamped envelope
AB	All before	GND	Ground	SED	Said
ABT	About	GUD	Good	SIG	Signature; signal
ADR	Address	HI	The telegraphic laugh; high	SINE	Operator's personal initials
AGN	Again	HR	Here, hear		or nickname
ANT	Antenna	HV	Have	SKED	Schedule
BCI	Broadcast interference	HW	How	SRI	Sorry
BCL	Broadcast listener	LID	A poor operator	SSB	Single sideband
BK	Break; break me; break in	MA, MILS	Milliamperes	SVC	Service; prefix to service message
BN	All between; been	MSG	Message; prefix to radiogram	T	Zero
BUG	Semi-automatic key	N	No	TFC	Traffic
B4	Before	NCS	Net control station	TMW	Tomorrow
C	Yes	ND	Nothing doing	TNX-TKS	Thanks
CFM	Confirm; I confirm	NIL	Nothing; I have nothing for you	TT	That
CK	Check	NM	No more	TU	Thank you
CL	I am closing my station; call	NR	Number	TVI	Television interference
CLD-CLG	Called; calling	NW	Now; I resume transmission	TX	Transmitter
CQ	Calling any station	OB	Old boy	TXT	Text
CUD	Could	OC	Old chap	UR-URS	Your; you're; yours
CUL	See you later	OM	Old man	VFO	Variable-frequency oscillator
CW	Continuous wave	OP-OPR	Operator	VY	Very
	(that is, radiotelegraphy)	OT	Old-timer; old top	WA	Word after
DE	From, this is	PBL	Preamble	WB	Word before
DLD-DLVD	Delivered	PSE	Please	WD-WDS	Word; words
DR	Dear	PWR	Power	WKD-WKG	Worked; working
DX	Distance, foreign countries	PX	Press	WL	Well; will
ES	And, &	R	Received as transmitted; are	WUD	Would
FB	Fine business, excellent	RCD	Received	WX	Weather
FM	Frequency modulation	RCVR (RX)	Receiver	XCVR	Transceiver
GA	Go ahead (or resume sending)	REF	Refer to; referring to; reference	XMTR (TX)	Transmitter
GB	Good-by	RFI	Radio frequency interference	XTAL	Crystal
GBA	Give better address	RIG	Station equipment	XYL (YF)	Wife
GE	Good evening	RPT	Repeat; I repeat	YL	Young lady
GG	Going	RTTY	Radioteletype	73	Best regards
GM	Good morning	RX	Receiver	88	Love and kisses

Common Procedural Signals (Prosigns)

$\overline{AR}$	End of transmission or end of message	$\overline{SK}$	End of contact
AS	Please stand by	CL	Closing. Going off the air
R	All received correctly	$\overline{BK}$	Break or Back to you
$\overline{K}$	Go ahead. Any station transmit	$\overline{DN}$	Slant mark, used to indicate portable, mobile or other
$\overline{KN}$	Only called station transmit		additional identifying information with your call sign

and your signals are weak in strength.

If you get a report of, say, "59 plus 20 dB," it means your received signal reads 20 decibels higher than signal strength 9 on the transceiver S meter. Decibels provide a convenient way to compare the power of signals. If one signal is twice as strong as another, there will be a 3-dB difference between them. When one signal is 10-dB stronger than another it means it is ten times stronger. A difference of 20 dB means one signal is 100 times stronger and 30 dB means one signal is 1000 times stronger. If you receive a signal report of 59 plus 20 dB, and your transmitter is operating at 100 watts, you could reduce power to 1 watt and still have a "strength 9" signal!

On FM repeaters, RS reports are not used. FM signal reports are generally given in terms of signal quieting. *Full quieting* means the received signal is strong enough to block all receiver noise.

A further word about signal reports, one that applies to all types of operating: If your signal report is *too* good, *reduce your power*. FCC rules say that amateurs must use the minimum power necessary to maintain communications. Whether you're operating through an FM repeater, on VHF or UHF simplex or on HF, if you don't have to use an amplifier or the highest power your transceiver is capable of, decrease your transmitting power. You'll be less likely to interfere with other stations (and if you're using a hand-held transceiver or other portable radio you'll conserve your battery).

Tips for Better CW Operating

The basic information is only transmitted once. The other station will request repeats if necessary. Notice too that $\overline{BT}$ (B and T run together) is used to separate portions

Table 6.4

The RST System

READABILITY
1—Unreadable.
2—Barely readable, occasional words distinguishable.
3—Readable with considerable difficulty.
4—Readable with practically no difficulty.
5—Perfectly readable.

SIGNAL STRENGTH
1—Faint signals barely perceptible.
2—Very weak signals.
3—Weak signals.
4—Fair signals.
5—Fairly good signals.
6—Good signals.
7—Moderately strong signals.
8—Strong signals.
9—Extremely strong signals.

TONE
1—Sixty-cycle ac or less, very rough and broad.
2—Very rough ac, very harsh and broad.
3—Rough ac tone, rectified but not filtered.
4—Rough note, some trace of filtering.
5—Filtered rectified ac but strongly ripple-modulated.
6—Filtered tone, definite trace of ripple modulation.
7—Near pure tone, trace of ripple modulation.
8—Near perfect tone, slight trace of modulation.
9—Perfect tone, no trace of ripple or modulation of any kind.

The "tone" report refers only to the purity of the signal. It has no connection with its stability or freedom from clicks or chirps. Most of the signals you hear will be a T-9. Other tone reports occur mainly if the power supply filter capacitors are not doing a thorough job. If so, some trace of ac ripple finds its way onto the transmitted signal. If the signal has the characteristic steadiness of crystal control, add X to the report (for example, RST 469X). If it has a chirp or "tail" (either on "make" or "break") add C (for example, 469C). If it has clicks or noticeable other keying transients, add K (for example, 469K). Of course a signal could have both chirps and clicks, in which case both C and K could be used (for example, RST 469CK).

of the text. This character is really the double dash (=), and is usually written as a long dash or hyphen on your copy paper. HW? means "how do you copy?" BK signifies that KA7XYZ is turning it over (back) to N2SN for his basic info. KA7XYZ does not sign both calls all over again. FCC rules require identification only at the end of a QSO, and once every 10 minutes.

At the end of the contact send **73** and sign off. 73 is a common abbreviation that means "Best regards." Most hams say "73" at the end of a **phone** contact, too. This is one of those CW abbreviations that has made its way into the mainstream of Amateur Radio lingo. You will also hear many hams say "seventy threes" or send 73s. This is a practice that can quickly identify you as a lid. 73 gives the other operator your best regards. You wouldn't say "best regardses," would you?

Conversation is a two-way phenomenon. There is no reason that an Amateur Radio QSO can't be a back-and-forth process. No one wants to listen to a long, unnecessary monologue. Propagation conditions might change, hampering the QSO. KA7XYZ and N2SN will relate better if each contributes equally. Sometimes there is interference or marginal copy because of weak signals. It may help to transmit your call sign when you are turning the conversation back to the other station.

In summary, here are the points to keep in mind:
- *Listen before transmitting.* Send QRL? ("Is this frequency in use?") before transmitting. Listen again! It's worth repeating: Listen!
- *Send short CQs* and listen between each.
- *Send no faster* than you can *reliably copy.*
- *Use standard abbreviations* whenever possible — become familiar with them.
- *Use prosigns and Q signals properly.*
- *Identify at the end of a QSO* (the entire contact, not each turnover) and *every 10 minutes.*
- *Use R only if you've received 100 percent* of what the other station sent.
- *Be courteous.*

Tuning Up

What is the most exciting, most memorable and perhaps most terrifying moment in your entire ham experience? Your first on-the-air contact with another station! Before you have that experience, you'll want to know how to operate your station equipment.

The best place to start is the instruction manual. Before you even turn on your radio, read the instructions carefully so you'll be familiar with each control. Without turning on the equipment, try adjusting the controls. Nothing will happen, but you'll learn the location and feel of each important control.

After studying the manual and finding the important controls, you'll be ready to tune up. Your FCC license

must have been granted before you can transmit or even tune up on the air!

If your transmitter requires tuning when you change bands, connect your transmitter output to a **dummy load** while you tune. This avoids on-the-air interference. Never tune up on the air because you could interfere with other hams.

Once you have tuned up the transceiver according to the instruction manual, disconnect the dummy load and connect the antenna (an antenna switch makes this easy). Now, you're ready to operate! If you use an antenna tuner, you may have to transmit a brief low-power signal to adjust the circuit.

Amateur Radio Internet Gateways

Amateur Radio applications using Voice Over Internet Protocol, better known as VoIP, are becoming a popular new way for Technician Class amateurs to participate in a new kind of "Internet-aided" DXing. This technology allows users to have voice conversations with other amateurs far beyond the range of their VHF or UHF FM transceivers. Higher class licensees who do not have ready access to HF ham stations at home can also benefit from this new technology. Amateurs wishing to access these Internet channels for ham communications would access a special type of amateur station known as a **gateway**. In other words, a gateway is used to connect other amateur stations with the Internet.

There are several different kinds of amateur VoIP in use today. Depending on how they are configured, these systems may involve repeater linking where two distant repeater systems share signals with each other as shown

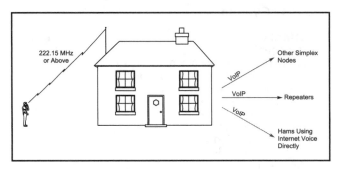

Figure 6.3 — A diagram of a VoIP simplex node. If a control operator is not physically present at the station location and the node is functioning with wireless remote control, the control link must operate above 222.15 MHz.

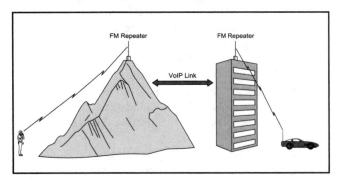

Figure 6.2 — Two FM repeaters linked via VoIP.

in **Figure 6.2**. Another application is called simplex linking where one or more users with handheld or mobile transceivers communicate directly with a "base" station (or node) that is linked to the Internet as shown in **Figure 6.3**. The one element common to all amateur VoIP systems is that the Internet acts as the relay between stations.

[Now turn to Chapter 11 and study questions T6A05, T6A06 and T6A08. You should also study questions T6A11, T6A13 and T6B05. Finally, study questions T6B07 through T6B12. Review this section if you have any difficulty with these questions.]

Bandwidth

The amount of space in the radio-frequency spectrum that a signal occupies is called its **bandwidth**. The bandwidth of a transmission is determined by the information rate. Thus, a pure, continuous, unmodulated carrier has a very small bandwidth with no sidebands. A television transmission, which contains a great deal of information, is about 6-megahertz wide.

Receiver Bandwidth

Receiver bandwidth determines how well you can receive one signal in the presence of another signal that is very close in frequency. The enjoyment you'll experience will depend greatly on how well you can isolate the signal you are receiving from all the others nearby.

Bandwidth is a measure of *selectivity*: how wide a range of frequencies is received with the receiver tuned to one frequency. For example, if you can hear signals as

much as 3 kHz above and 3 kHz below the frequency to which you are tuned, your receiver has a bandwidth of at least 6 kHz. If you cannot hear signals more than 200 Hz above or below the frequency to which you are tuned, the bandwidth is only 400 Hz. The narrower the bandwidth, the greater the selectivity and the easier it is to copy one signal when there is another one close by in frequency.

Selectivity is determined by special intermediate-frequency (IF) filters built into the receiver. Some receivers have several filters so you can choose different bandwidths. They are necessary because different **emission types** occupy a wider frequency range than others. A 250-Hz-bandwidth filter is excellent for separating CW signals on a crowded band, but it's useless for listening to SSB, AM or FM transmissions. A wider filter is needed to allow all the transmitted information to reach the detector.

Most receivers designed for single-sideband voice operation come standard with a filter selectivity of around

2.8 kHz. This is ideal for SSB, which usually has a bandwidth between 2 and 3 kHz. Your voice contains frequencies higher than 3 kHz, but all of the sounds necessary to understand speech are between about 300 Hz and 3000 Hz. Most amateur voice transmitters limit the bandwidth of a transmitted audio signal to between 300 and 3000 Hz. The difference between these limits is the bandwidth, 2700 Hz. By using a filter selectivity of 2.8 kHz (2800 Hz), you can see that your receiver will reproduce the full range of transmitted audio.

Although a bandwidth of 2.8 kHz is also usable on CW, a narrower bandwidth is needed to prevent adjacent CW signals from getting through at the same time. Many amateurs prefer a filter bandwidth of 500 Hz or even 250 Hz for CW operation. A radioteletype signal has a bandwidth that is a little wider than a CW signal, but a 500 Hz or 250-Hz filter serves nicely for that mode, too.

CW signals have the narrowest bandwidth of any amateur emissions. Radioteletype emissions are wider than CW, and SSB signals are even wider than that. **Figure 6.4** illustrates the relative bandwidths of CW, RTTY and SSB signals and the bandwidth of IF filters that might be used to receive these signals. FM, which we will consider next, can occupy even more bandwidth.

Bandwidth in FM

When you transmit **Frequency Modulated (FM) phone** (voice) emissions, the frequency of the transmitted RF signal varies an amount that depends on the strength of your voice. When you speak louder, the frequency changes a greater amount than when you speak softly. The frequency or pitch of your voice (or other signal used to modulate the transmitter) controls how fast the frequency changes. Higher-frequency tones make the frequency vary at a faster rate than low-frequency tones. *Frequency deviation* is the instantaneous change in frequency for a given signal. The frequency swings just as far in both directions, so the total frequency swing is equal to twice the deviation. In addition, there are sidebands that increase the bandwidth still further. A good estimate of the band-

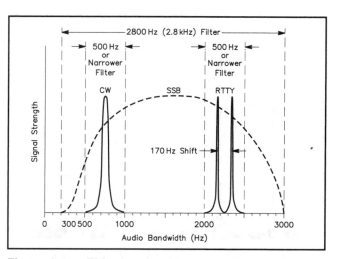

Figure 6.4 — This drawing illustrates the relative bandwidths of CW, RTTY and SSB signals. The bandwidths of filters that might be used in a receiver's intermediate frequency (IF) section to receive these signals are also shown.

width is twice the maximum frequency deviation plus the maximum modulating audio frequency:

$$Bw = 2 \times (D + M) \qquad \text{(Equation 6.1)}$$

where:
  Bw = bandwidth
  D = maximum frequency deviation
  M = maximum modulating audio frequency

An FM transmitter using 5-kHz deviation and a maximum audio frequency of 3 kHz uses a total bandwidth of about 16 kHz. The actual bandwidth of a typical FM signal may be somewhat greater than this. A good approximation is that the bandwidth of an FM voice signal is between 10 and 20 kHz.

[Now turn to Chapter 11 and study question T6B01 through T6B04. Review this section if you have any difficulty with those questions.]

Spurious Signals

An ideal transmitter emits a signal only on the operating frequency and nowhere else. Real-world transmitters radiate undesired signals, or **spurious emissions**, as well. Any transmitter can produce spurious emissions: it doesn't matter if you are using a 100-watt HF transceiver or a 2-watt hand-held VHF or UHF radio. Any signal produced by the radio that falls outside the band on which you are operating is a spurious emission. Using good design and construction practices, manufacturers and home builders can reduce spurious emissions so they cause no problems.

Harmonics

Harmonics are whole-number multiples of a given frequency. For example, the second harmonic of 100 Hz is 200 Hz. The fifth harmonic of 100 Hz is 500 Hz. Every oscillator generates harmonics in addition to a signal at its *fundamental frequency*. For example, consider an oscillator tuned to 7125 kHz in the 40-meter band. It also generates signals at 14,250 kHz (second harmonic), 21,375 kHz (third harmonic), 28,500 kHz (fourth harmonic), and so on. **Figure 6.5** shows a spectrum-analyzer display of the output of an oscillator that has many harmonics.

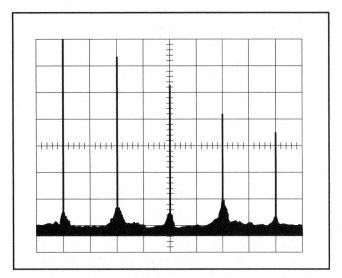

Figure 6.5 — Harmonics are signals that appear at whole number multiples of the resonant, or fundamental, frequency. This drawing represents a spectrum analyzer display screen, and shows a 2-MHz signal and some of its harmonics. A spectrum analyzer is an instrument that allows you to look at energy radiated over a wide range of fre-quencies. Here, the analyzer is adjusted to display all RF energy between 1 MHz and 11 MHz. Each vertical line in the background grid denotes an increment of 1 MHz. The first thick black vertical "pip" represents energy from the fundamental signal of a 2-MHz oscillator. The next pip, two vertical divisions later, is the second harmonic at 4 MHz (twice the fundamental frequency). The pip at the center of the photo is the third harmonic at 6 MHz (three times the fundamental frequency). This figure shows the second, third, fourth and fifth harmonics.

Calculating the frequency of the various harmonics of a fundamental, or desired, frequency is easy. Simply multiply by the whole number of the particular harmonic. For example, suppose you want to know the fourth harmonic of a 7160-kHz signal.

7160 kHz × 4 = 28,640 kHz

Harmonics can interfere with other amateurs or other users of the radio spectrum. The second through fourth harmonics of a 40-meter transmitter fall in the 20, 15 and 10-meter amateur bands. Imagine the interference (QRM) that would result if everyone transmitted two, four, six or more harmonics in addition to the desired signal! Suppose you receive a report from another amateur that your signals were heard on 28,640 kHz when you were operating your station on 7160 kHz. You should suspect that your transmitter is radiating excessive harmonic radiation. On some bands the harmonic signals will fall outside of any Amateur band, so you can cause interference to other radio services. The fourth harmonic of a 50.25 MHz signal is 201.00 MHz, for example.

To prevent the chaos that would occur if everyone transmitted harmonics, FCC regulations specify limits for harmonic and other spurious radiation. For example, if you are operating a 100-W-output transmitter, your harmonic signals can total no more than 10 milliwatts. As you can see, a transmitter that complies with the rules still generates some harmonic energy. Fortunately, that energy is so small that it is not likely to cause problems.

Good engineering calls for tuned circuits between stages in transmitters. These circuits reduce or eliminate spurious signals such as harmonics. The tuned circuits allow signals at the desired frequency to pass, but they *attenuate* (reduce) harmonics.

How can you be sure that your transmitter does not generate excessive harmonics? The FCC requires all transmitter manufacturers to prove that their equipment complies with its regulations. This means that commercially manufactured equipment usually produces clean signals. If you build a transmitter from a magazine or book article, check for information on harmonic radiation. ARRL requires that all transmitter projects published in *QST* and our technical books meet the FCC specifications for commercially manufactured equipment.

Other Causes for Spurious Emissions

We have been discussing spurious emissions caused by circuit problems in your transmitter. Your equipment can also cause spurious emissions if you operate it with some controls adjusted improperly. For example, if you operate an SSB transmitter with the microphone gain set too high you can cause **splatter**, or interference to frequencies near the one on which you are operating. Talking too loud into the microphone or having the microphone gain set too high causes the transmitter to overmodulate the signal. This means your transmitter may be putting out spurious emissions or splatter that could interfere with other stations when you operate it this way.

Many SSB transmitters include a speech processor to add extra "punch" to your voice, which will help another operator hear you under poor band conditions or interference. Too much speech processing can distort your audio and cause splatter interference on frequencies close to the one on which you are operating.

Even a hand-held FM transceiver can cause interference on nearby frequencies from spurious emissions if the microphone gain or deviation control is set too high. On an FM transmitter, the microphone gain or deviation control is usually inside the radio. You don't normally have to adjust this control, but if you consistently get reports that your audio is distorted or that you are causing splatter interference to nearby frequencies you may have to make an adjustment. You may also hear other operators say that you are *over-deviating*. This all means one thing: you need to correct the problem.

It may be that your voice characteristics and the microphone you are using require a small adjustment to the deviation control. This would be especially true if you change microphones from a mobile microphone to a base-station type microphone. Any time you change microphones you should make an on-the-air check with another station to ensure the quality of your signal.

Generally you should hold a microphone close to your mouth and speak in a normal voice. If you get reports that your FM transceiver is over deviating, you should try holding the microphone a bit farther from your mouth when you are talking. You may not need to adjust the deviation control if you try this.

Many operators tend to talk louder or even shout into the microphone, especially if the other station is having difficulty hearing you. This won't normally help, however, and may even make it more difficult. Shouting into the microphone may cause the radio to over deviate, distorting the transmitted audio.

If you have to remove the covers from your radio for any reason, be sure to reinstall them and tighten all the screws before operating the radio again. In addition to protecting the electronic components from physical damage, the covers also provide shielding to the circuit. Such shielding stops any spurious emissions or unwanted RF signals from being radiated.

Signal Purity

As a licensed Amateur Radio operator, you are responsible for the quality of the signal transmitted from your station. The rules require your transmitted signal to be stable in frequency and pure in tone or modulation. If your signal is not "clean," it is unpleasant to listen to. It may also cause interference to others using the band or other services.

Chirp can be a problem with some transmitters used for CW operation. Chirp occurs when the oscillator in your transmitter shifts frequency slightly whenever you close your telegraph key. The result is that other stations receive your transmitted signal as a chirping sound rather than as a pure tone. Your "dahdidahdit" will sound like "whoopwhiwhoopwhip." It isn't very much fun to copy a chirpy CW signal!

Chirp usually happens when the oscillator power supply voltage changes as you transmit. Your transmitter may also chirp if the load on the oscillator changes when you transmit. If the supply voltage changes, you must improve the *voltage regulation*. With better regulation, the voltage won't shift when you key your transmitter. Also, a bad filter capacitor in the transmitter power supply can cause a buzzing or hum in the signal of an amateur transmitter.

If it's not a voltage problem, then what? Amplifier stages after the oscillator may be loading it down and pulling its frequency. You may need a better buffer (isolation) or driver stage between the oscillator and the next stage in your transmitter. Some oscillators are sensitive to temperature changes. If there is too much current through the frequency-determining components, their temperature may increase and the resonant frequency will change.

Of course it is also possible for other signals to cause interference to your station. This can be frustrating because you may have to track down the source of the interference. One common source of interference that you probably won't have to go far to find is from your computer system.

Computers include a variety of oscillators and other noise sources. Add to this the many cables and connecting wires coming out of the back of your computer and you can see that there are many ways for unwanted signals to get to your radio. When you connect your computer equipment to your radio for HF data operation, be sure to include shielded cables. Also be sure to properly ground all your station equipment. This will help clear up any unwanted computer noise that might get into your receiver.

How to Get Help

Transmitting a signal with chirp, spurious emissions or that otherwise causes a problem is a violation of both the letter and spirit of the regulations governing Amateur Radio. The best way to find out if you have a bad-sounding signal is from the stations you work. If another operator tells you about a problem with your signal, don't be offended. He cares about the image of the Amateur Service and only wants to help you. You might never be aware of a problem otherwise.

Don't let this chapter scare you. Spurious signals, unwanted harmonics or other equipment difficulties can all be solved. So can interference to your station from other devices like computers. Two ARRL publications will be helpful: *The ARRL Handbook for Radio Amateurs* and *ARRL's RFI Book*. Check with your Amateur Radio instructor or any experienced ham for help. There's no substitute for experience. Another ham may know just how to solve your problem and return you to the air as soon as possible. If you'd like to set up a station in an area where RFI may be a real problem, you'll want to read *ARRL's Low Power Communication* and *Stealth Amateur Radio*. These books tell you how to enjoy Amateur Radio with few problems from an apartment, condo, dorm room, car or in the field.

Interference with Other Services

Radio frequency interference (RFI) has given radio amateurs headaches for years. It can occur whenever an electronic device is surrounded by RF energy. Your rig emits RF energy each time you transmit. This RF energy may interfere with your own or your neighbor's television set (causing **television interference — TVI**). You may also have problems with a stereo system, electronic organ, video cassette recorder, telephone or any other piece of consumer electronic equipment.

If you have a very visible antenna in your yard, your neighbors may blame you for any interference they experience, even when you're not on the air! If you have any problems with interference to your own equipment, it's a good bet that your neighbors do too. On the other hand, if you can show your neighbors that you don't interfere with your television, they may be more open to your suggestions for curing problems.

So what should you do if someone complains of interference? First, make sure that your equipment is operating properly. If the complaint is TVI, check for interference to your own TV. If you see it, stop operating and cure the problem before you go back on the air.

Even if you don't interfere with your own TV, don't stop there. Simply telling your neighbors you're not at fault can cause even more problems. Try to work with your neighbors to determine if your rig is actually causing the interference. If so, try to help solve the problem. A more-experienced ham can be a great help. If you don't know any other hams in your area, write to ARRL HQ. We'll try to help you find a knowledgeable local ham.

Receiver Overload

Receiver overload is a common type of TV and FM-broadcast interference. It happens most often to consumer electronic equipment near an amateur station or other transmitter. When the RF signal (at the fundamental frequency) enters the receiver, it overloads one or more circuits. The receiver front end (first RF amplifier stage after the antenna) is most commonly affected. For this reason, we sometimes call this interference **front-end overload** or **RF overload**.

A strong enough RF field may produce spurious signals in the receiver, which cause the interference. Receiver overload interference may occur in your neighbor's house or just your own. Receiver overload can result from transmitters operating on any frequency. It is the most-common interference problem caused by VHF and UHF transmitters. If you receive an RFI complaint, and determine that the problem exists no matter what frequency you operate on, you should suspect receiver overload.

Receiver overload usually has a dramatic effect on the television picture. Whenever you key your transmitter, the picture may be completely wiped out. The screen

may go black, or it might just become light with traces of color. The sound (audio) will probably be affected also. In an FM receiver, the audio may be blocked each time you transmit. More often than not, overload affects only TV channels 2 through 13. In cases of severe interference, however, it may also affect the UHF channels.

The objective in curing receiver overload is to prevent the amateur signal from entering the front end of the entertainment receiver. It is important to realize that there is nothing you can do to your transmitter to cure receiver overload. It is a fundamental problem with the receiving system, and the primary responsibility for curing the problem is with the equipment manufacturer and the owner.

The first step in trying to cure such a problem with a cable-TV receiver is to have the owner or a service technician tighten all connectors and inspect the cable system transmission line. Any loose connector or break in the transmission line of a cable TV system can allow amateur signals to leak into the line, causing interference to TV receivers. Such a leak in the system can also allow Cable TV signals to leak out of the system and cause interference to amateur receivers using that frequency. Cable TV systems use some amateur VHF/UHF frequencies to carry the signals along the cable. This causes no problems as long as there are no leaks in the system.

If the TV is not connected to a cable system, or if it is a stereo or other consumer electronic device receiving the interference, there are other steps you should take. Have the equipment owner or a qualified service technician install a **high-pass filter**. See **Figure 6.6**. The filter will block the amateur signal from coming in through the antenna feed line and reaching the receiver front-end components. This would also be the next step if tightening the cable TV connectors didn't help.

Install the filter at the TV or FM receiver input. The best location is where the antenna feed line connects to the TV or FM tuner. It is not usually a good idea for an Amateur Radio operator to install a filter on a neighbor's entertainment equipment. Only the owner or a qualified technician should install the filter. If you install the filter, you might later be blamed for other problems with the TV set. A high-pass filter is a tuned circuit that passes high frequencies (TV channels start at 54 MHz). The filter blocks low frequencies (the HF amateur bands are in the range of 1.8-30 MHz).

In addition to interference caused by amateur radio transmitters to home entertainment devices, there is another kind of interference caused by commercial and other kinds off high powered transmitters to amateur receivers. This interference can occur to amateur receivers in the 222 MHz band when they are in close proximity to a television transmitter on Channel 12 or 13. These two television channels are located just below the 222 MHz amateur band. If these high power transmitters are lo-

Figure 6.6 — A high-pass filter can prevent fundamental energy from an amateur signal from entering a television set. This type of high-pass filter goes in the 300-ohm feed line that connects the television to the antenna.

Figure 6.7 — Harmonics radiated from an amateur transmitter may cause "crosshatching."

Figure 6.8 — A low-pass filter. When connected in the coaxial cable feed line between an amateur transmitter and the antenna, a low-pass filter can reduce the strength of transmitted harmonics.

cated physically close to your ham station, you can experience interference and a loss of receiver sensitivity. One way to solve this problem is to use a **band-pass filter**, which blocks RF energy above and below the 222 MHz amateur band. The filter is connected to the output of your 222 MHz transceiver and must be designed to pass the transmitter power with negligible attenuation, but it must block any receiver interference above or below the amateur band. Although a simple low-pass filter would work in this situation, band-pass filters are commercially available which offer protection from strong signals both below and above the amateur band.

Harmonic Interference

Another problem for hams is harmonic interference to entertainment equipment. Harmonics are multiples of a given frequency. Your transmitter radiates undesired harmonics along with your signal. An HF transmitting frequency is much lower than the TV or FM channels. Some harmonics will fall within the home entertainment bands, however.

The entertainment receiver cannot distinguish between the TV or FM signals (desired signals) and your harmonics (undesirable intruders) on the same frequency. If your harmonics are strong enough, they can seriously interfere with the received signal. Harmonic interference shows up as a crosshatch or a herringbone pattern on the

TV screen. See **Figure 6.7**.

Unlike receiver overload, harmonic interference seldom affects all channels. Rather, it may bother the one channel that has a harmonic relationship to the band you're on. Generally, harmonics from amateur transmitters operating below 30 MHz affect the lower TV channels (2 through 6). Ten-meter transmitters usually bother channels 2 and 6, and channels 3 and 6 experience trouble from 15-meter transmitters.

Harmonic interference must be cured at your transmitter. As a licensed amateur, you must take steps to see that harmonics from your transmitter do not interfere with other services. All harmonics generated by your transmitter must be attenuated well below the strength of the fundamental frequency. If harmonics from your transmitting equipment exceed these limits, you are at fault.

In this section we will discuss some of the several possible cures for harmonic interference. Try each step in order and the chances are good that your problem will be solved quickly.

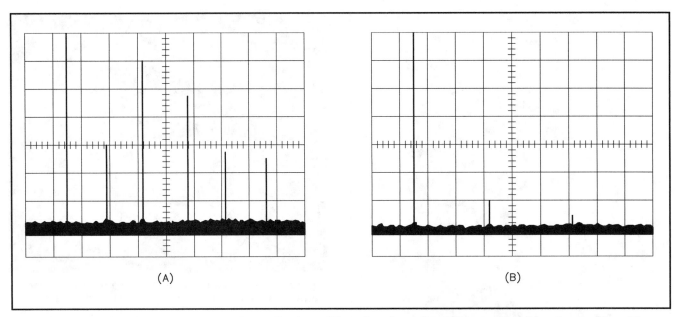

(A)

(B)

Figure 6.9 — A shows a spectrum-analyzer display of the signals emitted from an amateur transmitter. The pip at the left of the display (the one that extends to the top horizontal line) is the fundamental. All other pips represent harmonics. This particular transmitter generates several harmonics. On an analyzer display, stronger signals create taller pips. Here, the harmonic signals are quite strong. In fact, the third harmonic is about one-tenth as strong as the fundamental. The fundamental signal is 100 W, so the transmitter is radiating a potent 10-W signal at the third harmonic. Most of these harmonics will cause interference to other services. B shows the output of the same transmitter, operating at the same power level at the same frequency, after installation of a low-pass filter between the transmitter and the analyzer. The harmonics have all but disappeared from the display. The stronger of the two remaining harmonics is only about 100 microwatts – weak enough that it is unlikely to cause interference.

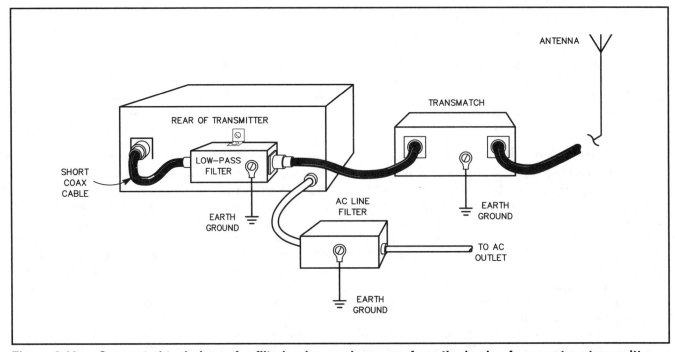

Figure 6.10 — Suggested techniques for filtering harmonic energy from the leads of an amateur transmitter.

The first step you should take is to install a **low-pass filter** like the one shown in **Figure 6.8**. The filter goes in the transmission line between your transmitter and antenna or antenna tuner. As the name implies, a low-pass filter is the opposite of a high-pass filter. A low-pass filter allows RF energy in the amateur bands to pass freely. It blocks very high frequency harmonics that can fall in the TV and FM bands. Low-pass filters usually have a specified cutoff frequency, often 40 MHz, above which they severely attenuate the passage of RF energy.

Even if your transmitter is working well within FCC specifications, you may need additional attenuation to reduce harmonics. Remember, your goal is to eliminate interference. Good-quality low-pass filters often attenuate signals falling in the entertainment bands by 70 or 80 dB. This is significantly better than the 40 to 50 dB typical of amateur transmitters. A decibel (dB) is a number (the logarithm of a ratio) used to describe how effective the filter is. Larger numbers indicate better filtering. **Figure 6.9** shows the output of a transmitter before and after filtering.

Another source of interference is RF energy from your transmitter that enters the ac power lines. The ac power-line filter is another kind of low-pass filter. It prevents RF energy from entering the ac line and radiating from power lines inside and near your house.

Telephone Interference

Interference to telephones and other audio devices from amateur radio transmitters is *not* the fault of the transmitter. As explained in the FCC's *Interference Handbook*, "Telephone interference generally happens because telephones are not designed to operate near radio transmitters, and the telephone improperly functions as a radio receiver." The major cause of interference to telephones from nearby radio transmitters is the fact that the telephone was not equipped with interference protection when it was manufactured. Cordless telephones, in particular, are highly susceptible to radio interference. Fortunately, commercially manufactured radio frequency interference filters are available that can be inserted in the telephone line where it connects to the telephone.

Multiband Antennas

You can also run into trouble if you use a multiband antenna. If your antenna works on two or three different bands, it will radiate any harmonics present on those frequencies. After all, we want the antenna to radiate energy at a given frequency. It cannot tell the difference between desired signal energy and unwanted harmonic energy.

This problem does not usually affect home entertainment equipment. It may cause interference to other amateurs or to other radio services operating near the amateur bands, however.

For example, a multiband dipole antenna that covers 80 and 40 meters may radiate 40-meter energy while you operate on 80 meters. The second harmonic of a 3.7-MHz signal falls above the 40-meter amateur band, at 7.4 MHz. If your transmitter is free of excessive harmonic output, you will probably not have a problem. (Note: Older, tube-type equipment can sometimes radiate excessive harmonics if it isn't "tuned up" properly. If you use a rig with a "plate tuning" control, be sure to adjust it according to the manufacturer's instructions.)

Proper shielding and grounding are essential to reduce harmonic and other spurious radiation. The only place you want RF to leave your transmitter is through the antenna connection. Your transmitter must be fully enclosed in a metal cabinet. The various shields that make up the metal cabinet should be securely screwed or welded together at the seams. You must also connect the transmitter to a good earth ground connection.

Remember: A low-pass filter will only block harmonics from reaching your antenna. It will do nothing for a poorly shielded transmitter that leaks stray RF from places other than the antenna connector. **Figure 6.10** summarizes the steps you can take to reduce harmonic radiation from your station.

More and more amateurs are using computers in their ham shacks. Most of the same steps you would take with your transceiver will also help reduce or eliminate interference from your computer. Yes, that's right! Your computer can cause interference to your receiver. A computer has a clock oscillator circuit that operates at a "radio" frequency. Do you have a 386/33, a 486/66 or a Pentium 200? The 33, 66 or 200 represents the clock frequency in megahertz!

Your computer should be in a metal cabinet with all screws securely attached, and you should use shielded cables with the shield connected to the equipment chassis. Be sure all your equipment is properly grounded. These steps will reduce to possibility of interference from your computer.

[Congratulations. You have completed your study of the material about good operating practices. Before you go on to Chapter 7, you should turn to Chapter 11 and study questions T2A02 and T2A05. Also study the questions numbered T6C01 through T6C12. Review this section if you have difficulty with any of these questions.]

BASIC COMMUNICATIONS ELECTRONICS

7

We can't see electricity as it flows through a circuit. We need some understanding of how it works, however, to design even a simple circuit.

This chapter introduces you to basic electronics and radio theory. The theory presented in this chapter will help you pass your Technician License exam. This theory will also help you to assemble and operate your amateur radio station.

There is much for you to learn, and most of the material presented here may be new to you. We will start with a description of the metric system of measure. Many of the measurements we make in electronics are based on metric units, so an understanding of this measuring system is important. Then we will cover some basic electrical principles. You'll learn the basics like voltage, current, conductors and insulators. Next, we will move on to electronics fundamentals. You will learn about resistance, Ohm's Law and power. You'll also learn about direct and alternating currents. And, you will learn about how alternating current applies to inductance and capacitance.

Three of the questions on your Technician class exam will be about the material in this chapter. These questions will come from syllabus topics T7A, T7B and T7C.

T7A Fundamentals of electricity; AC/DC power; units and definitions of current, voltage, resistance, inductance, capacitance and impedance; Rectification; Ohm's Law principle (simple math); Decibel; Metric system and prefixes (e.g., pico, nano, micro, milli, deci, centi, kilo, mega, giga).

T7B Basic electric circuits; Analog vs. digital communications; Audio/RF signal; Amplification.

T7C Concepts of Resistance/resistor; Capacitor/capacitance; Inductor/Inductance; Conductor/Insulator; Diode; Transistor; Semiconductor devices; Electrical functions of and schematic symbols of resistors, switches, fuses, batteries, inductors, capacitors, antennas, grounds and polarity; Construction of variable and fixed inductors and capacitors.

To get the most from this chapter, you should take it one section at a time. Study the material in each section and really know it before you go on to the next section. The sections build on each other, so you may find yourself referring to sections you've already studied from time to time. Don't be afraid to turn back to any section you have already studied. This review is helpful if you come across a term you are not sure about. You will probably not remember every bit of this theory just by reading the chapter once.

We use many technical terms in electronics. We have provided definitions that are as simple and to-the-point as possible. The first time these terms are used we have printed them in **boldface type**. The **Glossary of Key Words** at the end of this book includes these terms and their simple definitions, arranged alphabetically with the Key Words from all the other chapters in this book.

This chapter includes many drawings and illustrations to help you learn the material. Pay close attention to these graphics, and you'll find it easier to understand the text. We'll direct you to the Question Pool (Chapter 11) at appropriate points in the text. Use these directions to help you study the Technician Question Pool. When you can answer all of the questions, you are ready to move on.

If you have trouble understanding parts of this chapter, ask your instructor or another experienced ham for help. Many other books can help, too. ARRL's *Understanding Basic Electronics* is written for students with no previous electronics background. To study more advanced theory, you may want to purchase a copy of *The ARRL Handbook*. These publications are available from your local ham dealer or from ARRL Headquarters.

Take it slowly, section by section. Before you know it, you'll have learned what you need to know to pass your test and get on the air. Good luck!

The Metric System

We'll be talking about the units used to describe several electrical quantities later in this chapter. Before we do that, let's take a few minutes to become familiar with the **metric system**. This simple system is a standard system of measurement used all over the world. All the units used to describe electrical quantities are part of the metric system.

In the US, we use a measuring system known as the US Customary System for many physical quantities, such as distance, weight and volume. In this system there is no logical progression between the various units. For example, we have 12 inches in 1 foot, 3 feet in 1 yard and 1760 yards in 1 mile. For measuring the volume of liquids we have 2 cups in 1 pint, 2 pints in 1 quart and 4 quarts in 1 gallon. To make things even more difficult, we use some of these same names for different volumes when we measure dry materials! As you can see, this system of measurements can be very confusing. Even those who are very familiar with the system do not know all the units used for different types of measurements. Not many people know what a *slug* is, for example.

It is exactly this confusion that led scientists to develop the orderly system we know today as the metric system. This system uses a basic unit for each different type of measurement. For example, the basic unit of length is the meter. (This unit is spelled metre nearly everywhere in the world except the US!) The basic unit of volume is the liter (or litre). The unit for mass (or quantity of matter) is the gram. The newton is the metric unit of force, or weight, but we often use the gram to indicate how "heavy" something is. We can express larger or smaller quantities by multiplying or dividing the basic unit by factors of 10 (10, 100, 1000, 10,000 and so on). These multiples result in a standard set of prefixes, which can be used with all the basic units. **Table 7.1** summarizes the most-used **metric prefixes**. These same prefixes can be applied to any basic unit in the metric system. Even if you come across some terms you are not unfamiliar with, you will be able to recognize the prefixes.

We can write these prefixes as powers of 10, as shown in Table 7.1. The power of 10 (called the *exponent*) shows how many times you must multiply (or divide) the basic unit by 10. For example, we can see from the table that **kilo** means 10^3. Let's use the meter as an example. If you multiply a meter by 10 three times, you will have a *kilometer*. (1 meter $\times 10^3 = 1$ m $\times 10 \times 10 \times 10 = 1000$ meters, or 1 kilometer.) If you multiply 1 meter by 10 six times, you have a **mega**meter. (1 meter $\times 10^6 = 1$ m $\times 10 \times 10 \times 10 \times 10 \times 10 \times 10 = 1,000,000$ meters or 1 megameter.)

Notice that the exponent for some of the prefixes is a negative number. This indicates that you must *divide* the basic unit by 10 that number of times. If you divide a meter by 10, you will have a **deci**meter. (1 meter $\times 10^{-1} = 1$ m $\div 10 = 0.1$ meter, or 1 decimeter.) When we write 10^{-6}, it means you must divide by 10 six times. (1 meter $\times 10^{-6} = 1$ m $\div 10 \div 10 \div 10 \div 10 \div 10 \div 10 = 0.000001$ meter, or 1 **micro**meter.)

We can easily write very large or very small numbers with this system. We can use the metric prefixes with the basic units, or we can use powers of 10. Many of the quantities used in basic electronics are either very large or very small numbers, so we use these prefixes quite a bit. You should be sure you are familiar at least with the following prefixes and their associated powers of 10: **giga** (10^9), **mega** (10^6), **kilo** (10^3), **centi** (10^{-2}), **milli** (10^{-3}), **micro** (10^{-6}) and **pico** (10^{-12}).

Let's try an example. For this example, we'll use a term that you will run into quite often in your study of electronics: **hertz (abbreviated Hz)**. Hertz is a unit that refers to the frequency of a radio or television wave. We have a receiver dial calibrated in kilohertz (kHz), and it shows a signal at a frequency of 28450 kHz. Where would a dial calibrated in hertz show the signal? From Table 7.1 we see that kilo means times 1000. The basic unit of frequency is the hertz. That

Table 7-1

International System of Units (SI) — Metric Units

Prefix	Symbol	Multiplication Factor	
tera	T	10^{12}	= 1,000,000,000,000
giga	G	10^9	= 1,000,000,000
mega	M	10^6	= 1,000,000
kilo	k	10^3	= 1,000
hecto	h	10^2	= 100
deca	da	10^1	= 10
(unit)		10^0	= 1
deci	d	10^{-1}	= 0.1
centi	c	10^{-2}	= 0.01
milli	m	10^{-3}	= 0.001
micro	μ	10^{-6}	= 0.000001
nano	n	10^{-9}	= 0.000000001
pico	p	10^{-12}	= 0.000000000001

Figure 7.1 — This chart shows the symbols for all metric prefixes, with the power of ten that each represents. Write the abbreviations in decreasing order from left to right. The dots between certain prefixes indicate there are two decimal places between those prefixes. You must be sure to count a decimal place for each of these dots when converting from one prefix to another. When you change from a larger to a smaller prefix, you are moving to the right on the chart. The decimal point in the number you are changing also moves to the right. Likewise, when you change from a smaller to a larger prefix, you are moving to the left, and the decimal point also moves to the left.

10^{18}	10^{15}	10^{12}	10^{9}	10^{6}	10^{3}	10^{2}	10^{1}	10^{0}	10^{-1}	10^{-2}	10^{-3}	10^{-6}	10^{-9}	10^{-12}	10^{-15}	10^{-18}
E	·· P ··	T ··	G ··	M ··	k	h	da	U	d	c	m ··	μ ··	n ·	p ··	f ··	a

means that our signal is at 28450 kHz × 1,000 = 28,450,000 hertz. There are 1000 hertz in a kilohertz, so 28,450,000 divided by 1000 gives us 28,450 kHz.

How about another one? If we have a current of 3000 milliamperes, how many amperes is this? From Table 7.1 we see that milli means multiply by 0.001 or divide by 1000. Dividing 3000 milliamperes by 1000 gives us 3 amperes. The metric prefixes make it easy to use numbers that are a convenient size simply by changing the units. It is certainly easier to work with a measurement given as 3 amperes than as 3000 milliamperes!

Notice that it doesn't matter what the units are or what they represent. Meters, hertz, amperes, volts, farads or watts make no difference in how we use the prefixes. Each prefix represents a certain multiplication factor, and that value never changes.

With a little practice you should begin to understand how to change prefixes in the metric system. First write the number and find the proper power of ten (from memory or Table 7.1), and then move the decimal point to change to the basic unit. Then divide by the multiplication factor for the new prefix you want to use. With a little more practice you'll be changing prefixes with ease.

There is another method you can use to convert between metric prefixes, but it involves a little trick. Learn to write the chart shown in **Figure 7.1** on a piece of paper when you are going to make a conversion. Always start with the large prefixes on the left and go toward the right with the smaller ones. Sometimes you can make an abbreviated list, using only the units from kilo to milli. If you need the units larger than kilo or smaller than milli, be sure to include the dots as shown in Figure 7.1. (They mark the extra decimal places between the larger and smaller prefixes, which go in steps of 1000 instead of every 10.) Once you learn to write the chart correctly, it will be very easy to change prefixes.

Let's work through an example to show how to use this chart. Change 3725 kilohertz to hertz. Since we are starting with kilohertz (kilo), begin at the k on the chart. Now count each symbol to the right, until you come to the basic unit (U). Did you count three places? Well that's how many places you must move the decimal point to change from kilohertz (kHz) to hertz (Hz). Which way do you move the decimal point? Notice that you counted to the right on the chart. Move the decimal point in the same

direction. Now you can write the answer: 3725 kHz = 3,725,000 Hz!

Suppose a meter indicates a voltage of 3500 milli-volts (abbreviated mV) across a circuit. How many volts (abbreviated V) is that? First, write the list of metric prefixes. Since you won't need those smaller than milli or larger than kilo, you can write an abbreviated list. You don't have to write the powers of ten, if you remember what the prefixes represent. To change from milli to the unit, we count 3 decimal places toward the left. This tells us to move the decimal point in our number three places to the left.

3500 mV = 3.5 V

Let's try one more example for some extra practice changing metric prefixes by moving the decimal point in a number. What if someone told you to tune your radio receiver to 145,450,000 Hz? You probably won't find any radio receiver with a dial marking like this! To make the number more practical, we'll write the frequency with a prefix that's more likely to appear on a receiver dial.

Our first step is to select a new prefix to express the number. We can write the number with one, two or three digits to the left of the decimal point. It looks like we'll need the entire prefix chart for this one, so write it down as described earlier. (You can look at the chart in Figure 7.1, but you should practice writing it for those times when you don't have the book — like your exam!)

The next job is to count how many places you can move the decimal point. The number you end up with should have one, two or three digits to the left of the decimal point. Remember that metric prefixes larger than kilo represent multiples of 1000, or 10^3. Did you count six places to move the decimal point in our example, 145,450,000 Hz? That would leave us with 145.45×10^6 Hz.

Now go back to the chart and count six places to the left. (This is the same number of places and the same direction as we moved the decimal point.) The new spot on the chart indicates our new metric prefix, mega, abbreviated M. Replacing the power of ten with this prefix, we can write our frequency as 145.45 MHz.

[Before you go on to the next section, turn to Chapter 11. Be sure you can answer questions T7A17 through T7A21. Review this section if you have any difficulty.]

Basic Electrical Principles

In this section, you will learn what electricity is and how it works. We'll introduce you to the atom and the electron, the basic elements of electricity. There are no questions about atoms and electrons on the Technician exam, but understanding them will help you better understand the rest of this chapter.

Electricity

The word is a spine-tingling mystery. It's the force behind our space-age civilization. It's one of nature's greatest powers. We love it; we fear it. We use it in our work and play. But what is it?

Most of its mystery is because we can't see it. We only experience its effects on us and things around us. Actually, electricity is the marvelous stuff which, when untamed, we call lightning. One lightning bolt produces enough electricity to supply your needs for a lifetime. In another form, electricity is the power in a battery that cranks the engine to start your car. Electricity also ignites the gasoline in the engine. Yet, with all its power, electricity is the careful messenger carrying information from your brain to your muscles, enabling you to move your arms and legs. You can buy a small container of electricity no bigger than a dime (a battery). Electric utilities generate and transmit huge amounts of electricity every day. From lightning bolts to brain waves, it's all the same stuff: **electrons**.

Inside Atoms

Everything you can see and touch is made up of *atoms*. Atoms are the building blocks of nature. Atoms are too small to see, but the *subatomic particles* inside atoms are even smaller.

Each atom has a *nucleus* in its center. Other particles orbit around this central core. Think of the familiar maps of our solar system: planets orbit the sun. In an atom, charged particles orbit the central core (the nucleus). Other charged particles make up the nucleus. **Figure 7.2** is a simplified illustration of an atom's structure.

Some particles have *negative charges* while others have *positive charges*. The core of an atom contains positively charged particles. Negative particles, called **electrons**, orbit around the nucleus. Scientists have identified more than 100 different kinds of atoms. The number of positively and negatively charged particles in an atom determines what type of element that atom is. Different kinds of atoms combine to form various materials. For example, a hydrogen atom has one positively charged particle in its nucleus and one electron around the outside. An oxygen atom has eight positive particles in the nucleus and eight electrons around the outside. When two hydrogen atoms combine with one oxygen atom, we have water.

Have you ever tried to push the north poles of two

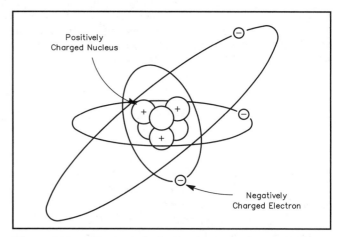

Figure 7.2 — Each atom is a microscopic particle composed of a central, dense, positively charged nucleus, surrounded by tiny negatively charged electrons. There are the same number of positive particles in the nucleus and negative electrons outside the nucleus.

magnets together? Remember that soft, but firm, pressure holding them apart? Similar poles in magnets repel each other; opposite poles attract each other. You can feel this if you experiment with a pair of small magnets.

Charged particles behave in a way similar to the two magnets. A positively charged particle and a negatively charged particle attract each other. Two positive or two negative particles repel each other. Like repels like; opposites attract.

Electrons stay near the central core, or nucleus, of the atom. The positive charge on the nucleus attracts the negative electrons. Meanwhile, since the electrons are all negatively charged, they repel each other. This makes the electrons move apart and fill the space around the nucleus. (Scientists sometimes refer to this area as an electron "cloud.") An atom has an equal balance of negative and positive charges and shows no electrical effect to the outside world. We say the atom is *neutral*.

Electron Flow

In many materials, especially metals, it's easy to dislodge an electron from an atom. When the atom loses an electron, it upsets the stability and electrical balance of the atom. With one particle of negative charge gone, the atom has an excess of positive charges. The free electron has a negative charge. We call the atom that lost the electron a positive *ion* because of its net positive charge. (An ion is a charged particle.) If there are billions of similar ions in one place, the quantity of charge becomes large enough to cause a noticeable effect.

Positively charged ions can pull negative particles (electrons) from neutral atoms. These electrons can move

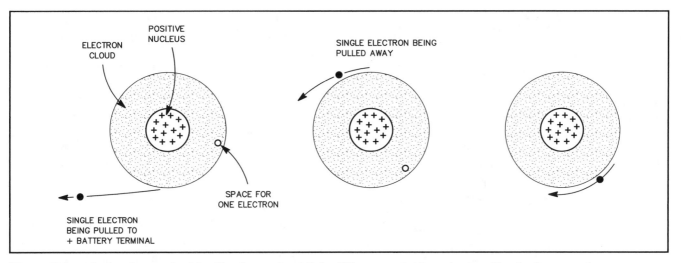

Figure 7.3 — An ion is an electrically charged particle. When an electron (a negative ion) moves from one atom to another, the atom losing the electron becomes a positive ion. This electron movement represents an electric current. The electrons are moving from right to left in this drawing.

across the space between the atom and the ion and orbit the positively charged ion. Now the positively charged ion has become a neutral atom again, and another atom has become a positively charged ion! If this process seems confusing, take a look at **Figure 7.3**. Here we show a series of atoms and positive ions, with electrons moving from one atom to the next. The electrons are moving from right to left in this diagram. We call this flow of electrons *electricity*. Electricity is nothing more than the flow of electrons.

How difficult is it for a positive ion to rip an electron away from an atom? That depends on the individual atoms making up a particular material. Some atoms hold firmly to their electrons and won't let them flow away easily. Other atoms keep only a loose grip on electrons and let them slip away easily. This means that some materials carry electricity better than others. **Conductors** are materials that keep only a loose grip on their electrons. We call those materials that hold tightly to their electrons **insulators**.

Demonstrating Electron Flow

Here's an easy way to see the power of electrical charges. On a dry day hang some metal foil from dry thread. Rub one end of a plastic comb on wool (or run it through your hair). Then bring the end of the comb near the metal foil.

Rubbing the comb on wool detaches electrons from the wool fibers, depositing them on the surface of the comb. When you bring the charged end of the comb near the foil, free electrons in the foil will be repelled by the negative charge on the comb. The free electrons will move as far from the comb as they can — on the edge farthest from the comb. This leaves the near edge of the foil with a shortage of electrons (in other words, with a positive charge). The near edge of the foil is then attracted to the negatively charged comb.

As soon as the foil touches the comb, some of the excess electrons on the comb flow onto the foil. (Electricity!) The foil will then have a net negative charge, as the comb does, and the foil will be repelled by the comb. This simple experiment shows the attraction, repulsion and flow of electrons — the heart of electricity.

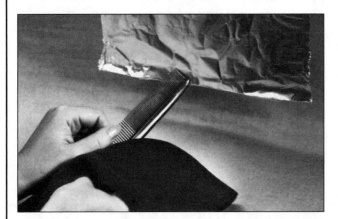

Why Do Electrons Flow?

There are many similarities between electricity flowing in a wire and water flowing through a pipe. Most people are familiar with what happens when you open a faucet and water comes out. We can use this to make a useful comparison between water flow and electron flow (electricity). Throughout this chapter we use examples of water flowing in a pipe to help explain electronics.

Do you know how your town's water system works? Chances are, there is a large supply of water stored somewhere. Some towns use a lake or river. Other towns get their water from wells and store it in a tank or reservoir. The system then uses gravity to pull the water down from the tank or reservoir. The water travels through a system of pipes to your house. Because the force of gravity is pulling down on the water in the tank, it exerts a pressure on the water in the pipes. This makes the water flow out of the faucets in your house with some force. If you have a well, you probably have a storage tank. The storage tank uses air pressure to push the water up to the top floor of your house.

In these water systems, a pump takes water from the large supply and puts it into a storage tank. Then the system uses air pressure or the force of gravity to push the water through pipes to the faucets in your home.

We can compare electrons flowing through wire to water flowing through a pipe. We need some force to make water flow through a pipe. What force exerts pressure to make electrons flow through a wire?

Voltage

The amount of pressure that it takes to push water to your house depends on the path the water has to take. If the water has to travel over hills along the way, more pressure will be required than if the water simply has to flow down off a mountain. The pressure required to make electrons flow in an electrical circuit also depends on the opposition that the electrons must overcome. The pressure that forces the electrons through the circuit is known as **electromotive force** or, simply, **EMF**.

EMF is similar to water pressure. More pressure moves more water. Similarly, more EMF moves more electrons. We measure EMF in a unit called the **volt** (abbreviated **V**), so we sometimes refer to the EMF as a voltage. If more voltage is applied to a circuit, more electrons will flow. We measure voltage with a device called a *voltmeter*.

An electric wall outlet in your home usually supplies about 120 volts. If you have an outlet for an electric stove or an electric clothes dryer in your home, that outlet probably provides 240 V. A car battery is normally rated at 12 volts. A single D-cell battery supplies 1.5 V. Voltage sources come in a wide variety of ratings, depending on their intended use. With our system of metric prefixes, we can express a thousand volts as 1 kilovolt or "1 kV."

Another way to think about this electrical voltage pushing electrons through a circuit is to remember that like-charged objects repel. If we have a large group of electrons, the negative charge of these electrons will act to repel, or push, other electrons through the circuit. In a similar way, a large group of positively charged ions attract, or pull, electrons through the circuit.

Because there are two types of electric charge (positive and negative), there are also two polarities associated with a voltage. A voltage source always has two terminals, or poles: the positive terminal and the negative terminal. The negative terminal repels electrons (negatively charged particles) and the positive terminal attracts electrons. If we connect a piece of wire between the two terminals of a voltage source, electrons will flow through the wire. We call this flow an electrical **current**.

Batteries

In our water system, a pump supplies pressure to pull water from the source and force it into the pipes. Similarly, electrical circuits require an electron source and a "pump" to move the electrons along.

A **battery** is one example of a power supply. We use a battery as both the source of electrons and the pump that moves them along. The battery is like the storage tank in our water system. A battery provides pressure to keep the electrons moving.

There is an excess of electrons at the negative terminal of a power supply. At the positive terminal there is an excess of positive ions. With a conducting wire connected between the two terminals, the electrical pressure (voltage) generated by the power supply will cause electrons to move through the conductor.

Batteries come in all shapes and sizes. Some batteries are tiny, like those used in hearing aids and cameras. Other batteries are larger than the one in your car. A battery is one kind of voltage source.

A battery changes chemical energy into electrical energy. When we connect a wire between the terminals of a battery, a chemical reaction takes place inside the battery. This reaction produces free electrons, and these electrons flow through the wire from the negative terminal to the positive terminal. Batteries may be small or large, round or square. Hearing aid and calculator batteries are tiny. The battery that starts your car is large by comparison, but batteries can be even larger than that. **Figure 7.4** shows several different batteries.

The basic unit of electromotive force (EMF) is the volt. The volt was named in honor of Alessandro Giuseppe Antonio Anastasio Volta (1745-1827). This Italian physicist invented the electric battery.

Figure 7.4 — Batteries come in all shapes and sizes. A battery changes chemical energy into electrical energy.

Batteries are made up of *cells*. Each cell has a positive electrode and a negative electrode. The cells produce a small voltage. The voltage a cell produces depends on the chemical process taking place inside the cell. Rechargeable nickel-cadmium cells produce about 1.2 volts per cell. Common zinc-acid and alkaline flashlight cells produce about 1.5 volts per cell. The lead-acid cells in a car battery each produce about 2 volts.

The number of cells in a battery depends on the voltage we want to get out of the battery. If we only need a low voltage the battery may contain only one cell. Small hearing-aid batteries, for example, usually contain only one cell. Part A of **Figure 7.5** shows the **schematic symbol** for a single-cell battery. Every circuit component has a schematic symbol. A schematic symbol is nothing more than a drawing used to represent a component. We use these symbols when we are making a circuit diagram, or wiring diagram, to show how the components connect for a specific pur-

pose. You will learn the schematic symbols for the circuit components discussed in this chapter. As you discover more about electronics, you will learn how these symbols can be used to illustrate practical circuit connections. The long line on the battery schematic symbol represents the positive terminal and the short line represents the negative terminal.

To produce a battery with a higher voltage, several cells must be connected in series so their outputs add. The battery manufacturer connects several cells in series to produce the desired battery voltage.

Part B of Figure 7.5 shows the schematic symbol for a multiple-cell battery. We use several lines to show the many cells in the battery. Again, the long line at one end represents the positive terminal, and the short line at the other end represents the negative terminal. The schematic symbol does not indicate the number of cells in the battery. Two sets of long and short lines represent any multiple-cell battery.

Current

You have probably heard the term "current" used to describe the flow of water in a stream or river. Similarly, we call the flow of electrons an electric **current**. Each electron is extremely small. It takes quintillions and quintillions of electrons to make your toaster heat bread or your TV to draw pictures. (A quintillion is a one with 18 zeros after it — 1,000,000,000,000,000,000. Using powers of 10, as described earlier, we could also write this as 1×10^{18}.)

When water flows from your home faucet, you don't try to count every drop. The numbers would be very large and unmanageable, and the drops are coming out much too fast to count! To measure water flow, you count larger quantities such as gallons and describe the flow in terms of gallons per minute. Similarly, we can't deal easily with large numbers of individual electrons, nor can we count them conveniently. We need a shorthand way to measure the number of electrons. So, as with gallons per minute of water, we have **amperes** of electric current. We abbreviate ampere **A**. We measure current with a device called an *ammeter*.

Suppose you are looking through a "window" into a wire, and can count electrons as they move past you. (See

Figure 7.5 — Some small batteries contain only one cell. We use the symbol at A for a single-cell battery. Manufacturers add several cells in series to produce more voltage. Part B is the schematic symbol for a multiple-cell battery.

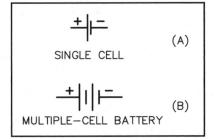

+ | | — (A)
SINGLE CELL

+ | | | — (B)
MULTIPLE-CELL BATTERY

The action of electric current on a magnet was first applied to telegraphy by André Marie Ampère (1775-1836) in 1820. An ampere is the basic unit of electrical current.

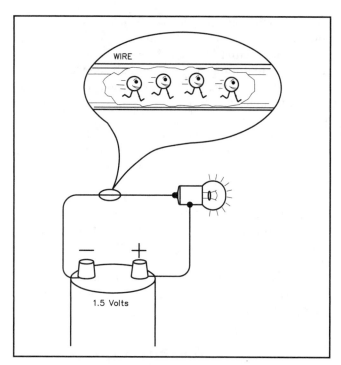

Figure 7.6 — A window like this into a wire might allow you to count electrons as they flow past, to measure the current. Even so, you would have to count 6.24 × 10^{18} electrons per second for a current of only 1 ampere!

Figure 7.6.) If you count 6,240,000,000,000,000,000 (6.24 × 10^{18}) electrons moving past your "window" each second, the circuit has a current of one **ampere**. (Don't worry! You won't have to remember this number.) So when you express a circuit's current in amperes, remember that it is a measure of the number of electrons flowing through the circuit. A circuit with a current of 2 amperes has twice as many electrons flowing out of the supply as a circuit with a current of 1 ampere.

Write "2 A" for two amperes or "100 mA" (milliamps) for 0.1 ampere (sometimes also abbreviated amp or amps). You can use all the metric prefixes with the ampere. Most of the time you will see currents expressed in amps, milliamps and microamps. See Table 7.1 to review the list of metric prefixes.

Conductors

As we pointed out earlier, some atoms have a firm grasp on their electrons and other atoms don't. More current can flow in materials made of atoms that have only a weak hold on their electrons. Some materials, then, conduct electricity better than others.

Silver is an excellent **conductor**. The loosely attached electrons in silver atoms require very little voltage (pressure) to produce an electric current. Copper is much less expensive than silver and conducts almost as well.

We can use copper to make wire needed in houses, and in radios and other electronic devices. Steel also conducts, but not as well as copper. In fact, most metals are fairly good conductors, so aluminum, mercury, zinc, tin and gold are all conductors.

Insulators

Other materials keep a very firm grip on their electrons. These materials do not conduct electricity very well, and are called **insulators**. Materials such as glass, rubber, plastic, ceramic, mica, wood and even air are poor conductors. Pure distilled water is a fairly good insulator. Most tap water is a good conductor, however, because it has minerals and other impurities dissolved in it. **Figure 7.7** may help you remember the difference between insulators and conductors.

The electric power company supplies 120 V on the wires into your home. That voltage is available for your use at electrical outlets or sockets. Why don't the electrons spill out of the sockets? The insulation between the two sides of the outlet prevents the electrons from flowing from one side to the other. The air around the socket acts as an insulator to stop them from flowing into the room.

Because insulators are *poor* conductors rather than *non*conductors, every insulator has a *breakdown voltage*. A voltage higher than the breakdown voltage will force electrons to move through the insulator. The insulator will start to conduct electricity. Depending on the material, it may be damaged if you exceed the breakdown voltage. Better insulators have higher breakdown voltages. Breakdown voltage also depends on the thickness of the insulat-

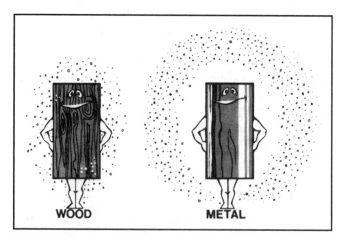

Figure 7.7 — Here's one way to show how an insulator differs from a conductor. Wood, on the left, holds onto its electrons pretty tightly, keeping them from flowing between its atoms. Metals, on the other hand, are more generous with their electrons. Electrons are more easily pulled away from the metal atoms, and the metal atoms are then left with a positive charge. If the metal atoms attract extra electrons from neighboring atoms, they become negatively charged.

ing material. A thin layer of one insulating material (like Teflon or mica) may be just as good as a much thicker layer of another material (like paper or air).

A good example of an insulator that will conduct at very high voltage is air. Air is a fine insulator at the voltages normally found in homes and industry. When a force of millions of volts builds up, however, there's enough pressure to send a bolt of electrons through the air — *lightning*. You can produce a voltage large enough to make a spark jump through a thin air layer by shuffling your feet across the carpet on a dry day. When you reach for a metal object like a doorknob, you can often feel the spark jump from your finger. If the room is darkened, you can also see the spark.

When you are insulating wires or components, always be sure to use the right insulating material. Make sure you use enough insulation for the voltages you're likely to encounter. Heat-shrinkable tubing or other insulating tubing is often convenient for covering a bare wire or a solder connection. You can also wrap the wire with electrical tape. Several layers of tape, wrapped so it overlaps itself, will provide enough insulation for up to a few hundred volts.

Resistance

Resistance is the property of preventing, or opposing the flow of electrons in a material. Even the best conductors have some resistance. Materials that are poorer conductors have more resistance, and materials that are better conductors have less resistance.

What if you partially blocked a water pipe with a sponge? Eventually, the water would get through the sponge, but it would have less pressure than before. The sponge opposes, or resists the water trying to flow through the pipe, and it takes pressure to overcome that resistance.

Similarly, materials that conduct electrical current also present some opposition, or **resistance**, to the movement of electrons. **Resistors** are devices that are especially designed to make use of this opposition. Resistors limit, or control the amount of current that flows through a circuit because they oppose the flow of electrons. **Figure 7.8** shows some common resistors.

In a water pipe, increasing the pressure forces more water through the sponge (the resistance). In an electrical circuit, increasing the voltage forces more current through the resistor. The relationship between voltage, current and resistance is predictable. We call this relationship **Ohm's Law**, and it is a basic electronics principle. You will learn more about Ohm's Law later in this chapter.

The **ohm** is the basic unit used to measure resistance. The abbreviation for ohms is Ω, the Greek capital letter omega. This unit is named for Georg Simon Ohm, a German physics teacher and mathematician. Of course we also use the metric prefixes with ohms, when appropriate. So you will often see resistors specified as having 47 kilohms or 1.2 megohms of resistance. Written with abbreviations, these resistors would be 47 kΩ and 1.2 MΩ. As you could probably guess, when you want to measure an amount of resistance, you will use an *ohmmeter*.

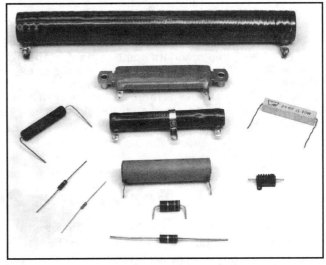

Figure 7.8 — This photograph shows some of the many types of resistors. Large power resistors are at the top of the photo. The small resistors are used in low-power transistor circuits.

When electrons flow from one point in a circuit to another point, there is *current* in that circuit. A perfect insulator would allow no electrons to flow through it (zero current), while a perfect conductor would allow infinite current (unlimited electrons flow). In practice, however, there is no such thing as a perfect conductor nor a perfect insulator. Some opposition to electron flow occurs when the electrons collide with other electrons or atoms in the conductor. The result is reduced current. The conductor is heated in this process.

The basic unit of resistance is the ohm, named in honor of Georg Simon Ohm (1787-1854).

Resistors

Resistors are important components in electronic circuits. A resistor opposes the flow of electrons. We can control the electron flow (the current) by varying the resistance in a circuit.

Resistors allow us to control the current in a circuit by controlling the opposition to electron flow. As they oppose the flow of electrons they dissipate electrical energy in the form of heat. The more energy a resistor dissipates, the hotter it will become.

Most resistors have standard fixed values, so they are called **fixed resistors**. **Variable resistors**, also called **potentiometers**, allow us to change the value of the resistance without removing and changing the component. They can be used to adjust the voltage, or potential, in a circuit. For example, potentiometers are used as the volume and tone controls in most stereo amplifiers.

Figure 7.9 shows two types of fixed resistors and a potentiometer. It also shows the schematic symbols for these resistors. When you look at these resistor symbols and see the zigzag lines you can just imagine how difficult it will be for the electrons to fight their way through these peaks and valleys!

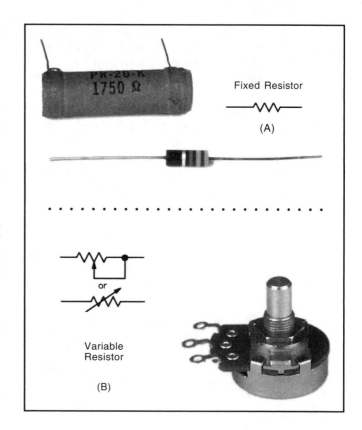

Figure 7.9 — Fixed resistors come in many standard values. Most of them look something like the ones shown at A. Variable resistors (also called potentiometers) are used wherever the value of resistance must be adjusted after the circuit is complete. Part B shows a potentiometer.

Series and Parallel Circuits

There are two basic ways that you can connect the parts in an electric circuit. If we hook several resistors together in a string, we call it a **series circuit**. If we connect several resistors side-by-side to the same voltage source, we call it a **parallel circuit**.

In our water-pipe example, what would happen to the current through the pipe if we placed another sponge in it? You're right: The second sponge would further reduce the flow. We could do the same thing with a single, larger sponge. The total resistance in a series circuit is the sum of all the resistances in the circuit.

In a series circuit, the same current flows through each resistor. The electrons have no other path to follow. **Figure 7.10A** shows the schematic diagram of three resistors connected in series with a battery. Resistors in series are connected end to end like a string of sausages.

Now let's look at the case of a parallel circuit. This is similar to having two water pipes running side by side. More water can flow through two parallel pipes of the same size than through a single one. With two pipes, the current is greater for a given pressure.

If these pipes had sponges in them, the flow would be reduced in each pipe. There are still two paths for the water to take. More water will flow than if there was a single pipe with a similar sponge in it. Now let's go back to electrical resistors and voltage. Adding a resistor in parallel with another one provides two paths for the electrical current to

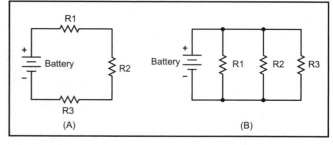

Figure 7.10 — Part A shows three resistors connected in series with a battery. Part B shows three resistors connected in parallel with a battery.

follow. This reduces the total resistance. You can connect more than two resistors in parallel, providing even more paths for the electrons. This will reduce the resistance still more. Figure 7.10B shows resistors connected in parallel with a battery. Resistors in parallel provide alternate paths for the current to take. Parallel resistors are side by side like a picket fence. The result is less total resistance in the circuit, and more current.

Why would you want to connect resistors in series or in parallel in a circuit? There will be times when you need a certain amount of resistance somewhere in a circuit. There may be no standard resistor value that will give the necessary resistance. Sometimes you may not have a certain value on hand. By combining resistors in parallel or series you can obtain the desired value.

When you connect resistors in series, as in Figure 7.10A, the total resistance is simply the sum of all the resistances. Resistors in series add.

$$R_{\text{Total in Series}} = R_1 + R_2 + R_3 + ... + R_n \qquad \text{(Equation 7.1)}$$

where n is the total number of resistors.

The total resistance of a string of resistors in series will always be greater than any individual resistor in the string. All the circuit current flows through each resistor in a series circuit. A series circuit with resistor values of 2 ohms, 3 ohms and 5 ohms would have a total resistance of 10 ohms. If a circuit has two equal-value resistors connected in series, the total resistance will be twice the value of either resistor alone.

In a parallel circuit, things are a bit different. When we connect two or more resistors in parallel, more than one path for current exists in the circuit. With more than one path, more electrons can flow. There is less resistance and a greater current.

The formula for calculating the total resistance of resistors connected in parallel is:

$$R_{\text{Total in Parallel}} = \cfrac{1}{\cfrac{1}{R_1} + \cfrac{1}{R_2} + \cfrac{1}{R_3} + ... + \cfrac{1}{R_n}}$$

(Equation 7.2)

where n is the total number of resistors. For example, if we connect three 300-ohm resistors in parallel, their total resistance is:

$$R_{\text{Total in Parallel}} = \cfrac{1}{\cfrac{1}{R_1} + \cfrac{1}{R_2} + \cfrac{1}{R_3}} = \cfrac{1}{\cfrac{1}{300\,\Omega} + \cfrac{1}{300\,\Omega} + \cfrac{1}{300\,\Omega}}$$

$$R_{\text{Total in Parallel}} = \cfrac{1}{\cfrac{3}{300\,\Omega}} = \cfrac{1}{\cfrac{1}{100\,\Omega}} = \cfrac{100\,\Omega}{1} = 100\,\Omega$$

To calculate the total resistance of two resistors in parallel, **Equation 7.2** reduces to the "product over sum" formula. Multiply the two resistor values and then divide by their sum:

$$R_{\text{Total in Parallel}} = \cfrac{R_1 \times R_2}{R_1 + R_2} \qquad \text{(Equation 7.3)}$$

If we connect two 100-ohm resistors in parallel, the total resistance would be:

$$R_{\text{Total in Parallel}} = \cfrac{R_1 \times R_2}{R_1 + R_2} = \cfrac{100\,\Omega \times 100\,\Omega}{100\,\Omega + 100\,\Omega} = \cfrac{10,000\,\Omega^2}{200\,\Omega}$$

$$= \cfrac{50\,\Omega^2}{1\,\Omega} = 50\,\Omega$$

From these two examples you can see that the total resistance of any resistors connected in parallel is always less than the value of any one of the resistors. You can use this fact to make a quick check of your calculations. The result you calculate should be smaller than the smallest value in the parallel combination. If it isn't, you've made a mistake somewhere!

[Turn to Chapter 11 now and study questions T7A06 through T7A08. Also study questions T7C01 through T7C03 and questions T7C11 through T7C13. Review this section if you can't answer any of those questions.]

Ohm's Law

In this section you will learn how to do some basic circuit calculations. We have kept the arithmetic simple. The text explains all of the steps in the solution. Associating numbers with a concept often makes the concept easier to understand. Read these examples and then try the calculations yourself. Be sure you can work the problems in the question pool when you study those questions.

The amount of water flowing through a pipe increases as we increase the pressure and decreases as we increase the resistance. If we replace "pressure" with "voltage," this same statement describes current through an electric circuit. We can write a mathematical relationship for an electric circuit:

$$\text{Current} = \cfrac{\text{Voltage}}{\text{Resistance}} \qquad \text{(Equation 7.4)}$$

This equation tells us the current through a circuit equals the voltage applied to the circuit divided by the circuit resistance.

If the voltage stays constant but more current flows in the circuit, we know there must be less resistance. The relationship between current and voltage is a measure of the resistance:

$$\text{Resistance} = \cfrac{\text{Voltage}}{\text{Current}} \qquad \text{(Equation 7.5)}$$

We can state this equation in words as: The circuit resistance is equal to the voltage applied to the circuit divided by the current through the circuit. This equation shows that if we apply a voltage of 1 volt to a circuit, and measure a current of 1 ampere through that circuit, then the circuit has a resistance of 1 ohm. This is one way to define a circuit with a resistance of 1 ohm.

Finally, we can determine the voltage if we know how much current is flowing and the resistance in the circuit:

Voltage = Current × Resistance   (Equation 7.6)

The voltage applied to a circuit is equal to the current through the circuit times the circuit resistance.

Scientists are always looking for shorthand ways of writing mathematical relationships. They use symbols to replace the words: E represents voltage (remember EMF?), current is I (from the French word *intensité*) and resistance is R. We can now express **Ohm's Law** in a couple of letters:

E = I R (volts = amperes × ohms)   (Equation 7.7)

This is the most common way to express Ohm's Law, but we can also write it as:

$$I = \frac{E}{R}$$ (amperes = volts divided by ohms)

(Equation 7.8)

and

$$R = \frac{E}{I}$$ (ohms = volts divided by amperes)

(Equation 7.9)

E is EMF in volts, I is the current in amperes and R is the resistance in ohms. If you know two of the numbers, you can calculate the third. If a circuit has an EMF of 1 volt applied to it, and the current through the circuit is 1 ampere, then the resistance of that circuit will be 1 ohm.

Figure 7.11 shows a diagram to help you solve Ohm's Law problems. Simply cover the symbol of the quantity that you do not know. If the remaining two are side-by-side, you must multiply them. If one symbol is above the other, then you must divide the quantity on top by the one on the bottom.

If you know current and resistance in a circuit, Ohm's Law will give you the voltage (**Equation 7.7**). For example, what is the voltage applied to the circuit if 2 amperes of current flows through 50 ohms of resistance? From Equation 7.7 or Figure 7.11, we see that we must multiply 2 amperes times 50 ohms to get the answer, 100 volts. The EMF in this circuit is 100 volts.

E = I R   (Equation 7.7)

E = 2 amperes × 50 ohms

E = 100 volts

Suppose you know voltage and resistance — 200 volts in the circuit to push electrons against 100 ohms of resis-

There Really Was an Ohm (1787-1854)

Although we take Ohm's Law for granted, it wasn't always so widely accepted. In 1827, Georg Simon Ohm finished his renowned work, *The Galvanic Circuit Mathematically Treated.* Scientists at first resisted Ohm's techniques. The majority of his colleagues were still holding to a non-mathematical approach. Finally, the younger physicists in Germany accepted Ohm's information in the early 1830s. The turning point for this basic electrical law came in 1841 when the Royal Society of London awarded Ohm the Copley Medal.

As the oldest son of a master locksmith, Georg received a solid education in philosophy and the sciences from his father. At the age of 16 he entered the University of Erlangen (Bavaria) and studied for three semesters. His father then forced him to withdraw because of alleged overindulgences in dancing, billiards and ice skating. After $4\frac{1}{2}$ years, his brilliance undaunted, Ohm returned to Erlangen to earn his PhD in mathematics.

Enthusiasm ran high at that time for scientific solutions to all problems. The first book Ohm wrote reflected his highly intellectualized views about the role of mathematics in education. These opinions changed, however, during a series of teaching positions. Oersted's discovery of electromagnetism in 1820 spurred Ohm to avid experiments, since he taught Physics and had a well-equipped lab. Ohm based his work on direct scientific observation and analyses, rather than on abstract theories.

One of Ohm's goals was to be appointed to a major university. In 1825 he started doing research with the thought of publishing his results. The following year he took a leave of absence from teaching and went to Berlin.

In Berlin, Ohm made his now-famous experiments. He ran wires between a zinc-copper battery and mercury-filled cups. While a Coulomb torsion balance (voltmeter) was across one leg of the series circuit, a "variable conductor" completed the loop. By measuring the loss in electromagnetic force for various lengths and sizes of wire, he had the basis for his formulas.

Because *The Galvanic Circuit* produced near-hostility, Ohm withdrew from the academic world for nearly six years before accepting a post in Nuremberg. English and French physicists do not seem to have been aware of the profound implications of Ohm's work until the late 1830s and early 1840s.

Following his belated recognition, Ohm became a corresponding member of the Berlin Academy. Late in 1849 he went to the University of Munich and in 1852, only two years before his death, he achieved his lifelong dream of a full professorship at a major university.

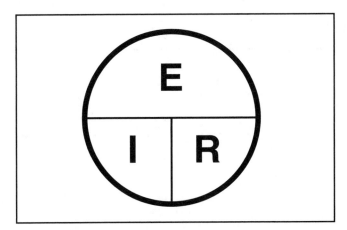

Figure 7.11 — This simple diagram will help you remember the Ohm's Law relationships. To find any quantity if you know the other two, simply cover the unknown quantity with your hand or a piece of paper. The positions of the remaining two symbols show if you have to multiply (when they are side by side) or divide (when they appear one over the other as a fraction).

tance. **Equation 7.8** gives the correct equation, or you can use the diagram in Figure 7.11. You must divide 200 volts by 100 ohms to find that 2 amperes of current is flowing.

$$I = \frac{E}{R} \qquad \text{(Equation 7.8)}$$

$$I = \frac{200 \text{ volts}}{100 \text{ ohms}}$$

$$I = 2 \text{ amperes}$$

If you know voltage and current in a circuit, you can calculate resistance. For example, suppose a current of 3 amperes flows through a resistor connected to 90 volts. This time **Equation 7.9** is the one to use, and you can also find this from Figure 7.11. 90 divided by 3 equals 30, so the resistance is 30 ohms.

$$R = \frac{E}{I} \qquad \text{(Equation 7.9)}$$

$$R = \frac{90 \text{ volts}}{3 \text{ amperes}}$$

$$R = 30 \text{ ohms}$$

If you know E and I, you can find R. If you know I and R, you can calculate E. If E and R are known, you can find I.

Put another way, if you know volts and amperes, you can calculate ohms. If amperes and ohms are known, volts can be found. Or if volts and ohms are known, amperes can be calculated. **Figure 7.12** illustrates some simple circuits and how Ohm's Law can be used to find an unknown quantity in the circuit. Make up a few problems of your own and test how well you understand this basic law of electricity. You'll soon find that this predictable relationship, symbolized by the repeatable equation of Ohm's Law, makes calculating values of components in electrical circuits easy. Ohm's Law is one electrical principle that you will use when working with almost any electronic circuit!

[Before you read further, turn to Chapter 11 and study questions T7A12 through T7A15. Review this section if you don't understand any of these questions.]

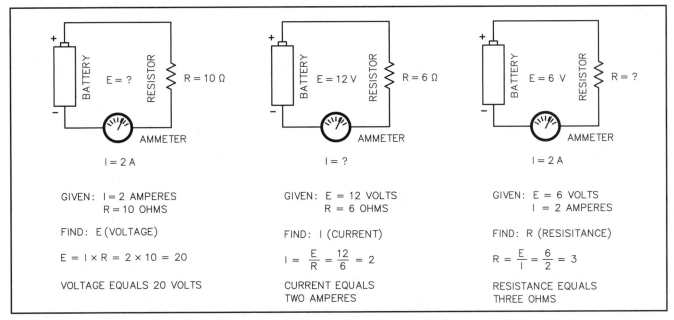

Figure 7.12 — This drawing shows some Ohm's Law problems and solutions.

Energy and Power

We define **energy** as the ability to do work. An object can have energy because of its position (like a rock ready to fall off the edge of a cliff). An object in motion also has energy (like the same rock as it falls to the bottom of the cliff). In electronics, a power supply or battery is the source of electrical energy. We can make use of that energy by connecting the supply to a light bulb, a radio or other circuit.

A voltage source pushes electrons through the resistance in an electric circuit. Suppose we have a circuit with two resistors connected so the current goes from the battery, through one resistor, then through the other and finally back to the battery. If we know how much current flows through the circuit, we can use Ohm's Law to calculate the voltage across each resistor. The example shown in **Figure 7.13** has two equal-value resistors, and each resistor has half the battery voltage because the total battery voltage is applied across both resistors. The voltage that appears across each individual resistor is called a *voltage drop*. In our example, after the current has gone through the first resistor, the voltage has dropped from 10 V to 5 V, and after the second resistor it has dropped to 0 V because it is back to the battery terminal at that time.

These voltage drops occur because electrical energy is "used up" or "consumed." Actually, we can't lose the electrical energy; it is just changed to some other form. The resistor heats up because of the current through it; the resistance converts electrical energy to heat energy. More current produces still more heat, and the resistor becomes warmer. If the current is too large the resistor might even catch fire!

As electrons flow through a light bulb, the resistance of the bulb converts some electrical energy to heat. The filament in the bulb gets so hot that it converts some of the electrical energy to light energy. Again, more current produces more light and heat.

You should get the idea that we can "use up" a certain amount of energy by having a small current go through a resistor for a long time or by having a larger current go through it for a shorter time. When you buy electricity from a power company, you pay for the electrical energy that you use each month. You might use all of the energy in one day, but you probably use a small amount every day. Your bill would be the same in either case, because the electric meter on your house just measures how much energy you use. The power company sends someone around to read the meter each month to determine how much electrical energy you used.

Sometimes it is important to know how fast a circuit can use energy. You might want to compare how bright two different light bulbs will be. If you're buying a new freezer, you might want to know how much electricity it will use in a month. You will have to know how fast the freezer or the light bulbs use electrical energy. We use the term **power** to define the rate of energy consumption. The

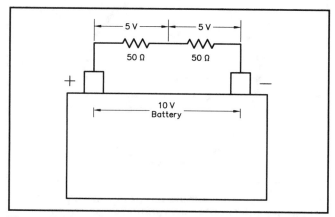

Figure 7.13 — When two resistors are connected in series with a battery, part of the battery voltage appears across each of the resistors. Here, each resistor has half the voltage because the two resistors have equal values.

basic unit for measuring power in the metric system is the **watt**. You have probably seen this term used to rate electrical appliances. You know that a light bulb rated at 75 watts will be brighter than one rated at 40 watts. (Sometimes we abbreviate watts with a capital W.) These same numbers tell us which light bulb uses more electrical energy each minute (or hour) that they are turned on. For example, if you turn on light bulbs of 60 watts, 75 watts and 100 watts, the 100-watt light bulb will use the most electrical energy in an hour.

Power and Decibels

The **decibel** is one unit that you will hear used (and misused) quite often in electronics. Just what does this term mean? First we'll define the term, and then we'll take a look at some of the ways we use decibels in electronics.

You have probably recognized *deci* as the metric prefix that means one tenth. So the unit we are really talking about here is the *bel*, and a decibel is just 1/10 of a bel. We often use a capital B to abbreviate bel. Since the lower case d is the abbreviation for deci, the proper abbreviation for a decibel is dB. The bel is named for Alexander Graham Bell. Most people remember Bell for his invention of the telephone. Bell was also very interested in working with deaf people and studying the way we hear sounds.

In electronics, we use the decibel as a comparison of power levels. A decibel is ten times the logarithm of a ratio of two power levels. We aren't going to get too technical or go into a lot of math here, so don't panic. A couple of examples will make this easier to understand. Suppose you are operating a transmitter with a power output of 5 watts. Now increase that output power to 10 watts. Find the ratio of these power levels by dividing the new (higher) power by the original value:

$$\text{Power Ratio} = \frac{10\ \text{W}}{5\ \text{W}} = 2$$

If you have a scientific calculator, you can find the logarithm (log) of 2, and the answer is 0.3. Now if we multiply that result by ten, we have our answer of 3 dB. So by going from 5 W to 10 W, we have increased our transmitter power by 3 dB.

Suppose you increased the power from 10 W to 20 W. Well, the ratio of those power levels is 2, so that is another 3 dB-increase in power.

Now you may be wondering how we would describe the change from 5 W to 20 W. Well in that case the ratio of output powers is:

$$\text{Power Ratio} = \frac{20\ \text{W}}{5\ \text{W}} = 4$$

Using your scientific calculator again, you can find that the log of 4 is 0.6. Multiply that answer by ten to find that this represents a 6-dB increase in power.

There is one more example that will give an an-

The basic unit of power is the watt. This unit is named after James Watt (1736-1819). Watt made engineering design changes to earlier steam engines, and developed a practical steam engine that helped create the industrial revolution.

Table 7.2
Some Common Decibel Values and Power Level Ratios

P_2/P_1	dB
0.1	−10
0.25	−6
0.5	−3
1	0
2	3
4	6
10	10

swer worth remembering. Suppose we increase that transmitter power from 5 W to 50 W. That new power is 10 times larger than the first power. The log of 10 is 1. So we have a 10-dB increase in power for this last example.

Every time you increase the power by a factor of 2 times, you have a 3-dB increase of power. Every 4 times increase of power is a 6-dB increase of power. When you increase the power by 10 times, you have a power increase of 10 dB. You can also use these same values for a decrease in power. Cut the power in half for a 3-dB loss of power. Reduce the power to ¼ the original value for a 6-dB loss in power. If you reduce the power to 1/10 of the original value you will have a 10-dB loss. The power-loss values are often written as negative values: −3, −6 or −10 dB. **Table 7.2** shows these common decibel values and power ratios.

[Before you go on to the next section in this chapter, turn to Chapter 11 and study questions T7A04 and T7A16. Review this section if you have any problems.]

Other Circuit Components

There are many electronic components, or parts used in the electronics devices we use every day. Batteries, resistors, capacitors, fuses, inductors, switches and transistors all are important. How do these components work and what do they do? So far in this chapter we have covered the basic operation of resistors and Ohm's Law. We have seen how batteries are used as a voltage source to push a current through circuits made with resistors. Now we will turn our attention to some of these other important parts that make up electronics circuits. You will find descriptions of several types of fuses, switches, capacitors and semiconductor devices. We combine these components with other devices to build practical electronic circuits.

Switches

How do you control the lights in your house? What turns on your car radio? A switch, of course.

The simplest kind of switch just connects or disconnects a single electrical contact. Two wires connect to the switch; when you turn the switch on, the two wires are connected. When you turn the switch off, the wires are disconnected. This is called a **single-pole, single-throw**

switch. It connects a single pair of wires (single pole) and has only two positions, on or off (single throw). Sometimes we abbreviate single pole, single throw as **SPST**. **Figure 7.14A** shows a simple SPST switch and the symbol we use to represent it on schematic diagrams.

A switch gives us a way to control the circuit. With the switch in the ON position, we have a **closed** or **complete circuit**. A closed circuit provides a complete path for the electrons to flow from the negative battery or supply terminal, through the circuit and return to the positive battery or supply terminal. A closed circuit has current through it.

With the switch in the OFF position, we have an **open circuit**. An open circuit does not provide a complete path for the electrons, so there is no current through the circuit.

The switches shown in Figure 7.14 are called *knife switches* because a metal blade pivots at one end to make or break the contact. These switches show the basic operation, and physically look like the schematic symbols. They can be dangerous if used with high-voltage circuits, however. Do not use a knife switch in a circuit that carries 120-volt house current unless it is enclosed and operated with an insulated handle designed for this purpose. Knife switches *are* available, however, and can be used in low-voltage circuits.

Most of the time you'll want to use switches with contacts sealed inside a protective case. When mounted in the wall or on a control panel, the switch lever is safely insulated from the circuit.

If we want to control more devices with a single switch, we need more contacts. If we add a second contact to a single-pole, single-throw switch we can select between two devices. This kind of switch is called a **single-pole, double-throw switch**. Sometimes we abbreviate single pole, double throw as **SPDT**. An SPDT switch connects a single wire (single pole) to one of two other contacts (double throw). The switch connects a center wire to one contact when the switch is in one position. When you flip the switch to the other position, the switch connects the center wire to the other contact. An SPDT switch connects one input to either of two outputs. Electric circuits that allow you to turn lights on or off from either of two locations use SPDT switches. Figure 7.14B shows an SPDT knife switch and the schematic symbol for any SPDT switch.

Suppose you want to switch two circuits on and off at the same time. Then you use a **double-pole, single-throw (DPST) switch**. This type of switch connects two input lines to their respective output lines at the same time. See Figure 7.14C for an example of this switch and its schematic-diagram symbol. When you look at the knife-switch drawing or the schematic symbol you can easily see that the DPST switch connects two inputs at the same time, one input to one output, and the other input to the other output.

We can add even more contacts to the switch. A **double-pole, double-throw switch** has two sets of three contacts. We use the abbreviation **DPDT** for double pole,

double throw. You can think of a DPDT switch as two SPDT switches in the same box with their handles connected. A DPDT switch has two center contacts. The switch connects each of these two center contacts (double pole) to one of two other contacts (double throw). Figure 7.14D shows a DPDT switch and its schematic symbol.

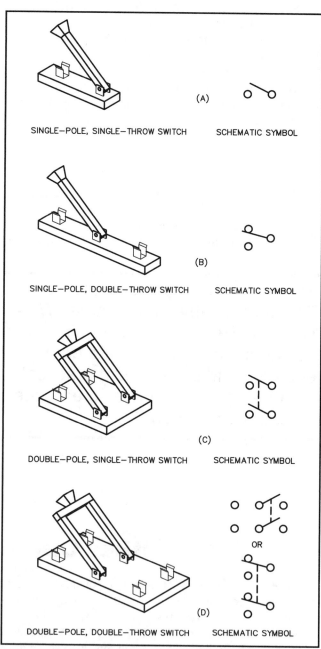

(A)

SINGLE-POLE, SINGLE-THROW SWITCH   SCHEMATIC SYMBOL

(B)

SINGLE-POLE, DOUBLE-THROW SWITCH   SCHEMATIC SYMBOL

(C)

DOUBLE-POLE, SINGLE-THROW SWITCH   SCHEMATIC SYMBOL

OR

(D)

DOUBLE-POLE, DOUBLE-THROW SWITCH   SCHEMATIC SYMBOL

Figure 7.14 — A single-pole, single-throw (SPST) switch can connect or disconnect one circuit. A single-pole, double-throw (SPDT) switch can connect one center contact to one of two other contacts. A double-pole, single-throw switch connects or disconnects two circuits at the same time. A double-pole, double-throw (DPDT) switch is like two SPDT switches in one package. Each half of the DPDT switch can connect one contact to two other contacts.

Antennas

Your receiver won't hear signals and no one will hear your transmitter without an **antenna**. The antenna is a very important part of any radio installation. Your antenna will pick radio signals out of the air for your receiver. It will also send your transmitter signals off into the atmosphere. We use the symbol shown in **Figure 7.15** to represent the antenna on a schematic diagram.

There are many types of antennas. You will learn more about the various kinds of antennas in Chapter 8. You will also learn how to choose antennas for various kinds of radio equipment.

Diodes and Transistors

Many of the great technological advances of recent times — men and women in space, computers in homes, ham radio stations tiny enough to be carried in a shirt pocket — all have been made possible by *semiconductor* electronics. Not simply a partial conductor as the name implies, a semiconductor has some of the properties of a conductor and some properties of an insulator.

Diodes and **transistors** are examples of two types of components made with semiconductor materials. These components are often called *solid-state devices* because

the materials have replaced vacuum tubes in most uses and created many new applications. Most semiconductor devices are much smaller than comparable tubes, and they produce less heat. Semiconductors are also usually less expensive than tubes.

Portable broadcast-band radios, which weighed several pounds and were an armful shortly after World War II, weigh ounces and can be carried in your pocket today. A complete ham radio station, which would have filled a room 50 years ago, now can be built into a container the size of a shoebox, or smaller. Solid-state technology has made all this possible.

There are two kinds of semiconductor material. They are known as *N-type material* and *P-type material*. The N refers to the way electrons, or negative electric charges, move through the material. The P refers to the way positive charges move through this material. (Don't worry about the details of how this works now. You can learn about how transistors actually work after you pass your license exam.)

If a manufacturer places a block of P-type material in contact with a block of N-type material, it creates a *PN junction* **diode**. Diodes have some very interesting and useful properties. If you connect the positive side of the battery to the P-type material and the negative side of the battery to the N-type material there will be current through the diode. See **Figure 7.16A**. In this case the diode is *forward biased*. If you reverse those connections, so the positive side of the battery connects to the N-type material and the negative side of the battery connects to the P-type material then there will be no current. Figure 7.16B shows the diode connected with this *reverse bias*. Diodes allow current to flow in only one direction. This is one way a diode can be used to control the current in a circuit.

Now suppose an alternating current source is connected

![antenna schematic symbol]

Figure 7.15 — Most receivers and transmitters are useless without an antenna. This schematic symbol represents the antenna in a circuit.

ANTENNA

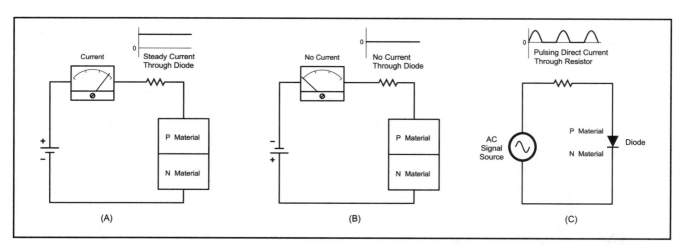

Figure 7.16 — Part A shows a layer of P-type semiconductor material and a layer of N-type semiconductor material connected to a battery. In this case the PN junction is forward biased, so current flows through the circuit. Part B shows the semiconductor materials connected to the battery so the PN junction is reverse biased. No current flows through the circuit. Part C shows the semiconductor materials connected to an alternating current signal source and a resistor. This time the PN junction is drawn using the schematic diagram symbol for a diode. The diode rectifies the ac signal. Pulses of direct current flow through the circuit because the diode only conducts during the positive half of the ac cycle.

to the diode. For half of the ac cycle, the diode will be forward biased, allowing current through the circuit. For the other half of the cycle the diode will be reverse biased, and there will be no current. The diode changes the alternating current signal into a varying direct current signal, as shown in Figure 7.16C. We say the diode will *rectify* the ac signal, so diodes are sometimes called *rectifiers*.

Transistors come in many shapes and sizes. **Figure 7.17** shows some of the more common case styles for transistors. One common type of transistor is the *bipolar* **transistor**. Bipolar transistors are made from the two different kinds of material (*bi* means two, as in *bi*cycle).

There also are two kinds of bipolar transistors. Each kind of bipolar transistor has a separate schematic symbol. **Figure 7.18** shows the schematic symbol for an **NPN transistor**. You can remember this symbol by remembering that the arrow is "*n*ot *p*ointing i*n*." An NPN transistor has a layer of P-type semiconductor material sandwiched between two layers of N-type material.

Figure 7.19 shows the symbol for the other kind of bipolar transistor, the **PNP transistor**. Remember this symbol by saying that the arrow "*p*oints i*n* *p*roudly." A PNP transistor has a layer of N-type semiconductor material sandwiched between two layers of P-type material.

The schematic symbols show that transistors have three leads, or electrodes. Each of the electrodes connects to a different part of the transistor. Transistors can amplify small signals; this is what makes them so useful. Usually, we use a low-voltage signal applied to the *base* of the transistor to control the current through the *collector* and *emitter*.

Figure 7.20A shows a simple NPN transistor amplifier circuit. Battery B_1 applies a positive voltage to the base of the transistor and battery B_2 applies a positive voltage to the collector. The emitter has a negative voltage applied. A small current flows through the emitter and base portion of the circuit. This small current controls a (usually larger) current from the negative emitter to the positive collector. If the base current decreases, the collector current also decreases. If the base current increases, so will the collector current. If you remove B_1 or other-

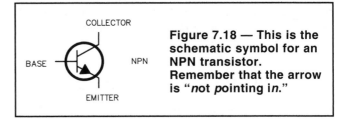

Figure 7.18 — This is the schematic symbol for an NPN transistor. Remember that the arrow is "*not pointing in.*"

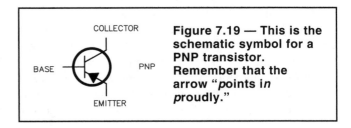

Figure 7.19 — This is the schematic symbol for a PNP transistor. Remember that the arrow "*points in proudly.*"

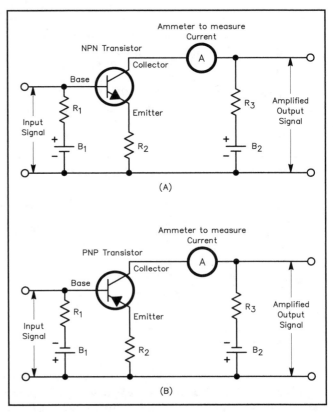

Figure 7.20 — These diagrams show simple transistor circuits for NPN and PNP transistors. Batteries B1 and B2 provide the proper operating voltages and polarities to produce a current through the collector/emitter part of each circuit.

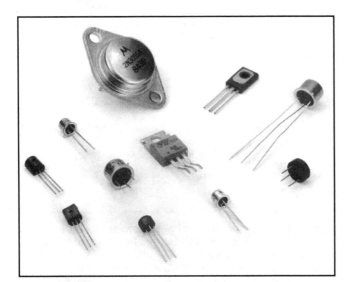

Figure 7.17 — Transistors are packaged in many different types of cases.

wise open the base circuit, there will be no collector current.

Figure 7.20B is a similar circuit for a PNP transistor. Notice this time B_1 applies a negative voltage to the transistor base lead and B_2 applies a negative voltage to the collector. Once again a small current through the base and emitter portion of the circuit controls the current through the collector and emitter part of the circuit.

These transistor circuits will amplify — or make a larger version of — a small signal. The voltages required to operate the circuit are relatively small, often 12 volts or less. Vacuum tube circuits can also be used to amplify small signals. Tubes usually require much higher operating voltages, however.

Integrated Circuits

No discussion of modern electronics would be complete without at least a brief mention of integrated circuits (ICs). An IC usually performs several circuit functions in one package, and sometimes an entire application requires only the addition of a few external components. Like transistors, ICs are made with semiconductor materials. They use low operating voltages and are generally low-power devices. **Figure 7.21** shows some examples of IC typical packages.

Figure 7.21 — Integrated circuits (ICs) come in a variety of package styles.

[This is a good time to take a break from reading the text. You should turn to Chapter 11 now and study questions T7A11, T7B10, T7B11, T7C09, T7C10, T7C14, T7C16, T7C18 and T7C19. Review this section if you have any problems with these questions.]

Inductors and Inductance

The motion of electrons produces magnetism. Every electric current creates a *magnetic field* around the wire in which it flows. A magnetic field is the area through which an invisible magnetic force acts. We can observe that force as the attraction and repulsion between magnets. Like invisible tubes, the magnetic field is positioned in concentric circles around the conductor. See **Figure 7.22A**. The field is created when the current flows, and collapses back into the conductor when the current stops. The field increases in strength when the current increases and decreases in strength as the current decreases. The force produced around a straight piece of wire by this magnetic field is usually very small. When the same wire is formed into a coil, the force is much greater. In coils, the magnetic field around each turn also affects the other turns. Together, the combined forces produce one large magnetic field, as shown in Figure 7.22B. Much of the energy in the magnetic field concentrates in the material in the center of the coil (the *core*). Most practical **inductors** consist of a length of wire wound on an iron core or a core made from a mixture of iron and other materials.

Figure 7.22 — A magnetic field surrounds a wire with a current through it. If the wire is formed into a coil, the magnetic field becomes much stronger as the lines of force add to reinforce each other.

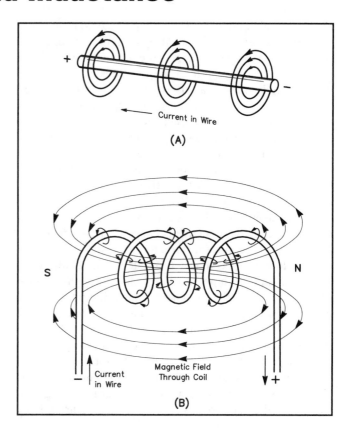

An inductor stores energy in a magnetic field. This property of a coil to store energy in a magnetic field is called **inductance**. Magnetic fields can also set electrons in motion. When a magnetic field increases in strength, the voltage on a conductor within that field increases. When the field strength decreases, so does the voltage.

Let's apply a dc voltage to an inductor. There is no current to start with, so the current begins to increase when the voltage is applied. This will establish an electrical current in the inductor, and this current produces a magnetic field. The magnetic field in turn *induces*, or creates, a voltage in the wire. The voltage induced by the magnetic field of the inductor opposes the applied voltage. Therefore, the inductor will oppose the increase in current. This is a basic property of inductors. Any changes in current through the inductor, whether increasing or decreasing, are opposed. A voltage is induced in the coil that opposes the applied voltage, and tries to prevent the current from changing. This is called induced EMF (voltage) or back EMF. Gradually a current will be produced by the applied voltage. (The term "gradually" is relative. In radio circuits, the time needed to produce the current in the circuit is often measured in microseconds or less.) The important point is that the current doesn't increase to its final value instantly when the voltage is first applied.

The "final" current that flows through the inductor is limited only by any resistance that might be in the circuit. There is very little resistance in the wire of most coils. The current will be quite large if there is no other resistance.

In the process of getting this current to flow, energy is stored. This energy is in the form of a magnetic field around the coil. When the applied current is shut off, the magnetic field collapses. The collapsing field returns energy to the circuit as a momentary current that continues to flow in the same direction as the original current. This current can be quite large for large values of inductance. The induced voltage can rise to many times the applied voltage. This can cause a spark to jump across switch or relay contacts when the circuit is broken to turn off the current. This effect is called "inductive kickback."

When an ac voltage is applied to an inductor, the current through the inductor will reverse direction every half cycle. This means the current will be constantly changing. The inductor will oppose this change. Energy is stored in the magnetic field while the current is increasing during the first half cycle. This energy will be returned to the circuit as the current starts to decrease. A new magnetic field will be produced during the second half cycle. The north and south poles of the field will be the reverse of the first half cycle. The energy stored in that field will be returned to the circuit as the current again starts to decrease. Then a new magnetic field will be produced on the next half cycle. This process keeps repeating, as long as the ac voltage is applied to the inductor.

We can summarize the actions of an inductor by considering two factors. Inductors store energy in magnetic fields, and they oppose any change in current through the inductor. Because an *electric current* produces a *magnetic field* we say the action of an inductor storing electrical energy is an *electromagnetic* process.

Inductors play several very important roles in electronic circuits. When an ac signal is applied to the inductor, the inductance will act to oppose or reduce the flow of ac. As we learned earlier, however, when a dc signal is applied to an inductor, the inductance will have little effect on the current, at least after that initial opposition. Inductors reduce the flow of ac signals but allow dc signals to flow freely. We use a capital L to represent the amount of inductance that a coil exhibits.

The basic unit of inductance is the henry (abbreviated H), named for the American physicist Joseph Henry. The henry is often too large for practical use in measurements. We use the millihenry (10^{-3}) abbreviated mH, or microhenry (10^{-6}) abbreviated μH.

An inductor's *core* refers to the area inside the inductor, where the magnetic field is concentrated. If we add an *iron* or *ferrite core* to the coil, the inductance increases as compared to a coil with air in the core. **Figure 7.23** shows some common schematic symbols for various inductors. Notice that if the inductor has a core material other than air, there are two parallel lines drawn next to coil in the schematic symbol.

There are several ways that the inductance of a coil can be varied. Figure 7.23 shows two methods. In one case, a metal "slug" or core can be threaded into or out of the center of the coil. Another way to adjust the inductance value is to simply attach a wire at some point in from one end. This is called an adjustable tap point. Variable inductors can be used to adjust the operating frequency of a circuit.

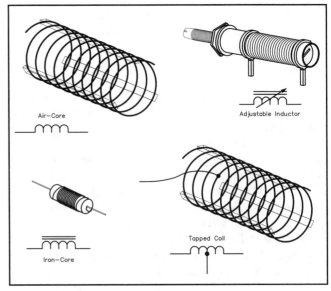

Figure 7.23 — **Various types of coils, and their schematic symbols. The adjustable inductor uses a movable powdered-iron core or slug. They are sometimes called slug-tuned or permeability-tuned inductors.**

Inductors in Series and Parallel

In circuits, inductors combine like resistors. The total inductance of several inductors connected in series is the sum of all the inductances:

$$L_{TOTAL} = L_1 + L_2 + L_3 + ... + L_n \qquad \text{(Equation 7.10)}$$

where n is the total number of inductors.

For two equal-value inductors connected in series, the total inductance will be twice the value of one of the inductors.

For parallel-connected inductors:

$$L_{\text{Total in Parallel}} = \cfrac{1}{\cfrac{1}{L_1} + \cfrac{1}{L_2} + \cfrac{1}{L_3} + ... + \cfrac{1}{L_n}}$$

$$\text{(Equation 7.11)}$$

You might recognize this equation from our study of combining resistors in parallel, and realize that for two parallel-connected inductors, **Equation 7.11** reduces to:

$$L_{\text{Total in Parallel}} = \frac{L_1 \times L_2}{L_1 + L_2} \qquad \text{(Equation 7.12)}$$

For two equal-value inductors connected in parallel, the total inductance will be half the value of one of the components.

[Turn to Chapter 11 now and study exam questions T7A09, T7C08 and T7C17. Review any material you have difficulty with before going on.]

Capacitors and Capacitance

A simple **capacitor** is formed by separating two conductor surfaces, or *plates*, with an insulating material. Let's conduct a small experiment to see how a capacitor works. First connect the capacitor to a battery and a switch, as shown in **Figure 7.24A.** One plate connects to the positive terminal of a voltage source. The other plate connects to the negative terminal. Close the switch, as shown in Part B. A surplus of electrons will start to build up on the side connected to the negative battery terminal, creating a negative charge on that capacitor plate. A positive charge will start to build up on the other capacitor plate, as Part B shows. At some point, the voltage across the capacitor will equal the applied voltage, and the capacitor is said to be charged. Part C shows this condition. There is no current flowing in the circuit when the capacitor is fully charged.

Now comes the interesting part of our experiment. Open the switch, as shown in Part D. The capacitor plates will hold the electric charge because there is no circuit for the electrons to flow through. The capacitor is storing electric energy in the form of the charges on the capacitor plates.

In an uncharged capacitor, the potential difference between the two plates is zero. As we charge the capacitor, this potential difference increases until it reaches the full applied voltage. The difference in potential creates an *electric field* between the two plates. Figure 7.24 shows that electric field by using dashed arrows drawn between the capacitor plates. A *field* is an invisible force of nature. (In the previous section we learned about the magnetic field around a wire with a current flowing through it.) We put energy into the capacitor by charging it. Until we dis-

charge it, or the charge leaks away somehow, the energy is stored in the electric field. When the field is not moving, we sometimes call it an *electrostatic field*. The basic property of a capacitor (called **capacitance**) is this ability to store a charge in an electric field.

The stored electric charge produces an *electric field*, which is an invisible electric force of attraction or repulsion acting between charged objects. (In this case the electric field is between the capacitor plates.) The capacitor stores energy as an electric field between the capacitor plates. Once the capacitor has charged to the full voltage of the applied signal, no more charge will flow onto the capacitor plates, so the current stops.

As we learned in our experiment, the charged capacitor will remain charged unless there is some path for the electrons to follow to get off the negative plate and back to the positive plate. If we connect a resistor across the charged capacitor plates, the charge will flow through the resistor, releasing the stored energy.

When the voltage across a capacitor increases, the capacitor stores more charge in reaction to the increased voltage. When the voltage decreases, the capacitor returns some of its stored charge. These actions tend to oppose any change in the voltage applied to a capacitor. This opposition to changes in *voltage* is called *capacitive reactance*.

We can summarize the operation of a capacitor by considering two factors. A capacitor stores electric energy in the form of an electrostatic field and it opposes any change in the applied voltage.

If we connect an ac signal to a capacitor, the plates will charge during one part of the ac cycle. After the signal

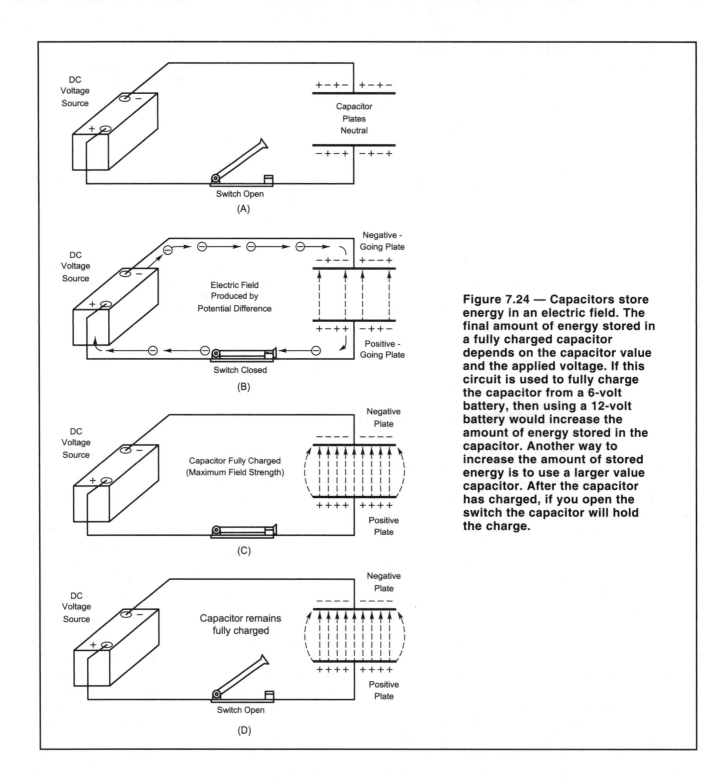

Figure 7.24 — Capacitors store energy in an electric field. The final amount of energy stored in a fully charged capacitor depends on the capacitor value and the applied voltage. If this circuit is used to fully charge the capacitor from a 6-volt battery, then using a 12-volt battery would increase the amount of energy stored in the capacitor. Another way to increase the amount of stored energy is to use a larger value capacitor. After the capacitor has charged, if you open the switch the capacitor will hold the charge.

reaches the peak voltage, however, the charge will start to flow back into the circuit in the opposite direction until the capacitor is charged with the opposite polarity during the second half of the ac cycle. This process of charging first one direction and then the other will continue as long as the ac signal is applied to the capacitor plates.

Capacitors play a role that is opposite to that of inductors. A capacitor will block direct current because as

soon as the capacitor charges to the applied voltage level, no more current can flow. A capacitor will pass alternating current with little or no opposition, however.

The basic unit of capacitance is the farad (abbreviated F), named for Michael Faraday. Like the henry, the farad is usually too large a unit for practical measurements. For convenience, we use microfarads (10^{-6}), abbreviated µF, or picofarads (10^{-12}), abbreviated pF.

Practical Capacitors

Practical capacitors are described by the material used for the insulating material used between the conducting plates. This insulating material is called a *dielectric*. Mica, ceramic, plastic-film, polystyrene, paper and electrolytic capacitors are in common use today. They each have properties that make them more or less suitable for a particular application. **Figure 7.25A** shows the symbol used to represent capacitors on schematic diagrams.

Electrolytic capacitors have a dielectric that is formed after the capacitor is manufactured. Two common types of electrolytic capacitors are aluminum-electrolytic capacitors and tantalum-dielectric capacitors.

Electrolytic capacitors can be made with a very high capacitance value in a small package. Electrolytic capacitors are polarized — dc voltages must be connected to the positive and negative capacitor terminals with the correct polarity. The positive and negative electrodes in an electrolytic capacitor are clearly marked. Connecting an electrolytic capacitor incorrectly causes gas to form inside the capacitor and the capacitor may actually explode. This can be very dangerous. At the very least the capacitor will be destroyed by connecting it incorrectly.

When we draw electrolytic capacitors on schematic diagrams, we must indicate the proper polarity for the capacitor. We do this by adding a + sign to the capacitor symbol, as Figure 7.25B shows.

Variable Capacitors

In some circuits we may want a way to vary the capacitance. An example is in the tuning circuit of a receiver or transmitter VFO. We would use a **variable capacitor** in that case. A basic air-dielectric variable capacitor is shown in **Figure 7.26A**. This figure also shows the schematic symbol for a variable capacitor. One set of plates is fixed in one position to the capacitor frame. These plates form the *stator*. The other set of plates rotates by turning the control shaft. The movable plates form the *rotor*. The rotation controls the amount of plate area shared by the two sets of plates. When the capacitor is fully meshed, all the rotor plates are down in between the stator plates. In this position, the capacitor will have its largest value of capaci-

tance. When the rotor is unmeshed, the value of capacitance is at a minimum. The capacitance can be varied smoothly between the maximum and minimum values.

Another type of variable capacitor is the compression variable capacitor shown in Figure 7.26B. In this type of variable capacitor, the spacing between the two plates is varied. There is a thin wafer of mica between each pair of capacitor plates. (Mica is a mineral that has very good insulating properties.) When the spacing is at its minimum, the capacitance is at a maximum value. When the spacing is adjusted to its maximum, the value of capacitance is at a minimum. This type of variable capacitor is normally used as a *trimmer capacitor*. A trimmer capacitor is a control used to peak or fine tune a part of a

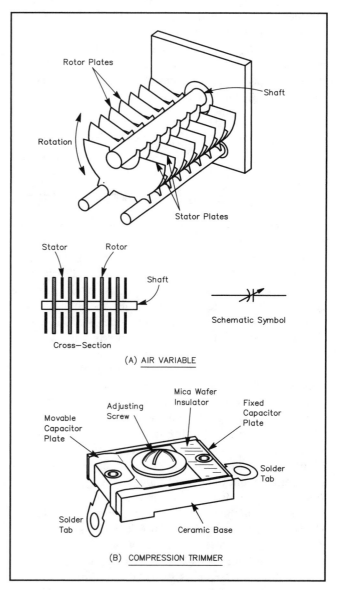

Figure 7.26 — Variable capacitors can be made with air as the dielectric, or with mica or ceramic dielectrics.

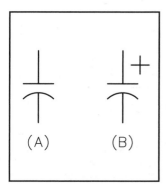

Figure 7.25 — Part A shows the schematic symbol representing fixed capacitors. This symbol has the appearance of two plates separated by an insulator. Part B shows the symbol representing electrolytic capacitors, which must be connected to dc voltages with the proper polarity.

circuit. It is usually left alone once adjusted to the correct value. You should use a plastic screwdriver-like adjusting tool when tuning a trimmer capacitor. The metal of a normal screwdriver can affect the capacitance and cause false readings as you try to adjust it.

Capacitors in Series and Parallel

If we connect capacitors in parallel with each other, the total area of the capacitor plates increases. This increases the value of capacitance. Parallel-connected capacitors act like one larger capacitor. The total capacitance of several parallel-connected capacitors is the sum of all the values.

$$C_{TOTAL} = C_1 + C_2 + C_3 + ... + C_n \qquad \text{(Equation 7.13)}$$

where n is the total number of capacitors.

If you connect two equal-value capacitors in parallel, the total capacitance of this combination will be twice the value of either capacitor alone.

Connecting capacitors in series has the effect of increasing the distance between the plates, thereby reducing the total capacitance. For capacitors in series, we use the familiar reciprocal formula:

$$C_{\text{Total in Series}} = \cfrac{1}{\cfrac{1}{C_1} + \cfrac{1}{C_2} + \cfrac{1}{C_3} + ...} \qquad \text{(Equation 7.14)}$$

When there are only two capacitors in series, **Equation 7.14** reduces to the product over sum formula:

$$C_{\text{Total in Series}} = \frac{C_1 \times C_2}{C_1 + C_2} \qquad \text{(Equation 7.15)}$$

Using this formula for two equal-value resistors or two equal-value inductors in *parallel*, we discovered the total value is half the value of either one. Two equal-value capacitors connected in *series* equals one-half the value of either single capacitor. The total capacitance will always be less than any of the individual capacitance values when you connect capacitors in series.

[Before going on to the last section of Chapter 7 you should turn to Chapter 11 and study questions T7A10, T7C04 through T7C07, and T7C15. Review any material you have difficulty with before going on.]

Analog and Digital Communications

Many electronics circuits are designed to perform some action on a signal that is fed into the circuit. The signal is changed in some way, and then passed on to the next circuit. For example, **Figure 7.27** shows a simple transistor amplifier circuit. A small signal is fed into the left side of the amplifier and a larger copy of that signal comes out the right side. At least within the limits of the amplifier, for any signal fed to the input there will be a larger copy at the output.

This amplifier processes **analog signals**. An analog signal is one with voltage or current values that vary continuously over some range. A sine wave is one example of a simple analog signal. Voice waveforms are more complicated examples of analog signals. As a simple experiment, suppose you speak into a microphone and display a picture of that voice signal. You will see that your voice changes frequency and amplitude, or strength over a wide range of values. **Figure 7.28** shows a voice signal.

Single-sideband (SSB) voice, frequency modulated (FM) voice, slow-scan television (SSTV) and fast-scan amateur television (FSTV or ATV) are all examples of analog communications modes. To transmit these modes, we combine the analog signals with a radio frequency (RF) carrier to create the transmitted radio signal.

Some electronics circuits are designed to perform some operation on signals that are either on or off. Within the limits of the circuits, the voltage or current value does not affect how the signal is processed. When the signal is on, we often assign that a value of 1, and when the signal is off we assign it a value of 0. A **digital signal** is one in which we only care if the signal is on (1) or off (0).

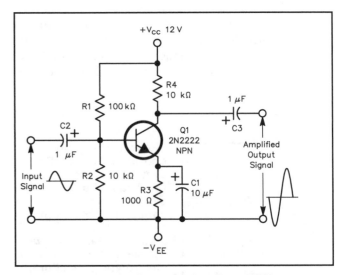

Figure 7.27 — This diagram shows an NPN common-emitter amplifier circuit. Notice that the output signal is a larger version of the input signal.

Figure 7.28 — This signal is a voice pattern. The graph is taken from part of a voice signal captured using a computer sound card and a sound-editing program.

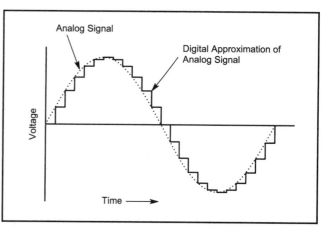

Figure 7.29 — This graph shows a sine wave ac signal drawn as an analog signal and as an approximation of that signal taken from the step values of a digital signal.

Amateur Radio operators use several communications methods that make use of digital signals. Morse code is a digital signal because the radio signal is turned on to form dots and dashes, and is off to form the spaces between the dots and dashes, spaces between letters and spaces between words. Many hams use the name CW to refer to Morse code communications. A radio frequency continuous wave signal is turned on to form the dots and dashes. It is turned off to form the spaces. Other communications modes that use digital signals include radioteletype (RTTY) as well as packet radio, PSK31 and other computer-generated signals.

Some electronics circuits represent the voltage or current value of an analog signal by assigning digital values. In this case the digital signal is an approximate representation of the analog signal values. **Figure 7.29** shows a sine wave analog signal along with a digital approximation of that signal. You can see that the digital signal has values of only specific steps over a range. An analog-to-digital converter would take the analog signal input and create the digital approximation values. A digi-

tal signal processing circuit can then perform operations on the digital signal. Later, we might use a digital-to-analog converter to change the signal back to an analog format. This process is a simple explanation of the operation of digital signal processing (DSP). Many of the latest Amateur Radio transceivers use some form of DSP to provide filtering options in the receiver.

[Congratulations. You have completed your study of this Basic Communications Electronics chapter. Before you move on to Chapter 8, you should turn to the question pool in Chapter 11 and study questions T7B01 through T7B04. Review this section if any of those questions give you difficulty.]

GOOD ENGINEERING PRACTICES

W1AW may be every ham's dream station, with all the latest equipment and lots of it. Don't expect your first station to look like this, but you can have plenty of fun with a simple station layout.

Your Technician exam will include six questions about the good engineering practices covered in this chapter. Those questions come from the following six syllabus groups:

T8A Basic amateur station apparatus; Choice of apparatus for desired communications; Setting up station; Constructing and modifying amateur station apparatus; Station layout for CW, SSB, FM, Packet and other popular modes.

T8B How transmitters work; Operation and tuning; VFO; Transceiver; Dummy load; Antenna switch; Power supply; Amplifier; Stability; Microphone gain; FM deviation; Block diagrams of typical stations.

T8C How receivers work, operation and tuning, including block diagrams; Super-heterodyne including Intermediate frequency; Reception; Demodulation or Detection; Sensitivity; Selectivity; Frequency standards; Squelch and audio gain (volume) control.

T8D How antennas work; Radiation principles; Basic construction; Half wave dipole length vs. frequency; Polarization; Directivity; ERP; Directional/non-directional antennas; Multiband antennas; Antenna gain; Resonant frequency; Loading coil; Electrical vs. physical length; Radiation pattern; Transmatch.

T8E How transmission lines work; Standing waves/SWR/SWR-meter; Impedance matching; Types of transmission lines; Feed point; Coaxial cable; Balun; Waterproofing Connections.

T8F Voltmeter/ammeter/ohmmeter/multi/S-meter, peak reading and RF watt meter; Building/modifying equipment; Soldering; Making measurements; Test instruments.

Home Stations

Once you have received your Technician class license, you have lots of options open to you in building "homebrew" equipment or modifying existing commercial gear so that you can get on the air and enjoy the wonderful hobby of Amateur Radio! Your Technician license is your FCC permission to build or modify your own Amateur Radio transmitting equipment.

Location

First, give some thought to the location of your station. Hams put their equipment in many places. Some use the basement or attic, while others choose the den, kitchen or a spare bedroom. Some hams with limited space build their station into a small closet. A foldout shelf and folding chair form the operating position.

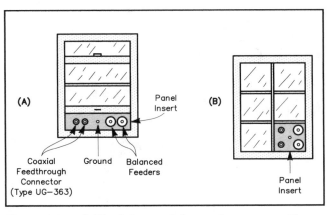

Figure 8.2 — A Plexiglas, metal, wood or composition panel can be used to replace a pane of glass in a window, as shown at A. Then feed-through connectors can be installed so feed lines can be attached on either side as a way to connect your antennas. A similar panel can also be placed in the window opening, and the window then closed on the new panel. Be sure to secure stop blocks or use another method to prevent the window from simply being slid open, allowing intruders to gain access to your equipment.

Figure 8.1 — How you arrange your station equipment is a matter of personal taste and available space. The most important considerations are safe operation and a pleasing and convenient layout.

Where you put your station depends on the room you have available and on your personal tastes. There are, however, several things to keep in mind while searching for the best place. The photos of **Figure 8.1** show several ways amateur stations can be arranged.

One often-overlooked requirement for a good station location is adequate electrical service. Eventually you will have several pieces of station equipment and accessories, many of which will require power to operate. Be sure that at least one, and preferably several, electrical outlets are located near your future operating position. Be sure the outlets

provide the proper voltage and current for your rig. Most modern radios require only a few amperes. You may run into problems, however, if your shack is on the same circuit as the air conditioner or washing machine. The total current drawn at any one time must not exceed rated limits. Someday you'll probably upgrade and may want to purchase a power amplifier. If so, you should have a 240-volt line in the shack, or the capability to add one.

Another must for your station is a good **ground connection**. A good ground not only reduces the possibility of electrical shock but also improves the performance of your station. By connecting all of your equipment to ground, you will help to avoid stray radio-frequency (RF) current in the shack. Stray RF can cause equipment to malfunction. A good ground can also help reduce the possibility of interference. The wire connecting your station to an earth ground should be as short as possible.

Basement and first-floor locations generally make it easier to provide a good ground connection for your station. You can also find a way to put your ham shack on the second or third floor or even on the top floor of a high-rise apartment, for that matter.

Your radio station will require a feed line of some sort to connect the antenna to the radio. So you will need a convenient means of getting the feed line into the shack. There are many ways of doing this, but one of the most effective requires only a window. Many hams simply replace the glass pane in a nearby window with a clear acrylic panel. You could also use a replacement panel made from wood or other composition material. The panel can be drilled to accept as many feed lines as needed. Special threaded "feed-through" connectors make the job easy. If you decide to relocate your station, the glass pane can be replaced. This will restore the window to its original condition.

A simpler, more temporary approach is to pass the feed lines through the open window and close it gently. Do this carefully, because crushed coaxial cable will give you nothing but trouble. You can add some foam or other soft material to close the gaps and keep "critters" out. Another method involves cutting a spacer from wood, acrylic or other suitable material to fit the width of the opening and drilling holes to pass the feed lines through. Place your spacer in the window opening and close the window on the spacer. Be sure to secure the window with a block of wood or some other "locking" device. Your new equipment, seen through an open window, may tempt an unwanted visitor! **Figure 8.2** illustrates these techniques.

For a more permanent installation you may want to consider a feed-through pipe in the wall. A piece of PVC pipe can be fit to an opening cut in the wall, and the feed lines pass through the pipe. Stuff the pipe with fiberglass insulation or other suitable material to prevent drafts and seal out "critters." You can caulk around the tube to seal the pipe to your house siding. You can use almost any size pipe, but if you select 3 or 4-inch PVC there will be plenty of room to add more feed lines as your "antenna farm" grows! See **Figure 8.3** for an example of how to make this installation.

Another important requirement for your station is comfort. The space should be large enough so you can spread out as needed. Operating from a telephone booth isn't much fun! Because you will probably be spending some time in your shack (an understatement!), be sure it will be warm in the winter and cool in the summer. It should also be as dry as possible. High humidity can cause such equipment problems as high-voltage arcing and switch-contact failure.

You will eventually want to operate late at night to snag the "rare ones" on 80 and 40 meters. Although a Morse code or voice contact is music to your ears, it may not endear you to a sleeping family. Putting your station in a bedroom shared with others may not be the best idea. You can keep the "music" to yourself, however, by using a good pair of headphones when operating your station.

Arranging Your Equipment

Before you set everything up and hook up the cables, think about where you want each piece of equipment. While there is no one best layout for a ham station, some general rules do apply. Of course, the location you've chosen for your station may limit your choices a bit. For example, if you're going to put the station in the basement, you may have a lot of space. If you'll be using a corner of the bedroom or den, however, you may have to keep the equipment in a small area.

Generally, the piece of gear that requires the most adjustment is the transceiver (or receiver if you have a separate one). Make sure you can conveniently reach its controls, keeping in mind which hand you're going to use to make the adjustments. It doesn't make much sense to put the transceiver on the left side of the desk or table if

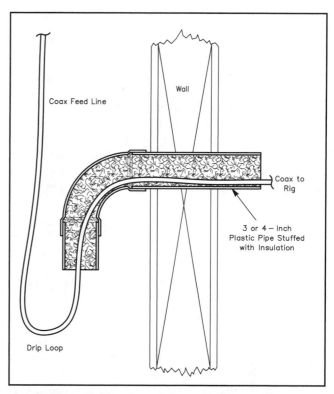

Figure 8.3 — Neither insects nor rain can get into your shack when you use this method to bring cables into your shack. Install a piece of PVC or other pipe through the wall into your shack. Use an elbow and short length of pipe on the outside to prevent rain from falling into the open end of the pipe. Run the feed lines through, then stuff the tube with fiberglass insulation or similar material. If you use a 3 or 4-inch pipe there will be plenty of room to add more feed lines later. Just remove the stuffing, add the new feed lines, and then replace the stuffing.

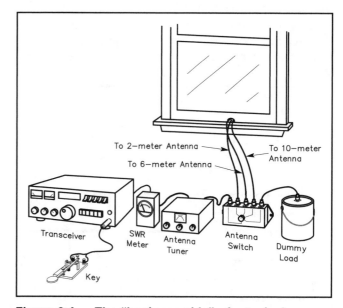

Figure 8.4 — The "business side" of a typical station. Some radios have built-in antenna tuners and keyers.

you're going to adjust it with your right hand. Once you've found the best location for the transceiver, you can position the rest of your equipment around it.

If you'll be using Morse code, placement of the sending device (key, keyer or keyboard) is also very important. It must be easy to reach with the hand you send with, and placed so your arm will be supported when you're using it. Try to position it away from anything dangerous, such as sharp corners and edges, rough surfaces and electrical wires.

If you have room for a desk or table long enough to hold all your gear, you might prefer to keep everything on one surface. If you're pressed for space, however, a shelf built above the desktop is a good solution. To ensure that there is adequate air circulation above your transceiver, leave at least 3 inches of space between the top of the tallest unit on the desktop and the bottom of your shelf. Try to restrict the shelf space to lightweight accessory items that you don't have to move very often, such as the station clock, SWR meter and antenna-rotator control box.

After you have a good idea of where you want everything, you can start connecting the cables. **Figure 8.4** shows how an amateur station, including some common accessories, can be connected. Some of these accessories are discussed in more detail later in this chapter.

Basic Station Layout

Figure 8.5 shows a block diagram of a very simple Amateur Radio station. Let's discuss the blocks one by one.

Transmitters

A transmitter is a device that produces a radio-frequency (RF) signal. Television and radio broadcast stations use powerful transmitters to put their signals into the air. Radio amateurs use lower-powered transmitters to send signals to each other. A transmitter produces an electrical signal that can be sent to a distant receiver.

We call the signal from a transmitter the **radio-frequency carrier** or RF carrier. To transmit Morse code, you could use a telegraph key as a switch to turn the carrier on and off in the proper code pattern. If you want to transmit voice signals, you need extra circuitry in the transmitter to add voice content to the carrier. We call this extra circuitry a **modulator**.

Amateur transmitters range from the simple to the elaborate. They generally have two basic stages, an oscillator and a power amplifier (PA). This section introduces the basic operation of a CW transmitter and an FM transmitter.

Separate receivers and transmitters have been replaced by transceivers in most amateur stations. A transceiver com-bines circuits necessary for receiving and transmitting in one package. Some circuit sections may perform both transmitting and receiving functions. Other sections are dedicated to transmit-only or receive-only functions. To simplify some of the following information, we will speak of transmitter or receiver circuits. The principles of operation are the same in transceivers. The transmitter topics apply to transceivers in the transmit mode. Receiver topics apply to transceivers in the receive mode.

CW Transmitters

Figure 8.6A shows a block diagram of a simple amateur transmitter. It produces CW (continuous-wave) radio signals when the key is closed. The simple crystal-controlled transmitter consists of a crystal oscillator followed by a driver stage and a power amplifier. A crystal

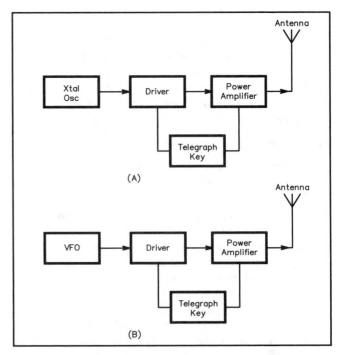

Figure 8.6 — Part A shows a block diagram of a basic crystal-controlled CW transmitter. Part B shows a simple VFO-controlled CW transmitter.

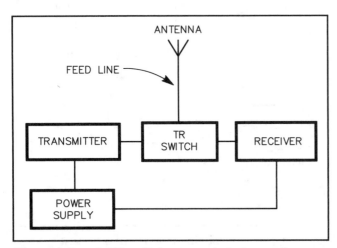

Figure 8.5 — A TR switch connects between the transmitter, receiver and antenna.

oscillator uses a quartz crystal to keep the frequency of the radio signal constant.

To transmit information, we must modulate the radio signal. This means we are making some change to the radio signal, and adding information to it. Pressing the key of a CW transmitter and holding it down produces a radio-frequency (RF) carrier. This is also called an unmodulated carrier. An RF carrier is a constant-amplitude, unmodulated, radio-frequency signal. When you use the key to turn the signal on and off to produce Morse code dots and dashes, however, you modulate the signal. Modulation is the process of varying an RF carrier in some way to send information.

Crystal oscillators may not be practical in all cases. A different crystal is needed for each operating frequency. After a while, this becomes quite expensive, as well as impractical. If we use a variable-frequency oscillator (VFO) in place of the crystal oscillator, as shown in Figure 8.6B, we can change the transmitter frequency whenever we want. So we can use either a crystal oscillator or a variable frequency oscillator to control the transmitter operating frequency.

The telegraph key may connect to one or more transmitter sections. Figure 8.6 shows the key connected to both the driver and power amplifier stages. You would not normally key the oscillator stage because this may cause the oscillator to change frequency slightly.

All transmitters also require some source of operating voltage. We have left the **power supply** block off the Figure 8.6 drawings for simplicity, but you should know that adequate filtering of the power supply is necessary to prevent **ac hum** on your CW signal.

FM Transmitters

When a radio signal or carrier is modulated, some characteristic of the radio signal is changed in order to convey information. We transmit information by modulating any property of a carrier. For example, we can modulate the frequency or phase of a carrier. **Frequency modulation (FM)** and **phase modulation (PM)** are closely related. The phase of a signal cannot be varied without also varying the frequency, and vice versa.

Phase modulation (PM) and frequency modulation (FM) are especially suited for channelized local UHF and VHF communication. They feature good audio fidelity and high signal-to-noise ratio. FM voice systems are more resistant to received noise, such as static, than AM systems, provided that the FM signal is above a minimum threshold level.

In practical FM systems, the carrier frequency is varied or modulated by changes in voltage that represent information to be transmitted. This information may originate from a **microphone**, a computer modem or even a video camera. The carrier frequency changes in proportion to the rise and fall of the modulating voltage.

In other words, a modulating voltage that is becoming more positive increases the carrier frequency. As the voltage becomes more negative, the carrier frequency decreases. The amount of increase or decrease in frequency depends on how

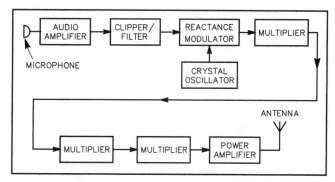

Figure 8.7 — This is a block diagram of a phase-modulated transmitter. The transmitted signal is identical to the output from a frequency-modulated transmitter, so this radio is sometimes called an FM transmitter.

much the voltage of the modulating signal changes. Speaking loudly into the microphone causes larger variations in carrier frequency than speaking in a normal voice. Speaking *too* loudly, though, may cause distortion.

One way to directly shift the frequency of an oscillator to create FM is to use a **reactance modulator**. A reactance modulator changes the capacitance or inductance of the oscillator resonant circuit. The changes occur in response to an input signal. The problem with a direct-modulated FM oscillator is frequency stability. Designs that allow the oscillator frequency to be easily modulated may have an unfortunate side effect of becoming more difficult to minimize unwanted frequency shifts arising from changes in temperature, supply voltage, vibration and so on. Any frequency multiplying stages also multiply drift or other instability problems in the oscillator.

Phase modulation produces what is called *indirect FM.* You won't be able to tell the difference between a phase-modulated signal and a frequency-modulated signal by listening to both types on your receiver. So the only real difference is in the electronics of how the signal is produced.

The most common method of generating a phase-modulated telephony signal is again a reactance modulator. An active device such as a transistor is connected so that it changes either the capacitance or inductance of a resonant circuit in response to an input signal. The RF carrier is passed through this resonant circuit. Changes in the resonant circuit caused by the reactance modulator causes phase shifts in the RF carrier. **Figure 8.7** shows a block diagram of a phase-modulated transmitter.

The weak signal from the microphone is first amplified and then passed through a clipper/filter. The clipper/filter sets the maximum amplitude of the audio signal going to the reactance modulator. If the signal exceeds the limit, the excess signal is simply *clipped,* or cut off. Otherwise, **over deviation** can occur and the spectrum occupied by the FM transmitter increases beyond what is necessary for communication. Over deviation can cause interference to users on nearby channels. If someone tells you that your radio is over deviating, try holding the microphone farther from your mouth when you talk. You can also talk a little softer.

The crystal oscillator in Figure 8.7 provides a stable operating frequency, and the reactance modulator varies the phase of that frequency with the signal picked up by the microphone. After the modulator there are usually frequency multiplication stages to reach the final desired operating frequency. Finally the signal is amplified before being sent to the antenna and radiated for others to receive. As with a direct-FM transmitter, if there is no modulation, the carrier frequency will be constant.

[Turn to Chapter 11 now and study questions T2B18 and T2B19. Also study questions T8A08, T8B02 through T8B06, T8B12, T8B13, T8C09 and T8F14. Review this section if you have difficulty with any of those questions.]

Receivers

The transmitter is a sending device. It sends a radio-frequency (RF) signal to a transmitting antenna, and the antenna radiates the signal into the air. Some distance away, the signal produces a voltage in a receiving antenna. That ac voltage goes from the receiving antenna into a **receiver**. The receiver converts the RF energy into an audio-frequency (AF) signal. You hear this AF signal in headphones or from a loudspeaker.

Just about everyone is familiar with receivers. Receivers take electronic signals out of the air and convert them into signals that we can see or hear. Your clock radio is a receiver and so is your television set. If you look around the room you're in right now, you'll probably see at least one receiver. The receiver is a very important part of an Amateur Radio station.

The main purpose of any radio receiver is to change radio-frequency signals (which we can't hear or see) to signals that we can hear or see. A good receiver can detect weak radio signals. It separates them from other signals and interference. Also, it stays tuned to one frequency without drifting. The ability of a receiver to detect weak signals is called **sensitivity**. **Selectivity** is the ability to separate (select) a desired signal from undesired signals. **Stability** is a measure of the ability of a receiver to stay tuned to a particular frequency. In general, then, a good receiver is very sensitive, selective and stable.

Amateur receivers can be simple or complex. You can build a simple receiver that will work surprisingly well. The *ARRL Handbook for Radio Communication* has receiver plans, including sources for parts and circuit boards.

Detection

The **detector** is the heart of a receiver. It is where we collect the information we want from the signal. "Crystal sets" using galena crystals and "cat's whiskers" were an early form of amplitude modulation (AM) detector. AM is generated by varying the amplitude of an RF signal in

response to a microphone or other signal source. The cat's whisker is just a thin, stiff piece of wire. With the galena crystal it forms a point-contact diode. See **Figure 8.8**.

Today, however, more sensitive and selective receivers are required. In addition, crystal sets cannot receive single sideband (SSB) and CW signals properly. The crystal set shows how simple a receiver can be, though. It is an excellent example of how detection works. Every receiver

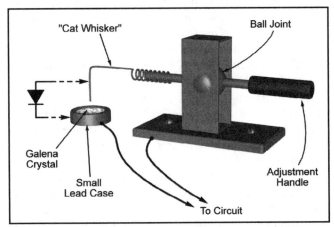

Figure 8.8 — Here is an example of a galena crystal and a cat's whisker, the detector in early crystal sets.

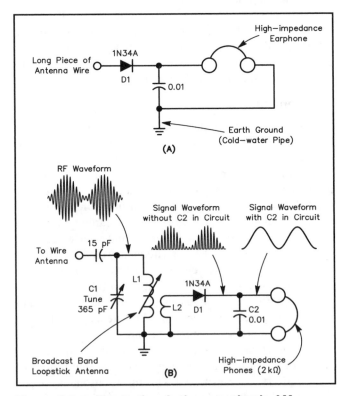

Figure 8.9 — Illustration A shows a simple AM receiver using a crystal detector. It consists only of a wire antenna, detector diode, capacitor, earphone and earth ground. The circuit at B has a tuned circuit that helps separate the broadcast-band signals, but otherwise operates the same as the circuit at A. If you have never listened to a simple crystal radio, this can be a fun project!

has some type of detector. **Figure 8.9A** shows a very simple receiver. Diode D1 does the same job as the cat's-whisker detector. If there is a strong AM broadcast station in your area you should hear the signals from that station in your earphones with this receiver.

A more practical receiver would have some way to tune different frequencies. The circuit shown in Figure 8.9B will be a better receiver because there is a tuned circuit at the input to select signals on different frequencies. This is a **tuned-radio-frequency (TRF)** receiver. An incoming signal causes current to flow from the antenna, through the resonant tuned circuit, to ground. The current induces a voltage with the same waveform in L2. The L1-C1 circuit resonates at the frequency of the incoming signal and tends to reject signals at other frequencies. The diode rectifies the RF signal, allowing only half the waveform to pass through. Capacitor C2 fills in and smoothes out the gaps between the cycles of the RF signal. Only the audio signal passes on to the headphones. Amplification can improve the sensitivity of this receiver, but other receiver types have much better selectivity.

Direct-Conversion Receivers

The next step up in receiver complexity is shown in **Figure 8.10**. Direct-conversion means the RF signal is converted directly to audio, in one step. The incoming

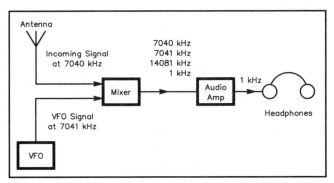

Figure 8.10 — A direct-conversion receiver converts RF signals directly to audio, using only one mixer.

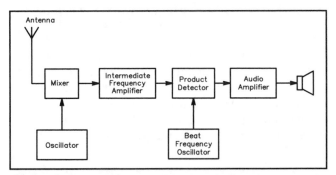

Figure 8.11 — This block diagram shows a superheterodyne SSB/CW receiver. A mixer converts the incoming signal to the intermediate frequency (IF). A second mixer, called a product detector, recovers the audio or Morse code and converts it into an audio signal.

signal is combined with a signal from a **variable-frequency oscillator (VFO)** in the **mixer** stage. In this example, we mix an incoming signal at 7040 kHz with a signal from the VFO at 7041 kHz. The output of the mixer contains signals at 7040 kHz, 7041 kHz, 14,081 kHz and 1 kHz (the original signals and their sum and difference frequencies). One of these signals (1 kHz) is within the range of human hearing. We use an audio amplifier and hear it in the headphones.

By changing the VFO frequency, other signals in the range of the receiver can be converted to audio signals. Direct-conversion receivers are capable of providing good usable reception with relatively simple, inexpensive circuits.

Superheterodyne Receivers

A block diagram of a simple **superheterodyne** receiver for CW and SSB is shown in **Figure 8.11**. The mixer produces a signal at the **intermediate frequency (IF)**, often 455 kHz in a single-conversion receiver. The amplifier after the mixer is designed for peak efficiency at the IF. The superhet receiver solves the selectivity/bandwidth problem by converting all signals to the same IF before filtering and amplification. Many receivers allow the operator to select different IF filters with different bandwidths customized for particular modes, such as SSB, CW, RTTY or FM.

To receive SSB and CW signals, a second mixer, called a **product detector**, is used. The product detector mixes the IF signal with a signal from the *beat-frequency oscillator (BFO)*. The BFO converts the received-signal information from the intermediate frequency to the audio range. The product-detector output contains audio that can be amplified and sent to a speaker or headphones.

Most modern commercially manufactured receivers (and the receiver stage in transceivers) have two or three intermediate frequency stages. Signals are often converted first to a high frequency, such as around 73 MHz, then — after some filtering and amplifications — converted to a second IF, often around 9 MHz. After further filtering and amplification the signal may be converted to a third IF — usually around 455 kHz — and then to audio. Some receivers may convert the signal to audio after the second IF. These extra conversions help solve some problems and limitations of single-conversion methods.

Most communications receivers include a means to hold down the amplitude of signals so that they don't overload the detector (and hurt the operator's ears). This circuitry is called the *Automatic Gain Control* (AGC). The IF signal is rectified and filtered to produce a dc control voltage, which in turn controls the gain of the IF and RF amplifiers. An **S meter** connected across the AGC line can be used to show relative signal strength, and is usually calibrated in "S units." An ideal S meter would read S9 with an input signal of 50 microvolts. Each S unit below S9 would represent a signal 6 dB lower ($\frac{1}{4}$ as strong) as the next higher number. An S8 signal would be $\frac{1}{4}$ as strong as S9, S7 $\frac{1}{4}$ as strong as S8 and so on. For a variety of reasons, no real S meter reaches this goal. Use your S meter to give a relative signal strength, compared to other signals.

In a superhet receiver that uses a number of oscillators, you might wonder whether all of them are actually operating on their designed frequencies. For many years hams have tuned to the **WWV/WWVH** frequency-standard stations run by NIST, the US National Institute of Standards and Technology, at 10, 15 and 20 MHz to make sure their radios are properly calibrated in frequency.

FM Receivers

An FM superheterodyne receiver is similar, but with a few different stages. It has a wider bandwidth filter and a different type of **detector**. One common FM detector is the **frequency discriminator**. The discriminator output varies in amplitude as the frequency of the incoming signal changes. If the frequency discrimator in an FM receiver stops working, there will be no audio output from the receiver.

Most FM receivers also have a **limiter** stage between the IF amplifier and the detector. The limiter makes the receiver less sensitive to amplitude variations and pulse noise than AM or SSB/CW receivers. As its name suggests, the limiter output remains almost constant when the signal level fluctuates. Noise pulses are also amplitude-modulated signals. The limiter does not pass them on to the detector. This feature makes FM popular for mobile and portable communications. **Figure 8.12** is a block diagram showing the main stages of an FM receiver. This receiver is a single-conversion superheterodyne receiver.

Suppose the oscillator of Figure 8.12 operates at 157.7 MHz and the intermediate frequency amplifier operates at 10.7 MHz. What frequencies could the radio receive? Using your knowledge of mixers, you can add the oscillator frequency and IF to get 168.4 MHz. You can also subtract those two frequencies to get 147.0 MHz.

Most FM receivers also include **squelch** circuitry after the FM detector that "squelches" or mutes the noise coming through the speaker when a FM carrier signal is not present. The operator usually sets a front-panel squelch control until the noise is just silenced. When the squelch is properly adjusted, weak signals can still be heard, while noise is muted by the squelch.

Transceivers

In many modern Amateur Radio stations, the transmitter and receiver are combined into one box. We call this combination a **transceiver**. It's really more than just a transmitter and receiver in one box, though. Some of the circuits in a transceiver are used for both transmitting and receiving. Transceivers generally take up less space than a separate transmitter and receiver.

Many modern radios require 12 V dc to operate. This makes them ideal for use in a car as part of a *mobile* radio station. You will need a separate **power supply** to operate such radios in your house. The power supply (usually) converts the 120 V ac from your wall sockets into 12 V dc

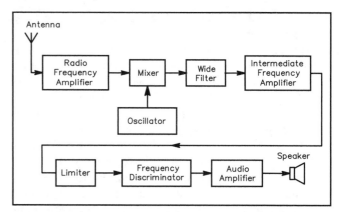

Figure 8.12 — This block diagram shows the main stages of a simple FM receiver. All receivers have some type of detector, and in the FM receiver the frequency discriminator serves as the detector, converting the received signal to audio.

to power the radios.

A 100-watt transceiver may draw 20 amps or more of current when it is transmitting. A *heavy-duty* power supply is usually required to provide the current needed to operate the radio in transmit. Some radios have built-in power supplies while others are designed only for 12-V operation, and require an extra power supply if you want to use them on 120 V ac.

Many hams operate their transceivers in the car and in the house. Some operators use a 12-volt battery in their homes to supply power to their transceivers, recharging the battery with a small automotive-style charger. But most hams use a 120 V ac to 12 V dc power supply at their home station, as mentioned above.

Elementary DC Power Troubleshooting

If you find that your radio works fine in your car, but does not work when you move it into your home, you should probably suspect a problem with the ac power supply. Measure the voltage with a test meter at the dc connector on the back panel of your radio to make sure it is 12 V dc, especially when transmitting, when it is drawing the heaviest dc current. You should first check any 12-V fuses if there is no voltage at all at the radio.

In your car you may hear annoying noises such as "alternator whine," impulse noises when you operate switches, or even RF radiating where it shouldn't go — creating audio squeals or oscillation — because of inadequate filtering on the power supply lines. In such cases, it may be important to filter the power lines for dc as well as for RF.

[Turn to Chapter 11 now and study questions T8A02, T8A09, T8B08 through T8B10, T8C01 through T8C08, T8C10 through T8C15, T8F09, T8F16 and T8F17. Review this section if you have difficulty with any of those questions.]

Radioteletype and Data Communications

Radioteletype (RTTY) and data communications are Amateur Radio transmissions that are designed to be received and printed automatically. Sometimes called *digital communications*, they often involve direct transfer of information (data) between computers. When you type information into your computer, the computer (with the help of some accessory equipment) processes the information. The computer then sends the information to your transmitter and the transmitter sends it out over the air. The station on the other end receives the signal, processes it and prints it out on a computer screen or printer. RTTY and data communications have become a popular form of ham radio communication. Here we will talk about setting up a station for radioteletype (RTTY) and packet radio communications.

Radioteletype

Radioteletype (RTTY) communications have been around for a long time. You may have seen big noisy **teleprinter** machines in old movies. A teleprinter is something like an electric typewriter. When you type on the teleprinter keys, however, the teleprinter sends out electrical codes that represent the letters you are typing. If we send these codes to another teleprinter machine, the second machine reproduces everything you type. Hams have been converting this equipment and using it on the air for years. You can also send and receive radioteletype with a computer. These

days computers are so cheap and readily available that they have just about replaced the old noisy teleprinters.

We use a **modem** for Amateur Radio digital communications. Modem is short for *mo*dulator-*dem*odulator. The modem accepts information from your computer and uses the information to modulate a transmitter. The modulated transmitter produces a signal that we send out over the air. When another station receives the signal, the other station uses a similar modem to demodulate the signal. The modem then passes the demodulated signal to a computer. The computer processes and displays the signal. On the HF bands most hams transmit RTTY by feeding the modem signal tones into the microphone input of an SSB transmitter. On the VHF and UHF bands they usually do the same thing with a conventional FM transmitter.

Sometimes hams use an older teleprinter instead of a computer. The teleprinter converts and displays information from the modem. A complete radioteletype station must have a computer or teleprinter, a modem and a transceiver. The modem connects between the computer and the transmitter, as shown in **Figure 8.13**.

Packet Radio

Packet radio uses a *terminal node controller (TNC)* as an interface between your computer and transceiver. We might call a TNC an "intelligent" modem. The TNC accepts information from your computer and breaks the data into small pieces called *packets*. Along with the information from your computer, each packet contains addressing, error-checking and control information.

The addressing information includes the call signs of the station sending the packet and the station the packet is being sent to. The address may also include call signs of stations that are being used to relay the packet. The receiving station uses the error-checking information to determine whether the received packets contain any errors. If the received packet contains errors, the receiving station asks for a retransmission. The retransmission and error checking continue until the receiving station gets the packet with no errors.

Breaking up the data into small parts allows several users to share a channel. Packets from one user are transmitted in the spaces between packets from other users. The addressing information allows each user's TNC to separate packets for that station from packets intended for other stations. The addresses also allow packets to be relayed through several stations before they reach their final destination. The error-checking information in each packet assures perfect copy.

A TNC connects to your station the same way a modem does. The TNC goes between the radio and the computer, as shown in **Figure 8.14**. Stations that don't use computers have a piece of equipment called a **terminal** that takes the place of a computer in a packet radio

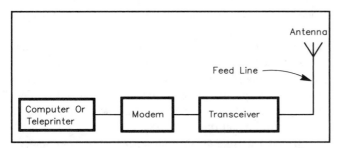

Figure 8.13 — In a typical radioteletype station the modem connects between the transceiver and the computer or teleprinter.

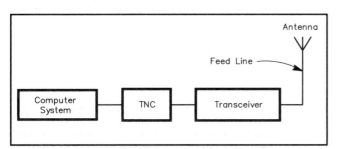

Figure 8.14 — In a packet radio station, the terminal node controller (TNC) connects between the transceiver and a computer.

station. Terminals are much less expensive than computers, but are not nearly as useful.

Although packet is used at HF, the most widely used packet radio systems are operated at VHF/UHF because higher-speed data can be handled in that part of the spectrum using FM. The transceiver in Figure 8.14 would thus most often be a VHF or UHF FM transceiver. The signal squelch control is set at a low enough threshold so that incoming packets are not lost, while squelching out noise that might falsely trigger the TNC as though the noise were a data carrier.

[Turn to Chapter 11 and study the questions numbered T8A03, T8A10, T8A12 and T8A13. If you have any problems, review this last section.]

Station Accessories

So far, we have been talking about very basic station layout. We showed you how to connect a transmitter, receiver and antenna switch to make a simple station. To communicate effectively, you also will need a few accessories. Let's look at what you need.

Connecting Many Antennas

What if you have more than one antenna? You could disconnect the antenna from your transmitter or receiver and reconnect another feed line. This can be very inconvenient. A simpler technique is to use an **antenna switch**. An antenna switch connects one transmitter, receiver or transceiver to several antennas. You can switch from one antenna to another with a simple flick of the switch.

The antenna switch connects at the point where the feed lines from all the antennas come into the station. An antenna switch connects one receiver, transmitter or transceiver to one of several antennas. Even if you only have one antenna you may find an antenna switch useful. Many amateurs use an antenna switch to select between the station antenna and a **dummy antenna**, used for transmitter tuning and testing. See **Figure 8.15**.

Monitoring the System with an SWR Meter

You may want to add an **SWR meter** to your station. This device is also called an SWR bridge. The SWR meter measures something called the *standing-wave ratio*. You don't need to know too much about SWR right now. We will go over it in more detail later in this chapter.

Standing-wave ratio is a good indicator of how well your antenna system is working. If you install an SWR meter in your station, you can keep an eye out for problems with your antenna. If you spot the problems early you can head them off before they damage your equipment.

The SWR meter can be connected at several points in your station. One good place to connect the meter is between the antenna switch and transceiver, as **Figure 8.16** shows. If you use a separate receiver and transmitter, you can connect the SWR meter between the TR switch and the rest of the antenna system. Most amateurs connect their SWR meter as close to the transmitter output as possible.

Antenna Tuners

Another useful accessory that you will see in many ham shacks is an **antenna tuner**, also known as an *impedance-matching network*. (Impedance is similar to resistance.) This device may let you use one antenna on several bands. The matching network may also allow you to use your antenna on a band it is not designed for. Sometimes we call the antenna tuner a *Transmatch*. The antenna tuner matches (tunes) the impedance of the load (the antenna and feed line) to the impedance of your transmitter. We usually connect the antenna tuner right where the antenna comes into the station.

If you are using an antenna tuner to tune your antenna system, you will need an SWR meter. Connect the SWR meter

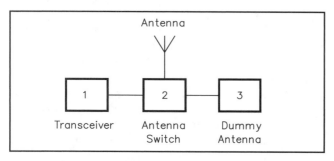

Figure 8.15 — You can use an antenna switch to connect either your station antenna or a dummy antenna (sometimes called a *dummy load*) to your transmitter or transceiver. A dummy antenna is useful for transmitter testing or adjustment without putting a radio signal on the air.

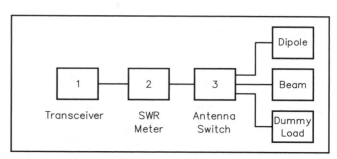

Figure 8.16 — An antenna switch can connect a transmitter to one of several antennas. Many operators place an SWR meter between the transmitter or transceiver and the antenna switch.

between the impedance-matching network and the transmitter or transceiver. See **Figure 8.17**. The SWR meter then indicates when the matching network is adjusted properly.

We'll be covering antenna tuners in more detail later in this chapter.

Morse Code Operation

Morse code is transmitted by switching the output of a transmitter on and off. Inventive radio operators have developed many devices over the years to make this switching easier.

The simplest kind of code-sending device is one

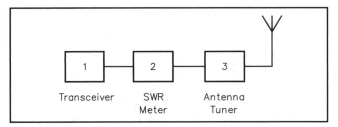

Figure 8.17 — An antenna tuner (or impedance-matching network) connects directly to the antenna feed line. Placing an SWR meter between the tuner and the transmitter or transceiver lets you see when the tuner is adjusted properly.

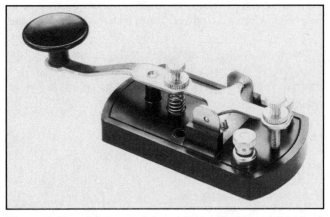

Figure 8.18 — A telegraph key (also called a *straight key*) is the simplest type of Morse code sending device.

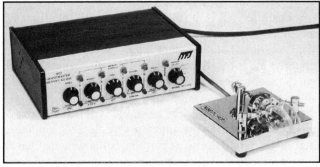

Figure 8.19 — You can produce perfect Morse code characters with an electronic keyer and a little practice.

you're probably already familiar with: the *straight key* or **telegraph key**. See **Figure 8.18**. A telegraph key is a simple switch. When you press down on the key, the contacts meet and the transmitter produces a signal.

The code you produce with a key is only as good as your "fist," or your ability to send well-timed code. An **electronic keyer**, like the one in **Figure 8.19**, makes it easier to send well-timed code. You must connect a *paddle* to the keyer. The paddle has two switches, one on each side. When you press one side of the paddle, one of the switches closes and the keyer sends a continuous string of dots. When you press the other side of the paddle, the keyer sends dashes. With a little practice and some rhythm, you can send perfectly timed code with a keyer. You may want to start out with a hand key, however. Using a hand key can help you develop the rhythm you need to send good code. When you can send good code with a hand key, you're ready to try a keyer. Both the telegraph key and the electronic keyer connect directly to the transmitter.

Microphones

If you want to transmit voice, you'll need a **microphone**. A microphone converts sound waves into electrical signals that can be used by a transmitter. All voice transmitters require a microphone of some kind. Like a code key, the microphone connects directly to the transmitter. The microphone in **Figure 8.20** connects to the transmit section of the transceiver.

The Duplexer

Multiband VHF/UHF radios have become quite popular in recent years, especially **multi-mode** radios that work on FM and packet, as well as on the SSB and CW **weak-signal** modes. You can buy one radio and operate on the popular 2-meter (144 to 148 MHz) band as well as either the 1.25-meter (222 to 225 MHz) band or the 70-cm (420 to 450 MHz) band. Multi-mode VHF/UHF radios are, however, more expensive than the more common FM-only transceivers.

The "dual band" combination of 2 meters and 70 cm is very popular on hand-held FM-only transceivers. The same combination of bands is popular on FM mopbile radios. Some of the mobile radios have separate antenna

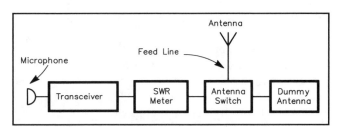

Figure 8.20 — A microphone connects directly to the transmitter or transceiver. You will need a microphone to transmit voice.

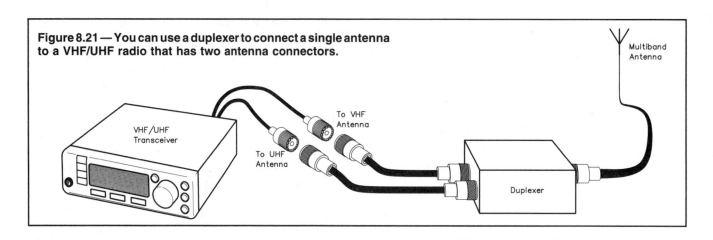

Figure 8.21 — You can use a duplexer to connect a single antenna to a VHF/UHF radio that has two antenna connectors.

connectors for each band and others have one connector used for both. With this type of radio you also have the option of using separate antennas for each band or a single antenna that is designed to operate on both bands. Your choices can lead to some interesting complications. How do you connect two antennas to a radio with only one antenna connector? Or how do you connect your **dual-band antenna** if your radio has two antenna connectors?

The solution to this problem may be a **duplexer**. You can think of a duplexer as a frequency-sensitive signal-steering device. Suppose you have a VHF/UHF radio with two antenna connectors, for example, and you want to connect them both to a single dual-band antenna. A duplexer will ensure that the signal coming out the 2-meter antenna connector goes to the antenna, but not back into the radio through the 70-cm antenna connector. When you are transmitting on 70 cm, it also protects the 2-meter section of the radio in the same way. Received signals coming in on the antenna are directed to the proper antenna connector on your radio. See **Figure 8.21**.

Power Amplifier

Most hams have a 2-meter hand-held transceiver and many have dual-band 2-meter and 70 cm hand-held transceivers. These radios are usually low power units, producing between 1 to perhaps 5 watts of output power.

There may be times when you'd like to get into a distant repeater, perhaps from inside your house, and the hand-held unit's low power is inadequate for that task. Here is where an external power amplifier may be very useful, especially when it uses the home station's outside antenna. There are a number of commercial and homemade power amplifiers available. Hams often call them "bricks" because they are rectangular in shape, like a brick. You can use an amplifier to boost the power output up to 100 watts or more.

[Now turn to Chapter 11. Study questions T8A01, T8A04 through T8A07, T8A11, T8A14, T8B01, T8B11, T8B14, T8B16, T8B17, T8B18, T8D22 and T8E05. Review this section if you have any problems.]

Wavelengths

We sometimes talk about our amateur bands in wavelengths. A **wavelength** relates to the operating frequency. You find the wavelength of a certain RF signal by dividing the speed of light by the operating frequency. Often you'll see the Greek letter lambda (λ) used as an abbreviation for wavelength.

$$\lambda \text{ (in meters)} = \frac{300}{f \text{ (MHz)}} \qquad \text{(Equation 8.1)}$$

Many people prefer to use the US Customary system of measurements, especially if they are going to measure a length with a ruler or tape measure. You can use the following equation to find the wavelength in feet, or in inches, for a specific frequency, in megahertz (MHz).

$$\lambda \text{ (in feet)} = \frac{984}{f \text{ (MHz)}} \qquad \text{(Equation 8.2)}$$

$$\lambda \text{ (in inches)} = \frac{11803}{f \text{ (MHz)}} \qquad \text{(Equation 8.2A)}$$

Let's say we wanted to know the wavelength for 52.15 MHz. We divide 984 by 52.15, and the answer is about 18.9 feet, which is 226.3 inches.

Equations 8.1 and **8.2** show a simple relationship between operating frequency and wavelength. The wavelength is shorter at the higher frequencies. Wavelength is longer at the lower frequencies. It is important to realize that these equations *do not* give the length of a wire to use for an antenna. These equations calculate the wavelength of the RF signal in *space*. The signal will actually travel more slowly through the antenna wire. In addition, other factors will combine to require an antenna wire that is shorter than the wavelength in space. Later in this chapter you will learn how to calculate the approximate length of wire needed to make various types of antennas.

Whenever we talk about an antenna, we specify its design frequency, or the amateur band it covers. Most popular ham antennas are less than 1 λ long. (A very popular antenna is a ½-λ **dipole antenna**. You'll learn how to build one later in this chapter.) We could talk about a "6-meter dipole," for example, as an antenna intended for operation in the 6-meter (50-54-MHz) band.

Antennas are tuned circuits. A simple antenna such as a ½-λ dipole or a ¼-λ **vertical** has a *resonant frequency*. Such antennas do best at their resonant frequency, as do most other tuned circuits. To change the resonant frequency of a tuned circuit, you vary the capacitor value or the inductor value. You can change the resonant frequency of an antenna by changing its length, which affects its capacitance *and* inductance.

Feed Lines

To get RF energy from your transmitter to an antenna you use **transmission line**. A transmission line is a special cable or arrangement of wires. Such lines are sometimes called **feed lines**. They feed power to the antenna, or feed a received signal from the antenna to the receiver.

Characteristic Impedance

One electrical property of a feed line is its *characteristic impedance*. Resistance is an opposition to electric current. **Impedance** is another form of opposition to electric current, but impedance includes resistance and factors related to the inductance and capacitance in an ac circuit.

The spacing between line conductors and the type of insulating material determines the characteristic impedance of a transmission line. Characteristic impedance is important because we want the feed line to take all the transmitter power and feed it to the antenna. For this to occur, the transmitter (source) must have the same impedance as its load (the feed line). In turn, the feed line must have the same impedance as its load (the antenna).

We can use special circuits called *matching devices* or *matching networks* if any of these impedances are different. *Network* just refers to a combination of inductors and capacitors that forms a special circuit. Still, careful selection of a feed line can minimize such matching problems.

Coaxial Cable

Several types of feed line are available for amateur use. The most common is **coaxial cable**. Called "coax" (pronounced *kó-aks*) for short, this feed line has one conductor inside the other. It's like a wire inside a flexible tube. The center conductor is surrounded by insulation, and the insulation is surrounded by a wire braid called the *shield*. The whole cable is then encased in a tough vinyl outer coating, which makes the cable weatherproof. See **Figure 8.22**. Coax comes in different sizes, with different electrical properties. Figure 8.22 shows several types of coaxial cables used by amateurs.

The most common types of coax have either a 50-ohm (Greek letter omega, Ω) or a 72-Ω characteristic impedance. Coax designated RG-58, RG-8 and RG-213 are 50-Ω cables. Some coax designations may also include a suffix such as /U, A/U or B/U, or bear the label "polyfoam." Feed line of this type may be used with most antennas. Cables labeled RG-59 or RG-11 are 75-Ω lines. Many hams use these types to feed dipole antennas.

The impedance of a ½-λ dipole far from other objects is about 73 Ω. Practical dipoles placed close to the Earth, trees, buildings or other objects, have an input impedance closer to 50 Ω. In any case, the small impedance mismatch caused by using 50 or 75-Ω cable as antenna feed line is unimportant.

In choosing the feed line for your installation, you'll have a trade-off between electrical characteristics and physical properties. The RG-58 and RG-59 types of cable are about ¼ inch in diameter, comparatively lightweight, and reasonably flexible. RG-8, RG-213 and RG-11 are about ½ inch in diameter, nearly three times heavier, and considerably less flexible. As far as operation goes, RG-8, RG-213 and RG-11 will handle much more power than RG-58 and RG-59.

Any line that feeds an antenna absorbs a small amount of transmitter power. That power is lost, because it serves no useful purpose. (The lost power warms the feed line slightly.) The loss occurs because the wires are not perfect conductors, and the insulating material is not a perfect insulator. Signal loss also increases slightly with higher SWR values, so we try to keep the SWR below 2:1 if possible.

Better-quality coaxial cables have lower loss than poor-quality cables. More of the transmitter power is lost as heat in a poor-quality coaxial cable. You usually get better-quality coax if you stick with name brands. You can also look at the shield braid on the coax. Better-quality cables have more complete coverage of the center insulator. If you can easily see through the holes in the braid, you should probably select another cable.

The larger coax types, RG-8, RG-213 and RG-11, have less signal loss than the smaller types. If your feed line is less than 100 feet long, you probably won't notice the small additional signal loss, at least on the HF bands. This, combined with lightweight and flexibility, is why many HF operators find the smaller coax better suited to their needs. Also, the smaller feed line costs about half as much per foot as the larger types.

On the VHF/UHF bands, however, you will find the losses in RG-58 and RG-59 more noticeable, especially if your feed line is longer than about 50 feet. On these bands, most amateurs use higher-quality RG-213 coax or even lower-loss special coaxial cables. It is also important to

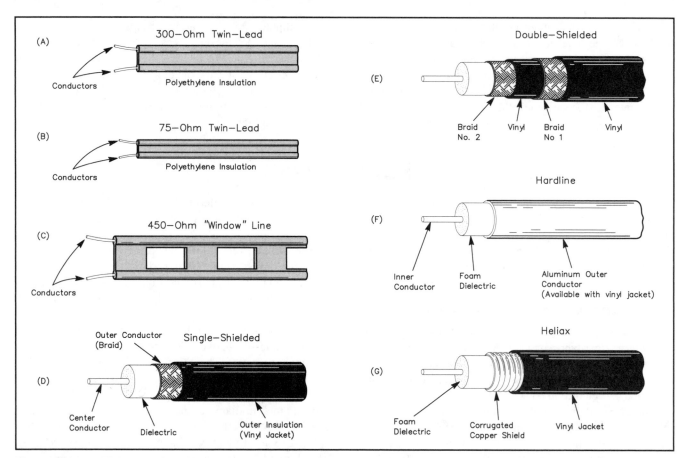

Figure 8.22 — This drawing illustrates some common types of open-wire and coaxial cables used by amateurs. Open-wire line has two parallel conductors separated by insulation. "Coax" has a center conductor surrounded by insulation. The second conductor, called the shield, goes around that. Plastic insulation covers the entire cable.

use good-quality connectors at VHF and UHF.

Coaxial cable has several advantages as a feed line. It is readily available, and is resistant to weather. Most common amateur antennas have characteristic impedances of about 50 Ω. Coax can be buried in the ground if necessary. It can be bent, coiled and run next to metal with little effect. Its major drawback is its cost.

Amateurs commonly use RG-8, RG-58, RG-174 and RG-213 coaxial cable. RG-8 and RG-213 are similar cables, and they have the least loss of the types listed here. RG-174 is only about 1/8-inch in diameter, and it has the highest loss of the cables listed here. RG-174 is normally used for cables that connect sections of a transmitter or receiver, or for short interconnecting cables in a low-power system. Some amateurs use RG-174 cable as the feed line for a low-power portable HF station because of its low weight.

Extra cable length increases attenuation. When using coaxial cable, you should try to use a feed line and antenna that have matched impedances. You should then be able to change feed line lengths without significantly affecting the antenna system. Your feed line has only to be long enough to reach your antenna. A low SWR on the line means that the impedance seen by the transmitter will

be about the same regardless of line length. You can cut off or shorten excess cable length to reduce attenuation of the signal caused by antenna-system loss. (This does not apply to multiple antennas in phased arrays or line sections used for impedance-matching purposes.)

Coaxial-cable connectors are an important part of a coaxial feed line. Your choice of connectors normally depends on the matching connectors on your radios. Most HF radios and many VHF radios use SO-239 connectors. The mating connector is called a PL-259. (These are military-type designations.) The PL-259 is sometimes called a *UHF connector,* although they are not the best choice for the UHF bands. **Figure 8.23** shows the SO-239 connector and its mating PL-259. PL-259 connectors are designed for use with RG-8 or RG-213 cables. Figure 8.23 also shows an adapter for use with the smaller diameter RG-58 coax.

Many VHF and UHF hand-held radios use BNC connectors. These connectors are designed for use with RG-58 coax. They produce a low-loss connection that is also weatherproof. **Figure 8.24** shows a pair of BNC connectors. BNC connectors are well suited for use with hand-held-radio antennas because they require only a quarter turn to install or remove, yet they lock securely in place.

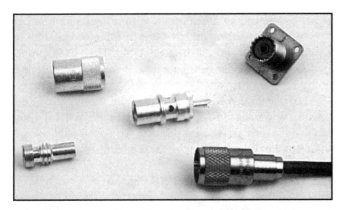

Figure 8.23 — This photo shows an SO-239 chassis connector and its mating PL-259. The PL-259 connector consists of a body and a connecting sleeve. The connector is designed for use with $\frac{1}{2}$-inch diameter coax such as RG-8 or RG-213. The adapter shown next to the connector body is used with $\frac{1}{4}$-inch diameter cable such as RG-58. There is another adapter with a larger center opening designed to be used by the slightly larger diameter RG-59 coax. Most HF equipment uses the SO-239/PL-259 connectors. Although they are sometimes called UHF connectors, the SO-239/PL-259 pair are not the lowest loss connectors you could use on the UHF bands.

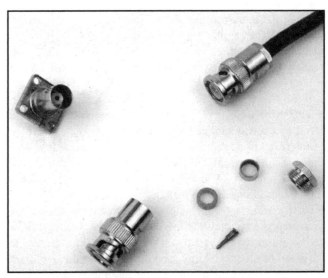

Figure 8.24 — This photo shows a BNC connector pair. Many hand-held radios use BNC connectors. They are also popular when a weatherproof connector is needed for RG-58 sized cable.

It is a good idea to check your coaxial connectors on a regular basis. Be sure they are clean and tight to minimize their resistance. If you suspect a bad solder connection, you should resolder the joints.

Open-Wire Transmission Lines

Another type of transmission line used by many hams is **open-wire line**. Two parallel wires are spaced a constant distance from each other by insulation of some kind to create open-wire line, also known as **parallel-conductor feed line**. The top three types of transmission line in Figure 8.22 are types of open-wire line. The "window" line is also known as "ladder" line, since it resembles a ladder.

One of the main advantages of open-wire transmission line is that the loss is less than that for coaxial cable. It will operate well even with a high SWR. (You will learn about SWR in the next section.) Open-wire line is also considerably cheaper than coax. But it has the disadvantage that it must be kept away from metallic objects, because, unlike coax, open-wire line doesn't have an outer shield that keeps stray currents from flowing on the line. Open-wire line is a *balanced* transmission line because of its symmetry, while coax cable is inherently an **unbalanced** transmission line, with the outer shield connected to ground.

[Now turn to Chapter 11 and study question T8E06 through T8E09, T8E12 and T8E13. Review this section if you have difficulty with any of these questions.]

Impedance-Matching and Balancing

Standing-Wave Ratio (SWR)

If an antenna system does not match the characteristic impedance of the transmitter, some of the transmitter energy is reflected from the antenna. The power traveling from the transmitter to the antenna is called **forward power**. When that power reaches the antenna in an unmatched system, some of the power is reflected back down the feed line toward the transmitter. Some of the power is also radiated from the antenna, which is what you want to happen. The power that returns to the transmitter from the antenna is called **reflected power**.

The forward power and the reflected power passing each other on the feed line cause voltage standing waves on the line. When this happens, the RF voltage and current are not uniform along the line. The **standing-wave ratio (SWR)** is the ratio of the maximum voltage on the line to the minimum voltage. (These two points will always be $\frac{1}{4}$ λ apart.) An **SWR meter** measures the relative impedance match between an antenna and its feed line. It does this by measuring the voltage of the RF signal on the line. Lower SWR values mean a better impedance match exists between the transmitter and the antenna system. If a perfect match exists, the SWR is 1:1. Your SWR meter thus gives a relative measure of how well the antenna system impedance matches that of the transmitter.

Modern transmitters are designed to match 50-Ω coaxial lines and antennas. Most commercial antennas are designed to have nearly the same characteristic impedance *when properly adjusted*. So, if your SWR is higher than 2:1, it means your antenna is not adjusted properly for the frequency you are using. We adjust the antenna for minimum SWR (not always 1:1) somewhere in the middle of the band of interest. On other frequencies, the SWR may be higher. If the antenna is assembled properly, an SWR of 2:1 or less is probably all right. An SWR measurement of 1.5:1 indicates a fairly good impedance match.

If you are using a matching device, such as an **antenna tuner**, you can probably adjust it so the SWR meter reads 1:1. The SWR on the transmission line between the tuner and the antenna will, however, be different. A matching device adjusts the impedance match between the transceiver and the transmission line.

SWR Meters

The most common **SWR meter** application is tuning an antenna to resonate on the frequency you want to use. (This discussion applies if you connect the feed line directly to the transmitter output, with no antenna tuner.)

An SWR reading of 2:1 or less is quite acceptable. A reading of 4:1 or more is unacceptable. This means there is a serious impedance mismatch between your antenna and your feed line.

To use the SWR meter, you transmit through it. (You must have a license to operate a transmitter! What if your license has not arrived by the time you are ready to test your antenna? Just invite a licensed ham over to operate the transmitter.)

How you measure the SWR depends on your type of meter. Some SWR meters have a SENSITIVITY control and a FORWARD-REFLECTED switch. If so, the meter scale usually gives you a direct SWR reading. To use the meter, first put the switch in the FORWARD position. Then adjust the SENSITIVITY control and the transmitter power output until the meter reads full scale. Some meters have a mark on the meter face labeled SET or CAL. The meter pointer should rest on this mark. Next, set the selector switch to the REFLECTED position. Do this without readjusting the transmitter power or the meter SENSITIVITY control. Now the meter pointer shows you the SWR value.

Most SWR meters are designed for operation on the

SWR: What Does It Mean?

You already know that SWR is defined as the ratio of the maximum voltage to the minimum voltage in the standing wave:

$$SWR = \frac{E_{max}}{E_{min}}$$

An SWR of 1:1 means you have no reflected power. The transmission line is said to be "flat." If the load is completely resistive (no reactance), then the SWR can be calculated. Divide the line characteristic impedance by the load resistance, or vice versa. Use whichever gives a value greater than one:

$$SWR = \frac{Z_0}{R} \quad or \quad SWR = \frac{R}{Z_0}$$

where
Z_0 = characteristic impedance of the transmission line
R = load resistance (not reactance)

For example, if you feed a 100-Ω antenna with 50-Ω transmission line, the SWR is 100/50 or 2:1. Similarly, if the impedance of the antenna is 25 Ω the SWR is 50/25 or 2:1.

When a high SWR exists, losses in the feed line are increased. This is because of the multiple reflections from the antenna and transmitter. Each time the transmitted power has to travel up and down the feed line, a little more energy is lost as heat.

This effect is not so great as some people believe, however. Some line losses are less than 2 dB (such as

for 100 feet of RG-213 or RG-58 cables up to about 30 MHz). The SWR would have to be greater than 3:1 to add an extra decibel of loss because of the SWR. (A high SWR will cause the output power to drop drastically with many solid-state transceivers. The drop in power is caused by internal circuits that sense the high SWR and automatically reduce output power to protect the transceiver.)

A transmission line should be terminated in a resistance equal to its characteristic impedance. Then maximum power is delivered to the antenna, and transmission line losses are minimized. This would be an ideal condition. Such a perfect match is seldom realized in a practical antenna system.

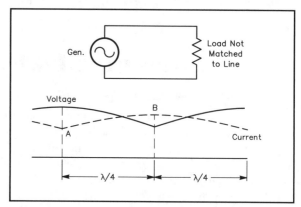

Figure A—The standing-wave ratio (SWR) is the ratio of the voltage amplitude at point A to the voltage amplitude at point B, or the ratio of the current amplitude at point B to the current amplitude of point A.

high-frequency (HF) bands. You may be able to use your SWR meter on the VHF bands if you are able to adjust the meter for a full-scale reading in the SET or CAL position. The readings may not be as accurate as the readings you obtain on the HF bands, but it may give an indication of the impedance match to your VHF antenna.

Wattmeters

A **wattmeter** is a device connected in the transmission line to measure the power (in watts) coming out of a transmitter. Wattmeters are designed to operate at a certain line impedance, normally 50 Ω. Make sure the feed-line impedance is the same as the design impedance of the wattmeter. If impedances are different, any measurements will be inaccurate.

Likewise, a power meter designed for use at 3-30 MHz (HF) will be inaccurate at VHF. For most accurate measurement, the wattmeter should be connected directly at the transceiver output (antenna) jack.

One type of wattmeter is a **directional wattmeter**. There are two kinds of directional wattmeters. One has a meter that reads forward power and another meter that reads reflected power. The other has a single meter that can be switched to read either forward or reflected power.

You can use a directional wattmeter to measure the output power from your transmitter. It is easy to become confused by the readings on your wattmeter, however. First measure and record the forward power, or power going from the transmitter to the antenna. Then measure the reflected power, which is any power coming back toward the transmitter from the antenna. To find the true power from your transmitter, you must subtract the reflected power from the forward reading. The power reflected from the antenna will again be reflected by the transmitter. This power adds to the forward power reading on the meter.

Suppose your transmitter power output is 100 watts and 10 watts of power is reflected from the antenna. Those 10 watts will be added into the forward reading on your wattmeter when they are reflected from the transmitter. Your forward wattmeter reading would indicate 110 watts, which is incorrect. To find true forward power you must subtract the reflected measurement from the forward power measurement:

True forward power = Forward power reading – Reflected power reading   (Equation 8.3)

For example, suppose you have a wattmeter connected in the line from your transmitter. It gives a forward-power reading of 90 watts and a reflected-power reading of 10 watts. What is the true power out of your transmitter?

True forward power = 90 W – 10 W = 80 W.

The main reason for using a wattmeter in your amateur station is to ensure that you are not exceeding the maximum power allowed by your license. The FCC specifies this maximum power in terms of peak envelope power or PEP. For this reason, the most accurate way to measure

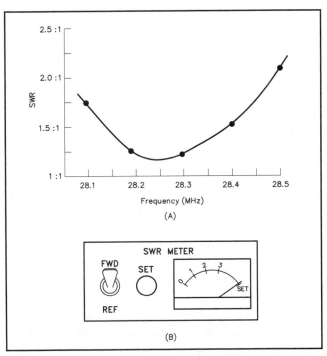

Figure 8.25 — To determine if your antenna is cut to the right length, measure the SWR at different points in the band. Plot these values and draw a curve, as shown in Part A. Use the curve to see if the antenna is too long or too short. Adjusting the length will bring the lowest SWR to the desired frequency. This graph shows how the SWR might vary across an amateur frequency band. The point of lowest SWR here is near the center of the band, so no further antenna-length adjustments are necessary. Part B shows a common SWR meter, with the measurement switch set to the FWD position (forward) and the SET control adjusted to produce a full-scale meter reading with a low-power signal from the transmitter. To measure SWR, stop transmitting and move the switch to the REF position (reflected) without changing the SET control. Briefly transmit a signal again and read the SWR on the meter.

your power is with a peak-reading RF wattmeter. Some wattmeters are calibrated to measure average power rather than peak power. You can use an average-reading meter, but you must be aware that if your *average power* is at or close to the maximum limit then your *peak envelope power* may be higher than the limit!

Using an SWR Meter

Find the **resonant frequency** of an antenna by connecting the meter between the feed line and your antenna and looking for the frequency where the SWR is lowest. This technique measures the relative impedance match between your antenna and its feed line. Ideally, you will measure the lowest SWR at the center of the band, with higher readings at each end. See **Figure 8.25**.

Sometimes it isn't practical to put your SWR meter at the antenna feed point, between the feed line and the antenna.

(The antenna feed point is where the feed line connects to the antenna.) Most hams just put the meter in their shack, at the transmitter, and make measurements there. You should realize that this is a compromise, however. You are measuring the relative impedance match between your transmitter and the antenna *system*, which includes the feed line.

This method works for dipoles or vertical antennas. It does not show antenna resonance if you have a matching device between the SWR meter and the antenna. Nor does it show resonance for antenna systems that include a matching device at the antenna. An SWR meter *will* show when you have adjusted the matching device properly, however. Use the settings that give you the lowest SWR at your preferred operating frequency.

If you are using an antenna tuner with your antenna system, you should place the SWR meter between the transmitter and the tuner. The meter then indicates when you have adjusted the antenna tuner to provide the best impedance match to your transmitter.

Finding Antenna Problems with an SWR Meter

Sometimes problems occur when you first install an antenna. Sometimes, problems show up only after the weather batters your antenna for weeks, months or years.

It's handy to have an SWR meter or wattmeter to help diagnose antenna problems. This section tells how to interpret SWR meter readings to solve specific problems. This information applies to any type of antenna. We assume the antenna you're using normally provides a good match to your feed line at the measurement frequency.

One common problem is a loose connection where the feed line from your station attaches to the antenna wire. Splices or joints are another possible failure point. Your SWR meter will tell if the problem you're experiencing is a poor connection somewhere in the antenna. Observe the SWR reading. It should remain constant. If it is erratic, jumping markedly, chances are you have a loose connection. This problem is very easy to see on windy days.

If your SWR reading is unusually high, greater than 10:1 or so, you probably have a worse problem. *Caution:* Do not operate your transmitter with a very high SWR any

longer than it takes to read the SWR! The problem could be an open connection or a short circuit. The most likely failure point is at the antenna feed point. The problem might also be at the connector attaching your feed line to your transmitter. Carefully check your connections and your feed line for damage. You can also get unusually high SWR readings if the antenna is far from the correct length. This would happen if you try to operate your antenna on the wrong amateur band!

Most hams leave an SWR meter in the line all the time. Any sudden changes in the SWR mean you have a problem, such as a broken wire or bad connection.

Antenna Tuners

Your transmitter won't operate very well if it is connected to a feed line that presents an impedance that is different from the transmitter output impedance. Your transmitter probably has an output circuit designed for a 50-Ω load. Your antenna system (the combination of your antenna and feed line) may not have an impedance of 50 Ω, though. An **impedance-matching device** or network will provide the proper impedance correction. For some mismatches, a suitable network might contain only an inductor and a capacitor.

An antenna tuner is a special type of matching device. Antenna tuners contain variable matching components (inductors and capacitors) and often a band switch. They offer the flexibility of matching a wide range of impedances over a wide frequency range. With an antenna tuner, it is possible to use one antenna on several bands. For example, you might use a center-fed wire (dipole) antenna. Each band will use its own tuner settings: one combination for 80, one for 40, one for 15, and one for 10 meters, for example.

Connect the antenna tuner between the antenna and the SWR meter, as **Figure 8.26** shows. (Remember that an SWR meter measures the impedance mismatch on the feed line between the two pieces of equipment it is connected to.) Adjust the controls on your antenna tuner for minimum SWR. Don't worry if you can't achieve a perfect match (1:1). Anything lower than 2:1 will work just fine.

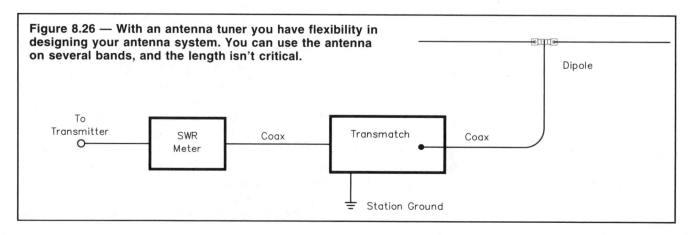

Figure 8.26 — With an antenna tuner you have flexibility in designing your antenna system. You can use the antenna on several bands, and the length isn't critical.

Baluns

A center-fed wire with open ends, such as a dipole, is a *balanced* antenna. In a balanced center-fed antenna, the current flowing into one half of the antenna is equal to the current in the other half. The two currents are also opposite in *phase*. (*Phase* refers to the relative positions of two points on a wave, or on two different waves at a particular instant of time. If the two currents are opposite in phase, one is in the positive half of the cycle when the other is in the negative half cycle.) You can think of a balanced antenna as one where neither side connects to ground. A balanced antenna is balanced with respect to ground.

If we feed a dipole at the center with coax, we upset the system balance. One side of the antenna connects to the coax inner, or center, conductor. The other side connects to the coax shield. The outside shield of coaxial cable is normally connected to ground at the transceiver. Coax, then, is an **unbalanced line**. This unbalanced condition may allow some antenna current to flow down the outside of the coax braid from the antenna. This can lead to several antenna problems, and should be avoided.

When connecting coaxial (*unbalanced*) feed lines to *balanced antennas*, many hams use a **balun**. Balun is a contraction for *bal*anced to *un*balanced. You install the balun at the antenna feed point, between the coaxial cable and the antenna.

Different types of baluns are available commercially, or you can make your own. A common type is a balun transformer, which uses wires wound on a toroidal core. Besides providing a balance, these baluns can transform an impedance, such as from 50 to 75 Ω. Another type is a bead or *choke* balun. Several ferrite beads go over the outside of the coax, one after the other. The beads tend to choke off any RF current that might otherwise flow on the outside of the shield.

You can easily make another type of choke balun from the coax transmission line itself. At the antenna feed point, coil up 10 turns of coax into a roll about 6 inches in diameter. Tape the coax turns together. The inductance of the coiled turns tends to choke off RF currents on the shield.

[Study questions T8E01 through T8E04, T8E10, T8E11, and T8E14 in Chapter 11 now. Also study questions T8F10 through T8F13. Review this section if you have difficulty answering these questions.]

Choosing an Antenna

As a new ham, you should quickly learn two antenna truths: 1) Any antenna is better than no antenna! 2) Time, effort and money invested in your antenna system generally will provide more improvement to your station than an equal investment to any other part of the station.

We know that a transmitter generates radio-frequency energy. We convert this electrical energy into radio waves with an **antenna**. An antenna may be just a piece of wire or other conductor designed to *radiate* the energy. An antenna converts current into an electromagnetic field (radio waves). The radio waves spread out or *propagate* from the antenna. You might relate their travel to the ever-expanding waves you get when you drop a pebble in water. Waves from an antenna radiate in all directions, though, not just in a flat plane.

It also works the other way. When a radio wave crosses an antenna, it generates a voltage in the antenna. That voltage isn't very strong, but it's enough to create a small current. That current travels through the **transmission line** to the receiver. The receiver detects the radio signal. In short, the antenna converts electrical energy to radio waves and radio waves to electrical energy. This process makes two-way radio communication possible with just one antenna.

Your success in making contacts depends heavily on your antenna. A good antenna can make a fair receiver seem like a champ. It can also make a few watts sound like a whole lot more. Remember, you'll normally use the same antenna to transmit and receive. Any improvements to your antenna make your transmitted signal stronger, and increase the strength of the signals you receive.

Assembling an antenna system gives you a chance to be creative. You may discover, for example, that property size or landlord restrictions rule out a traditional antenna. If so, you can innovate. *Simple and Fun Antennas for Hams* is an ARRL publication full of ideas for just these conditions. *The ARRL Antenna Book*, *The ARRL Antenna Compendium* series and similar publications also offer lots of antenna suggestions. This chapter contains a few suggestions, too.

Some antennas work better than others. Antenna design and construction have kept radio amateurs busy since the days of Marconi. You'll probably experiment with different antenna types over the years. Putting up a better antenna can be an inexpensive but rewarding way to improve your station.

Practical Antennas

Hams use many different kinds of antennas. There is no one best kind. Beginners usually prefer simpler, less expensive types. Some hams with more experience have antenna systems that cost thousands of dollars. Others have antennas that use several acres of property!

The Half-Wave Dipole Antenna

Probably the most common amateur antenna is a wire cut to ½ λ at the operating frequency. The feed line attaches across an insulator at the center of the wire. This is the **half-wave dipole**. We often refer to an antenna like this as a **dipole antenna**. (*Di* means two, so a dipole has two equal parts. A dipole could be a length other than ½ λ.) The total length of a half-wavelength dipole is ½ λ. The feed line connects to the center. This means that each side of this dipole is ¼-λ long.

Use Equation 8.4 to find the total length of a ½-λ dipole for a specific frequency. Notice that the frequency is given in megahertz and the antenna length is in feet for this equation.

$$\text{Length (in feet)} = \frac{468}{f \text{ (MHz)}}$$

(Equation 8.4)

If you look back at Equation 8.2, you will notice that it is similar to **Equation 8.4**. There is a different value in the top of the fraction, though. The smaller number (468) is not simply one-half of 984, since it takes into account that the radio signal travels slower in the wire than it does through space. It also takes into account other factors, often called *antenna effects*. Equation 8.4 gives the approximate length of wire to use when building a practical HF dipole antenna. The equation will not be as accurate for VHF/UHF antenna lengths. The element diameter is a larger percentage of the wavelength at VHF and higher frequencies. Other effects, such as *end effects* also make the equation less accurate at

Antenna Radiation Patterns

Often one desirable antenna feature is **directivity**. Directivity means the ability to pick up signals from one direction, while suppressing signals from other unwanted directions. Going hand in hand with directivity is **gain**. Gain tells how much signal a given antenna will pick up as compared with that from another antenna, usually a dipole.

An antenna that has directivity should also have gain. These two antenna properties are useful not only for picking up or receiving radio signals, but also for transmitting them. An antenna that has gain will boost your transmitted energy in the favored direction while suppressing it in other directions.

When you mention gain and directivity, most amateurs envision large antenna arrays, made from aluminum tubing, with many elements. Simple wire antennas can also be very effective, however, as illustrated in this antenna radiation pattern. Such patterns reveal both the gain and the directivity of a specific antenna.

Let's say we connect the antenna to a transmitter and send. The pattern shows the relative power received at a fixed distance from the antenna, in various compass directions. If you connect the antenna to a receiver, the pattern shows how the antenna responds to signals from various directions. In the direction where the antenna has gain, the incoming signals will be enhanced. The incoming signals will be suppressed in other directions.

Here is an important point to remember. You can never have antenna gain in one direction without a loss (signal suppression) in one or more other directions. Never! Another way to think of this is that an antenna cannot create power. It can only focus or beam the power supplied by the transmitter.

We call the long, thin lobes in a pattern the *major lobes*. The smaller lobes in a pattern are *minor lobes*. One or more major lobes mean directivity. An antenna with less directivity than this one would have fatter lobes. An antenna with no directivity at all

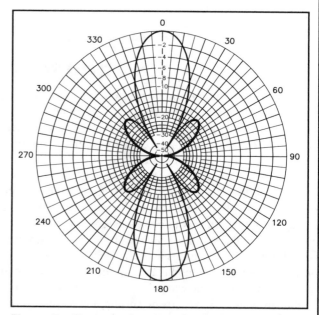

Figure B—The calculated or theoretical radiation pattern of an extended double Zepp antenna is shown here. In its favored directions, this antenna exhibits roughly 2 decibels of gain over a half-wavelength dipole. This would make a 200-watt signal as strong as 317 watts into a dipole. An extended double Zepp antenna may be made with a horizontal wire hanging between two supports. (The wire is 1.28-λ long at the operating frequency.) The wire axis is along the 90°/270° line shown in the chart.

would have a pattern that is a perfect circle. A theoretical antenna called an isotropic radiator has such a pattern. Radiation patterns are a very useful tool in measuring antenna capability.

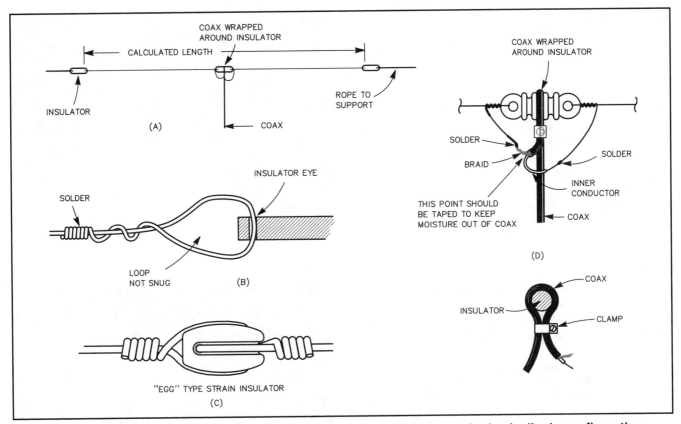

Figure 8.27 — Simple half-wave dipole antenna construction. Part A shows the basic dipole configuration. Parts B and C show how to connect the wire ends to various insulator types. Part D shows the feed-line connection at the center.

VHF and UHF. The values given by Equation 8.4 for 2 and 1.25 meters are only to serve as a starting point for building antennas for those bands, but they will probably be too long so that you can prune the length. A $\frac{1}{2}-\lambda$ dipole for 147 MHz will be about 37 inches long.

Equation 8.4 gives the following approximate lengths for $\frac{1}{2}-\lambda$ dipoles.

Wavelength	Frequency	Length
80 meters	3.725 MHz	125.6 feet
40 meters	7.125 MHz	66 feet
15 meters	21.125 MHz	22 feet
10 meters	28.150 MHz	16.6 feet
10 meters	28.475 MHz	16.4 feet
2 meters	147.0 MHz	3.18 feet = 37 inches
1.25 meters	223 MHz	2.1 feet = 25 inches

Figure 8.27A shows the construction of a basic $\frac{1}{2}-\lambda$ dipole antenna. Parts B through D show enlarged views of how to attach the insulators. You can use just about any kind of copper or copper-clad steel wire for your dipole. Most hardware or electrical supply stores carry suitable wire.

House wire and stranded wire will stretch with time, so a heavy-gauge copper-clad steel wire is best. This wire consists of a copper jacket over a steel core. Such construction provides the strength of steel combined with the excellent conducting properties of copper. You can sometimes find copper-clad steel wire at a radio store. This wire

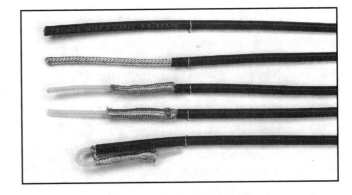

Figure 8.28 — Preparing coaxial cable for connection to antenna wire. A — Remove the outer insulation with a sharp knife or wire stripper. If you nick the braid, start over. B — Push the braid in accordion fashion against the outer jacket. C — Spread the shield strands at the point where the outer insulation ends. D — Fish the center conductor through the opening in the braid. Now strip the center conductor insulation back far enough to make the connection and tin (flow solder onto) both center conductor and shield. Be careful not to use too much solder, which will make the conductors inflexible. Also be careful not to apply too much heat, or you will melt the insulation. A pair of pliers used as a heat sink will help. The outer jacket removed in step A can be slipped over the braid as an insulator, if necessary. Be sure to slide it onto the braid before soldering the leads to the antenna wires.

is used for electric fences to keep farm animals in their place, so another place to try is a farm supply store.

Remember, you want a good conductor for the antenna, but the wire must also be strong. The wire must support itself *and* the weight of the feed line connected at the center.

We use wire gauge to rate wire size. Larger gauge numbers represent smaller wire diameters. Conversely, smaller gauge numbers represent larger wire diameters. Although you can make a dipole antenna from almost any size wire, #12 or #14 gauge is usually best. Smaller-diameter wires may stretch or break easily.

Cut your dipole according to the dimension found by Equation 9.4, but leave a little extra length to wrap the ends around the insulators. You'll need a feed line to connect it to your transmitter. For the reasons mentioned earlier, the most popular feed line for use with dipole antennas is co-axial cable. When you shop for coax, look for some with a heavy braided shield. If possible, get good quality cable that has at least 95 percent shielding. If you stick with name brand cable, you'll get a good quality feed line. **Figure 8.28** shows the steps required to prepare the cable end for attachment to the antenna wires at the center insulator.

The final items you'll need for your dipole are three insulators. You can purchase them from your local radio or hardware store (**Figure 8.29**). You can also make your own insulators from plastic or Teflon blocks. See **Figure 8.30**. One insulator goes on each end and another holds the two wires together in the center. **Figure 8.31** shows some examples of how the feed line can attach to the antenna wires at a center insulator.

Dipole antennas send radio energy best in a direction that is 90° to the antenna wire. For example, suppose you install a dipole antenna so the ends of the wire run in an east/west direction. Assuming it was well off the ground (preferably ½ λ high), this antenna would send stronger signals in north and south directions. A dipole also sends radio energy straight up and straight down. Of course the dipole also sends some energy in directions off the ends of the wire, but these signals won't be as strong. So you will be able to contact stations to the east and west with this

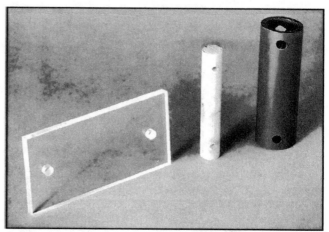

Figure 8.30 — Some ideas for homemade antenna insulators.

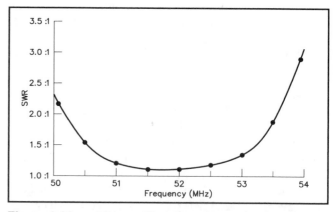

Figure 8.31 — Some dipole center insulators have connectors for easy feed-line removal. Others have a direct solder connection to the feed line.

Figure 8.32 — After cutting the wire to the length given by the equation, you will have to adjust the tuning of your antenna for the best operation. Put the antenna in its final location and check the SWR at various frequencies across the band. Plot the SWR values on a graph with frequency and draw a smooth curve between the points. Your graph will indicate if the antenna is too long or too short. If the SWR is much higher at the low-frequency end of the band your antenna is too short. If the SWR is much higher at the high-frequency end of the band, the antenna is too long. When the antenna is properly tuned, the lowest SWR values should be around the frequency you plan to operate most.

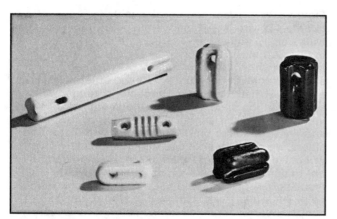

Figure 8.29 — Various commercially made antenna insulators.

antenna, but you will find that the signals are stronger with stations to the north and south.

Tuning a Dipole Antenna

When you build an antenna, you cut it to the length given by an equation. This length is just a first approximation. Nearby trees, buildings or large metal objects and height above ground all affect the antenna resonant frequency. An SWR meter can help you determine if you should shorten or lengthen the antenna. The correct length provides the best impedance match for your transmitter.

The first step is to measure the SWR at the bottom, middle and top of the band. On 6 meters, for example, you could check the SWR at 50.05, 52. 00 and 53.95 MHz. Check other frequencies in between, too. Graph the readings, as shown in **Figure 8.32**. You could be lucky — no further antenna adjustments may be necessary, depending on your transmitter.

Many tube-type transmitters include an output-tuning network. They will usually operate fine with an SWR of 3:1 or less. Most solid-state transmitters (using all transistors and integrated circuits) do not include such an output-tuning network. These no-tune radios begin to shut down — the power output drops off — with any SWR higher than 1.5:1. In any event, most hams like to prune their antennas for the lowest SWR they can get at the center of the band. With a full-size dipole 30 or 40 feet high, your SWR should be less than 2:1. If you can get the SWR down to 1.5:1, great! It's not worth the time and effort to do any better than that.

Sometimes your antenna may resonate far off frequency. In this situation you will not get a "dip" in SWR readings with frequency. Instead, your readings will increase as you change frequency from one end of the band to the other. For example, you might read 2.5:1 at the low-frequency band edge, and the reading might increase across the band to 5:1 at the high-frequency end. This

means antenna resonance is closer to the low-frequency end of the band than the high. It also means that resonance is below the low-frequency band edge. For a dipole or vertical antenna, this condition exists when the antenna is too long. Trimming the length will correct the problem.

Suppose the readings were 5:1 at the low-frequency end of the band and decreased across the band to 2.5:1 at the high end. See **Figure 8.33**. Here, the antenna is too short. Adding to the antenna length will correct this problem. Adjusting the antenna length for resonance in this way is what we call *tuning the antenna*.

If the SWR is lower at the low-frequency end of the band, your antenna is probably too long. Making the antenna *shorter* will *increase* the resonant frequency. Disconnect the transmitter and try shortening your dipole antenna at each end. The amount to trim off depends on two things. First is which band the antenna is operating on, and, second, how much you want to change the resonant frequency. Let's say the antenna is cut for the 80-meter band. You'll probably need to cut 8 or 10 inches off each end to move the resonant frequency 50 kHz. You may have to trim only an inch or less for small frequency changes on the 6 or 10-meter bands. Measure the SWR again (remember to recheck the calibration). If the SWR went down, keep shortening the antenna until the SWR at the center of the band is less than 2:1.

If the SWR is lower at the high-frequency end of the band, your antenna was probably too short to begin with. If so, you must add more wire until the SWR is acceptable. Making the antenna *longer* will *decrease* the resonant frequency. Before you solder more wire on the antenna ends, try attaching a 12-inch wire on each end. Use alligator clips, as **Figure 8.34** shows. You don't need to move the insulators yet. Clip a wire on each end and again measure the SWR. Chances are the antenna will now be too long. You will need to shorten it a little at a time until the SWR is below 2:1.

Once you know how much wire you need to add, cut two pieces and solder them to the ends of the antenna. When you add wire, be sure to make a sound mechanical connection before soldering. **Figure 8.35** shows how. Remember that these joints must bear the weight of the antenna and the feed line. After you solder the wire, reinstall the insulators at the antenna ends, past the solder connections.

If the SWR is very high, you may have a problem that

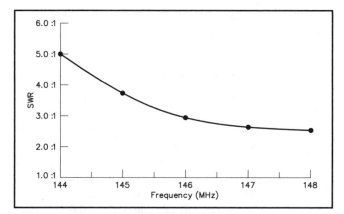

Figure 8.33 — **This SWR and frequency graph indicates that the antenna is too short. Lengthen the antenna by a small amount (probably ¼ to ½ inch at a time for this 2-meter antenna) and check the SWR again until the antenna is tuned for the lowest SWR at your desired operating frequency.**

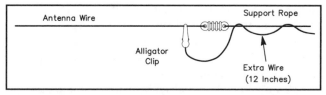

Figure 8.34 — **If your antenna is too short, attach an extra length of wire to each end with an alligator clip. Then shorten the extra length a little at a time until you get the correct length for the antenna. Finally, extend the length inside the insulators with a soldered connection. (See Figure 8.35.)**

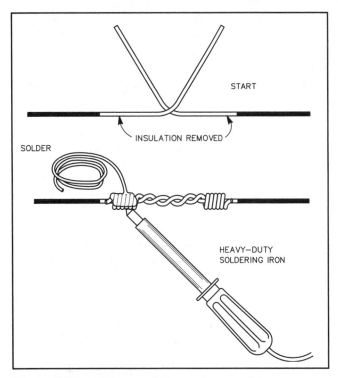

Figure 8.35 — When splicing antenna wire, remember that the connection must be strong mechanically and good electrically.

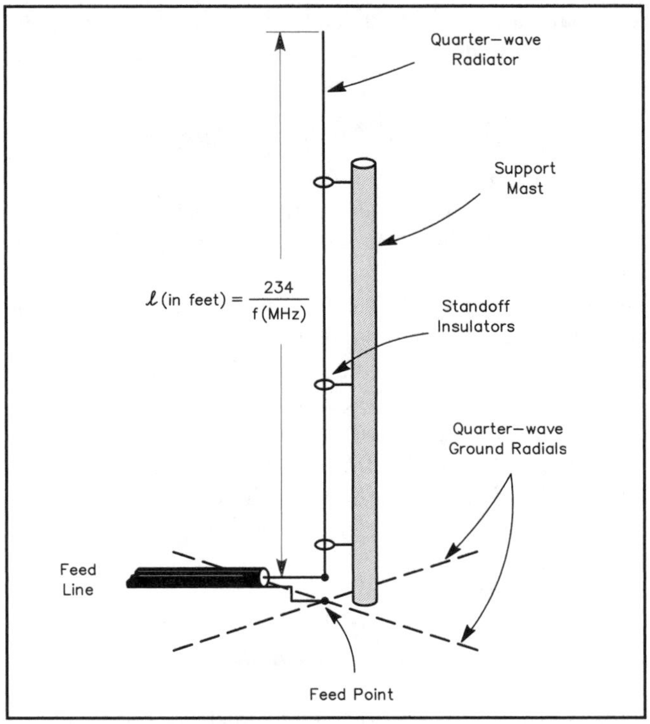

Figure 8.36 — The quarter-wave vertical antenna has a center radiator and four or more radials spread out from the base. These radials form a ground plane.

$$\ell \text{ (in feet)} = \frac{234}{f \text{ (MHz)}}$$

can't be cured by simple tuning. A very high SWR may mean that your feed line is open or shorted. Perhaps a connection isn't making good electrical contact. It could also be that your antenna is touching metal. A metal mast, the rain gutter on your house or some other conductor would add considerable length to the antenna. If the SWR is very high, check all connections and feed lines, and be sure the antenna clears surrounding objects.

Now you have enough information to construct, install and adjust your dipole antenna. You'll normally need a separate dipole antenna for each band on which you expect to operate.

Multiband Dipole Operation

The single-band dipole is fine if you operate on only one band. If you want to operate on more than one band, however, you could build and install a dipole for each band. What if you don't have supports for all these dipoles? Or what if you don't want to spend the money for extra coaxial cable? A multiband dipole will enable you to operate on more than one band with a single feed line.

A single-band dipole can be converted into a *multiband antenna* without too much difficulty. All you need to do is connect two additional ¼-λ wires for each additional band you want to use. Each added wire connects to the same feed line as the original dipole. The result is a single antenna system, fed with a single coaxial cable that

works on several different bands without adjustment. There is one potential problem with this antenna, though. The antenna will radiate signals on two or more bands simultaneously, so make sure your transmitter is adjusted properly. A poorly adjusted transmitter may produce harmonics of the desired output. If so, energy from your transmitter may show up on more than one band. The FCC takes a dim view of such operation!

[Now turn to Chapter 11 and study questions T8D03, T8D04, T8D15 and T8D20. Review this section if you have difficulty with any of these questions.]

The Quarter-Wavelength Vertical Antenna

The **quarter-wavelength vertical antenna** is easy to build. This helps make this type of antenna very popular. It requires only one element and one support, and can be very effective. On the HF bands (80-10 meters) it is often used for DX work. Vertical antennas send radio energy equally well in all compass directions. This is why we sometimes call them *nondirectional antennas* or *omnidirectional antennas*. They also tend to concentrate the signals toward the horizon. Vertical antennas do not generally radiate strong signals straight up, like horizontal dipoles close to the ground do.

Because they concentrate signals toward the horizon, they have a *low-angle radiation pattern*. This gives vertical antennas **gain** as compared to a dipole. Gain always refers to a comparison with some another antenna. A dipole is one common comparison antenna for stating antenna gain.

Figure 8.36 shows a simple vertical antenna you can make. This **vertical antenna** has a radiator that is ¼-λ long. Use **Equation 8.5** to find the approximate length for the radiator. The frequency is given in megahertz and the length is in feet or inches in this equation.

$$\text{Length(in feet)} = \frac{234}{f \text{ (in MHz)}} \qquad \text{(Equation 8.5)}$$

$$\text{Length (in inches)} = \frac{2808}{f(\text{MHz})} \qquad \text{(Equation 8.5A)}$$

If you compare **Equation 8.5** with Equation 8.4 you will notice that the 234 is half of the 468 value used in Equation 8.4. This should make sense when you realize that ¼-λ is ½ the length of a ½-λ dipole. Equation 8.5 gives us the approximate length for the radiator and each ground radial of a ¼-λ vertical. This equation is most accurate for frequencies up to around 30 MHz. One reason for this frequency limitation is because the ratio of wavelength to element diameter is larger at VHF and higher frequencies. Another reason is because of effects commonly known as *end effects*. So the values given below for the VHF and UHF bands are only for comparison purposes. These lengths might serve as a starting point for building antennas for 2 meters, 1.25 meters, 70 cm or 23 cm, but they will probably be too long.

Wavelength	Frequency	Length
80 meters	3.700 MHz	63.24 feet
40 meters	7.125 MHz	32.8 feet
15 meters	21.125 MHz	11.1 feet
10 meters	28.150 MHz	8.3 feet
10 meters	28.4 MHz	8.2 feet
6 meters	52.5 MHz	4.5 feet
2 meters	146.0 MHz	1.6 feet (19.25 inches)
1.25 meters	223.0 MHz	1.05 feet (12.6 inches)
70 cm	440.0 MHz	0.53 feet (6.4 inches)
23 cm	1282.5 MHz	0.18 feet (2.2 inches)

As with ½-λ dipoles, the resonant frequency of a ¼-λ vertical decreases as the length increases. Shorter antennas have higher resonant frequencies, but you can lower the resonant frequency by *loading* the antenna with a **loading coil**. Loading coils are typically placed either at the base of a vertical for easy access and pruning, or about halfway up the antenna, where the efficiency of the antenna is improved but access for fine-tuning is more difficult. A loading coil can be used to reduce the physical length of an antenna without changing its resonant frequency.

The ¼-λ vertical also has radials. For operation on 80 through 10 meters, the vertical may be at ground level and the radials placed on the ground. The key to successful operation with a ground-mounted vertical antenna is a good radial system. The best radial system uses *many* ground radials. Lay them out like the spokes of a wheel, with the

vertical at the center. Some hams have buried ground radial systems containing over 100 individual wires.

Ideally, these wires would be ¼-λ long or more at the lowest operating frequency. With such a system, earth or ground losses will be negligible. When the antenna is mounted at ground level, radial length is not very critical, however. Studies show that with fewer radials you can use shorter lengths, but with a corresponding loss in antenna efficiency.[1,2] Some of your transmitter power does no more than warm the earth beneath your antenna. With 24 radials, there is no point in making them longer than about ⅛ λ. With 16 radials, a length greater than 0.1 λ is unwarranted. Four radials should be considered an absolute minimum. Don't put the radials more than about an inch below the ground surface.

Compared with 120 radials of 0.4 λ, antenna efficiency with 24 radials is roughly 63%. For 16 radials, the efficiency is roughly 50%. So it pays to put in as many radials as you can.

If you place the vertical above ground, you reduce earth losses drastically. Here, the wires should be cut to ¼ λ for the band you plan to use. Above ground, you need only a few radials — two to five. If you install a multiband vertical antenna above ground, perhaps on a roof, use separate ground radials for each band you plan to use. These lengths are more critical than for a ground-mounted vertical. You can also mount a vertical on a pipe driven into the ground, on a chimney or on a tower.

The radials at the bottom of a vertical antenna mounted above ground form a surface that acts like the ground under the antenna. These antennas are sometimes called *ground-plane antennas*.

Ground-plane antennas are popular mobile antennas because the car body can serve as the ground plane. You can place a magnetic-base whip antenna on the roof of your car, for example. This type of antenna is often used on the VHF and UHF bands for FM voice communication. Because it is a vertical antenna, it sends radio energy out equally well in all compass directions.

For HF operation you need low radiation angles — for DX work up to about 30° above the horizon. A horizontally polarized antenna can deliver low-angle radiation, provided that it is mounted high (in terms of wavelength) above ground. For example, a 15-meter dipole mounted 50 feet in the air will perform well for long-distance (DX) contacts. This antenna is 1 λ high on 21.1 MHz.

Things become a lot more challenging on the lower-frequency HF bands. On 80 meters, 1 λ is 280 feet high! Many DXers use vertically polarized antennas on the 80- and 40-meter bands because these can generate sig-

[1] J. O. Stanley, "Optimum Ground Systems for Vertical Antennas," *QST*, December 1976, pp 14-15.
[2] B. Edward, "Radial Systems for Ground-Mounted Vertical Antennas," *QST*, June 1985, pp 28-30.

nals at low elevation angles without having to raise the base of the antenna high off ground.

At VHF and UHF, however, it pays to get your antenna up high. This is true whether you use a vertically polarized omnidirectional antenna or a horizontally polarized dipole. At these frequencies you want the antenna higher than even distant obstructions, such as mountains or tall buildings.

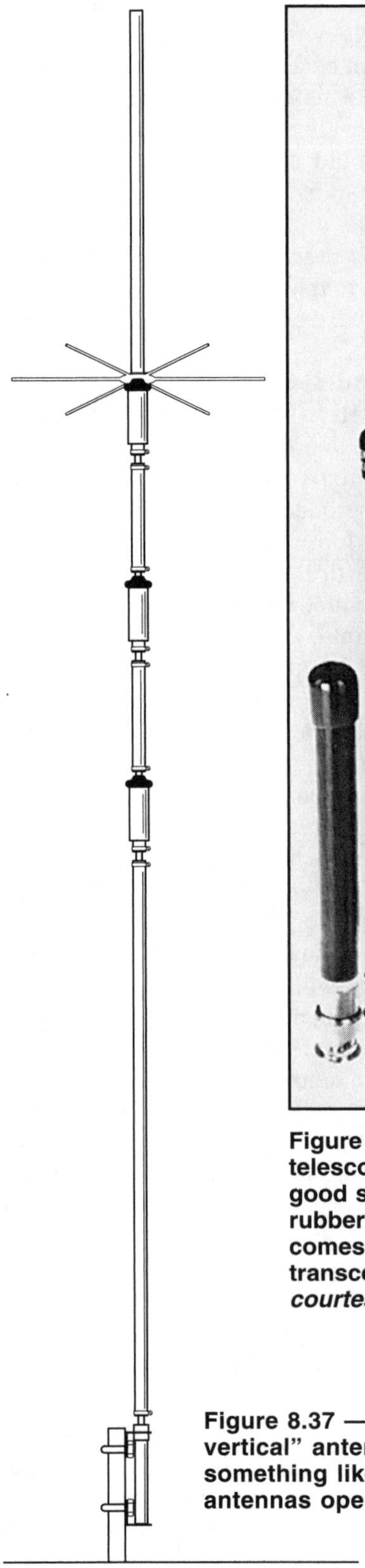

Most vertical antennas used at lower frequencies are ¼ λ long. For VHF and UHF, antennas are physically short enough that longer verticals may be used. A popular mobile antenna is a ⅝-λ vertical, often called a "five-eighths whip." This antenna is popular because it may concentrate more of the radio energy toward the horizon than a ¼-λ vertical. Mounted on the roof of a car, a ⅝-λ vertical may provide more gain than a ¼-λ vertical. Simply stated, gain means a concentration of transmitter power in some direction. A ⅝-λ vertical concentrates the power toward the horizon. Naturally, this is the most useful direction, unless you want to talk to airplanes or satellites. At 222 MHz, a ⅝-λ whip is only 28½ inches long.

Don't use any of the equations in this chapter to calculate the length of a ⅝-λ whip. The equations won't give the correct answer because of a variety of antenna factors. In addition, there is an impedance-matching device needed at the antenna feed point, where the feed line attaches to the antenna itself. See *The ARRL Antenna Book* for complete construction details.

A ⅝-λ vertical is great for mobile operation because it is omnidirectional. That means it radiates a signal equally well in all compass directions. This is especially useful for mobile operation because you change direction often. One minute you may be driving toward the repeater, and the next minute you may be driving away from it.

Vertical antennas that are ½-λ long can be used without ground radials. This may sometimes be a definite advantage because it takes less wire and occupies less horizontal space. To find the size of a ½-λ vertical antenna, double the lengths given above in the table of ¼-λ verticals.

Commercially made vertical antennas need a coax feed line, usually with a PL-259 connector. Just as with the dipole antenna, you can use RG-8, RG-11 or RG-58 coax. The instructions that accompany the antenna should provide details for attaching both the feed line and the ground radials.

Some manufacturers offer *trap verticals*. **Traps** are tuned circuits that change the antenna electrical length. They allow the antenna to work on several bands, making it a multiband antenna. Some manufacturers even offer 20- to 30-foot-high vertical antennas that cover all HF bands. **Figure 8.37** shows one such antenna.

Antennas for Hand-Held Transceivers

When you buy a new VHF hand-held transceiver, it will have a flexible rubber antenna commonly called a "**rubber duck**." This antenna is inexpensive, small, lightweight and difficult to break. On the other hand, it has some disadvantages: It is a compromise design that is inefficient and thus does not perform as well as larger antennas. A full-size antenna will always work better than a rubber duck antenna, and an outdoor antenna in the clear will always work better than an indoor antenna (particularly an antenna inside a car). Two

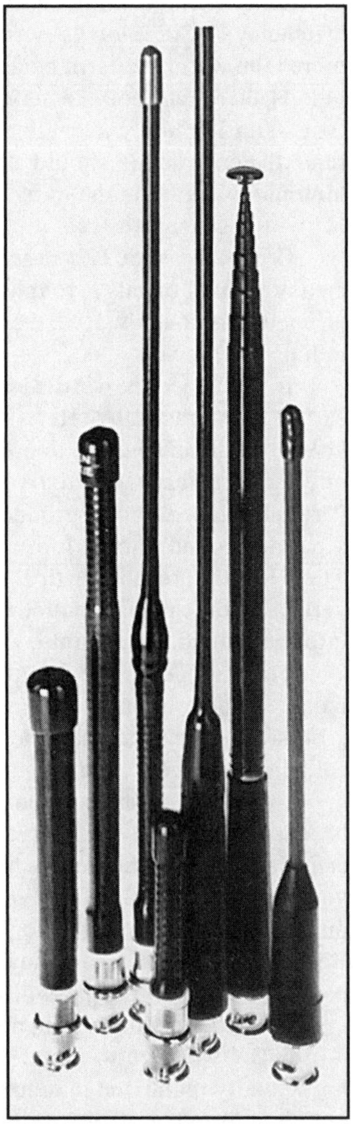

Figure 8.38 — The ¼-λ telescoping antenna is a good substitute for the rubber flex antenna that comes with most hand-held transceivers. (Photo courtesy Larsen Electronics)

Figure 8.37 — Commercial "trap vertical" antennas generally look something like this. These antennas operate on several bands.

better-performing antennas are the ¼ and ⁵/₈-λ telescoping types (see **Figure 8.38**).

Vertical Antennas for 146, 222 and 440 MHz

For FM and packet radio operation with nearby stations, the ease of construction and low cost of a ¼-λ vertical make it an ideal choice. Three different types of construction are shown in **Figures 8.39** through **8.41**. The choice of construction method depends on the materials available and the desired style of antenna mounting.

The 146-MHz model shown in Figure 8.39 uses a flat piece of sheet aluminum, to which radials are connected with machine screws. A 45° bend is made in each of the radials. This bend can be made with an ordinary bench vise. An SO-239 chassis connector is mounted at the center of the aluminum plate with the threaded part of the connector facing down. The vertical portion of the antenna is made of #12 copper wire soldered directly to the center pin of the SO-239 connector.

The 222-MHz version in Figure 8.40 uses a slightly differ-

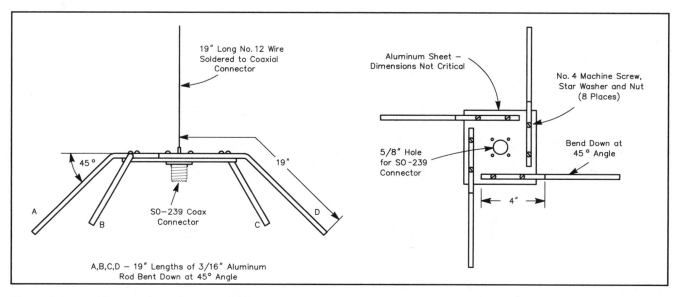

Figure 8.39 — These drawings show the dimensions for a 146-MHz ground-plane antenna. The radials are bent down at a 45° angle.

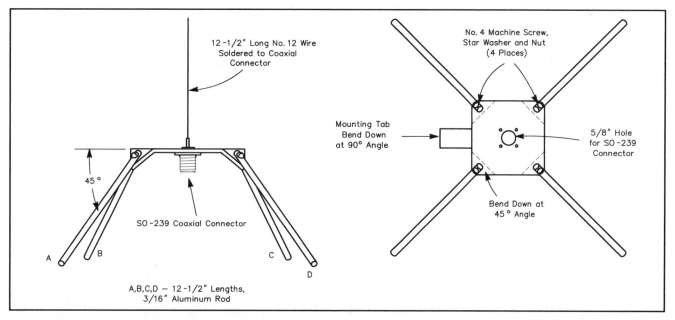

Figure 8.40 — Dimensional information for a 222-MHz ground-plane antenna. Lengths for A, B, C and D are the total distances measured from the center of the SO-239 connector. The corners of the aluminum plate are bent down at a 45° angle rather than bending the aluminum rod as in the 146-MHz model. Either method is suitable for these antennas.

ent technique for mounting and sloping the radials. In this case the corners of the aluminum plate are bent down at a 45° angle with respect to the remainder of the plate. The four radials are held to the plate with machine screws, lock washers and nuts. A mounting tab is included in the design of this antenna as part of the aluminum base. A compression type of hose clamp could be used to secure the antenna to a mast. As with the 146-MHz

version, the vertical portion of the antenna is soldered directly to the SO-239 connector.

A very simple method of construction, shown in Figure 8.41 and **Figure 8.42**, requires nothing more than an SO-239 connector and some 4-40 hardware. A small loop formed at the inside end of each radial is used to attach the radial directly to the mounting holes of the coaxial connector. After the radial is fastened to the SO-239 with no. 4-40 hardware, a large soldering iron or propane torch is used to solder the radial and the mounting hardware to the coaxial connector. The radials are bent to a 45° angle and the vertical portion is soldered to the center pin to complete the antenna. You can mount the antenna by passing the feed line through a mast of ¾-inch ID plastic or aluminum tubing. Use a compression hose clamp to secure the PL-259 connector, attached to the feed line, in the end of the mast. Dimensions for the

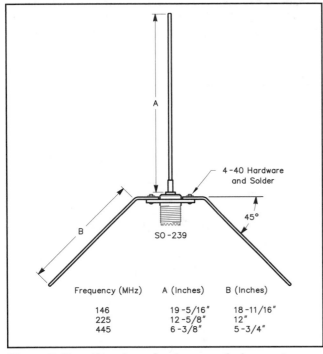

Frequency (MHz)	A (Inches)	B (Inches)
146	19-5/16"	18-11/16"
225	12-5/8"	12"
445	6-3/8"	5-3/4"

Figure 8.41 — Here is a simple ground-plane antenna for the 146, 222 and 440-MHz bands. The vertical element and radials are ³/₃₂ or ¹/₁₆-in. brass welding rod. Although ³/₃₂-in. rod is preferred for the 146-MHz antenna, #10 or #12 copper wire can also be used.

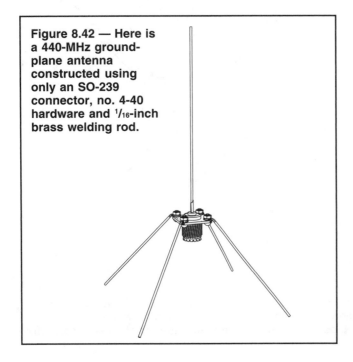

Figure 8.42 — Here is a 440-MHz ground-plane antenna constructed using only an SO-239 connector, no. 4-40 hardware and ¹/₁₆-inch brass welding rod.

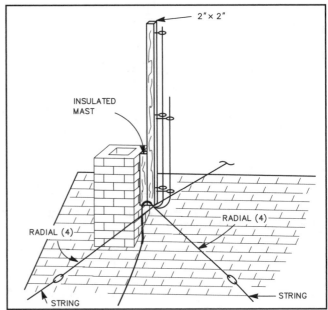

Figure 8.43 — This is a simple vertical antenna design. The text gives the dimensions to build an antenna for use on 10 and 15 meters.

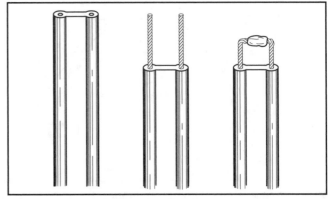

Figure 8.44 — For each length of twin lead, strip back the insulation from both ends, connect the two wires, and solder them.

146, 222, and 440-MHz bands are given in Figure 8.41.

If these antennas are to be mounted outside it is wise to apply a small amount of RTV sealant or similar material around the areas of the center pin of the connector to waterproof the assembly, preventing the entry of water into the connector and coax line.

A Simple 10 and 15 Meter Vertical

Figure 8.43 shows a simple, inexpensive vertical antenna for 10 and 15 meters. The antenna requires very little space and it's great for working DX. A few materials make up the entire antenna.

12-foot piece of clean 2 × 2 pine from the local lumberyard
20 feet of flat four-wire rotator control cable
20 feet of regular TV twin lead
Several TV standoff insulators

Cut the twin lead into lengths of 11 feet 3 inches, and 8 feet 6 inches. Remove 1 inch of insulation from both wires at both ends on each twin-lead length. Wrap the two wires together securely at each end, as **Figure 8.44** shows, and solder. Cover one end of each length of twin lead with electrical tape.

Mount the TV standoff insulators at regular intervals on opposite sides of the 2 × 2. These will support the two pieces of twin lead. Separate the control cable into two pieces of two-conductor cable. Do this by slitting the cable a small amount at one end, then pulling the two pieces apart like a zipper.

Carefully cut the rotator cable as **Figure 8.45** shows. Separate the pieces between the center cuts to make four

identical sets of two-conductor cable. These make up the radials for the antenna system. Strip about 1 inch of insulation from each wire on the evenly cut end. The unevenly cut ends will be away from the antenna.

Attach a suitable length of RG-58 coaxial cable to the antenna. Connect the coax center conductor to the two wires on the 2 × 2. Then attach the cable braid to all the radial ends soldered together. **Figure 8.46** shows the antenna construction. Make all the connections waterproof.

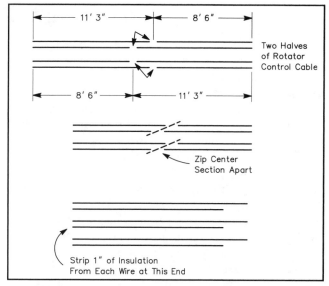

Figure 8.45 — Cut some flat TV rotator-control cable to make the radials.

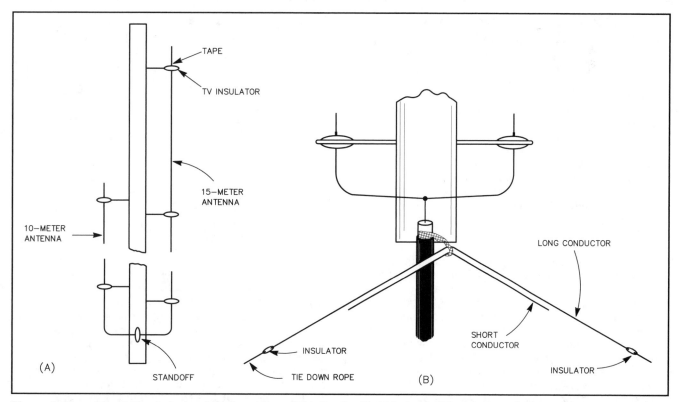

Figure 8.46 — Attach the twin lead to the sides of the 2 × 2 with TV standoff insulators. A illustrates how to do this. Then connect the feed line to both twin-lead lengths at the base, as shown in Part B.

Now install the 2 × 2. You can do this in different ways. You could clamp it with U bolts to a TV mast, or hang it with a hook over a high branch. Or you might mount it on your house, at the side, near the roof peak. Mount the antenna as high as possible. Hang the radials at about a 45° angle away from the antenna base. For example, you could clamp the wood to your chimney with TV chimney-mount hardware. Let the radials follow the roof slope. Tie them off at the four corners. Unless you are surrounded by buildings or high hills, this antenna should perform well on 10 and 15 meters.

[Now turn to Chapter 11 and study questions numbered T8D01, T8D02, T8D05, T8D06, and T8D21. Review this section if you have difficulty with any of these questions.]

Antenna Polarization

For VHF and UHF base-station operation, most amateurs use a vertical antenna or a beam antenna. For VHF and UHF FM and repeater operation, almost everyone uses vertical **polarization**.

Polarization refers to the electrical-field characteristic of a radio wave. You can think of it as how the antenna is positioned. An antenna that is parallel to the Earth's surface (like a dipole antenna) produces horizontally polarized radio waves. One that is perpendicular (at a 90° angle) to the earth's surface, such as a ¼-λ vertical, produces vertically polarized waves.

Polarization is most important when installing antennas for VHF or UHF. Propagation at these frequencies is mostly line of sight. The polarization of a terrestrial (on the ground, as opposed to out in space) VHF or UHF signal does not change from transmitting antenna to receiving antenna.

Best signal reception occurs when both transmitting and receiving stations use the same polarization. The polarization of an HF signal may change randomly many times as it passes through the ionosphere. Antenna polarization at HF is not important for skywave communications.

A beam antenna is impractical for VHF and UHF FM mobile operation. Most hams use a vertical of some kind. Mobile antennas are available in several varieties. Most mount on the automobile roof or trunk lid, but some even mount on a glass window.

Most VHF/UHF FM and data communications is done with vertically polarized antennas. Vertically polarized antennas are more popular for repeaters and other VHF/UHF FM communications, because the antennas used on cars are almost always verticals. Vertical antennas are also more useful for repeaters and home-station

---

Antenna Polarization

The signal sent from an amateur station depends on the antenna type and how it is oriented. A horizontal antenna, parallel to the earth's surface (like a dipole), will produce a *horizontally polarized signal*. A Yagi antenna with horizontal elements will also produce a horizontally polarized signal. See Part A in the drawing.

A vertical antenna (perpendicular to the earth's surface) will produce a *vertically polarized signal*. A Yagi with vertical elements also produces vertical polarization. See Part B in the drawing.

Most communications on the HF bands (80 through 10 meters) use horizontal polarization. Polarization on the HF bands is not critical, however. As a signal travels through the ionosphere, its polarization can change.

On the VHF/UHF bands, most FM communications use vertical polarization. Here, the polarization is important. The signals retain their polarization from transmitter to receiver. If you use a horizontal antenna, you will have difficulty working through a repeater with a vertical antenna.

Since the antennas on orbiting satellites are normally *circularly polarized*, earth-based antennas that are used for satellite communications should also be circularly polarized. One type of circularly polarized antenna is the crossed-Yagi, shown in Part C in the drawing.

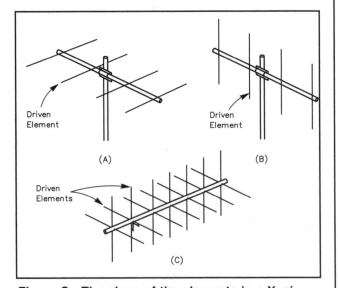

Figure C—The plane of the elements in a Yagi antenna determines the transmitted-signal polarization. If the elements are horizontal, as shown at A, the signal will have horizontal polarization. Vertical mounting, shown at B, produces a vertically polarized wave. An antenna with elements that are both horizontal and vertical, shown at C, produce signals that are circularly polarized.

use on these bands because they are not directional.

For long-distance FM operating, a vertically polarized beam is the best antenna. Data communication on the VHF/UHF bands is also mostly done with vertically polarized antennas. Most people operating VHF/UHF CW or SSB (the so-called "weak-signal" modes), however, use horizontally polarized antennas.

If you plan to do both VHF weak-signal and FM repeater work, you'll probably need separate antennas for each. This is because at VHF and UHF, signal strength suffers greatly if your antenna has different polarization than the station you're trying to work.

Yagi beam antennas can have either horizontal or vertical polarization. If the antenna elements are parallel to the earth, or horizontal, the antenna will produce horizontally polarized waves.

If the Yagi elements are turned perpendicular to the earth, the antenna will produce vertically polarized waves. See the Antenna Polarization Sidebar. The antenna at A produces horizontally polarized waves and the one at B produces vertically polarized waves. Notice that the boom is horizontal in both cases.

The quarter-wavelength vertical antenna is a popular HF antenna because it provides low-angle radiation when a beam or dipole cannot be placed far enough above ground. Low-angle radiation refers to signals that travel closer to the horizon, rather than signals that are high above the horizon. Low-angle radiation is usually better when you are trying to contact distant stations. Vertical antennas of any length radiate vertically polarized waves.

Most man-made noise tends to be vertically polarized, however. Thus, a horizontally polarized antenna will receive less noise of this type than will a vertical antenna.

Circular Polarization

There is one more type of polarization: **circular**. Signals from orbiting satellites are circularly polarized, so the ground-based antennas that receive these signals should also be circularly polarized. Part C of the diagram in the Antenna Polarization Sidebar shows an example of a circularly polarized antenna.

[Now turn to Chapter 11 and study questions T8D13, T8D14, T8D16 through T8D18. Review this section if you have any difficulty answering these questions.]

Antenna Location

Once you have assembled your dipole or vertical antenna, find a good place to put it. *Never* put your antenna or feed line under—or over the top of—electrical power lines. *Never* place a vertical antenna where it could fall against the electrical power lines. If power lines ever come into contact with your antenna, you could be electrocuted. Avoid running your antenna parallel to power lines that come close to your station. Otherwise you may receive unwanted electrical noise. Sometimes power-line noise can cover up all but the strongest signals your receiver hears. You'll also want to avoid running your antenna too close to metal objects. These could be rain gutters, metal beams, metal siding, or even electrical wiring in the attic of your house. Metal objects tend to shield your antenna, reducing its capability.

The key to good dipole operation is height. How high? One wavelength (1 λ) above ground is good, and this ranges from about 35 feet on 10 meters to about 240 feet on 80 meters. On the 2-meter band, one wavelength is only about 7 feet. You should try to install the antenna higher, to get it clear of buildings and trees. Of course very few people can get their antennas 240 feet in the air, so 40 to 60 feet is a good average height for an 80-meter dipole. Don't despair if you can get your antenna up only 20 feet or so, though. Low antennas can work well. Generally, the higher above ground and surrounding objects you can get your antenna, the greater the success you'll have. You'll find this to be true even if you can get only part of your antenna up high.

Normally you will support the dipole at both ends. The supports can be trees, buildings, poles or anything else high enough. Sometimes, however, there is just no way you can put your dipole high in the air at both ends. If you're faced with this problem, you have two reasonably good alternatives. You can support your dipole in the middle or at one end.

If you choose to support the antenna in the middle, both ends will droop toward the ground. This antenna, known as an *inverted-V dipole*, works best when the angle between the wires is greater than 90°. See **Figure 8.47B**. If you use an inverted-V dipole, make sure the ends are high enough that no one can touch them. When you transmit, the high voltages present at the ends of a dipole can cause an *RF burn*. Yes, radio energy can burn your skin.

If you support your antenna at only one end, you'll have what is known as a *sloper*. This antenna also works well. As with the inverted-V dipole, be sure the low end is high enough to prevent anyone from touching it.

If you don't have the room to install a dipole in the standard form, don't be afraid to experiment a little. You can get away with bending the ends to fit your property, or even making a horizontal V-shaped antenna. Many hams have enjoyed countless hours of successful operating with antennas bent in a variety of shapes and angles.

On the 6 and 2-meter bands, dipoles for FM or packet operation work much better if they are installed vertically. Now you need only one support. The coax should come away from the antenna at a right angle for as far as

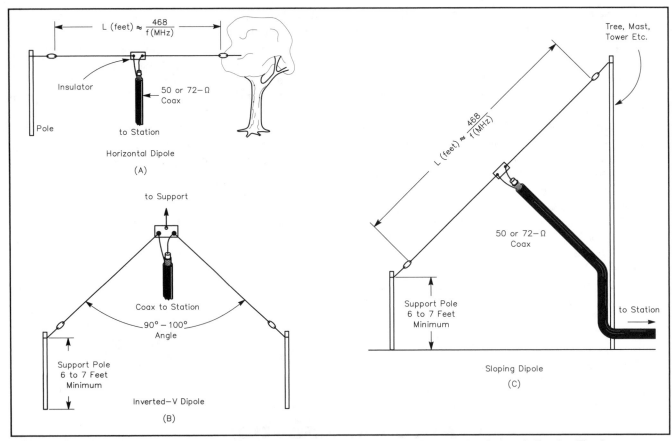

$$L \text{ (feet)} \approx \frac{468}{f \text{ (MHz)}}$$

Insulator

50 or 72–Ω Coax

Pole

to Station

Horizontal Dipole

(A)

to Support

Coax to Station

90° – 100° Angle

Support Pole 6 to 7 Feet Minimum

Inverted–V Dipole

(B)

Tree, Mast, Tower Etc.

$$L \text{ (feet)} \approx \frac{468}{f \text{ (MHz)}}$$

50 or 72–Ω Coax

Support Pole 6 to 7 Feet Minimum

to Station

Sloping Dipole

(C)

Figure 8.47 — These are simple but effective wire antennas. Part A shows a horizontal dipole. The legs can be drooped to form an inverted-V dipole, as at Part B. Part C illustrates a sloping dipole (sloper). The feed line should come away from the sloper at a 90° angle for best results. If the supporting mast is metal, the antenna will have some directivity in the direction of the slope.

possible, so it doesn't interfere with the radiation from the antenna. Dipoles are not often used on frequencies above the 2-meter band. Beam antennas are physically small and easy to build for the UHF bands.

Antenna Installation

After you've built your antenna and chosen its location, how do you get it up into the air? There are many schools of thought on putting up antennas. Can you support at least one end of your antenna on a mast, tower, building or in an easily climbed tree? If so, you have solved some of your problems. Unfortunately, this is not always the case. Hams use several methods to get antenna support ropes into trees. Most methods involve a weight attached to a rope or line. You might be able to tie a rope around a rock and throw it over the intended support. This method works for low antennas. Even a major league pitcher, however, would have trouble getting an antenna much higher than 40 feet with this method.

A better method is to use a bow and arrow, a fishing rod or even a slingshot to launch the weight and rope. See **Figures 8.48** and **8.49**. You'll find that strong, lightweight fishing line is the best line to attach to the weight. (Lead fishing weights are a good choice.) Regular rope is too

Figure 8.48 — There are many ways to get an antenna support rope into a tree. These hams use a bow and arrow to shoot a lightweight fishing line over the desired branch. Then they attach the support rope to the fishing line and pull it up into the tree.

heavy to shoot any great distance. When you have successfully cleared the supporting tree, remove the weight. Then tie the support rope to the fishing line and reel it in.

If your first attempt doesn't go over the limb you were hoping for, try again. Don't just reel in the line, however. Let the weight down to the ground first and take it off the line. Then you can reel the line in without getting the weight tangled in the branches.

You can put antenna supports in trees 120 feet and higher with this method. As with any type of marksmanship, make sure all is clear downrange before shooting. Your neighbors will not appreciate stray arrows, sinkers or rocks falling in their yards! Be sure the line is strong enough to withstand the shock of shooting the weight. Always check the bow and arrow or slingshot to ensure they are in good working order.

When your support ropes are in place, attach them to the ends of the dipole and haul it up. Pull the dipole reasonably tight, but not so tight that it is under a lot of strain. Tie the ends off so they are out of reach of passersby. Be sure to leave enough rope so you can let the dipole down temporarily if necessary. Dacron rope is resistant to the sun's ultraviolet radiation and other weather effects, and is a good choice for an antenna-support rope. Nylon is strong, but slowly deteriorates in sunlight. Inexpensive polypropylene rope is a poor choice because it disintegrates rapidly when exposed to sunlight and weather.

Just one more step and your antenna installation is complete. After routing the coaxial cable to your station, cut it to length and install the proper connector for your rig. Usually this connector will be a PL-259, sometimes called a UHF connector. **Figure 8.50** shows how to attach one of these fittings to RG-8 or RG-11 cable. Follow the step-by-step instructions exactly as illustrated and you should have no trouble. Be sure to place the coupling ring on the cable *before* you install the connector body! If you are using RG-58 or RG-59 cable, use an adapter to fit the cable to the connector. **Figure 8.51** illustrates the steps for installing the connector with adapter. The PL-259 is standard on most rigs. If you require another kind of connector, consult your radio instruction manual or *The ARRL*

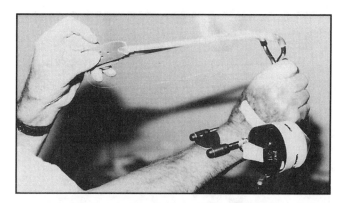

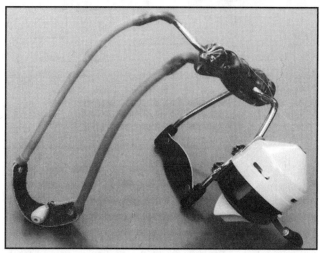

Figure 8.49 — Here is another method for getting an antenna support into a tree. Small hose clamps attach a casting reel to the wrist bracket of a slingshot. Monofilament fishing line attached to a 1-ounce sinker is easily shot over almost any tree. Remove the sinker and rewind the line for repeated shots. When you find a suitable path through the tree, use the fishing line to pull a heavier line over the tree.

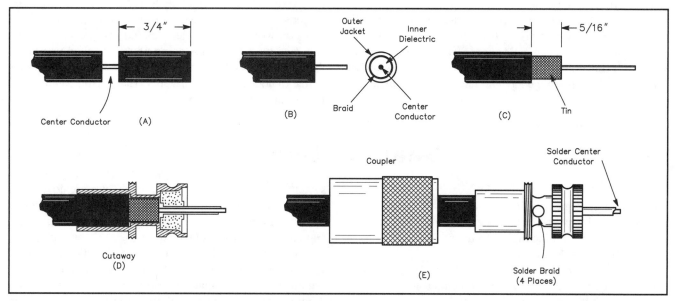

Figure 8.50 — The PL-259 or UHF connector is almost universal for amateur HF work. It is also popular for equipment operating in the VHF range. Steps A through E illustrate how to install the connector properly. Despite its name, the UHF connector is rarely used on frequencies above 225 MHz.

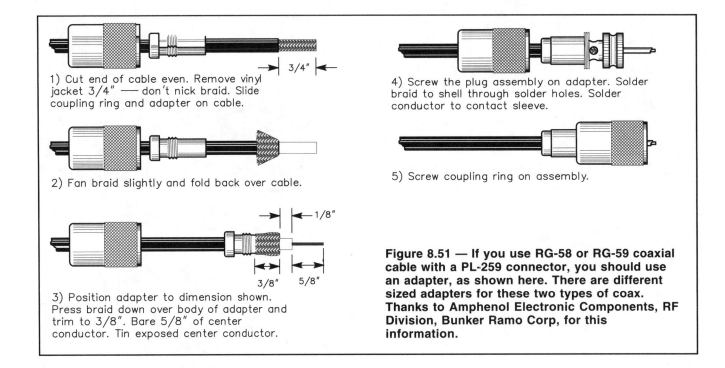

1) Cut end of cable even. Remove vinyl jacket 3/4" — don't nick braid. Slide coupling ring and adapter on cable.

2) Fan braid slightly and fold back over cable.

3) Position adapter to dimension shown. Press braid down over body of adapter and trim to 3/8". Bare 5/8" of center conductor. Tin exposed center conductor.

4) Screw the plug assembly on adapter. Solder braid to shell through solder holes. Solder conductor to contact sleeve.

5) Screw coupling ring on assembly.

Figure 8.51 — If you use RG-58 or RG-59 coaxial cable with a PL-259 connector, you should use an adapter, as shown here. There are different sized adapters for these two types of coax. Thanks to Amphenol Electronic Components, RF Division, Bunker Ramo Corp, for this information.

Handbook for installation information.

Antenna work sometimes requires that someone climb up on a tower, into a tree or onto the roof. Never work alone! Work slowly, thinking out each move before you make it. The person on the ladder, tower, tree or roof-top should always wear a safety belt, and keep it securely anchored. Before each use, inspect the belt carefully for damage such as cuts or worn areas. If your safety belt is made of leather, be sure it is not dried and cracked or brittle. Such an old belt could break unexpectedly. The belt will make it much easier to work on the antenna and will also prevent an accidental fall. A hard hat and safety glasses are also important safety equipment.

Before climbing a tower, inspect the guy lines and all hardware. Be sure there is no broken or worn hardware, loose bolts or frayed cable. Be sure to have a helper on the ground. Inspect the tower from the ground and think about how you will step around any antennas or other obstacles attached to the tower.

Never try to climb a tower carrying tools or antenna components in your hands. Carry what you can with a tool belt, including a long rope leading back to the ground. Then use the rope to pull other needed objects up to your workplace after securing your safety belt. It is helpful (and safe) to tie strings or lightweight ropes to all tools. You can save much time in retrieving dropped tools if you tie them to the tower. This also reduces the chances of injuring a helper on the ground.

Helpers on the ground should never stand directly under the work being done. All ground helpers should wear hard hats and safety glasses for protection. Even a small tool can make quite a dent if it falls from 50 or 60 feet. A ground helper should always observe the tower work carefully. Have you ever wondered why electric utility crews seem to have someone on the ground "doing nothing"? Now you know that for safety's sake, a ground observer with no other duties is free to notice potential hazards. That person could save a life by shouting a warning.

Beam Antennas

Yagis

Although generally impractical on 80 meters, and very large and expensive on 40 meters, *directional antennas* often see use on the higher frequency bands, such as 15 and 10 meters. Most operators use some type of directional antenna on the VHF and UHF bands. The most common directional antenna that amateurs use is the **Yagi antenna**, but there are other types, too.

Generally called **beams**, these directional antennas have two important advantages over dipole and vertical

systems. First, a beam antenna concentrates most of its transmitted signal in one compass direction. The antenna provides **gain** or *directivity* in the direction it is pointed. Gain makes your signal sound stronger to other operators, and their signals sound stronger to you, when compared with non-directional antennas. Suppose one antenna has a gain of 3 dB compared to another antenna, such as a dipole. This antenna will double the effective radiated power going in the desired direction.

The second important advantage is that the antenna

Figure 8.52 — Yagi beams at W1AW. A single beam sits atop the tower at left. Three stacked beams adorn the taller tower at the right.

reduces the strength of signals coming from directions other than where you point it. This increases your operating enjoyment by reducing the interference from stations in other directions.

A graph of an antenna's gain and directivity shows its *radiation pattern*. **Figure 8.52** shows some of the Yagi beams at W1AW, the station located at ARRL Headquarters in Newington, Connecticut. **Figure 8.53** shows the radiation pattern of a typical Yagi beam.

A Yagi beam antenna has several elements attached to a central *boom*, as **Figure 8.54** shows. The elements are parallel to each other and are placed in a straight line along the boom. Although several factors affect the amount of gain of a Yagi antenna, *boom length* has the largest effect: The longer the boom, the higher the gain.

The feed line connects to only one element. We call this element the **driven element**. On a 3-element Yagi like the one shown in Figure 8.54, the driven element is in the middle. The element at the front of the antenna (toward the favored direction) is a **director**. Behind the driven element is the **reflector** element. The driven element is about ½ λ long at the antenna design frequency. The director is a bit shorter than ½ λ, and the reflector a bit longer.

Yagi beams can have more than three elements. Seldom is there more than one reflector. Instead, the added

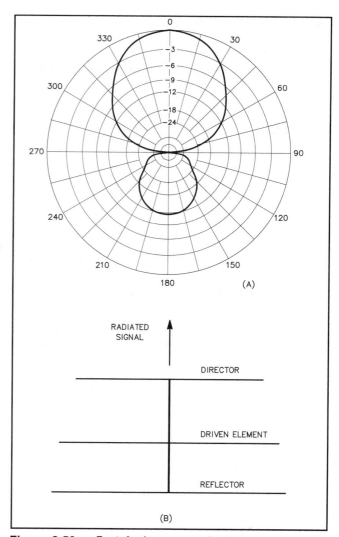

Figure 8.53 — Part A shows a typical radiation pattern for a Yagi beam antenna. Part B shows the direction the beam is pointing. The transmitted signal is stronger in the forward direction than in others.

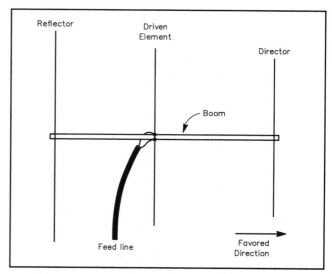

Figure 8.54 — A three-element Yagi antenna has a director, a driven element and a reflector. A boom supports the elements.

elements are directors. A 4-element Yagi has a reflector, a driven element and two directors. Directors and reflectors are called **parasitic elements**, since they are not fed directly. Beams are sometimes called **parasitic beam antennas.**

The direction of maximum radiation from a parasitic beam antenna is from the reflector through the driven element to the director. The term *major lobe* refers to the region of maximum radiation from a directional antenna. The major lobe is also sometimes referred to as the *main lobe*. Communication in different directions may be achieved by rotating the array in the *azimuthal, or horizontal, plane*, to point it in different compass directions.

Because beams are directional, you'll need something to turn them. A single-band beam for 6 or 2 meters can be mounted in the same manner as a TV antenna. You can use a TV mast, hardware and rotator. You could plan to buy a large triband beam for use on 10 and 15 meters as a Technician with credit for passing a Morse code exam. It will also cover 20 meters when you upgrade to a General or Amateur Extra class license. For such a big antenna you'll need a heavy-duty mount and rotator. Most amateurs who use HF beam antennas mount them on a tower. You can get good advice about the equipment you'll need from your instructor or from local hams.

Other Types of Beam Antennas

Cubical Quad Antennas

The **cubical quad antenna** is another type of beam antenna that uses parasitic elements. This antenna is sometimes simply called a *quad*. The elements of a quad antenna are usually wire loops. The total length of the wire in the driven element is approximately one electrical wavelength. A typical quad, shown in **Figure 8.55**, has two elements — a *driven element* and a *reflector*. A two-element quad could also use a driven element with a *director*. You can add more elements, such as a reflector and one or more directors. The radiation pattern of a typical quad is similar to that of the Yagi shown in Figure 8.53.

The elements of the quad are usually square. Each

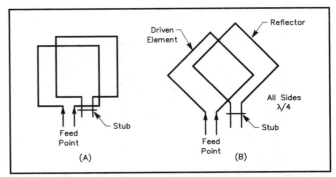

Figure 8.56 — The feed point of a quad antenna determines the polarization. Fed in the middle of the bottom side (as shown at A) or at the bottom corner (as shown at B), the antenna produces a horizontally polarized wave. Vertical polarization is produced by feeding the antenna at the side in either case.

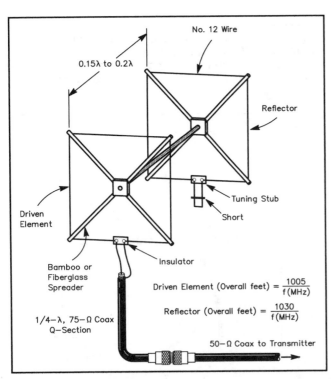

Figure 8.55 — The cubical quad antenna. The total length of the driven element is about one wavelength. This antenna can be fed directly with coaxial cable.

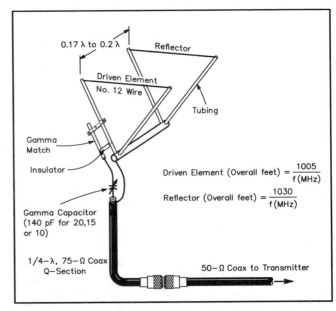

Figure 8.57 — A delta loop antenna. The total length of each element is approximately one wavelength, the same as a quad antenna. The antenna is fed with a gamma match.

loop is about an electrical wavelength long. Each side of the square is about ¼-λ long.

The polarization of the signal from a quad antenna can be changed. Polarization is determined by where the feed point is located on the driven element. See **Figure 8.56**. If the feed point is located in the center of a horizontal side, parallel to the earth's surface, the transmitted wave will be horizontally polarized. When the antenna is fed in the center of a vertical side, the transmitted wave is vertically polarized. We can turn the antenna 45°, so it looks like a diamond. When the antenna is fed at the bottom corner, the transmitted wave is horizontally polarized. If the antenna is fed at a side corner, the transmitted wave is vertically polarized.

Delta Loop Antennas

The **delta loop antenna**, shown in **Figure 8.57**, is similar to the quad. A delta loop antenna has triangular elements, rather than square. The total loop length is still one wavelength. Divide the total length by 3 to find the length of each side of the elements. The radiation pattern of a delta loop is similar to that of the quad and Yagi, shown in Figure 8.53.

[This completes your study of antennas for your Technician exam. You will want to learn more about antennas later. After you pass the exam and have your license you'll be able to experiment with lots of antenna types. You only have to learn about a few pieces of test equipment to complete your study of this Good Engineering Practices chapter. Now turn to Chapter 11 and study questions T8D07 through T8D12 and T8D19. Also study questions T0B03 through T0B10. Review this section as needed.]

Test Equipment

Safety

This is a good point to pause and consider some more safety issues. First, when you are using test equipment, you should follow the old rule of "one hand behind the back." You can't easily make yourself into a path for current to flow from fingertip to fingertip (and thus through your heart) if one hand is safely tucked behind your back, can you?

A second safety consideration not directly related to using test equipment, but very often associated with test and measurement issues is to observe proper safety measures when you are soldering. The soldering iron is *hot*, so make very sure you don't touch it — let a soldering iron cool down for at least 10 minutes before touching the hot part. You should always wear safety glasses when soldering. Splashes of molten solder can do real damage! Make sure also that the area where you're doing your soldering is well ventilated because fumes from the flux used in soldering can be hazardous.

The Voltmeter

The **voltmeter** is an instrument used to measure voltage. It is a basic meter movement with a resistor in series, as shown in **Figure 8.58**. The series resistor limits the current that can flow through the meter movement. Commercial voltmeters usually have several resistors inside the meter case. A switch selects the appropriate resistor to set the measurement range of the meter.

A high value resistor provides a high impedance input for the meter. (Impedance refers to the opposition to current flowing in a circuit. It includes resistance and the effects of capacitors and inductors to alternating current.) An ideal voltmeter would have an infinite input imped-ance. It would not draw any current from the circuit, and would not affect the circuit under test in any way. Real-world voltmeters, however, have a finite value of input impedance. There is a possibility that the voltage you are measuring will change when the meter is connected to the circuit. This is because the meter adds some load to the circuit when you connect the voltmeter.

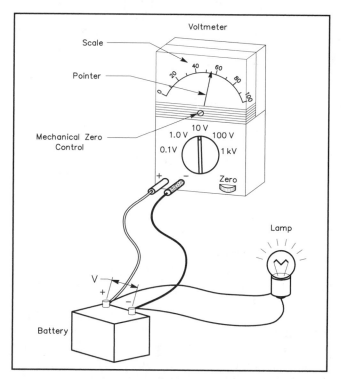

Figure 8.58—When you use a voltmeter to measure voltage, the meter must be connected in parallel with the voltage you want to measure.

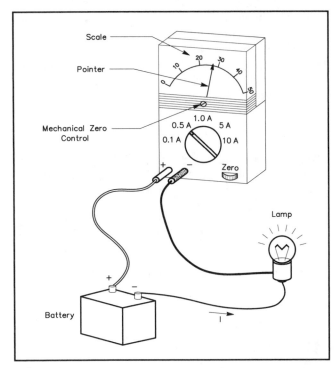

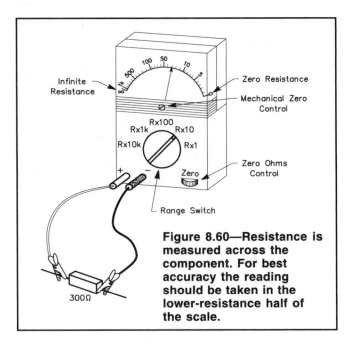

Figure 8.60—Resistance is measured across the component. For best accuracy the reading should be taken in the lower-resistance half of the scale.

Figure 8.59—To measure current you must break the circuit at some point and connect the meter in series at the break. A shunt resistor expands the scale of the meter to measure higher currents than it could normally handle.

Use a voltmeter with a very high input impedance compared with the impedance of the circuit you are measuring. This prevents the voltmeter from drawing too much current from the circuit. Excessive current drawn from the circuit would significantly affect circuit operation. The input impedance of an inexpensive voltmeter is about 20 kΩ per volt. Voltage measurements are made by placing the meter in parallel with the circuit voltage to be measured.

You should always be sure to select a voltage range on your meter that is higher than the voltage you expect to measure. If you select a range that is much lower than the circuit voltage, the meter could draw too much current. This would burn out the meter movement, destroying the meter circuitry.

The Ammeter

The **ammeter** depends on a current flowing through it to deflect the needle. The ammeter is placed in series with the circuit. That way, all the current flowing in the circuit must pass through the meter. Many times the meter cannot handle all the current. The range of the meter can be extended by placing resistors in parallel with the meter to provide a path for part of the current. A shunt resistor is shown in **Figure 8.59**. Selecting different shunt resistors changes the current-measuring range.

Commercial ammeters usually have several shunt resistors inside the meter case. A switch selects the appropriate resistor to set the measurement range of the meter. The shunt-resistor values are calculated so the total circuit current can be read on the meter. You must be sure to select a current measuring range that is greater than the current you expect to find in the circuit. For example, if you were to set your ammeter to measure microamps and then connect it to a circuit that draws 5 amps, you will probably burn out the meter, destroying the circuitry. The safest approach is always to start with the highest meter setting, and then switch to lower ranges as needed.

Most ammeters have very low resistance, but low-impedance circuits require caution. There is a chance that the slight additional resistance of the series ammeter will disturb circuit operation.

Multimeters

A **multimeter** is a piece of test equipment that most amateurs should know how to use. The simplest kind of multimeter is the volt-ohm-milliammeter (VOM). As its name implies, a VOM measures voltage, resistance and current. VOMs use one basic meter movement for all functions. The movement requires a fixed amount of current (often 1 mA) for a full-scale reading. As shown in the two previous sections, resistors are connected in series or parallel to provide the proper voltage or current meter reading. In a VOM, a switch selects various ranges for voltage, resistance and current measurements. This switch places high-value *multiplier* resistors in series with the meter movement for voltage measurement. It connects low-value *shunt* resistors in parallel with the movement for current measurement. These parallel and series resistors extend the range of the basic meter movement.

If you are going to purchase a VOM, buy one with the

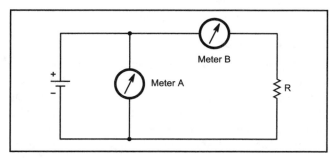

Figure 8.61—This schematic diagram shows how a voltmeter (meter A) and an ammeter (meter B) can be used to monitor circuit conditions.

Figure 8.62—A dummy antenna like this one uses a liquid coolant, often transformer oil, to dissipate heat. Dry dummy antennas dissipate heat into the air.

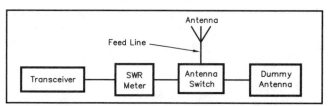

Figure 8.63—A dummy antenna is just a resistance that provides your transmitter with a proper load when you are tuning up and don't want to radiate a signal. Connect it to your antenna switch.

highest ohms-per-volt rating that you can find. Stay away from meters rated under 20,000 ohms per volt if you can.

Measuring resistance with a meter — that is, using an **ohmmeter** — involves placing the meter leads across the component or circuit you wish to measure. Make sure to select the proper resistance scale. The full-scale-reading multipliers vary from 1 to 1000 and higher. The scale is usually compressed on the higher end of the range. See **Figure 8.60**. For best accuracy, keep the reading in the lower-resistance half of the scale. On most meters this is the right-hand side. Thus, if you want to measure a resistance of about 5000 Ω, select the R × 1000 scale. Then the meter will indicate 5.

A multimeter includes a battery for resistance measurements. The battery supplies a small current through the resistor or other component you are testing. You should never try to measure resistance in a circuit that has power applied to it. Ideally you will only measure resistance for components that are removed from the circuit. Trying to measure resistance of a part in a circuit will give an inexact measurement at best. If you have your meter connected in a circuit to make a voltage measurement, with power applied to the circuit, and then switch your meter to a resistance scale, you could burn out the moving-needle meter movement. This would destroy the meter circuitry.

Another type of meter is a field-effect transistor volt-ohm-milliammeter (FET VOM). This instrument uses a field-effect transistor (FET) to isolate the indicating meter from the circuit to be measured. FET VOMs have an input impedance of several megohms.

Figure 8.61 shows a schematic diagram of a simple circuit. Meter A is connected to measure the battery voltage. Meter B is connected to measure the current through the resister. In Chapter 7 you learned to calculate the power in circuit. One way to find the power used by the resistor in the circuit is to multiply the resistor value in ohms by the square of the current, as read on meter B.

Dummy Antenna

A **dummy antenna**, sometimes called a *dummy load*, is an important piece of test equipment. It really is noth-

ing more than a large resistor. It replaces your antenna when you want to operate your transmitter without radiating a signal. The dummy antenna safely converts the RF energy coming out of your transmitter into heat. The heat goes into the air or into the coolant, depending on the type of dummy antenna. It does all this while presenting your transmitter with a constant 50-Ω load. Dummy antennas are used to make test transmissions, or to make tuning adjustments to your radio. Be sure the one you choose is rated for the type of operating (HF or VHF/UHF) and power level you'll be using.

Relatively inexpensive, a dummy antenna is one of the most useful accessories you can own. Every conscientious amateur should own one. You can build your own or buy one that's ready to use (see **Figure 8.62**). The container, often a one-gallon paint can, acts as a shield to keep RF energy from being radiated. When filled with transformer oil, it allows the dummy antenna to dissipate large amounts of RF power. You can use an antenna switch to connect the dummy antenna to the transmitter. See **Figure 8.63**.

With a dummy antenna connected to the transmitter, you can make off-the-air tests — no signal goes out over the air. For transmitter tests, remember that a dummy antenna is a resistor. It must be capable of safely dissipating the entire (continuous) power output of the transmitter. A dummy antenna will often get warm during use, since the RF energy from the transmitter is turned into heat.

A dummy antenna should provide the transmitter with a perfect load. This usually means that it has a pure resistance (with no reactance) of approximately 50 Ω. (Reactance is the effect of capacitors and inductors on alternating current.) The resistors used to construct dummy antennas must be noninductive. Composition resistors are usable, but wire-wound resistors are not. A single high-power resistor is best. Several lower-power resistors can be connected in parallel to obtain a 50-Ω load capable of dissipating high power. You must be sure the dummy antenna is able to handle the full transmitter power. For example, for a 100-watt SSB transmitter, you will need a dummy antenna that is rated to handle at least 100 watts of power.

Some older amateur literature suggested using a standard light bulb as a dummy antenna. A 100-watt light bulb would be used for a 100-watt transmitter, for example. The transmitter would be adjusted for maximum brightness of the bulb. While this was probably an acceptable dummy antenna for a tube-type radio, it should not be used with a modern transistorized radio. The impedance of the light bulb changes significantly as bulb heats up.

Signal Generator

As we pointed out in the section on superheterodyne receivers, there are a number of RF signals at different frequencies in a modern radio. A **signal generator** is an instrument that can generate RF at various frequencies and at various amplitude levels. This is a very handy instrument for troubleshooting a radio as well as for measuring its performance capabilities — such as the sensitivity of a receiver, the bandwidth of a filter or the ability of a receiver to discriminate against strong adjacent-channel unwanted signals.

[Congratulations. You have completed your study of this Good Engineering Practice chapter. Before you go on to Chapter 9, turn to Chapter 11 and study questions T8B07, T8B15, T8F01 through T8F08, T8F15 and T8F18 through T8F21. Review the material in this section if you have any difficulty with these questions.]

SPECIAL OPERATIONS

When you receive your new Technician-class license, you'll be anxious to make your first contact on the air! You'll probably operate through a VHF/UHF FM repeater.

Your Technician exam will include two questions about the special operations covered in this chapter. Those questions come from the following two syllabus groups:

T9A How an FM Repeater Works; Repeater operating procedures; Available frequencies; Input/output frequency separation; Repeater ID requirements; Simplex operation; Coordination; Time out; Open/closed repeater; Responsibility for interference.

T9B Beacon, satellite, space, EME communications; Radio control of models; Autopatch; Slow scan television; Telecommand; CTCSS tone access; Duplex/crossband operation.

VHF and UHF FM Voice Operation

Any **voice communication** mode is known as **phone** under FCC Rules. AM, **single sideband (SSB)** and **frequency-modulated (FM) voice** are all phone **emission types**.

More hams use FM voice than any other communications mode. Most hams have an FM rig of some type. They use it to keep in touch with their local friends. Hams often pass the time during their morning and evening commutes talking on the air. In most communities, amateurs interested in a specialized topic (such as chasing DX) have an FM frequency where they meet regularly to exchange information. At flea markets and conventions, hand-held FM units are in abundance as hams compare notes with their buddies on the latest bargain they've found.

FM voice operation is well-suited to local VHF/UHF radio communication because the audio signal from an FM receiver is not affected by static-type electrical noise. Car engines and ignition systems produce quite a bit of static electrical noise, and many hams like to operate their FM radios while they are driving or riding in a car. (This is called **mobile** operation.) An AM or SSB receiver is affected much more by static-type electrical noise.

Generally, it's a good idea to use VHF or UHF for all local communications. The HF bands should be reserved for longer-distance contacts. This will help reduce interference on the HF bands. VHF and UHF FM voice operation takes two forms: **repeater** and **simplex**.

Repeaters

The communications range for VHF and UHF FM simplex is usually limited to your local area. If you live high on a mountain and use a high-gain directional antenna, you may be able to extend your range considerably. Unfortunately, most of us do not enjoy the luxury of ideal VHF/UHF operating conditions. Often, we want to make contacts even though we live in a valley, are driving in a car or are using a low-power, hand-held transceiver.

Enter the **repeater**. A repeater receives a signal and retransmits it, usually with higher power, better antennas and from a superior location, to provide a larger communications range. Often located atop a tall building or high mountain, VHF and UHF repeaters greatly extend the operating range of amateurs using mobile and hand-held transceivers. See **Figure 9.1**. If a repeater serves an area, it's not necessary for everyone to live on a hilltop. You only have to be able to hear the repeater's transmitter and reach the repeater's receiver with your transmitted signal.

A repeater receives a signal on one frequency and simultaneously retransmits (repeats) it on another frequency. The frequency it receives on is called the **input frequency**, and the frequency it transmits on is called the **output frequency**. Repeaters identify themselves periodically using Morse code.

To use a repeater, you must have a transceiver that can transmit on the repeater's input frequency and receive on the repeater's output frequency. The input and output frequencies are separated by a predetermined amount that is different for each band. This separation is called the **offset** (sometimes called the **split**). For example, the standard offset on 1.25 meters is 1.6 MHz. A repeater on 1.25 meters might have its input on 222.32 MHz and its output on 223.92 MHz. Repeater frequencies are often specified in terms of the output frequency (the frequency you set your receiver to listen on) and the offset. Your transmitter operates on a frequency that is different from the receive frequency by the offset amount.

You will find repeater stations on each of the VHF and UHF bands. **Table 9.1** summarizes the **standard frequency offset** between the repeater input and output frequencies on each band. Since the offset is different for each band, it is helpful for you to know the standard offsets. For example, on the 2-meter (144 to 148 MHz) band, most repeaters use an input/output frequency separation of 600 kHz. On the 1.25-meter (222 to 225 MHz) band, the standard offset is 1.6 MHz and on the 70-cm (420 to 450 MHz) band it is 5.0 MHz. You can see that when there is more space available on the band, a wider offset is chosen. By providing more space between the input and output frequencies there is less chance for interference or interaction between the two.

Some specialized repeaters receive on one amateur

Table 9.1
Repeater Input/Output Offsets

Band	Offset
6 meters	1 MHz
2 meters	600 kHz
1.25 meters	1.6 MHz
70 cm	5 MHz
33 cm	12 MHz
23 cm	20 MHz

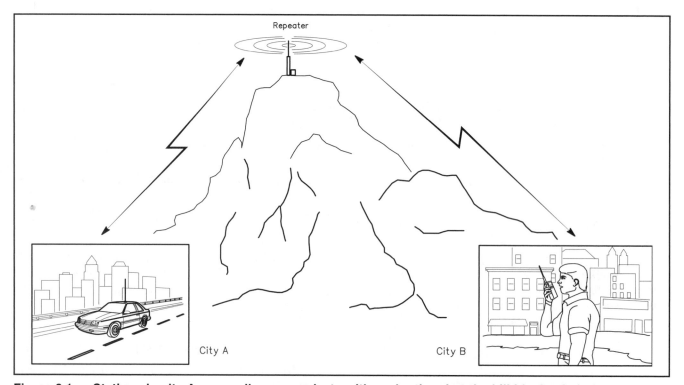

Figure 9.1 — Stations in city A can easily communicate with each other, but the hill blocks their communications with city B. The hilltop repeater enables the groups to communicate with each other.

band and retransmit on another amateur band. These are called **crossband** repeaters. Because they use widely separated frequencies, crossband repeaters can even be used for **duplex** operation, much like a regular telephone allows the user to talk and listen simultaneously. A crossband repeater might receive on the 70-cm band and retransmit on the 2-meter band, for example.

A typical use of a crossband repeater might be when an operator on foot needs to communicate with a wide-area 2-meter simplex emergency net using a low-power 70-cm hand-held radio. A car-mounted dual-band radio can function as a crossband repeater, receiving the hand-held's 70-cm signal and retransmitting it (at higher power through an efficient mobile antenna) on 2 meters. Search and Rescue groups covering a wide geographic area often benefit from such crossband capabilities to boost the communications range.

You should always consider other repeater users when selecting an operating frequency. You can easily select another frequency or move a conversation to a simplex frequency so you don't cause interference to the repeater. Try to stay off repeater frequencies when testing your radios. For example, if you want to test a pair of hand-held transceivers on your workbench you should select an unoccupied simplex frequency rather than tying up the local repeater.

Most transceivers designed for FM repeater operation are set up for the correct offset. They usually have a switch to change between **simplex** operation (transmit and receive on the same frequency — we'll cover operating simplex in more detail later) and **duplex** operation (transmit and receive on different frequencies).

When you have the correct frequency and offset dialed in, just key your microphone button to transmit through (*access*) the repeater. Most repeaters are **open repeaters** — that is, they are available for use by anyone in range. Some repeaters, however, have limited access. Remember that a repeater site may well be rented, and the repeater hardware and antenna are usually funded and maintained by either an individual or a club on a voluntary basis. The owner or owners may decide to restrict access to a small group, perhaps just the members of a club. If you wish to join a group that sponsors such a **closed repeater**, contact the repeater control operator or club.

Many repeaters require the transmission of a subaudible tone-controlled squelch or a short "burst" of tones for access. These are called **CTCSS** (continuous tone-coded squelch system) or **PL** (Private Line — PL is a Motorola trademark) tones. The reason for requiring access tones for "open" repeaters is to prevent interference by extraneous transmissions that might accidentally key the repeater. Sometimes a repeater receives interference from other nearby strong signals. For example, the repeater may be located at a commercial communications site. The repeater antenna may share tower space with many other antennas. If the repeater requires a certain CTCSS signal to activate the transmitter, then only the desired signals will be repeated.

Suppose your local repeater operates on the 146.67/146.07 MHz repeater frequency pair. There may be another repeater using this same frequency pair that is located, say, 75 miles away. Normally, the operators using the two repeaters don't hear each other. Occasionally, however, some of the stations using the other repeater may key up your club's repeater. Operating through this interference can become more than a minor annoyance, especially if it occurs during a public service activity or some type of emergency. This is a good example of why many repeaters use a CTCSS system. As long as the hams using the other repeater don't transmit the tone to access your club repeater, they won't key it up when they transmit.

Finding a Repeater

Most communities in the United States are served by repeaters. While the majority of repeaters (over 9000) are on 2 meters, there are more than 1800 repeaters on 222 MHz, more than 7000 on 440 MHz, over 125 on 902 MHz and more than 350 on 1270 MHz. More repeaters are being put into service all the time. Repeater frequencies are selected through consultation with **frequency coordinators** — individuals or groups that recommend repeater frequencies based on potential interference and other factors. (We'll get more into the subject of frequency coordination later in this chapter.)

There are several ways to find local repeater(s). Ask local amateurs or contact the nearest radio club. Each year, the ARRL publishes *The ARRL Repeater Directory*, a comprehensive listing of repeaters throughout the United States, Canada, Central and South America and the Caribbean. Besides finding out about local repeater activity, the *Directory* is handy for finding repeaters to use during vacations and business trips. See **Figure 9.2**. ARRL also publishes the *North American Repeater Atlas*, a book with maps for each state, Canadian province, Mexico, Central America and the Caribbean. *TravelPlus For Repeaters* is a CD-ROM version of the *Repeater Directory* database. It also includes a printable map feature that can show the locations of repeaters along your travel route.

Certain segments of each band are set aside for FM operation. For example, on the 2 meter band, repeater inputs are found between 144.60 and 144.90 MHz, 146.01 and 146.37 MHz, and between 147.60 and 147.99 MHz. The corresponding repeater outputs are found between 145.20 and 145.50 MHz, and between 146.61 and 147.39 MHz. There are frequencies for packet radio operation, FM simplex and other frequencies for single sideband (SSB) and Morse code (CW) operation.

On 1.25 meters, repeater inputs are found between 222.32 and 223.28 MHz. The corresponding outputs are between 223.92 and 224.98 MHz. Frequencies between 223.42 and 223.9 MHz are set aside for simplex operation.

On 70 cm, voice repeater inputs and outputs can be found from 442.00 to 445.00 MHz, and 447.00 to

PENNSYLVANIA

Location	Output	Input	Call	Notes	Sponsor
New Knsngtn	146.6400	–	K3MJW	OAE 131.8	Skyview
New Knsngtn	145.3700	–	WA3WOM	OE(CA)t	WA3WOM
Pgh/Baldwin	145.3300	–	W3PGH	O	GPVHFS
Pgh/Carrick	146.6100	–	W3PGH	OAELZ	GPVHFS
Pgh/Hzlwood	145.4700	–	WA3PBD	OAEX	GtwyFM
Pgh/Hmstead	146.7300	–	WA3PBD	OAEX	GtwyFM
Pgh/N Hills	147.0900	+	W3EXW	OR(CA)	NHARC
Pgh/N Hills	146.8800	–	W3EXW	OR(CA)	NHARC
SCHUYLKILL					
Delano	145.3700	–	W3EEK	o(ca)e Wxt	SARA
SNYDER					
Middleburg	146.8200	–	WA3DTV	oRWx	SnderCoEM
Selinsgrove	147.1800	+	NR3U	o(ca)RA Wx	SVARC
SOMERSET 123.0					
Central City	146.6250	–	WA3MYA	OLZ(CA) 123.0	W3KKC
Meyersdale	145.2700	–	WV3A	OLZ(CA)	AHRA
Seven Spngs	146.8350	–	W3KKC	OLRXZ 123.0	AHRA
Somerset	147.1950	+	K3SMT	OAERZ	SARC
SOUTH CENTRAL 123.0					
Bedford	145.4900	–	K3SAK	O	BCARS
Blue Knob	147.1500	+	K3OIH	OAELR ZX	BKRA
Chmbersburg	147.1200	+	W3ACH	O	CVARC
Fort Loudon	147.2250	+	K3PQX	O	K3PQX
SOUTHWEST 131.8					
Acme	146.6700	–	W3SII	OAERZ	LHVHFS
Bentleyville	147.2700	+	WA3DIQ	Oy	WA3DIQ
California	145.1100	–	KA3FLU	OEA	
Connellsville	145.1700	–	WB3LUC	WB3JNP	
Connellsville	146.8950	–	KB3BJZ	OER	CCRC
Derry	145.1500	–	W3CRC	OEARy 131.8TT	CRARC
Greensburg	147.1800	+	W3LWW	O(CA) ETT325	FARC
Indian Head	147.2250	+	KA3BFI	OA	KA3BFI
Indiana	146.9100	–	W3BMD	O	ICARC
Mt. Pleasant	147.0150	+	KA3JSD	OELX (CA)	KA3JSD
Uniontown	147.0450	+	W3PIE	OAX	UARC
Uniontown	147.2550	+	W3PIE	O	UARC
Washington	145.4900	–	W3CYO	OA	W3CYO
Washington	146.7900	–	K3PSP	OA	K3PSP
Waynesburg	146.4300	147.4300	N3LIF	OE131.8	GCARA
SULLIVAN					
Laporte	146.8950	–	N3CDC	o(ca)el RARBWxLi	S.C.D.E.S.
SUSQUEHANNA					
Elk Mountain	147.2400	+	N3HPY	o(ca)eA RBWxLiTZ	B&B

Figure 9.2 — Anyone who operates on VHF FM should have a copy of *The ARRL Repeater Directory*. Directory information includes the repeater call sign, location, frequency and sponsor.

450.00 MHz. There are many local options for voice-repeater frequencies, as well as simplex voice communication and control-link frequencies. The national simplex frequency is 446.00 MHz. The 70-cm band is the lowest-frequency amateur band that allows wideband **Amateur Television** (ATV) operation, either simplex or through ATV repeaters.

On 23 cm, repeater inputs run between 1270 and 1276 MHz, with corresponding outputs between 1282 and 1288 MHz. Simplex operation is between 1294 and 1295 MHz.

Most of these frequency segments are part of the ARRL and ITU *band plans*. Band plans are agreements between operators about how to use the band, rather than FCC regulations. Good operators are familiar with the band plans and try to follow them.

[Before you go on to the next section, turn to Chapter 11 and study the questions with numbers T9A01, T9A05, T9A09 through T9A12, T9A18, T9A19 and T9B19 through T9B21. Review this section if you have difficulty with any of these questions.]

Repeater Operating Procedures

Before you make your first FM repeater contact, you should learn some repeater operating techniques. It's worth a few minutes to listen and familiarize yourself with the procedures used by other hams in your area. Accepted procedures can vary slightly from repeater to repeater.

Your First Transmission

Making your first transmission on a repeater is as simple as signing your call. If the repeater is quiet, just say "N1GZO" or "N1GZO listening" — to attract someone's attention. After you stop transmitting, you will usually hear the unmodulated repeater carrier for a second or two, followed by a short burst of noise. This *squelch tail* lets you know that the repeater is working. Someone interested in talking to you will call you after your initial transmission. Some repeaters have specific rules for making yourself heard. In general, however, your call sign is all you need.

Don't call CQ to initiate a conversation on a repeater. It takes longer to complete a CQ than to transmit your call sign. (In some areas, a solitary "CQ" is permissible.) Efficient communication is the goal. You are not on HF, trying to attract the attention of someone who is casually tuning across the band. In the FM mode, stations are either monitoring their favorite frequency or not. Except for scanner operation, there is not much tuning across the repeater bands.

To join a conversation in progress, transmit your call sign during a break between transmissions. The station that transmits next will usually acknowledge you. Don't use the word "break" to join a conversation — unless you want to use the repeater to help in an **emergency**. To make a distress call over a repeater, say *break break* and then your call sign to alert all stations to stand by while you deal with the emergency.

A further word about emergencies: Regardless of the band, mode or your class of license, FCC rules specify that, in case of emergency, the normal rules can be suspended. If you hear an emergency call for help, you should do whatever you can to establish contact with the station needing assistance, and immediately pass the information on to the proper authorities. If you are talking with another station and you hear an emergency call for help, stop your QSO immediately and take the emergency call.

To call another station when the repeater is not in use, just give both calls. For example, "N1II, this is N1BKE" or shorter still, "N1II N1BKE" (with a short space between the two call signs). If the repeater is in use, but the conversation sounds like it is about to end, wait before calling another station. If the conversation sounds like it is going to continue for a while, however, transmit only your call sign between their transmissions. After you are acknowledged, ask to make a quick call. Usually, the other stations will stand by. Make your call short. If your friend responds, try to meet on another repeater or on a simplex frequency. Otherwise, ask your friend to stand by until the present conversation ends.

Use plain language on a repeater. If you want to know someone's location, say "Where are you?" If you want to know whether someone you're talking with is using a mobile rig or a hand-held radio, just ask: "What kind of radio are you using?" You get the idea.

Courtesy Counts

If you are in the midst of a conversation and another station transmits his or her call sign between transmissions, the next station in line to transmit should acknowledge the new station and permit the new arrival to make a call or join the conversation. It is impolite not to acknowledge new stations, or to acknowledge them but not let them speak. The calling station may need to use the repeater immediately. He or she may have an emergency to handle, so let him or her make a transmission promptly.

When you wish to break into a conversation on a repeater, the proper procedure is to give your call sign as soon as one of the stations stops transmitting, while the other station pauses to listen for any breakers. If you are one of the people involved in an ongoing conversation, make sure you briefly pause before you begin each transmission. This allows other stations to break in — there could be an emergency. Don't key your microphone as soon as someone else releases theirs. If your exchanges are too quick, you can prevent other stations from getting in.

The **courtesy tone** found on some repeaters prompts users to leave a space between transmissions. The beeper sounds a second or two after each transmission to permit new stations to transmit their call signs in the intervening time. The conversation may continue only after the beeper sounds. If a station is too quick and begins transmitting before the beeper sounds, the repeater may indicate the violation, sometimes by shutting down!

Keep transmissions as short as possible, so more people can use the repeater. Again, long transmissions could prevent someone with an emergency from getting the chance to call for help through the repeater. All repeaters encourage short transmissions by "timing out" (shutting down for a few minutes) when someone gets longwinded. The **time-out timer** also prevents the repeater from transmitting continuously, due to distant signals or interference. Because it has such a wide coverage area, a continuously transmitting repeater could cause unnecessary interference. Continuous operation can also damage the repeater.

You must transmit your call sign at the end of a contact and at least every 10 minutes during the course of any communication. You do not have to transmit the call sign of the station to whom you are transmitting.

Never transmit without identifying. For example, keying your microphone to turn on the repeater without saying your station call sign is illegal. If you do not want to engage in conversation, but simply want to check if you are able to access a particular repeater, simply say something like "N1KB testing."

Fixed Stations and Prime Time

Repeaters were originally intended to enhance mobile communications. During commuter rush hours, **mobile** stations still have preference over fixed stations on some repeaters. During mobile prime time, fixed stations should generally yield to mobile stations. When you're operating as a fixed station, don't abandon the repeater completely, though. Monitor the mobiles: your assistance may be needed in an emergency. Use good judgment: Rush hours are not the time to test your radio extensively or to join a net that doesn't deal with the weather, highway conditions or other subjects related to commuting. Third-party communications nets also should not be conducted on a repeater during prime commuting hours.

Autopatch: Use it Wisely

An **autopatch** allows repeater users to make telephone calls through the repeater. To use most repeater autopatches, you generate the standard telephone company tones to access and dial through the system. The tones are usually generated with a telephone-type tone pad connected to the transceiver. Tone pads are available from equipment manufacturers as standard or optional equipment. They are often mounted on the front of a portable transceiver or on the back of a fixed or mobile transceiver's microphone. Whatever equipment you use, the same autopatch operating procedures apply.

There are strict guidelines for autopatch use. The first question you should ask is "Is the call necessary?" If it is an emergency, there is no problem — just do it! Calling for an ambulance or a tow truck is okay. Other reasons may fall into a gray area. As a result, some repeater groups expressly forbid autopatch use, except for emergencies.

Don't use an autopatch where regular telephone service is available. One example of poor operating practice can be heard most evenings in any metropolitan area. Someone will call home to announce departure from the office. Why not make that call from work before leaving?

Never use the autopatch for anything that could be considered business communications. The FCC strictly forbids you to conduct communications in Amateur Radio for your business or for your employer. You may, however, use Amateur Radio to conduct your own personal communications. The rules don't forbid you to use the autopatch to call your doctor or dentist to make an appointment, or to order food, for example. Some repeater groups may prefer that you not use their autopatch for such calls, however. It is always best to ask someone in the club about their autopatch guidelines.

Don't use an autopatch just to avoid a toll call. Autopatch operation is a privilege granted by the FCC. Abuses of autopatch privileges may lead to their loss for everyone.

You have a legitimate reason to use the autopatch? Here's how most systems operate. First, you must access (turn on) the autopatch, usually by pressing a designated key on the tone pad. Ask the other hams on a repeater how to learn the access code. Many clubs provide this information only to club members. When you hear a dial tone, you know that you have successfully accessed the autopatch. Now, simply punch in the telephone number you wish to call.

Once a call is established, remember that you are still on the air. Unlike a normal telephone call, only one party at a time may speak. Both you and the other person should use the word "over" to indicate that you are finished talking and expect a reply. Keep the call short. Many repeaters shut off the autopatch after a certain time.

Turning off the autopatch is similar to accessing it. A key or combination of keys must be punched to return the repeater to normal operation. Ask the repeater group sponsoring the autopatch for specific information about access and turn-off codes, as well as timer specifics. Don't forget to identify your station. Most groups expect you to give your call sign, the date and time just before accessing the autopatch and just after turning it off.

Repeater Frequency Coordination

Repeaters in the same area that use the same or similar frequencies can interfere with each other. As more and more repeater stations have been set up, there have been more and more cases of repeater interference. One effective way of dealing with the problem is **frequency coordination**. Volunteer frequency coordinators have been appointed to ensure that new repeaters use frequencies that will tend not to interfere with existing repeaters in the same area. The FCC encourages frequency coordination, but the process is organized and run by hams and groups of hams who use repeaters.

The FCC has ruled in favor of coordinated repeaters if there is harmful interference between two repeaters. In such a case, if a frequency coordinator has coordinated one but not the other, the licensee of the *uncoordinated* repeater is responsible for solving the interference problem. If both repeaters are coordinated, or if neither is, then both licensees are equally responsible for resolving the interference.

[Before you go on to the next section, turn to Chapter 11 and study the questions with numbers T6A04, T9A02 through T9A04, T9A06 through T9A08, T9A16, T9A17, T9A20, T9B13 and T9B14. Review this section if you have difficulty with any of these questions.]

Simplex Operation

Simplex operation means the stations are talking to each other directly, on the same frequency. This is similar to making a contact on the HF bands. After you have made a contact on a repeater, move the conversation to a *simplex* frequency if possible. The repeater is not a soapbox. You may like to listen to yourself, but others who may

need to use the repeater will not appreciate your tying up the repeater unnecessarily. The easiest way to determine if you are able to communicate with the other station on simplex is to listen to the *repeater input frequency*. Since this is the frequency the other station uses to transmit to the repeater, if you can hear his signals there, you should be able to use simplex. Many radios include a *reverse* feature. With the push of a button or other control you can listen on the normal transmit frequency. This is a very useful feature for checking to see if you can operate simplex with the other station.

As mentioned previously, if you want to perform an on-the-air test of a pair of hand-held radios, you should select an unoccupied simplex frequency. That way you can perform your tests without interfering with repeater users.

The function of a repeater is to provide communications between stations that can't otherwise communicate because of terrain, equipment limitations or both. It follows that stations able to communicate without a repeater should not use one. That way, the repeater is available for stations that need it. (Besides, communication on simplex offers a degree of privacy impossible to achieve on a repeater. On simplex you can usually have extensive conversations without interruption.)

Select a frequency designated for FM simplex operation. Otherwise, you may interfere with stations operating in other modes without realizing it. (The reason for this is simple: Changing to a simplex frequency is far easier than changing the frequencies a repeater uses.) **Table 9.2** lists the common simplex frequencies for popular VHF/UHF amateur bands. Each band has a designated national FM simplex calling frequency, which is the

---

Table 9.2

Common VHF/UHF FM Simplex Frequencies

2-Meter Band	1.25-Meter Band	70-cm Band
146.52*	223.42	446.0*
146.535	223.44	
146.55	223.46	*33-cm Band*
146.565	223.48	906.5*
146.58	223.50*	
146.595	223.52	*23-cm Band*
147.42		1294.5*
147.435		1294.000
147.45		1294.025
147.465		Every 25 kHz to 1295
147.48		
147.495		
147.51		
147.525		
147.54		
147.555		
147.57		
147.585		

*National Simplex Frequency

center for most simplex operation. The 2-meter national simplex calling frequency is 146.52 MHz. On the 1¼-meter band this is at 223.50 MHz. On the 23-cm band the national simplex calling frequency is 1294.50 MHz.

[Before you go on to the next section, turn to Chapter 11 and study the questions with numbers T9A13 through T9A15. Review this section if you have difficulty with any of these questions.]

Amateur Satellite Operations

Amateur Radio operators have built many satellites since the first one was launched in 1961. Amateurs use these *Orbiting Satellites Carrying Amateur Radio* (OSCARs) to communicate with other amateurs around the world. Any licensed Amateur can operate through a satellite using the VHF and UHF bands.

Radio signals on the VHF/UHF bands normally go right through the ionosphere. The satellites retransmit signals to provide greater communications range than would normally be possible on those bands. While it is possible to use HF signals for satellite operation (and some satellites do), more of the HF signal energy may be bent back to the Earth rather than going through to the satellite. (And these HF signals already provide long-distance communication.)

Since satellite communication uses line-of-sight propagation, two amateurs can communicate through a satellite as long as the satellite is in view of both stations. **Figure 9.3** shows how a satellite can relay an amateur's signals. Notice that stations 1 and 2 can communicate through the satellite at this time, but neither station could communicate with station 3 at this time. Later, as the satellite orbits the Earth, stations 2 and 3 will be able to use the satellite, but not station 1.

A satellite's orbit around the Earth is usually shaped like an *ellipse*. In fact, a perfectly circular orbit is one kind of ellipse. Most orbits however are not perfectly circular. The distance from the center of the Earth to a satellite's closest approach to the Earth is called the **perigee**, and the farthest distance from the center of the Earth in a satellite's orbit is called the **apogee**. The location of a particular satellite from any point on the Earth can be computed using a set of mathematical parameters called **Keplerian elements**.

Most hams use computer programs to calculate where exactly to point their directional antennas in the direction of the "bird." This requires that you be able to aim your antenna in different compass directions (azimuth) as well as change the elevation angle to keep the antenna pointed at the satellite as it moves through space. When the satellite is almost directly overhead, and you can point your antenna at the satellite, relatively low power is required. It is even possible to operate through

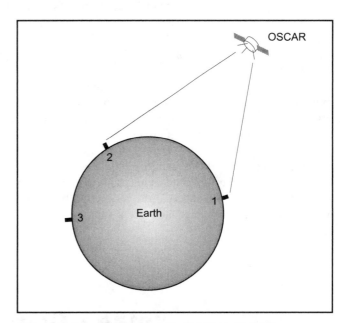

Figure 9.3 — Amateurs use Orbiting Satellites Carrying Amateur Radio (OSCARs) to relay signals. Both stations must be able to "see" the satellite for direct communications to take place. With the satellite in the position shown, stations 1 and 2 can communicate, but station 3 cannot. As the satellite orbits the Earth, stations 2 and 3 may be able to communicate, but not station 1.

some satellites using simple vertical antennas and low-power hand-held radios. When the satellite is near the horizon, however, you may need more power even if you can point your gain antenna directly at the bird. This is primarily because your signal must travel a longer distance through the relatively dense air close to the Earth.

The **Doppler effect** shifts the apparent frequency of a satellite transmission due to the relative motion between the satellite and the earth station. As the satellite moves towards you, the frequency of the signal transmitted from the satellite appears to shift higher. As the satellite passes directly overhead and then moves away from you, the frequency will shift downwards — this is similar to how the pitch of a car's horn changes as the car moves towards you, passes you and then moves away from you. The Doppler effect requires you to tune your receiver to match the frequency changes as the satellite moves in its orbit.

Contacts from a well-equipped ground station with the **International Space Station** (ISS) — which is really just a big satellite — typically last from 4 to 6 minutes for each pass, since it has a fairly low, nearly circular orbit with a period of about 90 minutes.

Earth-Moon-Earth (Moonbounce) Communications

The concept behind **Earth-Moon-Earth — EME** or **Moonbounce** — communication is really quite simple: Stations that can simultaneously see the Moon communicate by reflecting VHF or UHF signals off the Moon's surface! Those stations can be separated by more than 11,000 miles on the Earth's surface.

There is one drawback to this communications method, however. The Moon's average distance from the Earth is 239,000 miles, and EME signals must travel twice the distance to the Moon. Path losses are huge when compared to "local" VHF paths. Path loss refers to the total signal loss between the transmitting and receiving stations as compared to the total radiated signal energy. In addition to the long distance to the Moon and back, the Moon's surface is irregular and not a particularly effi-

cient reflector of radio waves. Because signals received from the Moon are very weak, most operators use CW, with narrow receiving filters.

A typical EME station also uses high-gain antennas and a high-power amplifier. For example, a high-gain array of stacked Yagi or collinear antennas would be good choice for a moonbounce station. Or you might elect to use a large parabolic dish. You would not even want to try moonbounce with a low-gain antenna like a simple ground-plane antenna, no matter how much transmitter power you had!

[Turn to Chapter 11 and study questions T9B03 through T9B11. Review this section if you have difficulty with any of those questions.]

Image Communications

Amateur TV (ATV)

Amateur TV (ATV) is ham television that uses the same standards as broadcast TV. It is often called "fast-scan television" to distinguish it from "slow-scan television" described in the next section. Several cable-TV channels operate at frequencies in the Amateur 420 to 450 MHz band. Cable channels 57 through 61 are in that band. (Note: These are *cable* channels, not *broadcast* channels.) So a cable-ready TV set to receive one of those channels should be able to pick up any local ATV activity when used with a good outdoor antenna — not your Cable TV feed line, of course!

Transmitting ATV involves using an AM (double sideband) transmitter and a video source, usually an inexpensive camera or a VCR. **Figure 9.4** shows a block diagram from *The ARRL Handbook* of a complete ATV station using a homemade 20-W ATV transceiver.

Slow-Scan Television (SSTV)

Slow-Scan Television (SSTV) is the transmission of still pictures over radio. The picture is transmitted using a

process that turns an image into audio tones. These tones go into the microphone input of the radio. The object is to use the minimum bandwidth allowed by the FCC Rules for the phone mode in use. SSTV is popular on 20-meter HF using SSB, and it is also used on VHF/UHF with FM radios. Some 2-meter voice repeaters also allow SSTV operation on their machines. (Because SSTV transmissions can take almost two minutes for color pictures, you should get permission to use a repeater before you attempt to use it for SSTV operation, as a matter of courtesy.)

Figure 9.5 from *The ARRL Handbook* shows a block diagram of a simple PC-based SSTV station. The SSTV interface is a very simple circuit using several transformers and a single op-amp working through the COM port of a computer. *The ARRL Image Communications Handbook* also has more information on how you can send/receive SSTV pictures.

[Turn to Chapter 11 and study questions T9B15 and T9B16. Review this section if you have difficulty with either of those questions.]

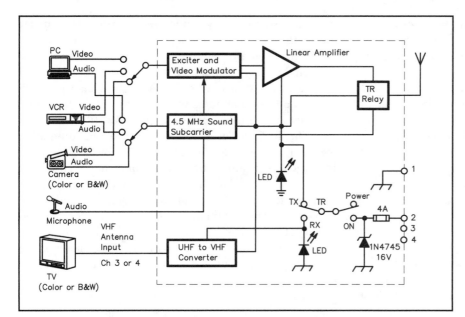

Figure 9.4 — Block diagram of a complete ATV station using a 20-W transceiver. For more detailed information, see the 2003 Edition of *The ARRL Handbook,* Chapter 12.

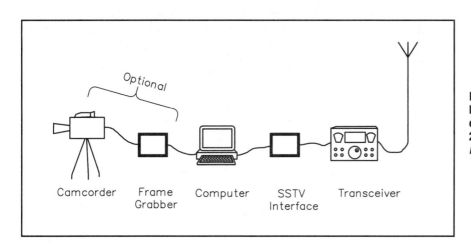

Figure 9.5 — A modern, PC-based SSTV station. For more detailed information, see the 2003 Edition of *The ARRL Handbook,* Chapter 12.

One-Way Communications

Amateur Radio is a two-way communications service. Amateur Radio stations may *not* engage in **broadcasting**. Broadcasting normally means the transmission of information intended for reception by the general public. There are also restrictions regulating **one-way communications** or transmissions of information of general interest to other amateurs. Amateur stations may transmit one-way signals for **beacon** operation or radio-control **telecommand** operation. Since normal restrictions are suspended when life or property is in immediate danger, one-way transmissions

are not considered broadcasting (which is not allowed) under emergency conditions.

Beacon Stations

A **beacon** station is simply a transmitter that alerts listeners to its presence. In the amateur service, beacons are used primarily for the study of radio-wave propagation — to allow amateurs to tell when a band is open to different parts of the country or world. The FCC defines a beacon station as an amateur station transmitting communications for the purposes of observation of propagation and reception or other related experimental activities.

The FCC Rules address beacon operation this way:

- Automatically controlled beacon stations are limited to certain parts of the 28, 50, 144, 222 and 432-MHz amateur bands, and all amateur bands above 450 MHz.
- The transmitter power of a beacon must not exceed 100 W.
- Technician and higher class licensees can operate a beacon station.

Telecommand

Telecommand means literally "command from a distance." Telecommand operation is a one-way transmission to initiate, modify or terminate functions of a device at a distance. A familiar example is remote control of a model aircraft or boat, but telecommand operation can also include control of an amateur satellite or a remotely located amateur station. Control of the remote device or station can be by means of a wire line (even fiber optic) or a radio control link. The system must be protected so that only authorized transmissions under the control of the control operator can be made.

When you are operating an amateur transmitter by telecommand, you must post a copy of your station license at the transmitter site. You must also post the name, address and telephone number of at least one designated control operator at that location.

The FCC Rules for telecommand operation of a model craft don't require that identification be used, since identification is impractical in that application. However, there must be an identification label with the station call sign and the licensee's name and address affixed to the transmitter. The maximum transmitter power for this kind of operation is 1 W. Since you are holding the transmitter in your hands while you control the model craft, you don't have to attach a copy of your actual license to the transmitter.

[Congratulations! You have completed all of the material about special operations for your Technician class license exam. Before you go on to Chapter 10, turn to Chapter 11 and study questions T9B01, T9B02, T9B12, T9B17 and T9B18. Review this section if you have difficulty with any of those questions.]

Electrical, Antenna Structure and RF Safety Practices

10

Safety is always your first concern. As a Technician licensee, you must know how to install and operate your Amateur Radio station without harming yourself or others. You probably won't install a station with towers and antennas like we have at W1AW, ARRL Headquarters.

A mateur Radio is similar to many everyday pastimes. There are potential dangers all around us. To a careless or uneducated person, these dangers can be significant — even deadly! Careful and knowledgeable hams control the risks and operate without hurting themselves or those around them. You must be aware of the dangers of electrically operated equipment and the hazards of antenna installation and tower safety. Someone is sure to ask you about the dangers of lightning striking that antenna when they see you hanging it in the air. Others may share concerns about the possible heating of body tissue from radio frequency energy when you transmit. The information in this chapter will help you answer the questions and demonstrate that your station is safe. You are responsible for all aspects of safety around your Amateur Radio station.

Your Element 2 Technician license exam will include six questions about various safety aspects around your station. Those six questions will be taken from the six groups of topics in the T0 exam subelement:

T0A Sources of electrical danger in amateur stations: lethal voltages, high current sources, fire; avoiding electrical shock; Station wiring; Wiring a three wire electrical plug; Need for main power switch; Safety interlock switch; Open/short circuit; Fuses; Station grounding.

T0B Lightning protection; Antenna structure installation safety; Tower climbing Safety; Safety belt/hard hat/safety glasses; Antenna structure limitations.

T0C Definition of RF radiation; Procedures for RF environmental safety; Definitions and guidelines.

T0D Radiofrequency exposure standards; Near/far field, Field strength; Compliance distance; Controlled/Uncontrolled environment.

T0E RF Biological effects and potential hazards; Radiation exposure limits; OET Bulletin 65; MPE (Maximum permissible exposure).

T0F Routine station evaluation.

Open and Short Circuits

A **closed**, or **complete circuit** has an uninterrupted path for the current to follow. This allows the circuit to work as it was intended. Turning a switch on, for example, closes or completes the circuit, allowing current to flow. **Figure 10.1A** shows a properly operating complete circuit.

You've probably heard the term **short circuit** before. A short circuit happens when the current flowing through the components doesn't follow the path we expect it to. Instead, the current finds another path — a shorter one — between the terminals of the power source. This is why we call this path a short circuit. There is less opposition to the flow of electrons, so there is a larger current. Often the current through the new (short) path is so large that the wires or components can't handle it. When this happens, the wires and components can be damaged. Figure 10.1B shows a bare wire causing a short circuit.

Some people think that a short circuit occurs when there is no resistance in the connection between the positive and negative terminals of the power supply. Actually there will always be some resistance but it may be such a small amount that it can be ignored.

In the extreme case, if a short circuit develops in our house wiring, the wire may overheat and can even start a fire. This is why it is important to have a properly rated fuse connected in line with a circuit. We will describe fuses in more detail later in this chapter.

Current flows *through* the circuit, but the same current that flows out of a battery or other power supply will flow back into the supply at the other terminal. You can imagine electrons leaving the negative battery terminal and flowing through the circuit. All the electrons that leave the battery eventually return to the positive terminal. A short circuit usually allows more current than the circuit was designed to handle.

Too much current is a relative term. A short circuit draws more current than is intended. If you connect two or three electric space heaters and a few lights to one 15-amp household circuit, they may draw too much current. This will blow a fuse or trip a circuit breaker, but it does not mean you have a short circuit. Each heater is drawing the current it is designed to draw.

The opposite of a short circuit is an **open circuit**. In an open circuit the current is interrupted, just as it is when you turn a light switch off. There is no current through an open circuit. The switch *breaks* (opens) the circuit, putting a layer of insulating air in the way so no current can flow. This break in the current path presents an extremely high resistance. An open circuit can be good, as when you turn the ON/OFF switch to OFF. An open circuit can be bad if it's an unwanted condition caused by a broken wire or a bad component. Figure 10.1C illustrates an open circuit.

When a fuse blows or a circuit breaker trips it creates an open circuit. We use fuses or circuit breakers in our house wiring and in electrical equipment to protect against the large current drawn by a short circuit or an overloaded circuit. It is much better to blow the fuse or trip the circuit

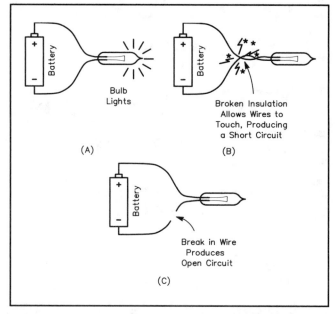

Figure 10.1 — Part A shows a light bulb in a working circuit. This is a closed or complete circuit. In Part B, the insulation covering the wires has broken, and the two wires are touching. This is a short circuit. In Part C, one wire has broken, preventing the current from flowing through the bulb. This is an example of an open circuit.

breaker and create an open circuit than to cause a fire because the wires overheated!

Sometimes the resistance in the circuit path is so large that it is impractical to measure it. When this is true, we say that there is an infinite resistance in the path, creating an open circuit.

Fuses

What would happen if part of your receiver suddenly developed a short circuit? The current, flowing without opposition through portions of the circuit, could easily damage components not built to withstand such high current.

To protect against unexpected short circuits and other problems, most electronic equipment includes one or more fuses. A **fuse** is simply a device made of metal that will heat up and melt when there is a certain amount of current through it. The manufacturer determines the amount of current that causes each fuse to melt, or "blow." When the fuse (usually placed in the main power line to the equipment) blows, it creates an open circuit, stopping the current.

Fuses come in many shapes and sizes. **Figure 10.2** shows some of the more common fuse types. This figure also shows the three common symbols used to represent a fuse on schematic diagrams. Notice that two of these symbols seem to have a small wire through the center and

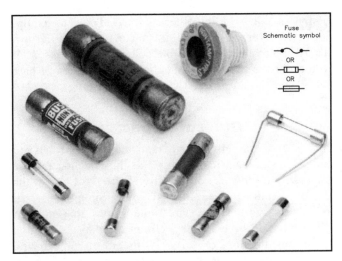

Figure 10.2 — This photo shows some common fuses. Fuses protect circuits from excessive current. The inset drawing shows common fuse schematic symbols.

Figure 10.3 — To protect your mobile equipment against being "zapped" install fuses on both the positive and negative leads, close to the battery terminals.

one is open through the center. That should help remind you that if there is too much current through the fuse, the wire will melt and produce an open circuit. Remember that fuses are designed to protect against too much current, not voltage.

Most people use circuit breakers instead of fuses to protect their house circuits from overload. Circuit breakers use a spring-loaded mechanism that unlatches and pops open if there is too much current through the breaker. To reset the breaker you simply move the lever to the OFF position and then back to the ON position. Circuit breakers are also available for use on circuit boards and other applications where you need to protect against having too much current in the circuit.

If you are building a piece of equipment that will be powered from the ac line voltage, always include a fuse in the hot lead. That fuse should be located right at the point where the power line enters the equipment cabinet. The hot line should go to the fuse first, and then to the power switch. Never use a fuse in the neutral or ground side of the ac line. If that fuse were to blow, you would still have the full line voltage present inside the equipment, creating a dangerous shock hazard.

The best way to install the power wiring for your mobile radio is to connect heavy-gauge positive and negative power wires directly to the car battery. This minimizes any voltage drop and electrical noise. Although the negative side of the battery connects to the car frame, you should still run both positive and negative wires directly to the battery. Add fuses in both the positive and negative power leads, as close to the battery as possible. There is an important reason for including a fuse in the negative lead of a mobile installation. Under some circumstances your radio and this negative lead could become part of the current path for the starter motor of your car. The huge current required to turn this motor to start your car engine would quickly destroy the radio. See **Figure 10.3** for an example of the battery connections and fuses.

Electrical Safety

It is important to arrange your home, portable or mobile station so it is safe for you and for any visitors. All wiring should be neat and out of the way. This includes all antenna feed lines and any cables connecting pieces of equipment. Make sure there is no way you can tangle your feet in loose wires. Don't leave any voltage (regardless of how low) exposed.

A main power switch allows you to turn all station equipment on or off at once. This saves needless wear on the equipment power switches and, more importantly, is a highly recommended safety item. Make sure every member of your family knows how to turn off the power to your workbench and operating position. If you ever receive an electrical shock

and cannot free yourself, the main disconnect switch will help your rescuer come to your aid quickly.

You must take special safety precautions if young children can come into your shack. Locking your station into its own room is an ideal solution. Few of us have this luxury, however. There are other ways to secure your equipment so unauthorized persons won't be able to use it. For example, you can build your station into a closet or cabinet that can be locked. If the equipment is in a nonsecure area, even a simple toggle switch — if well-hidden — can help keep your station secure.

The same principles apply if you set up your station for public display. FCC rules require that only a licensed control operator may put the station on the air. To ensure that unauthorized persons will not be able to transmit, you may have to remove a microphone or control cable temporarily while the equipment is left unattended.

Whether you use commercially built equipment or homemade gear, you should never operate the equipment without proper shielding over all circuit components. Dangerous voltages may be exposed on the chassis-mounted components. Therefore, all equipment should have a protective shield on the top, the bottom and all sides. An enclosure also prevents unwanted signals from entering a receiver, or from being radiated by a transmitter.

There should be a device that turns power off automatically if you remove the shielding. Such a **safety interlock** reduces the danger of electrical shock from high voltages when you open the cabinet. The safety interlock switch should control the voltage applied to the power supply circuit. Any equipment that connects to the 120 V or 240 V ac supply should include such a safety switch.

Of course, just because the power has been turned off inside the equipment doesn't guarantee that it is safe to work on the circuit. If the power cord is plugged in, the ac supply voltage will still be present on the wires where they connect to the fuse and power switch or safety interlock switch. There may also be high-voltage capacitors that are still charged. Remember that capacitors store a charge until there is some path to discharge them. Don't allow your body to be part of that path! The charge remaining on a capacitor after the voltage source has been removed is called a *residual charge*.

In arranging your station, always think of safety as well as comfort and convenience. After you've arranged things where you think they should be, try to find fault with your layout. Don't feel satisfied with your station until you can't find anything to improve.

Your station equipment makes use of ac line voltage. This voltage can be dangerous. The equipment also generates additional potentially lethal voltages of its own. You should be familiar with some basic precautions. Your own safety and that of others depends on it.

You should make sure everyone in your family knows where the main electrical box is located in your home. This box contains the fuses or circuit breakers for each electrical circuit in your home. Every one should know how to turn off the electricity to your house in an emergency.

Three-Wire 120-V Power Cords

State and national electrical-safety codes require three-wire power cords on many 120-V tools and appliances. Power supplies and station equipment use similar connections. Two of the conductors (the "hot" and "neutral" wires) power the device. The third conductor (the safety ground wire) connects to the metal frame of the device. See **Figure 10.4**. The "hot" wire is usually black or red. The "neutral" wire is white. The frame/ground wire is green or sometimes bare. These colors are the most

common. You may find other colors used on some equipment, however, especially if it is made for sale in Europe. There are a variety of possible color combinations, so if you don't see the red or black, white, and green or bare wires you should proceed with extreme caution.

Current Capacity

There is another factor to take into account when you are wiring an electrical circuit. It is the current-handling capability (*ampacity*) of the wire. **Table 10.1** shows the current-handling capability of some common in-wall residential wire sizes. The table shows that number 14 wire could be used for a circuit carrying 15 A. You must use number 12 (or larger) wire for a circuit carrying 20 A. Wires smaller than number 14 may not be used

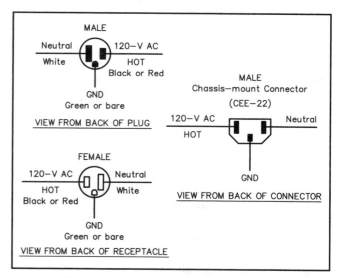

Figure 10.4 — Correct wiring technique for 120 V ac power cords and receptacles. The white wire is neutral, the green wire is the safety ground and the black or red wire is the hot lead. Notice that the receptacles are shown viewed from the back, or wiring side.

Table 10.1

Current-Carrying Capability of Some Common Wire Sizes

Copper Wire Size (AWG)	Allowable Ampacity (A)	Max Fuse or Circuit Breaker (A)
6	55	50
8	40	40
10	30	30
12	25 (20)[1]	20
14	20 (15)[1]	15

[1]The National Electrical Code limits the fuse or circuit breaker size (and as such, the maximum allowable circuit load current) to 15 A for #14 AWG copper wire and to 20 A for #12 AWG copper wire conductors.

for in-wall residential wiring.

To remain safe, don't overload the ac circuits in your home. The circuit breaker or fuse rating is the maximum load for the line at any one time. Simple addition can be used to calculate the current drawn on the circuit serving your ham radio equipment. Most equipment has the power requirements printed on the back. If not, the owner's manual should contain such information. Calculations must include any other household equipment or appliances on the same line (lighting, air-conditioning, fans, and so on). The sum of all the power requirements connected to the same circuit must not exceed the permissible loads shown in Table 10.1.

Do not put a larger fuse in an existing circuit — too much current could be drawn. (See Table 10.1 for the maximum fuse or circuit breaker rating for the existing wire size.) The wires would become hot and a fire could result. If your transceiver blows a fuse in the main ac power line, you should find out what caused the fuse to blow and repair the problem. Replace the fuse only with another one of the same rating. For example if you replaced a 5-amp fuse with one rated for 30 amps the transceiver could draw too much current, causing the wires to overheat and even starting a fire.

Even in an automotive circuit, you must be sure all equipment has the proper current rating and appropriate fuses. If the main power switch in your radio became defective, you should check the current and voltage ratings of the original switch before replacing it. Buying an inexpensive switch rated for 1 amp is a bad idea if the transceiver draws 8 amps on transmit. Again, the new switch could overheat and become a safety hazard.

You should never underestimate the potential hazard when working with electricity. **Table 10.2** shows some of the effects of electric current — as little as 100 milliamps (mA), or 1/10 amps (A), can be fatal! As the saying goes, "It's volts that jolts, but it's mills that kills." Low-voltage power supplies may seem safe, but even battery-powered equipment should be treated with respect. The minimum

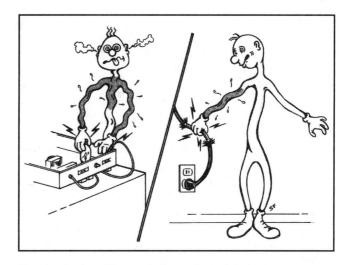

Figure 10.5 — The path from the electrical source to ground affects how severe an electrical shock will be. The most dangerous path (from hand to hand directly through the heart) is shown at the left. The path from one finger to another on the same hand shown at the right is not quite so dangerous.

voltage considered dangerous to humans is 30 volts. These voltage and current ratings are only general guidelines. Automobile batteries are designed to provide very high current (as much as 200 A) for short periods when starting a car. This much current can kill you, even at 12 volts. You will feel pain if the shock current is in the range of 30 to 50 mA. Even a current as small as 2 mA ($^1/_{500}$ A) will give you a tingling sensation that might feel like pain.

A few factors affect just how little voltage and current can be considered dangerous. One factor is skin resistance. The lower the resistance of the path, the more current that will pass through it. If you perspire heavily, you may get quite a bit more severe shock than if your skin were dry. Another factor is the path through the body to ground. As **Figure 10.5** shows, the most dangerous path is from one hand to the other or through one arm to the opposite leg. This path passes directly through a person's heart. Even a very minimal current can cause heart failure and death. Current passing from one finger to another on the same hand will not have quite such a serious effect. For this reason, if you must troubleshoot a live circuit, keep one hand behind your back or in your pocket. If you do slip, the shock may not be as severe as if you were using both hands.

If you should discover someone who is being burned by high voltage, immediately turn off the power, call for help and give cardio-pulmonary resuscitation (CPR). Be sure all family members know how to turn off power at the main power switch. These measures could save the life of a friend or family member.

[Now turn to Chapter 11 and study questions T0A01 through T0A05 and T0A07 through T0A13. Review this section if you have difficulty with any of these questions.]

Table 10.2

Effects of Electric Current Through the Body of an Average Person

Current (1 Second Contact)	Effect
1 mA	Just Perceptible.
5 mA	Maximum harmless current.
10 - 20 mA	Lower limit for sustained muscular contractions.
30 - 50 mA	Pain
50 mA	Pain, possible fainting. "Can't let go" current.
100 - 300 mA	Normal heart rhythm disrupted. Electrocution if sustained current.
6 A	Sustained heart contractions. Burns if current density is high.

Ground

You should connect all the equipment in your station to a good Earth ground. There are really two kinds of ground connections: **chassis ground** and **Earth ground**. The metal box that your radio is built on is called a chassis. Most manufacturers use the chassis as a common connection for all the places in the circuit that connect to the negative side of the power supply. This common connection is called the chassis ground. **Figure 10.6A** shows the schematic symbol for a chassis ground. When you look at this symbol you can visualize the box shape that represents the chassis.

To keep your station safe, you should also connect the chassis ground to a good Earth ground. This connection is called an Earth ground because it goes into the Earth. An Earth ground has a different schematic symbol than a chassis ground. Figure 10.6B shows the schematic symbol for

an Earth ground. When you look at the lines at the bottom of this symbol it might remind you of the point on a garden spade shovel. If you think about pushing that spade into the ground, you will remember the Earth ground.

What is a Good Ground?

Since **station grounding** is a good idea for several reasons, it's worth discussing in detail. All station equipment should be tied to a good ground. Most amateurs connect their equipment to a **ground rod** driven into the ground as close to the shack as possible. For a few dollars you can purchase a ½ or ⅝-inch-diameter, 8-foot-long ground rod at any electrical supply store. (Eight feet is the shortest practical length for a station ground rod. In some locations you may need more than one ground rod to make a good ground.) Drive this copper-clad steel rod into the ground outside of your house, as close to your station location as possible. (Don't settle for the short, thin "ground rods" sold by some discount electronics stores. The copper cladding on the outside of most of these steel rods is very thin. They begin to rust almost immediately when they are put in the ground.)

Run a heavy copper wire (number 8 or larger) from your shack and attach it to the rod with a clamp. You can purchase the clamp when you buy the ground rod. Heavy copper strap or flashing (sold at hardware or roofing-supply stores) is even better. The braid from a piece of RG-8 coaxial cable also makes a good ground cable. **Figure 10.7** shows one method of grounding each piece of equipment in your station. It's important to connect the chassis of each piece of station equipment to an effective ground con-

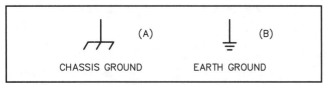

CHASSIS GROUND (A)   EARTH GROUND (B)

Figure 10.6 — The metal chassis of a radio is sometimes used to make a common ground connection for all the circuit points that connect to the negative side of the power supply. We use the symbol shown at A to show those connections on a schematic diagram. Your radio equipment should be connected to a ground rod or a copper cold-water pipe that goes into the ground, for safety. We use the symbol at B to show an Earth-ground connection.

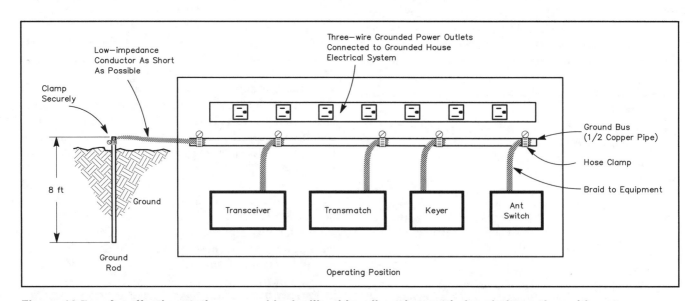

Figure 10.7 — An effective station ground looks like this: all equipment is bonded together with a strong conductor such as copper flashing or coaxial cable braid. It then ties into a good Earth ground — an 8-foot ground rod located as close to the station as possible is the minimum you should use. More than one ground rod may be needed in some locations.

nection. Keep the cable between your station and the earth ground as short as possible. Such a ground connection is an important safety measure. It can protect you from electrical shock if something breaks down in your equipment. This is the most important reason to connect all of your station equipment to ground. It also helps reduce interference problems from RF signals going places they shouldn't be.

The **National Electrical Code** requires all ground rods to be connected to form a single grounding system. These connections must use number 8 or larger copper wire. Have a qualified electrician perform this work if you are not familiar with the National Electrical Code and common wiring practices.

The National Electrical Code (NEC) describes safe grounding practices for electrical wiring, antennas and other electrical equipment. Published by The National Fire Protection Association, the NEC forms the basis for most local building codes regarding electrical wiring practices. It is a good idea to check with local building officials and the requirements of the National Electrical Code to ensure that your antenna installation meets all safety requirements.

Some hams ground their station equipment by connecting the ground wire to a cold-water pipe. Caution is in order here. If you live in an apartment or have your shack in an attic, be careful. The cold-water pipe near your transmitter may follow such a long and winding path to the earth that it may not act as a ground at all! It may, in fact, act as an antenna, radiating RF energy — exactly what you don't want it to do.

Beware, too, of nonmetallic cold-water pipes. PVC and other plastic pipes are effective insulators. There may be a piece of copper water pipe running close to your station. If there is a piece of PVC pipe connected between that spot and where the water line enters your house, however, you will not have a ground connection!

Lightning Protection

The lightning hazard from an antenna is often exaggerated. Ordinary amateur antennas are no more likely to be hit by a direct strike than any other object of the same height in the neighborhood. Just the same, lightning does strike thousands of homes each year, so it doesn't hurt to be careful. When your station is not being used, you should ground all antennas, feed lines and rotator cables for effective **lightning protection**. An ungrounded antenna can pick up large electrical charges from storms in the area. These charges can damage your equipment (particularly receivers) if you don't take precautions. You should also unplug your equipment.

Most commercial beam and vertical antennas are grounded for lightning protection through the tower itself. Of course, the tower must be grounded, too. If you use a roof mount, run a heavy ground wire from the mount to a ground rod. Dipoles and end-fed wires are not grounded. Use an antenna switch that grounds all unused inputs. Keep one input position unused so you can set the

switch to that position to ground all your antennas. You can also disconnect the antenna feed line from your equipment and use an alligator-clip lead to connect both sides of the feed line to your station ground.

Storm clouds often carry dangerous electrical charges that are coupled into high objects (like amateur antennas) without visible lightning. You may be operating and suddenly hear a "SNAP!" in your antenna tuner, or your receiver may go dead. You can usually hear an increase in static crashes in your receiver well in advance of a thunderstorm. Be safe. When it sounds like a thunderstorm is headed your way, get off the air. If the weather forecast is for thunderstorms, don't operate! Snow and rain also generate static charges on antennas, but usually not enough to damage equipment.

The best protection against lightning is to disconnect all antennas and rotator control cables and connect them to ground. You should also form the habit of unplugging all power cords when you aren't on the air. It takes time to hook up everything when you want to operate again, but you will protect your station and your home if you follow this simple precaution. By the way, power companies recommend that you unplug *all* electronic appliances, including TVs, VCRs and computers, when a storm threatens.

Why unplug your equipment if the antennas are disconnected? Lightning can still find its way into your equipment through the power cord. Power lines can act as long antennas, picking up sizable charges during a storm. Simply turning off the main circuit breaker is not enough — lightning can easily jump over the circuit breaker contacts and find its way into your equipment.

You may decide to leave your antennas connected and your equipment plugged in except during peak thunderstorm months. If so, you can still protect the equipment from unexpected storms. One simple step you can take is to install a grounding switch, as shown in **Figure 10.8**. A

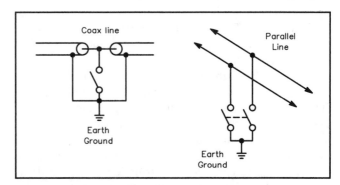

Figure 10.8 — A heavy-duty knife switch can be used to connect the wires in your antenna feed line to ground. A clip lead to a ground wire can be used instead of the switch. This will prevent a large static-electricity build-up on your antenna. It will also prevent equipment damage caused by voltage on your antenna produced by a nearby lightning strike. There is no sure way to prevent a direct hit by lightning, however.

small knife switch will allow you to ground your feed line when you are not on the air. It will not disturb the normal operation of your station (with the switch open, of course) if the lead from the feed line to the switch is no more than a couple of inches long. An alligator clip can be used instead of the switch. Whatever you use, don't forget to disconnect the ground when you transmit. This precaution is useful only on the HF bands. The switch will cause high SWR if used at VHF and UHF.

Another device that can help protect your equipment in an electrical storm is a *lightning arrestor*. This device connects permanently between your feed line and the ground. When the charge on your antenna builds up to a large enough potential, the lightning arrestor will "fire." This shorts the charge to ground — not through your sta-tion. A lightning arrestor can help prevent serious damage to your equipment. Most, however, don't work fast enough to protect your station completely. Lightning arrestors are useful for commercial stations and public service (fire and police) stations that must remain on the air regardless of the weather. Unless you are actually handling emergency communications, you shouldn't rely on them alone to protect your equipment, home or life. Turn off the equipment, pull the plug and disconnect and ground your antennas when a storm approaches.

[Now it is time to study the following questions in Chapter 11: T0A06, T0B01 and T0B02. Review this section if you have any difficulty with these questions.]

RF Environmental Safety Practices

FCC Rules require all amateurs to meet certain maximum permissible exposure limits for RF radiation from their stations. In the remainder of this chapter, you will learn how to evaluate your station to be sure you meet these important safety requirements.

Amateur Radio is basically a safe activity. In recent years, however, there has been considerable discussion and concern about the possible hazards of electromagnetic radiation (EMR), including both RF energy and power-frequency (50-60 Hz) electromagnetic fields. FCC regulations set limits on the maximum permissible exposure (MPE) allowed from the operation of radio transmitters. These regulations do not take the place of RF-safety practices, however. This section deals with the topic of **RF safety**. See the sidebar, "FCC RF-Exposure Regulations," for specific information about the rules.

Extensive research on RF safety is underway in many countries. This final section of Chapter 10 was prepared by members of the ARRL RF Safety Committee and coordinated by Dr Robert E. Gold, WBØKIZ. It summarizes what is now known and offers safety precautions based on the research to date.

All life on Earth has adapted to survive in an environment of weak, natural, low-frequency electromagnetic fields (in addition to the Earth's static geomagnetic field). Natural low-frequency EM fields come from two main sources: the sun, and thunderstorm activity. But in the last 100 years, man-made fields at much higher intensities and with a very different spectral distribution have altered this natural EM background in ways that are not yet fully understood. Much more research is needed to assess the biological effects of EMR.

Both RF and 60-Hz fields are classified as **nonionizing radiation** because the frequency is too low for there to be enough photon energy to ionize atoms. (**Ionizing radiation**, such as X-rays, gamma rays and even some ultraviolet radiation has enough energy to knock elec-trons loose from their atoms. When this happens, positive and negative ions are formed.) Still, at sufficiently high power densities, EMR poses certain health hazards. It has been known since the early days of radio that RF energy can cause injuries by heating body tissue. (Anyone who has ever touched an improperly grounded radio chassis or energized antenna and received an **RF burn** will agree that this type of injury can be quite painful. You do not have to actually *touch* the chassis to get an RF burn.) In extreme cases, RF-induced heating in the eye can result in cataract formation and can even cause blindness. Excessive RF heating of the reproductive organs can cause sterility. Other serious health problems can also result from RF heating. These heat-related health hazards are called *thermal effects*. In addition, there is evidence that magnetic fields may produce biologic effects at energy levels too low to cause body heating. The proposition that these *athermal effects* may produce harmful health consequences has produced a great deal of research.

In addition to the ongoing research, much else has been done to address this issue. For example, FCC regulations set limits on exposure from radio transmitters. The Institute of Electrical and Electronics Engineers, the American National Standards Institute and the National Council for Radiation Protection and Measurement, among others, have recommended voluntary guidelines to limit human exposure to RF energy. The ARRL has established the RF Safety Committee, a committee of concerned medical doctors and scientists, serving voluntarily to monitor scientific research in the fields and to recommend safe practices for radio amateurs.

Thermal Effects of RF Energy

Body tissues that are subjected to very high levels of RF energy may suffer serious heat damage. These effects depend upon the frequency of the energy, the power density of the RF field that strikes the body, and even on factors such as the polarization of the wave.

At frequencies near the body's natural resonant frequency, RF energy is absorbed more efficiently, and maximum heating occurs. In adults, this frequency usually is about 35 MHz if the person is grounded, and about 70 MHz if the person's body is insulated from the ground. Also, body parts may be resonant; the adult head, for example is resonant around 400 MHz, while a baby's smaller head resonates near 700 MHz. Body size thus determines the frequency at which most RF energy is absorbed. As the frequency is increased above resonance, less RF heating generally occurs. However, additional longitudinal resonances occur at about 1 GHz near the body surface. **Specific absorption rate (SAR)** is a term that describes the rate at which RF energy is absorbed into the human body. Maximum permissible exposure (MPE) limits are based on whole-body SAR values. This helps explain why these safe exposure limits vary with frequency.

Nevertheless, thermal effects of RF energy should not be a major concern for most radio amateurs because of the relatively low RF power we normally use and the intermittent nature of most amateur transmissions. Amateurs spend more time listening than transmitting, and many amateur transmissions such as CW and SSB use low-duty-cycle modes. (With FM or RTTY, though, the RF is present continuously at its maximum level during each transmission.) In any event, it is rare for radio amateurs to be subjected to RF fields strong enough to produce thermal effects unless they are fairly close to an energized antenna or unshielded power amplifier. Specific suggestions for avoiding excessive exposure are offered later.

[Turn to Chapter 11 now and study questions T0C10, T0C17, T0C18, T0D02, T0E07, T0E08, T0E09 and T0E11. Review this section as needed.]

Athermal Effects of EMR

Nonthermal effects of EMR may be of greater concern to most amateurs because they involve lower level energy fields. Research about possible health effects resulting from exposure to the lower level energy fields — the athermal effects — has been of two basic types: epidemiological research and laboratory research.

Scientists conduct laboratory research into biological mechanisms by which EMR may affect animals, including humans. Epidemiologists look at the health patterns of large groups of people using statistical methods. These epidemiological studies have been inconclusive. By their basic design, these studies do not demonstrate cause and effect, nor do they postulate mechanisms of disease. Instead, epidemiologists look for associations between an environmental factor and an observed pattern of illness. For example, in the earliest research on malaria, epidemiologists observed the association between populations with high prevalence of the disease and the proximity of mos-

quito infested swamplands. It was left to the biological and medical scientists to isolate the organism causing malaria in the blood of those with the disease and identify the same organisms in the mosquito population.

In the case of athermal effects, some studies have identified a weak association between exposure to EMF at home or at work and various malignant conditions including leukemia and brain cancer. A larger number of equally well designed and performed studies, however, have found no association. A risk ratio of between 1.5 and 2.0 has been observed in positive studies (the number of observed cases of malignancy being 1.5 to 2.0 times the "expected" number in the population). Epidemiologists generally regard a risk ratio of 4.0 or greater to be indicative of a strong association between the cause and effect under study. For example, men who smoke one pack of cigarettes per day increase their risk for lung cancer tenfold compared to nonsmokers, and two packs per day increase the risk to more than 25 times the nonsmokers' risk.

Epidemiological research by itself is rarely conclusive, however. Epidemiology only identifies health patterns in groups—it does not ordinarily determine their cause. And there are often confounding factors: Most of us are exposed to many different environmental hazards that may affect our health in various ways. Moreover, not all studies of persons likely to be exposed to high levels of EMR have yielded the same results.

There has also been considerable laboratory research about the biological effects of EMR in recent years. For example, it has been shown that even fairly low levels of EMR can alter the human body's circadian rhythms, affect the manner in which cancer-fighting T lymphocytes function in the immune system, and alter the nature of the electrical and chemical signals communicated through the cell membrane and between cells, among other things.

Much of this research has focused on low-frequency magnetic fields, or on RF fields that are keyed, pulsed or modulated at a low audio frequency (often below 100 Hz). Several studies suggested that humans and animals can adapt to the presence of a steady RF carrier more readily than to an intermittent, keyed or modulated energy source. There is some evidence that while EMR may not directly cause cancer, it may sometimes combine with chemical agents to promote its growth or inhibit the work of the body's immune system.

None of the research to date conclusively proves that low-level EMR causes adverse health effects. Given the fact that there is a great deal of ongoing research to examine the health consequences of exposure to EMF, the American Physical Society (a national group of highly respected scientists) issued a statement in May 1995 based on its review of available data pertaining to the possible connections of cancer to 60-Hz EMF exposure. This report is exhaustive and should be reviewed by anyone with a serious interest in the field. Among its general conclusions were the following:

1. "The scientific literature and the reports of reviews by other panels show no consistent, significant link be-

tween cancer and powerline fields."

2. "No plausible biophysical mechanisms for the systematic initiation or promotion of cancer by these extremely weak 60-Hz fields has been identified."

3. "While it is impossible to prove that no deleterious health effects occur from exposure to any environmental factor, it is necessary to demonstrate a consistent, significant, and causal relationship before one can conclude that such effects do occur."

The APS study is limited to exposure to 60-Hz EMF. Amateurs will also be interested in exposure to EMF in the RF range. A 1995 publication entitled *Radio Frequency and ELF Electromagnetic Energies, A Handbook for Health Professionals* includes a chapter called "Biologic Effects of RF Fields." In it, the authors state: "In conclusion, the data do not support the finding that exposure to RF fields is a causal agent for any type of cancer" (page 176). Later in the same chapter they write: "Although the data base has grown substantially over the past decades, much of the information concerning nonthermal effects is generally inconclusive, incomplete, and sometimes contradictory. Studies of human populations have not demonstrated any reliably effected end point." (page 186).

Readers may want to follow this topic as further studies are reported. Amateurs should be aware that exposure to RF and ELF (60 Hz) electromagnetic fields at all power levels and frequencies may not be completely safe. Prudent avoidance of any avoidable EMR is always a good idea. An Amateur Radio operator should not be fearful of using his or her equipment, however. If any risk does exist, it will almost surely fall well down on the list of causes that may be harmful to your health (on the other end of the list from your automobile).

Safe Exposure Levels

How much EM energy is safe? Scientists and regulators have devoted a great deal of effort to deciding upon safe RF-exposure limits. This is a very complex problem, involving difficult public health and economic considerations. The recommended safe levels have been revised downward several times in recent years—and not all scientific bodies agree on this question even today. An Institute of Electrical and Electronics Engineers (IEEE) standard for recommended EM exposure limits went into effect in 1991. It replaced a 1982 IEEE and American National-Standards Institute (ANSI) standard that permitted somewhat higher exposure levels. The newer IEEE standard was adopted by ANSI in 1992.

The IEEE standard recommends frequency-dependent and time-dependent maximum permissible exposure levels. Unlike earlier versions of the standard, the 1991 standard recommends different RF exposure limits in **controlled environments** (that is, where energy levels can be accurately determined and everyone on the premises is aware of the presence of EM fields) and in **uncontrolled environments** (where energy levels are not known or where some persons present may not be aware of the EM fields).

The graph in **Figure 10.9** depicts the maximum permissible exposure limits set by the 1991 IEEE standard. It is necessarily a complex graph because the standards differ not only for controlled and uncontrolled environments but also for electric fields (E fields) and magnetic fields

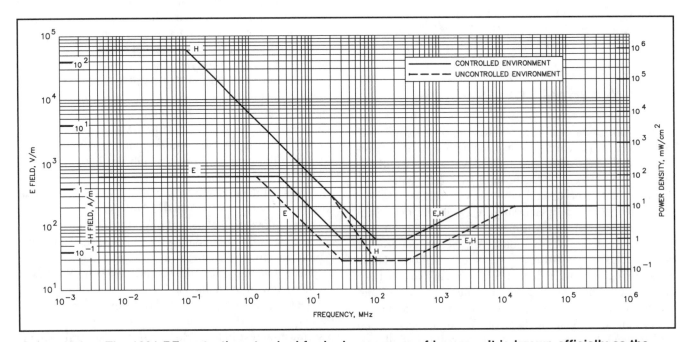

Figure 10.9 — The 1991 RF protection standard for body exposure of humans. It is known officially as the "IEEE Standard for Safety Levels with Respect to Human Exposure to Radio Frequency Electromagnetic Fields, 3 kHz to 300 GHz." (Note that the exposure levels set by this standard are not the same as the FCC maximum permissible exposure limits.)

(H fields). Basically, the lowest E-field exposure limits occur at frequencies between 30 and 300 MHz. The lowest H-field exposure levels occur at 100 to 300 MHz. The standard sets the maximum E-field limits between 30 and 300 MHz at a power density of 1 mW/cm² (61.4 V/m) in controlled environments—but at one-fifth that level (0.2 mW/cm² or 27.5 V/m) in uncontrolled environments. The H-field limit drops to 1 mW/cm² (0.163 A/m) at 100-300 MHz in controlled environments and 0.2 mW/cm² (0.0728 A/m) in uncontrolled environments. Higher power densities are permitted at frequencies below 30 MHz (below 100 MHz for H fields) and above 300 MHz, based on the concept that the body will not be resonant at those frequencies and will therefore absorb less energy.

In general, the 1991 IEEE standard requires averaging the power level over time periods ranging from 6 to 30 minutes for power-density calculations, depending on the frequency and other variables. The exposure limits for uncontrolled environments are lower than those for controlled environments, but to compensate for that the standard allows exposure levels in those environments to be averaged over much longer time periods (generally 30 minutes). This long averaging time means that an intermittently operating RF source (such as an Amateur Radio transmitter) will show a much lower power density than a continuous-duty station for a given power level and antenna configuration.

Time averaging is based on the concept that the human body can withstand a greater rate of body heating (and thus, a higher level of RF energy) for a short time than for a longer period.

The IEEE standard excludes any transmitter with an output below 7 W because such low-power transmitters would not be able to produce significant whole-body heating. (Recent studies show that hand-held transceivers often produce power densities in excess of the IEEE standard within the head.)

There is disagreement within the scientific community about these RF exposure guidelines. A small but significant number of researchers now believe athermal effects should also be taken into consideration. Several European countries have adopted stricter standards than the recently updated IEEE standard.

Cardiac Pacemakers and RF Safety

It is a widely held belief that cardiac pacemakers may be adversely affected in their function by exposure to electromagnetic fields. Amateurs with pacemakers may ask whether their operating might endanger themselves or visitors to their shacks who have a pacemaker. Because of this and similar concerns regarding other sources of electromagnetic fields, pacemaker manufacturers apply design methods that for the most part shield the pacemaker circuitry from even relatively high EM field strengths.

It is recommended that any amateur who has a pacemaker or is being considered for one discuss this matter with his or her physician. The physician will probably put the amateur into contact with the technical representative of the pacemaker manufacturer. These representatives are generally excellent resources and may have data from laboratory or "in the field" studies with pacemaker units of the type the amateur needs to know about.

One study examined the function of a modern (dual chamber) pacemaker in and around an Amateur Radio station. The pacemaker generator has circuits that receive and process electrical signals produced by the heart and also generate electrical signals that stimulate (pace) the heart. In one series of experiments the pacemaker was connected to a heart simulator. The system was placed on top of the cabinet of a 1-kW HF linear amplifier during SSB and CW operation. In addition, the system was placed in close proximity to several 1 to 5-W 2-meter hand-held transceivers. The test pacemaker connected to the heart simulator was also placed on the ground 9 meters below and 5 meters in front of a three-element Yagi HF antenna. No interference with pacemaker function was observed in this experimental system.

Although the possibility of interference cannot be entirely ruled out by these few observations, these tests represent more severe exposure to EM fields than would ordinarily be encountered by an amateur with an average amount of common sense. Of course prudence dictates that amateurs with pacemakers using hand-held VHF transceivers keep the antenna as far from the site of the implanted pacemaker generator as possible and use the lowest transmitter output required for adequate communication. For high power HF transmission, the antenna should be as far from the operating position as possible and all equipment should be properly grounded.

Low-Frequency Fields

Recently, much concern about EMR has focused on low-frequency energy rather than RF. Amateur Radio

Table 10.3

Typical 60-Hz Magnetic Fields Near Amateur Radio Equipment and AC-Powered Household Appliances

Item	Field	Distance
	Values are in milligauss	
Electric blanket	30-90	Surface
Microwave oven	10-100	Surface
	1-10	12"
IBM personal	5-10	Atop monitor
computer	0-1	15" from screen
Electric drill	500-2000	At handle
Hair dryer	200-2000	At handle
HF transceiver	10-100	Atop cabinet
	1-5	15" from front
1-kW RF	80-1000	Atop cabinet
amplifier	1-25	15" from front

(Source: measurements made by members of the ARRL RF Safety Committee)

equipment can be a significant source of low-frequency magnetic fields, although there are many other sources of this kind of energy in the typical home. Magnetic fields can be measured relatively accurately with inexpensive 60-Hz dosimeters that are made by several manufacturers.

Table 10.3 shows typical magnetic field intensities of Amateur Radio equipment and various household items. Because these fields dissipate rapidly with distance, "prudent avoidance" would mean staying perhaps 12 to 18 inches away from most Amateur Radio equipment (and 24 inches from power supplies with 1-kW RF amplifiers) whenever the ac power is turned on. The old custom of leaning over a linear amplifier on a cold winter night to keep warm may not be the best idea! There are currently no non-occupational US standards for exposure to low-frequency fields.

Determining RF Power Density

Unfortunately, determining the power density of the RF fields generated by an amateur station is not as simple as measuring low-frequency magnetic fields. Although sophisticated instruments can be used to measure RF power densities quite accurately, they are costly and require frequent recalibration. Most amateurs don't have access to such equipment, and the inexpensive field-strength meters that we do have are not suitable for measuring RF power density. The best we can usually do is to estimate our own RF power density based on measurements made by others or, given sufficient computer programming skills, use computer modeling techniques. The FCC has prepared a bulletin, "Amateur Supplement to OET Bulletin 65: Evaluating Compliance With FCC-Specified Guidelines for Human Exposure to Radio Frequency Radiation," that contains charts and tables that amateurs can use to estimate compliance with the rules. A copy of this bulletin is included in the ARRL publication *RF Exposure and You.*

Table 10.4 shows a sampling of measurements made at Amateur Radio stations by the Federal Communications Commission and the Environmental Protection Agency in 1990. As this table indicates, a good antenna well removed from inhabited areas poses no hazard under any of the various exposure guidelines. The FCC/EPA survey also indicates, however, that amateurs must be careful about using indoor or attic-mounted antennas, mobile antennas, low directional arrays or any other antenna that is close to inhabited areas, especially when moderate to high power is used.

Ideally, before using any antenna that is in close proximity to an inhabited area, you should measure the RF power density. If that is not feasible, the next best option is to make the installation as safe as possible by observing the safety suggestions listed in **Table 10.5**.

It is also possible, of course, to calculate the probable power density near an antenna using simple equations. Such calculations have many pitfalls. For one, most of the situations in which the power density would be high enough to be of concern are in the near field. The boundary between the near field and the far field of an antenna is approximately several wavelengths from the antenna. In the near field, ground interactions and other variables produce power densities that cannot be determined by simple arithmetic. In the far field, conditions become easier to predict with simple calculations. It is difficult to accurately evaluate the effects of **RF radiation** exposure in the near field. The boundary between the near field and the far field depends on the wavelength of the transmitted signal and the physical size and configuration of the antenna.

Computer antenna-modeling programs such as *MININEC* or other codes derived from *NEC* (Numerical

Table 10.4

Typical RF Field Strengths Near Amateur Radio Antennas

A sampling of values as measured by the Federal Communications Commission and Environmental Protection Agency, 1990

Antenna Type	Freq (MHz)	Power (W)	E Field (V/m)	Location
Dipole in attic	14.15	100	7-100	In home
Discone in attic	146.5	250	10-27	In home
Half sloper base	21.5	1000	50	1 m from
Dipole at 7-13 ft	7.14	120	8-150	1-2 m from earth
Vertical	3.8	800	180	0.5 m from base
5-element Yagi at 60 ft	21.2	1000	10-20	In shack
			14	12 m from base
3-element Yagi at 25 ft	28.5	425	8-12	12 m from base
Inverted V at 22-46 ft	7.23	1400	5-27	Below antenna
Vertical on roof	14.11	140	6-9	In house
			35-100	At antenna tuner
Whip on auto roof	146.5	100	22-75	2 m from antenna
			15-30	In vehicle
			90	Rear seat
5-element Yagi at 20 ft	50.1	500	37-50	10 m from antenna

Table 10.5

RF Awareness Guidelines

These guidelines were developed by the ARRL RF Safety Committee, based on the FCC/EPA measurements of Table 10.4 and other data.

- Although antennas on towers (well away from people) pose no exposure problem, make certain that the RF radiation is confined to the antennas' radiating elements themselves. Provide a single, good station ground (earth), and eliminate radiation from transmission lines. Use good coaxial cable, not open-wire lines or end-fed antennas that come directly into the transmitter area.
- No person should ever be near any transmitting antenna while it is in use. This is especially true for mobile or ground-mounted vertical antennas. Avoid transmitting with more than 25 W in a VHF mobile installation unless it is possible to first measure the RF fields inside the vehicle. At the 1-kW level, both HF and VHF directional antennas should be at least 35 ft above inhabited areas. Avoid using indoor and attic-mounted antennas if at all possible.
- Don't operate high-power amplifiers with the covers removed, especially at VHF/UHF.
- In the UHF/SHF region, never look into the open end of an activated length of waveguide or microwave feed-horn antenna or point it toward anyone. (If you do, you may be exposing your eyes to more than the maximum permissible exposure level of RF radiation.) Never point a high-gain, narrow-band-width antenna (a paraboloid, for instance) toward people. Use caution in aiming an EME (moonbounce) array toward the horizon; EME arrays may deliver an effective radiated power of 250,000 W or more.
- With hand-held transceivers, keep the antenna away from your head and use the lowest power possible to maintain communications. Use a separate microphone and hold the rig as far away from you as possible. This will reduce your exposure to the RF energy.
- Don't work on antennas that have RF power applied.
- Don't stand or sit close to a power supply or linear amplifier when the ac power is turned on. Stay at least 24 inches away from power transformers, electrical fans and other sources of high-level 60-Hz magnetic fields.

Electromagnetics Code) are suitable for estimating RF magnetic and electric fields around amateur antenna systems. (See Chapter 2 of *The ARRL Antenna Book* for more information about *NEC* and *MININEC*.) These programs also have limitations. Ground interactions must be considered in estimating near-field power densities. Also, computer modeling is not sophisticated enough to predict "hot spots" in the near field — places where the field intensity may be far higher than would be expected.

Intensely elevated but localized fields often can be detected by professional measuring instruments. These "hot spots" are often found near wiring in the shack and metal objects such as antenna masts or equipment cabinets. But even with the best instrumentation, these measurements may also be misleading in the near field.

One need not make precise measurements or model the exact antenna system, however, to develop some idea of the relative fields around an antenna. Computer modeling using close approximations of the geometry and power input of the antenna will generally suffice. Those who are familiar with *MININEC* can estimate their power densities by computer modeling, and those who have access to professional power-density meters can make useful measurements.

While our primary concern is ordinarily the intensity of the signal radiated by an antenna, we should also remember that there are other potential energy sources to be considered. You can also be exposed to RF radiation directly from a power amplifier if it is operated without proper shielding. Transmission lines may also radiate a significant amount of energy under some conditions.

Further RF Exposure Suggestions

Potential exposure situations should be taken seriously. Based on the FCC/EPA measurements and other data, the "RF awareness" guidelines of Table 10.5 were developed by the ARRL RF Safety Committee. A longer version of these guidelines, along with a complete list of references, appeared in a *QST* article by Ivan Shulman, MD, WC2S. "Is Amateur Radio Hazardous to Our Health" in the October 1989 issue of *QST* provides useful information. In addition, *QST* carries information regarding the latest developments for RF safety precautions and regulations at the local and federal levels.

Limiting RF Exposure

You must always take care to position your amateur antennas in a manner so they cannot harm you or anyone else. The simplest way to do this is to always install them high and in the clear, away from buildings or other locations where people might be close to them. To prevent **RF burns** you must be sure no one can reach the antenna while you are transmitting into it. It doesn't matter what type of antenna it is, or how much power you are running. If you or someone else can touch the antenna, it is too close.

Of course the one exception to this is the antenna on a hand-held radio. You aren't likely to receive an RF burn from touching the antenna on your hand-held radio because the transmitter power is quite low. You should still keep the antenna as far from you or anyone else as possible, however, to minimize your exposure to the RF electromagnetic fields from the radiated signal.

As you learned in the previous section of this chapter, even if you can't touch the antenna, the RF fields can still produce some heating of your body tissue. You will learn more about how to estimate a safe distance to minimize any RF heating later in this chapter.

The combination of electric and magnetic waves of energy that are produced by your transmitter are called electromagnetic radiation. Electromagnetic radiation with frequencies between about 3 kHz and 300 GHz is called **radio frequency (RF) radiation**. (Higher-frequency electromagnetic waves, such as light, ultraviolet radiation and even gamma rays and X-rays are all above the RF range.)

The FCC has established limits for the maximum exposure that people can receive from transmitted electric and magnetic fields. You must ensure that people in and around your amateur station do not receive more than the maximum permissible exposure from your station. FCC Rules may require you to perform a routine RF radiation exposure evaluation to show that your station meets these requirements. You should have a basic understanding of some factors that can affect the strength of the RF fields that radiate from your antenna. This will help you understand the procedures you can follow to perform such an evaluation, and the steps you can take to minimize exposure.

Higher transmitter power will produce stronger radiated RF fields. So using the minimum power necessary to carry out your communications will minimize the exposure of anyone near your station. Reducing power is one effective way of meeting the FCC MPE limits.

An antenna that is higher and farther away from people also reduces the strength of the radiated fields that anyone will be exposed to. If you can raise your antenna higher in the air or move it farther from your neighbor's property line you will reduce exposure.

A half-wavelength dipole antenna that is only 5 meters above the ground would generally create a stronger RF field on the ground beneath the antenna than many other antennas. For example, a horizontal loop, a 3-element Yagi antenna or a 3-element Quad antenna all have significantly more gain than a dipole. Yet at a height of 30 meters each of these antennas would produce a smaller RF field strength on the ground beneath the antenna than would the low dipole. As a general rule, place your antenna at least as high as necessary to ensure that you meet the FCC radiation exposure guidelines.

You can also use the radiation pattern of the antenna to your advantage in controlling exposure. For example, if you position your dipole antenna (with maximum radiation off the sides of the antenna and minimum radiation off the ends) so the ends are pointed at your neighbor's house (or your house) you will reduce the exposure. A beam antenna can have an even more dramatic effect on reducing the exposure. Simply do not point the antenna in the direction where people will most likely be located.

Even your choice of operating frequency can have an affect. Humans absorb less RF energy at some frequencies (and the MPE is higher at those frequencies). You can reduce exposure by selecting an operating frequency with a higher MPE.

Everything else being equal, some emission modes will result in less RF radiation exposure than others. For example, modes like RTTY or FM voice transmit at full power during the entire transmission. On CW, you transmit at full power during dots and dashes and at zero power during the space between these elements. A single-sideband (SSB) phone signal generally produces the lowest radiation exposure because the transmitter is at full power for only a small percentage of the time during a single transmission. The **duty cycle** of an emission takes into account the amount of time a transmitter is operating at full power during a single transmission. An emission with a lower duty cycle produces less RF radiation exposure for the same PEP output.

Lower duty cycles, then, result in lower RF radiation exposures. That also means the antenna can be closer to people without exceeding their MPE limits. Compared to a 100% duty-cycle mode, people can be closer to your antenna if you are using a 50% duty-cycle mode.

Another step you can take to limit your RF radiation exposure is by reducing your actual transmitting time. The FCC regulations specify time averaged MPE limits. For a controlled RF exposure environment, the exposure is averaged over any 6-minute period. For an uncontrolled RF exposure environment, the exposure is averaged over any 30-minute period. So if your routine RF radiation exposure evaluation indicates that you might exceed the MPE limits for a controlled RF environment, reduce your actual transmit time during any 6-minute period. If you might exceed the MPE limits for an uncontrolled environment, reduce your actual transmit time during any 30-minute period.

[You have been studying some very important information. Let's review what you have learned before going on to more new material. Turn to Chapter 11 and study questions T0C01 through T0C04, T0C06 through T0C09, T0C11 through T0C16 and T0C19. Also study questions T0D06, T0E03 through T0E06, T0F05 and T0F12. Review this section if any of those questions give you trouble.]

General Safety Recommendations

There are a few additional RF safety points that you should be aware of when operating your Amateur Radio station. This section includes some general guidelines to help keep you and anyone near your station safe while you are operating your station.

Hand-held radios are very popular for VHF and UHF operation, especially with FM repeaters. They transmit with less than 7-watts of power, which is generally considered safe. Because the radios are designed to be operated with an antenna that is within 20 centimeters of your body, they are classified as **portable devices** by the FCC. Some special considerations are in order to ensure safe operation. This is especially true because hand-held radios generally place the antenna close to your head. Try to position the radio so the antenna is as far from your head (and especially your eyes) while transmitting. An external speaker microphone can be helpful. See **Figure 10.10**.

A **mobile device** is a transceiver that is designed to be mounted in a vehicle. Mobile devices are normally intended to be operated with an antenna that is at least 20 cm from any person. Mobile operations also require some special considerations. For example, you should try to mount the antenna in the center of the metal roof of your vehicle, if possible. This will use the metal body of the vehicle as an RF shield to protect people inside the car. Glass-mounted antennas can result in higher exposure levels, as can antennas mounted on a trunk lid or front fender. Glass does not form a good RF shield.

Although mobile transceivers usually transmit with higher power levels than hand-held radios, the mobile unit often produces less RF radiation exposure. This is because an antenna mounted on a metal vehicle roof is generally well shielded from vehicle occupants.

Don't operate RF power amplifiers or transmitters with the covers or shielding removed. This practice helps you avoid both electric shock hazards and RF safety hazards. A safety interlock prevents the gear from being turned on accidentally while the shielding is off. (If your equipment does not have such a safety interlock you should take other steps to ensure that the amplifier cannot be turned on accidentally.) This is especially important for VHF and UHF equipment. When reassembling transmitting equipment, replace all the screws that hold the RF compartment shielding in place. Tighten all the screws securely before applying power to the equipment.

Another area you should pay attention to is the feed line connecting your transmitter to your antenna. If you are using poor-quality coax, with shielding that is inadequate, or if there are other causes leading to signals radiating from your feed line, you should consider corrective measures. (Use only good-quality coax and be sure your connectors are installed properly.) Improper grounding can also lead to a condition known as RF in the shack. This is especially a problem with stations installed in the second or third floor (or higher) where the ground lead begins to act more like an antenna. If you notice that your SWR reading changes as you touch your equipment, or if you feel a tingling sensation in your fingers when you touch the radio or microphone, these may be indicators of RF in the shack. You will have to take some steps to correct these conditions to ensure a safe operating environment.

If you are installing a repeater or other transmitter in a location that includes antennas and transmitters operating in other services, you must be aware that the total site installation must meet the FCC RF radiation MPE limits. This means your signal is only one part of the total RF radiation from that location. You will probably have to cooperate with the licensees for the other transmitters to determine the total exposure.

Figure 10.10 — Keep the antenna of a hand-held radio as far from your head (especially your eyes) as possible while transmitting. A remote microphone allows you to hold the radio farther away.

[You should turn to Chapter 11 now and study questions T0C05, T0D01, T0D03 and T0F13. Review this section if you don't understand the answers to any of these questions.]

FCC RF-Exposure Regulations

FCC regulations control the amount of RF exposure that can result from your station's operation (§§97.13, 1.1307 (b)(c)(d), 1.1310 and 2.1093). The regulations set limits on the maximum permissible exposure (MPE) allowed from operation of transmitters in all radio services. They also require that certain types of stations be evaluated to determine if they are in compliance with the MPEs specified in the rules. The FCC has also required that questions on RF environmental safety practices be included on the Technician and General class examinations.

The material presented here is only an overview of this topic.

The Rules
Maximum Permissible Exposure (MPE)

The regulations control *exposure* to RF fields, not the *strength* of RF fields. There is no limit to how strong a field can be as long as no one is being exposed to it, although FCC regulations require that amateurs use the minimum necessary power at all times (§97.313 [a]). All radio stations must comply with the requirements for MPEs, even QRP stations running only a few watts or less. The MPEs vary with frequency, as shown in **Table 10.6**.

MPE limits are specified in maximum electric and magnetic fields for frequencies below 30 MHz, in power density for frequencies above 300 MHz and all three ways for frequencies from 30 to 300 MHz. For compliance purposes, all of these limits must be considered separately—if any one is exceeded, the station is not in compliance. For example, your 2-meter (146 MHz) station radiated electric field strength and power density may be less than the maximum allowed. If the radiated magnetic field strength exceeds that limit, however, your station does not meet the requirements.

Environments

In the latest rules, the FCC has defined two exposure environments—controlled and uncontrolled. A **controlled environment** is one in which the people who are being exposed are aware of that exposure and can take steps to minimize that exposure, if appropriate. In an **uncontrolled environment**, the people being exposed are not normally aware of the exposure. The uncontrolled environment limits are more stringent than the controlled environment limits.

Although the controlled environment is usually intended as an occupational environment, the FCC has determined that it generally applies to amateur operators and members of their immediate households. In most cases, controlled-environment limits can be applied to your home and property to which you can control physical access. The uncontrolled environment is intended for areas that are accessible by the general public, normally your neighbors' properties and the public sidewalk areas around your home. In either case, you can apply the more restrictive limits, if you choose.

Station Evaluations

The FCC requires that certain amateur stations be evaluated for compliance with the MPEs. This will help ensure a safe operating environment for amateurs, their families and neighbors. Although an amateur can have someone else do the evaluation, it is not difficult for hams to evaluate their own stations. FCC Office of Engineering and Technology (OET) Bulletin 65 and the Amateur Supplement to that Bulletin contain basic information about the regulations and a number of tables that show compliance distances for specific antennas and power levels. Generally, hams will use these tables to evaluate their stations. If they choose, however, they can do more extensive calculations, use a computer to model their antenna and exposure, or make actual measurements.

In most cases, hams will be able to use an FCC table that best describes their station's operation to determine the minimum compliance distance for their specific operation. Such tables are included in the FCC OET Bulletin 65 and the Amateur Supplement. More extensive tables are also included in ARRL's *RF Exposure and You*. The tables show the compliance distances for controlled and uncontrolled environments for a particular type of antenna at a particular height. The power levels shown in a table can be adjusted for the duty cycle of the operating mode being used, and operating on and off time. The data can be averaged over 6 minutes for controlled environments or 30 minutes for uncontrolled environments.

Categorical Exemptions

Some types of amateur stations do not need to be evaluated, but these stations must still comply with the MPE limits. The station licensee remains responsible for ensuring that the station meets these requirements.

The FCC has exempted these stations from the evaluation requirement because their output power, operating mode and frequency are such that they are presumed to be in compliance with the rules.

Amateur station licensees are not required to perform a routine RF environmental evaluation if the transmitter output PEP is less than or equal to the limits specified in Section 97.13(c) of the FCC Rules. (This section is printed on page 10.18.)

Certain repeater stations are also exempt. If you are (or become) a repeater licensee, read the FCC Rules carefully to determine if you are required to perform an RF evaluation for your repeater station.

Hand-held radios and vehicle-mounted mobile radios that operate using a push-to-talk (PTT) button are also categorically exempt from performing the routine evaluation.

Correcting Problems

Most hams are already in compliance with the MPE requirements. Some amateurs, especially those using indoor antennas or high-power, high-duty-cycle modes such as a RTTY bulletin station and specialized stations for moonbounce operations and the like may need to make adjustments to their station or operation to be in compliance.

The FCC permits amateurs considerable flexibility in complying with these regulations. Hams can adjust their operating frequency, mode or power to comply with the MPE limits. They can also adjust their operating habits or control the direction their antenna is pointing. For example, if an amateur were to discover that the MPE limits had been exceeded for uncontrolled exposure after 28 minutes of transmitting, the FCC would consider it perfectly acceptable to take a 2-minute break after 28 minutes.

Ongoing Developments

As with all FCC Rules, the RF Exposure Rules are subject to change from time to time. Check *QST*, W1AW bulletins and the RF Exposure News page on *ARRLWeb* (**http://www.arrl.org/news/rfsafety**).

Table 10.6

(From §1.1310) Limits for Maximum Permissible Exposure (MPE)

(A) Limits for Occupational/Controlled Exposure				
Frequency Range (MHz)	**Electric Field Strength (V/m)**	**Magnetic Field Strength (A/m)**	**Power Density (mW/cm²)**	**Averaging Time (minutes)**
0.3-3.0	614	1.63	(100)*	6
3.0-30	1842/f	4.89/f	(900/f²)*	6
30-300	61.4	0.163	1.0	6
300-1500	—	—	f/300	6
1500-100,000	—	—	5	6
f = frequency in MHz				
* = Plane-wave equivalent power density (see Note 1).				

(B) Limits for General Population/Uncontrolled Exposure				
Frequency Range (MHz)	**Electric Field Strength (V/m)**	**Magnetic Field Strength (A/m)**	**Power Density (mW/cm²)**	**Averaging Time (minutes)**
0.3-1.34	614	1.63	(100)*	30
1.34-30	824/f	2.19/f	(180/f²)*	30
30-300	27.5	0.073	0.2	30
300-1500	—	—	f/1500	30
1500-100,000	—	—	1.0	30
f = frequency in MHz				
* = Plane-wave equivalent power density (See Note 1.)				

Note 1: This means the equivalent far-field strength that would have the E or H-field component calculated or measured. It does not apply well in the near field of an antenna. The equivalent far-field power density can be found in the near or far field regions from the relationships:

$$P_d = |E_{total}|^2/3770 \text{ mW/cm}^2 \text{ or from } P_d = |H_{total}|^2 \times 37.7 \text{ mW/cm}^2$$

FCC Maximum Permissible Exposure (MPE) Limits

In the first part of this chapter, we described the 1991 IEEE standard, which ANSI adopted in 1992, as well as the National Council for Radiation Protection and Measurement (NCRP) recommended exposure guidelines. When the FCC adopted RF radiation protection rules in 1996, they chose a blend of these guidelines. **Table 10.6** (on the two previous pages) in the RF Exposure Regulations sidebar lists the FCC Maximum Permissible Exposure limits for both the controlled and uncontrolled radiation environments at various frequencies.

Amateurs normally look only to Part 97 for the exact Rules governing Amateur Radio. There are other Parts to the FCC Rules, though, and in the case of the RF radiation exposure limits, you will have to look in Part 1 to find the exact limits. If we look in Part 97 for information about the exposure limits we find:

§97.13(c) Before causing or allowing an amateur station to transmit from any place where the operation of the station could cause human exposure to levels of radiofrequency (RF) radiation in excess of that allowed under § 1.1310 of this chapter, the licensee is required to take certain actions.

(1) The licensee must perform the routine RF environmental evaluation prescribed by § 1.1307(b) of this chapter if the power of the licensee's station exceeds the limits given in the following table:

Wavelength Band		Evaluation Required if Power* (watts) Exceeds:
MF	160 m	500
HF	80 m	500
	75 m	500
	40 m	500
	30 m	425
	20 m	225
	17 m	125
	15 m	100
	12 m	75
	10 m	50
VHF (all bands)		50
UHF	70 cm	70
	33 cm	150
	23 cm	200
	13 cm	250
SHF (all bands)		250
EHF (all bands)		250
Repeater stations (all bands)		Non-building-mounted antennas: height above ground level to lowest point of antenna < 10 m and power > 500 W ERP. Building-mounted antennas: power > 500 W ERP

(2) If the routine environmental evaluation indicates that the RF electromagnetic fields could exceed the limits contained in §1.1310 of this chapter in accessible areas, the licensee must take action to prevent human exposure to such RF electromagnetic fields. Further information on evaluating compliance with these limits can be found in the OET Bulletin Number 65, "Evaluating Compliance with FCC-Specified Guidelines for Human Exposure to Radio Frequency Electromagnetic Fields."

As mentioned in the last line, FCC's Office of Engineering and Technology (OET) Bulletin 65 also lists the specific MPE limits and provides some information that will help amateurs evaluate their stations. Table 10.6 will help you determine the MPE limits that apply to your amateur operations. If you will only be using one or two bands, you will only have to perform a station evaluation for those bands. If you will be using a variety of bands over the HF, VHF and UHF ranges, you will have to perform an evaluation for each band you will be using. Don't worry about trying to memorize the table. You will have a copy of it included with your exam papers, so you only have to know how to read the table to find the information you need.

For some frequency ranges, the MPE limits are given as constant values. For example, over the VHF (30 to 300 MHz) range, the **controlled environment** MPE limits are 61.4 V/m for the electric field and 0.163 A/m for the magnetic field. The plane-wave equivalent power density is 1.0 mW/cm². Look at Section B of Table 10.6 to find the **uncontrolled environment** limits over the VHF range (30 to 300 MHz). Here you will notice that the electric field MPE is 27.5 V/m and the magnetic field MPE is 0.073 A/m. The plane-wave equivalent (far field) power density is 0.2 mW/cm². These same values apply to the amateur 2-meter (146-MHz) band as well as the 1.25-meter (222-MHz) band.

If you want to know the MPE limits for the HF bands, you will have some simple calculations to perform. Simply use the equations listed in Table 10.6 Section A and the three in Section B for the frequency range you want to evaluate. For example, the controlled environment power density MPE limit on 3.7 MHz is:

HF Controlled Environment Plane-Wave Equivalent
(Equation 10.1)

$$\text{Power Density (MPE)} = \frac{900}{(f(\text{MHz}))^2}$$

HF Controlled Environment Plane-Wave Equivalent

$$\text{Power Density (MPE)} = \frac{900}{(3.7)^2} = \frac{900}{13.69} = 65.7 \frac{\text{mW}}{\text{cm}^2}$$

This value is called the *plane-wave equivalent power density* or the *equivalent far-field power density* because power density values are only defined in an antenna's far-field radiation zone. You will learn more about the near field and far-field zones of an antenna shortly.

Suppose you wanted to know the MPE limits for an uncontrolled environment at 28.4 MHz. Again, just perform the calculations indicated in Table 10.6 Section B for the HF range.

HF Uncontrolled Environment Plane-Wave

$$\text{Equivalent Power Density (MPE)} = \frac{180}{(f(\text{MHz}))^2}$$

(Equation 10.2)

HF Uncontrolled Environment Plane-Wave
Equivalent Power Density (MPE) =

$$\frac{180}{(28.4)^2} = \frac{180}{806.56} = 0.223 \; \frac{\text{mW}}{\text{cm}^2}$$

In the UHF (300 to 1500 MHz) and SHF (1500 to 100,000 MHz) ranges, the FCC only specifies MPE limits in plane-wave equivalent power densities. This makes it easier for you to determine if your station meets the safe exposure limits because you only have to consider this one value, rather than electric field, magnetic field and power density values. Suppose you wanted to know the controlled environment MPE limit for the 70-cm (440-MHz) band or the 1270-MHz band. Look at Section A of Table 10.6 and find the 300 to 1500-MHz value. This is another one that varies with frequency, so you are given an equation: divide the operating frequency in megahertz by 300.

UHF Controlled Environment Plane-Wave

$$\text{Equivalent Power Density (MPE)} = \frac{f(\text{MHz})}{300}$$

(Equation 10.3)

UHF Controlled Environment Plane-Wave
Equivalent Power Density (MPE) =

$$\frac{1270}{300} = 4.2 \; \frac{\text{mW}}{\text{cm}^2}$$

To find the MPE limits for uncontrolled environments over this frequency range, you will have to look at Section B of Table 10.6. Here you can find the maximum power density by dividing the operating frequency by 1500.

UHF Uncontrolled Environment Plane-Wave

$$\text{Equivalent Power Density (MPE)} = \frac{f(\text{MHz})}{1500}$$

(Equation 10.4)

Determining the Field Strengths Around Your Antenna

You have just learned that the FCC maximum permissible exposure limits are given in terms of electric and magnetic field strengths. So how do you determine if the transmitted signal from your station is within these RF exposure limits? You must analyze, measure or otherwise determine your transmitted field strengths and power density. This means there are a number of ways you can perform the required routine RF radiation evaluation.

One way to do this is by making direct measurements of the electric and magnetic field strengths around your antenna while transmitting a signal. If you happen to have a calibrated field-strength meter with a calibrated field-strength sensor, you can make accurate measurements. Unfortunately, such calibrated meters are expensive and not normally found in an amateur's toolbox. The relative field strength meters many amateurs use are not accurate enough to make this type of measurement.

Even if you do have access to a laboratory-grade calibrated field-strength meter, you must be aware of factors that can upset your readings. Reflections from ground and nearby conductors (power lines, other antennas, house wiring, etc) can easily confuse field strength readings. For example, the measuring probe and the person making the measurement can interact with the antenna radiation if they are in the near-field zone. In addition, you must know the frequency response of the test equipment and probes, and use them only within the appropriate range. Even the orientation of the test probe with respect to the test antenna polarization is important.

A wide-bandwidth instrument used to measure RF fields is calibrated over a wide frequency range and responds instantly to any signal within that range. The nice thing about a wide-bandwidth instrument is that it requires no tuning over its entire operating range. A narrow-bandwidth instrument, on the other hand, may be able to cover a wide frequency range, but would have a bandwidth of perhaps only a few kilohertz at any instant. You have to tune the instrument to the particular frequency of interest before making your measurements.

Why should we be concerned with the separation between the source antenna and the field-strength meter, which has its own receiving antenna? One important reason is that if you place a receiving antenna very close to an antenna when you measure the field strength, *mutual coupling* between the two antennas may actually alter the radiation from the antenna you are trying to measure.

This sort of mutual coupling can occur in the region very close to the antenna under test. This region is called the *reactive near-field* region. The term "reactive" refers to the fact that the mutual impedance between the transmitting and receiving antennas can be either capacitive or inductive in nature. The reactive near field is sometimes called the "induction field," meaning that the magnetic field usually is predominant over the electric field in this region. The antenna acts as though it were a rather large, lumped-constant inductor or capacitor, storing energy in the reactive near field rather than propagating it into space.

For simple wire antennas, the reactive near field is considered to be within about a half wavelength from an antenna's radiating center. For making field-strength measurements, we do not want to be too close to the antenna being measured.

The strength of the reactive near field decreases in a complicated fashion as you increase the distance from the antenna. Beyond the reactive near field, the antenna's radiated field is divided into two other regions: the *radiating near field* and the *radiating far field*. Nearly any metal object or other conductor that is located within the radiating near field can alter the radiation pattern of the antenna. Conductors such as telephone wiring or aluminum siding on a building that is located in the radiating near field will interact with the theoretical electric and magnetic fields to add or subtract intensity. This results in areas of varying field strength. Although you have measured the fields in the general area around your antenna and found that your station meets the MPE limits, there may still be "hot spots" or areas of higher field strengths within that region. In the near field of an antenna, the field strength varies in a way that depends on the type of antenna and other nearby objects as you move farther away from the antenna.

There is no clear boundary between the reactive near field, the radiating near field and the radiating far field areas around an antenna. It is a rather "fuzzy" description that just tries to help identify the conditions around the antenna. **Figure 10.11** shows the three fields around of a simple wire antenna.

The radiating far-field forms the traveling electromagnetic waves. Far-field radiation is distinguished by the fact that the power density is proportional to the inverse square of the distance. (That means if you double the distance from the antenna, the power density will be one fourth as strong.) The electric and magnetic fields are perpendicular to each other in the wave front, and are in time phase. The total energy is equally divided between the electric and magnetic fields. Beyond several wavelengths from the antenna, these are the only fields we need to consider. For accurate measurement of radiation patterns, we must place our measuring instruments at least several wavelengths away from the antenna under test.

If you don't have the necessary measuring equipment, you can perform some calculations to determine the electric and magnetic field strengths from your station. This is normally done using computer programs, which take into account the gain and directivity of an antenna. There are a variety of programs available. The most reliable ones are based on the Numerical Electromagnetic Code (NEC) program that uses the Method of Moments analysis. (MININEC is a variation of the original program shortened to run on personal computers.) While these are powerful analysis tools, you must be careful to accurately model the antenna and all conductors that might be within a few wavelengths of the antenna for reliable results. Some simple analysis methods ignore the effects of ground conductivity on the field strengths. For the best analysis, however, you must account for the ground conductivity and how that interacts with your antenna radiation pattern.

In this section you have learned that you can conduct the required routine station evaluation by measuring the field strength directly. You can also perform some calculations, either directly or by using a computer program. Bulletin 65 from the FCC Office of Engineering and Technology has more detailed information about how you can perform the calculations if you prefer to use that method. You can also perform the required station evaluation without performing any calculations, either by hand or by computer. You can evaluate your station by finding the appropriate entries in published tables. You will learn about using tables in the next section. The FCC does not specify any mandatory (required) procedures that you must follow to evaluate your station. The FCC only requires that your station does not exceed the maximum permissible exposure limits.

The FCC does not require you to keep any records of your routine RF radiation exposure evaluation. It is a good idea to keep them, however. They may prove useful if the FCC would ask for documentation to substantiate (prove) that an evaluation has been performed. The FCC will ask you to demonstrate that you have read and understood the FCC Rules about RF-radiation exposure by indicating that understanding on FCC Form 605 when you apply for your license.

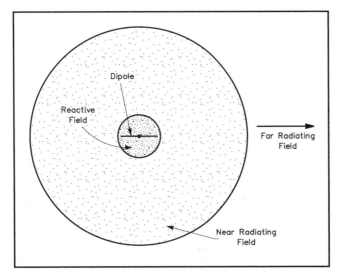

Figure 10.11 — This drawing illustrates the reactive near field, the radiating near field and the far field around a half-wavelength dipole antenna.

[Turn to Chapter 11 now and study questions T0D04, T0D05, T0D07, T0D08, T0D09, T0E01, T0E02, T0F01 through T0F04, T0F06 through T0F11, T0F14 and T0F15. Review this section as needed.]

Routine Evaluation by Tables

There is one more method of performing a routine RF radiation exposure evaluation that you should be aware of. In fact, this is probably the method most amateurs will use. It involves the use of some tables created to help you determine safe exposure distances from your antennas. You simply look through the tables to find the station and antenna configuration that is most like your station and then read the minimum recommended distances for controlled and uncontrolled environments. The tables are generated by using a computer analysis and modeling of various station configurations.

The FCC has published such tables in the Amateur Supplement to their Office of Engineering and Technology (OET) Bulletin 65. Amateurs can use the information in that bulletin and supplement to evaluate their stations. The ARRL book *RF Exposure and You* also includes tables from a large number of computer calculations for various station configurations.

Table 10.7 shows an antenna table for a 3-element 10-meter Yagi taken from ARRL's *RF Exposure and You*. This particular table is for an antenna mounted 30 feet above ground. The data for the table was calculated using the NEC-4 computer program to analyze this antenna over average ground.

You can use this table by selecting the maximum transmitter power that you use, and then reading the minimum horizontal distance from the antenna to the nearest possible human. As long as no one can come closer to the antenna than the listed uncontrolled environment distance, you will be in compliance with the FCC maximum permissible exposure (MPE) limits. Notice that you and your family should come no closer to the antenna than the distance listed in the controlled environment column. **Figure 10.12** shows how to calculate the horizontal distance at ground level and higher floors in a building.

As an example of reading this table, suppose you operate with no more than 100 watts on 10 meters. Anyone can safely be directly beneath this antenna at any height from the ground up to 20 feet. The third floor of your house, at 30 feet above ground, must be at least 10.5 feet from the antenna. Your neighbor's house would have to be 18.5 feet from the antenna in this case.

Table 10.8 shows a similar table that was prepared for a 2-meter ground-plane antenna, also mounted 30 feet above ground. If you normally use 50 watts of power on

Table 10.7
10-meter band horizontal, 3-element Yagi, Frequency = 29.7 MHz, Antenna height = 30 feet

Horizontal distance (feet) from any part of the antenna for compliance with occupational/controlled or general population/uncontrolled exposure limits*

Power** (watts)	6 feet		12 feet		20 feet		30 feet	
	con.	unc.	con.	unc.	con.	unc.	con.	unc.
10	0	0	0	0	0	0	8	9
25	0	0	0	0	0	0	8.5	11
50	0	0	0	0	0	0	9	13.5
100	0	0	0	0	0	0	10.5	18.5
200	0	0	0	0	0	21.5	12.5	25
250	0	0	0	0	0	25	13.5	27.5
300	0	0	0	0	0	28.5	14.5	30
400	0	0	0	39	0	35	16.5	34
500	0	0	0	47	0	48	18.5	37.5
600	0	0	0	52.5	0	59.5	20	40.5
750	0	36	0	59	16.5	70.5	22	45.5
1000	0	46.5	0	67	21.5	82.5	25	61.5
1250	0	53	0	73.5	25	91.5	27.5	95.5
1500	0	58.5	0	79	28.5	99	30	108

Height above ground (feet) where exposure occurs

* 0 feet indicates that the exposure at the height in the column above or below the antenna is in compliance.
** Power = Average power input to the antenna.

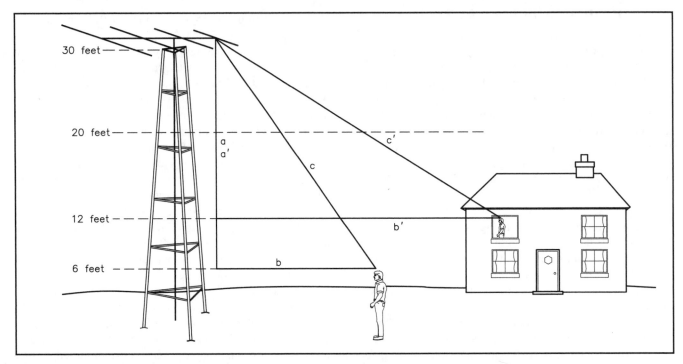

Figure 10.12 — This drawing shows how to calculate the horizontal distances between an antenna and the areas being evaluated. To use Tables 10.7 and 10.8 for worst-case horizontal compliance distances you must consider the antenna height, the height of the exposure point and the horizontal distance between the antenna and the exposure point. Use the a' and b' triangle sides for the second-story exposure. From there, you can use the formula: $c = \sqrt{a^2 + b^2}$

Table 10.8
2-meter band ground plane, 45-degree radials, Frequency = 146.0 MHz, Height above ground = 30 feet

Horizontal distance (feet) from any part of the antenna for compliance with occupational/controlled or general population/uncontrolled exposure limits*

Power**					*Height above ground (feet) where exposure occurs*				
	6 feet		**12 feet**		**20 feet**		**30 feet**	
(watts)	con.	unc.	con.	unc.	con.	unc.	con.	unc.
10	0	0	0	0	0	0	2	3
25	0	0	0	0	0	0	2.5	4
50	0	0	0	0	0	0	3	6
100	0	0	0	0	0	0	3.5	8.5
200	0	0	0	0	0	0	5.5	12
250	0	0	0	0	0	0	6	13.5
300	0	0	0	0	0	0	6.5	14.5
400	0	0	0	0	0	0	7.5	17
500	0	0	0	0	0	0	8.5	19
600	0	0	0	0	0	0	9.5	20.5
750	0	0	0	0	0	0	10.5	23
1000	0	0	0	0	0	20	12	27.5
1250	0	0	0	0	0	24	13.5	29.5
1500	0	0	0	0	0	32.5	14.5	31.5

* 0 feet indicates that the exposure at the height in the column above or below the antenna is in compliance.
** Power = Average power input to the antenna.

Figure 10.13 — These tables are included with the question pool graphics. There will be a copy of these tables included with your exam. Several questions ask you to select the correct minimum safe distance for a certain antenna and transmitter power.

Figure T0-2

Estimated distances to meet RF power density guidelines with a horizontal half-wave dipole antenna (estimated gain, 2 dBi). Calculations include the EPA ground reflection factor of 2.56.

Frequency: 7 MHz
Estimated antenna gain: 2 dBi
Controlled limit: 18.37 mw/cm^2
Uncontrolled limit: 3.67 mw/cm^2

Transmitter power (watts)	Distance to controlled limit	Distance to uncontrolled limit
100	1.4'	3.1'
500	3.1'	6.9'
1000	4.3'	9.7'
1500	5.3'	11.9'

Estimated distances to meet RF power density guidelines in the main beam of a typical 3-element "triband" Yagi for the 14, 21 and 28 MHz amateur radio bands. Calculations include the EPA ground reflection factor of 2.56.

Frequency: 28 MHz
Antenna gain: 8 dBi
Controlled limit: 1.15 mw/cm^2
Uncontrolled limit: 0.23 mw/cm^2

Transmitter power (watts)	Distance to controlled limit	Distance to uncontrolled limit
100	11'	24.5'
500	24.5'	54.9'
1000	34.7'	77.6'
1500	42.5'	95.1'

Estimated distances to meet RF power density guidelines in the main beam of a 17-element Yagi on a five-wavelength boom designed for weak signal communications on the 144 MHz amateur radio band (estimated gain, 16.8 dBi). Calculations include the EPA ground reflection factor of 2.56.

Frequency: 144 MHz
Estimated antenna gain: 16.8 dBi
Controlled limit: 1 mw/cm^2
Uncontrolled limit: 0.2 mw/cm^2

Transmitter power (watts)	Distance to controlled limit	Distance to uncontrolled limit
10	10.2'	22.9'
100	32.4'	72.4'
500	72.4'	162'
1500	125.5'	280.6'

Estimated distances to meet RF power density guidelines with a VHF quarter-wave ground plane or mobile whip antenna (estimated gain, 1 dBi). Calculations include the EPA ground reflection factor of 2.56.

Frequency: 146 MHz
Estimated antenna gain: 1 dBi
Controlled limit: 1 mw/cm^2
Uncontrolled limit: 0.2 mw/cm^2

Transmitter power (watts)	Distance to controlled limit	Distance to uncontrolled limit
10	1.7'	3.7'
50	3.7'	8.3'
150	6.4'	14.4'

Estimated distances to meet RF power density guidelines in the main beam of UHF 5/8 ground plane or mobile whip antenna (estimated gain, 4 dBi). Calculations include the EPA ground reflection factor of 2.56.

Frequency: 446 MHz
Estimated antenna gain: 4 dBi
Controlled limit: 1.49 mw/cm^2
Uncontrolled limit: 0.3 mw/cm^2

Transmitter power (watts)	Distance to controlled limit	Distance to uncontrolled limit
10	1.9'	4.3'
50	4.3'	9.6'
150	7.5'	16.7'

this band, you must be at least 3 feet from the antenna when you are 30 feet above ground. Your neighbor or any other person who does not know you are transmitting radio signals must be at least 6 feet from the antenna.

You should notice that there are a lot of zeros in the columns of Tables 10.7 and 10.8. Basically, the tables are telling you that the vertical distance between you (or your neighbors) and your antenna is all the separation you need. Someone standing at the base of the tower or antenna support structure will receive less than the maximum permissible exposure to RF radiation. Common sense should also apply. No one should stand close enough to touch an antenna while it is transmitting. If someone did touch the antenna they could receive an RF burn.

On your Technician exam, you will be given a set of tables that use a condensed format and not quite as much information as Tables 10.7 and 10.8. **Figure 10.13** shows that set of tables. The most important thing about using any tables to evaluate your station or answer questions on your exam is to be sure you select the correct table. For example, if you are evaluating a horizontal half-wave dipole on 40 meters (7 MHz) then you would use the information in the first block. Select the proper transmitter power and look for the column representing either the controlled environment or the uncontrolled environment as appropriate.

This section is only intended to introduce you to the concept of how to evaluate your station using tables. We could not include the tables for all possible station configurations in this book. ARRL's *RF Exposure and You* includes tables for many more antenna types at a variety of heights.

When you are looking for a configuration that matches your station you must be careful to read all the notes and the complete antenna description, so you are sure to select the proper table. Be sure you read the appropriate column for either the controlled or uncontrolled environment distances. Also be careful to select the appropriate power level. If there is no listing for the power

you normally use, then select the next higher value. This will recommend a farther distance for safety, and will provide a higher margin for error.

Of course you have many ways to ensure that no one receives more than the maximum permissible exposure of RF radiation from your station. For example, you might simply take steps to ensure that you can't transmit with your antenna pointed directly at your neighbor's house. You can also reduce operating power, select an operating mode with a lower duty cycle or even limit your transmit time during any 30-minute averaging period.

You also have the option of restricting access to any areas of high RF radiation levels. This might mean putting up a fence around your property to ensure that no one can wander too close to your antennas while you are transmitting.

[Congratulations! You have now studied all the RF safety material for your Technician license exam. If you have studied the material in this book in the order it was presented, then you have also completed your study of all the material for your license exam. You aren't quite done yet, though. You should turn to Chapter 11 now and study one last group of questions: T0D10 through T0D14 and T0E10. You will want to review any areas that gave you particular difficulty before going for your exam. Good luck with the test!]

TECHNICIAN (ELEMENT 2) QUESTION POOL —WITH ANSWERS

The questions in this chapter will help you review your understanding of the material in the first 10 chapters. The questions will help you prepare for your exam. Your Technician class license exam will consist of 35 questions from the Element 2 Question Pool printed in this chapter.

DON'T START HERE!

This chapter contains the complete question pool for the Element 2 exam. Element 2 is the Technician class Amateur Radio license exam. To earn a Technician class license, you must pass a 35-question written exam. The Technician license does not require a Morse code test. If you do pass the 5-words-per-minute Morse code exam then your Technician license will allow you to operate on several high-frequency bands.

Before you read the questions and answers printed in this chapter, *be sure to read the text in the previous chapters*. Use these questions as review exercises, when the text tells you to study them. (Paper clips make excellent place markers to help you find your place in the text and the question pool as you study.) Don't try to memorize all the questions and answers.

This question pool, prepared by the Volunteer Examiner Coordinators' Question Pool Committee, is for use on exams beginning July 1, 2003. The pool is scheduled to be used through June 30, 2007. Changes to FCC Rules and other factors may result in earlier revisions. Such changes will be announced in *QST* and other Amateur Radio publications. Normally, the Question Pool Committee will simply withdraw outdated questions.

The material presented in this book has been carefully written and presented to guide you step-by-step through the learning process. By understanding the electronics principles and Amateur Radio concepts as they are presented, your in-

sight into our hobby and your appreciation for the privileges granted by an Amateur Radio license will be greatly enhanced.

How Many Questions?

The FCC specifies that an Element 2 exam must include 35 questions. This question pool is divided into ten sections, called subelements. (A subelement is a portion of the exam element, in this case Element 2.) The VEC Question Pool Committee specifies the number of questions from each subelement that should appear on your test. For example, there must be five questions from the FCC Rules section, Subelement T1. **Table 11.1** summarizes the number of questions to be selected from each subelement to make up a Technician class (Element 2) exam. The number of questions to be used from each subelement also appears at the beginning of that subelement in the question pool.

The Volunteer Examiner Coordinators' Question Pool Committee has broken the subelements into smaller groups. Each subelement has the same number of groups as there are questions from that subelement on the exam. This means there are five groups for the FCC Rules subelement and three groups for the Basic Communications Electronics subelement. The Question Pool Committee intends one question from each smaller group be used on the exam. This is not an FCC requirement, however.

There is a list of topics printed in **bold** type at the begin-

Table 11.1

Technician Exam Content

Subelement	Topic	Number of Questions
T1	FCC Rules	5
T2	Methods of Communication	2
T3	Radio Phenomena	2
T4	Station Licensee Duties	3
T5	Control Operator Duties	3
T6	Good Operating Practices	3
T7	Basic Communications Electronics	3
T8	Good Engineering Practice	6
T9	Special Operations	2
T0	Electrical, Antenna Structure and RF Safety Practices	6

ning of each small group of questions. This list of topics for each subelement forms the *syllabus*, or study guide topics for that section. The entire Technician syllabus is printed at the end of the Introduction chapter.

The small groups are labeled alphabetically within each subelement. The five groups in the FCC Rules subelement are labeled T1A through T1E. Three exam questions come from the Control Operator Duties subelement, so that subelement has sections labeled T5A through T5C.

The question numbers used in the question pool relate to the syllabus or study guide printed at the end of the Introduction, before Chapter 1 of this book. The syllabus is an outline of topics covered by the exam. Each question number begins with a T to indicate the question is from the Technician class question pool. Next is a number to indicate from which of the ten subelements the question is taken. These numbers will range from 1 through 9 and 0. Following this number is a letter to indicate which group the question is from in that subelement. Each question number ends with a two-digit number to specify its position in the set. So question T2A01 is the first question in the A group of the second subelement. Question T9B08 is the eighth question in the B group of the ninth subelement.

Who Picks the Questions?

The FCC allows Volunteer Examiner Teams to select the questions that will be used on amateur exams. If your test is coordinated by the ARRL/VEC, your test will be prepared by the VEC, or by using a computer program supplied by the VEC. All VECs and Examiners must use the questions, answers and distracters (incorrect answers) printed here. The positions of the answers may be scrambled on the exam, though. This means that you can't be sure the correct answer to question T1A01 will always be B. The correct answer may appear in location A, B, C or D.

This question pool contains more than ten times the number of questions necessary to make up an exam. This ensures that the examiners have sufficient questions to choose from when they make up an exam.

Who Gives the Test?

All Amateur Radio license exams are given by teams of three or more Volunteer Examiners (VEs). Each of the examiners is accredited by a Volunteer Examiner Coordinator (VEC) to give exams under their program. A VEC is an organization that has entered into an agreement with the FCC to coordinate the efforts of VEs. The VEC reviews the paperwork for each exam session, and then forwards the information to the FCC. The FCC then issues new or upgraded Amateur Radio licenses to those who qualify for them.

Question Pool Format

The rest of this chapter contains the entire Element 2 question pool. We have printed the answer key to these questions along the edge of the page. There is a line to indicate where you can fold the page to hide the answer key while you study. (Fold the edge of the page *under* rather than *over* the page, so you don't cover part of the questions on the page.) After making your best effort to answer the questions, you can look at the answers to check your understanding.

We have also included page references along with the answers. These page numbers indicate where in this book you will find the text discussion related to each question. If you have any problems with a question, refer to the page listed for that question. You may have to study beyond the listed page number to review all the related material. With questions that relate directly to Federal Communications Commission (FCC) Rules, we have also included references to the sections of Part 97 of the FCC Rules. We have included the text of the rules from Part 97 where appropriate. All of the questions in subelement 1, FCC Rules, include such references. There are also questions in some of the other subelements that relate directly to the FCC Rules. This book does *not* include a complete copy of Part 97, however. For the complete text of the FCC Rules governing Amateur Radio, we recommend a copy of *The ARRL's FCC Rule Book*. That book includes the complete text for Part 97, along with text to explain all the rules. *The ARRL's FCC Rule Book* is updated regularly to reflect changes to the Rules.

The VEC Question Pool Committee included a set of drawings used in some of the questions. We placed a copy of these drawings at the beginning of the question pool, for your information. You may receive a one or two-page handout similar to this with your exam papers, so you will have the figures available if your exam includes any of the questions that reference them. Some Volunteer Examiner Coordinators (such as the ARRL/VEC) may place the appropriate figures with those exam questions that require them, rather than use the entire graphics sheet with each exam. Either way, you will have the necessary drawings for reference if your exam includes one of those questions. For your convenience, we also placed the individual figures near the questions that refer to them in the question pool.

Good luck with your studies. With a bit of time devoted to reviewing this book, you'll soon be ready for your Technician class exam!

Element 2 (Technician) Graphics – For use on/after July 1, 2003

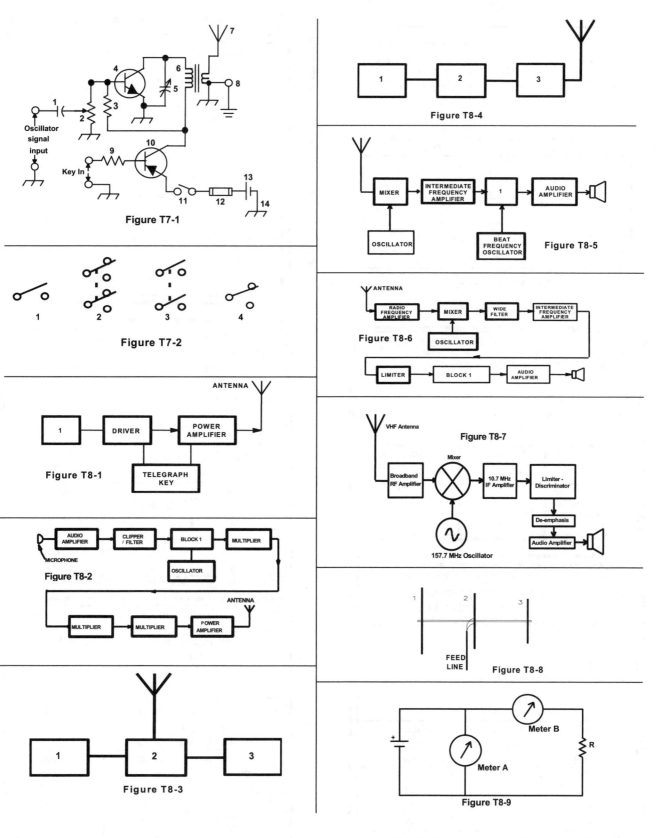

Figure T7-1

Figure T7-2

Figure T8-1

Figure T8-2

Figure T8-3

Figure T8-4

Figure T8-5

Figure T8-6

Figure T8-7

Figure T8-8

Figure T8-9

Figure TO- 1

(A) Limits for Occupational/Controlled Exposure				
Frequency Range (MHz)	Electrical Field Strength (V/m)	Magnetic Field Strength (A/m)	Power Density (mW/cm^2)	Averaging Time (minutes)
0.3-3.0	614	1.63	(100)*	6
3.0-30	1842/f	4.89/f	(900/f^2)*	6
30-300	61.4	0.163	1.0	6
300-1500	----	----	f/300	6
1500-100,000	----	----	5	6
(B) Limits for General Population/Uncontrolled Exposure				
Frequency Range (MHz)	Electrical Field Strength (V/m)	Magnetic Field Strength (A/m)	Power Density (mW/cm^2)	Averaging Time (minutes)
0.3-1.34	614	1.63	(100)*	30
1.34-30	824/f	2.19/f	(180/f^2)*	30
30-300	27.5	0.073	0.2	30
300-1500	----	----	f/1500	30
1500-100,000	----	----	1.0	30

f=frequency in MHz   *=Plane-wave equivalent power density

Figure TO- 2

Estimated distances to meet RF power density guidelines with a horizontal half-wave dipole antenna (estimated gain, 2 dBi). Calculations include the EPA ground reflection factor of 2.56.

Frequency: 7 MHz
Estimated antenna gain: 2 dBi
Controlled limit: 18.37 mw/cm^2
Uncontrolled limit: 3.67 mw/cm^2

Transmitter power (watts)	Distance to controlled limit	Distance to uncontrolled limit
100	1.4'	3.1'
500	3.1'	6.9'
1000	4.3'	9.7'
1500	5.3'	11.9'

Estimated distances to meet RF power density guidelines in the main beam of a typical 3-element "triband" Yagi for the 14, 21 and 28 MHz amateur radio bands. Calculations include the EPA ground reflection factor of 2.56.

Frequency: 28 MHz
Antenna gain: 8 dBi
Controlled limit: 1.15 mw/cm^2
Uncontrolled limit: 0.23 mw/cm^2

Transmitter power (watts)	Distance to controlled limit	Distance to uncontrolled limit
100	11'	24.5'
500	24.5'	54.9'
1000	34.7'	77.6'
1500	42.5'	95.1'

Estimated distances to meet RF power density guidelines in the main beam of a 17-element Yagi on a five-wavelength boom designed for weak signal communications on the 144 MHz amateur radio band (estimated gain, 16.8 dBi). Calculations include the EPA ground reflection factor of 2.56.

Frequency: 144 MHz
Estimated antenna gain: 16.8 dBi
Controlled limit: 1 mw/cm^2
Uncontrolled limit: 0.2 mw/cm^2

Transmitter power (watts)	Distance to controlled limit	Distance to uncontrolled limit
10	10.2'	22.9'
100	32.4'	72.4'
500	72.4'	162'
1500	125.5'	280.6'

Estimated distances to meet RF power density guidelines with a VHF quarter-wave ground plane or mobile whip antenna (estimated gain, 1 dBi). Calculations include the EPA ground reflection factor of 2.56.

Frequency: 146 MHz
Estimated antenna gain: 1 dBi
Controlled limit: 1 mw/cm^2
Uncontrolled limit: 0.2 mw/cm^2

Transmitter power (watts)	Distance to controlled limit	Distance to uncontrolled limit
10	1.7'	3.7'
50	3.7'	8.3'
150	6.4'	14.4'

Estimated distances to meet RF power density guidelines in the main beam of UHF 5/8 ground plane or mobile whip antenna (estimated gain, 4 dBi). Calculations include the EPA ground reflection factor of 2.56.

Frequency: 446 MHz
Estimated antenna gain: 4 dBi
Controlled limit: 1.49 mw/cm^2
Uncontrolled limit: 0.3 mw/cm^2

Transmitter power (watts)	Distance to controlled limit	Distance to uncontrolled limit
10	1.9'	4.3'
50	4.3'	9.6'
150	7.5'	16.7'

Technician Class (Element 2)
Question Pool — With Answers

As released by the National Conference of Volunteer Examiner Coordinators' Question Pool Committee for use on exams starting July 1, 2003 through June 30, 2007.

SUBELEMENT T1 - FCC Rules
[5 Exam Questions — 5 Groups]

T1A **Definition and purpose of Amateur Radio Service, Amateur-Satellite Service in places where the FCC regulates these services and elsewhere; Part 97 and FCC regulation of the amateur services; Penalties for unlicensed operation and for violating FCC rules; Prohibited transmissions.**

T1A01
Who makes and enforces the rules for the amateur service in the United States?
A. The Congress of the United States
B. The Federal Communications Commission (FCC)
C. The Volunteer Examiner Coordinators (VECs)
D. The Federal Bureau of Investigation (FBI)

T1A01
(B)
[97]
Page 1.3

T1A02
What are two of the five fundamental purposes for the amateur service in the United States?
A. To protect historical radio data, and help the public understand radio history
B. To help foreign countries improve communication and technical skills, and encourage visits from foreign hams
C. To modernize radio schematic drawings, and increase the pool of electrical drafting people
D. To increase the number of trained radio operators and electronics experts, and improve international goodwill

T1A02
(D)
[97.1]
Page 1.4

T1A03
What is the definition of an amateur station?
A. A radio station in a public radio service used for radiocommunications
B. A radio station using radiocommunications for a commercial purpose
C. A radio station using equipment for training new broadcast operators and technicians
D. A radio station in the amateur service used for radiocommunications

T1A03
(D)
[97.3a5]
Page 1.5

T1A04
When is an amateur station authorized to transmit information to the general public?
A. Never
B. Only when the operator is being paid
C. Only when the broadcast transmission lasts less than 1 hour
D. Only when the broadcast transmission lasts longer than 15 minutes

T1A04
(A)
[97.113b]
Page 1.19

T1A05
When is an amateur station authorized to transmit music?
A. Amateurs may not transmit music, except as an incidental part of an authorized rebroadcast of space shuttle communications
B. Only when the music produces no spurious emissions
C. Only when the music is used to jam an illegal transmission
D. Only when the music is above 1280 MHz, and the music is a live performance

T1A05
(A)
[97.113a4, 97.113e]
Page 1.20

T1A06
(C)
[97.113a4,
97.211b,
97.217]
Page 1.20

T1A06
When is the transmission of codes or ciphers allowed to hide the meaning of a message transmitted by an amateur station?
A. Only during contests
B. Only during nationally declared emergencies
C. Codes and ciphers may not be used to obscure the meaning of a message, although there are special exceptions
D. Only when frequencies above 1280 MHz are used

T1A07
(B)
[97.3a10,
97.113b]
Page 1.19

T1A07
Which of the following one-way communications may NOT be transmitted in the amateur service?
A. Telecommand to model craft
B. Broadcasts intended for reception by the general public
C. Brief transmissions to make adjustments to the station
D. Morse code practice

T1A08
(C)
[97.3a40]
Page 1.20

T1A08
What is an amateur space station?
A. An amateur station operated on an unused frequency
B. An amateur station awaiting its new call letters from the FCC
C. An amateur station located more than 50 kilometers above the Earth's surface
D. An amateur station that communicates with the International Space Station

T1A09
(B)
[97.207a]
Page 1.20

T1A09
Who may be the control operator of an amateur space station?
A. An amateur holding an Amateur Extra class operator license grant
B. Any licensed amateur operator
C. Anyone designated by the commander of the spacecraft
D. No one unless specifically authorized by the government

T1A10
(A)
[97.113a4]
Page 1.20

T1A10
When may false or deceptive signals or communications be transmitted by an amateur station?
A. Never
B. When operating a beacon transmitter in a "fox hunt" exercise
C. When playing a harmless "practical joke"
D. When you need to hide the meaning of a message for secrecy

T1A11
(C)
[97.119a]
Page 1.20

T1A11
When may an amateur station transmit unidentified communications?
A. Only during brief tests not meant as messages
B. Only when they do not interfere with others
C. Only when sent from a space station or to control a model craft
D. Only during two-way or third-party communications

T1A12
(A)
[97.119a]
Page 1.20

T1A12
What is an amateur communication called that does NOT have the required station identification?
A. Unidentified communications or signals
B. Reluctance modulation
C. Test emission
D. Tactical communication

T1A13
(B)
[97.3a23]
Page 1.20

T1A13
What is a transmission called that disturbs other communications?
A. Interrupted CW
B. Harmful interference
C. Transponder signals
D. Unidentified transmissions

T1A14
What does the term broadcasting mean?
A. Transmissions intended for reception by the general public, either direct or relayed
B. Retransmission by automatic means of programs or signals from non-amateur stations
C. One-way radio communications, regardless of purpose or content
D. One-way or two-way radio communications between two or more stations

T1A15
Why is indecent and obscene language prohibited in the Amateur Service?
A. Because it is offensive to some individuals
B. Because young children may intercept amateur communications with readily available receiving equipment
C. Because such language is specifically prohibited by FCC Rules
D. All of these choices are correct

T1A16
Which of the following is a prohibited amateur radio transmission?
A. Using an autopatch to seek emergency assistance
B. Using an autopatch to pick up business messages
C. Using an autopatch to call for a tow truck
D. Using an autopatch to call home to say you are running late

T1B International aspect of Amateur Radio; International and domestic spectrum allocation; Spectrum sharing; International communications; reciprocal operation.

T1B01
What are the frequency limits of the 6-meter band in ITU Region 2?
A. 52.0 - 54.5 MHz
B. 50.0 - 54.0 MHz
C. 50.1 - 52.1 MHz
D. 50.0 - 56.0 MHz

T1B02
What are the frequency limits of the 2-meter band in ITU Region 2?
A. 144.0 - 148.0 MHz
B. 145.0 - 149.5 MHz
C. 144.1 - 146.5 MHz
D. 144.0 - 146.0 MHz

T1B03
What are the frequency limits of the 1.25-meter band in ITU Region 2?
A. 225.0 - 230.5 MHz
B. 222.0 - 225.0 MHz
C. 224.1 - 225.1 MHz
D. 220.0 - 226.0 MHz

T1B04
What are the frequency limits of the 70-centimeter band in ITU Region 2?
A. 430.0 - 440.0 MHz
B. 430.0 - 450.0 MHz
C. 420.0 - 450.0 MHz
D. 432.0 - 435.0 MHz

T1A14
(A)
[97.3a10]
Page 1.19

T1A15
(D)
[97.113a4]
Page 1.20

T1A16
(B)
[97.113a3]
Page 1.19

T1B01
(B)
[97.301a]
Page 1.14

T1B02
(A)
[97.301a]
Page 1.14

T1B03
(B)
[97.301f]
Page 1.14

T1B04
(C)
[97.301a]
Page 1.14

T1B05
(D)
[97.301a]
Page 1.14

T1B05
What are the frequency limits of the 33-centimeter band in ITU Region 2?
A. 903 - 927 MHz
B. 905 - 925 MHz
C. 900 - 930 MHz
D. 902 - 928 MHz

T1B06
(B)
[97.301a]
Page 1.14

T1B06
What are the frequency limits of the 23-centimeter band in ITU Region 2?
A. 1260 - 1270 MHz
B. 1240 - 1300 MHz
C. 1270 - 1295 MHz
D. 1240 - 1246 MHz

T1B07
(A)
[97.301a]
Page 1.14

T1B07
What are the frequency limits of the 13-centimeter band in ITU Region 2?
A. 2300 - 2310 MHz and 2390 - 2450 MHz
B. 2300 - 2350 MHz and 2400 - 2450 MHz
C. 2350 - 2380 MHz and 2390 - 2450 MHz
D. 2300 - 2350 MHz and 2380 - 2450 MHz

T1B08
(C)
[97.303]
Page 1.15

T1B08
If the FCC rules say that the amateur service is a secondary user of a frequency band, and another service is a primary user, what does this mean?
A. Nothing special; all users of a frequency band have equal rights to operate
B. Amateurs are only allowed to use the frequency band during emergencies
C. Amateurs are allowed to use the frequency band only if they do not cause harmful interference to primary users
D. Amateurs must increase transmitter power to overcome any interference caused by primary users

T1B09
(C)
[97.101b]
Page 1.15

T1B09
What rule applies if two amateur stations want to use the same frequency?
A. The station operator with a lesser class of license must yield the frequency to a higher-class licensee
B. The station operator with a lower power output must yield the frequency to the station with a higher power output
C. Both station operators have an equal right to operate on the frequency
D. Station operators in ITU Regions 1 and 3 must yield the frequency to stations in ITU Region 2

T1B10
(D)
[97.301e]
Page 2.5

T1B10
If you are operating on 28.400 MHz, in what amateur band are you operating?
A. 80 meters
B. 40 meters
C. 15 meters
D. 10 meters

T1B11
(D)
[97.301f]
Page 1.14

T1B11
If you are operating on 223.50 MHz, in what amateur band are you operating?
A. 15 meters
B. 10 meters
C. 2 meters
D. 1.25 meters

T1B12

When are you allowed to communicate with an amateur in a foreign country?

A. Only when the foreign amateur uses English
B. Only when you have permission from the FCC
C. Only when a third party agreement exists between the US and the foreign country
D. At any time, unless it is not allowed by either government

T1B12
(D)
[97.111a1]
Page 1.18

T1B13

If you are operating FM phone on the 23-cm band and learn that you are interfering with a radiolocation station outside the US, what must you do?

A. Stop operating or take steps to eliminate this harmful interference
B. Nothing, because this band is allocated exclusively to the amateur service
C. Establish contact with the radiolocation station and ask them to change frequency
D. Change to CW mode, because this would not likely cause interference

T1B13
(A)
[97.303h]
Page 1.16

T1B14

What does it mean for an amateur station to operate under reciprocal operating authority?

A. The amateur is operating in a country other than his home country
B. The amateur is allowing a third party to talk to an amateur in another country
C. The amateur has permission to communicate in a foreign language
D. The amateur has permission to communicate with amateurs in another country

T1B14
(A)
[97.107]
Page 1.18

T1B15

What are the frequency limits for the amateur radio service for stations located north of Line A in the 70-cm band?

A. 430 - 450 MHz
B. 420 - 450 MHz
C. 432 - 450 MHz
D. 440 - 450 MHz

T1B15
(A)
[97.301(f)(1)]
Page 1.16

T1C   All about license grants; Station and operator license grant structure including responsibilities, basic differences; Privileges of the various operator license classes; License grant term; Modifying and renewing license grant; Grace period.

T1C01

Which of the following is required before you can operate an amateur station in the US?

A. You must hold an FCC operator's training permit for a licensed radio station
B. You must submit an FCC Form 605 together with a license examination fee
C. The FCC must grant you an amateur operator/primary station license
D. The FCC must issue you a Certificate of Successful Completion of Amateur Training

T1C01
(C)
[97.5a]
Page 1.5

T1C02

What are the US amateur operator licenses that a new amateur might earn?

A. Novice, Technician, General, Advanced
B. Technician, Technician Plus, General, Advanced
C. Novice, Technician Plus, General, Advanced
D. Technician, Technician with Morse code, General, Amateur Extra

T1C02
(D)
[97.9a]
Page 1.8

T1C03

How soon after you pass the examination elements required for your first Amateur Radio license may you transmit?

A. Immediately
B. 30 days after the test date
C. As soon as the FCC grants you a license and the data appears in the FCC's ULS data base
D. As soon as you receive your license from the FCC

T1C03
(C)
[97.5a]
Page 1.6

T1C04
(A)
[97.21a3i]
Page 1.6

T1C04
How soon before the expiration date of your license may you send the FCC a completed Form 605 or file with the Universal Licensing System on the World Wide Web for a renewal?
A. No more than 90 days
B. No more than 30 days
C. Within 6 to 9 months
D. Within 6 months to a year

T1C05
(C)
[97.25a]
Page 1.6

T1C05
What is the normal term for an amateur station license grant?
A. 5 years
B. 7 years
C. 10 years
D. For the lifetime of the licensee

T1C06
(A)
[97.21b]
Page 1.6

T1C06
What is the "grace period" during which the FCC will renew an expired 10-year license?
A. 2 years
B. 5 years
C. 10 years
D. There is no grace period

T1C07
(D)
[97.103a]
Page 1.18

T1C07
What is your responsibility as a station licensee?
A. You must allow another amateur to operate your station upon request
B. You must be present whenever the station is operated
C. You must notify the FCC if another amateur acts as the control operator
D. You are responsible for the proper operation of the station in accordance with the FCC rules

T1C08
(B)
[97.5d]
Page 1.5

T1C08
Where does a US amateur license allow you to operate?
A. Anywhere in the world
B. Wherever the amateur service is regulated by the FCC
C. Within 50 km of your primary station location
D. Only at the mailing address printed on your license

T1C09
(B)
[97.111a3,4]
Page 1.18

T1C09
Under what conditions are amateur stations allowed to communicate with stations operating in other radio services?
A. Never; amateur stations are only permitted to communicate with other amateur stations
B. When authorized by the FCC or in an emergency
C. When communicating with stations in the Citizens Radio Service
D. When a commercial broadcast station is using Amateur Radio frequencies for newsgathering during a natural disaster

T1C10
(B)
Page 1.9

T1C10
To what distance limit may Technician class licensees communicate?
A. Up to 200 miles
B. There is no distance limit
C. Only to line of sight contacts distances
D. Only to contacts inside the USA

T1C11
(A)
Page 1.6

T1C11
If you forget to renew your amateur license and it expires, may you continue to transmit?
A. No, transmitting is not allowed
B. Yes, but only if you identify using the suffix "GP"
C. Yes, but only during authorized nets
D. Yes, any time for up to two years (the "grace period" for renewal)

T1D **Qualifying for a license; General eligibility; Purpose of examination; Examination elements; Upgrading operator license class; Element credit; Provision for physical disabilities.**

T1D01
Who can become an amateur licensee in the US?
A. Anyone except a representative of a foreign government
B. Only a citizen of the United States
C. Anyone except an employee of the US government
D. Anyone

T1D01
(A)
[97.5b1]
Page 1.9

T1D02
What age must you be to hold an amateur license?
A. 14 years or older
B. 18 years or older
C. 70 years or younger
D. There are no age limits

T1D02
(D)
[97.5b1]
Page 1.9

T1D03
What government agency grants your amateur radio license?
A. The Department of Defense
B. The State Licensing Bureau
C. The Department of Commerce
D. The Federal Communications Commission

T1D03
(D)
Page 1.8

T1D04
What element credit is earned by passing the Technician class written examination?
A. Element 1
B. Element 2
C. Element 3
D. Element 4

T1D04
(B)
[97.501c]
Page 1.8

T1D05
If you are a Technician licensee who has passed a Morse code exam, what is one document you can use to prove that you are authorized to use certain amateur frequencies below 30 MHz?
A. A certificate from the FCC showing that you have notified them that you will be using the HF bands
B. A certificate showing that you have attended a class in HF communications
C. A Certificate of Successful Completion of Examination showing that you have passed a Morse code exam
D. No special proof is required

T1D05
(C)
[97.9b]
Page 1.9

T1D06
What is a Volunteer Examiner (VE)?
A. A certified instructor who volunteers to examine amateur teaching manuals
B. An FCC employee who accredits volunteers to administer amateur license exams
C. An amateur, accredited by one or more VECs, who volunteers to administer amateur license exams
D. An amateur, registered with the Electronic Industries Association, who volunteers to examine amateur station equipment

T1D06
(C)
[97.509a]
Page 1.10

T1D07
What minimum examinations must you pass for a Technician amateur license?
A. A written exam, Element 1 and a 5 WPM code exam, Element 2
B. A 5 WPM code exam, Element 1 and a written exam, Element 3
C. A single 35 question multiple choice written exam, Element 2
D. A written exam, Element 2 and a 5 WPM code exam, Element 4

T1D07
(C)
[97.503b1]
Page 1.13

T1D08
(D)
[VE
Instructions]
Page 1.13

T1D08
How may an Element 1 exam be administered to an applicant with a physical disability?
A. It may be skipped if a doctor signs a statement saying the applicant is too disabled to pass the exam
B. By holding an open book exam
C. By lowering the exam's pass rate to 50 percent correct
D. By using a vibrating surface or flashing light

T1D09
(A)
[97.503a]
Page 1.10

T1D09
What is the purpose of the Element 1 examination?
A. To test Morse code comprehension at 5 words-per-minute
B. To test knowledge of block diagrams
C. To test antenna-building skills
D. To test knowledge of rules and regulations

T1D10
(A)
[97.505(A)
(6)]
Page 1.13

T1D10
If a Technician class licensee passes only the 5 words-per-minute Morse code test at an exam session, how long will this credit be valid for license upgrade purposes?
A. 365 days
B. Until the current license expires
C. Indefinitely
D. Until two years following the expiration of the current license

T1D11
(D)

T1D11
This question has been withdrawn.

T1E   Amateur station call sign systems including Sequential, Vanity and Special Event; ITU Regions; Call sign formats.

T1E01
(C)
Page 1.16

T1E01
Which of the following call signs is a valid US amateur call?
A. UZ4FWD
B. KBL7766
C. KB3TMJ
D. VE3BKJ

T1E02
(B)
Page 1.16

T1E02
What letters must be used for the first letter in US amateur call signs?
A. K, N, U and W
B. A, K, N and W
C. A, B, C and D
D. A, N, V and W

T1E03
(D)
Page 1.16

T1E03
What numbers are normally used in US amateur call signs?
A. Any two-digit number, 10 through 99
B. Any two-digit number, 22 through 45
C. A single digit, 1 though 9
D. A single digit, 0 through 9

T1E04

In which ITU region is Alaska?
A. ITU Region 1
B. ITU Region 2
C. ITU Region 3
D. ITU Region 4

T1E04
(B)
Page 1.14

T1E05

In which ITU region is Guam?
A. ITU Region 1
B. ITU Region 2
C. ITU Region 3
D. ITU Region 4

T1E05
(C)
Page 1.14

T1E06

What must you transmit to identify your amateur station?
A. Your "handle"
B. Your call sign
C. Your first name and your location
D. Your full name

T1E06
(B)
[97.119a]
Page 1.16

T1E07

How might you obtain a call sign made up of your initials?
A. Under the vanity call sign program
B. In a sequential call sign program
C. In the special event call sign program
D. There is no provision for choosing a call sign

T1E07
(A)
[97.19]
Page 1.17

T1E08

This question has been withdrawn.

T1E08

T1E09

How may an amateur radio club obtain a station call sign?
A. You must apply directly to the FCC in Gettysburg, PA
B. You must apply through a Club Station Call Sign Administrator
C. You must submit FCC Form 605 to FCC in Washington, DC
D. You must notify VE team on NCVEC Form 605

T1E09
(B)
[97.17b2]
Page 1.18

T1E10

Amateurs of which license classes are eligible to apply for temporary use of a 1-by-1 format Special Event call sign?
A. Only Amateur Extra class amateurs
B. 1-by-1 format call signs are not authorized in the US Amateur Service
C. Any FCC-licensed amateur
D. Only trustees of amateur radio clubs

T1E10
(C)
Page 1.18

T1E11

How does the FCC issue new amateur radio call signs?
A. By call sign district in random order
B. The applicant chooses a call sign no one else is using
C. By ITU prefix letter(s), call sign district numeral and a suffix in strict alphabetic order
D. The Volunteer Examiners who gave the exams choose a call sign no one else is using

T1E11
(C)
[97.17d]
Page 1.16

T1E12
Which station call sign format groups are available to Technician Class amateur radio operators?
A. Group A
B. Group B
C. Only Group C
D. Group C and D

SUBELEMENT T2 — Methods of Communication
[2 Exam Questions — 2 Groups]

T2A How Radio Works; Electromagnetic spectrum; Magnetic/Electric Fields; Nature of Radio Waves; Wavelength; Frequency; Velocity; AC Sine wave/ Hertz; Audio and Radio frequency.

T2A01
What happens to a signal's wavelength as its frequency increases?
A. It gets shorter
B. It gets longer
C. It stays the same
D. It disappears

T2A02
How does the frequency of a harmonic compare to the desired transmitting frequency?
A. It is slightly more than the desired frequency
B. It is slightly less than the desired frequency
C. It is exactly two, or three, or more times the desired frequency
D. It is much less than the desired frequency

T2A03
What does 60 hertz (Hz) mean?
A. 6000 cycles per second
B. 60 cycles per second
C. 6000 meters per second
D. 60 meters per second

T2A04
What is the name for the distance an AC signal travels during one complete cycle?
A. Wave speed
B. Waveform
C. Wavelength
D. Wave spread

T2A05
What is the fourth harmonic of a 50.25 MHz signal?
A. 201.00 MHz
B. 150.75 MHz
C. 251.50 MHz
D. 12.56 MHz

T2A06
What is a radio frequency wave?
A. Wave disturbances that take place at less than 10 times per second
B. Electromagnetic oscillations or cycles that repeat between 20 and 20,000 times per second
C. Electromagnetic oscillations or cycles that repeat more than 20,000 times per second
D. None of these answers are correct

T2A07
What is an audio-frequency signal?
A. Wave disturbances that cannot be heard by the human ear
B. Electromagnetic oscillations or cycles that repeat between 20 and 20,000 times per second
C. Electromagnetic oscillations or cycles that repeat more than 20,000 times per second
D. Electric energy that is generated at the front end of an AM or FM radio receiver

T2A08
In what radio-frequency range do amateur 2-meter communications take place?
A. UHF, Ultra High Frequency range
B. MF, Medium Frequency range
C. HF, High Frequency range
D. VHF, Very High Frequency range

T2A09
Which of the following choices is often used to identify a particular radio wave?
A. The frequency or the wavelength of the wave
B. The length of the magnetic curve of wave
C. The time it takes for the wave to travel a certain distance
D. The free-space impedance of the wave

T2A10
How is a radio frequency wave identified?
A. By its wavelength, the length of a single radio cycle from peak to peak
B. By its corresponding frequency
C. By the appropriate radio band in which it is transmitted or received
D. All of these choices are correct

T2A11
How fast does a radio wave travel through space (in a vacuum)?
A. At the speed of light
B. At the speed of sound
C. Its speed is inversely proportional to its wavelength
D. Its speed increases as the frequency increases

T2A12
What is the standard unit of frequency measurement?
A. A megacycle
B. A hertz
C. One thousand cycles per second
D. EMF, electromagnetic force

T2A13
What is the basic principle of radio communications?
A. A radio wave is combined with an information signal and is transmitted; a receiver separates the two
B. A transmitter separates information to be received from a radio wave
C. A DC generator combines some type of information into a carrier wave so that it may travel through space
D. The peak-to-peak voltage of a transmitter is varied by the sidetone and modulated by the receiver

T2A06
(C)
Page 2.3

T2A07
(B)
Page 2.3

T2A08
(D)
Page 2.4

T2A09
(A)
Page 2.4

T2A10
(D)
Page 2.4

T2A11
(A)
Page 2.3

T2A12
(B)
Page 2.2

T2A13
(A)
Page 2.7

T2A14
(B)
Page 2.4

T2A14
How is the wavelength of a radio wave related to its frequency?
A. Wavelength gets longer as frequency increases
B. Wavelength gets shorter as frequency increases
C. There is no relationship between wavelength and frequency
D. The frequency depends on the velocity of the radio wave, but the wavelength depends on the bandwidth of the signal

T2A15
(D)
Page 2.2

T2A15
What term means the number of times per second that an alternating current flows back and forth?
A. Pulse rate
B. Speed
C. Wavelength
D. Frequency

T2A16
(A)
Page 2.2

T2A16
What is the basic unit of frequency?
A. The hertz
B. The watt
C. The ampere
D. The ohm

T2B   Frequency privileges granted to Technician class operators; Amateur service bands; Emission types and designators; Modulation principles; AM/FM/Single sideband/upper-lower, international Morse code (CW), RTTY, packet radio and data emission types; Full quieting.

T2B01
(B)
[97.301e]
Page 2.5

T2B01
What are the frequency limits of the 80-meter band in ITU Region 2 for Technician class licensees who have passed a Morse code exam?
A. 3500 - 4000 kHz
B. 3675 - 3725 kHz
C. 7100 - 7150 kHz
D. 7000 - 7300 kHz

T2B02
(C)
[97.301e]
Page 2.5

T2B02
What are the frequency limits of the 10-meter band in ITU Region 2 for Technician class licensees who have passed a Morse code exam?
A. 28.000 - 28.500 MHz
B. 28.100 - 29.500 MHz
C. 28.100 - 28.500 MHz
D. 29.100 - 29.500 MHz

T2B03
(C)
[97.3c2]
Page 2.5

T2B03
What name does the FCC use for telemetry, telecommand or computer communications emissions?
A. CW
B. Image
C. Data
D. RTTY

T2B04
What does "connected" mean in a packet-radio link?
A. A telephone link is working between two stations
B. A message has reached an amateur station for local delivery
C. A transmitting station is sending data to only one receiving station; it replies that the data is being received correctly
D. A transmitting and receiving station are using a digipeater, so no other contacts can take place until they are finished

T2B05
What emission types are Technician control operators who have passed a Morse code exam allowed to use from 7100 to 7150 kHz in ITU Region 2?
A. CW and data
B. Phone
C. Data only
D. CW only

T2B06
What emission types are Technician control operators who have passed a Morse code exam allowed to use on frequencies from 28.3 to 28.5 MHz?
A. All authorized amateur emission privileges
B. CW and data
C. CW and single-sideband phone
D. Data and phone

T2B07
What emission types are Technician control operators allowed to use on the amateur 1.25-meter band in ITU Region 2?
A. Only CW and phone
B. Only CW and data
C. Only data and phone
D. All amateur emission privileges authorized for use on the band

T2B08
What term describes the process of combining an information signal with a radio signal?
A. Superposition
B. Modulation
C. Demodulation
D. Phase-inversion

T2B09
What is the name of the voice emission most used on VHF/UHF repeaters?
A. Single-sideband phone
B. Pulse-modulated phone
C. Slow-scan phone
D. Frequency-modulated phone

T2B10
What does the term "phone transmissions" usually mean?
A. The use of telephones to set up an amateur contact
B. A phone patch between amateur radio and the telephone system
C. AM, FM or SSB voice transmissions by radiotelephony
D. Placing the telephone handset near a transceiver's microphone and speaker to relay a telephone call

T2B04
(C)
Page 2.9

T2B05
(D)
[97.305,
97.307f9]
Page 2.5

T2B06
(C)
[97.305,
97.307f10]
Page 2.5

T2B07
(D)
[97.305]
Page 2.7

T2B08
(B)
Page 2.7

T2B09
(D)
Page 2.8

T2B10
(C)
Page 2.7

T2B11
(A)
Page 2.8

T2B11
Which sideband is commonly used for 10-meter phone operation?
A. Upper sideband
B. Lower sideband
C. Amplitude-compandored sideband
D. Double sideband

T2B12
(C)
[97.313c2]
Page 2.5

T2B12
What is the most transmitter power a Technician control operator with telegraphy credit may use on the 10-meter band?
A. 5 watts PEP output
B. 25 watts PEP output
C. 200 watts PEP output
D. 1500 watts PEP output

T2B13
(D)
[97.3c5]
Page 2.7

T2B13
What name does the FCC use for voice emissions?
A. RTTY
B. Data
C. CW
D. Phone

T2B14
(B)
[97.305c]
Page 1.16

T2B14
What emission privilege is permitted a Technician class operator in the 219 MHz - 220 MHz frequency range?
A. Slow-scan television
B. Point-to-point digital message forwarding
C. FM voice
D. Fast-scan television

T2B15
(A)
Page 2.8

T2B15
Which sideband is normally used for VHF/UHF SSB communications?
A. Upper sideband
B. Lower sideband
C. Double sideband
D. Double sideband, suppressed carrier

T2B16
(A)
Page 2.8

T2B16
Which of the following descriptions is used to describe a good signal through a repeater?
A. Full quieting
B. Over deviation
C. Breaking up
D. Readability zero

T2B17
(B)
Page 2.9

T2B17
What is the typical bandwidth of PSK31 digital communications?
A. 500 kHz
B. 31 Hz
C. 5 MHz
D. 600 kHz

T2B18
(D)
Page 8.5

T2B18
What emissions do a transmitter using a reactance modulator produce?
A. CW
B. Test
C. Single-sideband, suppressed-carrier phone
D. Phase-modulated phone

T2B19

What other emission does phase modulation most resemble?

A. Amplitude modulation
B. Pulse modulation
C. Frequency modulation
D. Single-sideband modulation

T2B19
(C)
Page 8.5

SUBELEMENT T3 - Radio Phenomena
[2 Exam Questions - 2 Groups]

Subelement
T3

T3A How a radio signal travels; Atmosphere/troposphere/ionosphere and ionized layers; Skip distance; Ground (surface)/sky (space) waves; Single/multihop; Path; Ionospheric absorption; Refraction.

T3A01

What is the name of the area of the atmosphere that makes long-distance radio communications possible by bending radio waves?

A. Troposphere
B. Stratosphere
C. Magnetosphere
D. Ionosphere

T3A01
(D)
Page 3.2

T3A02

Which ionospheric region is closest to the Earth?

A. The A region
B. The D region
C. The E region
D. The F region

T3A02
(B)
Page 3.5

T3A03

Which region of the ionosphere is mainly responsible for absorbing MF/HF radio signals during the daytime?

A. The F2 region
B. The F1 region
C. The E region
D. The D region

T3A03
(D)
Page 3.5

T3A04

Which region of the ionosphere is mainly responsible for long-distance sky-wave radio communications?

A. D region
B. E region
C. F1 region
D. F2 region

T3A04
(D)
Page 3.6

T3A05

When a signal travels along the surface of the Earth, what is this called?

A. Sky-wave propagation
B. Knife-edge diffraction
C. E-region propagation
D. Ground-wave propagation

T3A05
(D)
Page 3.3

T3A06
(C)
Page 3.3

T3A06
What type of solar radiation is most responsible for ionization in the outer atmosphere?
A. Thermal
B. Non-ionized particle
C. Ultraviolet
D. Microwave

T3A07
(C)
Page 3.4

T3A07
What is the usual cause of sky-wave propagation?
A. Signals are reflected by a mountain
B. Signals are reflected by the Moon
C. Signals are bent back to Earth by the ionosphere
D. Signals are retransmitted by a repeater

T3A08
(B)
Page 3.3

T3A08
What type of propagation has radio signals bounce several times between Earth and the ionosphere as they travel around the Earth?
A. Multiple bounce
B. Multi-hop
C. Skip
D. Pedersen propagation

T3A09
(A)
Page 3.6

T3A09
What effect does the D region of the ionosphere have on lower-frequency HF signals in the daytime?
A. It absorbs the signals
B. It bends the radio waves out into space
C. It refracts the radio waves back to earth
D. It has little or no effect on 80-meter radio waves

T3A10
(C)
Page 3.7

T3A10
How does the signal loss for a given path through the troposphere vary with frequency?
A. There is no relationship
B. The path loss decreases as the frequency increases
C. The path loss increases as the frequency increases
D. There is no path loss at all

T3A11
(A)
Page 3.4

T3A11
When a signal is returned to Earth by the ionosphere, what is this called?
A. Sky-wave propagation
B. Earth-Moon-Earth propagation
C. Ground-wave propagation
D. Tropospheric propagation

T3A12
(B)
Page 3.3

T3A12
How does the range of sky-wave propagation compare to ground-wave propagation?
A. It is much shorter
B. It is much longer
C. It is about the same
D. It depends on the weather

T3B **HF vs. VHF vs. UHF characteristics; Types of VHF-UHF propagation; Daylight and seasonal variations; Tropospheric ducting; Line of sight; Maximum usable frequency (MUF); Sunspots and sunspot Cycle, Characteristics of different bands.**

T3B01
When a signal travels in a straight line from one antenna to another, what is this called?
A. Line-of-sight propagation
B. Straight line propagation
C. Knife-edge diffraction
D. Tunnel ducting

T3B02
What can happen to VHF or UHF signals going towards a metal-framed building?
A. They will go around the building
B. They can be bent by the ionosphere
C. They can be reflected by the building
D. They can be polarized by the building's mass

T3B03
Ducting occurs in which region of the atmosphere?
A. F2
B. Ecosphere
C. Troposphere
D. Stratosphere

T3B04
What causes VHF radio waves to be propagated several hundred miles over oceans?
A. A polar air mass
B. A widespread temperature inversion
C. An overcast of cirriform clouds
D. A high-pressure zone

T3B05
In which of the following frequency ranges does sky-wave propagation least often occur?
A. LF
B. UHF
C. HF
D. VHF

T3B06
Why should local amateur communications use VHF and UHF frequencies instead of HF frequencies?
A. To minimize interference on HF bands capable of long-distance communication
B. Because greater output power is permitted on VHF and UHF
C. Because HF transmissions are not propagated locally
D. Because signals are louder on VHF and UHF frequencies

T3B07
How does the number of sunspots relate to the amount of ionization in the ionosphere?
A. The more sunspots there are, the greater the ionization
B. The more sunspots there are, the less the ionization
C. Unless there are sunspots, the ionization is zero
D. Sunspots do not affect the ionosphere

T3B01
(A)
Page 3.7

T3B02
(C)
Page 3.7

T3B03
(C)
Page 3.8

T3B04
(B)
Page 3.8

T3B05
(B)
Page 3.7

T3B06
(A)
Page 3.7

T3B07
(A)
Page 3.4

T3B08
(C)
Page 3.4

T3B08
How long is an average sunspot cycle?
A. 2 years
B. 5 years
C. 11 years
D. 17 years

T3B09
(B)
Page 3.9

T3B09
Which of the following frequency bands is most likely to experience summertime sporadic-E propagation?
A. 23 centimeters
B. 6 meters
C. 70 centimeters
D. 1.25 meters

T3B10
(A)
Page 3.7

T3B10
Which of the following emission modes are considered to be weak-signal modes and have the greatest potential for DX contacts?
A. Single sideband and CW
B. Packet radio and RTTY
C. Frequency modulation
D. Amateur television

T3B11
(D)
Page 3.6

T3B11
What is the condition of the ionosphere above a particular area of the Earth just before local sunrise?
A. Atmospheric attenuation is at a maximum
B. The D region is above the E region
C. The E region is above the F region
D. Ionization is at a minimum

T3B12
(A)
Page 3.3

T3B12
What happens to signals that take off vertically from the antenna and are higher in frequency than the critical frequency?
A. They pass through the ionosphere
B. They are absorbed by the ionosphere
C. Their frequency is changed by the ionosphere to be below the maximum usable frequency
D. They are reflected back to their source

T3B13
(A)
Page 3.4

T3B13
In relation to sky-wave propagation, what does the term "maximum usable frequency" (MUF) mean?
A. The highest frequency signal that will reach its intended destination
B. The lowest frequency signal that will reach its intended destination
C. The highest frequency signal that is most absorbed by the ionosphere
D. The lowest frequency signal that is most absorbed by the ionosphere

SUBELEMENT T4 — Station Licensee Duties
[3 Exam Questions — 3 Groups]

T4A Correct name and mailing address on station license grant; Places from where station is authorized to transmit; Selecting station location; Antenna structure location; Stations installed aboard ship or aircraft.

T4A01
When may you operate your amateur station aboard a cruise ship?
A. At any time
B. Only while the ship is not under power
C. Only with the approval of the master of the ship and not using the ship's radio equipment
D. Only when you have written permission from the cruise line and only using the ship's radio equipment

T4A02
When may you operate your amateur station somewhere in the US besides the address listed on your license?
A. Only during times of emergency
B. Only after giving proper notice to the FCC
C. During an emergency or an FCC-approved emergency practice
D. Whenever you want to

T4A03
What penalty may the FCC impose if you fail to provide your correct mailing address?
A. There is no penalty if you do not provide the correct address
B. You are subject to an administrative fine
C. Your amateur license could be revoked
D. You may only operate from your address of record

T4A04
Under what conditions may you transmit from a location different from the address printed on your amateur license?
A. If the location is under the control of the FCC, whenever the FCC Rules allow
B. If the location is outside the United States, only for a time period of less than 90 days
C. Only when you have written permission from the FCC Engineer in Charge
D. Never; you may only operate at the location printed on your license

T4A05
Why must an amateur operator have a current US postal mailing address?
A. So the FCC has a record of the location of each amateur station
B. To follow the FCC rules and so the licensee can receive mail from the FCC
C. Because all US amateurs must be US residents
D. So the FCC can publish a call-sign directory

T4A06
What is one way to notify the FCC if your mailing address changes?
A. Fill out an FCC Form 605 using your new address, attach a copy of your license, and mail it to your local FCC Field Office
B. Fill out an FCC Form 605 using your new address, attach a copy of your license, and mail it to the FCC office in Gettysburg, PA
C. Call your local FCC Field Office and give them your new address over the phone
D. Call the FCC office in Gettysburg, PA, and give them your new address over the phone

T4A01
(C)
[97.11a]
Page 4.3

T4A02
(D)
Page 4.3

T4A03
(C)
[97.23]
Page 4.2

T4A04
(A)
Page 4.3

T4A05
(B)
[97.23]
Page 4.1

T4A06
(B)
[97.21a1]
Page 4.1

T4A07
(A)
[97.15(A)]
Page 4.3

T4A07
What do FCC rules require you to do if you plan to erect an antenna whose height exceeds 200 feet?
A. Notify the Federal Aviation Administration and register with the FCC
B. FCC rules prohibit antenna structures above 200 feet
C. Alternating sections of the supporting structure must be painted international airline orange and white
D. The antenna structure must be approved by the FCC and DOD

T4A08
(D)
[97.13c] [OET Bulletin 65 Supplement B] ["RF Exposure and You", W1RFI]
Page 4.3

T4A08
Which of the following is NOT an important consideration when selecting a location for a transmitting antenna?
A. Nearby structures
B. Height above average terrain
C. Distance from the transmitter location
D. Polarization of the feed line

T4A09
(B)
[97.15b]
Page 4.3

T4A09
What is the height restriction the FCC places on Amateur Radio Service antenna structures without registration with the FCC and FAA?
A. There is no restriction by the FCC
B. 200 feet
C. 300 feet
D. As permitted by PRB-1

T4A10
(C)
[97.11a]
Page 4.3

T4A10
When may you operate your amateur station aboard an aircraft?
A. At any time
B. Only while the aircraft is on the ground
C. Only with the approval of the pilot in command and not using the aircraft's radio equipment
D. Only when you have written permission from the airline and only using the aircraft's radio equipment

T4B   Designation of control operator; FCC presumption of control operator; Physical control of station apparatus; Control point; Immediate station control; Protecting against unauthorized transmissions; Station records; FCC Inspection; Restricted operation.

T4B01
(C)
[97.3a12]
Page 4.3

T4B01
What is the definition of a control operator of an amateur station?
A. Anyone who operates the controls of the station
B. Anyone who is responsible for the station's equipment
C. Any licensed amateur operator who is responsible for the station's transmissions
D. The amateur operator with the highest class of license who is near the controls of the station

T4B02
(D)
[97.3a12]
Page 4.3

T4B02
What is the FCC's name for the person responsible for the transmissions from an amateur station?
A. Auxiliary operator
B. Operations coordinator
C. Third-party operator
D. Control operator

T4B03
When must an amateur station have a control operator?
A. Only when training another amateur
B. Whenever the station receiver is operated
C. Whenever the station is transmitting
D. A control operator is not needed

T4B03
(C)
[97.7]
Page 4.4

T4B04
What is the term for the location at which the control operator function is performed?
A. The operating desk
B. The control point
C. The station location
D. The manual control location

T4B04
(B)
[97.3a13]
Page 4.4

T4B05
What is the control point of an amateur station?
A. The on/off switch of the transmitter
B. The input/output port of a packet controller
C. The variable frequency oscillator of a transmitter
D. The location at which the control operator function is performed

T4B05
(D)
[97.3a13]
Page 4.4

T4B06
When you operate your transmitting equipment alone, what is your official designation?
A. Engineer in Charge
B. Commercial radio operator
C. Third party
D. Control operator

T4B06
(D)
[97.3a12]
Page 4.4

T4B07
When does the FCC assume that you authorize transmissions with your call sign as the control operator?
A. At all times
B. Only in the evening hours
C. Only when operating third party traffic
D. Only when operating as a reciprocal operating station

T4B07
(A)
[97.103b]
Page 4.4

T4B08
What is the name for the operating position where the control operator has full control over the transmitter?
A. Field point
B. Auxiliary point
C. Control point
D. Access point

T4B08
(C)
[97.3a13]
Page 4.4

T4B09
When is the FCC allowed to conduct an inspection of your amateur station?
A. Only on weekends
B. At any time
C. Never, the FCC does not inspect stations
D. Only during daylight hours

T4B09
(B)
[97.103c]
Page 4.4

T4B10
How many transmitters may an amateur licensee control at the same time?
A. Only one
B. No more than two
C. Any number
D. Any number, as long as they are transmitting in different bands

T4B10
(C)
[97.5d]
Page 4.4

T4B11
(A)
[97.121]
Page 4.4

T4B11
If you have been informed that your amateur radio station causes interference to nearby radio or television broadcast receivers of good engineering design, what operating restrictions can FCC rules impose on your station?
A. Require that you discontinue operation on frequencies causing interference during certain evening hours and on Sunday morning (local time)
B. Relocate your station or reduce your transmitter's output power
C. Nothing, unless the FCC conducts an investigation of the interference problem and issues a citation
D. Reduce antenna height so as to reduce the area affected by the interference

T4B12
(B)
Page 4.4

T4B12
How could you best keep unauthorized persons from using your amateur station at home?
A. Use a carrier-operated relay in the main power line
B. Use a key-operated on/off switch in the main power line
C. Put a "Danger - High Voltage" sign in the station
D. Put fuses in the main power line

T4B13
(A)
Page 4.4

T4B13
How could you best keep unauthorized persons from using a mobile amateur station in your car?
A. Disconnect the microphone when you are not using it
B. Put a "do not touch" sign on the radio
C. Turn the radio off when you are not using it
D. Tune the radio to an unused frequency when you are done using it

T4C Providing public service; emergency and disaster communications; Distress calling; Emergency drills and communications; Purpose of RACES.

T4C01
(D)
[97.405a]
Page 4.6

T4C01
If you hear a voice distress signal on a frequency outside of your license privileges, what are you allowed to do to help the station in distress?
A. You are NOT allowed to help because the frequency of the signal is outside your privileges
B. You are allowed to help only if you keep your signals within the nearest frequency band of your privileges
C. You are allowed to help on a frequency outside your privileges only if you use international Morse code
D. You are allowed to help on a frequency outside your privileges in any way possible

T4C02
(C)
[97.403]
Page 4.6

T4C02
When may you use your amateur station to transmit an "SOS" or "MAYDAY"?
A. Never
B. Only at specific times (at 15 and 30 minutes after the hour)
C. In a life- or property-threatening emergency
D. When the National Weather Service has announced a severe weather watch

T4C03
(A)
[97.401a]
Page 4.5

T4C03
If a disaster disrupts normal communication systems in an area where the FCC regulates the amateur service, what kinds of transmissions may stations make?
A. Those that are necessary to meet essential communication needs and facilitate relief actions
B. Those that allow a commercial business to continue to operate in the affected area
C. Those for which material compensation has been paid to the amateur operator for delivery into the affected area
D. Those that are to be used for program production or newsgathering for broadcasting purposes

T4C04

What information is included in an FCC declaration of a temporary state of communication emergency?

A. A list of organizations authorized to use radio communications in the affected area
B. A list of amateur frequency bands to be used in the affected area
C. Any special conditions and special rules to be observed during the emergency
D. An operating schedule for authorized amateur emergency stations

T4C04
(C)
[97.401c]
Page 4.6

T4C05

If you are in contact with another station and you hear an emergency call for help on your frequency, what should you do?

A. Tell the calling station that the frequency is in use
B. Direct the calling station to the nearest emergency net frequency
C. Call your local Civil Preparedness Office and inform them of the emergency
D. Stop your QSO immediately and take the emergency call

T4C05
(D)
Page 4.6

T4C06

What is the proper way to interrupt a repeater conversation to signal a distress call?

A. Say "BREAK" once, then your call sign
B. Say "HELP" as many times as it takes to get someone to answer
C. Say "SOS," then your call sign
D. Say "EMERGENCY" three times

T4C06
(A)
Page 4.6

T4C07

What is one reason for using tactical call signs such as "command post" or "weather center" during an emergency?

A. They keep the general public informed about what is going on
B. They are more efficient and help coordinate public-service communications
C. They are required by the FCC
D. They increase goodwill between amateurs

T4C07
(B)
Page 4.7

T4C08

What type of messages concerning a person's well being are sent into or out of a disaster area?

A. Routine traffic
B. Tactical traffic
C. Formal message traffic
D. Health and welfare traffic

T4C08
(D)
Page 4.7

T4C09

What are messages called that are sent into or out of a disaster area concerning the immediate safety of human life?

A. Tactical traffic
B. Emergency traffic
C. Formal message traffic
D. Health and welfare traffic

T4C09
(B)
Page 4.7

T4C10

Why is it a good idea to have a way to operate your amateur station without using commercial AC power lines?

A. So you may use your station while mobile
B. So you may provide communications in an emergency
C. So you may operate in contests where AC power is not allowed
D. So you will comply with the FCC rules

T4C10
(B)
Page 4.6

T4C11
What is the most important accessory to have for a hand-held radio in an emergency?
A. An extra antenna
B. A portable amplifier
C. Several sets of charged batteries
D. A microphone headset for hands-free operation

T4C12
Which type of antenna would be a good choice as part of a portable HF amateur station that could be set up in case of an emergency?
A. A three-element quad
B. A three-element Yagi
C. A dipole
D. A parabolic dish

T4C13
How must you identify messages sent during a RACES drill?
A. As emergency messages
B. As amateur traffic
C. As official government messages
D. As drill or test messages

T4C14
With what organization must you register before you can participate in RACES drills?
A. A local Amateur Radio club
B. A local racing organization
C. The responsible civil defense organization
D. The Federal Communications Commission

SUBELEMENT T5 - Control Operator Duties
[3 Exam Questions — 3 Groups]

T5A Determining operating privileges, Where control operator must be situated while station is locally or remotely controlled; Operating other amateur stations.

T5A01
If you are the control operator at the station of another amateur who has a higher-class license than yours, what operating privileges are you allowed?
A. Any privileges allowed by the higher license
B. Only the privileges allowed by your license
C. All the emission privileges of the higher license, but only the frequency privileges of your license
D. All the frequency privileges of the higher license, but only the emission privileges of your license

T5A02
Assuming you operate within your amateur license privileges, what restrictions apply to operating amateur equipment?
A. You may operate any amateur equipment
B. You may only operate equipment located at the address printed on your amateur license
C. You may only operate someone else's equipment if you first notify the FCC
D. You may only operate store-purchased equipment until you earn your Amateur Extra class license

T5A03
When an amateur station is transmitting, where must its control operator be, assuming the station is not under automatic control?
A. At the station's control point
B. Anywhere in the same building as the transmitter
C. At the station's entrance, to control entry to the room
D. Anywhere within 50 km of the station location

T5A04
Where will you find a detailed list of your operating privileges?
A. In the OET Bulletin 65 Index
B. In FCC Part 97
C. In your equipment's operating instructions
D. In Part 15 of the Code of Federal Regulations

T5A05
If you transmit from another amateur's station, who is responsible for its proper operation?
A. Both of you
B. The other amateur (the station licensee)
C. You, the control operator
D. The station licensee, unless the station records show that you were the control operator at the time

T5A06
If you let another amateur with a higher class license than yours control your station, what operating privileges are allowed?
A. Any privileges allowed by the higher license, as long as proper identification procedures are followed
B. Only the privileges allowed by your license
C. All the emission privileges of the higher license, but only the frequency privileges of your license
D. All the frequency privileges of the higher license, but only the emission privileges of your license

T5A07
If a Technician class licensee uses the station of a General class licensee, how may the Technician licensee operate?
A. Within the frequency limits of a General class license
B. Within the limits of a Technician class license
C. Only as a third party with the General class licensee as the control operator
D. A Technician class licensee may not operate a General class station

T5A08
What type of amateur station does not require the control operator to be present at the control point?
A. A locally controlled station
B. A remotely controlled station
C. An automatically controlled station
D. An earth station controlling a space station

T5A09
Why can't unlicensed persons in your family transmit using your amateur station if they are alone with your equipment?
A. They must not use your equipment without your permission
B. They must be licensed before they are allowed to be control operators
C. They must first know how to use the right abbreviations and Q signals
D. They must first know the right frequencies and emissions for transmitting

T5A03
(A)
[97.109b]
Page 5.1

T5A04
(B)
Page 5.2

T5A05
(A)
[97.103a]
Page 5.1

T5A06
(A)
[97.105b]
Page 5.1

T5A07
(B)
[97.105b]
Page 5.1

T5A08
(C)
[97.109d]
Page 5.2

T5A09
(B)
[97.109b]
Page 5.2

T5A10
(C)
Page 5.2

T5A10
If you own a dual-band mobile transceiver, what requirement must be met if you set it up to operate as a crossband repeater?
A. There is no special requirement if you are licensed for both bands
B. You must hold an Amateur Extra class license
C. There must be a control operator at the system's control point
D. Operating a crossband mobile system is not allowed

T5B   Transmitter power standards; Interference to stations providing emergency communications; Station identification requirements.

T5B01
(C)
[97.119a]
Page 5.2

T5B01
How often must an amateur station be identified?
A. At the beginning of a contact and at least every ten minutes after that
B. At least once during each transmission
C. At least every ten minutes during and at the end of a contact
D. At the beginning and end of each transmission

T5B02
(C)
[97.119a]
Page 5.3

T5B02
What identification, if any, is required when two amateur stations end communications?
A. No identification is required
B. One of the stations must transmit both stations' call signs
C. Each station must transmit its own call sign
D. Both stations must transmit both call signs

T5B03
(B)
[97.119a]
Page 5.2

T5B03
What is the longest period of time an amateur station can operate without transmitting its call sign?
A. 5 minutes
B. 10 minutes
C. 15 minutes
D. 30 minutes

T5B04

T5B04
This question has been withdrawn.

T5B05
(D)
[97.3b6]
Page 5.4

T5B05
What is the term for the average power supplied to an antenna transmission line during one RF cycle at the crest of the modulation envelope?
A. Peak transmitter power
B. Peak output power
C. Average radio-frequency power
D. Peak envelope power

T5B06

T5B06
This question has been withdrawn.

T5B07
What amount of transmitter power must amateur stations use at all times?
A. 25 watts PEP output
B. 250 watts PEP output
C. 1500 watts PEP output
D. The minimum legal power necessary to communicate

T5B07
(D)
[97.313a]
Page 5.4

T5B08
If you are using a language besides English to make a contact, what language must you use when identifying your station?
A. The language being used for the contact
B. The language being used for the contact, provided the US has a third-party communications agreement with that country
C. English
D. Any language of a country that is a member of the International Telecommunication Union

T5B08
(C)
[97.119b2]
Page 5.3

T5B09
If you are helping in a communications emergency that is being handled by a net control operator, how might you best minimize interference to the net once you have checked in?
A. Whenever the net frequency is quiet, announce your call sign and location
B. Move 5 kHz away from the net's frequency and use high power to ask for other emergency communications
C. Do not transmit on the net frequency until asked to do so by the net operator
D. Wait until the net frequency is quiet, then ask for any emergency traffic for your area

T5B09
(C)
Page 5.2

T5B10
What are the station identification requirements for an amateur transmitter used for telecommand (control) of model craft?
A. Once every ten minutes
B. Once every ten minutes, and at the beginning and end of each transmission
C. At the beginning and end of each transmission
D. Station identification is not required if the transmitter is labeled with the station licensee's name, address and call sign

T5B10
(D)
[97.215a]
Page 5.3

T5B11
Why is transmitting on a police frequency as a "joke" called harmful interference that deserves a large penalty?
A. It annoys everyone who listens
B. It blocks police calls that might be an emergency and interrupts police communications
C. It is in bad taste to communicate with non-amateurs, even as a joke
D. It is poor amateur practice to transmit outside the amateur bands

T5B11
(B)
[97.3a23]
Page 5.2

T5B12
If you are using a frequency within a band assigned to the amateur service on a secondary basis, and a station assigned to the primary service on that band causes interference, what action should you take?
A. Notify the FCC's regional Engineer in Charge of the interference
B. Increase your transmitter's power to overcome the interference
C. Attempt to contact the station and request that it stop the interference
D. Change frequencies; you may be causing harmful interference to the other station, in violation of FCC rules

T5B12
(D)
[97.303]
Page 5.2

T5C   Authorized transmissions, Prohibited practices; Third party communications; Retransmitting radio signals; One way communications.

T5C01
(D)
[97.119a]
Page 5.3

T5C01
If you answer someone on the air and then complete your communication without giving your call sign, what type of communication have you just conducted?
A. Test transmission
B. Tactical signal
C. Packet communication
D. Unidentified communication

T5C02
(A)
[97.111(B) (3)]
Page 1.20

T5C02
What is one example of one-way communication that Technician class control operators are permitted by FCC rules?
A. Transmission for radio control of model craft
B. Use of amateur television for surveillance purposes
C. Retransmitting National Weather Service broadcasts
D. Use of amateur radio as a wireless microphone for a public address system

T5C03
(D)
[97.11a2]
Page 5.5

T5C03
What kind of payment is allowed for third-party messages sent by an amateur station?
A. Any amount agreed upon in advance
B. Donation of repairs to amateur equipment
C. Donation of amateur equipment
D. No payment of any kind is allowed

T5C04
(A)
[97.3a44]
Page 5.5

T5C04
What is the definition of third-party communications?
A. A message sent between two amateur stations for someone else
B. Public service communications for a political party
C. Any messages sent by amateur stations
D. A three-minute transmission to another amateur

T5C05
(D)
[97.115a2]
Page 5.5

T5C05
When are third-party messages allowed to be sent to a foreign country?
A. When sent by agreement of both control operators
B. When the third party speaks to a relative
C. They are not allowed under any circumstances
D. When the US has a third-party agreement with the foreign country or the third party is qualified to be a control operator

T5C06
(A)
[97.115b1]
Page 5.5

T5C06
If you let an unlicensed third party use your amateur station, what must you do at your station's control point?
A. You must continuously monitor and supervise the third-party's participation
B. You must monitor and supervise the communication only if contacts are made in countries that have no third-party communications agreement with the US
C. You must monitor and supervise the communication only if contacts are made on frequencies below 30 MHz
D. You must key the transmitter and make the station identification

T5C07
Besides normal identification, what else must a US station do when sending third-party communications internationally?
A. The US station must transmit its own call sign at the beginning of each communication, and at least every ten minutes after that
B. The US station must transmit both call signs at the end of each communication
C. The US station must transmit its own call sign at the beginning of each communication, and at least every five minutes after that
D. Each station must transmit its own call sign at the end of each transmission, and at least every five minutes after that

T5C08
If an amateur pretends there is an emergency and transmits the word "MAYDAY," what is this called?
A. A traditional greeting in May
B. An emergency test transmission
C. False or deceptive signals
D. Nothing special; "MAYDAY" has no meaning in an emergency

T5C09
If an amateur transmits to test access to a repeater without giving any station identification, what type of communication is this called?
A. A test emission; no identification is required
B. An illegal unmodulated transmission
C. An illegal unidentified transmission
D. A non-communication; no voice is transmitted

T5C10
When may you deliberately interfere with another station's communications?
A. Only if the station is operating illegally
B. Only if the station begins transmitting on a frequency you are using
C. Never
D. You may expect, and cause, deliberate interference because it can't be helped during crowded band conditions

T5C11
If an amateur repeatedly transmits on a frequency already occupied by a group of amateurs in a net operation, what type of interference is this called?
A. Break-in interference
B. Harmful or malicious interference
C. Incidental interference
D. Intermittent interference

T5C12
What device is commonly used to retransmit amateur radio signals?
A. A beacon
B. A repeater
C. A radio controller
D. A duplexer

T5C07
(B)
[97.115c]
Page 5.3

T5C08
(C)
[97.113a4]
Page 5.3

T5C09
(C)
[97.119a]
Page 5.3

T5C10
(C)
[97.101d]
Page 5.3

T5C11
(B)
[97.3a22]
Page 5.3

T5C12
(B)
Page 5.2

SUBELEMENT T6 - Good Operating Practices
[3 Exam Questions — 3 Groups]

T6A Calling another station; Calling CQ; Typical amateur service radio contacts; Courtesy and respect for others; Popular Q-signals; Signal reception reports; Phonetic alphabet for voice operations.

T6A01
(A)
[97.119b2]
Page 6.3

T6A01
What is the advantage of using the International Telecommunication Union (ITU) phonetic alphabet when identifying your station?
A. The words are internationally recognized substitutes for letters
B. There is no advantage
C. The words have been chosen to represent Amateur Radio terms
D. It preserves traditions begun in the early days of Amateur Radio

T6A02
(A)
[97.119b2]
Page 6.3

T6A02
What is one reason to avoid using "cute" phrases or word combinations to identify your station?
A. They are not easily understood by non-English-speaking amateurs
B. They might offend English-speaking amateurs
C. They do not meet FCC identification requirements
D. They might be interpreted as codes or ciphers intended to obscure the meaning of your identification

T6A03
(A)
Page 6.4

T6A03
What should you do before you transmit on any frequency?
A. Listen to make sure others are not using the frequency
B. Listen to make sure that someone will be able to hear you
C. Check your antenna for resonance at the selected frequency
D. Make sure the SWR on your antenna feed line is high enough

T6A04
(B)
Page 9.4

T6A04
How do you call another station on a repeater if you know the station's call sign?
A. Say "break, break 79," then say the station's call sign
B. Say the station's call sign, then identify your own station
C. Say "CQ" three times, then say the station's call sign
D. Wait for the station to call "CQ," then answer it

T6A05
(D)
Page 6.7

T6A05
What does RST mean in a signal report?
A. Recovery, signal strength, tempo
B. Recovery, signal speed, tone
C. Readability, signal speed, tempo
D. Readability, signal strength, tone

T6A06
(D)
Page 6.8

T6A06
What is the meaning of: "Your signal report is five nine plus 20 dB..."?
A. Your signal strength has increased by a factor of 100
B. Repeat your transmission on a frequency 20 kHz higher
C. The bandwidth of your signal is 20 decibels above linearity
D. A relative signal-strength meter reading is 20 decibels greater than strength 9

T6A07
(D)
Page 6.3

T6A07
What is the meaning of the procedural signal "CQ"?
A. Call on the quarter hour
B. New antenna is being tested (no station should answer)
C. Only the called station should transmit
D. Calling any station

T6A08
What is a QSL card in the amateur service?
A. A letter or postcard from an amateur pen pal
B. A Notice of Violation from the FCC
C. A written acknowledgment of communications between two amateurs
D. A postcard reminding you when your license will expire

T6A08
(C)
Page 6.6

T6A09
What is the correct way to call CQ when using voice?
A. Say "CQ" once, followed by "this is," followed by your call sign spoken three times
B. Say "CQ" at least five times, followed by "this is," followed by your call sign spoken once
C. Say "CQ" three times, followed by "this is," followed by your call sign spoken three times
D. Say "CQ" at least ten times, followed by "this is," followed by your call sign spoken once

T6A09
(C)
Page 6.4

T6A10
How should you answer a voice CQ call?
A. Say the other station's call sign at least ten times, followed by "this is," then your call sign at least twice
B. Say the other station's call sign at least five times phonetically, followed by "this is," then your call sign at least once
C. Say the other station's call sign at least three times, followed by "this is," then your call sign at least five times phonetically
D. Say the other station's call sign once, followed by "this is," then your call sign given phonetically

T6A10
(D)
Page 6.4

T6A11
What is the meaning of: "Your signal is full quieting..."?
A. Your signal is strong enough to overcome all receiver noise
B. Your signal has no spurious sounds
C. Your signal is not strong enough to be received
D. Your signal is being received, but no audio is being heard

T6A11
(A)
Page 6.8

T6A12
What is meant by the term "DX"?
A. Best regards
B. Distant station
C. Calling any station
D. Go ahead

T6A12
(B)
Page 6.5

T6A13
What is the meaning of the term "73"?
A. Long distance
B. Best regards
C. Love and kisses
D. Go ahead

T6A13
(B)
Page 6.9

T6B **Occupied bandwidth for emission types; Mandated and voluntary band plans; CW operation.**

T6B01
Which list of emission types is in order from the narrowest bandwidth to the widest bandwidth?
A. RTTY, CW, SSB voice, FM voice
B. CW, FM voice, RTTY, SSB voice
C. CW, RTTY, SSB voice, FM voice
D. CW, SSB voice, RTTY, FM voice

T6B01
(C)
Page 6.11

T6B02
(D)
Page 6.11

T6B02
What is the usual bandwidth of a single-sideband amateur signal?
A. 1 kHz
B. 2 kHz
C. Between 3 and 6 kHz
D. Between 2 and 3 kHz

T6B03
(C)
Page 6.11

T6B03
What is the usual bandwidth of a frequency-modulated amateur signal?
A. Less than 5 kHz
B. Between 5 and 10 kHz
C. Between 10 and 20 kHz
D. Greater than 20 kHz

T6B04
(B)
Page 6.10

T6B04
What is the usual bandwidth of a UHF amateur fast-scan television signal?
A. More than 6 MHz
B. About 6 MHz
C. About 3 MHz
D. About 1 MHz

T6B05
(A)
Page 6.10

T6B05
What name is given to an amateur radio station that is used to connect other amateur stations with the Internet?
A. A gateway
B. A repeater
C. A digipeater
D. FCC regulations prohibit such a station

T6B06
(A)
Page 6.2

T6B06
What is a band plan?
A. A voluntary guideline beyond the divisions established by the FCC for using different operating modes within an amateur band
B. A guideline from the FCC for making amateur frequency band allocations
C. A plan of operating schedules within an amateur band published by the FCC
D. A plan devised by a club to best use a frequency band during a contest

T6B07
(C)
Page 6.6

T6B07
At what speed should a Morse code CQ call be transmitted?
A. Only speeds below five WPM
B. The highest speed your keyer will operate
C. Any speed at which you can reliably receive
D. The highest speed at which you can control the keyer

T6B08
(A)
Page 6.6

T6B08
What is the meaning of the procedural signal "DE"?
A. "From" or "this is," as in "W0AIH DE KA9FOX"
B. "Directional Emissions" from your antenna
C. "Received all correctly"
D. "Calling any station"

T6B09
(B)
Page 6.6

T6B09
What is a good way to call CQ when using Morse code?
A. Send the letters "CQ" three times, followed by "DE," followed by your call sign sent once
B. Send the letters "CQ" three times, followed by "DE," followed by your call sign sent three times
C. Send the letters "CQ" ten times, followed by "DE," followed by your call sign sent twice
D. Send the letters "CQ" over and over until a station answers

T6B10
How should you answer a Morse code CQ call?
A. Send your call sign four times
B. Send the other station's call sign twice, followed by "DE," followed by your call sign twice
C. Send the other station's call sign once, followed by "DE," followed by your call sign four times
D. Send your call sign followed by your name, station location and a signal report

T6B11
What is the meaning of the procedural signal "K"?
A. "Any station transmit"
B. "All received correctly"
C. "End of message"
D. "Called station only transmit"

T6B12
What is one meaning of the Q signal "QRS"?
A. "Interference from static"
B. "Send more slowly"
C. "Send RST report"
D. "Radio station location is"

T6C TVI and RFI reduction and elimination, Band/Low/High pass filter, Out of band harmonic Signals, Spurious Emissions, Telephone Interference, Shielding, Receiver Overload.

T6C01
What is meant by receiver overload?
A. Too much voltage from the power supply
B. Too much current from the power supply
C. Interference caused by strong signals from a nearby source
D. Interference caused by turning the volume up too high

T6C02
What type of filter might be connected to an amateur HF transmitter to cut down on harmonic radiation?
A. A key-click filter
B. A low-pass filter
C. A high-pass filter
D. A CW filter

T6C03
What type of filter should be connected to a TV receiver as the first step in trying to prevent RF overload from an amateur HF station transmission?
A. Low-pass
B. High-pass
C. Band pass
D. Notch

T6B10
(B)
Page 6.7

T6B11
(A)
Page 6.7

T6B12
(B)
Page 6.6

T6C01
(C)
Page 6.14

T6C02
(B)
Page 6.17

T6C03
(B)
Page 6.14

T6C04
(C)
Page 6.14

T6C04
What effect might a break in a cable television transmission line have on amateur communications?
A. Cable lines are shielded and a break cannot affect amateur communications
B. Harmonic radiation from the TV receiver may cause the amateur transmitter to transmit off-frequency
C. TV interference may result when the amateur station is transmitting, or interference may occur to the amateur receiver
D. The broken cable may pick up very high voltages when the amateur station is transmitting

T6C05
(A)
Page 6.14

T6C05
If you are told that your amateur station is causing television interference, what should you do?
A. First make sure that your station is operating properly, and that it does not cause interference to your own television
B. Immediately turn off your transmitter and contact the nearest FCC office for assistance
C. Connect a high-pass filter to the transmitter output and a low-pass filter to the antenna-input terminals of the television
D. Continue operating normally, because you have no reason to worry about the interference

T6C06
(C)
Page 6.15

T6C06
If harmonic radiation from your transmitter is causing interference to television receivers in your neighborhood, who is responsible for taking care of the interference?
A. The owners of the television receivers are responsible
B. Both you and the owners of the television receivers share the responsibility
C. You alone are responsible, since your transmitter is causing the problem
D. The FCC must decide if you or the owners of the television receivers are responsible

T6C07
(D)
Page 6.14

T6C07
If signals from your transmitter are causing front-end overload in your neighbor's television receiver, who is responsible for taking care of the interference?
A. You alone are responsible, since your transmitter is causing the problem
B. Both you and the owner of the television receiver share the responsibility
C. The FCC must decide if you or the owner of the television receiver are responsible
D. The owner of the television receiver is responsible

T6C08
(A)
Page 6.15

T6C08
What circuit blocks RF energy above and below certain limits?
A. A band-pass filter
B. A high-pass filter
C. An input filter
D. A low-pass filter

T6C09
(D)
Page 6.11

T6C09
If someone tells you that signals from your hand-held transceiver are interfering with other signals on a frequency near yours, what may be the cause?
A. You may need a power amplifier for your hand-held
B. Your hand-held may have chirp from weak batteries
C. You may need to turn the volume up on your hand-held
D. Your hand-held may be transmitting spurious emissions

T6C10
(B)
Page 6.12

T6C10
What may happen if an SSB transmitter is operated with the microphone gain set too high?
A. It may cause digital interference to computer equipment
B. It may cause splatter interference to other stations operating near its frequency
C. It may cause atmospheric interference in the air around the antenna
D. It may cause interference to other stations operating on a higher frequency band

T6C11
What may cause a buzzing or hum in the signal of an HF transmitter?
A. Using an antenna that is the wrong length
B. Energy from another transmitter
C. Bad design of the transmitter's RF power output circuit
D. A bad filter capacitor in the transmitter's power supply

T6C12
What is the major cause of telephone interference?
A. The telephone ringer is inadequate
B. Tropospheric ducting at UHF frequencies
C. The telephone was not equipped with interference protection when it was manufactured.
D. Improper location of the telephone in the home

SUBELEMENT T7 Basic Communications Electronics
[3 Exam Questions — 3 Groups]

T7A   Fundamentals of electricity; AC/DC power; units and definitions of current, voltage, resistance, inductance, capacitance and impedance; Rectification; Ohm's Law principle (simple math); Decibel; Metric system and prefixes (e.g., pico, nano, micro, milli, deci, centi, kilo, mega, giga).

T7A01
What is the name for the flow of electrons in an electric circuit?
A. Voltage
B. Resistance
C. Capacitance
D. Current

T7A02
What is the name of a current that flows only in one direction?
A. An alternating current
B. A direct current
C. A normal current
D. A smooth current

T7A03
What is the name of a current that flows back and forth, first in one direction, then in the opposite direction?
A. An alternating current
B. A direct current
C. A rough current
D. A steady state current

T7A04
What is the basic unit of electrical power?
A. The ohm
B. The watt
C. The volt
D. The ampere

T6C11
(D)
Page 6.13

T6C12
(C)
(Reference: FCC CIB Telephone Interference Bulletin)
Page 6.17

Subelement
T7

T7A01
(D)
Page 2.2, 7.7

T7A02
(B)
Page 2.2

T7A03
(A)
Page 2.2

T7A04
(B)
Page 7.14

T7A05
(C)
Page 2.2

T7A05
What is the basic unit of electric current?
A. The volt
B. The watt
C. The ampere
D. The ohm

T7A06
(A)
Page 7.6

T7A06
How much voltage does an automobile battery usually supply?
A. About 12 volts
B. About 30 volts
C. About 120 volts
D. About 240 volts

T7A07
(D)
Page 7.9

T7A07
What limits the current that flows through a circuit for a particular applied DC voltage?
A. Reliance
B. Reactance
C. Saturation
D. Resistance

T7A08
(D)
Page 7.9

T7A08
What is the basic unit of resistance?
A. The volt
B. The watt
C. The ampere
D. The ohm

T7A09
(C)
Page 7.20

T7A09
What is the basic unit of inductance?
A. The coulomb
B. The farad
C. The henry
D. The ohm

T7A10
(A)
Page 7.22

T7A10
What is the basic unit of capacitance?
A. The farad
B. The ohm
C. The volt
D. The henry

T7A11
(B)
Page 7.18

T7A11
Which of the following circuits changes an alternating current signal into a varying direct current signal?
A. Transformer
B. Rectifier
C. Amplifier
D. Director

T7A12
(A)
Page 7.12

T7A12
What formula shows how voltage, current and resistance relate to each other in an electric circuit?
A. Ohm's Law
B. Kirchhoff's Law
C. Ampere's Law
D. Tesla's Law

T7A13
If a current of 2 amperes flows through a 50-ohm resistor, what is the voltage across the resistor?
A. 25 volts
B. 52 volts
C. 100 volts
D. 200 volts

T7A14
If a 100-ohm resistor is connected to 200 volts, what is the current through the resistor?
A. 1 ampere
B. 2 amperes
C. 300 amperes
D. 20,000 amperes

T7A15
If a current of 3 amperes flows through a resistor connected to 90 volts, what is the resistance?
A. 3 ohms
B. 30 ohms
C. 93 ohms
D. 270 ohms

T7A16
If you increase your transmitter output power from 5 watts to 10 watts, what decibel (dB) increase does that represent?
A. 2 dB
B. 3 dB
C. 5 dB
D. 10 dB

T7A17
If an ammeter marked in amperes is used to measure a 3000-milliampere current, what reading would it show?
A. 0.003 amperes
B. 0.3 amperes
C. 3 amperes
D. 3,000,000 amperes

T7A18
How many hertz are in a kilohertz?
A. 10
B. 100
C. 1000
D. 1,000,000

T7A19
If a dial marked in megahertz shows a reading of 3.525 MHz, what would it show if it were marked in kilohertz?
A. 0.003525 kHz
B. 35.25 kHz
C. 3525 kHz
D. 3,525,000 kHz

T7A20
How many microfarads is 1,000,000 picofarads?
A. 0.001 microfarads
B. 1 microfarad
C. 1000 microfarads
D. 1,000,000,000 microfarads

T7A13
(C)
Page 7.12

T7A14
(B)
Page 7.12

T7A15
(B)
Page 7.13

T7A16
(B)
Page 7.14

T7A17
(C)
Page 7.3

T7A18
(C)
Page 7.3

T7A19
(C)
Page 7.3

T7A20
(B)
Page 7.3

T7A21
(B)
Page 7.3

T7A21
If you have a hand-held transceiver with an output of 500 milliwatts, how many watts would this be?
A. 0.02
B. 0.5
C. 5
D. 50

T7B Basic electric circuits; Analog vs. digital communications; Audio/RF signal; Amplification.

T7B01
(A)
Page 7.24

T7B01
What type of electric circuit uses signals that can vary continuously over a certain range of voltage or current values?
A. An analog circuit
B. A digital circuit
C. A continuous circuit
D. A pulsed modulator circuit

T7B02
(B)
Page 7.24

T7B02
What type of electric circuit uses signals that have voltage or current values only in specific steps over a certain range?
A. An analog circuit
B. A digital circuit
C. A step modulator circuit
D. None of these choices is correct

T7B03
(C)
Page 7.24

T7B03
Which of the following is an example of an analog communications method?
A. Morse code (CW)
B. Packet Radio
C. Frequency-modulated (FM) voice
D. PSK31

T7B04
(D)
Page 7.25

T7B04
Which of the following is an example of a digital communications method?
A. Single-sideband (SSB) voice
B. Amateur Television (ATV)
C. FM voice
D. Radioteletype (RTTY)

T7B05
(B)
Page 2.3

T7B05
Most humans can hear sounds in what frequency range?
A. 0 - 20 Hz
B. 20 - 20,000 Hz
C. 200 - 200,000 Hz
D. 10,000 - 30,000 Hz

T7B06
(B)
Page 2.3

T7B06
Why do we call electrical signals in the frequency range of 20 Hz to 20,000 Hz audio frequencies?
A. Because the human ear cannot sense anything in this range
B. Because the human ear can sense sounds in this range
C. Because this range is too low for radio energy
D. Because the human ear can sense radio waves in this range

T7B07
What is the lowest frequency of electrical energy that is usually known as a radio frequency?
A. 20 Hz
B. 2,000 Hz
C. 20,000 Hz
D. 1,000,000 Hz

T7B07
(C)
Page 2.3

T7B08
Electrical energy at a frequency of 7125 kHz is in what frequency range?
A. Audio
B. Radio
C. Hyper
D. Super-high

T7B08
(B)
Page 2.3

T7B09
If a radio wave makes 3,725,000 cycles in one second, what does this mean?
A. The radio wave's voltage is 3725 kilovolts
B. The radio wave's wavelength is 3725 kilometers
C. The radio wave's frequency is 3725 kilohertz
D. The radio wave's speed is 3725 kilometers per second

T7B09
(C)
Page 2.2

T7B10
Which component can amplify a small signal using low voltages?
A. A PNP transistor
B. A variable resistor
C. An electrolytic capacitor
D. A multiple-cell battery

T7B10
(A)
Page 7.18

T7B11
Which component can amplify a small signal but normally uses high voltages?
A. A transistor
B. An electrolytic capacitor
C. A vacuum tube
D. A multiple-cell battery

T7B11
(C)
Page 7.19

T7C   Concepts of Resistance/resistor; Capacitor/capacitance; Inductor/ Inductance; Conductor/Insulator; Diode; Transistor; Semiconductor devices; Electrical functions of and schematic symbols of resistors, switches, fuses, batteries, inductors, capacitors, antennas, grounds and polarity; Construction of variable and fixed inductors and capacitors.

T7C01
Which of the following lists include three good electrical conductors?
A. Copper, gold, mica
B. Gold, silver, wood
C. Gold, silver, aluminum
D. Copper, aluminum, paper

T7C01
(C)
Page 7.8

T7C02
What is one reason resistors are used in electronic circuits?
A. To block the flow of direct current while allowing alternating current to pass
B. To block the flow of alternating current while allowing direct current to pass
C. To increase the voltage of the circuit
D. To control the amount of current that flows for a particular applied voltage

T7C02
(D)
Page 7.9

T7C03
(D)
Page 7.11

T7C03

If two resistors are connected in series, what is their total resistance?

A. The difference between the individual resistor values
B. Always less than the value of either resistor
C. The product of the individual resistor values
D. The sum of the individual resistor values

T7C04
(A)
Page 7.22

T7C04

What is one reason capacitors are used in electronic circuits?

A. To block the flow of direct current while allowing alternating current to pass
B. To block the flow of alternating current while allowing direct current to pass
C. To change the time constant of the applied voltage
D. To change alternating current to direct current

T7C05
(A)
Page 7.24

T7C05

If two equal-value capacitors are connected in parallel, what is their total capacitance?

A. Twice the value of one capacitor
B. Half the value of one capacitor
C. The same as the value of either capacitor
D. The value of one capacitor times the value of the other

T7C06
(B)
Page 7.21

T7C06

What does a capacitor do?

A. It stores energy electrochemically and opposes a change in current
B. It stores energy electrostatically and opposes a change in voltage
C. It stores energy electromagnetically and opposes a change in current
D. It stores energy electromechanically and opposes a change in voltage

T7C07
(D)
Page 7.23

T7C07

Which of the following best describes a variable capacitor?

A. A set of fixed capacitors whose connections can be varied
B. Two sets of insulating plates separated by a conductor, which can be varied in distance from each other
C. A set of capacitors connected in a series-parallel circuit
D. Two sets of rotating conducting plates separated by an insulator, which can be varied in surface area exposed to each other

T7C08
(C)
Page 7.20

T7C08

What does an inductor do?

A. It stores energy electrostatically and opposes a change in voltage
B. It stores energy electrochemically and opposes a change in current
C. It stores energy electromagnetically and opposes a change in current
D. It stores energy electromechanically and opposes a change in voltage

T7C09
(C)
Page 7.17

T7C09

What component controls current to flow in one direction only?

A. A fixed resistor
B. A signal generator
C. A diode
D. A fuse

T7C10
(A)
Page 7.19

T7C10

What is one advantage of using ICs (integrated circuits) instead of vacuum tubes in a circuit?

A. ICs usually combine several functions into one package
B. ICs can handle high-power input signals
C. ICs can handle much higher voltages
D. ICs can handle much higher temperatures

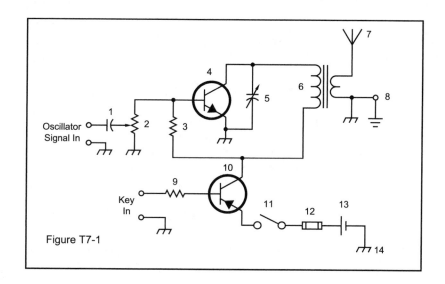

Figure T7-1

T7C11
Which symbol of Figure T7-1 represents a fixed resistor?
A. Symbol 1
B. Symbol 2
C. Symbol 3
D. Symbol 5

T7C11
(C)
Page 7.10

T7C12
In Figure T7-1, which symbol represents a variable resistor or potentiometer?
A. Symbol 1
B. Symbol 2
C. Symbol 3
D. Symbol 12

T7C12
(B)
Page 7.10

T7C13
In Figure T7-1, which symbol represents a single-cell battery?
A. Symbol 1
B. Symbol 6
C. Symbol 12
D. Symbol 13

T7C13
(D)
Page 7.7

T7C14
In Figure T7-1, which symbol represents an NPN transistor?
A. Symbol 2
B. Symbol 4
C. Symbol 10
D. Symbol 12

T7C14
(B)
Page 7.18

T7C15
Which symbol of Figure T7-1 represents a fixed-value capacitor?
A. Symbol 1
B. Symbol 3
C. Symbol 5
D. Symbol 13

T7C15
(A)
Page 7.23

T7C16
(B)
Page 7.17

T7C16
In Figure T7-1, which symbol represents an antenna?
A. Symbol 5
B. Symbol 7
C. Symbol 8
D. Symbol 14

T7C17
(A)
Page 7.20

T7C17
In Figure T7-1, which symbol represents a fixed-value iron-core inductor?
A. Symbol 6
B. Symbol 9
C. Symbol 11
D. Symbol 12

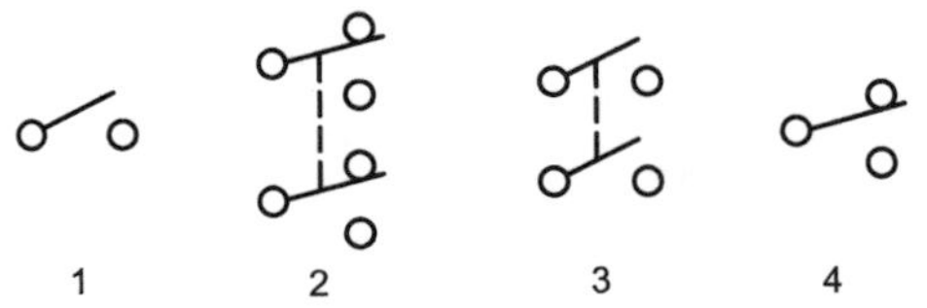

Figure T7-2

T7C18
(D)
Page 7.16

T7C18
In Figure T7-2, which symbol represents a single-pole, double-throw switch?
A. Symbol 1
B. Symbol 2
C. Symbol 3
D. Symbol 4

T7C19
(C)
Page 7.16

T7C19
In Figure T7-2, which symbol represents a double-pole, single-throw switch?
A. Symbol 1
B. Symbol 2
C. Symbol 3
D. Symbol 4

**Subelement
T8**

SUBELEMENT T8 - Good Engineering Practice
[6 Exam Questions - 6 Groups]

**T8A   Basic amateur station apparatus; Choice of apparatus for desired
communications; Setting up station; Constructing and modifying
amateur station apparatus; Station layout for CW, SSB, FM, Packet
and other popular modes.**

T8A01
(C)
Page 8.11

T8A01
What two bands are most commonly used by "dual band" hand-held transceivers?
A. 6 meters and 2 meters
B. 2 meters and 1.25 meters
C. 2 meters and 70 cm
D. 70 cm and 23 cm

T8A02

If your mobile transceiver works in your car but not in your home, what should you check first?

A. The power supply
B. The speaker
C. The microphone
D. The SWR meter

T8A02
(A)
Page 8.8

T8A03

Which of the following devices would you need to conduct Amateur Radio communications using a data emission?

A. A telegraph key
B. A computer
C. A transducer
D. A telemetry sensor

T8A03
(B)
Page 8.9

T8A04

Which of the following devices would be useful to create an effective Amateur Radio station for weak-signal VHF communication?

A. A hand-held VHF FM transceiver
B. A multi-mode VHF transceiver
C. An Omni-directional antenna
D. A mobile VHF FM transceiver

T8A04
(B)
Page 8.11

T8A05

What would you connect to a transceiver for voice operation?

A. A splatter filter
B. A terminal-voice controller
C. A receiver audio filter
D. A microphone

T8A05
(D)
Page 8.11

T8A06

What would you connect to a transceiver to send Morse code?

A. A key-click filter
B. A telegraph key
C. An SWR meter
D. An antenna switch

T8A06
(B)
Page 8.11

T8A07

What do many amateurs use to help form good Morse code characters?

A. A key-operated on/off switch
B. An electronic keyer
C. A key-click filter
D. A DTMF keypad

T8A07
(B)
Page 8.11

T8A08

Why is it important to provide adequate power supply filtering for a CW transmitter?

A. It isn't important, since CW transmitters cannot be modulated by AC hum
B. To eliminate phase noise
C. It isn't important, since most CW receivers can easily suppress any hum by using narrow filters
D. To eliminate modulation of the RF signal by AC hum

T8A08
(D)
Page 8.5

T8A09

Why is it important to provide adequate DC source supply filtering for a mobile transmitter or transceiver?

A. To reduce AC hum and carrier current device signals
B. To provide an emergency power source
C. To reduce stray noise and RF pick-up
D. To allow the use of smaller power conductors

T8A09
(C)
Page 8.8

T8A10
(A)
Page 8.9

T8A10
What would you connect to a transceiver for RTTY operation?
A. A modem and a teleprinter or computer system
B. A computer, a printer and a RTTY refresh unit
C. A data-inverter controller
D. A modem, a monitor and a DTMF keypad

T8A11
(B)
Page 8.10

T8A11
What might you connect between your transceiver and an antenna switch connected to several antennas?
A. A high-pass filter
B. An SWR meter
C. A key-click filter
D. A mixer

T8A12
(A)
Page 8.10

T8A12
What might happen if you set your receiver's signal squelch too low while attempting to receive packet mode transmissions?
A. Noise may cause the TNC to falsely detect a data carrier
B. Weaker stations may not be received
C. Transmission speed and throughput will be reduced
D. The TNC could be damaged

T8A13
(D)
Page 8.9

T8A13
What is one common method of transmitting RTTY on VHF/UHF bands?
A. Frequency shift the carrier to indicate mark and space at the receiver
B. Amplitude shift the carrier to indicate mark and space at the receiver
C. Key the transmitter on to indicate space and off for mark
D. Modulate a conventional FM transmitter with a modem

T8A14
(D)
Page 8.12

T8A14
What would you use to connect a dual-band antenna to a mobile transceiver that has separate VHF and UHF output connectors?
A. A dual-needle SWR meter
B. A full-duplex phone patch
C. Twin high-pass filters
D. A duplexer

T8B   How transmitters work; Operation and tuning; VFO; Transceiver; Dummy load; Antenna switch; Power supply; Amplifier; Stability; Microphone gain; FM deviation; Block diagrams of typical stations.

T8B01
(B)
Page 8.11

T8B01
Can a transceiver designed for FM phone operation also be used for single sideband in the weak-signal portion of the 2-meter band?
A. Yes, with simple modification
B. Only if the radio is a "multimode" radio
C. Only with the right antenna
D. Only with the right polarization

T8B02
(B)
Page 8.5

T8B02
How is a CW signal usually transmitted?
A. By frequency-shift keying an RF signal
B. By on/off keying an RF signal
C. By audio-frequency-shift keying an oscillator tone
D. By on/off keying an audio-frequency signal

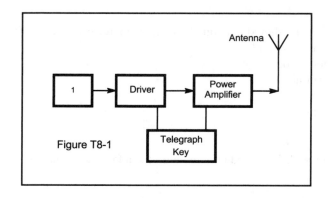

Figure T8-1

T8B03
What purpose does block 1 serve in the simple CW transmitter pictured in Figure T8-1?
A. It detects the CW signal
B. It controls the transmitter frequency
C. It controls the transmitter output power
D. It filters out spurious emissions from the transmitter

T8B04
What circuit is pictured in Figure T8-1 if block 1 is a variable-frequency oscillator?
A. A packet-radio transmitter
B. A crystal-controlled transmitter
C. A single-sideband transmitter
D. A VFO-controlled transmitter

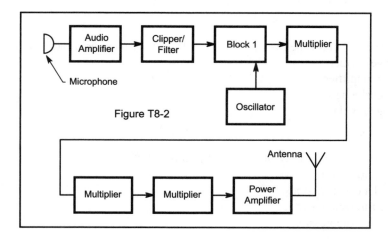

Figure T8-2

T8B05
What circuit is shown in Figure T8-2 if block 1 represents a reactance modulator?
A. A single-sideband transmitter
B. A double-sideband AM transmitter
C. An FM transmitter
D. A product transmitter

T8B06
How would the output of the FM transmitter shown in Figure T8-2 be affected if the audio amplifier failed to operate (assuming block 1 is a reactance modulator)?
A. There would be no output from the transmitter
B. The output would be 6-dB below the normal output power
C. The transmitted audio would be distorted but understandable
D. The output would be an unmodulated carrier

T8B03
(B)
Page 8.5

T8B04
(D)
Page 8.4

T8B05
(C)
Page 8.5

T8B06
(D)
Page 8.6

T8B07
(A)
Page 8.39

T8B07
What minimum rating should a dummy antenna have for use with a 100-watt, single-sideband-phone transmitter?
A. 100 watts continuous
B. 141 watts continuous
C. 175 watts continuous
D. 200 watts continuous

T8B08
(B)
Page 8.8

T8B08
A mobile radio may be operated at home with the addition of which piece of equipment?
A. An alternator
B. A power supply
C. A linear amplifier
D. A rhombic antenna

T8B09
(C)
Page 8.8

T8B09
What might you use instead of a power supply for home operation of a mobile radio?
A. A filter capacitor
B. An alternator
C. A 12-volt battery
D. A linear amplifier

T8B10
(C)
Page 8.8

T8B10
What device converts 120 V AC to 12 V DC?
A. A catalytic converter
B. A low-pass filter
C. A power supply
D. An RS-232 interface

T8B11
(B)
Page 8.12

T8B11
What device could boost the low-power output from your hand-held radio up to 100 watts?
A. A voltage divider
B. A power amplifier
C. A impedance network
D. A voltage regulator

T8B12
(B)
Page 8.5

T8B12
What is the result of over deviation in an FM transmitter?
A. Increased transmitter power
B. Out-of-channel emissions
C. Increased transmitter range
D. Poor carrier suppression

T8B13
(D)
Page 8.5

T8B13
What can you do if you are told your FM hand-held or mobile transceiver is over deviating?
A. Talk louder into the microphone
B. Let the transceiver cool off
C. Change to a higher power level
D. Talk farther away from the microphone

T8B14
(B)
Page 8.10

T8B14
In Figure T8-3, if block 1 is a transceiver and block 3 is a dummy antenna, what is block 2?
A. A terminal-node switch
B. An antenna switch
C. A telegraph key switch
D. A high-pass filter

Figure T8-3

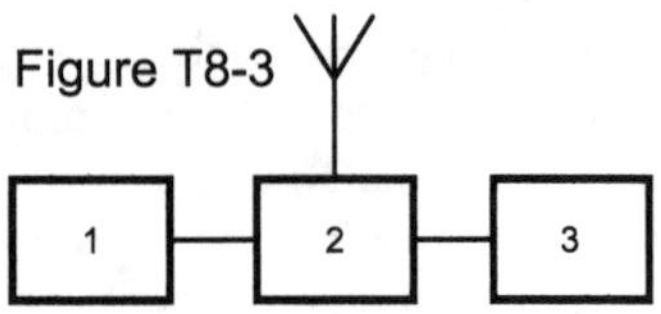

T8B15
In Figure T8-3, if block 1 is a transceiver and block 2 is an antenna switch, what is block 3?
A. A terminal-node switch
B. An SWR meter
C. A telegraph key switch
D. A dummy antenna

T8B15
(D)
Page 8.39

T8B16
In Figure T8-4, if block 1 is a transceiver and block 2 is an SWR meter, what is block 3?
A. An antenna switch
B. An antenna tuner
C. A key-click filter
D. A terminal-node controller

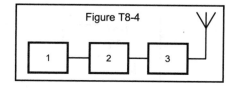

Figure T8-4

T8B16
(B)
Page 8.11

T8B17
In Figure T8-4, if block 1 is a transceiver and block 3 is an antenna tuner, what is block 2?
A. A terminal-node switch
B. A dipole antenna
C. An SWR meter
D. A high-pass filter

T8B17
(C)
Page 8.10

T8B18
In Figure T8-4, if block 2 is an SWR meter and block 3 is an antenna tuner, what is block 1?
A. A terminal-node switch
B. A power supply
C. A telegraph key switch
D. A transceiver

T8B18
(D)
Page 8.11

T8C   How receivers work, operation and tuning, including block diagrams; Super-heterodyne including Intermediate frequency; Reception; Demodulation or Detection; Sensitivity; Selectivity; Frequency standards; Squelch and audio gain (volume) control.

T8C01
What type of circuit does Figure T8-5 represent if block 1 is a product detector?
A. A simple phase modulation receiver
B. A simple FM receiver
C. A simple CW and SSB receiver
D. A double-conversion multiplier

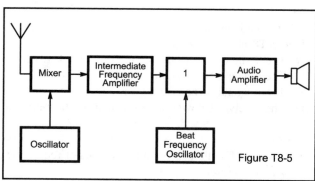

Figure T8-5

T8C01
(C)
Page 8.7

T8C02
If Figure T8-5 is a diagram of a simple single-sideband receiver, what type of circuit should be shown in block 1?
A. A high pass filter
B. A ratio detector
C. A low pass filter
D. A product detector

T8C02
(D)
Page 8.7

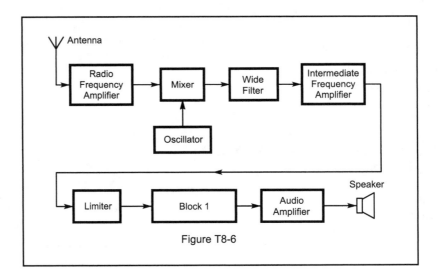

Figure T8-6

T8C03
(D)
Page 8.8

T8C03
What circuit is pictured in Figure T8-6, if block 1 is a frequency discriminator?
A. A double-conversion receiver
B. A variable-frequency oscillator
C. A superheterodyne receiver
D. An FM receiver

T8C04
(A)
Page 8.8

T8C04
What is block 1 in the FM receiver shown in Figure T8-6?
A. A frequency discriminator
B. A product detector
C. A frequency-shift modulator
D. A phase inverter

T8C05
(B)
Page 8.8

T8C05
What would happen if block 1 failed to function in the FM receiver diagram shown in Figure T8-6?
A. The audio output would sound loud and distorted
B. There would be no audio output
C. There would be no effect
D. The receiver's power supply would be short-circuited

T8C06
(C)
Page 8.6

T8C06
What circuit function is found in all types of receivers?
A. An audio filter
B. A beat-frequency oscillator
C. A detector
D. An RF amplifier

T8C07
(C)
Page 8.8

T8C07
What is one accurate way to check the calibration of your receiver's tuning dial?
A. Monitor the BFO frequency of a second receiver
B. Tune to a popular amateur net frequency
C. Tune to one of the frequencies of station WWV or WWVH
D. Tune to another amateur station and ask what frequency the operator is using

T8C08

What circuit combines signals from an IF amplifier stage and a beat-frequency oscillator (BFO), to produce an audio signal?
A. An AGC circuit
B. A detector circuit
C. A power supply circuit
D. A VFO circuit

T8C09

Why is FM voice so effective for local VHF/UHF radio communications?
A. The carrier is not detectable
B. It is more resistant to distortion caused by reflected signals than the AM modes
C. It has audio that is less affected by interference from static-type electrical noise than the AM modes
D. Its RF carrier stays on frequency better than the AM modes

T8C10

Why do many radio receivers have several IF filters of different bandwidths that can be selected by the operator?
A. Because some frequency bands are wider than others
B. Because different bandwidths help increase the receiver sensitivity
C. Because different bandwidths improve S-meter readings
D. Because some emission types need a wider bandwidth than others to be received properly

T8C11

What is the function of a mixer in a superheterodyne receiver?
A. To cause all signals outside of a receiver's passband to interfere with one another
B. To cause all signals inside of a receiver's passband to reinforce one another
C. To shift the frequency of the received signal so that it can be processed by IF stages
D. To interface the receiver with an auxiliary device, such as a TNC

T8C12

What frequency or frequencies could the radio shown in Figure T8-7 receive?
A. 136.3 MHz
B. 157.7 MHz and 10.7 MHz
C. 10.7 MHz
D. 147.0 MHz and 168.4 MHz

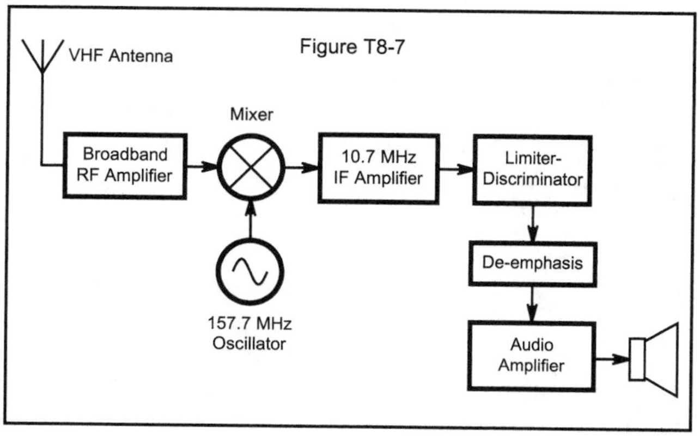

Figure T8-7

T8C13

What type of receiver is shown in Figure T8-7?
A. Direct conversion
B. Superregenerative
C. Single-conversion superheterodyne
D. Dual conversion superheterodyne

T8C14

What emission mode could the receiver in Figure T8-7 detect?
A. AM
B. FM
C. Single sideband (SSB)
D. CW

T8C08
(B)
Page 8.7

T8C09
(C)
Page 8.5

T8C10
(D)
Page 8.7

T8C11
(C)
Page 8.7

T8C12
(D)
Page 8.7

T8C13
(C)
Page 8.7

T8C14
(B)
Page 8.8

T8C15
Where should the squelch be set for the proper operation of an FM receiver?
A. Low enough to hear constant background noise
B. Low enough to hear chattering background noise
C. At the point that just silences background noise
D. As far beyond the point of silence as the knob will turn

T8D How antennas work; Radiation principles; Basic construction; Half wave dipole length vs. frequency; Polarization; Directivity; ERP; Directional/non-directional antennas; Multiband antennas; Antenna gain; Resonant frequency; Loading coil; Electrical vs. physical length; Radiation pattern; Transmatch.

T8D01
Which of the following will improve the operation of a hand-held radio inside a vehicle?
A. Shielding around the battery pack
B. A good ground to the belt clip
C. An external antenna on the roof
D. An audio amplifier

T8D02
Which is true of "rubber duck" antennas for hand-held transceivers?
A. The shorter they are, the better they perform
B. They are much less efficient than a quarter-wavelength telescopic antenna
C. They offer the highest amount of gain possible for any hand-held transceiver antenna
D. They have a good long-distance communications range

T8D03
What would be the length, to the nearest inch, of a half-wavelength dipole antenna that is resonant at 147 MHz?
A. 19 inches
B. 37 inches
C. 55 inches
D. 74 inches

T8D04
How long should you make a half-wavelength dipole antenna for 223 MHz (measured to the nearest inch)?
A. 112 inches
B. 50 inches
C. 25 inches
D. 12 inches

T8D05
How long should you make a quarter-wavelength vertical antenna for 146 MHz (measured to the nearest inch)?
A. 112 inches
B. 50 inches
C. 19 inches
D. 12 inches

T8D06
How long should you make a quarter-wavelength vertical antenna for 440 MHz (measured to the nearest inch)?
A. 12 inches
B. 9 inches
C. 6 inches
D. 3 inches

T8D07

Which of the following factors has the greatest effect on the gain of a properly designed Yagi antenna?
A. The number of elements
B. Boom length
C. Element spacing
D. Element diameter

T8D07
(B)
Page 8.34

T8D08

Approximately how long is the driven element of a Yagi antenna?
A. 1/4 wavelength
B. 1/3 wavelength
C. 1/2 wavelength
D. 1 wavelength

T8D08
(C)
Page 8.34

T8D09

In Figure T8-8, what is the name of element 2 of the Yagi antenna?
A. Director
B. Reflector
C. Boom
D. Driven element

T8D09
(D)
Page 8.35

FEED LINE   Figure T8-8

T8D10

In Figure T8-8, what is the name of element 3 of the Yagi antenna?
A. Director
B. Reflector
C. Boom
D. Driven element

T8D10
(A)
Page 8.35

T8D11

In Figure T8-8, what is the name of element 1 of the Yagi antenna?
A. Director
B. Reflector
C. Boom
D. Driven element

T8D11
(B)
Page 8.35

T8D12

What is a cubical quad antenna?
A. Four straight, parallel elements in line with each other, each approximately 1/2-electrical wavelength long
B. Two or more parallel four-sided wire loops, each approximately one-electrical wavelength long
C. A vertical conductor 1/4-electrical wavelength high, fed at the bottom
D. A center-fed wire 1/2-electrical wavelength long

T8D12
(B)
Page 8.36

T8D13

What does horizontal wave polarization mean?
A. The magnetic lines of force of a radio wave are parallel to the Earth's surface
B. The electric lines of force of a radio wave are parallel to the Earth's surface
C. The electric lines of force of a radio wave are perpendicular to the Earth's surface
D. The electric and magnetic lines of force of a radio wave are perpendicular to the Earth's surface

T8D13
(B)
Page 8.30

T8D14
(C)
Page 8.30

T8D14

What does vertical wave polarization mean?

A. The electric lines of force of a radio wave are parallel to the Earth's surface
B. The magnetic lines of force of a radio wave are perpendicular to the Earth's surface
C. The electric lines of force of a radio wave are perpendicular to the Earth's surface
D. The electric and magnetic lines of force of a radio wave are parallel to the Earth's surface

T8D15
(C)
Page 8.22

T8D15

If the ends of a half-wavelength dipole antenna (mounted at least a half-wavelength high) point east and west, which way would the antenna send out radio energy?

A. Equally in all directions
B. Mostly up and down
C. Mostly north and south
D. Mostly east and west

T8D16
(B)
Page 8.30

T8D16

What electromagnetic wave polarization do most repeater antennas have in the VHF and UHF spectrum?

A. Horizontal
B. Vertical
C. Right-hand circular
D. Left-hand circular

T8D17
(C)
Page 8.31

T8D17

What electromagnetic wave polarization is used for most satellite operation?

A. Only horizontal
B. Only vertical
C. Circular
D. No polarization

T8D18
(B)
Page 8.30

T8D18

Which antenna polarization is used most often for weak signal VHF/UHF SSB operation?

A. Vertical
B. Horizontal
C. Right-hand circular
D. Left-hand circular

T8D19
(C)
Page 8.34

T8D19

How will increasing antenna gain by 3 dB affect your signal's effective radiated power in the direction of maximum radiation?

A. It will cut it in half
B. It will not change
C. It will double it
D. It will quadruple it

T8D20
(A)
Page 8.24

T8D20

What is one advantage to using a multiband antenna?

A. You can operate on several bands with a single feed line
B. Multiband antennas always have high gain
C. You can transmit on several frequencies simultaneously
D. Multiband antennas offer poor harmonic suppression

T8D21

What could be done to reduce the physical length of an antenna without changing its resonant frequency?

A. Attach a balun at the feed point
B. Add series capacitance at the feed point
C. Use thinner conductors
D. Add a loading coil

T8D21
(D)
Page 8.25

T8D22

What device might allow use of an antenna on a band it was not designed for?

A. An SWR meter
B. A low-pass filter
C. An antenna tuner
D. A high-pass filter

T8D22
(C)
Page 8.10

T8E   How transmission lines work; Standing waves/SWR/SWR-meter; Impedance matching; Types of transmission lines; Feed point; Coaxial cable; Balun; Waterproofing Connections.

T8E01

What does standing-wave ratio mean?

A. The ratio of maximum to minimum inductances on a feed line
B. The ratio of maximum to minimum capacitances on a feed line
C. The ratio of maximum to minimum impedances on a feed line
D. The ratio of maximum to minimum voltages on a feed line

T8E01
(D)
Page 8.15

T8E02

What instrument is used to measure standing wave ratio?

A. An ohmmeter
B. An ammeter
C. An SWR meter
D. A current bridge

T8E02
(C)
Page 8.15

T8E03

What would an SWR of 1:1 indicate about an antenna system?

A. That the antenna was very effective
B. That the transmission line was radiating
C. That the antenna was reflecting as much power as it was radiating
D. That the impedance of the antenna and its transmission line were matched

T8E03
(D)
Page 8.15

T8E04

What does an SWR reading of 4:1 mean?

A. An impedance match that is too low
B. An impedance match that is good, but not the best
C. An antenna gain of 4
D. An impedance mismatch; something may be wrong with the antenna system

T8E04
(D)
Page 8.16

T8E05

What does an antenna tuner do?

A. It matches a transceiver output impedance to the antenna system impedance
B. It helps a receiver automatically tune in stations that are far away
C. It switches an antenna system to a transceiver when sending, and to a receiver when listening
D. It switches a transceiver between different kinds of antennas connected to one feed line

T8E05
(A)
Page 8.10

T8E06
(D)
Page 8.13

T8E06
What is a coaxial cable?
A. Two wires side-by-side in a plastic ribbon
B. Two wires side-by-side held apart by insulating rods
C. Two wires twisted around each other in a spiral
D. A center wire inside an insulating material covered by a metal sleeve or shield

T8E07
(A)
Page 8.13

T8E07
Why should you use only good quality coaxial cable and connectors for a UHF antenna system?
A. To keep RF loss low
B. To keep television interference high
C. To keep the power going to your antenna system from getting too high
D. To keep the standing-wave ratio of your antenna system high

T8E08
(B)
Page 8.15

T8E08
What is parallel-conductor feed line?
A. Two wires twisted around each other in a spiral
B. Two wires side-by-side held apart by insulating material
C. A center wire inside an insulating material that is covered by a metal sleeve or shield
D. A metal pipe that is as wide or slightly wider than a wavelength of the signal it carries

T8E09
(D)
Page 8.15

T8E09
Which of the following are some reasons to use parallel-conductor, open-wire feed line?
A. It has low impedance and will operate with a high SWR
B. It will operate well even with a high SWR and it works well when tied down to metal objects
C. It has a low impedance and has less loss than coaxial cable
D. It will operate well even with a high SWR and has less loss than coaxial cable

T8E10
(D)
Page 8.19

T8E10
What does "balun" mean?
A. Balanced antenna network
B. Balanced unloader
C. Balanced unmodulator
D. Balanced to unbalanced

T8E11
(A)
Page 8.19

T8E11
Where would you install a balun to feed a dipole antenna with 50-ohm coaxial cable?
A. Between the coaxial cable and the antenna
B. Between the transmitter and the coaxial cable
C. Between the antenna and the ground
D. Between the coaxial cable and the ground

T8E12
(C)
Page 8.13

T8E12
What happens to radio energy when it is sent through a poor quality coaxial cable?
A. It causes spurious emissions
B. It is returned to the transmitter's chassis ground
C. It is converted to heat in the cable
D. It causes interference to other stations near the transmitting frequency

T8E13
(C)
Page 8.15

T8E13
What is an unbalanced line?
A. A feed line with neither conductor connected to ground
B. A feed line with both conductors connected to ground
C. A feed line with one conductor connected to ground
D. All of these answers are correct

T8E14
What point in an antenna system is called the feed point?
A. The antenna connection on the back of the transmitter
B. Halfway between the transmitter and the feed line
C. At the point where the feed line joins the antenna
D. At the tip of the antenna

T8F   Voltmeter/ammeter/ohmmeter/multi/S-meter, peak reading and RF watt meter; Building/modifying equipment; Soldering; Making measurements; Test instruments.

T8F01
Which instrument would you use to measure electric potential or electromotive force?
A. An ammeter
B. A voltmeter
C. A wavemeter
D. An ohmmeter

T8F02
How is a voltmeter usually connected to a circuit under test?
A. In series with the circuit
B. In parallel with the circuit
C. In quadrature with the circuit
D. In phase with the circuit

T8F03
What happens inside a voltmeter when you switch it from a lower to a higher voltage range?
A. Resistance is added in series with the meter
B. Resistance is added in parallel with the meter
C. Resistance is reduced in series with the meter
D. Resistance is reduced in parallel with the meter

T8F04
How is an ammeter usually connected to a circuit under test?
A. In series with the circuit
B. In parallel with the circuit
C. In quadrature with the circuit
D. In phase with the circuit

T8F05
Which instrument would you use to measure electric current?
A. An ohmmeter
B. A wavemeter
C. A voltmeter
D. An ammeter

T8F06
What test instrument would be useful to measure DC resistance?
A. An oscilloscope
B. A spectrum analyzer
C. A noise bridge
D. An ohmmeter

T8E14
(C)
Page 8.19

T8F01
(B)
Page 8.37

T8F02
(B)
Page 8.37

T8F03
(A)
Page 8.37

T8F04
(A)
Page 8.37

T8F05
(D)
Page 8.37

T8F06
(D)
Page 8.38

T8F07
(C)
Page 8.38

T8F07
What might damage a multimeter that uses a moving-needle meter?
A. Measuring a voltage much smaller than the maximum for the chosen scale
B. Leaving the meter in the milliamps position overnight
C. Measuring voltage when using the ohms setting
D. Not allowing it to warm up properly

T8F08
(D)
Page 8.38

T8F08
For which of the following measurements would you normally use a multimeter?
A. SWR and power
B. Resistance, capacitance and inductance
C. Resistance and reactance
D. Voltage, current and resistance

T8F09
(A)
Page 8.7

T8F09
What is used to measure relative signal strength in a receiver?
A. An S meter
B. An RST meter
C. A signal deviation meter
D. An SSB meter

T8F10
(A)
Page 8.15

T8F10
With regard to a transmitter and antenna system, what does "forward power" mean?
A. The power traveling from the transmitter to the antenna
B. The power radiated from the top of an antenna system
C. The power produced during the positive half of an RF cycle
D. The power used to drive a linear amplifier

T8F11
(B)
Page 8.15

T8F11
With regard to a transmitter and antenna system, what does "reflected power" mean?
A. The power radiated down to the ground from an antenna
B. The power returned towards the source on a transmission line
C. The power produced during the negative half of an RF cycle
D. The power returned to an antenna by buildings and trees

T8F12
(B)
Page 8.17

T8F12
At what line impedance do most RF watt meters usually operate?
A. 25 ohms
B. 50 ohms
C. 100 ohms
D. 300 ohms

T8F13
(B)
Page 8.17

T8F13
If a directional RF wattmeter reads 90 watts forward power and 10 watts reflected power, what is the actual transmitter output power?
A. 10 watts
B. 80 watts
C. 90 watts
D. 100 watts

T8F14
(B)
Page 8.1

T8F14
What is the minimum FCC certification required for an amateur radio operator to build or modify their own transmitting equipment?
A. A First-Class Radio Repair License
B. A Technician class license
C. A General class license
D. An Amateur Extra class license

T8F15

What safety step should you take when soldering?

A. Always wear safety glasses

B. Ensure proper ventilation

C. Make sure no one can touch the soldering iron tip for at least 10 minutes after it is turned off

D. All of these choices are correct

T8F15
(D)
Page 8.37

T8F16

Where would you connect a voltmeter to a 12-volt transceiver if you think the supply voltage may be low when you transmit?

A. At the battery terminals

B. At the fuse block

C. Midway along the 12-volt power supply wire

D. At the 12-volt plug on the chassis of the equipment

T8F16
(D)
Page 8.8

T8F17

If your mobile transceiver does not power up, what might you check first?

A. The antenna feed point

B. The coaxial cable connector

C. The microphone jack

D. The 12-volt fuses

T8F17
(D)
Page 8.8

T8F18

What device produces a stable, low-level signal that can be set to a desired frequency?

A. A wavemeter

B. A reflectometer

C. A signal generator

D. An oscilloscope

T8F18
(C)
Page 8.39

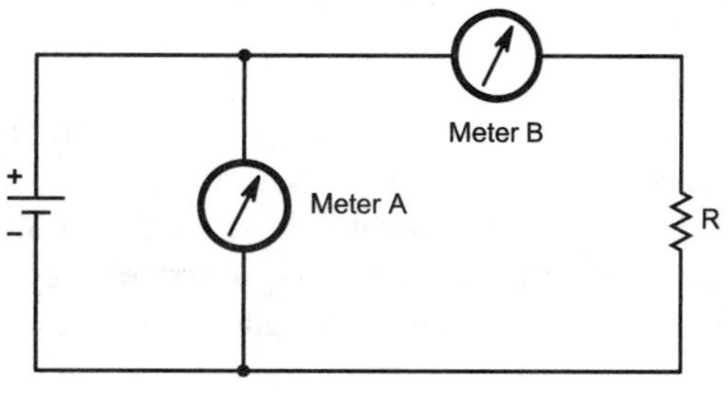

T8F19

In Figure T8-9, what circuit quantity would meter B indicate?

A. The voltage across the resistor

B. The power consumed by the resistor

C. The power factor of the resistor

D. The current flowing through the resistor

T8F19
(D)
Page 8.39

Meter B

Meter A

R

Figure T8-9

T8F20

In Figure T8-9, what circuit quantity is meter A reading?

A. Battery current

B. Battery voltage

C. Battery power

D. Battery current polarity

T8F20
(B)
Page 8.39

T8F21

In Figure T8-9, how would the power consumed by the resistor be calculated?

A. Multiply the value of the resistor times the square of the reading of meter B

B. Multiply the value of the resistor times the reading of meter B

C. Multiply the reading of meter A times the value of the resistor

D. Multiply the value of the resistor times the square root of the reading of meter B

T8F21
(A)
Page 8.39

**SUBELEMENT T9 - Special Operations
[2 Exam Questions — 2 Groups]**

T9A **How an FM Repeater Works; Repeater operating procedures; Available frequencies; Input/output frequency separation; Repeater ID requirements; Simplex operation; Coordination; Time out; Open/closed repeater; Responsibility for interference.**

T9A01
(B)
Page 9.2

T9A01
What is the purpose of repeater operation?
A. To cut your power bill by using someone else's higher power system
B. To help mobile and low-power stations extend their usable range
C. To transmit signals for observing propagation and reception
D. To communicate with stations in services other than amateur

T9A02
(B)
Page 9.5

T9A02
What is a courtesy tone, as used in repeater operations?
A. A sound used to identify the repeater
B. A sound used to indicate when a transmission is complete
C. A sound used to indicate that a message is waiting for someone
D. A sound used to activate a receiver in case of severe weather

T9A03
(D)
Page 9.5

T9A03
During commuting rush hours, which type of repeater operation should be discouraged?
A. Mobile stations
B. Low-power stations
C. Highway traffic information nets
D. Third-party communications nets

T9A04
(D)
Page 9.4

T9A04
Which of the following is a proper way to break into a conversation on a repeater?
A. Wait for the end of a transmission and start calling the desired party
B. Shout, "break, break!" to show that you're eager to join the conversation
C. Turn on an amplifier and override whoever is talking
D. Say your call sign during a break between transmissions

T9A05
(A)
Page 9.2

T9A05
When using a repeater to communicate, which of the following do you need to know about the repeater?
A. Its input frequency and offset
B. Its call sign
C. Its power level
D. Whether or not it has an autopatch

T9A06
(C)
Page 9.5

T9A06
Why should you pause briefly between transmissions when using a repeater?
A. To check the SWR of the repeater
B. To reach for pencil and paper for third-party communications
C. To listen for anyone wanting to break in
D. To dial up the repeater's autopatch

T9A07
(A)
Page 9.5

T9A07
Why should you keep transmissions short when using a repeater?
A. A long transmission may prevent someone with an emergency from using the repeater
B. To see if the receiving station operator is still awake
C. To give any listening non-hams a chance to respond
D. To keep long-distance charges down

T9A08

How could you determine if a repeater is already being used by other stations?

A. Ask if the frequency is in use, then give your call sign
B. If you don't hear anyone, assume that the frequency is clear to use
C. Check for the presence of the CTCSS tone
D. If the repeater identifies when you key your transmitter, it probably was already in use

T9A08
(A)
Page 9.4

T9A09

What is the usual input/output frequency separation for repeaters in the 2-meter band?

A. 600 kHz
B. 1.0 MHz
C. 1.6 MHz
D. 5.0 MHz

T9A09
(A)
Page 9.2

T9A10

What is the usual input/output frequency separation for repeaters in the 70-centimeter band?

A. 600 kHz
B. 1.0 MHz
C. 1.6 MHz
D. 5.0 MHz

T9A10
(D)
Page 9.2

T9A11

What does it mean to say that a repeater has an input and an output frequency?

A. The repeater receives on one frequency and transmits on another
B. The repeater offers a choice of operating frequency, in case one is busy
C. One frequency is used to control the repeater and another is used to retransmit received signals
D. The repeater must receive an access code on one frequency before retransmitting received signals

T9A11
(A)
Page 9.2

T9A12

What is the most likely reason you might hear Morse code tones on a repeater frequency?

A. Intermodulation
B. An emergency request for help
C. The repeater's identification
D. A courtesy tone

T9A12
(C)
Page 9.2

T9A13

What is the common amateur meaning of the term "simplex operation"?

A. Transmitting and receiving on the same frequency
B. Transmitting and receiving over a wide area
C. Transmitting on one frequency and receiving on another
D. Transmitting one-way communications

T9A13
(A)
Page 9.6

T9A14

When should you use simplex operation instead of a repeater?

A. When the most reliable communications are needed
B. When a contact is possible without using a repeater
C. When an emergency telephone call is needed
D. When you are traveling and need some local information

T9A14
(B)
Page 9.6

T9A15

If you are talking to a station using a repeater, how would you find out if you could communicate using simplex instead?

A. See if you can clearly receive the station on the repeater's input frequency
B. See if you can clearly receive the station on a lower frequency band
C. See if you can clearly receive a more distant repeater
D. See if a third station can clearly receive both of you

T9A15
(A)
Page 9.6

T9A16
(D)
Page 9.6

T9A16
What is it called if the frequency coordinator recommends that you operate on a specific repeater frequency pair?
A. FCC type acceptance
B. FCC type approval
C. Frequency division multiplexing
D. Repeater frequency coordination

T9A17
(D)
Page 9.5

T9A17
What is the purpose of a repeater time-out timer?
A. It lets a repeater have a rest period after heavy use
B. It logs repeater transmit time to predict when a repeater will fail
C. It tells how long someone has been using a repeater
D. It limits the amount of time a repeater can transmit continuously

T9A18
(A)
Page 9.3

T9A18
What should you do if you hear a closed repeater system that you would like to be able to use?
A. Contact the control operator and ask to join
B. Use the repeater until told not to
C. Use simplex on the repeater input until told not to
D. Write the FCC and report the closed condition

T9A19
(B)
Page 9.3

T9A19
Who pays for the site rental and upkeep of most repeaters?
A. All amateurs, because part of the amateur license examination fee is used
B. The repeater owner and donations from its users
C. The Federal Communications Commission
D. The federal government, using money granted by Congress

T9A20
(D)
[97.205c]
Page 9.6

T9A20
If a repeater is causing harmful interference to another amateur repeater and a frequency coordinator has recommended the operation of both repeaters, who is responsible for resolving the interference?
A. The licensee of the repeater that has been recommended for the longest period of time
B. The licensee of the repeater that has been recommended the most recently
C. The frequency coordinator
D. Both repeater licensees

T9B   Beacon, satellite, space, EME communications; Radio control of models; Autopatch; Slow scan television; Telecommand; CTCSS tone access; Duplex/crossband operation.

T9B01
(A)
[97.3a9]
Page 9.9

T9B01
What is an amateur station called that transmits communications for the purpose of observation of propagation and reception?
A. A beacon
B. A repeater
C. An auxiliary station
D. A radio control station

T9B02
(D)
[97.203c,d,g]
Page 9.9

T9B02
Which of the following is true of amateur radio beacon stations?
A. Automatic control is allowed in certain band segments
B. One-way transmissions are permitted
C. Maximum output power is 100 watts
D. All of these choices are correct

T9B03
The control operator of a station communicating through an amateur satellite must hold what class of license?
A. Amateur Extra or Advanced
B. Any class except Novice
C. Any class
D. Technician with satellite endorsement

T9B03
(C)
[97.209a]
Page 9.7

T9B04
How does the Doppler effect change an amateur satellite's signal as the satellite passes overhead?
A. The signal's amplitude increases or decreases
B. The signal's frequency increases or decreases
C. The signal's polarization changes from horizontal to vertical
D. The signal's circular polarization rotates

T9B04
(B)
Page 9.7

T9B05
Why do many amateur satellites operate on the VHF/UHF bands?
A. To take advantage of the skip zone
B. Because VHF/UHF equipment costs less than HF equipment
C. To give Technician class operators greater access to modern communications technology
D. Because VHF and UHF signals easily pass through the ionosphere

T9B05
(D)
Page 9.7

T9B06
Which antenna system would NOT be a good choice for an EME (moonbounce) station?
A. A parabolic-dish antenna
B. A multi-element array of collinear antennas
C. A ground-plane antenna
D. A high-gain array of Yagi antennas

T9B06
(C)
Page 9.8

T9B07
What does the term "apogee" refer to when applied to an Earth satellite?
A. The closest point to the Earth in the satellite's orbit
B. The most distant point from the Earth in the satellite's orbit
C. The point where the satellite appears to cross the equator
D. The point when the Earth eclipses the satellite from the sun

T9B07
(B)
Page 9.7

T9B08
What does the term "perigee" refer to when applied to an Earth satellite?
A. The closest point to the Earth in the satellite's orbit
B. The most distant point from the Earth in the satellite's orbit
C. The time when the satellite will be on the opposite side of the Earth
D. The effect that causes the satellite's signal frequency to change

T9B08
(A)
Page 9.7

T9B09
What mathematical parameters describe a satellite's orbit?
A. Its telemetry data
B. Its Doppler shift characteristics
C. Its mean motion
D. Its Keplerian elements

T9B09
(D)
Page 9.7

T9B10
What is the typical amount of time an amateur has to communicate with the International Space Station?
A. 4 to 6 minutes per pass
B. An hour or two per pass
C. About 20 minutes per pass
D. All day

T9B10
(A)
Page 9.8

T9B11
(A)
Page 9.8

T9B11
Which of the following would be the best emission mode for two-way EME contacts?
A. CW
B. AM
C. FM
D. Spread spectrum

T9B12
(C)
[97.215a]
Page 9.10

T9B12
What minimum information must be on a label affixed to a transmitter used for telecommand (control) of model craft?
A. Station call sign
B. Station call sign and the station licensee's name
C. Station call sign and the station licensee's name and address
D. Station call sign and the station licensee's class of license

T9B13
(C)
Page 9.5

T9B13
What is an autopatch?
A. An automatic digital connection between a US and a foreign amateur
B. A digital connection used to transfer data between a hand-held radio and a computer
C. A device that allows radio users to access the public telephone system
D. A video interface allowing images to be patched into a digital data stream

T9B14
(C)
Page 9.6

T9B14
Which of the following statements about Amateur Radio autopatch usage is true?
A. The person called using the autopatch must be a licensed radio amateur
B. The autopatch will allow only local calls to police, fire and ambulance services
C. Communication through the autopatch is not private
D. The autopatch should not be used for reporting emergencies

T9B15
(B)
Page 9.8

T9B15
Which of the following will allow you to monitor Amateur Television (ATV) on the 70-cm band?
A. A portable video camera
B. A cable ready TV receiver
C. An SSTV converter
D. A TV flyback transformer

T9B16
(A)
Page 9.8

T9B16
When may slow-scan television be transmitted through a 2-meter repeater?
A. At any time, providing the repeater control operator authorizes this unique transmission
B. Never; slow-scan television is not allowed on 2 meters
C. Only after 5:00 PM local time
D. Never; slow-scan television is not allowed on repeaters

T9B17
(C)
[97.3a43]
Page 9.10

T9B17
What is the definition of telecommand?
A. All communications using the telephone or telegraphy with space stations
B. A one way transmission to initiate conversation with astronauts aboard a satellite or space station
C. A one way transmission to initiate, modify or terminate functions of a device at a distance
D. Two way transmissions to initiate, modify or terminate functions of a device at a distance

T9B18
(D)
[97.213a,b,c]
Page 9.10

T9B18
What provisions must be in place for the legal operation of a telecommand station?
A. The station must have a wire line or radio control link
B. A photocopy of the station license must be posted in a conspicuous location
C. The station must be protected so that no unauthorized transmission can be made
D. All of these choices are correct

T9B19
What is a continuous tone-coded squelch system (CTCSS) tone (sometimes called PL — a Motorola trademark)?
A. A special signal used for telecommand control of model craft
B. A sub-audible tone, added to a carrier, which may cause a receiver to accept the signal
C. A tone used by repeaters to mark the end of a transmission
D. A special signal used for telemetry between amateur space stations and Earth stations

T9B19
(B)
Page 9.3

T9B20
What does it mean if you are told that a tone is required to access a repeater?
A. You must use keypad tones like your phone system to operate it
B. You must wait to hear a warbling two-tone signal to operate it
C. You must wait to hear a courtesy beep tone at the end of another's transmission before you can operate it
D. You must use a subaudible tone-coded squelch with your signal to operate it

T9B20
(D)
Page 9.3

T9B21
What is the term that describes a repeater that receives signals on one band and retransmits them on another band?
A. A special coordinated repeater
B. An illegally operating repeater
C. An auxiliary station
D. A crossband repeater

T9B21
(D)
Page 9.2

SUBELEMENT T0 - Electrical, Antenna Structure and RF Safety Practices
[6 Exam Questions - 6 Groups]

Subelement
T0

T0A **Sources of electrical danger in amateur stations: lethal voltages, high current sources, fire; avoiding electrical shock; Station wiring; Wiring a three wire electrical plug; Need for main power switch; Safety interlock switch; Open/short circuit; Fuses; Station grounding.**

T0A01
What is the minimum voltage that is usually dangerous to humans?
A. 30 volts
B. 100 volts
C. 1000 volts
D. 2000 volts

T0A01
(A)
Page 10.5

T0A02
Which electrical circuit draws high current?
A. An open circuit
B. A dead circuit
C. A closed circuit
D. A short circuit

T0A02
(D)
Page 10.2

T0A03
What could happen to your transceiver if you replace its blown 5 amp AC line fuse with a 30 amp fuse?
A. The 30-amp fuse would better protect your transceiver from using too much current
B. The transceiver would run cooler
C. The transceiver could use more current than 5 amps and a fire could occur
D. The transceiver would not be able to produce as much RF output

T0A03
(C)
Page 10.5

T0A04
(A)
Page 10.5

T0A04
How much electrical current flowing through the human body will probably be fatal?
A. As little as 1/10 of an ampere
B. Approximately 10 amperes
C. More than 20 amperes
D. Current through the human body is never fatal

T0A05
(A)
Page 10.5

T0A05
Which body organ can be fatally affected by a very small amount of electrical current?
A. The heart
B. The brain
C. The liver
D. The lungs

T0A06
(B)
Page 10.6

T0A06
For best protection from electrical shock, what should be grounded in an amateur station?
A. The power supply primary
B. All station equipment connected to a common ground
C. The antenna feed line
D. The AC power mains

T0A07
(D)
Page 10.4

T0A07
Which potential does the green wire in a three-wire electrical plug represent?
A. Neutral
B. Hot
C. Hot and neutral
D. Ground

T0A08
(C)
Page 10.3

T0A08
What is an important consideration for the location of the main power switch?
A. It must always be near the operator
B. It must always be as far away from the operator as possible
C. Everyone should know where it is located in case of an emergency
D. It should be located in a locked metal box so no one can accidentally turn it off

T0A09
(A)
Page 10.4

T0A09
What circuit should be controlled by a safety interlock switch in an amateur transceiver or power amplifier?
A. The power supply
B. The IF amplifier
C. The audio amplifier
D. The cathode bypass circuit

T0A10
(C)
Page 10.2

T0A10
What type of electrical circuit is created when a fuse blows?
A. A closed circuit
B. A bypass circuit
C. An open circuit
D. A short circuit

T0A11
(D)
Page 10.4

T0A11
Why would it be unwise to touch an ungrounded terminal of a high voltage capacitor even if it's not in an energized circuit?
A. You could damage the capacitor's dielectric material
B. A residual charge on the capacitor could cause interference to others
C. You could damage the capacitor by causing an electrostatic discharge
D. You could receive a shock from a residual stored charge

T0A12

What safety equipment item should you always add to home built equipment that is powered from 110 volt AC lines?

A. A fuse or circuit breaker in series with the equipment
B. A fuse or circuit breaker in parallel with the equipment
C. Install Zener diodes across AC inputs
D. House the equipment in a plastic or other non-conductive enclosure

T0A13

When fuses are installed in 12-volt DC wiring, where should they be placed?

A. At the radio
B. Midway between voltage source and radio
C. Fuses aren't required for 12-volt DC equipment
D. At the voltage source

T0B   Lightning protection; Antenna structure installation safety; Tower climbing Safety; Safety belt/hard hat/safety glasses; Antenna structure limitations.

T0B01

How can an antenna system best be protected from lightning damage?

A. Install a balun at the antenna feed point
B. Install an RF choke in the antenna feed line
C. Ground all antennas when they are not in use
D. Install a fuse in the antenna feed line

T0B02

How can amateur station equipment best be protected from lightning damage?

A. Use heavy insulation on the wiring
B. Never turn off the equipment
C. Disconnect the ground system from all radios
D. Disconnect all equipment from the power lines and antenna cables

T0B03

Why should you wear a hard hat and safety glasses if you are on the ground helping someone work on an antenna tower?

A. So you won't be hurt if the tower should accidentally fall
B. To keep RF energy away from your head during antenna testing
C. To protect your head from something dropped from the tower
D. So someone passing by will know that work is being done on the tower and will stay away

T0B04

What safety factors must you consider when using a bow and arrow or slingshot and weight to shoot an antenna-support line over a tree?

A. You must ensure that the line is strong enough to withstand the shock of shooting the weight
B. You must ensure that the arrow or weight has a safe flight path if the line breaks
C. You must ensure that the bow and arrow or slingshot is in good working condition
D. All of these choices are correct

T0B05

Which of the following is the best way to install your antenna in relation to overhead electric power lines?

A. Always be sure your antenna wire is higher than the power line, and crosses it at a 90-degree angle
B. Always be sure your antenna and feed line are well clear of any power lines
C. Always be sure your antenna is lower than the power line, and crosses it at a small angle
D. Only use vertical antennas within 100 feet of a power line

T0A12
(A)
Page 10.3

T0A13
(D)
Page 10.3

T0B01
(C)
Page 10.7

T0B02
(D)
Page 10.7

T0B03
(C)
Page 8.34

T0B04
(D)
Page 8.33

T0B05
(B)
Page 8.31

T0B06
(C)
Page 8.34

T0B06
What should you always do before attempting to climb an antenna tower?
A. Turn on all radio transmitters that use the tower's antennas
B. Remove all tower grounding to guard against static electric shock
C. Put on your safety belt and safety glasses
D. Inform the FAA and the FCC that you are starting work on a tower

T0B07
(D)
Page 8.31

T0B07
What is the most important safety precaution to take when putting up an antenna tower?
A. Install steps on your tower for safe climbing
B. Insulate the base of the tower to avoid lightning strikes
C. Ground the base of the tower to avoid lightning strikes
D. Look for and stay clear of any overhead electrical wires

T0B08
(A)
Page 8.34

T0B08
What should you consider before you climb a tower with a leather climbing belt?
A. If the leather is old, it is probably brittle and could break unexpectedly
B. If the leather is old, it is very tough and is not likely to break easily
C. If the leather is old, it is flexible and will hold you more comfortably
D. An unbroken old leather belt has proven its holding strength over the years

T0B09
(D)
Page 8.34

T0B09
What should you do before you climb a guyed tower?
A. Tell someone that you will be up on the tower
B. Inspect the tower for cracks or loose bolts
C. Inspect the guy wires for frayed cable, loose cable clamps, loose turnbuckles or loose guy anchors
D. All of these choices are correct

T0B10
(D)
Page 8.34

T0B10
What should you do before you do any work on top of your tower?
A. Tell someone that you will be up on the tower
B. Bring a variety of tools with you to minimize your trips up and down the tower
C. Inspect the tower before climbing to become aware of any antennas or other obstacles that you may need to step around
D. All of these choices are correct

T0C   Definition of RF radiation; Procedures for RF environmental safety; Definitions and guidelines.

T0C01
(A)
Page 10.14

T0C01
What is radio frequency radiation?
A. Waves of electric and magnetic energy between 3 kHz and 300 GHz
B. Ultra-violet rays emitted by the sun between 20 Hz and 300 GHz
C. Sound energy given off by a radio receiver
D. Beams of X-Rays and Gamma rays emitted by a radio transmitter

T0C02
(B)
Page 10.13

T0C02
Why is it a good idea to adhere to the FCC's Rules for using the minimum power needed when you are transmitting with your hand-held radio?
A. Large fines are always imposed on operators violating this rule
B. To reduce the level of RF radiation exposure to the operator's head
C. To reduce calcification of the NiCd battery pack
D. To eliminate self-oscillation in the receiver RF amplifier

T0C03
Which of the following units of measurement are used to specify the power density of a radiated RF signal?
A. Milliwatts per square centimeter
B. Volts per meter
C. Amperes per meter
D. All of these choices are correct

T0C03
(A)
Page 10.10

T0C04
Over what frequency range are the FCC Regulations most stringent for RF radiation exposure?
A. Frequencies below 300 kHz
B. Frequencies between 300 kHz and 3 MHz
C. Frequencies between 3 MHz and 30 MHz
D. Frequencies between 30 MHz and 300 MHz

T0C04
(D)
Page 10.17

T0C05
Which of the following categories describes most common amateur use of a hand-held transceiver?
A. Mobile devices
B. Portable devices
C. Fixed devices
D. None of these choices is correct

T0C05
(B)
Page 10.15

T0C06
From an RF safety standpoint, what impact does the duty cycle have on the minimum safe distance separating an antenna and people in the neighboring environment?
A. The lower the duty cycle, the shorter the compliance distance
B. The compliance distance is increased with an increase in the duty cycle
C. Lower duty cycles subject people in the environment to lower radio-frequency radiation
D. All of these answers are correct

T0C06
(D)
Page 10.14

T0C07
Why is the concept of "duty cycle" one factor used to determine safe RF radiation exposure levels?
A. It takes into account the amount of time the transmitter is operating at full power during a single transmission
B. It takes into account the transmitter power supply rating
C. It takes into account the antenna feed line loss
D. It takes into account the thermal effects of the final amplifier

T0C07
(A)
Page 10.14

T0C08
What factors affect the resulting RF fields emitted by an amateur transceiver that expose people in the environment?
A. Frequency and power level of the RF field
B. Antenna height and distance from the antenna to a person
C. Radiation pattern of the antenna
D. All of these answers are correct

T0C08
(D)
Page 10.14

T0C09
What unit of measurement specifies RF electric field strength?
A. Coulombs (C) at one wavelength from the antenna
B. Volts per meter (V/m)
C. Microfarads (uF) at the transmitter output
D. Microhenrys (uH) per square centimeter

T0C09
(B)
Page 10.12

T0C10
(D)
Page 10.8

T0C10
Which of the following is considered to be non-ionizing radiation?
A. X-radiation
B. Gamma radiation
C. Ultra violet radiation
D. Radio frequency radiation

T0C11
(C)
Page 10.16

T0C11
What do the FCC RF radiation exposure regulations establish?
A. Maximum radiated field strength
B. Minimum permissible HF antenna height
C. Maximum permissible exposure limits
D. All of these choices are correct

T0C12
(C)
Page 10.14

T0C12
Which of the following steps would help you to comply with RF-radiation exposure guidelines for uncontrolled RF environments?
A. Reduce transmitting times within a 6-minute period to reduce the station duty cycle
B. Operate only during periods of high solar absorption
C. Reduce transmitting times within a 30-minute period to reduce the station duty cycle
D. Operate only on high duty cycle modes

T0C13
(C)
Page 10.14

T0C13
Which of the following steps would help you to comply with RF-exposure guidelines for controlled RF environments?
A. Reduce transmitting times within a 30-minute period to reduce the station duty cycle
B. Operate only during periods of high solar absorption
C. Reduce transmitting times within a 6-minute period to reduce the station duty cycle
D. Operate only on high duty cycle modes

T0C14
(B)
Page 10.14

T0C14
To avoid excessively high human exposure to RF fields, how should amateur antennas generally be mounted?
A. With a high current point near ground
B. As far away from accessible areas as possible
C. On a nonmetallic mast
D. With the elements in a horizontal polarization

T0C15
(D)
Page 10.14

T0C15
What action can amateur operators take to prevent exposure to RF radiation in excess of the FCC-specified limits?
A. Alter antenna patterns
B. Relocate antennas
C. Revise station technical parameters, such as frequency, power, or emission type
D. All of these choices are correct

T0C16
(C)
Page 10.14

T0C16
Which of the following radio frequency emissions will result in the least RF radiation exposure if they all have the same peak envelope power (PEP)?
A. Two-way exchanges of phase-modulated (PM) telephony
B. Two-way exchanges of frequency-modulated (FM) telephony
C. Two-way exchanges of single-sideband (SSB) telephony
D. Two-way exchanges of Morse code (CW) communication

T0C17

Why is the concept of "specific absorption rate (SAR)" one factor used to determine safe RF radiation exposure levels?

A. It takes into account the overall efficiency of the final amplifier
B. It takes into account the transmit/receive time ratio during normal amateur communication
C. It takes into account the rate at which the human body absorbs RF energy at a particular frequency
D. It takes into account the antenna feed line loss

T0C17
(C)
Page 10.9

T0C18

Why must the frequency of an RF source be considered when evaluating RF radiation exposure?

A. Lower-frequency RF fields have more energy than higher-frequency fields
B. Lower-frequency RF fields penetrate deeper into the body than higher-frequency fields
C. Higher-frequency RF fields are transient in nature, and do not affect the human body
D. The human body absorbs more RF energy at some frequencies than at others

T0C18
(D)
Page 10.9

T0C19

What is the maximum power density that may be emitted from an amateur station under the FCC RF radiation exposure limits?

A. The FCC Rules specify a maximum emission of 1.0 milliwatt per square centimeter
B. The FCC Rules specify a maximum emission of 5.0 milliwatts per square centimeter
C. The FCC Rules specify exposure limits, not emission limits
D. The FCC Rules specify maximum emission limits that vary with frequency

T0C19
(C)
Page 10.14

T0D   Radiofrequency exposure standards; Near/far field, Field strength; Compliance distance; Controlled/Uncontrolled environment.

T0D01

What factors must you consider if your repeater station antenna will be located at a site that is occupied by antennas for transmitters in other services?

A. Your radiated signal must be considered as part of the total RF radiation from the site when determining RF radiation exposure levels
B. Each individual transmitting station at a multiple transmitter site must meet the RF radiation exposure levels
C. Each station at a multiple-transmitter site may add no more than 1% of the maximum permissible exposure (MPE) for that site
D. Amateur stations are categorically excluded from RF radiation exposure evaluation at multiple-transmitter sites

T0D01
(A)
Page 10.15

T0D02

Why do exposure limits vary with frequency?

A. Lower-frequency RF fields have more energy than higher-frequency fields
B. Lower-frequency RF fields penetrate deeper into the body than higher-frequency fields
C. The body's ability to absorb RF energy varies with frequency
D. It is impossible to measure specific absorption rates at some frequencies

T0D02
(C)
Page 10.9

T0D03

Why might mobile transceivers produce less RF radiation exposure than hand-held transceivers in mobile operations?

A. They do not produce less exposure because they usually have higher power levels.
B. They have a higher duty cycle
C. When mounted on a metal vehicle roof, mobile antennas are generally well shielded from vehicle occupants
D. Larger transmitters dissipate heat and energy more readily

T0D03
(C)
Page 10.15

T0D04
(C)
Page 10.20

T0D04
In the far field, as the distance from the source increases, how does power density vary?
A. The power density is proportional to the square of the distance
B. The power density is proportional to the square root of the distance
C. The power density is proportional to the inverse square of the distance
D. The power density is proportional to the inverse cube of the distance

T0D05
(D)
Page 10.19

T0D05
In the near field, how does the field strength vary with distance from the source?
A. It always increases with the cube of the distance
B. It always decreases with the cube of the distance
C. It varies as a sine wave with distance
D. It depends on the type of antenna being used

T0D06
(A)
Page 10.13

T0D06
Why should you never look into the open end of a microwave feed horn antenna while the transmitter is operating?
A. You may be exposing your eyes to more than the maximum permissible exposure of RF radiation
B. You may be exposing your eyes to more than the maximum permissible exposure level of infrared radiation
C. You may be exposing your eyes to more than the maximum permissible exposure level of ultraviolet radiation
D. All of these choices are correct

T0D07
(A)
Page 10.19

T0D07
What factors determine the location of the boundary between the near and far fields of an antenna?
A. Wavelength and the physical size of the antenna
B. Antenna height and element length
C. Boom length and element diameter
D. Transmitter power and antenna gain

T0D08
(A)
Page 10.18

T0D08
Referring to Figure T0-1, which of the following equations should you use to calculate the maximum permissible exposure (MPE) on the Technician (with code credit) HF bands for a controlled RF radiation exposure environment?
A. Maximum permissible power density in mW per square cm equals 900 divided by the square of the operating frequency, in MHz
B. Maximum permissible power density in mW per square cm equals 180 divided by the square of the operating frequency, in MHz
C. Maximum permissible power density in mW per square cm equals 900 divided by the operating frequency, in MHz
D. Maximum permissible power density in mW per square cm equals 180 divided by the operating frequency, in MHz

Figure T0- 1

(A) Limits for Occupational/Controlled Exposure				
Frequency Range (MHz)	Electrical Field Strength (V/m)	Magnetic Field Strength (A/m)	Power Density (mW/cm ^{2})	Averaging Time (minutes)
0.3-3.0	614	1.63	(100)*	6
3.0-30	1842/f	4.89/f	$(900/f^2)$*	6
30-300	61.4	0.163	1.0	6
300-1500	----	----	f/300	6
1500-100,000	----	----	5	6
(B) Limits for General Population/Uncontrolled Exposure				
Frequency Range (MHz)	Electrical Field Strength (V/m)	Magnetic Field Strength (A/m)	Power Density (mW/cm ^{2})	Averaging Time (minutes)
0.3-1.34	614	1.63	(100)*	30
1.34-30	824/f	2.19/f	$(180/f^2)$*	30
30-300	27.5	0.073	0.2	30
300-1500	----	----	f/1500	30
1500-100,000	----	----	1.0	30

f=frequency in MHz *=Plane-wave equivalent power density

T0D09

Referring to Figure T0-1, what is the formula for calculating the maximum permissible exposure (MPE) limit for uncontrolled environments on the 2-meter (146 MHz) band?

A. There is no formula, MPE is a fixed power density of 1.0 milliwatt per square centimeter averaged over any 6 minutes
B. There is no formula, MPE is a fixed power density of 0.2 milliwatt per square centimeter averaged over any 30 minutes
C. The MPE in milliwatts per square centimeter equals the frequency in megahertz divided by 300 averaged over any 6 minutes
D. The MPE in milliwatts per square centimeter equals the frequency in megahertz divided by 1500 averaged over any 30 minutes

T0D09
(B)
Page 10.18

T0D10

What is the minimum safe distance for a controlled RF radiation environment from a station using a half-wavelength dipole antenna on 7 MHz at 100 watts PEP, as specified in Figure T0-2?

A. 1.4 foot
B. 2 feet
C. 3.1 feet
D. 6.5 feet

T0D10
(A)
Page 10.24

Figure T0-2

Estimated distances to meet RF power density guidelines with a horizontal half-wave dipole antenna (estimated gain, 2 dBi). Calculations include the EPA ground reflection factor of 2.56.

Frequency: 7 MHz
Estimated antenna gain: 2 dBi
Controlled limit: 18.37 mw/cm²
Uncontrolled limit: 3.67 mw/cm²

Transmitter power (watts)	Distance to controlled limit	Distance to uncontrolled limit
100	1.4'	3.1'
500	3.1'	6.9'
1000	4.3'	9.7'
1500	5.3'	11.9'

Estimated distances to meet RF power density guidelines in the main beam of a typical 3-element "triband" Yagi for the 14, 21 and 28 MHz amateur radio bands. Calculations include the EPA ground reflection factor of 2.56.

Frequency: 28 MHz
Antenna gain: 8 dBi
Controlled limit: 1.15 mw/cm²
Uncontrolled limit: 0.23 mw/cm²

Transmitter power (watts)	Distance to controlled limit	Distance to uncontrolled limit
100	11'	24.5'
500	24.5'	54.9'
1000	34.7'	77.6'
1500	42.5'	95.1'

Estimated distances to meet RF power density guidelines in the main beam of a 17-element Yagi on a five-wavelength boom designed for weak signal communications on the 144 MHz amateur radio band (estimated gain, 16.8 dBi). Calculations include the EPA ground reflection factor of 2.56.

Frequency: 144 MHz
Estimated antenna gain: 16.8 dBi
Controlled limit: 1 mw/cm²
Uncontrolled limit: 0.2 mw/cm²

Transmitter power (watts)	Distance to controlled limit	Distance to uncontrolled limit
10	10.2'	22.9'
100	32.4'	72.4'
500	72.4'	162'
1500	125.5'	280.6'

Estimated distances to meet RF power density guidelines in the main beam of UHF 5/8 ground plane or mobile whip antenna (estimated gain, 4 dBi). Calculations include the EPA ground reflection factor of 2.56.

Frequency: 446 MHz
Estimated antenna gain: 4 dBi
Controlled limit: 1.49 mw/cm²
Uncontrolled limit: 0.3 mw/cm²

Transmitter power (watts)	Distance to controlled limit	Distance to uncontrolled limit
10	1.9'	4.3'
50	4.3'	9.6'
150	7.5'	16.7'

Estimated distances to meet RF power density guidelines with a VHF quarter-wave ground plane or mobile whip antenna (estimated gain, 1 dBi). Calculations include the EPA ground reflection factor of 2.56.

Frequency: 146 MHz
Estimated antenna gain: 1 dBi
Controlled limit: 1 mw/cm²
Uncontrolled limit: 0.2 mw/cm²

Transmitter power (watts)	Distance to controlled limit	Distance to uncontrolled limit
10	1.7'	3.7'
50	3.7'	8.3'
150	6.4'	14.4'

T0D11
(C)
Page 10.23

T0D11
What is the minimum safe distance for an uncontrolled RF radiation environment from a station using a 3-element "triband" Yagi antenna on 28 MHz at 100 watts PEP, as specified in Figure T0-2?
A. 7 feet
B. 11 feet
C. 24.5 feet
D. 34 feet

T0D12
(A)
Page 10.23

T0D12
What is the minimum safe distance for a controlled RF radiation environment from a station using a 146 MHz quarter-wave whip antenna at 10 watts, as specified in Figure T0-2?
A. 1.7 feet
B. 2.5 feet
C. 1.2 feet
D. 2 feet

T0D13
(D)
Page 10.23

T0D13
What is the minimum safe distance for a controlled RF radiation environment from a station using a 17-element Yagi on a five-wavelength boom on 144 MHz at 100 watts, as specified in Figure T0-2?
A. 72.4 feet
B. 78.5 feet
C. 101 feet
D. 32.4 feet

T0D14
(B)
Page 10.23

T0D14
What is the minimum safe distance for an uncontrolled RF radiation environment from a station using a 446 MHz 5/8-wave ground plane vertical antenna at 10 watts, as specified in Figure T0-2?
A. 1 foot
B. 4.3 feet
C. 9.6 feet
D. 6 feet

T0E   RF Biological effects and potential hazards; Radiation exposure limits; OET Bulletin 65; MPE (Maximum permissible exposure).

T0E01
(A)
Page 10.12

T0E01
If you do not have the equipment to measure the RF power densities present at your station, what might you do to ensure compliance with the FCC RF radiation exposure limits?
A. Use one or more of the methods included in the amateur supplement to FCC OET Bulletin 65
B. Call an FCC-Certified Test Technician to perform the measurements for you
C. Reduce power from 200 watts PEP to 100 watts PEP
D. Operate only low-duty-cycle modes such as FM

T0E02
(C)
Page 10.18

T0E02
Where will you find the applicable FCC RF radiation maximum permissible exposure (MPE) limits defined?
A. FCC Part 97 Amateur Service Rules and Regulations
B. FCC Part 15 Radiation Exposure Rules and Regulations
C. FCC Part 1 and Office of Engineering and Technology (OET) Bulletin 65
D. Environmental Protection Agency Regulation 65

T0E03
To determine compliance with the maximum permitted exposure (MPE) levels, safe exposure levels for RF energy are averaged for an "uncontrolled" RF environment over what time period?
A. 6 minutes
B. 10 minutes
C. 15 minutes
D. 30 minutes

T0E04
To determine compliance with the maximum permitted exposure (MPE) levels, safe exposure levels for RF energy are averaged for a "controlled" RF environment over what time period?
A. 6 minutes
B. 10 minutes
C. 15 minutes
D. 30 minutes

T0E05
Why are Amateur Radio operators required to meet the FCC RF radiation exposure limits?
A. The standards are applied equally to all radio services
B. To ensure that RF radiation occurs only in a desired direction
C. Because amateur station operations are more easily adjusted than those of commercial radio services
D. To ensure a safe operating environment for amateurs, their families and neighbors

T0E06
At what frequencies do the FCC's RF radiation exposure guidelines incorporate limits for Maximum Permissible Exposure (MPE)?
A. All frequencies below 30 MHz
B. All frequencies between 20,000 Hz and 10 MHz
C. All frequencies between 300 kHz and 100 GHz
D. All frequencies above 300 GHz

T0E07
On what value are the maximum permissible exposure (MPE) limits based?
A. The square of the mass of the exposed body
B. The square root of the mass of the exposed body
C. The whole-body specific gravity (WBSG)
D. The whole-body specific absorption rate (SAR)

T0E08
What is one biological effect to the eye that can result from RF exposure?
A. The strong magnetic fields can cause blurred vision
B. The strong magnetic fields can cause polarization lens
C. It can cause heating, which can result in the formation of cataracts
D. It can cause heating, which can result in astigmatism

T0E09
Which of the following effects on the human body are a result of exposure to high levels of RF energy?
A. Very rapid hair growth
B. Very rapid growth of fingernails and toenails
C. Possible heating of body tissue
D. High levels of RF energy have no known effect on the human body

T0E03
(D)
Page 10.14

T0E04
(A)
Page 10.14

T0E05
(D)
Page 10.14

T0E06
(C)
Page 10.17

T0E07
(D)
Page 10.9

T0E08
(C)
Page 10.8

T0E09
(C)
Page 10.8

T0E10
(D)
Page 10.24

T0E10
Why should you not stand within reach of any transmitting antenna when it is being fed with 1500 watts of RF energy?
A. It could result in the loss of the ability to move muscles
B. Your body would reflect the RF energy back to its source
C. It could cause cooling of body tissue
D. You could accidentally touch the antenna and be injured

T0E11
(B)
Page 10.8

T0E11
What is one effect of RF non-ionizing radiation on the human body?
A. Cooling of body tissues
B. Heating of body tissues
C. Rapid dehydration
D. Sudden hair loss

T0F   Routine station evaluation.

T0F01
(D)
Page 10.16

T0F01
Is it necessary for you to perform mathematical calculations of the RF radiation exposure if your VHF station delivers more than 50 watts peak envelope power (PEP) to the antenna?
A. Yes, calculations are always required to ensure greatest accuracy
B. Calculations are required if your station is located in a densely populated neighborhood
C. No, calculations may not give accurate results, so measurements are always required
D. No, there are alternate means to determine if your station meets the RF radiation exposure limits

T0F02
(A)
Page 10.19

T0F02
What is one method that amateur radio licensees may use to conduct a routine station evaluation to determine whether the station is within the Maximum Permissible Exposure guidelines?
A. Direct measurement of the RF fields
B. Indirect measurement of the energy density at the limit of the controlled area
C. Estimation of field strength by S-meter readings in the controlled area
D. Estimation of field strength by taking measurements using a directional coupler in the transmission line

T0F03
(A)
Page 10.20

T0F03
What document establishes mandatory procedures for evaluating compliance with RF exposure limits?
A. There are no mandatory procedures
B. OST/OET Bulletin 65
C. Part 97 of the FCC rules
D. ANSI/IEEE C95.1—1992

T0F04
(B)
Page 10.18

T0F04
Which category of transceiver is NOT excluded from the requirement to perform a routine station evaluation?
A. Hand-held transceivers
B. VHF base station transmitters that deliver more than 50 watts peak envelope power (PEP) to an antenna
C. Vehicle-mounted push-to-talk mobile radios
D. Portable transceivers with high duty cycles

T0F05

Which of the following antennas would (generally) create a stronger RF field on the ground beneath the antenna?
A. A horizontal loop at 30 meters above ground
B. A 3-element Yagi at 30 meters above ground
C. A 1/2 wave dipole antenna 5 meters above ground
D. A 3-element Quad at 30 meters above ground

T0F06

How may an amateur determine that his or her station complies with FCC RF-exposure regulations?
A. By calculation, based on FCC OET Bulletin No. 65
B. By calculation, based on computer modeling
C. By measurement, measuring the field strength using calibrated equipment
D. Any of these choices

T0F07

Below what power level at the input to the antenna are amateur radio operators categorically excluded from routine evaluation to predict if the RF exposure from their VHF station could be excessive?
A. 25 watts peak envelope power (PEP)
B. 50 watts peak envelope power (PEP)
C. 100 watts peak envelope power (PEP)
D. 500 watts peak envelope power (PEP)

T0F08

Above what power level is a routine RF radiation evaluation required for a VHF station?
A. 25 watts peak envelope power (PEP) measured at the antenna input
B. 50 watts peak envelope power (PEP) measured at the antenna input
C. 100 watts input power to the final amplifier stage
D. 250 watts output power from the final amplifier stage

T0F09

What must you do with the records of a routine RF radiation exposure evaluation?
A. They must be sent to the nearest FCC field office
B. They must be sent to the Environmental Protection Agency
C. They must be attached to each Form 605 when it is sent to the FCC for processing
D. Though not required, records may prove useful if the FCC asks for documentation to substantiate that an evaluation has been performed

T0F10

Which of the following instruments might you use to measure the RF radiation exposure levels in the vicinity of your station?
A. A calibrated field strength meter with a calibrated field strength sensor
B. A calibrated in-line wattmeter with a calibrated length of feed line
C. A calibrated RF impedance bridge
D. An amateur receiver with an S meter calibrated to National Bureau of Standards and Technology station WWV

T0F11

What effect does the antenna gain have on a routine RF exposure evaluation?
A. Antenna gain is part of the formulas used to perform calculations
B. The maximum permissible exposure (MPE) limits are directly proportional to antenna gain
C. The maximum permissible exposure (MPE) limits are the same in all locations surrounding an antenna.
D. All of these choices are correct

T0F05
(C)
Page 10.14

T0F06
(D)
Page 10.16

T0F07
(B)
Page 10.18

T0F08
(B)
Page 10.18

T0F09
(D)
Page 10.20

T0F10
(A)
Page 10.19

T0F11
(A)
Page 10.20

T0F12 (C) Page 10.14	**T0F12** As a general rule, what effect does antenna height above ground have on the RF exposure environment? A. Power density is not related to antenna height or distance from the RF exposure environment B. Antennas that are farther above ground produce higher maximum permissible exposures (MPE) C. The higher the antenna the less the RF radiation exposure at ground level D. RF radiation exposure is increased when the antenna is higher above ground
T0F13 (C) Page 10.15	**T0F13** Why does the FCC consider a hand-held transceiver to be a portable device when evaluating for RF radiation exposure? A. Because it is generally a low-power device B. Because it is designed to be carried close to your body C. Because it's transmitting antenna is generally within 20 centimeters of the human body D. All of these choices are correct
T0F14 (C) Page 10.20	**T0F14** Which of the following factors must be taken into account when using a computer program to model RF fields at your station? A. Height above sea level at your station B. Ionization level in the F2 region of the ionosphere C. Ground interactions D. The latitude and longitude of your station location
T0F15 (C) Page 10.20	**T0F15** In which of the following areas is it most difficult to accurately evaluate the effects of RF radiation exposure? A. In the far field B. In the cybersphere C. In the near field D. In the low-power field

Appendix

In this Appendix you'll find an array of data tables, charts and other information to aid your review before the exam—and assist you after you've passed.

Helpful Data Tables

Standard Resistance Values

Numbers in **bold** type are ± 10% values. Others are 5% values.

Ohms

1.0	3.6	**12**	43	**150**	510	**1800**	6200	**22000**	75000	*Megohms*						
1.1	**3.9**	13	**47**	160	**560**	2000	**6800**	24000	**82000**	0.24	0.62	1.6	4.3	11.0		
1.2	4.3	**15**	51	**180**	620	**2200**	7500	**27000**	91000	0.27	**0.68**	1.8	**4.7**	**12.0**		
1.3	**4.7**	16	**56**	200	**680**	2400	**8200**	30000	**100000**	0.30	0.75	2.0	5.1	13.0		
1.5	5.1	**18**	62	**220**	750	**2700**	9100	**33000**	110000	**0.33**	**0.82**	**2.2**	**5.6**	**15.0**		
1.6	**5.6**	20	**68**	240	**820**	3000	**10000**	36000	**120000**	0.36	0.91	2.4	6.2	16.0		
1.8	6.2	**22**	75	**270**	910	**3300**	11000	**39000**	130000	**0.39**	**1.0**	**2.7**	**6.8**	**18.0**		
2.0	**6.8**	24	**82**	300	**1000**	3600	**12000**	43000	**150000**	0.43	1.1	3.0	7.5	20.0		
2.2	7.5	**27**	91	**330**	1100	**3900**	13000	**47000**	160000	**0.47**	**1.2**	**3.3**	**8.2**	**22.0**		
2.4	**8.2**	30	**100**	360	**1200**	4300	**15000**	51000	**180000**	0.51	1.3	3.6	9.1			
2.7	9.1	**33**	110	**390**	1300	**4700**	16000	**56000**	200000	0.56	1.5	**3.9**	**10.0**			
3.0	**10.0**	36	**120**	430	**1500**	5100	**18000**	62000	**220000**							
3.3	11.0	**39**	130	**470**	1600	**5600**	20000	**68000**								

Standard Values for 1000-V Disc-Ceramic Capacitors

pF	pF	pF	pF
3.3	39	250	1000
5	47	270	1200
6	50	300	1500
6.8	51	330	1800
8	56	360	2000
10	68	390	2500
12	75	400	2700
15	82	470	3000
18	100	500	3300
20	120	510	3900
22	130	560	4700
24	150	600	5000
25	180	680	5600
27	200	750	6800
30	220	820	8200
33	240	910	10000

Resistor Color Code

Color	Sig. Figure	Decimal Multiplier	Tolerance (%)	Color	Sig. Figure	Decimal Multiplier	Tolerance (%)
Black	0	1		Violet	7	10,000,000	
Brown	1	10		Gray	8	100,000,000	
Red	2	100		White	9	1,000,000,000	
Orange	3	1,000		Gold	—	0.1	5
Yellow	4	10,000		Silver	—	0.01	10
Green	5	100,000		No color	—		20
Blue	6	1,000,000					

Common Values for Small Electrolytic Capacitors

μF	V*	μF	V*
33	6.3	10	35
33	10	22	35
100	10	33	35
220	10	47	35
330	10	100	35
470	10	220	35
10	16	330	35
22	16	470	35
33	16	1000	35
47	16	1	50
100	16	2.2	50
220	16	3.3	50
470	16	4.7	50
1000	16	10	50
2200	16	33	50
4.7	25	47	50
22	25	100	50
33	25	220	50
47	25	330	50
100	25	470	50
220	25	10	63
330	25	22	63
470	25	47	63
1000	25	1	100
2200	25	10	100
4.7	35	33	100

*Working voltage

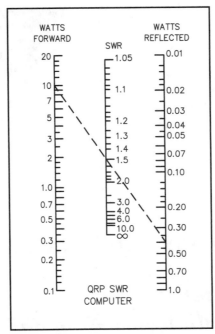

Nomograph of SWR versus forward and reflected power for levels up to 20 watts. Dashed line shows an SWR of 1.5:1 for 10 W forward and 0.4 W reflected.

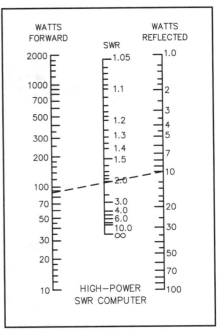

Nomograph of SWR versus forward and reflected power for levels up to 2000 watts. Dashed line shows an SWR of 2:1 for 90 W forward and 10 W reflected.

Fractions of an Inch with Metric Equivalents

Fractions Of An Inch	Decimals Of An Inch	Millimeters	Fractions Of An Inch	Decimals Of An Inch	Millimeters
1/64	0.0156	0.397	33/64	0.5156	13.097
1/32	0.0313	0.794	17/32	0.5313	13.494
3/64	0.0469	1.191	35/64	0.5469	13.891
1/16	0.0625	1.588	9/16	0.5625	14.288
5/64	0.0781	1.984	37/64	0.5781	14.684
3/32	0.0938	2.381	19/32	0.5938	15.081
7/64	0.1094	2.778	39/64	0.6094	15.478
1/8	0.1250	3.175	5/8	0.6250	15.875
9/64	0.1406	3.572	41/64	0.6406	16.272
5/32	0.1563	3.969	21/32	0.6563	16.669
11/64	0.1719	4.366	43/64	0.6719	17.066
3/16	0.1875	4.763	11/16	0.6875	17.463
13/64	0.2031	5.159	45/64	0.7031	17.859
7/32	0.2188	5.556	23/32	0.7188	18.256
15/64	0.2344	5.953	47/64	0.7344	18.653
1/4	0.2500	6.350	3/4	0.7500	19.050
17/64	0.2656	6.747	49/64	0.7656	19.447
9/32	0.2813	7.144	25/32	0.7813	19.844
19/64	0.2969	7.541	51/64	0.7969	20.241
5/16	0.3125	7.938	13/16	0.8125	20.638
21/64	0.3281	8.334	53/64	0.8281	21.034
11/32	0.3438	8.731	27/32	0.8438	21.431
23/64	0.3594	9.128	55/64	0.8594	21.828
3/8	0.3750	9.525	7/8	0.8750	22.225
25/64	0.3906	9.922	57/64	0.8906	22.622
13/32	0.4063	10.319	29/32	0.9063	23.019
27/64	0.4219	10.716	59/64	0.9219	23.416
7/16	0.4375	11.113	15/16	0.9375	23.813
29/64	0.4531	11.509	61/64	0.9531	24.209
15/32	0.4688	11.906	31/32	0.9688	24.606
31/64	0.4844	12.303	63/64	0.9844	25.003
1/2	0.5000	12.700	1	1.0000	25.400

Schematic Symbols

Schematic Symbols Used in Circuit Diagrams

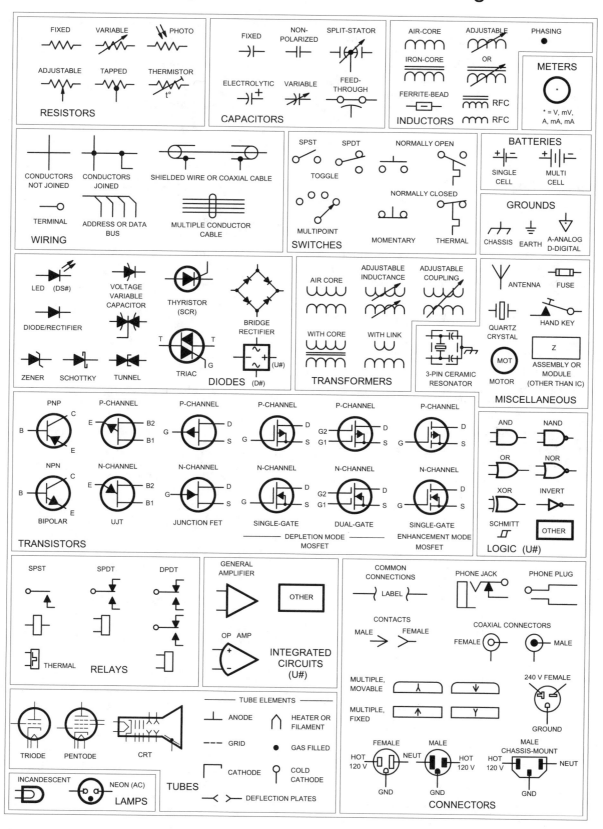

US Customary to Metric Conversions

International System of Units (SI)—Metric Prefixes

Prefix	Symbol		Multiplication Factor
exa	E	10^{18} =	1 000 000 000 000 000 000
peta	P	10^{15} =	1 000 000 000 000 000
tera	T	10^{12} =	1 000 000 000 000
giga	G	10^{9} =	1 000 000 000
mega	M	10^{6} =	1 000 000
kilo	k	10^{3} =	1 000
hecto	h	10^{2} =	100
deca	da	10^{1} =	10
(unit)		10^{0} =	1
deci	d	10^{-1} =	0.1
centi	c	10^{-2} =	0.01
milli	m	10^{-3} =	0.001
micro	μ	10^{-6} =	0.000001
nano	n	10^{-9} =	0.000000001
pico	p	10^{-12} =	0.000000000001
femto	f	10^{-15} =	0.000000000000001
atto	a	10^{-18} =	0.000000000000000001

Linear
1 metre (m) = 100 centimetres (cm) = 1000 millimetres (mm)

Area
$1 \ m^2 = 1 \times 10^4 \ cm^2 = 1 \times 10^6 \ mm^2$

Volume
$1 \ m^3 = 1 \times 10^6 \ cm^3 = 1 \times 10^9 \ mm^3$
1 litre (l) = 1000 cm^3 = 1×10^6 mm^3

Mass
1 kilogram (kg) = 1 000 grams (g)
(Approximately the mass of 1 litre of water)
1 metric ton (or tonne) = 1 000 kg

US Customary Units

Linear Units
12 inches (in) = 1 foot (ft)
36 inches = 3 feet = 1 yard (yd)
1 rod = $5^1/_2$ yards = $16^1/_2$ feet
1 statute mile = 1 760 yards = 5 280 feet
1 nautical mile = 6 076.11549 feet

Area
$1 \ ft^2 = 144 \ in^2$
$1 \ yd^2 = 9 \ ft^2 = 1 \ 296 \ in^2$
$1 \ rod^2 = 30^1/_4 \ yd^2$
$1 \ acre = 4840 \ yd^2 = 43 \ 560 \ ft^2$
$1 \ acre = 160 \ rod^2$
$1 \ mile^2 = 640 \ acres$

Volume
$1 \ ft^3 = 1 \ 728 \ in^3$
$1 \ yd^3 = 27 \ ft^3$

Liquid Volume Measure
1 fluid ounce (fl oz) = 8 fluidrams = 1.804 in^3
1 pint (pt) = 16 fl oz
1 quart (qt) = 2 pt = 32 fl oz = $57^3/_4$ in^3
1 gallon (gal) = 4 qt = 231 in^3
1 barrel = $31^1/_2$ gal

Dry Volume Measure
1 quart (qt) = 2 pints (pt) = 67.2 in^3
1 peck = 8 qt
1 bushel = 4 pecks = 2 150.42 in^3

Avoirdupois Weight
1 dram (dr) = 27.343 grains (gr) or (gr a)
1 ounce (oz) = 437.5 gr
1 pound (lb) = 16 oz = 7 000 gr
1 short ton = 2 000 lb, 1 long ton = 2 240 lb

Troy Weight
1 grain troy (gr t) = 1 grain avoirdupois
1 pennyweight (dwt) or (pwt) = 24 gr t
1 ounce troy (oz t) = 480 grains
1 lb t = 12 oz t = 5 760 grains

Apothecaries' Weight
1 grain apothecaries' (gr ap) = 1 gr t = 1 gr a
1 dram ap (dr ap) = 60 gr
1 oz ap = 1 oz t = 8 dr ap = 480 fr
1 lb ap = 1 lb t = 12 oz ap = 5 760 gr

Multiply $\longrightarrow$

Metric Unit = Conversion Factor $\times$ US Customary Unit

$\longleftarrow$ Divide

Metric Unit $\div$ Conversion Factor = US Customary Unit

Metric Unit =	Conversion Factor	$\times$	US Unit	Metric Unit =	Conversion Factor	$\times$	US Unit
(Length)				**(Volume)**			
mm	25.4		inch	mm^3	16387.064		in^3
cm	2.54		inch	cm^3	16.387		in^3
cm	30.48		foot	m^3	0.028316		ft^3
m	0.3048		foot	m^3	0.764555		yd^3
m	0.9144		yard	ml	16.387		in^3
km	1.609		mile	ml	29.57		fl oz
km	1.852		nautical mile	ml	473		pint
				ml	946.333		quart
(Area)				l	28.32		ft^3
mm^2	645.16		$inch^2$	l	0.9463		quart
cm^2	6.4516		in^2	l	3.785		gallon
cm^2	929.03		ft^2	l	1.101		dry quart
m^2	0.0929		ft^2	l	8.809		peck
cm^2	8361.3		yd^2	l	35.238		bushel
m^2	0.83613		yd^2	**(Mass)**	**(Troy Weight)**		
m^2	4047		acre	g	31.103		oz t
km^2	2.59		mi^2	g	373.248		lb t
(Mass)	**(Avoirdupois Weight)**			**(Mass)**	**(Apothecaries' Weight)**		
grams	0.0648		grains	g	3.387		dr ap
g	28.349		oz	g	31.103		oz ap
g	453.59		lb	g	373.248		lb ap
kg	0.45359		lb				
tonne	0.907		short ton				
tonne	1.016		long ton				

US Amateur Bands

ARRL *The national association for* **AMATEUR RADIO**

June 1, 2003   Novice, Advanced and Technician Plus Allocations

New Novice, Advanced and Technician Plus licenses are no longer being issued, but *existing* Novice, Technician Plus and Advanced class licenses are unchanged. Amateurs can continue to renew these licenses. Technicians who pass the 5 wpm Morse code exam *after* that date have Technician Plus privileges, although their license says Technician. They must retain the 5 wpm Certificate of Successful Completion of Examination (CSCE) as proof. The CSCE is valid indefinitely for operating authorization, but is valid only for 365 days for upgrade credit.

160 METERS

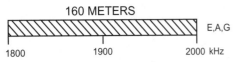

E,A,G

1800   1900   2000 kHz

Amateur stations operating at 1900-2000 kHz must not cause harmful interference to the radiolocation service and are afforded no protection from radiolocation operations.

80 METERS

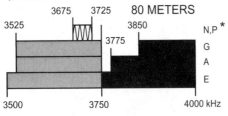

N,P *
G
A
E

3500   3750   4000 kHz

60 METERS

General, Advanced, and Amateur Extra licensees may use the following five channels on a secondary basis with a maximum effective radiated power of 50 W PEP relative to a half wave dipole. Only upper sideband suppressed carrier voice transmissions may be used. The frequencies are 5330.5, 5346.5, 5366.5, 5371.5 and 5403.5 kHz. The occupied bandwidth is limited to 2.8 kHz centered on 5332, 5348, 5368, 5373, and 5405 kHz respectively.

40 METERS

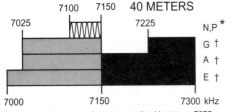

N,P *
G †
A †
E †

7000   7150   7300 kHz

† Phone and Image modes are permitted between 7075 and 7100 kHz for FCC licensed stations in ITU Regions 1 and 3 and by FCC licensed stations in ITU Region 2 West of 130 degrees West longitude or South of 20 degrees North latitude. See Sections 97.305(c) and 97.307(f)(11). Novice and Technician Plus licensees outside ITU Region 2 may use CW only between 7050 and 7075 kHz. See Section 97.301(e). These exemptions do not apply to stations in the continental US.

30 METERS

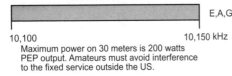

E,A,G

10,100   10,150 kHz

Maximum power on 30 meters is 200 watts PEP output. Amateurs must avoid interference to the fixed service outside the US.

20 METERS

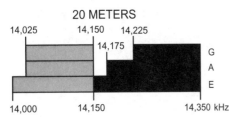

G
A
E

14,000   14,150   14,350 kHz

17 METERS

E,A,G

18,068   18,110   18,168 kHz

15 METERS

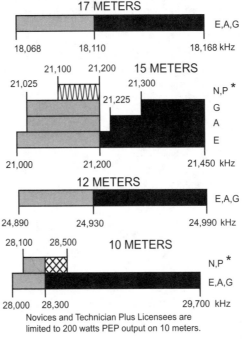

N,P *
G
A
E

21,000   21,200   21,450 kHz

12 METERS

E,A,G

24,890   24,930   24,990 kHz

10 METERS

N,P *
E,A,G

28,000   28,300   29,700 kHz

Novices and Technician Plus Licensees are limited to 200 watts PEP output on 10 meters.

6 METERS

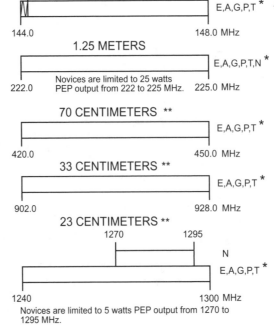

E,A,G,P,T *

50.0   54.0 MHz

2 METERS

E,A,G,P,T *

144.0   148.0 MHz

1.25 METERS

E,A,G,P,T,N *

222.0   225.0 MHz

Novices are limited to 25 watts PEP output from 222 to 225 MHz.

70 CENTIMETERS **

E,A,G,P,T *

420.0   450.0 MHz

33 CENTIMETERS **

E,A,G,P,T *

902.0   928.0 MHz

23 CENTIMETERS **

N
E,A,G,P,T *

1240   1300 MHz

Novices are limited to 5 watts PEP output from 1270 to 1295 MHz.

US AMATEUR POWER LIMITS

At all times, transmitter power should be kept down to that necessary to carry out the desired communications. Power is rated in watts PEP output. Unless otherwise stated, the maximum power output is 1500 W. Power for all license classes is limited to 200 W in the 10,100-10,150 kHz band and in all Novice subbands below 28,100 kHz. Novices and Technicians are restricted to 200 W in the 28,100-28,500 kHz subbands. In addition, Novices are restricted to 25 W in the 222-225 MHz band and 5 W in the 1270-1295 MHz subband.

Operators with Technician class licenses and above may operate on all bands above 50 MHz. For more detailed information see *The ARRL FCC Rule Book.*

KEY

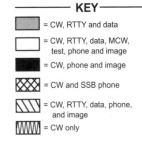

= CW, RTTY and data

= CW, RTTY, data, MCW, test, phone and image

= CW, phone and image

= CW and SSB phone

= CW, RTTY, data, phone, and image

= CW only

E = EXTRA CLASS
A = ADVANCED
G = GENERAL
P = TECHNICIAN PLUS
T = TECHNICIAN
N = NOVICE

*Technicians who have passed the 5 wpm Morse code exam are indicated as "P".

**Geographical and power restrictions apply to all bands with frequencies above 420 MHz. See *The ARRL FCC Rule Book* for more information about your area.

All licensees except Novices are authorized all modes on the following frequencies:

2300-2310 MHz
2390-2450 MHz
3300-3500 MHz
5650-5925 MHz
10.0-10.5 GHz
24.0-24.25 GHz
47.0-47.2 GHz
75.5-76.0, 77.0-81.0 GHz
119.98-120.02 GHz
142-149 GHz
241-250 GHz
All above 300 GHz

For band plans and sharing arrangements, see *The ARRL FCC Rule Book.*

Glossary of Key Words

AC hum — Unwanted 60- or 120-Hz modulation of a RF signal due to inadequate filtering in a power supply.

Alternating current (ac) — Electrical current that flows first in one direction in a wire and then in the other. The applied voltage is also changing polarity. This direction reversal continues at a rate that depends on the frequency of the ac.

Amateur operator — A person holding a written authorization to be the control operator of an amateur station.

Amateur Radio Emergency Service (ARES)— Sponsored by the ARRL and provides emergency communications in working with groups such as the American Red Cross and local Emergency Operations Centers.

Amateur service — A radiocommunication service for the purpose of self-training, intercommunication and technical investigations carried out by amateurs, that is, duly authorized persons interested in radio technique solely with a personal aim and without **pecuniary** interest.

Amateur station — A station licensed in the amateur service, including necessary equipment, used for amateur communication.

Amateur Television (ATV) — A wideband TV system that can use commercial transmission standards. ATV is only permitted on the 70-cm band (420 to 450 MHz) and higher frequencies.

Ammeter — A test instrument that measures current.

Ampere (A) — The basic unit of electrical current. Current is a measure of the electron flow through a circuit. If we could count electrons, we would find that if there are 6.24×10^{18} electrons moving past a point in one second, we have a current of one ampere.[1] We abbreviate amperes as amps.

Amplitude modulation (AM) — A method of combining an information signal and an RF (radio-frequency) carrier. In double-sideband voice AM transmission, we use the voice information to vary (modulate) the amplitude of an RF carrier. Shortwave broadcast stations use this type of AM, as do stations in the Standard Broadcast Band (535-1710 kHz). Few amateurs use double-sideband voice AM, but a variation, known as single sideband, is very popular.

Analog signals — A signal (usually electrical) that can have any amplitude (voltage or current) value, and that amplitude can vary smoothly over time. Also see **digital signals**.

Antenna — A device that picks up or sends out radio frequency energy.

Antenna structure — The assembly or structure that includes one or more antennas, any tower supports or other attachments.

Antenna switch — A switch used to connect one transmitter, receiver or transceiver to several different antennas.

Antenna tuner — A device that matches the antenna system input impedance to the transmitter, receiver or transceiver output impedance. Also called an *antenna-matching network, impedance-matching network* or *Transmatch*.

Apogee — That point in a satellite's orbit (such as the Moon) when it is farthest from the Earth.

Atmosphere — The mass of air surrounding the Earth. Radio signals travel through the atmosphere, and different conditions in the atmosphere affect how those signal travel or propagate.

Audio frequency (AF) signal — Your ears respond to air pressure vibrations approximately in the range of 20 herts to 20,000 hertz. An electrical signal in that same frequency range will produce sounds you can hear if it is connected to a speaker (and if it is strong enough). So electrical signals in the range of 20 hertz to 20 kilohertz (20,000 hertz) are called audio frequency signals.

Autopatch — A device that allows repeater users to make telephone calls through a repeater.

Automatic Gain Control (AGC) — Receiver circuitry used to maintain a constant level of audio output.

Balun — Contraction for balanced to unbalanced. A device to couple a balanced load to an unbalanced source, or vice versa.

Band-pass filter — A circuit that allows signals to go through it only if they are within a certain range of frequencies. It attenuates signals above and below this range.

Bandwidth — The width of a frequency band outside of which the mean power is attenuated at least 26 dB below the mean power of the total emission, including allowances for transmitter drift or Doppler shift. Bandwidth describes the range of frequencies that a radio transmission occupies.

Battery — A device that converts chemical energy into electrical energy.

Beacon station — An amateur station transmitting communications for the purposes of observation of propagation and reception or other related experimental activities.

Beam antenna — A directional antenna. A beam antenna must be rotated to provide coverage in different directions.

Block diagram — A drawing using boxes to represent sections of a complicated device or process. The block diagram shows the connections between sections.

Broadcasting — Transmissions intended to be received by the general public, either direct or relayed.

Capacitance — A measure of the ability of a capacitor to store energy in an *electric field*.

Capacitor — An electrical component usually formed by separating two conductive plates with an insulating material. A capacitor stores energy in an *electric field*.

Centi — The metric prefix for 10^{-2}, or divide by 100.

Chassis ground — The common connection for all parts of a circuit that connect to the negative side of the power supply.

Chirp — A slight shift in transmitter frequency each time you key the transmitter.

Closed repeater — A repeater that restricts access to only include members of a certain group of amateurs.

Closed circuit — An electrical circuit with an uninterrupted path for the current to follow. Turning a switch on, for example, closes or completes the circuit, allowing current to flow. Also called a **complete circuit**.

Coaxial cable — Coax (pronounced kó-aks). A type of feed line with one conductor inside the other.

Color code — A system in which numerical values are assigned to various colors. Colored stripes are painted on the body of resistors and sometimes other components to show their value.

Communications emergency — A situation in which communications is required for immediate safety of human life or protection of property.

Complete circuit — An electrical circuit with an uninterrupted path for the current to follow. Turning a switch on, for example, closes or completes the circuit, allowing current to flow. Also called a **closed circuit**.

Conductor — A material that has a loose grip on its electrons, so an electrical current can pass through it.

Connected — The condition in which two packet-radio stations are sending information to each other. Each is acknowledging when the data has been received correctly.

Continuous wave (CW) — Radio communications transmitted by on/off keying of a continuous radio-frequency signal. Another name for international Morse code.

Control operator — An amateur operator designated by the licensee of a station to be responsible for the transmissions of an amateur station.

Control point — The locations at which the control operator function is performed.

Controlled environment — Any area in which an RF signal may cause radiation exposure to people who are aware of the radiated electric and magnetic fields and who can exercise some control over their exposure to these fields. The FCC generally considers amateur operators and their families to be in a controlled RF exposure environment to determine the maximum permissible exposure levels.

Courtesy tone — A tone or beep transmitted by a repeater to indicate that it is okay for the next station to begin transmitting. The courtesy tone is designed to allow a pause between transmissions on a repeater, so other stations can call. It also indicates that the **time-out timer** has been reset.

CQ — "Calling any station": the general call when requesting a conversation with anyone.

Critical frequency — The highest frequency at which a radio wave sent vertically through the atmosphere will return. Above the critical frequency radio signals will pass through the ionosphere instead of returning to Earth.

Crossband — Able to receive and transmit on different amateur frequency bands. For example, a repeater might retransmit at 2 meters a signal received on 70 cm.

Crystal oscillator — A device that uses a quartz crystal to keep the frequency of a transmitter constant.

Crystal-controlled transmitter — A simple type of transmitter that consists of a crystal oscillator followed by driver and power amplifier stages.

CTCSS — Continuous tone coded squelch system. A sub-audible tone system used on some repeaters. When added to a carrier, a CTCSS tone allows a receiver to accept a signal. Also called **PL**.

Cubical quad antenna — An antenna built with its elements in the shape of four-sided loops.

Current — A flow of electrons in an electrical circuit.

CW (Morse code) — Radio communications transmitted by on/off keying of a continuous radio-frequency signal. Another name for international Morse code.

D region — The lowest region of the ionosphere. The D region contributes very little to short-wave radio propagation. It acts mainly to absorb energy from radio waves as they pass through it. This absorption has a significant effect on signals below about 7.5 MHz during daylight.

Data — Computer-based communications modes, such as **packet radio**, which can be used to transmit and receive computer files, or digital information.

DE — The Morse code abbreviation for "from" or "this is."

Deceptive signals — Transmissions that are intended to mislead or confuse those who may receive the transmissions. For example, distress calls transmitted when there is no actual emergency are false or deceptive signals.

Decibel (dB) — The smallest change in sound level that can be detected by the human ear. In electronics we use decibels to compare power levels. A decibel is ten times the logarithm of a ratio of two power levels.

Deci — The metric prefix for 10^{-1}, or divide by 10.

Delta loop antenna — A variation of the cubical quad with triangular elements.

Detector — The stage in a receiver in which the modulation (voice or other information) is recovered from the RF signal.

Deviation — The change in frequency of an FM carrier due to a modulating signal.

Digipeater — A packet-radio station used to retransmit signals that are specifically addressed to be retransmitted by that station.

Digital communications — Computer-based communications modes. This can include **data** modes like **packet radio** and text-only modes like **radioteletype (RTTY)**.

Digital signal — A signal (usually electrical) that can only have certain specific amplitude values, or steps. If a digital signal is used to represent an **analog signal**, the amplitude values only change by the allowed steps, rather than the smooth variation of an analog signal.

Diode — An electronic component that allows electric current to flow in only one direction. A *PN junction* diode is made with one layer of P-type semiconductor material and one layer of N-type semiconductor material.

Dipole antenna — See **Half-wave dipole**. A dipole need not be $\frac{1}{2}$ wavelength long.

Direct current (dc) — Electrical current that flows in one direction only.

Directional wattmeter (see **Wattmeter**)

Director — An element in front of the driven element in a Yagi and some other directional antennas.

Doppler shift — A change in observed frequency of a signal caused by relative motion between the transmitter and receiver. Your ears hear Doppler shift when a race car drives past you and you hear the pitch of the engine noise change. You will have to adjust your receive frequency to hear a satellite as it passes overhead because of Doppler shift.

Double-pole, double-throw (DPDT) switch — A switch that has six contacts. The DPDT switch has two center contacts. The two center contacts can each be connected to one of two other contacts.

Double-pole, single-throw (DPST) switch — A switch that connects two contacts to another set of contacts. A DPST switch turns two circuits on or off at the same time.

Doubling — The undesirable act of two or more operators transmitting at the same time on the same frequency. Both operators are usually unaware of the other's presence, sometimes during the entire transmission!

Driven element — The part of an antenna that connects directly to the feed line.

Dual-band antenna — An antenna designed for use on two different Amateur Radio bands.

Dummy antenna — A station accessory that allows you to test or adjust transmitting equipment without sending a signal out over the air. Also called **dummy load**.

Dummy load — A station accessory that allows you to test or adjust transmitting equipment without sending a signal out over the air. Also called **dummy antenna**.

Duplex — A mode of communications (also known as *full duplex*) in which a user transmits on one frequency and receives on another frequency simultaneously. This is in contrast to half duplex, where the user transmits at one time and receives at another time.

Duplexer — A device that allows a dual-band radio to use a single dual-band antenna.

Duty cycle — A measure of the amount of time a transmitter is operating at full output power during a single transmission. A lower duty cycle means less **RF radiation** exposure for the same PEP output.

DX — Distance, foreign countries.

E region — The second lowest ionospheric region, the E region exists only during the day. Under certain conditions, it may refract radio waves enough to return them to Earth.

Earth ground — A circuit connection to a ground rod driven into the Earth or to a cold-water pipe made of copper that goes into the ground.

Earth station — An amateur station located on, or within 50 km of, the Earth's surface intended for communications with space stations or with other Earth stations by means of one or more other objects in space.

Earth-Moon-Earth (EME) or Moonbounce — A method of communicating with other stations by reflecting radio signals off the Moon's surface.

Electric field — An invisible force of nature. An electric field exists in a region of space if an electrically charged object placed in the region is subjected to an electrical force.

Electromotive force (EMF) — The force or pressure that pushes a current through a circuit.

Electron — A tiny, negatively charged particle, normally found in an area surrounding the nucleus of an atom. Moving electrons make up an electrical current.

Electronic keyer — A device that makes it easier to send well-timed Morse code. It sends either a continuous string of dots or dashes, depending on which side of the *paddle* is pressed.

Emergency — A situation where there is a danger to lives or property.

Emergency communications — Communications conducted under adverse conditions where normal channels of communications are not available.

Emergency traffic – Messages with life and death urgency or requests for medical help and supplies that leave an area shortly after an emergency.

Emission — The transmitted signal from an amateur station.

Emission privilege — Permission to use a particular emission type (such as Morse code or voice).

Emission types — Term for the different modes authorized for use on the Amateur Radio bands. Examples are CW, SSB, RTTY and FM.

Energy — The ability to do work; the ability to exert a force to move some object.

F region — A combination of the two highest ionospheric regions, the F1 and F2 regions. The F region refracts radio waves and returns them to Earth. Its height varies greatly depending on the time of day, season of the year and amount of sunspot activity.

False or deceptive signals — Transmissions that are intended to mislead or confuse those who may receive the transmissions. For example, distress calls transmitted when there is no actual emergency are false or deceptive signals.

Federal Communications Commission (FCC) — Federal agency in the United States that regulates use and allocation of the frequency spectrum among many different services, including Amateur Radio.

Feed line — The wires or cable used to connect a transmitter, receiver or transceiver to an antenna. The feed line connects to an antenna at its feed point. Also see **Transmission line**.

Filter — A circuit that will allow some signals to pass through it but will greatly reduce the strength of others.

Fixed resistor — An electronic component specifically designed to oppose or control current through a circuit. The **resistance** value of a fixed resistor cannot be changed or adjusted.

Form 605 — An FCC form that serves as the application for your Amateur Radio license, or for modifications to an existing license.

Forward power — The power traveling from the transmitter to the antenna along a transmission line.

Frequency — The number of complete cycles of an alternating current that occur per second.

Frequency bands — A group of frequencies where amateur communications are authorized.

Frequency coordination — Allocating repeater input and output frequencies to minimize interference between repeaters and to other users of the band.

Frequency coordinator – An individual or group that recommends repeater frequencies to reduce or eliminate interference between repeaters operating on or near the same frequency in the same geographical area.

Frequency discriminator — A type of detector used in some FM receivers.

Frequency modulated (FM) phone — The type of signals used to communicate by voice (phone) over most repeaters. FM broadcast stations and most professional communications (police, fire, taxi) use FM. VHF/UHF FM phone is the most popular amateur mode.

Frequency modulation (FM) — FM is a method of combining an RF carrier with an information signal, such as voice. The voice information (or data) changes the RF carrier frequency in the **modulation** process. We use voice or data to vary the frequency of the transmitted signal.

Frequency privilege — Permission to use a particular group of frequencies.

Front-end overload — Interference to a receiver caused by a strong signal that overpowers the receiver RF amplifier ("front end"). See also **receiver overload**.

Fuse — A thin metal strip mounted in a holder. When too much current passes through the fuse, the metal strip melts and opens the circuit.

Gain — Gain makes your signal sound stronger to other operators and their signals sound stronger to you, when compared with non-directional antennas. Gain in one direction means that gain in other directions is diminished.

Giga — The metric prefix for 10^9, or times 1,000,000,000.

Grace period — The time FCC allows following the expiration of an amateur license to renew that license without having to retake an examination. Those who hold an expired license may not operate an amateur station until the license is reinstated.

Ground connection — A connection made to the earth for electrical safety. This connection can be made inside (to a metal cold-water pipe) or outside (to a **ground rod**).

Ground rod — A copper or copper-clad steel rod that is driven into the earth. A heavy copper wire from the ham shack connects all station equipment to the ground rod.

Ground-wave propagation — The method by which radio waves travel along the Earth's surface.

Half-wave dipole — A basic antenna used by radio amateurs. It consists of a length of wire or tubing, opened and fed at the center. The entire antenna is $1/2$ wavelength long at the desired operating frequency.

Hand-held radio — A VHF or UHF transceiver that can be carried in the hand or pocket.

Harmful interference — Interference that seriously degrades, obstructs or repeatedly interrupts a radiocommunication service operating in accordance with the Radio Regulations. [§97.3 (a) (22)]

Harmonics — Signals from a transmitter or oscillator occurring on whole-number multiples (2×, 3×, 4×, etc) of the desired operating frequency.

Health and Welfare traffic – Messages about the well being of individuals in a disaster area. Such messages must wait for **Emergency** and **Priority traffic** to clear, and results is advisories to those outside the disaster area awaiting news from family and friends.

Hertz (Hz) — An alternating-current frequency of one cycle per second. The basic unit of frequency.

High frequency (HF) — The term used for the frequency range between 3 MHz and 30 MHz. The Amateur HF bands are where you are most likely to make long-distance (worldwide) contacts.

High-pass filter — A filter designed to pass high-frequency signals, while blocking lower-frequency signals.

Impedance — The opposition to electric current in a circuit. Impedance includes factors other than resistance, and applies to alternating currents. Ideally, the characteristic impedance of a feed line is the same as the transmitter output impedance and the antenna input impedance.

Impedance-matching device — A device that matches one impedance level to another. For example, it may match the impedance of an antenna system to the impedance of a transmitter or receiver. Amateurs also call such devices a Transmatch, impedance-matching network or antenna tuner.

Inductance — A measure of the ability of a coil to store energy in a *magnetic field*.

Inductor — An electrical component usually composed of a coil of wire wound on a central core. An inductor stores energy in a *magnetic field*.

Input frequency — A repeater's receiving frequency. To use a repeater, transmit on the input frequency and receive on the **output frequency**.

Insulator — A material that maintains a tight grip on its electrons, so that an electric current cannot pass through it (within voltage limits).

Intermediate frequency (IF) — The output frequency of a mixing stage in a superheterodyne receiver. The subsequent stages in the receiver are tuned for maximum efficiency at the IF.

Ionizing radiation — Electromagnetic radiation that has sufficient energy to knock electrons free from their atoms, producing positive and negative ions. X-rays, gamma rays and ultraviolet radiation are examples of ionizing radiation.

Ionosphere — A region of electrically charged (ionized) gases high in the atmosphere. The ionosphere bends radio waves as they travel through it, returning them to Earth. Also see **sky-wave propagation**.

K — The Morse code abbreviation for "any station respond."

Keplerian elements — Mathematical values for a satellite's orbit that can be used to compute the position of a satellite at any point in time, for any position on Earth.

Kilo — The metric prefix for 10^3, or times 1000.

Lightning protection — There are several ways to help prevent lightning damage to your equipment (and your house), among them unplugging equipment, disconnecting antenna feed lines and using a lightning arrestor.

Limiter — A stage of an FM receiver that makes the receiver less sensitive to amplitude variations and pulse noise.

Line-of-sight propagation — The term used to describe VHF and UHF propagation in a straight line directly from one station to another.

Loading coil — An inductor placed at the base or at the center of an antenna to resonate it. Most often, the antenna is a vertical that is physically shorter than a quarter-wavelength long.

Log — The documents or log of a station that detail operation of the station. They can be used as supporting evidence, and for troubleshooting interference-related problems or complaints.

Lower sideband (LSB)—The common single-sideband operating mode on the 40, 80 and 160-meter amateur bands.

Low-pass filter — A filter that allows signals below the cutoff frequency to pass through and attenuates signals above the cutoff frequency.

Malicious (harmful) interference — Intentional, deliberate obstruction of radio transmissions.

Maximum useable frequency (MUF) –- The highest-frequency radio signal that will reach a particular destination using **sky-wave propagation**, or *skip*. The MUF may vary for radio signals sent to different destinations.

MAYDAY — From the French *m'aidez* (help me), MAYDAY is used when calling for emergency assistance in voice modes.

Mega — The metric prefix for 10^6, or times 1,000,000.

Metric prefixes — A series of terms used in the metric system of measurement. We use metric prefixes to describe a quantity as compared to a basic unit. The metric prefixes indicate multiples of 10.

Metric system — A system of measurement developed by scientists and used in most countries of the world. This system uses a set of prefixes that are multiples of 10 to indicate quantities larger or smaller than the basic unit.

Micro — The metric prefix for 10^{-6}, or divide by 1,000,000.

Microphone — A device that converts sound waves into electrical energy.

Milli — The metric prefix for 10^{-3}, or divide by 1000.

Mixer — Circuitry used in a receiver to convert an incoming signal to an intermediate frequency. In a transmitter a mixer converts an IF signal to the desired output frequency.

Mobile station —A radio transmitter designed to be mounted in a vehicle. A push-to-talk (PTT) switch generally activates the transmitter. Any station that can be operated on the move, typically in a car, but also on a boat, a motorcycle, truck or RV.

Modem — Short for *mo*dulator/*dem*odulator. A modem modulates a radio signal to transmit data and demodulates a received signal to recover transmitted data.

Modulate — To vary the amplitude, frequency, or phase of a radio-frequency signal.

Modulation — The process of varying an RF carrier in some way (the amplitude or the frequency, for example) to add an information signal to be transmitted.

Monitor mode — One type of packet radio receiving mode. In monitor mode, everything transmitted on a packet frequency is displayed by the monitoring TNC. This occurs whether or not the transmissions are addressed to the monitoring station.

Morse code (see **CW**).

Multiband antenna — An antenna capable of operating on more than one amateur frequency band, usually using a single feed line.

Multihop propagation — Long-distance radio propagation using several skips or hops between the Earth and the ionosphere.

Multimeter — An electronic test instrument used to measure current, voltage and resistance in a circuit. Describes all meters capable of making these measurements, such as the volt-ohm-milliammeter (VOM), vacuum-tube voltmeter (VTVM) and field-effect transistor VOM (FET VOM).

Multimode radio—Transceiver capable of SSB, CW and FM operation.

National Electrical Code — A set of guidelines governing electrical safety, including antennas.

Network — A term used to describe several packet stations linked together to transmit data over long distances.

Nonionizing radiation — Electromagnetic radiation that does not have sufficient energy to knock electrons free from their atoms. Radio frequency (RF) radiation is nonionizing.

NPN transistor — A transistor that has a layer of P-type semiconductor material sandwiched between layers of N-type semiconductor material.

Offset frequency — The difference between a repeater's transmitter and receiver frequencies. Also known as the *split*.

Ohm — The basic unit of electrical resistance, used to describe the amount of opposition to current.

Ohm's Law — A basic law of electronics. Ohm's Law gives a relationship between voltage (E), current (I) and resistance (R). The voltage applied to a circuit is equal to the current through the circuit times the resistance of the circuit (E = IR).

Ohmmeter — A device used to measure resistance.

One-way communications — Radio signals not directed to a specific amateur radio station, or for which no reply is expected. The FCC Rules provide for limited types of one-way communications on the amateur bands. [§97.111 (b)]

Open circuit — An electrical circuit that does not have a complete path, so current can't flow through the circuit.

Open repeater — A repeater that can be used by all hams who have a license that authorizes operation on the repeater frequencies.

Operator/primary station license — An amateur license actually includes two licenses in one. The operator license is that portion of an Amateur Radio license that gives permission to operate an amateur station. The **primary station license** is that portion of an Amateur Radio license that authorizes an amateur station at a specific location. The station license also lists the call sign of that station.

Output frequency — A repeater's transmitting frequency. To use a repeater, transmit on the **input frequency** and receive on the output frequency.

Packet radio — A system of digital communication whereby information is broken into short bursts. The bursts ("packets") also contain addressing and error-detection information.

Parallel circuit — An electrical circuit in which the electrons follow more than one path in going from the negative supply terminal to the positive terminal.

Parallel-conductor line — A type of transmission line that uses two parallel wires spaced apart from each other by insulating material. Also known as *open-wire line*.

Parasitic beam antenna — Another name for the **beam antenna**.

Parasitic element — Part of a directive antenna that derives energy from mutual coupling with the driven element. Parasitic elements are not connected directly to the feed line.

Peak envelope power (PEP) — The average power of a signal at its largest amplitude peak.

Pecuniary — Payment of any type, whether money or other goods. Amateurs may not operate their stations in return for any type of payment.

Perigee — That point in the orbit of a satellite (such as the Moon) when it is closest to the Earth.

Phone — Another name for voice communications.

Phone emission — The FCC name for voice or other sound transmissions.

Phonetic alphabet — Standard words used on voice modes to make it easier to understand letters of the alphabet, such as those in call signs. The call sign KA6LMN stated phonetically is *Kilo Alfa Six Lima Mike November.*

Pico — The metric prefix for 10^{-12}, or divide by 1,000,000,000,000.

PL (see **CTCSS**) Private Line — PL is a Motorola trademark.

PNP transistor — A transistor that has a layer of N-type semiconductor material sandwiched between layers of P-type semiconductor material.

Polarization — The electrical-field characteristic of a radio wave. An antenna that is parallel to the surface of the earth, such as a dipole, produces horizontally polarized waves. One that is perpendicular to the earth's surface, such as a quarter-wave vertical, produces vertically polarized waves. An antenna that has both horizontal and vertical polarization is said to be circularly polarized.

Portable device — A radio transmitting device designed to have a transmitting antenna that is generally within 20 centimeters of a human body.

Potentiometer — Another name for a **variable resistor**. The value of a potentiometer can be changed over a range of values without removing it from a circuit.

Power — The rate of energy consumption. We calculate power in an electrical circuit by multiplying the voltage applied to the circuit times the current through the circuit ($P = IE$).

Power supply — A circuit that provides a direct-current output at some desired voltage from an ac input voltage.

Primary service — When a frequency band is shared among two or more different radio services, the primary service is preferred. Stations in the **secondary service** must not cause harmful interference to, and must accept interference from stations in the primary service. [§97.303]

Primary station license — An amateur license actually includes two licenses in one. The **operator license** is that portion of an Amateur Radio license that gives permission to operate an amateur station. The primary station license is that portion of an Amateur Radio license that authorizes an amateur station at a specific location. The station license also lists the call sign of that station.

Priority traffic – Emergency-related messages, but not as important as **Emergency traffic**.

Procedural signal (prosign) — One or two letters sent as a single character. Amateurs use prosigns in CW contacts as a short way to indicate the operator's intention. Some examples are K for "Go Ahead," or $\overline{AR}$ for "End of Message." (The bar over the letters indicates that we send the prosign as one character.)

Product detector — A device that allows a receiver to process CW and SSB signals.

Propagation — The study of how radio waves travel.

Q signals — Three-letter symbols beginning with Q. Used on CW to save time and to improve communication. Some examples are QRS (send slower), QTH (location), QSO (ham conversation) and QSL (acknowledgment of receipt).

QRL? — Ham radio Q signal meaning "Is this frequency in use?"

QSL card — A postcard that serves as a confirmation of communication between two hams.

QSO — A conversation between two radio amateurs.

Quarter-wavelength vertical antenna — An antenna constructed of a quarter-wavelength long radiating element placed perpendicular to the earth.

Radio Amateur Civil Emergency Service (RACES) — A part of the Amateur Service that provides radio communications for civil preparedness organizations during local, regional or national civil emergencies.

Radio frequency (RF) radiation — Electromagnetic energy that travels through space without wires. FCC Rules establish maximum permissible exposure (MPE) values for humans to RF radiation. [§1.1310 and §97.13 (c)]

Radio frequency (RF) waves — Electromagnetic energy that travels through space without wires. RF waves are generally considered to be any electromagnetic waves with a frequency higher than 20,000 Hz, up to 300 GHz. Above 300 GHz are the infrared waves, visible light, ultraviolet waves, X-rays and then gamma rays.

Radio-frequency interference (RFI) — Disturbance to electronic equipment caused by radio-frequency signals.

Radioteletype (RTTY) — Radio signals sent from one teleprinter machine to another machine. Anything that one operator types on his teleprinter will be printed on the other machine. Also known as narrow-band direct-printing telegraphy.

Receiver—A device that converts radio waves into signals we can hear or see.

Receiver overload — Interference to a receiver caused by a strong RF signal that forces its way into the equipment. A signal that overloads the receiver RF amplifier (front end) causes front-end overload. Receiver overload is sometimes called RF overload.

Reciprocal operating authority — Permission for amateur radio operators from another country to operate in the US using their home license. This permission is based on various treaties between the US government and the governments of other countries.

Reflected power — The power that returns to the transmitter from the antenna along a transmission line.

Reflection — Signals that travel by **line-of-sight propagation** are reflected by large objects like buildings.

Reflector — An element behind the driven element in a Yagi and some other directional antennas.

Refract — Bending of an electromagnetic wave as it travels through materials with different properties. Light refracts as it travels from air into water. Radio waves refract as they travel through the ionosphere. If the radio waves refract enough they will return to Earth. This is the basis for long-distance communication on the **HF bands**.

Repeater station — An amateur station that receives the signals of other stations and retransmits them for greater range.

Resistance — The ability to oppose an electric current.

Resistor — Any material that opposes a current in an electrical circuit. An electronic component specifically designed to oppose or control current through a circuit.

Resonant frequency — The desired operating frequency of a tuned circuit. In an antenna, the resonant frequency is one where the feed-point impedance contains only resistance.

RF burn — A burn produced by coming in contact with exposed RF voltages.

RF carrier — A steady radio frequency signal that is modulated to add an information signal to be transmitted. For example, a voice signal is added to the RF carrier to produce a **phone emission** signal.

RF overload — Another term for receiver overload.

RF radiation — Waves of electric and magnetic energy. Such electromagnetic radiation with frequencies as low as 3 kHz and as high as 300 GHz are considered to be part of the RF region.

RF safety — Preventing injury or illness to humans from the effects of radio-frequency energy.

Rig—The radio amateur's term for a transmitter, receiver or transceiver.

RST — A system of numbers used for signal reports: R is readability, S is strength and T is tone. (On single-sideband phone, only R and S reports are used.)

Rubber duck antenna — A flexible rubber-coated antenna that is inexpensive, small, lightweight and difficult to break. Rubber ducks are used mainly with hand-held VHF or UHF transceivers.

S meter — A meter that provides an indication of the relative strength of received signals.

Safety interlock — A switch that automatically turns off ac power to a piece of equipment when the top cover is removed.

Scattering — Several factors may cause some energy from a radio signal to follow a path other than the idealized "straight line." Scattering can take place from the Earth's ionospheric and other atmospheric regions as well as from objects in the wave path.

Schematic symbol — A drawing used to represent a circuit component on a wiring diagram.

Secondary service — When a frequency band is shared among two or more different radio services, the **primary service** is preferred. Stations in the secondary service must not cause harmful interference to, and must accept interference from stations in the primary service. [§97.303]

Series circuit — An electrical circuit in which all the electrons must flow through every part of the circuit. There is only one path for the electrons to follow.

Shack — The room where an Amateur Radio operator keeps his or her station equipment.

Short circuit — An electrical circuit in which the current does not take the desired path, but finds a shortcut instead. Often the current goes directly from the negative power-supply terminal to the positive one, bypassing the rest of the circuit.

Sidebands — The sum or difference frequencies generated when an RF carrier is mixed with an audio signal. Single-sideband phone (SSB) signals have an upper sideband (USB — that part of the signal above the carrier) and a lower sideband (LSB — the part of the signal below the carrier). SSB transceivers allow operation on either USB or LSB.

Signal generator — A device that produces a low-level signal that can be set to a desired frequency.

Simplex operation — Receiving and transmitting on the same frequency.

Single sideband (SSB) phone — A common mode of voice operation on the amateur bands. SSB is a form of amplitude modulation.The amplitude of the transmitted signal varies with the voice signal variations.

Single-pole, double-throw (SPDT) switch — A switch that connects one center contact to one of two other contacts.

Single-pole, single-throw (SPST) switch — A switch that only connects one center contact to another contact.

Skip zone — An area of poor radio communication, too distant for ground waves and too close for sky waves.

Sky-wave propagation — The method by which radio waves travel through the ionosphere and back to Earth. Sometimes called *skip*, sky-wave propagation has a far greater range than **line-of-sight** and **ground-wave propagation**.

Slow-Scan Television (SSTV) — A television system used by amateurs to transmit pictures within a signal bandwidth allowed on the HF or VHF/UHF bands by the FCC. It takes approximately 8 seconds to send a single black and white SSTV frame, and between 12 seconds and 4½ minutes for the various color systems currently in use on the HF bands.

SOS — A Morse code call for emergency assistance.

Space station — An amateur station located more than 50 km above the Earth's surface.

Specific absorption rate (SAR) — A term that describes the rate at which RF energy is absorbed into the human body. Maximum permissible exposure (MPE) limits are based on whole-body SAR values.

Splatter — A type of interference to stations on nearby frequencies. Splatter occurs when a transmitter is overmodulated.

Sporadic E — A form of enhanced radio-wave propagation that occurs when radio signals are reflected from small, dense ionization patches in the E region of the ionosphere. Sporadic E is observed on the 15, 10, 6 and 2-meter bands, and occasionally on the 1.25-meter band.

Spurious emissions — Signals from a transmitter on frequencies other than the operating frequency.

Squelch — Circuitry that mutes an FM receiver when no signal is received.

SSB — Abbreviation for the **single sideband phone** mode of communication. This is the most widely used mode for phone operation on the HF bands.

Standard frequency offset — The standard transmitter/receiver frequency offset used by a repeater on a particular amateur band. For example, the standard offset on 2 meters is 600 kHz. Also see **Offset frequency**.

Standing-wave ratio (SWR) — Sometimes called voltage standing-wave ratio (VSWR). A measure of the impedance match between the feed line and the antenna. Also, with a Transmatch in use, a measure of the match between the feed line from the transmitter and the antenna system. The system includes the Transmatch and the line to the antenna. VSWR is the ratio of maximum voltage to minimum voltage along the feed line. Also the ratio of antenna impedance to feed-line impedance when the antenna is a purely resistive load.

Station grounding — Connecting all station equipment to a good earth ground improves both safety and station performance.

Station license — An amateur license actually includes two licenses in one. The **operator license** is that portion of an Amateur Radio license that gives permission to operate an amateur station. The primary station license is that portion of an Amateur Radio license that authorizes an amateur station at a specific location. The station license also lists the call sign of that station.

Station records/station log — The documents or log of a station that detail operation of the station. They can be used as supporting evidence, and for troubleshooting interference-related problems or complaints.

Stratosphere — The part of the Earth's atmosphere that extends from about 7 miles to 30 miles above the earth. Clouds rarely form in the stratosphere.

Sunspot cycle — The number of **sunspots** increases and decreases in a predictable cycle that lasts about 11 years.

Sunspots — Dark spots on the surface of the sun. When there are few sunspots, long-distance radio propagation is poor on the higher-frequency bands. When there are many sunspots, long-distance HF propagation improves.

Superheterodyne receiver — A receiver that converts all signals to the same IF before filtering and amplification. This provides good performance over a wide range of radio frequencies.

Switch — A device used to connect or disconnect electrical contacts.

SWR meter — A measuring instrument that can indicate when an antenna system is working well. A device used to measure SWR.

Tactical call signs – Names used to identify a location or function during local emergency communications.

Tactical communications—A first-response communications under emergency conditions that involves a few people in a small area.

Telecommand operation — A one-way radio transmission to start, change or end functions of a device at a distance.

Telegraph key — A telegraph key (also called a *straight key*) is the simplest type of Morse code sending device.

Teleprinter — A machine that can convert keystrokes (typing) into electrical impulses. The teleprinter can also convert the proper electrical impulses back into text. Computers have largely replaced teleprinters for amateur radioteletype work.

Television interference (TVI) — Interruption of television reception caused by another signal.

Temperature inversion — A condition in the atmosphere in which a region of cool air is trapped beneath warmer air.

Temporary state of communications emergency — When a disaster disrupts normal communications in a particular area, the FCC can declare this type of emergency. Certain rules may apply for the duration of the emergency.

Terminal — An inexpensive piece of equipment that can be used in place of a computer in a packet radio station.

Third-party communications — Messages passed from one amateur to another on behalf of a third person.

Third-party communications agreement — An official understanding between the United States and another country that allows amateurs in both countries to participate in third-party communications.

Third-party participation — The way an unlicensed person can participate in amateur communications. A control operator must ensure compliance with FCC rules.

Ticket—A common name for an Amateur Radio license.

Time-out timer — A device that limits the amount of time any one person can talk through a repeater.

Transceiver — A radio transmitter and receiver combined in one unit.

Transistor — A solid-state device made of three layers of semiconductor material. See **NPN transistor** and **PNP transistor**.

Transmission line — The wires or cable used to connect a transmitter or receiver to an antenna. Also called **feed line**.

Transmitter — A device that produces radio-frequency signals.

Troposphere — The region in Earth's atmosphere just above the Earth's surface and below the ionosphere.

Tropospheric bending — When radio waves are bent in the troposphere, they return to Earth farther away than the visible horizon.

Tropospheric ducting — A type of VHF propagation that can occur when warm air overruns cold air (a temperature inversion).

Ultra high frequency (UHF) — The term used for the frequency range between 300 MHz and 3000 MHz (3 GHz). Technician licensees have full privileges on all Amateur UHF bands.

Ultraviolet (UV) — Electromagnetic waves with frequencies higher than visible light. Literally, "above violet," which is the high-frequency end of the the visible range.

Unbalanced line — Feed line with one conductor at ground potential, such as coaxial cable.

Uncontrolled environment — Any area in which an RF signal may cause radiation exposure to people who may not be aware of the radiated electric and magnetic fields. The FCC generally considers members of the general public and an amateur's neighbors to be in an uncontrolled **RF radiation** exposure environment to determine the maximum permissible exposure levels.

Unidentified communications or signals — Signals or radio communications in which the transmitting station's call sign is not transmitted.

Universal Licensing System (ULS) — FCC database for all FCC radio services.

Upper sideband (USB)—The common single-sideband operating mode on the 20, 17, 15, 12 and 10-meter HF amateur bands, and all the VHF and UHF bands.

Variable resistor — A resistor whose value can be adjusted over a certain range, without removing it from a circuit.

Variable-frequency oscillator (VFO) — An oscillator used in receivers and transmitters. The frequency is set by a tuned circuit using capacitors and inductors. The frequency can be changed by adjusting the components in the tuned circuit.

Vertical antenna — A common amateur antenna, often made of metal tubing. The radiating element is vertical. There are usually four or more radial elements parallel to or on the ground.

Very high frequency (VHF) — The term used for the frequency range between 30 MHz and 300 MHz. Technician licensees have full privileges on all Amateur VHF bands.

Visible horizon — The most distant point one can see by line of sight.

Voice — Any of the several methods used by amateurs to transmit speech.

Voice communications — Hams can use several voice modes, including FM and SSB.

Volt (V) — The basic unit of electrical pressure or EMF.

Voltage — The EMF or pressure that causes electrons to move through an electrical circuit.

Voltmeter — A test instrument used to measure voltage.

Volunteer Examiner (VE) — A licensed amateur who is accredited by a Volunteer Examiner Coordinator (VEC) to administer amateur license examinations.

Volunteer Examiner Coordinator (VEC) — An organization that has entered into an agreement with the FCC to coordinate amateur license examinations.

Watt (W) — The unit of power in the metric system. The watt describes how fast a circuit uses electrical energy.

Wattmeter — Also called a *power meter*, a test instrument used to measure the power output (in watts) of a transmitter. A directional wattmeter measures both forward and reflected power.

Wavelength — Often abbreviated λ. The distance a radio wave travels in one RF cycle. The wavelength relates to frequency. Higher frequencies have shorter wavelengths.

Weak-signal modes — Usually SSB or CW modes, used in relation to operating on the VHF and UHF bands, where many amateurs only operate FM phone.

WWV/WWVH — Radio stations run by the US NIST (National Institute of Standards and Technology) to provide accurate time and frequencies.

Yagi antenna — The most popular type of amateur directional (beam) antenna. It has one driven element and one or more additional elements.

73 — Ham lingo for "best regards." Used on both phone and CW toward the end of a contact.

About the ARRL

The seed for Amateur Radio was planted in the 1890s, when Guglielmo Marconi began his experiments in wireless telegraphy. Soon he was joined by dozens, then hundreds, of others who were enthusiastic about sending and receiving messages through the air—some with a commercial interest, but others solely out of a love for this new communications medium. The United States government began licensing Amateur Radio operators in 1912.

By 1914, there were thousands of Amateur Radio operators—hams—in the United States. Hiram Percy Maxim, a leading Hartford, Connecticut inventor and industrialist, saw the need for an organization to band together this fledgling group of radio experimenters. In May 1914 he founded the American Radio Relay League (ARRL) to meet that need.

Today ARRL, with approximately 170,000 members, is the largest organization of radio amateurs in the United States. The ARRL is a not-for-profit organization that:
- promotes interest in Amateur Radio communications and experimentation
- represents US radio amateurs in legislative matters, and
- maintains fraternalism and a high standard of conduct among Amateur Radio operators.

At ARRL headquarters in the Hartford suburb of Newington, the staff helps serve the needs of members. ARRL is also International Secretariat for the International Amateur Radio Union, which is made up of similar societies in 150 countries around the world.

ARRL publishes the monthly journal *QST*, as well as newsletters and many publications covering all aspects of Amateur Radio. Its headquarters station, W1AW, transmits bulletins of interest to radio amateurs and Morse code practice sessions. The ARRL also coordinates an extensive field organization, which includes volunteers who provide technical information and other support services for radio amateurs as well as communications for public-service activities. In addition, ARRL represents US amateurs with the Federal Communications Commission and other government agencies in the US and abroad.

Membership in ARRL means much more than receiving *QST* each month. In addition to the services already described, ARRL offers membership services on a personal level, such as the ARRL Volunteer Examiner Coordinator Program and a QSL bureau.

Full ARRL membership (available only to licensed radio amateurs) gives you a voice in how the affairs of the organization are governed. ARRL policy is set by a Board of Directors (one from each of 15 Divisions). Each year, one-third of the ARRL Board of Directors stands for election by the full members they represent. The day-to-day operation of ARRL HQ is managed by an Executive Vice President and his staff.

No matter what aspect of Amateur Radio attracts you, ARRL membership is relevant and important. There would be no Amateur Radio as we know it today were it not for the ARRL. We would be happy to welcome you as a member! (An Amateur Radio license is not required for Associate Membership.) For more information about ARRL and answers to any questions you may have about Amateur Radio, write or call:

ARRL—The national association for Amateur Radio
225 Main Street
Newington CT 06111-1494
Voice: 860-594-0200
    Fax: 860-594-0259
    E-mail: **hq@arrl.org**
    Internet: **www.arrl.org/**

Prospective new amateurs call (toll-free):
800-32-NEW HAM (800-326-3942)
You can also contact us via e-mail at **newham@arrl.org**
or check out *ARRLWeb* at **http://www.arrl.org/**

Index

Welcome to Amateur Radio!

Congratulations! You've taken your first step into a hobby—and a service—that knows no limits. Amateur Radio is a worldwide network of people from various cultures, united by a common love of wireless communication. Amateur Radio is as old as radio itself, and its future is no less fantastic than its past.

For most people, Amateur Radio is a lifelong pursuit. We want to make sure you get a good start, which is why we've published this book. But first, who are "we"?

ARRL—The National association for Amateur Radio: What's in it for You?

◆ **Help for New Hams**: Are you a beginning ham looking for help in getting started in your new hobby? The hams at ARRL HQ in Newington, Connecticut, will be glad to assist you. Call 800-32-NEWHAM. ARRL maintains a computer data base of ham clubs and ham radio "helpers" from across the country who've told us they're interested in helping beginning hams. There are probably several clubs in your area! Contact us for more information.

◆ **Licensing Classes**: If you're going to become a ham, you'll need to find a local license exam opportunity sooner or later. ARRL Registered Instructors teach licensing classes all around the country, and ARRL-sponsored Volunteer Examiners are right there to administer your exams. To find the locations and dates of Amateur Radio Licensing classes and test sessions in your area, call the New Ham Desk at 800-32-NEWHAM.

◆ **Clubs**: As a beginning ham, one of the best moves you can make is to join a local ham club. Whether you join an all-around group or a special-interest club (repeaters, DXing, and so on), you'll make new friends, have a lot of fun, and you can tap into a ready reserve of ham radio knowledge and experience. To find the ham clubs in your area, call HQ's New Ham Desk at 800-32-NEWHAM.

◆ **Technical Information Service**: Do you have a question of a technical nature? (What new ham doesn't?) Contact the Technical Information Service (TIS) at HQ. Our resident technical experts will help you over the phone, send you specific information on your question (antennas, interference and so on) or refer you to your local ARRL Technical Coordinator or Technical Specialist. It's expert information—and it doesn't cost Members an extra cent!

◆ **Regulatory Information**: Need help with a thorny antenna zoning problem? Having trouble understanding an FCC regulation? Vacationing in a faraway place and want to know how to get permission to operate your ham radio there? HQ's Regulatory Information Branch has the answers you need!

◆ **Operating Awards**: Like to collect "wallpaper"? The ARRL sponsors a wide variety of certificates and Amateur Radio achievement awards. For information on awards you can qualify for, contact the Membership Services Department at HQ.

◆ **Equipment Insurance**: When it comes to protecting their Amateur Radio equipment investments, ARRL Members travel First Class. A. H. Wohlers Company provides ARRL's "all-risk" equipment insurance plan. (It can protect your ham radio computer, too.) It's comprehensive and cost effective, and it's available only to ARRL Members. Why worry about losing your valuable radio equipment when you can protect it for only a few dollars a year?

◆ **Amateur Radio Emergency Service**: If you're interested in providing public service and emergency communications for your community, you can join more than 25,000 other hams who have registered their communications capabilities with local Emergency Coordinators. Your EC will call on you and other ARES members for vital assistance if disaster should strike your community. Contact the Field Services Department at HQ for information.

◆ **Audio-Visual Programs**: Need a program for your next ham club meeting, informal get-together or public display? ARRL Affililated clubs can buy tapes from ARRL's video programs. There are many to choose from, including popular titles on Amateur Radio's role in Operation Desert Storm and space shuttle activities. Contact Field & Educational Services at HQ for a complete list or to order a tape.

◆ **Blind, Disabled Ham Help**: For a list of available resources and information on the Courage HANDI-HAM System, contact the ARRL Program for the Disabled at HQ.

With your membership you also receive the monthly journal *QST*. Each issue is packed with valuable information you can use—including a special *QST Workbench* section with information of special interest to new hams! And *QST* Product Reviews are the most respected source of information to help you get the most for your Amateur Radio equipment dollar. (For many hams, *QST* alone is worth far more than the cost of ARRL membership.)

The ARRL also publishes newsletters and dozens of books covering all aspects of Amateur Radio. Our Headquarters station, W1AW, transmits bulletins of interest to radio amateurs and Morse Code practice sessions.

When it comes to representing Amateur Radio's best interests in our nation's capital, ARRL's team in Washington, DC, is constantly working with the FCC, Congress and industry to protect and foster your privileges as a ham operator.

Regardless of your Amateur Radio interests, ARRL Membership is relevant and important. We will be happy to welcome you as a Member. Use the Invitation to Membership on the next page to **join today**. And don't hesitate to contact us if you have any questions!

Invitation to Membership

You've got questions? we've got answers!

Now you've got what you need to go after your own Amateur Radio license and call sign! But you've probably still got a question or two. Does anyone in my area teach classes? Where can I find a person who can give me my exam? Where in my area can I buy equipment? Which is better from my location, a dipole antenna or a vertical antenna? If I decide to learn Morse code, where can I find someone to help me practice? Can someone check my station to see if I've set up everything correctly? Who do I turn to for answers? ARRL's New Ham Desk can send you a list of Amateur Radio clubs, instructors, examiners and Elmers who live in your area and enjoy helping newcomers. Here's your first question and answer: What's an Elmer? An Elmer is a person who helps you with whatever you need; an Elmer is another Amateur Radio tradition of hams helping others. For your list, send a postcard to ARRL NewHam Desk, 225 Main St, Newington, CT 06111, or call us at 1-800-32NEWHAM.

Notes

Resistors resist current flow... series ↑, parallel ↓

Coils oppose changes in current (block AC)
series ↑, parallel ↓

Capacitors oppose changes in voltage (block DC)
series ↓, parallel ↑   smooth out waveform, gaps between cycles
(see p. 8.6)

Notes

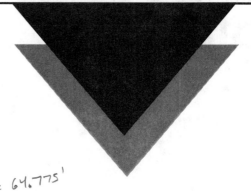

65.4545

7.150

7.300   64.1096

7.225 = 64.775'

14.175   33.0159   14.260   = 32.8191

              32.6132

14.350

Notes

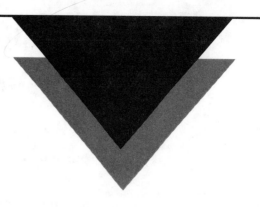

Index of Advertisers

MFJ *Deluxe* Antenna Tuner

Tune your antenna for minimum SWR!
Works 1.8 to 30 MHz on dipoles, verticals, inverted vees, random wires, beams, mobile whips, shortwave receiving antennas . . . Use coax, random wire, balanced lines. Has heavy duty 4:1 balun for balanced lines.

Custom designed inductor switch, 1000 volt tuning capacitors, *Teflon*(R) insulating

MFJ-949E **$149⁹⁵** washers and proper L/C ratio gives you *arc-free* no worries operation with up to 300 Watts PEP transceiver input power.

The MFJ-949E inductor switch was *custom* designed to withstand the extremely high RF voltages and currents that are developed in your tuner.

Antenna switch lets you select two coax fed antennas, random wire/balanced line or dummy load through your MFJ-949E or direct to your transceiver.

Full size 3-inch lighted Cross-Needle Meter. Lets you easily read SWR, *peak* or average forward and reflected power simul-

taneously. Has 300 Watt or 30 Watt ranges.

MFJ's *QRM-Free PreTune*™ lets you pre-tune your MFJ-949E *off-the-air* into its built-in dummy load! Makes tuning your actual antenna faster and easier.

Full size built-in non-inductive 50 Ohm dummy load, scratch-proof Lexan multi-colored front panel, 10⁵/₈x3¹/₂x7 in. Superior cabinet construction and more!

MFJ HF thru 6 Meter Antenna Tuner
Covers 1.8-30 MHz *and* 6 Meters. *Lighted* Cross-Needle SWR/Wattmeter. Lamp and RF bypass switches. 300 Watts xcvr input. 8wx2Hx6D inches.

MFJ-945E **$109⁹⁵**

MFJ Switching Power Supplies

Tiny 3.7 lb. switching power supply powers any transceiver! 25 Amps maximum or 22 Amps continuous. 5³/₄Wx4¹/₂Hx6D in. *No RF Hash!* Has Over Voltage and Over Current protection circuits. Front-panel has easy access heavy duty 5-way binding posts and convenient cigarette lighter socket. Variable 9 to 15 Volts DC. Works anywhere in the world, 85 to 135 VAC or 170 to 260 VAC. Replaceable fuse. 35 mV peak-to-peak ripple under 25 amp full load. Load regulation is better than 1.5% under full load.

MFJ-4125, $109.95. Super tiny 5¹/₂Wx2¹/₂Hx5³/₄D inches. Like MFJ-4225MV. No meters or cigarette lighter socket.

MFJ-4225MV **$149⁹⁵**

MFJ 1.8-170 MHz SWRAnalyzer

The world's most popular antenna analyzer gives you a complete picture of your antenna performance 1.8 to 170 MHz. Super easy-to-use -- makes tuning your antenna quick and easy. Read antenna SWR, complex impedance, return loss, reflection coefficient. Determine velocity factor, coax cable loss in dB, length of coax and distance to a short or open in feet. Read inductance in uH and capacitance in pF at RF frequencies. Large easy-to-read two line LCD screen and side-by-side meters clearly display your information. Built-in frequency counter, Ni-Cad charger circuit, battery saver, low battery warning and smooth reduction drive tuning.

MFJ-259B **$259⁹⁵**

MFJ 6-Band Vertical Antenna

Work lots of DX on 6 bands: 40, 20, 15, 10, 6, 2 Meters. No radials or ground needed!

MFJ-1796 **$209⁹⁵**

Only 12 feet high, tiny 24 inch footprint! Mount anywhere -- ground level to tower top -- apartments, small lots. Goes together in an afternoon.

Efficient end-loading, no lossy traps. Entire length is always radiating. Full size halfwave on 2/6 Meters.

Automatic bandswitching, low radiation angle, omni-directional, handles 1500 Watts PEP.

High power air-wound choke balun eliminates feedline radiation. No tuning interaction.

MFJ Hamshack Essentials

MFJ-1702C, $29.95. 2 position antenna coax switch. New center ground, lightning arrestor. 2.5 kW PEP, 1 kW CW. Loss below .2 dB. 50 dB isolation @ 450 MHz. 50 Ohms. 3x2x3".
MFJ-1704, $69.95. Like MFJ-1702C. 4 positions. 6¹/₄x 4¹/₄x1¹/₄ in. 50 dB isolation at 500 MHz. Center Ground/Lightning arrestor.

MFJ-281, $12.95. Communications speaker makes copying easier! Enhances speech and CW, improves intelligibility, reduces noise, static, hum.
MFJ-862, $54.95. Covers 144, 220, 440 MHz. *Cross-Needle Meter* 30/300 Watts forward, 6/60 Watts reflected ranges. Lighted meter, single sensor.

MFJ-108B, $19.95. Dual 24/12 hour-clock. Read UTC and local time simultaneously. Huge high-contrast 5/8 inch LCD, brushed aluminum frame. Includes long-life battery. 4¹/₂Wx1Dx2H inches.
MFJ-260C, $34.95. Dry 300 Watt HF/VHF dummy load. SWR 1.1:1 to 30 MHz; 1.5:1, 30-650 MHz. SO-239. 2¹/₄x2¹/₄x7 in.

MFJ All-Band G5RV Antenna

Covers all bands, 160-10 Meters with antenna tuner. 102 feet long, shorter than 80 Meter dipole. Use as inverted vee or sloper to be more compact. Use on 160 Meters as Marconi with tuner and ground. Handles full legal limit power. Add coax and some rope and you're *on the air!*

MFJ-1778 **$39⁹⁵**

MFJ-1778M, $34.95. MFJ *G5RV Junior* covers 10 through 40 Meters with tuner, handles 1500 Watts, 52 feet long. *New!*

MFJ . . . For All Your CW Needs . . .

MFJ-461, $79.95. Place this tiny MFJ Morse Code Reader near your receiver's speaker . . . Watch CW turn into solid text messages as they scroll across an LCD display.

MFJ-418, $79.95. Learn Morse code anywhere with MFJ's pocket tutor! Follows ARRL/VEC format. Go from zero code speed to CW Pro! Use earphones/built-in speaker.

MFJ-557, $29.95. Adjustable Morse key, code practice oscillator and speaker mounted on heavy steel base -- stays put. Earphone jack, tone, volume controls.

MFJ-407D, $69.95. MFJ Deluxe electronic CW keyer. Send 5-65 wpm. Front panel speed, weight, tone, volume controls. "Bug" mode. Tune switch. Sidetone, speaker. RFI proof. 7Wx2Hx6D inches.

MFJ-564, $49.95. Chrome. Deluxe MFJ *Iambic Paddles*™. Tension and contact spacing adjustments. Heavy precision machined base, non-skid feet. Self-adjusting bearings. MFJ-564B (black).

MFJ VHF/UHF Headquarters

MFJ-1717, $21.95. World's best-selling dual band *HT antenna!* 144/440 MHz flexible duck antenna is thin, super strong and flexible! Choose BNC or SMA. Hearty 2.15 dBi gain!

MFJ-1724B, $16.95. Dual band 144/440 MHz *magnet mount mobile* antenna. 19" radiator, 300W, 3¹/₂" super strong magnet, *free* BNC adapter, 15' coax.

MFJ-1750, $24.95. 2 Meter, 300 Watt 5/8 wave *maximum gain* ground plane *base antenna.* Easy to put up, U-bolt included, strong lightweight aluminum.

MFJ-295, $15.95. Tiny top-quality speaker mic for tiny HTs. Earphone jack, swivel lapel clip, 3¹/₂ foot coiled cord. Black. Specify Yaesu, Icom, Kenwood, others.

FREE manual downloads: *http://www.mfjenterprises.com*

Icom Base, Mobiles, & HTs...

Coming Soon!

IC-208H*

2M/70CM • 55W VHF/50W UHF • CTCSS/DTCS Encode/Decode w/ Tone Scan • Wide Band RX† 118-999.990 MHz • 500 Alphanumeric Memories • Remote Control Mic • DMS • DTMF Encode • 10dB Attenuator

Coming Soon!

IC-703*

• HF/6M • 10W~0.1W@13.5V SSB, CW, RTTY, FM / 4W ~ 0.1W @ 13.5V AM • Newly Designed PA Unit • Internal Antenna Tuner • Detachable, Remotable Control Panel • DSP with Auto Notch Filter & Noise Reduction • Automatic Battery Save Mode • Automatic Power Scale Meter • Low Current Mode • High Sensitivity

Coming Soon!

ID-1

• 1.2GHz • 10W/1W Selectable • FM (Analog Voice)/GMSK (Digital Voice/Data) • 128K Data • USB Control Interface • 10 BASE-T Ethernet Port • AMBE 2.4kbps • 105 Alphanumeric Memories • CTCSS Encode/Decode w/Tone Scan • PC Control

AO-40 Ready!

IC-910H

2M/70CM/1.2GHz*¹ • 100W VHF/75W UHF Variable Output • Works Two Bands at Once • 9600 bps High Speed PACKET Port • All Mode • .11 uV Sensitivity • Main & Sub Band Functions • Versatile Scanning Functions • CTCSS Encode/Decode/Tone Scan • Built-in Keyer • Memory Pad • Normal/Reverse Satellite Functions • Optional DSP • Optional AG-2400 Downlink Converter • Optional 1200 MHz Band Unit (*¹required for 1.2Ghz operation)

Proven Performer!

IC-706MKIIG

• 160-10M/6M/2M/70CM • HF/6M @ 100W, 2M @ 50W, 70CM @ 20W • AM, FM, WFM, SSB, CW, RTTY; w/DSP • 107 Alphanumeric Memories • CTCSS Encode/Decode w/Tone Scan • Auto Repeater • Plug-n-Play Filters • Backlit Function Keys • Built-in Keyer • IF-Shift • Tone Squelch • Remote Head Operation with Optional Equipment

V/V, U/U, V/U Operation!

IC-2720H

• 2M/70CM • 50W VHF/35W UHF Output • 212 Memories • Remote Control Mic • Wide Band RX† 118-549, 810-999.990 MHz • CTCSS/DTCS Encode/Decode w/Tone Scan • Auto Repeater

High Power 2M!

IC-V8000

• 2M • 75W Output • 207 Alphanumeric Memories • Remote Control Mic • FM Narrow Mode • CTCSS/DTCS Encode/Decode w/Tone Scan • Weather Alert & Channel Scan

2M On a Budget!

IC-2100H 25N

• 2M • 50W Output • 113 Alphanumeric Memories • Remote Control Mic • MIL SPEC • CTCSS Encode/Decode w/Tone Scan • Auto Repeater • Large Keys and Knobs

...Fun for Everyone!

Small Size, Big Sound!

Mini Multiband, Marvel!

High End 2M!

Rugged, Easy to Use!

2M On a Budget!

True Dual Band Performance!

IC-Q7A
- 2M/70CM @350mW/300mW
- Wide Band RX† 30-1300 MHz
- 200 Memory Channels
- Auto Squelch
- CTCSS Encode/Decode

IC-T90A
- 6M/2M/70CM @ 5.5W
- Wide Band RX†.495 - 999.99MHz
- 500 Alphanumeric Memories
- CTCSS & DTCS Encode/Decode w/Tone Scan
- Weather Alert
- PC Programmable††

IC-T22A
- 2M @ 5W
- RX 118-174 MHz Inc. Air Band RX
- 40 Alphanumeric Memories
- Auto Low Power & Power Saver
- Auto Repeater Function
- PC Programmable††

IC-V8
- 2M @ 5.5W
- 144-148 MHz (TX), 136-174 MHz (RX)
- 100 Alphanumeric Memories
- CTCSS & DTCS Encode/Decode w/Tone Scan
- Auto Repeater Function
- PC Programmable††

IC-T2H Sport
- 2M @ 6W
- 40 Alphanumeric Memories
- Alkaline Case
- CTCSS Encode/Decode w/Tone Scan
- Auto Repeater Function
- PC Programmable††

IC-W32A
- 2M/70CM @ 5W
- 200 Alphanumeric Memories
- V/V, U/U, V/U Operation
- Crossband Operation
- True Simultaneous Receive
- DTMF Auto Dialer w/Memory
- Auto Repeater Function
- PC Programmable††

Heard it. Worked it. Logged it!

IC-756PROII

HF/6M • 32 Bit Floating Point IF DSP & 24 BIT AD/DA Converter • Selectable Digital IF Filter Shapes for SSB & CW • Improved 3rd Order Intercept Point • All Mode • CW Memory Keyer • VOX • Auto Antenna Tuner • AGC Loop Management • Auto & Manual Notch • Digital Twin Passband Tuning • Built-in RTTY Demodulator & Decoder • 5" TFT Color Display • Separate RX Only Antenna Jack • Transverter I/O Port • Live Band Scope • Digital & Analog Meter • Dual Receive • Digital Voice Recorder

Supercharged Performance!

IC-746PRO

HF/6M/2M • 32 Bit Floating Point IF DSP & 24 BIT AD/DA Converter • Selectable Digital IF Filter Shapes for SSB & CW • Improved 3rd Order Intercept Point • All Mode • CW Memory Keyer • VOX • Auto Antenna Tuner • AGC Loop Management • Auto & Manual Notch • Digital Twin Passband Tuning • Built-in RTTY Demodulator & Decoder • LCD Display • 9600 Baud Packet Capable • Digital Meter • RX Audio Equalizer • SWR Analyzer • Sweeping Scope

HF On a Budget!

IC-718

• HF • 100W (40W on AM) • One Touch Band Switching • All Mode • Direct Frequency Input • VOX • Auto Tuning Steps • Auto Notch • Mic Compressor • IF Shift • Adjustable Noise Blanker • Built-in Keyer • Optional Voice Sythesizer • Optional DSP

Step out and up with Icom!

www.icomamerica.com

ICOM®

12 Store Buying Power!

HAM RADIO OUTLET
WORLDWIDE DISTRIBUTION

Call For Our Specials

YAESU

FT-897 VHF/UHF/HF Transceiver
- HF/6M/2M/70CM • DSP Built-in
- HF 100W (20W battery)
- Optional P.S. + Tuner

Call Now For Our Low Pricing!

FT-1000MP MKV HF Transceiver
- Enhanced Digital Signal Processing
- Dual RX
- Collins SSB filter built-in
- 200W, External power supply

FT1000MP MKV field unit 100w w/built-in power supply in stock

Call For Low Price!

FT-100D HF/6M/2M/70CM Transceiver
- Compact Transceiver w/detachable front panel
- Rx 100kHz to 970mHz (cell blocked)
- Tx 100W 160-6M, 50w 2M, 20W 70CM
- Built-in DSP, Vox, CW keyer
- 300 Memories

Call Now For Low Pricing!

FT-817 HF/VHF/UHF TCVR
- 5W @13.8V ext DC • USB, LSB, CW, AM, FM
- Packet (1200/9600 Baud FM) • 200 mems
- built in CTCSS/DCS • TX 160-10M, 6M, 2M, 440
- Compact 5.3" x 1.5" x 6.5", 2.6 lbs
- 9.6v Nicad or 8 AA battery capable

Call Now For Low Pricing!

FT-2800M 2M Mobile
- 65w • Ruggedly Built
- Alpha Numeric Memory System
- Direct Keypad Frequency Entry
- Bullet-proof Front End

Call Now For Low Intro Pricing!

VX-7R/VX-7R Black
50/2M/220/440 HT
- Wideband RX - 900 Memories
- 5W TX (300mw 220Mhz)
- Li-Ion Battery
- Fully Submersible to 3 ft.
- Built-in CTCSS/DCS
- Internet WIRES compatible

Now available in Black!
Great Price, Call Today!

VX-5R/VX-5RS
50/2M/440HT
- Wideband RX • 6M-2M-440TX
- 5W output • Li-Ion Battery
- 220 mems, opt. barometer unit
- Alpha Numeric Display
- CTCSS/DCS built-in

Call For Low Price!

FT-50RD
2M/440mHz Compact HT
- DVR, Decode, Paging Built-in
- Alpha numeric display
- Wide Band receive
- Battery Saver • 112 Mems
- Mil-Spec • HiSpeed scanning

Call For Your Low Price!

FT-857
Ultra compact HF, VHF, UHF
- 100w HF/6M, 50w 2M, 20w UHF
- DSP • 32 color display
- 200 mems • Detachable front panel (YSK-857 required)

Call for Low Intro Price!

FT-90R
2M/440 Mini Dualbander Transceiver
- 50w 2m, 40w 440mHz
- Wide Rx • Detachable Front Panel
- Packet Ready 1200/9600 Baud
- Built-in CTCSS/DCS Encoder/Decoder
- Less than 4" wide!

Call for Your Low Price!

FT-920 HF+6M Transceiver
- 100w 160-6M, 12VDC
- Built-in DVR, CW Memory Keyer
- DSP, Auto-Notch • 99 Memories
- Computer controllable, CAT System

Call For Low Pricing!

FT-8900R Quadband Transceiver
- 10M/6M/2M/70CM • Wires capable
- 800+ memories • Built-in CTCSS/DCS
- Remotable w/optional YSK-8900

Call Now For Special Pricing

Building your station is half the fun. Elecraft makes it easy!

At Elecraft, we believe in *hands-on* ham radio. That's why we created a line of easy-to-build, high-performance transceiver kits and accessories. When you build your own K1, K2, or K2/100 transceiver, you'll discover what our thousands of customers already know: there's no substitute for the thrill of operating a modern, feature-rich station that you put together yourself. Our kits are ideal for first-time builders, with built-in test equipment, modular assembly, and comprehensive manuals. We also provide unmatched customer support, and you'll have access to an e-mail forum monitored by knowledgeable builders who can answer just about any question.

K2 160-10 meter SSB/CW Transceiver

KAT100

Why pay $2000+ for a world-class HF transceiver? Starting at only $599, the K2 ranks near the top in every performance category, and is the rig of choice for many contesting and DX enthusiasts. It's also the perfect Field-Day rig, weighing only 3.3 pounds and offering far lower current drain than competing transceivers. The basic K2 puts out over 10 watts, and you can complete the K2 as a 100-watt K2/100 at any time. Options include the 150-watt KAT100 automatic antenna tuner (above). Visit our web site for more information.

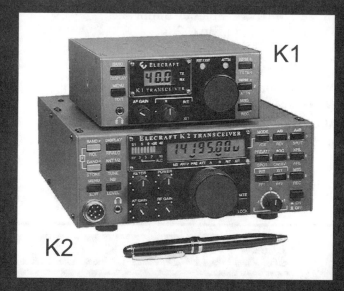
K1
K2

"I am absolutely taken by the K2. No comparison in the way of performance, feel, and all-around operating pleasure.... a fantastic piece of engineering." – Jim, K9FI

"In 42 years of hamming, I have never had so much consistent good luck with customer service from a ham radio manufacturer.... in my experience, Elecraft is tops on the list." – Brian, K7RE

"This K1 is a piece of art. The integration of form and function is superb. The care taken to make it buildable is unmatched." – Mike, W1MU

K1 Four-Band CW Transceiver

With its small size, low current drain, and 5-watt+ output, the K1 is a great rig for home, field, or travel. The four-band KFL1-4 module (shown at right) covers 40, 30, 20, and your choice of 17 or 15 meters. Dual-band modules cover any two bands of your choice (80-15 m). Other options include internal antenna tuner and internal AA battery pack. Starts at $289.

KFL1-4

www.elecraft.com

 ELECRAFT

P.O. Box 69
Aptos, CA 95001-0069

Phone: (831) 662-8345
sales@elecraft.com

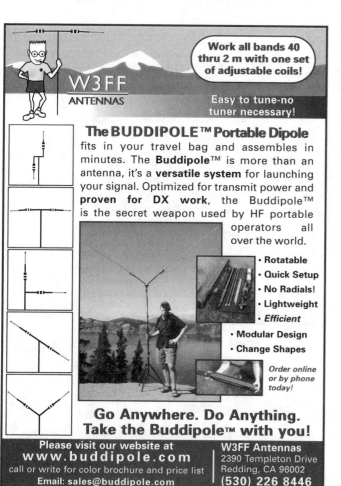

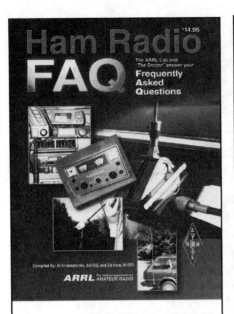

FEEDBACK

Please use this form to give us your comments on this book and what you'd like to see in future editions, or e-mail us at **pubsfdbk@arrl.org** (publications feedback). If you use e-mail, please include your name, call, e-mail address and the book title, edition and printing in the body of your message. Also indicate whether or not you are an ARRL member.

Please check the box that best answers these questions:

How well did this book prepare you for your exam? ☐ Very well   ☐ Fairly well   ☐ Not very well

How well did this book teach you about ham radio? ☐ Very well   ☐ Fairly well   ☐ Not very well

Which exam did you take (or will you be taking)? ☐ Technician ☐ Technician with code Did you pass? ☐ Yes ☐ No

If you checked Technician: Do you expect to learn Morse code at some point?   ☐ Yes   ☐ No

Which operating modes do you plan to use first?

☐ SSB   ☐ FM   ☐ Packet   ☐ RTTY   ☐ Image   ☐ Morse code   ☐ Other _____

Where did you purchase this book? ☐ From ARRL directly   ☐ From an ARRL dealer

Is there a dealer who carries ARRL publications within:

☐ 5 miles   ☐ 15 miles   ☐ 30 miles of your location? ☐ Not sure.

Name _____ ARRL member? ☐ Yes ☐ No

_____ Call Sign _____

Address _____

City, State/Province, ZIP/Postal Code _____

Daytime Phone (   ) _____ Age _____

If licensed, how long? _____

Other hobbies _____ E-mail _____

_____

Occupation _____

From _____

_____

_____

Please affix postage. Post Office will not deliver without postage.

EDITOR, NOW YOU'RE TALKING!
ARRL—THE NATIONAL ASSOCIATION FOR AMATEUR RADIO
225 MAIN STREET
NEWINGTON CT 06111-1494

— — — — — — — — — — please fold and tape — — — — — — — — — —